ASCENT
CENTER FOR TECHNICAL KNOWLEDGE

Creo Parametric 7.0 Advanced Assembly Design and Management

Learning Guide
1st Edition

ASCENT - Center for Technical Knowledge®
Creo Parametric 7.0
Advanced Assembly Design and Management
1st Edition

Prepared and produced by:

ASCENT Center for Technical Knowledge
630 Peter Jefferson Parkway, Suite 175
Charlottesville, VA 22911

866-527-2368
www.ASCENTed.com

ASCENT

CENTER FOR TECHNICAL KNOWLEDGE

Contents

Preface vii

In This Guide ix

Practice Files xi

Chapter 1: Advanced Component Selection 1-1

   1.1   Search Using the Find Command 1-2

   1.2   Search Using the Model Tree 1-6

   1.3   3D Box Selection 1-11

   Practice 1a Assembly Selection 1-14

   Practice 1b Model Tree Search 1-26

   Chapter Review Questions 1-38

Chapter 2: Advanced Component Placement 2-1

   2.1   Repeating Components 2-2

   2.2   Reference Patterns 2-5

   2.3   Component Interfaces 2-7
       Auto Place 2-9

   2.4   Flexible Components 2-10

   2.5   Copy and Paste 2-14
       Paste Special 2-15

   Practice 2a Repeating Components 2-16

   Practice 2b Using Component Interfaces 2-28

   Practice 2c Using Flexible Components 2-43

   Practice 2d Copy and Paste 2-50

   Chapter Review Questions 2-59

Chapter 3: Assembly Management **3-1**

3.1 Layers in Assembly Mode **3-2**

Add Part Level Features to a Layer 3-5

Display Status 3-6

Layer Info 3-7

Save Status 3-8

Editing Layers 3-8

Default Layers 3-9

3.2 Suppress and Resume **3-10**

3.3 Restructure **3-14**

3.4 Move to New Subassembly **3-17**

Practice 3a Working with Layers **3-19**

Practice 3b Assembly Restructure **3-30**

Chapter Review Questions **3-37**

Chapter 4: Assembly Family Tables **4-1**

4.1 Creating Assembly Family Tables **4-2**

Component Manipulation 4-7

Pattern.. 4-8

Controlling Lower Level Items.. 4-10

Instance Index 4-10

4.2 Modifying Family Tables **4-11**

Modifying Non-family Tables 4-12

Adding Components to the Generic Model 4-12

Adding Components to an Instance 4-13

Deleting Components from an Instance 4-14

Deleting Components from the Generic 4-15

Practice 4a Assembly Family Tables **4-16**

Practice 4b (Optional) Model Plane **4-24**

Chapter Review Questions **4-38**

Chapter 5: View Manager **5-1**

5.1 Component Display Styles **5-2**

Appearance States.. 5-8

5.2 Simplified Representations **5-9**

5.3 Automatic Representations **5-10**

5.4 Additional System-Defined Simplified Representations **5-12**

5.5 User-Defined Simplified Representations **5-14**

5.6 Opening Simplified Representations **5-19**

Practice 5a Using Component Display Styles **5-22**

Practice 5b Simplified Representations **5-33**

Practice 5c Automatic Simplified Representations **5-43**

Practice 5d (Optional) Define a Simplified Rep Without Loading the Model **5-56**

Chapter Review Questions **5-59**

Chapter 6: Advanced View Manager **6-1**

6.1 **Advanced Simplified Reps** **6-2**
Definition Rules 6-2
External Simplified Representations 6-4

6.2 **Zones** **6-7**

6.3 **Envelopes** **6-11**

Practice 6a Rule-Based Simplified Reps **6-16**

Practice 6b Zone-Based Simplified Reps **6-30**

Practice 6c (Optional) Substitute by Envelope **6-38**

Chapter Review Questions **6-45**

Chapter 7: Interchange Assemblies **7-1**

7.1 **Functional Components** **7-2**

7.2 **Simplified Components** **7-6**

7.3 **Simplifying Using Shrinkwrap Features** **7-13**
Replace 7-13
Simplified Representation Substitution 7-13

7.4 **Case Studies** **7-14**
Example 1 7-14
Example 2 7-15
Example 3 7-16

Practice 7a Functional Interchange Assemblies I **7-17**

Practice 7b Functional Interchange Assemblies II **7-26**

Chapter Review Questions **7-35**

Chapter 8: Skeleton Models **8-1**

8.1 **Skeleton Models** **8-2**
Parent/Child Relationships 8-2
Incorporating Motion 8-3
Spatial Claims 8-3

8.2 **Geometry Creation** **8-5**

8.3 **Skeleton Properties** **8-8**

8.4 **Motion Skeletons** **8-9**

Practice 8a Creating a Skeleton Part.. 8-16

Practice 8b Using Motion Skeletons 8-27

Practice 8c (Optional) Adding Components Using Package 8-49

Chapter Review Questions.. 8-58

Chapter 9: Designing in Context.. 9-1

  9.1   **External References**.. 9-2

  9.2   **Creating Parts in Assembly** 9-3

  9.3   **Creating Assembly Features**.. 9-7

  9.4   **Creating Models from a Motion Skeleton** 9-13

Practice 9a Assembly Features 9-15

Practice 9b Designing in Context 9-24

Practice 9c Adding Components to Motion Skeletons..................... 9-37

Chapter Review Questions.. 9-42

Chapter 10: Distributing Design Information 10-1

  10.1 **External Reference Control in Current Assembly**................. 10-2

  10.2 **Global External References** 10-5

       Rule Conflicts 10-8

  10.3 **Copy Geometry Features** 10-9

  10.4 **Publish Geometry Feature** 10-15

  10.5 **Shrinkwrap Features**.. 10-18

       Large Assembly Management 10-18

       Incoming Vendor Models 10-19

       Outgoing Models 10-19

       Swept Volume Analysis.. 10-19

Practice 10a Designing Parts in Assembly..................................... 10-26

Practice 10b Using Shrinkwrap Features.. 10-46

Practice 10c Component Geometry from Motion Skeletons......... 10-50

Chapter Review Questions.. 10-72

Chapter 11: Managing External References............................ 11-1

  11.1 **Investigating External References** 11-2

       Model Tree.. 11-2

       Model Information 11-3

  11.2 **Reference Viewer** 11-5

       Displaying Circular References 11-7

       Breaking Dependencies 11-10

       Checking Memory 11-10

       Message Window 11-10

11.3 Severing External References **11-11**
Sketched Features 11-11
Coaxial Holes 11-12
Copied Surfaces 11-12
Depth Options 11-12
Merged Features 11-12
Independent Copy Geometry Features 11-13

Practice 11a Severing External References **11-14**

Chapter Review Questions **11-24**

Chapter 12: Intelligent Fasteners Lite **12-1**

12.1 Intelligent Fastener Extension **12-2**

12.2 Assemble on Reference **12-3**
Two Aligning Surfaces 12-5
Two Opposing Surfaces 12-10

12.3 Assemble by Mouse Click **12-13**

12.4 Inserting Heli-Coils in IFX **12-15**

Practice 12a Assembling Intelligent Fasteners **12-17**

Chapter Review Questions **12-37**

Chapter 13: Advanced Assembly Operations **13-1**

13.1 Mirroring Components (Method 1) **13-2**
Mirroring Parts 13-2
Mirroring Subassemblies 13-7

13.2 Mirroring Components (Method 2) **13-11**
Mirroring Parts 13-11
Mirroring Subassemblies 13-12

13.3 Boolean Operations (Merge, Cut, and Intersect) **13-15**

13.4 Part Intersections **13-20**

13.5 Dragging **13-22**
Detecting Collision 13-25

13.6 Assembly Relations **13-27**

Practice 13a Mirroring Components **13-34**

Practice 13b Assembly Merge **13-42**

Practice 13c Mirroring an Assembly **13-51**

Practice 13d Dragging Components **13-57**

Practice 13e Assembly Relations **13-62**

Chapter Review Questions **13-69**

Preface

Understand the full assembly functionality of the Creo Parametric 7.0 software while concentrating on techniques that maximize large assembly management capabilities, as well as an introduction to Top Down Design. *Creo Parametric 7.0: Advanced Assembly Design and Management* is a hands-on learning guide with a substantial amount of time dedicated to practices.

Topics Covered

- Advanced Component Selection and Placement
- Top Down Design
- Managing External References
- Assembly Management
- Skeleton and Motion Skeleton Models
- Assembly Duplication Tools
- Assembly Family Tables
- Display Styles, Layers and Suppression
- Restructure
- Intelligent Fasteners Lite
- Creating Parts and Features in an Assembly
- Merge and Cut Out, Intersections
- Copy Geometry Features
- Inheritance Features
- Simplified Representations
- Interchange Assemblies

Prerequisites

- Access to the Creo Parametric 7.0 software. The practices and files included with this guide might not be compatible with prior versions. Practice files included with this guide are compatible with the commercial version of the software, but not the student edition.

- *Creo Parametric 7.0: Introduction to Solid Modeling* or equivalent Creo Parametric experience.

Note on Software Setup

This guide assumes a standard installation of the software using the default preferences during installation. Lectures and practices use the standard software templates and default options for the Content Libraries.

In This Guide

The following highlights the key features of this guide.

Feature	Description
Practice Files	The Practice Files page includes a link to the practice files and instructions on how to download and install them. The practice files are required to complete the practices in this guide.
Chapters	A chapter consists of the following - Learning Objectives, Instructional Content, Practices, Chapter Review Questions, and Command Summary. • **Learning Objectives** define the skills you can acquire by learning the content provided in the chapter. • **Instructional Content**, which begins right after Learning Objectives, refers to the descriptive and procedural information related to various topics. Each main topic introduces a product feature, discusses various aspects of that feature, and provides step-by-step procedures on how to use that feature. Where relevant, examples, figures, helpful hints, and notes are provided. • **Practice** for a topic follows the instructional content. Practices enable you to use the software to perform a hands-on review of a topic. It is required that you download the practice files (using the link found on the Practice Files page) prior to starting the first practice. • **Chapter Review Questions**, located close to the end of a chapter, enable you to test your knowledge of the key concepts discussed in the chapter.

Practice Files

To download the practice files for this guide, use the following steps:

1. Type the URL *exactly as shown below* into the address bar of your Internet browser, to access the Course File Download page.

   Note: If you are using the ebook, you do not have to type the URL. Instead, you can access the page simply by clicking the URL below.

   https://www.ascented.com/getfile/id/aulonocaraPF

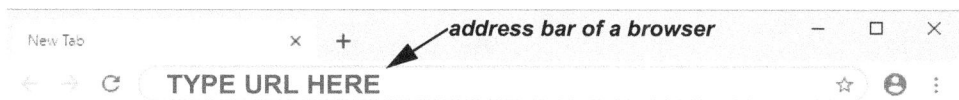

2. On the Course File Download page, click the **DOWNLOAD NOW** button, as shown below, to download the .ZIP file that contains the practice files.

3. Once the download is complete, unzip the file and extract its contents.

   The recommended practice files folder location is:
   C:\Creo Parametric Advanced Assembly Design Practice Files

   Note: It is recommended that you do not change the location of the practice files folder. Doing so may cause errors when completing the practices.

Stay Informed!

To receive information about upcoming events, promotional offers, and complimentary webcasts, visit:

www.ASCENTed.com/updates

Advanced Component Selection

As assemblies grow larger, finding components and features can be difficult. Search tools can be used to find and select items in the assembly based on predefined or user-defined criteria. Consider using search tools to locate references for component placement or selecting components for layers, simplified representations, etc.

Learning Objectives in This Chapter

- Use the **Find** command to search and select items in an assembly using rules.
- Use the **Search** options in the Model Tree to conduct predefined searches or user-defined searches to locate or select components in an assembly.
- Use the 3D Box Select tool to select all components that fall within the boundaries of the box.

1.1 Search Using the Find Command

The **Find** command enables you to search and select items using the search rules and is available in all of the modes of Creo Parametric. You can search for items by their attributes, history, status, or geometry.

How To: Perform a Search

1. Click 🔍 (Find) at the bottom of the window or click 🔍 (Find) in the *Tools* tab to open the Search Tool, as shown in Figure 1–1.

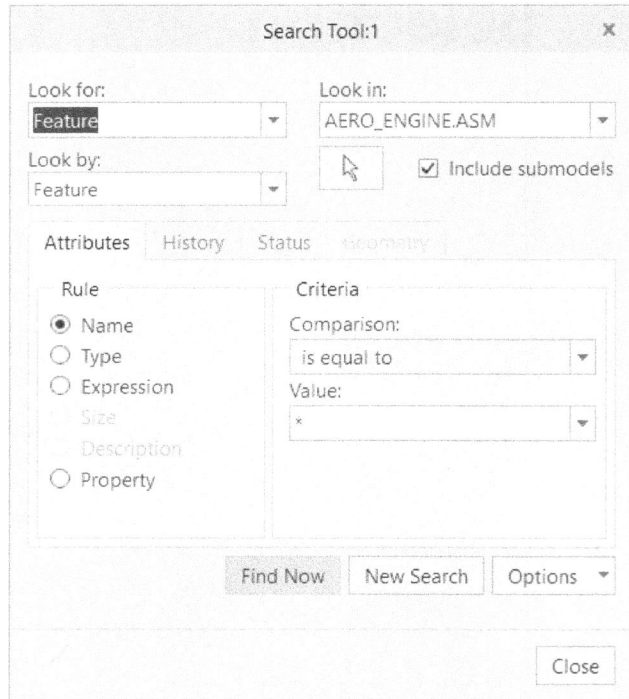

Figure 1–1

2. To filter the type of items to search, select an option in the **Look for** menu, as shown in Figure 1–2. In addition, you can select the component that you want to search for in the *Look in* area or items in the *Look by* area. Filtering enables you to search for specific items and components, narrowing the number of results.

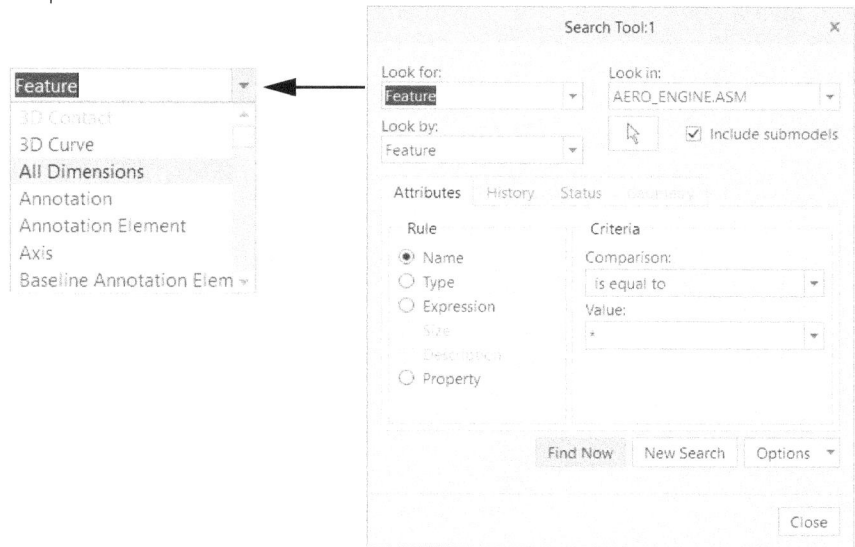

Figure 1–2

*The Geometry tab is only available in Assembly mode when the **Look for** area is set to **Component**.*

3. Select the type of rule in the *Attributes*, *History*, or *Status* tabs. Select the type of rule in the Comparison drop-down list (e.g., **is equal to**, **is not equal to**, etc.), and enter a value to describe the rule. Wildcards are permitted. For example, **D*** selects all of the applicable items in the model with a name beginning with D. The rule options for each tab are shown in Figure 1–3.

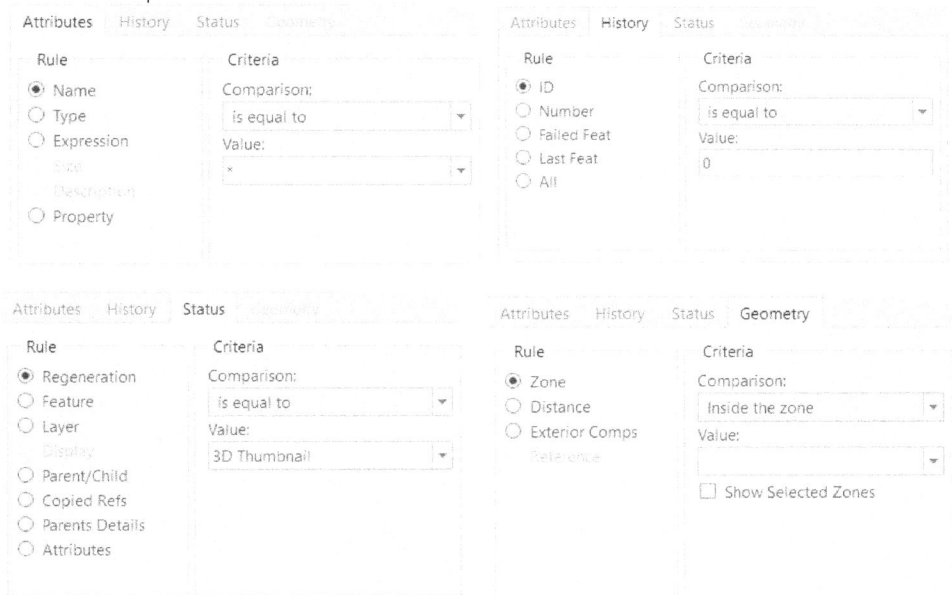

Figure 1–3

*To begin a new search, click **New Search**.*

To combine multiple rules, click **Options>Build Query**. The Search Tool dialog box expands to include the area shown in Figure 1–4. Rules can be added, removed, or updated as required. To complete the query, select the **and/or** operator for each query.

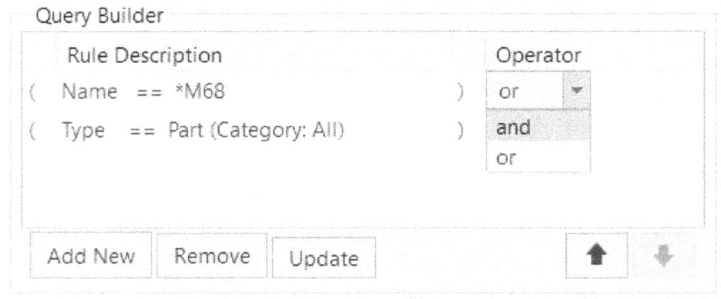

Query Builder

Rule Description		Operator
(Name == *M68	)	or ▼
(Type == Part (Category: All)	)	and
		or

Add New   Remove   Update   ⬆ ⬇

Figure 1–4

*Click **Options>Filter Tree** to set the Model Tree to only display the selected items.*

4. Click **Find Now** to start the search. All of the items that fit the criteria are listed at the bottom of the dialog box in the *Items Found* column, as shown in Figure 1–5.

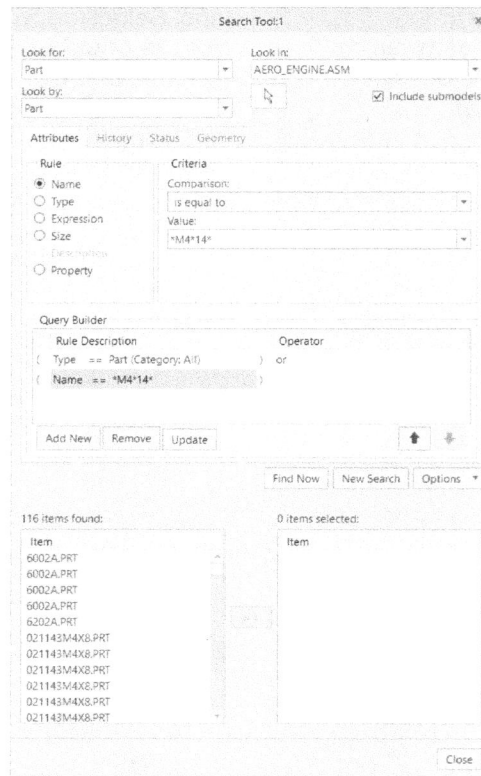

Figure 1–5

By default, the resulting items are not selected. To select an item, select it in the *Items Found* column and click ≫ (Add Item) to move the item to the selected column.

5. To save the search results in a new layer, click **Options> Save Query**. Enter the name of the layer in the Save Rules dialog box.

6. Click **Close** to close the dialog box. The items that meet the criteria are selected in the Model Tree.

1.2 Search Using the Model Tree

The **Apply Search** tool enables you to search and select items in the Model Tree. This tool is only available in assembly mode. You can search for items by name or status by entering the information and applying the search. The predefined status options are available in the flyout menu.

To specify the search, you can select a predefined search option as shown in Figure 1–6.

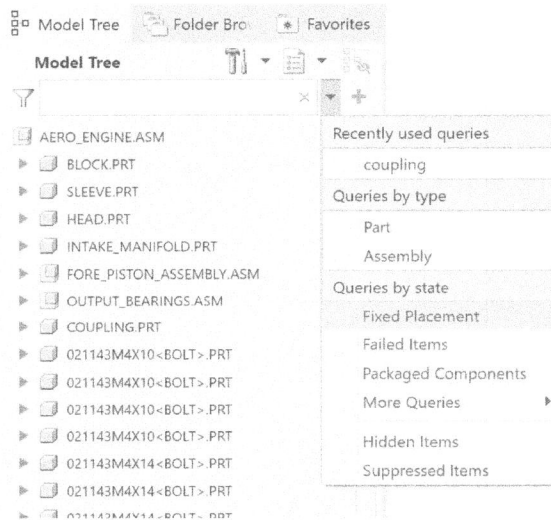

Figure 1–6

Additionally, you can search for items in the tree by entering a value as shown in Figure 1–7.

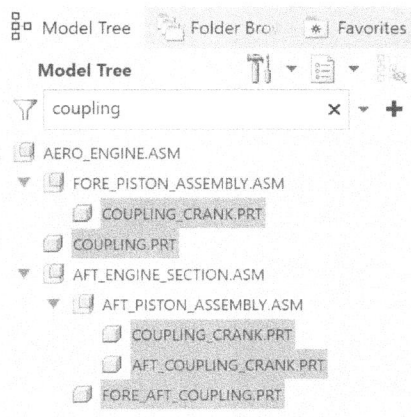

Figure 1–7

When using the Model Tree search tool, the Model Tree filters and updates dynamically as you type, as shown in Figure 1–8.

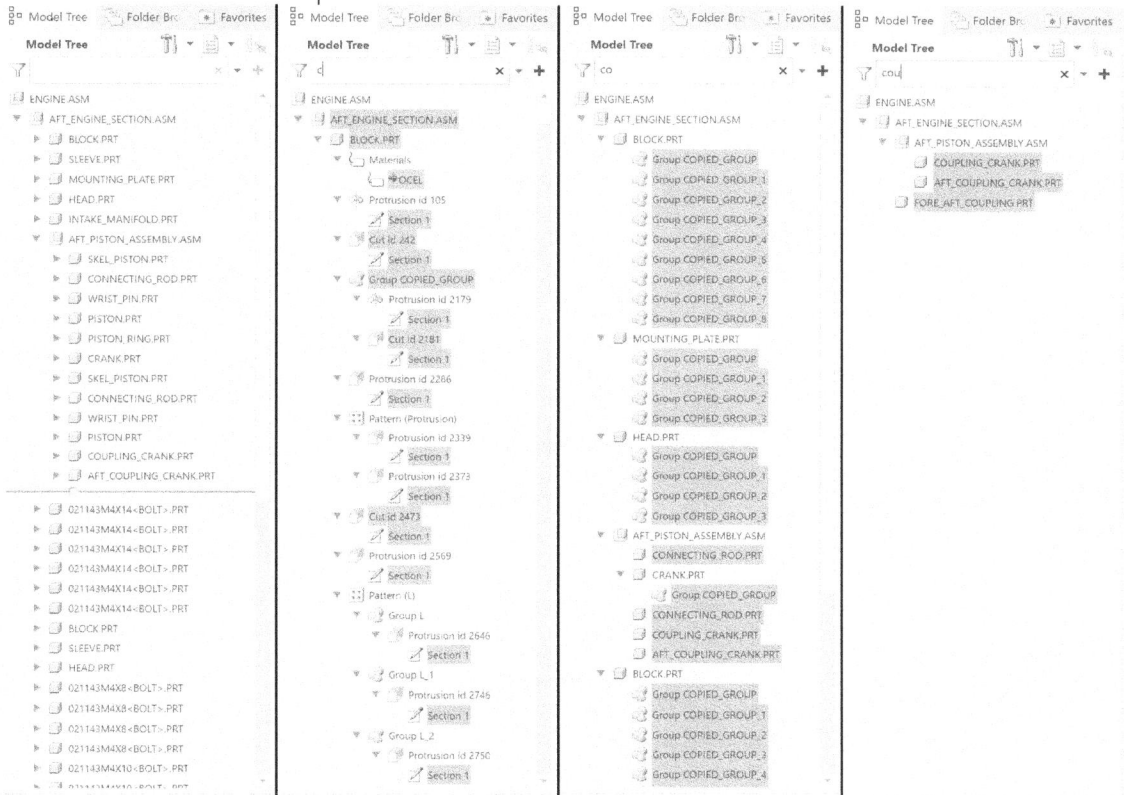

Figure 1–8

In addition to searching text, you can also search for conditions, query types, and wild cards. By default, the Model Tree filters as you type and highlights objects in the graphics area. These settings can be controlled by right-clicking in the Search bar and enabling or disabling the **Dynamic Filter/Search** or **Highlight in Graphics** options, shown in Figure 1–9.

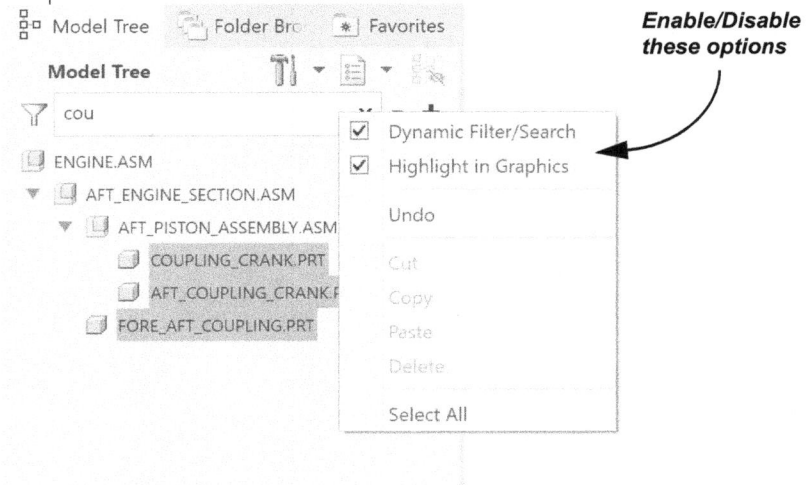

Figure 1–9

You can also filter using values from any columns you add to the Model Tree display. If you add columns to the Model Tree (as shown in Figure 1–10), you can right-click in the search box and select one or more of those columns from the shortcut menu.

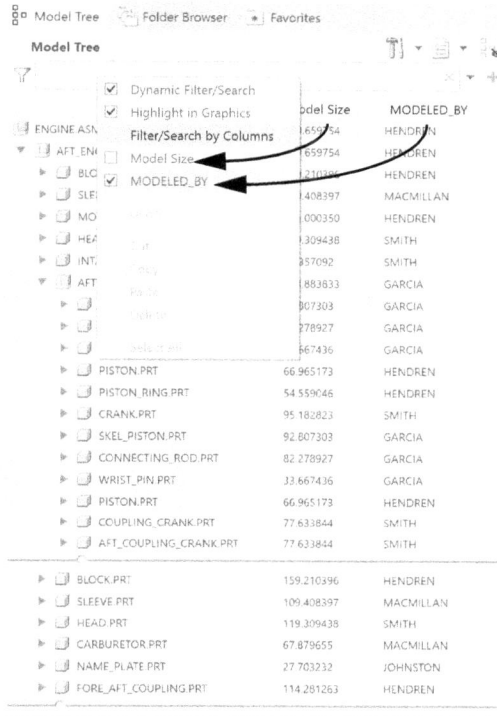

Figure 1–10

When you type values in the search field, the Model Tree filters based on the columns you selected, as Figure 1–11.

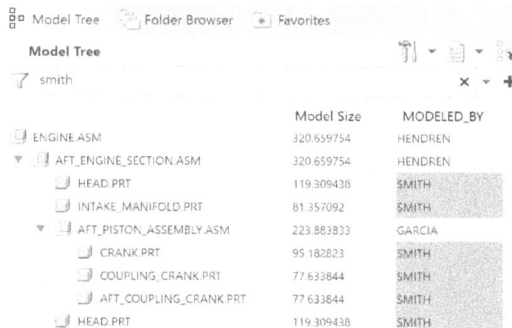

Figure 1–11

To select the objects that are highlighted by your search, click

✚ (Add Marked) in the Model Tree. Once items have been added to the selection buffer, you can perform a variety of tasks, such as suppress, delete, and regenerate.

If you want to search without filtering, click the 🝐 (Filter) next to the search bar. The icon changes to 🔍 (Search) and the found objects are highlighted but not filtered, as shown in Figure 1–12.

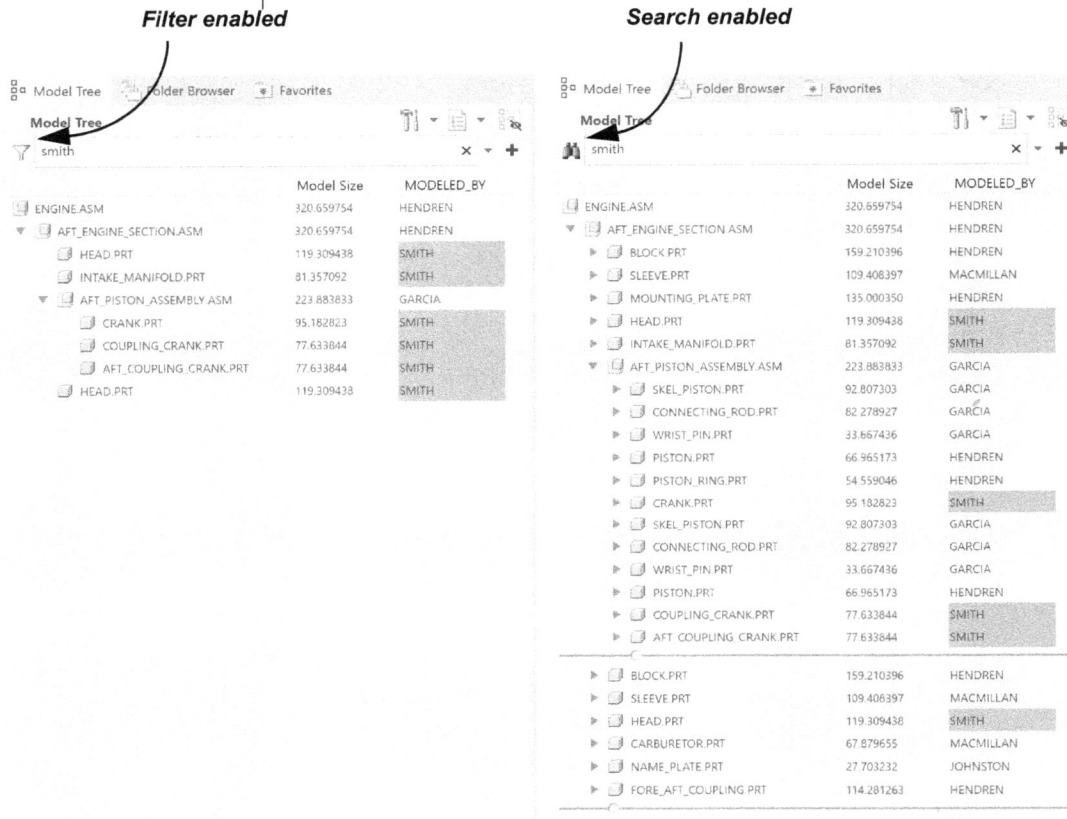

Filter enabled

Search enabled

	Model Size	MODELED_BY
ENGINE.ASM	320.659754	HENDREN
AFT_ENGINE_SECTION.ASM	320.659754	HENDREN
HEAD.PRT	119.309438	SMITH
INTAKE_MANIFOLD.PRT	81.357092	SMITH
AFT_PISTON_ASSEMBLY.ASM	223.883833	GARCIA
CRANK.PRT	95.182823	SMITH
COUPLING_CRANK.PRT	77.633844	SMITH
AFT_COUPLING_CRANK.PRT	77.633844	SMITH
HEAD.PRT	119.309438	SMITH

	Model Size	MODELED_BY
ENGINE.ASM	320.659754	HENDREN
AFT_ENGINE_SECTION.ASM	320.659754	HENDREN
BLOCK.PRT	159.210396	HENDREN
SLEEVE.PRT	109.408397	MACMILLAN
MOUNTING_PLATE.PRT	135.000350	HENDREN
HEAD.PRT	119.309438	SMITH
INTAKE_MANIFOLD.PRT	81.357092	SMITH
AFT_PISTON_ASSEMBLY.ASM	223.883833	GARCIA
SKEL_PISTON.PRT	92.807303	GARCIA
CONNECTING_ROD.PRT	82.278927	GARCIA
WRIST_PIN.PRT	33.667436	GARCIA
PISTON.PRT	66.965173	HENDREN
PISTON_RING.PRT	54.559046	HENDREN
CRANK.PRT	95.182823	SMITH
SKEL_PISTON.PRT	92.807303	GARCIA
CONNECTING_ROD.PRT	82.278927	GARCIA
WRIST_PIN.PRT	33.667436	GARCIA
PISTON.PRT	66.965173	HENDREN
COUPLING_CRANK.PRT	77.633844	SMITH
AFT_COUPLING_CRANK.PRT	77.633844	SMITH
BLOCK.PRT	159.210396	HENDREN
SLEEVE.PRT	109.408397	MACMILLAN
HEAD.PRT	119.309438	SMITH
CARBURETOR.PRT	67.879655	MACMILLAN
NAME_PLATE.PRT	27.703232	JOHNSTON
FORE_AFT_COUPLING.PRT	114.281263	HENDREN

Figure 1–12

1.3 3D Box Selection

Components can be selected using a dynamic bounding box.

Click ▢ (3D Box Select) near the selection filter in the lower right of the Creo Parametric window.

Select a surface to define the initial location of the bounding box, as shown in Figure 1–13.

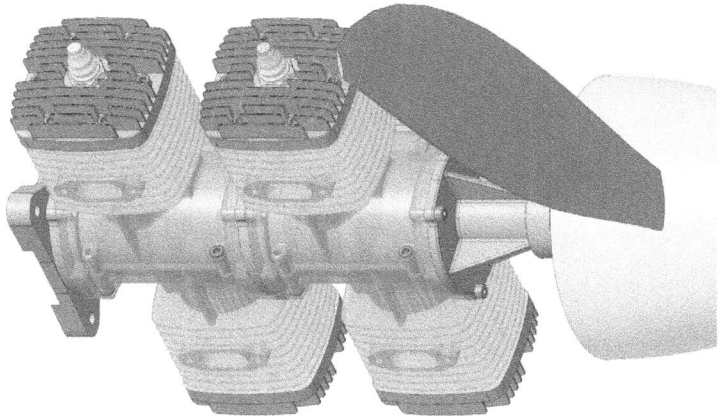

Figure 1–13

Click to define the first corner of a rectangle, then move the cursor and click to define the other corner, as shown in Figure 1–14.

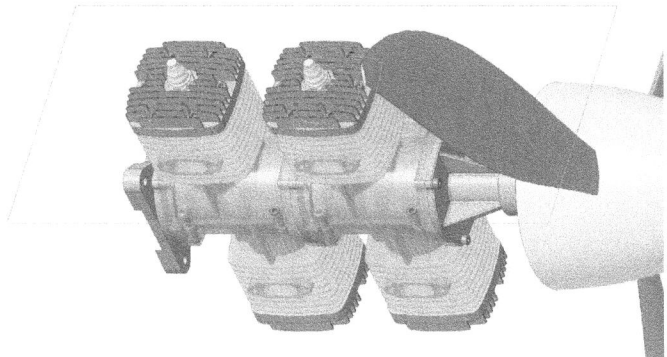

Figure 1–14

The system then defines the 3D selection box, that selects components within its boundaries, dependent on the direction the box is drawn. The 3D selection box has similar functionality as the 2D selection box used in drawings. If the box is drawn left to right, it will select only items that completely fall within the boundary, as shown in Figure 1–15.

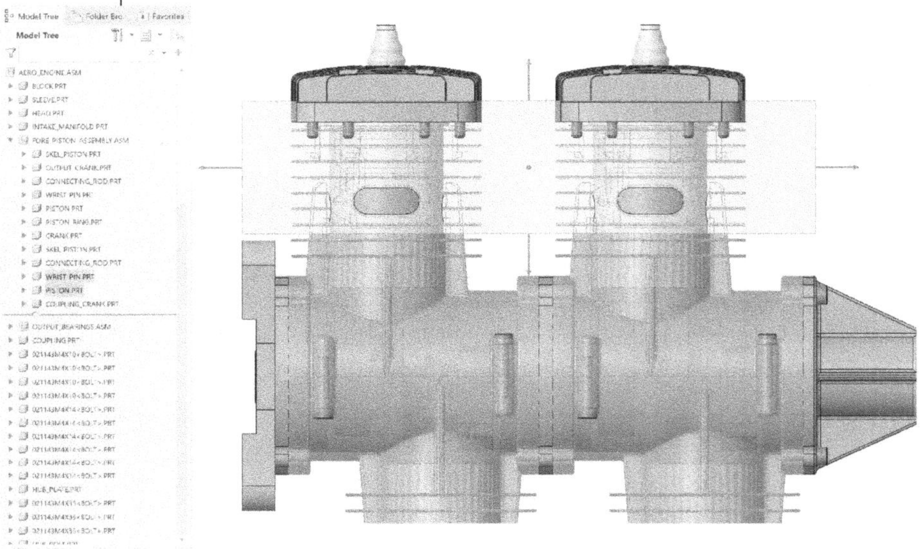

Figure 1–15

Drawing the box right to left will select anything that even partially enters the space as shown in Figure 1–16.

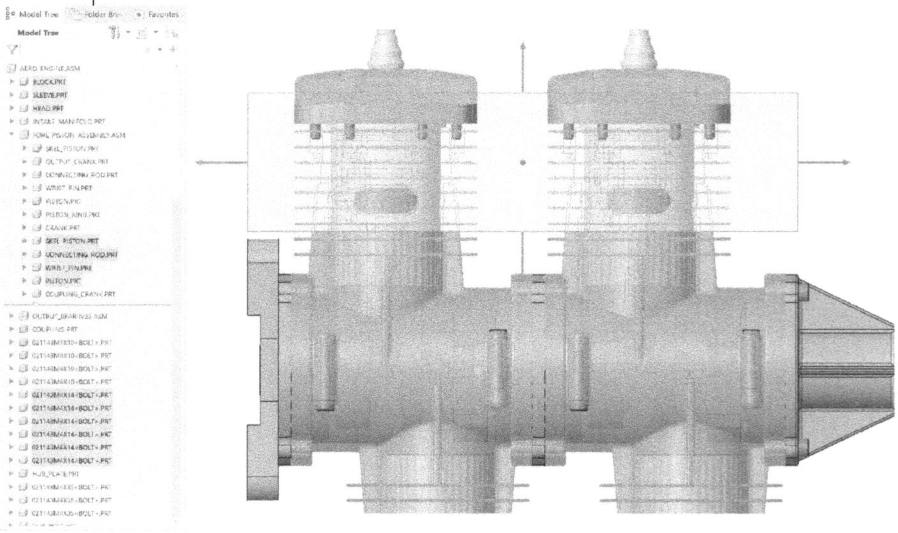

Figure 1–16

You can select and drag the direction arrows to increase or decrease the size of the bounding box, and therefore change the objects that are selected, as shown in Figure 1–17.

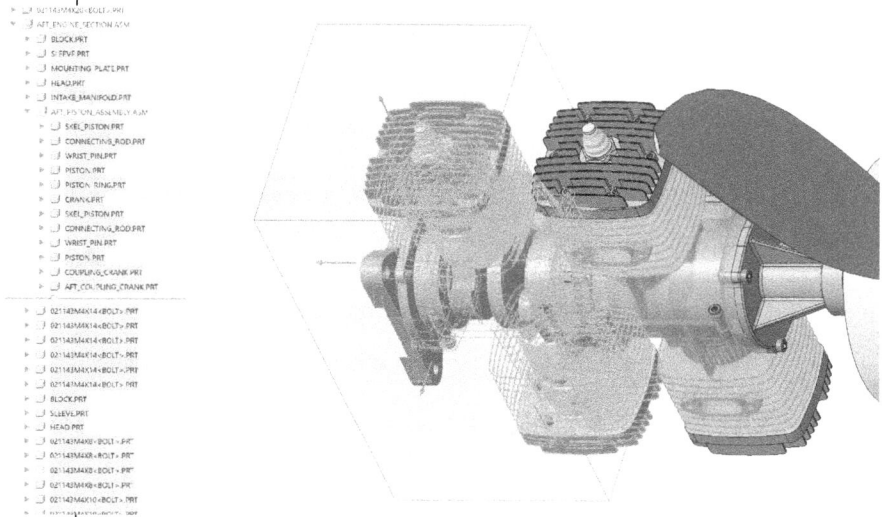

Figure 1–17

The selected components can then be suppressed, replaced, deleted, and so on.

Practice 1a | Assembly Selection

Practice Objective

- Use several search tools to select components.

In this practice, you will use several search tools such as Find and Model Tree search to select components.

Task 1 - Open an assembly file.

1. Set the working directory to the *Assembly_Selection* folder.

2. Open **aero_engine.asm**.

3. Set the model display as follows:

  - ⚝ *(Datum Display Filters)*: All Off

  - ⤳ *(Spin Center)*: Off

  - ▱ *(Display Style)*: ▱ (Shading With Edges)

Task 2 - Use the search tool to select all subassemblies.

1. In the lower right of the Creo Parametric window, click ▦ (Find) to open the Search Tool dialog box.

2. In the Look for drop-down list, select **Component**.

3. In the *Attributes tab*, in the *Rule* area, select **Type**.

4. From the Value drop-down list, select **Assembly**. The Search Tool displays as shown in Figure 1–18.

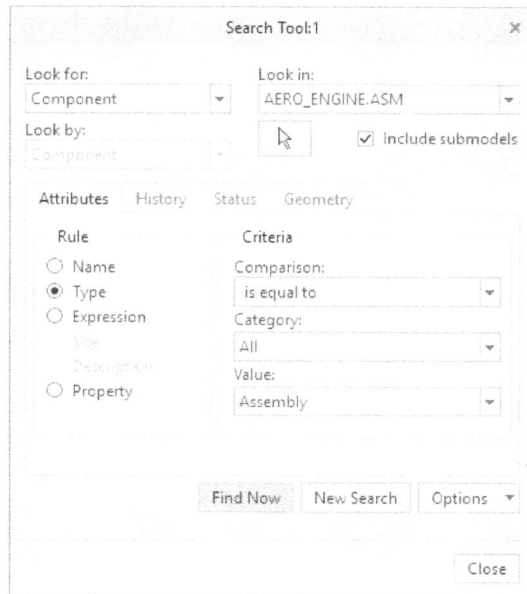

Figure 1–18

5. Click **Find Now**. The dialog box updates as shown in Figure 1–19.

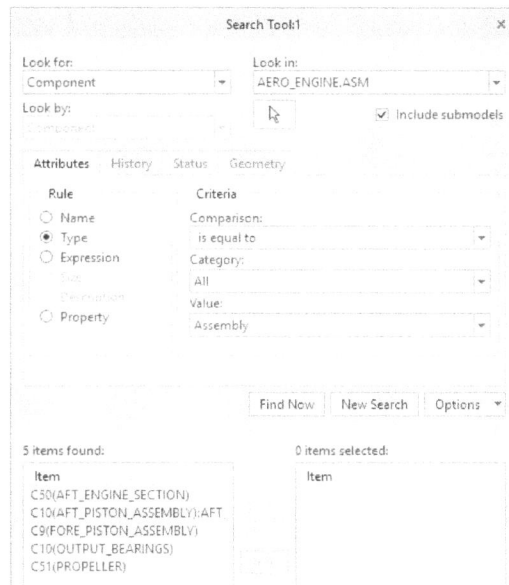

Figure 1–19

Note that this can be useful in very large assemblies, as the system automatically expands subassemblies in the tree when required.

6. Select the 5 objects in the *items found* list and click ≫ (Add Item) to move them to the *items selected* list.

7. Note that the objects are selected on screen and in the Model Tree. A partial Model Tree is shown in Figure 1–20.

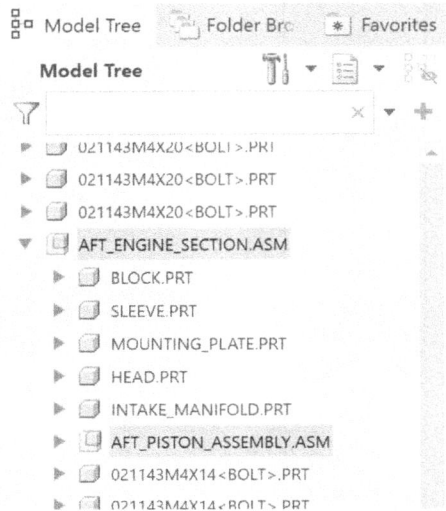

Figure 1–20

8. Select all objects except *C51(PROPELLER)* in the *items selected* list.

9. Right-click and select **Remove**.

10. Click **Close**.

11. The propeller assembly is highlighted, as shown in Figure 1–21.

Figure 1–21

12. Right-click and select ▰ (Suppress) in the mini toolbar.

13. Click **OK** in the Suppress dialog box. The model displays as shown in Figure 1–22.

Figure 1–22

14. Click on the screen to clear any selections.

Task 3 - Find all of the objects with "head" in the name.

1. In the lower right of the Creo Parametric window, click 🔍 (Find).

2. In the *Rule* area, select **Name**.

3. In the *Value* field, type ***head***.

4. Click **Find Now**. The Search Tool dialog box updates as shown in Figure 1–23.

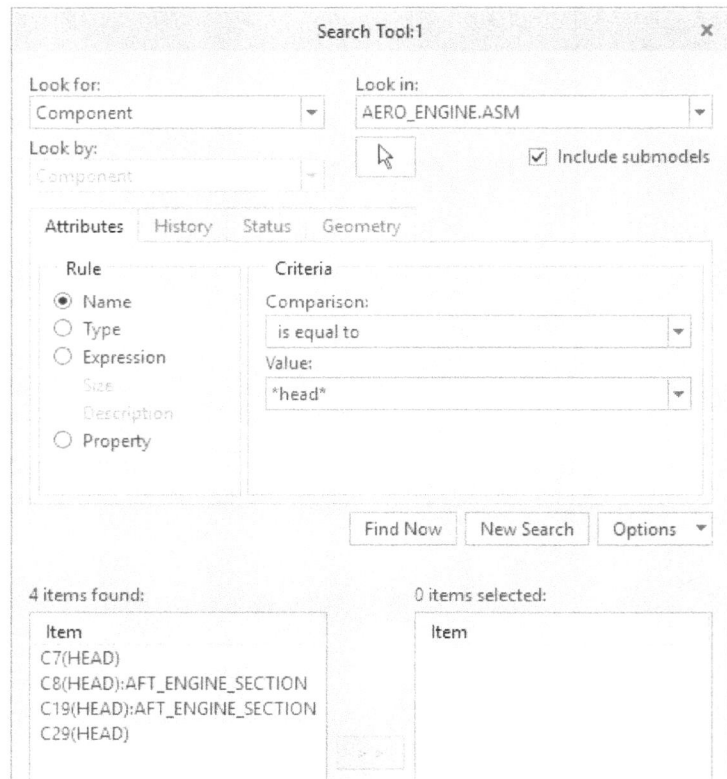

Figure 1–23

5. Select all of the objects in the *items found* list and click ≫ (Add Item) to select them.

6. Click **Close**.

7. Right-click and select ✎ (Hide) in the mini toolbar. The model updates as shown in Figure 1–24.

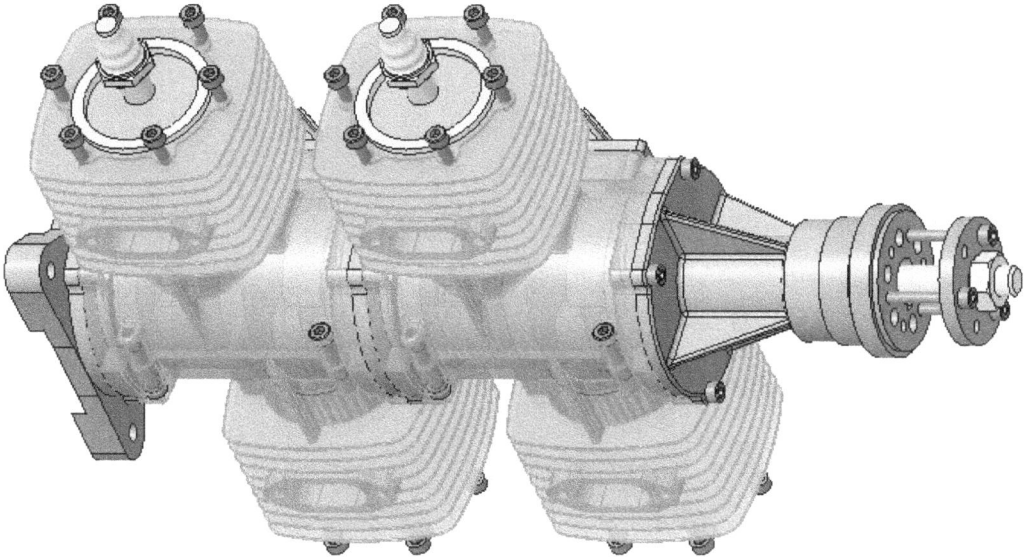

Figure 1–24

Task 4 - Create a query to search by size and name to remove several bolts from the assembly.

---

1. In the lower right of the Creo Parametric window, click 🔍 (Find).

2. Click **Options>Build Query**.

3. From the Look for drop-down list, select **Part**.

4. From the *Rule* area, select **Size**.

5. In the *Criteria* area, set the following:

   • *Type*: **Absolute**
   • *Comparison*: **is less than**
   • *Value*: **25**

6. Select **Include All Models**.

7. Click **Add New** to add the rule, as shown in Figure 1–25.

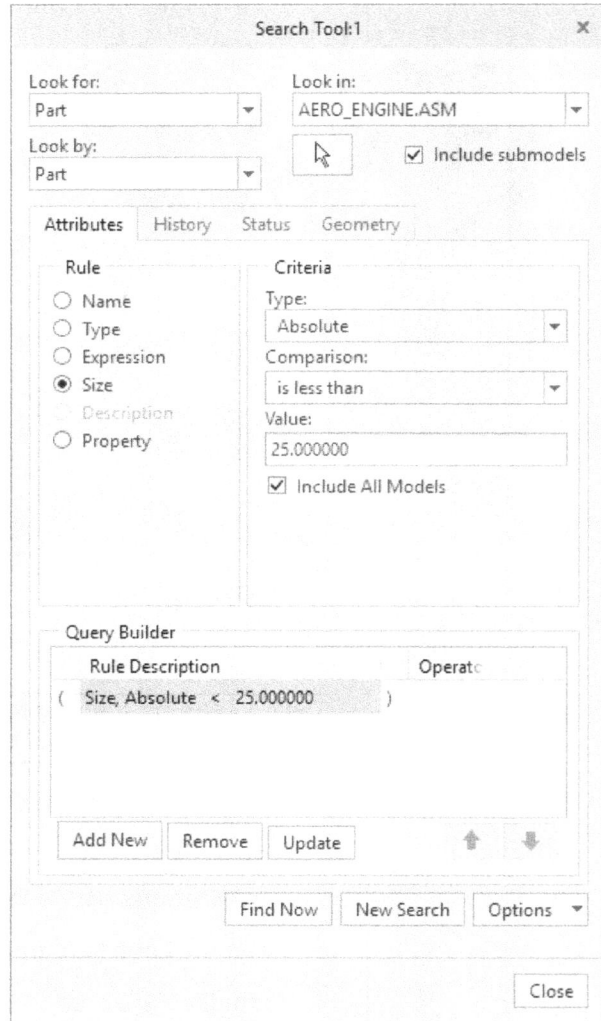

Figure 1–25

8. In the *Rule* area, select **Name**.

9. In the *Value* field, type ***bolt***.

10. Click **Add New** to add the rule, as shown in Figure 1–26.

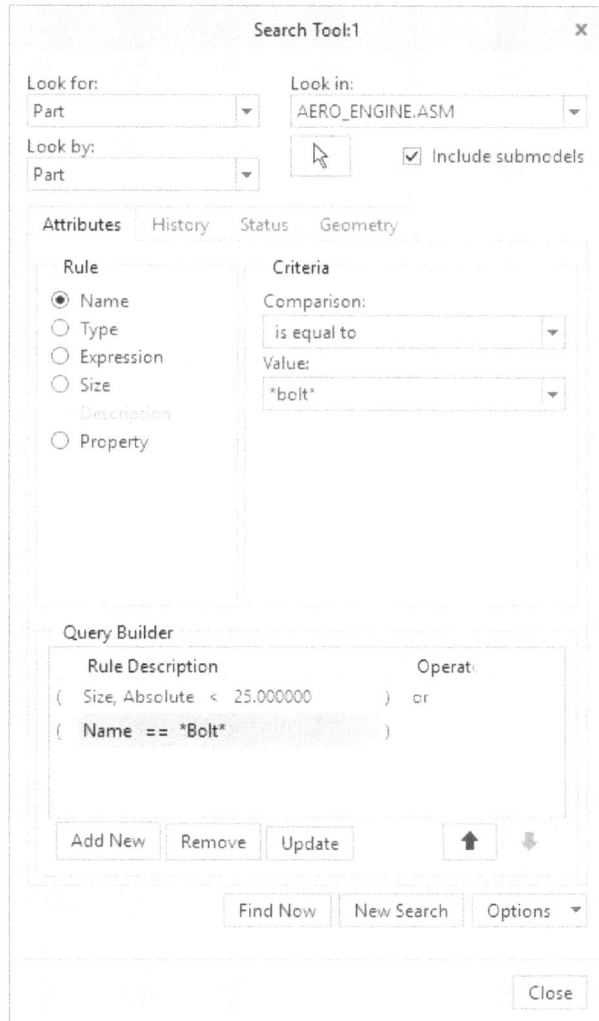

| Search Tool:1 | ✕ |

Look for:
Part ▾

Look in:
AERO_ENGINE.ASM ▾

Look by:
Part ▾

☑ Include submodels

Attributes | History | Status | Geometry

Rule
- ⦿ Name
- ○ Type
- ○ Expression
- ○ Size
- Description
- ○ Property

Criteria
Comparison:
is equal to ▾
Value:
bolt ▾

Query Builder

Rule Description	Operat
(Size, Absolute < 25.000000	) or
(Name == *Bolt*	)

Add New | Remove | Update | ⬆ ⬇

Find Now | New Search | Options ▾

Close

Figure 1–26

11. Click **Find Now**.

12. Select all of the 45 objects in the *items found* list and click
    ⟫ (Add Item) to select them.

13. Click **Close**.

14. Right-click and select 🗎 (Suppress) in the mini toolbar.

15. Click **OK** in the Suppress dialog box. The model updates as shown in Figure 1–27.

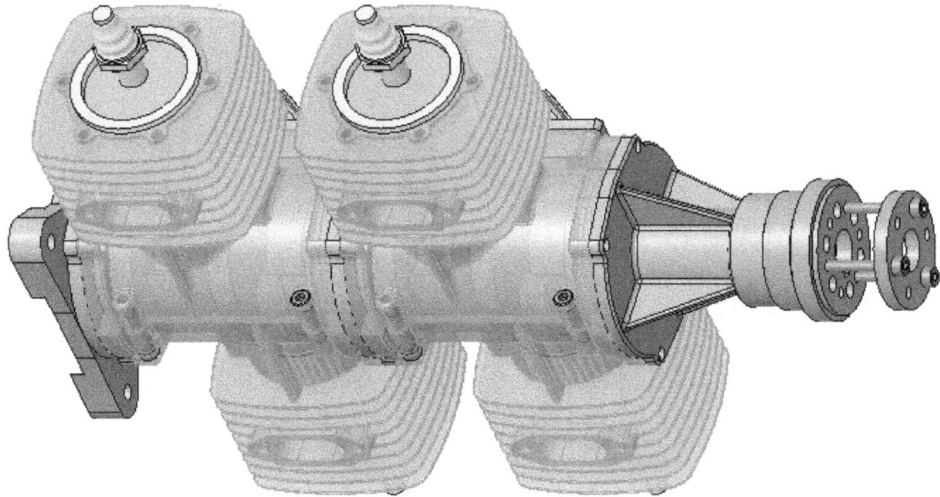

Figure 1–27

Task 5 - Use the Model Tree search tool to select all components with "piston" in their name.

1. In the Model Tree, type **piston**, as shown in Figure 1–28.

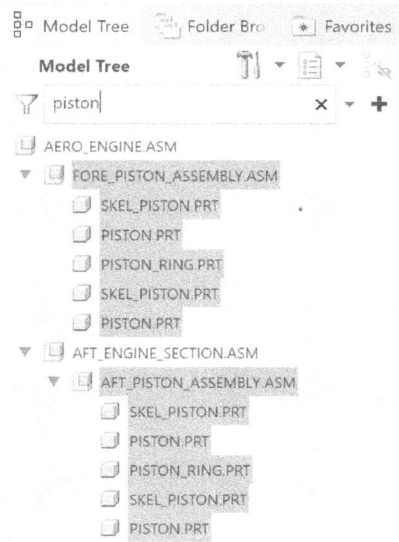

Figure 1–28

2. Click ✚ (Add Marked) to add the components to the selection buffer.

3. Right-click and select ✎ (Hide) in the mini toolbar.

4. In the Model Tree, click ✕ (Clear Search) to deactivate it, as shown in Figure 1–29.

Figure 1–29

Task 6 - Use the 3D Box Select tool to select components.

1. In the lower right of the Creo Parametric window, click ▭ (3D Box Select).

2. Select the surface shown in Figure 1–30.

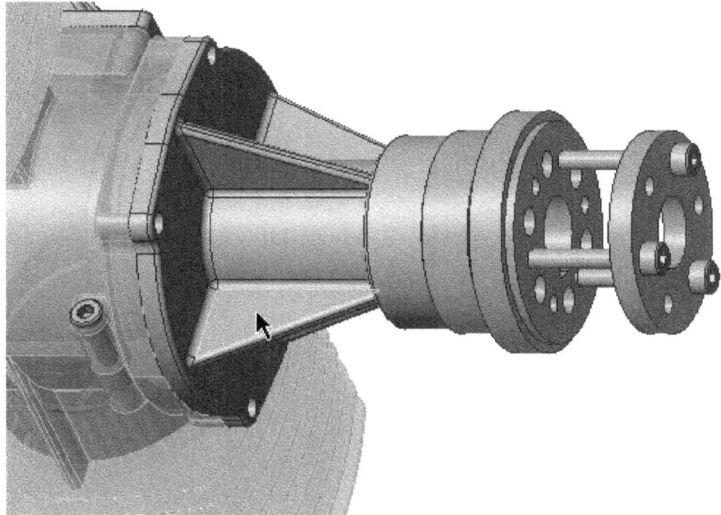

Figure 1–30

3. Click the two locations shown in Figure 1–31 to create a rectangle. **Note:** Select the corner on the right first.

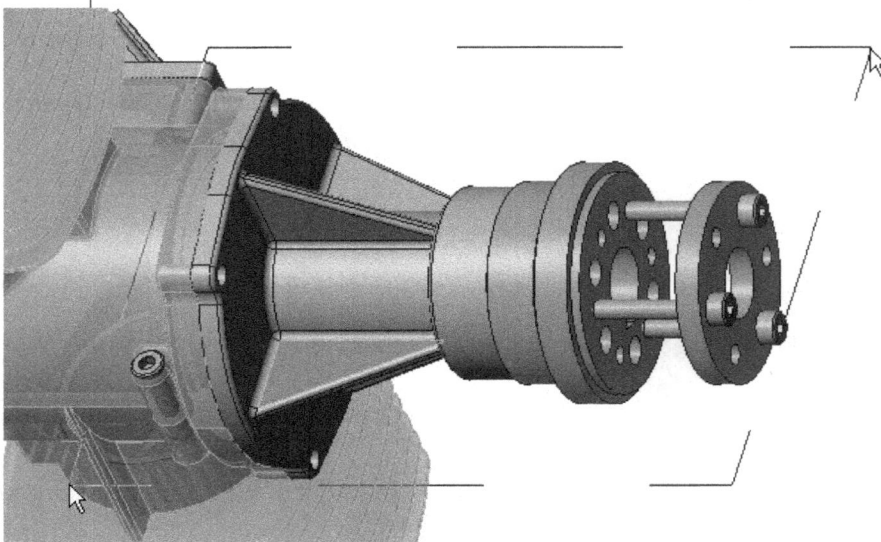

Figure 1–31

4. The selection box displays as shown in Figure 1–32.

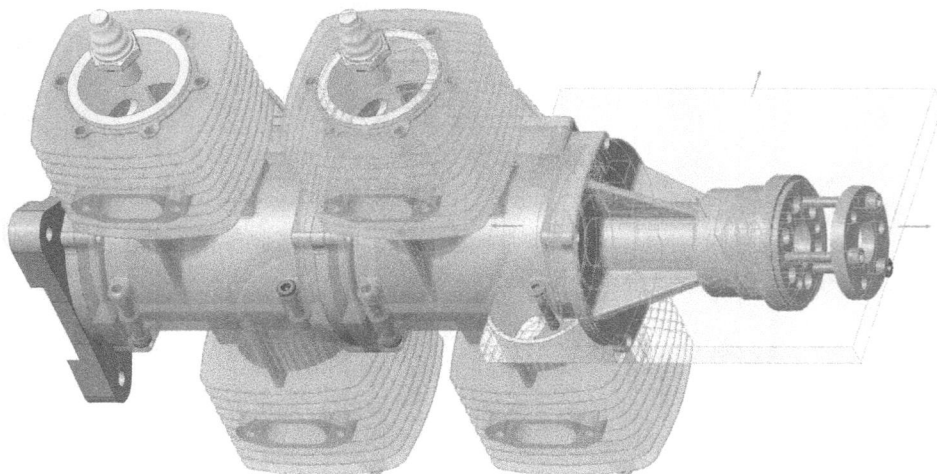

Figure 1–32

5. Select and drag the arrows until only the components shown in Figure 1–33 highlight.

You might have to drag the down arrow to select all of the bolts.

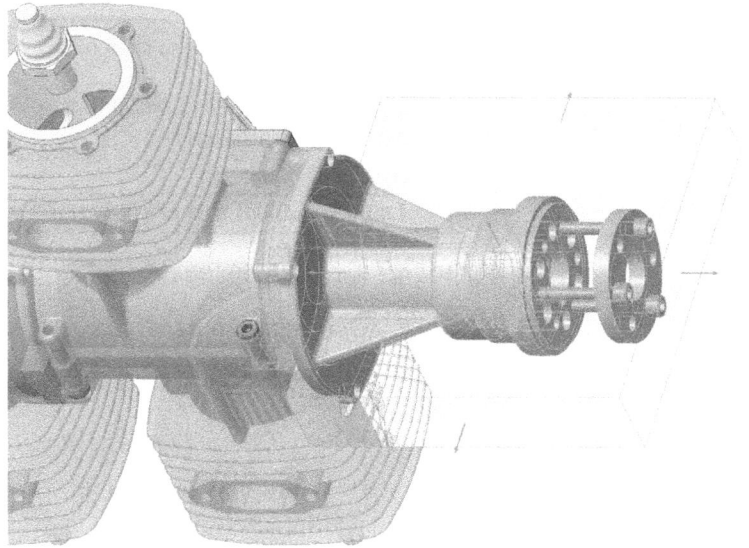

Figure 1–33

6. Right-click and select ✎ (Hide) in the mini toolbar. The model displays as shown in Figure 1–34.

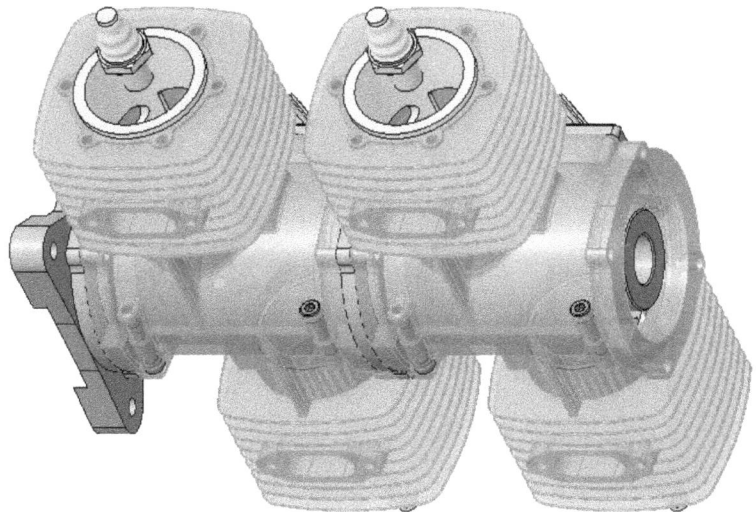

Figure 1–34

7. Save the assembly and erase it from memory.

Practice 1b | Model Tree Search

Practice Objective

- Use the Model Tree to search.

In this practice, you will use the Model Tree to search the contents of a model.

Task 1 - Open the engine.asm model.

1. Set the working directory to *Assembly_MT_Search*.

2. Open **engine.asm**.

3. Set the model display as follows:

- ⁕ *(Datum Display Filters)*: All Off
- ⅜ *(Spin Center)*: Off
- ⬚ *(Display Style)*: ⬚ (Shading With Edges)

The model displays as shown in Figure 1–35.

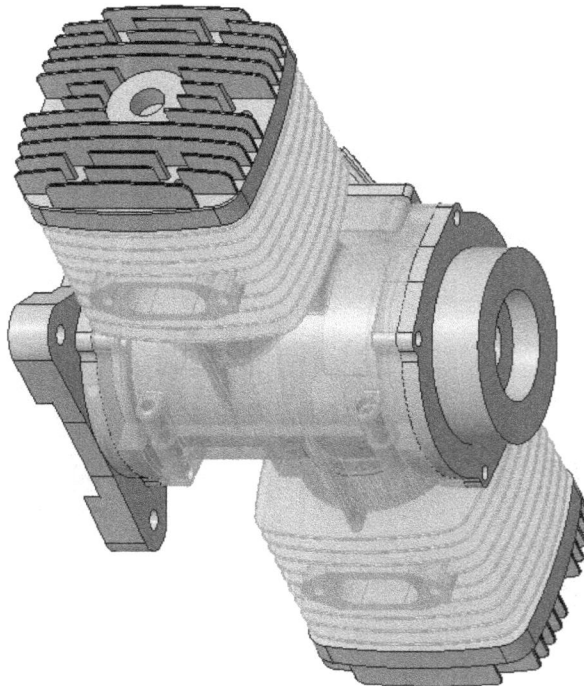

Figure 1–35

Task 2 - Review the enhanced Model Tree search and filtering.

Note the objects with those letters in the name are highlighted, the tree filters to only those objects, and they are also highlighted in the model itself.

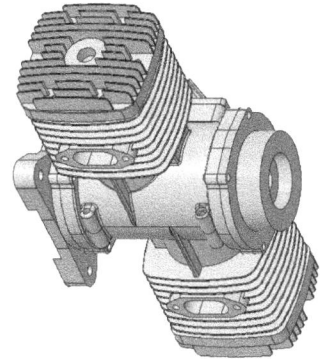

1. In the Model Tree, expand the **AFT_ENGINE_SECTION.ASM** and **AFT_PISTON_ASSEMBLY.ASM** nodes to see all of the components in the assembly.

2. Search for objects with *coupling* in the name. In the Model Tree search bar, type **co**, as shown in Figure 1–36.

Figure 1–36

3. Complete the word **coupling** and note that only objects containing coupling are filtered, as shown in Figure 1–37.

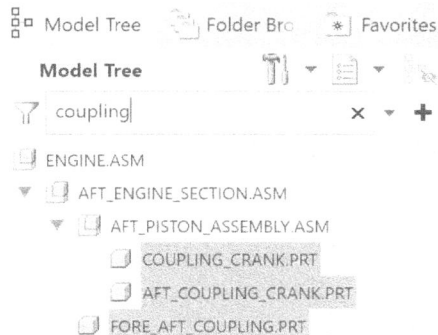

Figure 1–37

4. To see the found objects without filtering, click ⊽ (Filter) next to the search bar and the Model Tree updates as shown in Figure 1–38.

Note the ⊽ (Filter) icon switches to 🔍 (Search), indicating that search results are no longer filtered.

Figure 1–38

5. In the Model Tree, click 🔍 (Search) to return to filter mode.

6. In the Model Tree, click ✛ (Add Marked) to select the found objects.

7. Note that the highlight color changes, indicating that they are now selected, as shown in Figure 1–39.

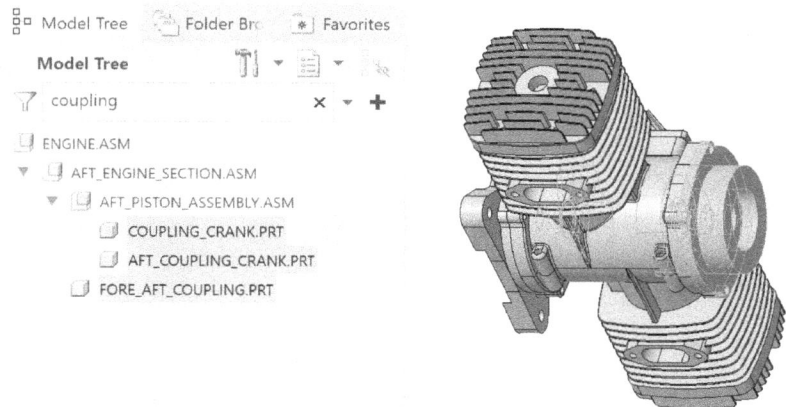

Figure 1–39

8. Click anywhere on the screen to remove the objects from selection, but note that they are still filtered.

9. Click ✕ (Clear Search) to cancel.

Task 3 - Hide objects using the new options.

1. In the Model Tree, click ⌄ (Show Recent Queries) next to the search bar, and note that any recent searches are available, as shown in Figure 1–40.

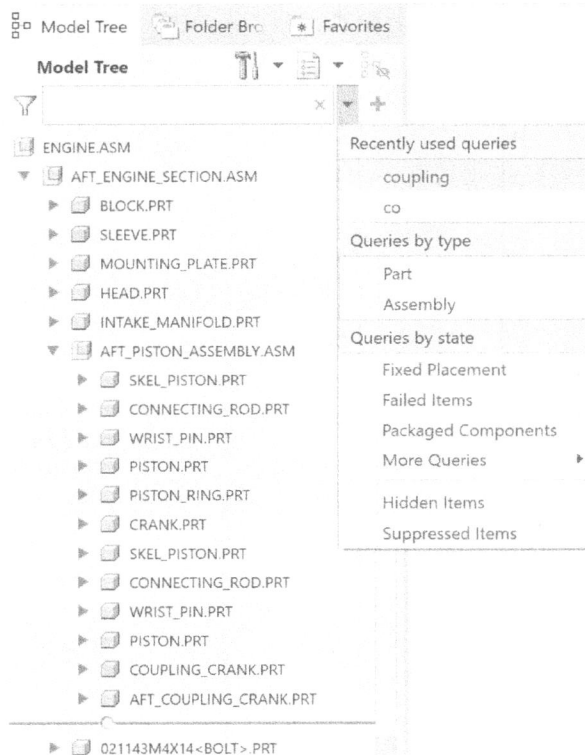

Figure 1–40

2. Select coupling from the list to filter the Model Tree.

3. Click ✛ (Add Marked) to select the components.

4. Right-click and select 👁 (Show Only). The model updates as shown in Figure 1–41.

Only the selected components are displayed when you use 👁 *(Show Only).*

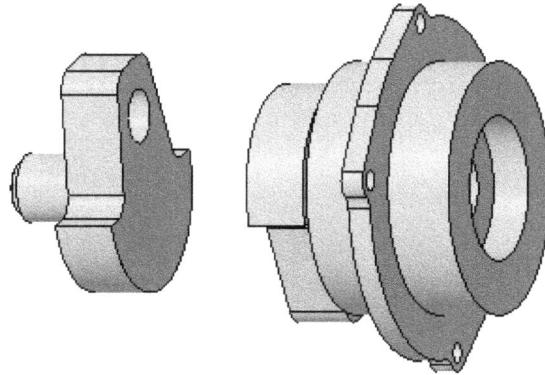

Figure 1–41

5. Click ✕ (Clear Search).

6. To quickly select all of the parts, use a predefined query. In the Model Tree, click ▾ (Show Recent Queries) and in the *Queries by state* section, select **Hidden Items**, as shown in Figure 1–42.

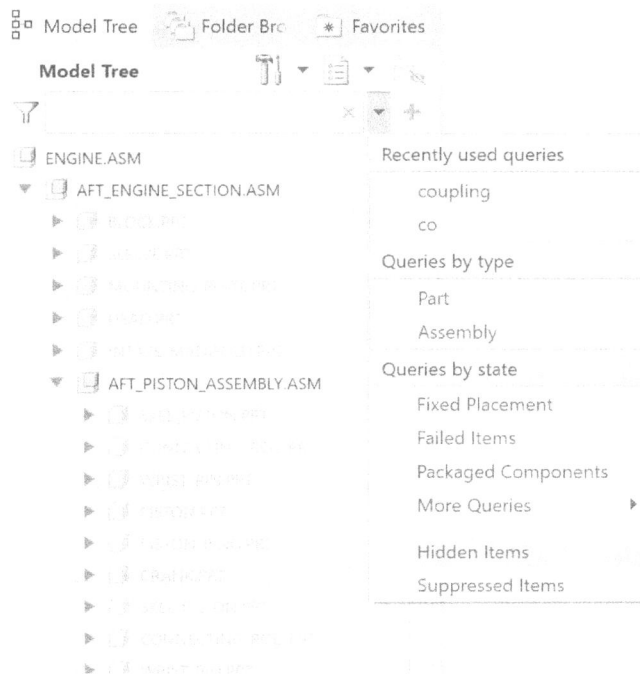

Figure 1–42

7. All of the objects that are hidden are found. Click ✛ (Add Marked).

8. Right-click and select ◉ (Show).

9. Click ✕ (Clear Search) and select anywhere on the screen to clear all selections.

10. Click ▾ (Show Recent Queries) and select **coupling**.

11. Click ✛ (Add Marked).

12. Right-click and select ▨ (Show All Except). The model updates as shown in Figure 1–43.

Note that in this case, the selected objects are removed from display.

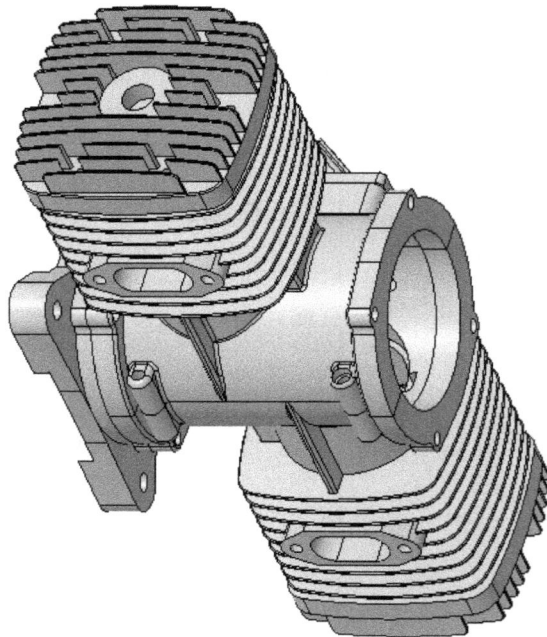

Figure 1–43

13. The objects should still be filtered in the Model Tree. Click ✛ (Add Marked).

14. Right-click and select ◉ (Show).

15. Click ✕ (Clear Search) and select anywhere on the screen to clear all selections.

Task 4 - Search the Model Tree to find objects developed by a specific designer using values found in the Model Tree columns.

1. In the Model Tree, click 🛠 ▾ (Settings)>**Tree Columns**. The Model Tree Columns dialog box opens, as shown in Figure 1–44.

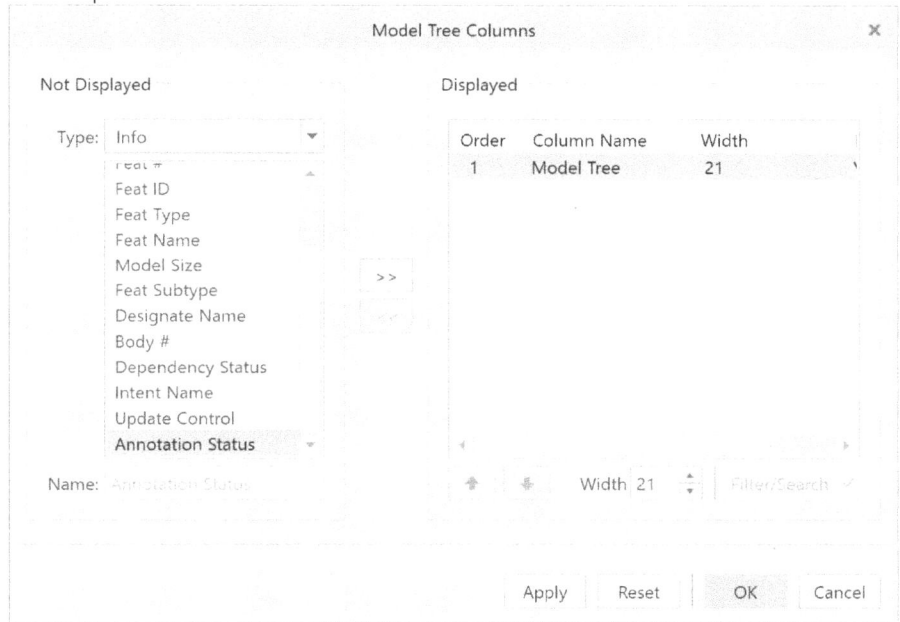

Model Tree Columns ✕

Not Displayed   Displayed

Type: Info   ▾   Order   Column Name   Width
      Feat #   1   Model Tree   21
      Feat ID
      Feat Type
      Feat Name
      Model Size
      Feat Subtype   >>
      Designate Name
      Body #
      Dependency Status
      Intent Name
      Update Control
      Annotation Status   ▾

Name: Annotation Status   ↑   ↓   Width 21 ⇕   Filter/Search ▾

                        Apply   Reset   OK   Cancel

Figure 1–44

2. In the Type drop-down list, select **Model Params**.

3. In the list of parameters, select **MODELED_BY** and click ≫ (Add Column).

4. Edit the *Width* to **8**.

5. Click **OK**. The Model Tree updates as shown in Figure 1–45.

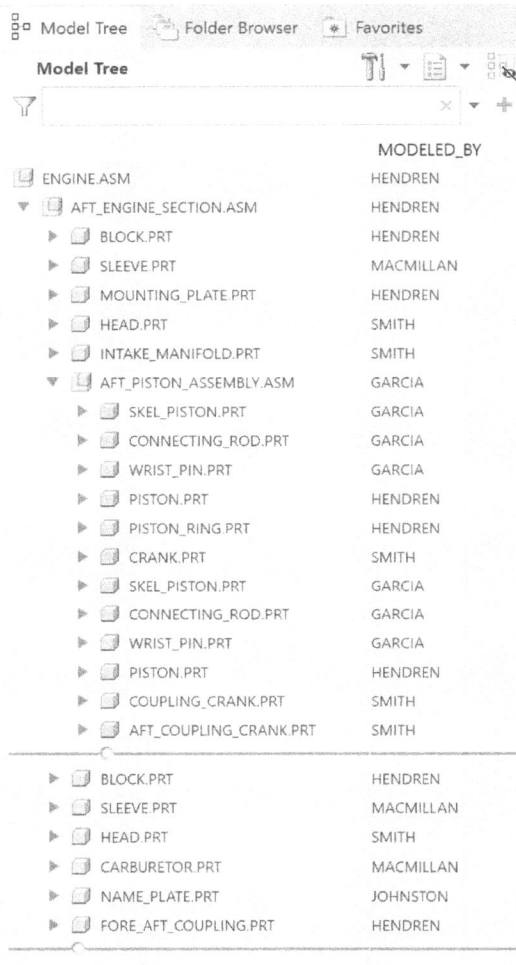

	MODELED_BY
⬛ ENGINE.ASM	HENDREN
▼ ⬛ AFT_ENGINE_SECTION.ASM	HENDREN
▶ ⬛ BLOCK.PRT	HENDREN
▶ ⬛ SLEEVE.PRT	MACMILLAN
▶ ⬛ MOUNTING_PLATE.PRT	HENDREN
▶ ⬛ HEAD.PRT	SMITH
▶ ⬛ INTAKE_MANIFOLD.PRT	SMITH
▼ ⬛ AFT_PISTON_ASSEMBLY.ASM	GARCIA
▶ ⬛ SKEL_PISTON.PRT	GARCIA
▶ ⬛ CONNECTING_ROD.PRT	GARCIA
▶ ⬛ WRIST_PIN.PRT	GARCIA
▶ ⬛ PISTON.PRT	HENDREN
▶ ⬛ PISTON_RING.PRT	HENDREN
▶ ⬛ CRANK.PRT	SMITH
▶ ⬛ SKEL_PISTON.PRT	GARCIA
▶ ⬛ CONNECTING_ROD.PRT	GARCIA
▶ ⬛ WRIST_PIN.PRT	GARCIA
▶ ⬛ PISTON.PRT	HENDREN
▶ ⬛ COUPLING_CRANK.PRT	SMITH
▶ ⬛ AFT_COUPLING_CRANK.PRT	SMITH
▶ ⬛ BLOCK.PRT	HENDREN
▶ ⬛ SLEEVE.PRT	MACMILLAN
▶ ⬛ HEAD.PRT	SMITH
▶ ⬛ CARBURETOR.PRT	MACMILLAN
▶ ⬛ NAME_PLATE.PRT	JOHNSTON
▶ ⬛ FORE_AFT_COUPLING.PRT	HENDREN

Figure 1–45

6. Right-click in the search bar and enable **MODELED_BY**, as shown in Figure 1–46.

By enabling
MODELED_BY, *any*
search is applied to the
values found in the
MODELED_BY column,
rather than part names.

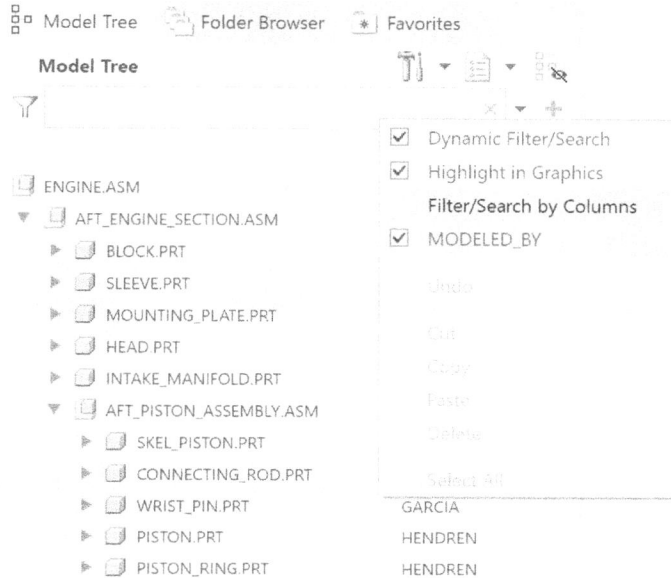

Model Tree   Folder Browser   Favorites

Model Tree

☑ Dynamic Filter/Search
☑ Highlight in Graphics
   Filter/Search by Columns
☑ MODELED_BY
   Undo
   Cut
   Copy
   Paste
   Delete
   Select All

ENGINE.ASM
  ▼ AFT_ENGINE_SECTION.ASM
    ▶ BLOCK.PRT
    ▶ SLEEVE.PRT
    ▶ MOUNTING_PLATE.PRT
    ▶ HEAD.PRT
    ▶ INTAKE_MANIFOLD.PRT
    ▼ AFT_PISTON_ASSEMBLY.ASM
      ▶ SKEL_PISTON.PRT
      ▶ CONNECTING_ROD.PRT
      ▶ WRIST_PIN.PRT   GARCIA
      ▶ PISTON.PRT   HENDREN
      ▶ PISTON_RING.PRT   HENDREN

Figure 1–46

7. In the search field, type **SMITH** and note that the Model Tree filters as shown in Figure 1–47.

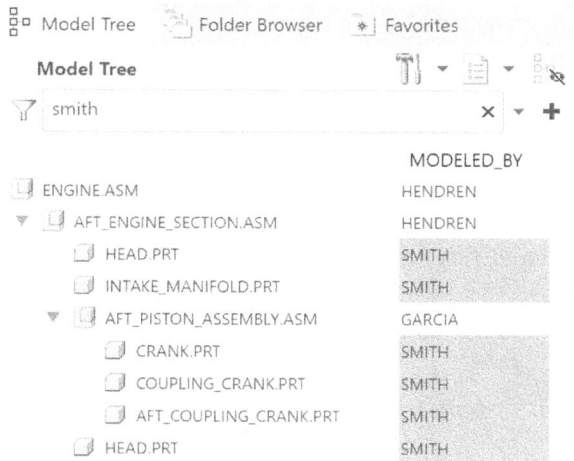

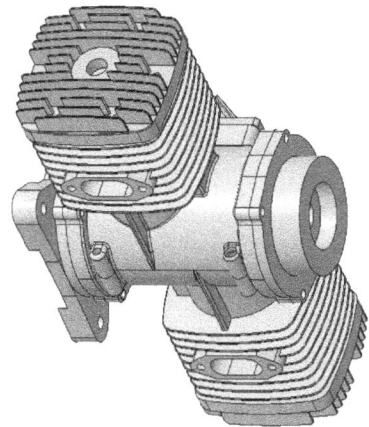

Model Tree   Folder Browser   Favorites

Model Tree

smith

	MODELED_BY
ENGINE.ASM	HENDREN
▼ AFT_ENGINE_SECTION.ASM	HENDREN
HEAD.PRT	SMITH
INTAKE_MANIFOLD.PRT	SMITH
▼ AFT_PISTON_ASSEMBLY.ASM	GARCIA
CRANK.PRT	SMITH
COUPLING_CRANK.PRT	SMITH
AFT_COUPLING_CRANK.PRT	SMITH
HEAD.PRT	SMITH

Figure 1–47

8. Select the first instance of **HEAD.PRT** and click 📂 (Open) from the mini toolbar.

9. In the In-graphics toolbar, enable λ_{σ} (Csys Display). The model displays as shown in Figure 1–48.

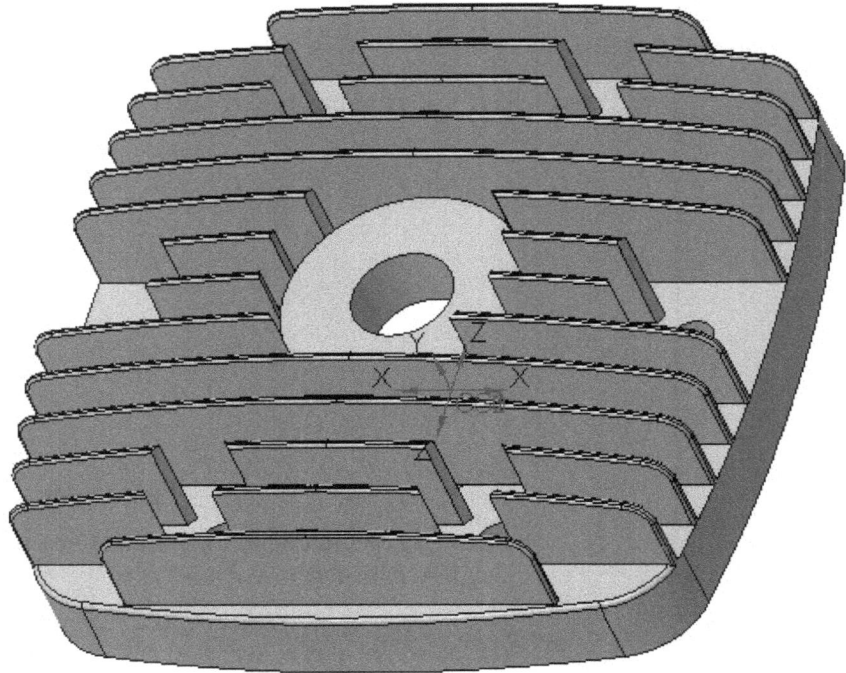

Figure 1–48

Task 5 - Search the Model Tree for coordinate system features and hide them.

---

1. In the Model Tree, type **CS** in the search field and note that the Model Tree filters as shown in Figure 1–49.

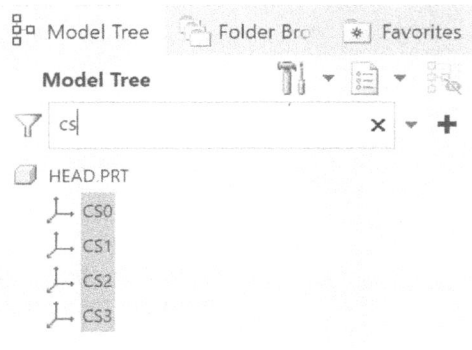

Figure 1–49

2. Click ✛ (Add Marked) to select the components.

3. Right-click and select ✎ (Hide). The model updates as shown in Figure 1–50.

The search capabilities work for components and features.

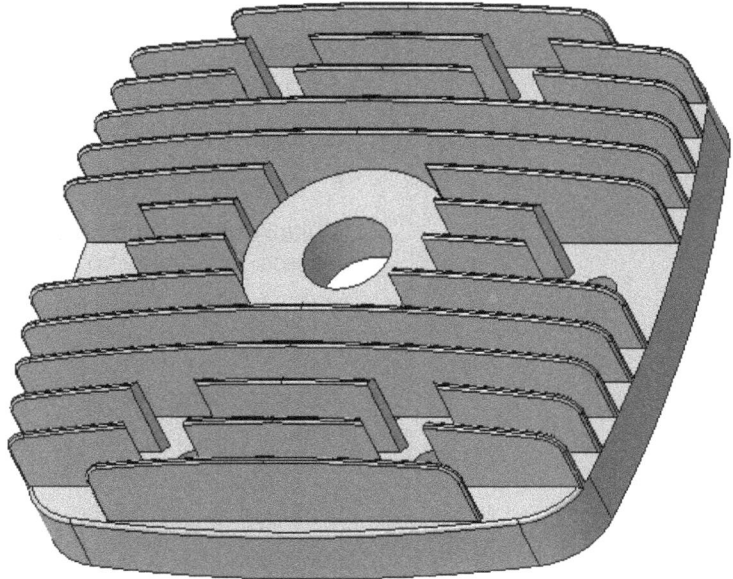

Figure 1–50

4. Close the part window.

5. In the assembly window, in the Model Tree, click ▯ ⌄ (Settings)>**Reset Tree Settings**>**Reset Tree Settings**.

6. Close all files and erase them from memory.

Chapter Review Questions

1. Which of the following Attributes can you search by in the Search Tool dialog box?

   a. Feature

   b. Size

   c. Name

   d. Type

   e. All of the above

2. Multiple rules can be combined by building a Query in the Search Tool dialog box.

   a. True

   b. False

3. You can search for values directly in the Model Tree search field.

   a. True

   b. False

4. Once you click a rectangle to define a 3D bounding box for selection, you can no longer change its size.

   a. True

   b. False

5. By default, when you enter text in the Model Tree search field, the system searches parameter values as well.

   a. True

   b. False

Answers: 1.e, 2.a, 3.a, 4.b, 5.b

Advanced Component Placement

Components are placed in an assembly using assembly constraints. Some advanced techniques are available that can be used to make component placement more efficient. These techniques involve referencing an existing component in an assembly to assemble the same component again. Alternatively, you can use component interfaces to set up a standard set of constraints that are always used when that component is assembled. Flexible components enable you to display a component in different geometric states, while still reporting it in the Bill of Materials as the same component.

Learning Objectives in This Chapter

- Use the **Repeat** command to quickly add the same component multiple times in the same assembly.
- Use the **Reference** pattern option to pattern a component that is constrained to a part or subassembly that has previously been patterned.
- Use the **Component Interface** option to predefine constraints and references.
- Place the component by selecting a location or using the **Auto Place** command.
- Learn to display a component using different geometric representations using the Flexible option.
- Learn to use the **Copy**, **Paste**, and **Paste Special** commands to duplicate a part or subassembly in an assembly.

2.1 Repeating Components

In many cases, components are duplicated in the assembly using the same assembly constraints, with small variations in the references or offset values. Creo Parametric provides an option that enables you to repeat constraints and make the required modifications.

How To: Repeat the Placement of an Existing Component

1. To access the ↺ (Repeat) command, you must select the part. Begin by setting the selection filter to **Part** before selecting, and then use the following options to repeat an existing component in an assembly, as shown in Figure 2–1:

   • Select the component and click ↺ (Repeat) in the *Model* tab.

   • Select the component in the graphics window, right-click, and select **Repeat**.

   • In the Model Tree, right-click on the component and select **Repeat**. This method does not require you to change the selection filter.

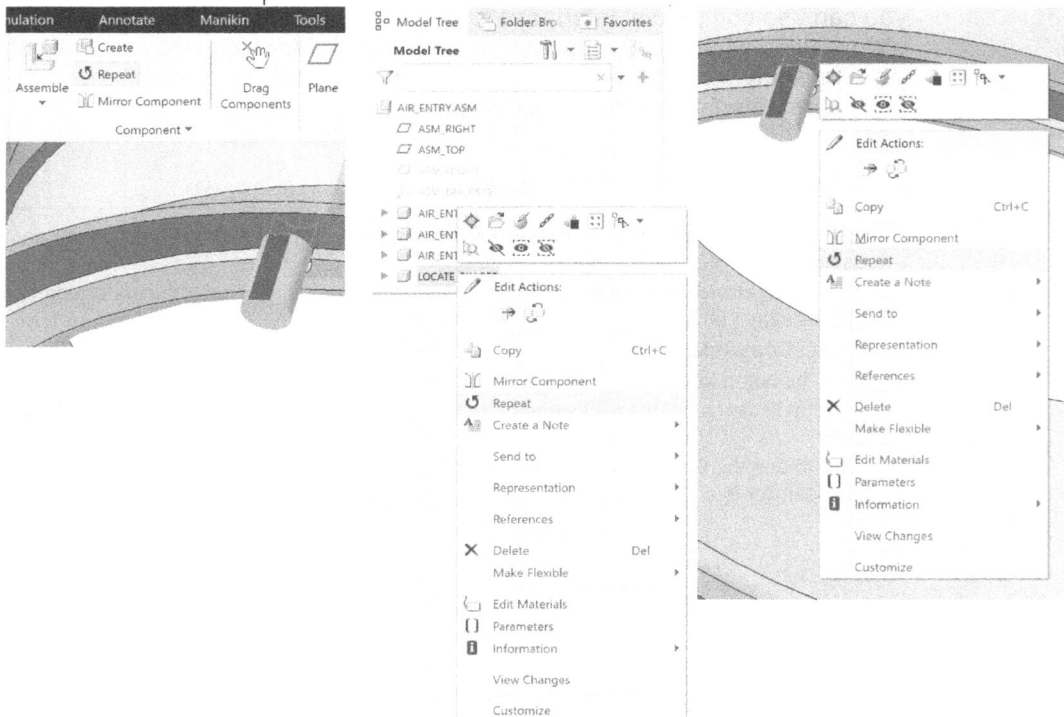

Figure 2–1

The Repeat Component dialog box opens as shown in Figure 2–2. The constraints and references used to assemble the selected component are listed in the *Variable Assembly Refs* area in the dialog box.

The LOCATE_PIN was assembled using two Coincident and one Parallel constraints

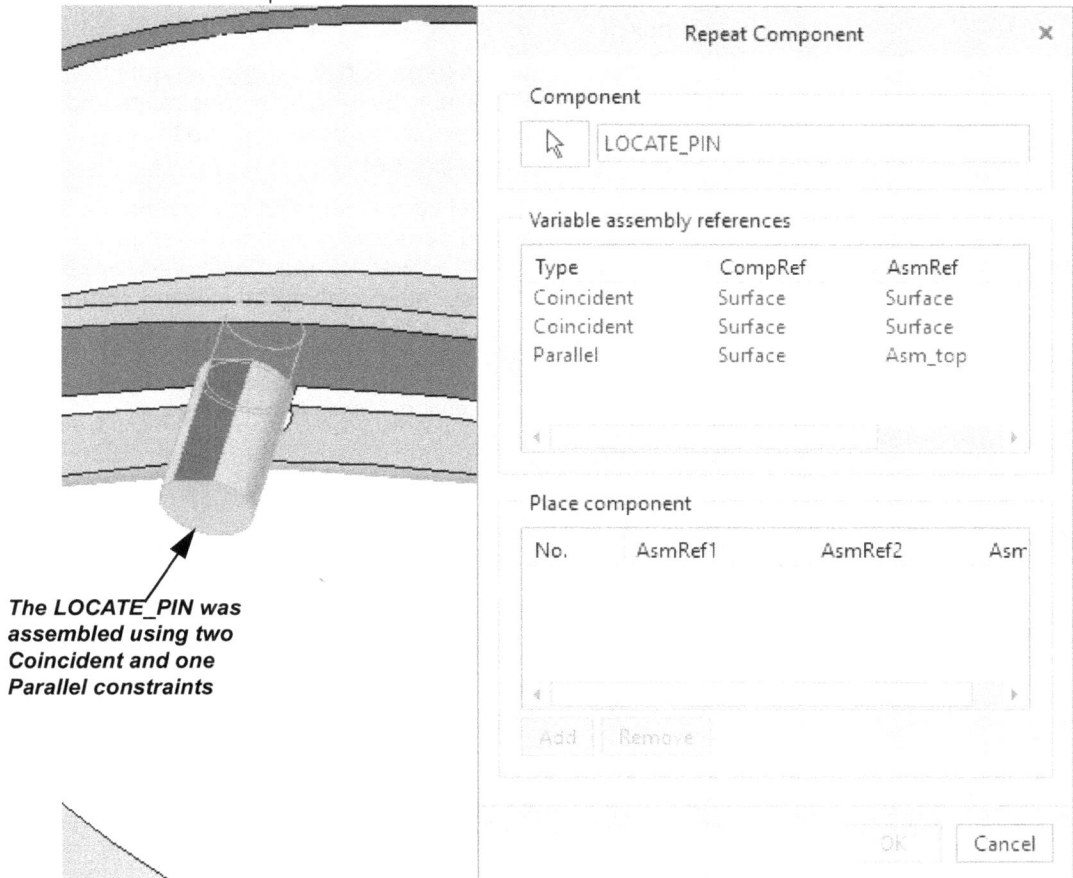

Figure 2–2

2. To reuse the constraints listed in the *Variable Assembly References* area, select the constraints and click **Add**. The system prompts you for a new assembly reference for each constraint. Once the references have been selected, the instance is listed in the *Place Component* area in the dialog box.

Figure 2–3 shows three additional components that were added to the assembly by repeating constraints and selecting new references from those used to place the original **LOCATE_PIN** component.

- Each additional component that is repeated must use the same selected constraints as the first repeated component. If you want to reuse a different combination of constraints, you must confirm the existing components and click ↺ to repeat the additional component.

Three additional LOCATE_PIN components are repeated by selecting a new alignment reference for each instance. The second Coincident reference is maintained, as indicated in the Place Component area.

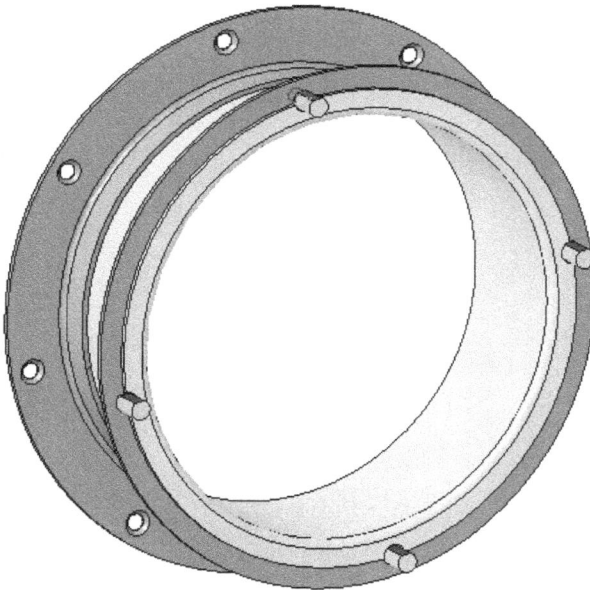

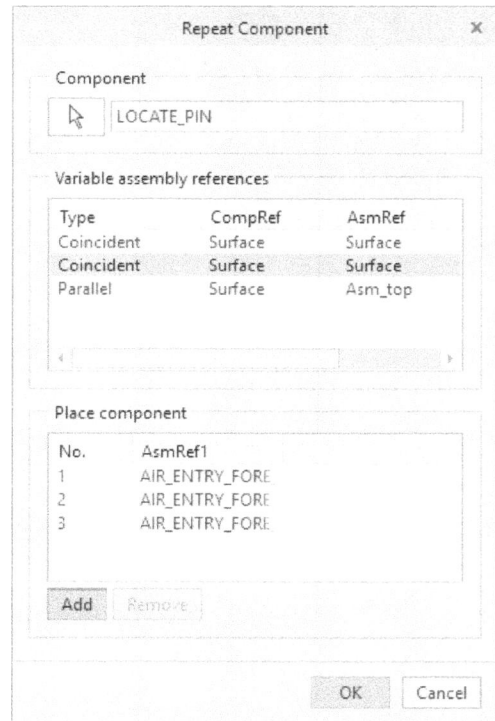

Figure 2–3

3. Once the new references have been selected, click **OK** to complete the **Repeat** operation.

2.2 Reference Patterns

All of the pattern types that you learned about for parts (e.g., tables, fill, etc.) can also be used for Assembly mode components.

Reference patterns enable you to reference an existing pattern of a component or feature pattern. The **Reference** option is only available when the component to be patterned references the leader of the original pattern.

Figure 2–4 shows an example of a reference pattern. The bolt is constrained to the assembly using the leader of the existing component (the washer) that was patterned.

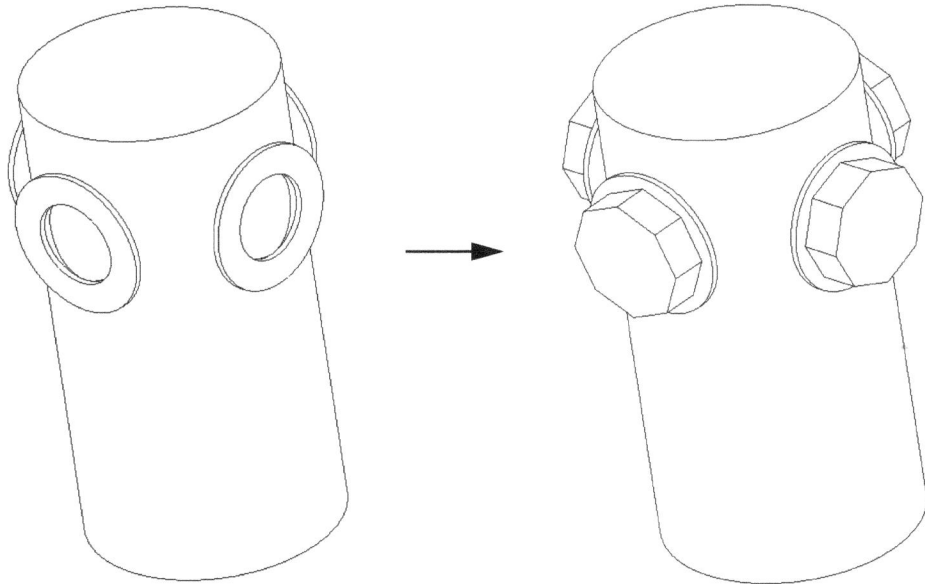

Figure 2–4

How To: Create a Reference Pattern

1. To start the creation of a pattern, select the component to be patterned and click ⊞ (Pattern).
2. If the component being patterned references another pattern, the **Reference** pattern type is selected by default. If not already selected, select **Reference** in the **Pattern Type** menu, as shown in Figure 2–5.

Figure 2–5

Reference patterns do not provide modifiable parameters for the number of instances or the increment values. The pattern is dependent on the parent pattern. However, you can, exclude any unwanted members by selecting the black hotspots.

3. Click ✔ (OK) to complete the pattern. The reference pattern is created automatically.

2.3 Component Interfaces

Component interfaces enable you to predefine constraints and references in a part or subassembly. When you assemble a component with a predefined interface, you are prompted to select an interface or manually assemble an interface.

How To: Create a New Interface

1. To create an interface in a part or subassembly, click
   (Component Interface) in the *Model* tab. The
   COMPONENT INTERFACE dialog box opens as shown in
   Figure 2–6.

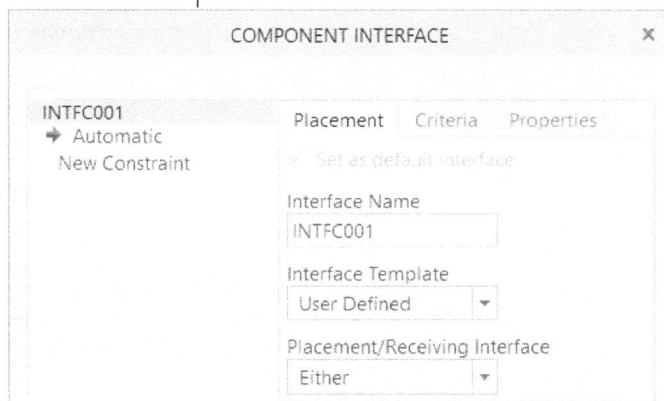

Adds and removes interfaces. Multiple interfaces can be defined. It also sets the interface that is available by default when assembled.

Adds connections for use in MDX.

Figure 2–6

2. Enter a meaningful name for the interface using the *Interface Name* field or accept the default name. Select the constraint type in the Constraint Type drop-down list, as shown at the top in Figure 2–7. If required, enter an *Offset* value. Select the type and enter an offset value for the constraint, if required. Select the reference on the model (e.g., surface, edge, axis, etc.). Add any additional constraints as required to fully define the interface.

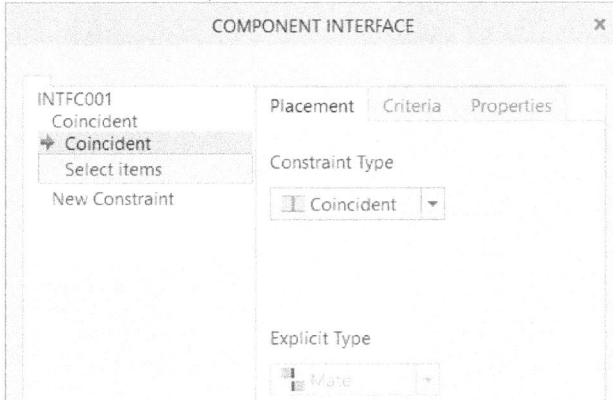

COMPONENT INTERFACE

INTFC001
  Coincident
→ Coincident
  Select items
  New Constraint

Placement   Criteria   Properties

Constraint Type

⊥ Coincident ▼

Explicit Type

≡ Mate ▼

Adds and removes the constraints and component references that are used when the component is assembled into a top-level assembly. Multiple constraints can be defined for a component.

Figure 2–7

*To set placement preferences for use with the component interface, select **File> Options>Assembly**.*

3. (Optional) Select the *Criteria* tab, as shown at the bottom in Figure 2–8. Define the conditions to refine the selection of the assembly reference (e.g., Name = A_1 would assign an **A_1** reference from the assembly).

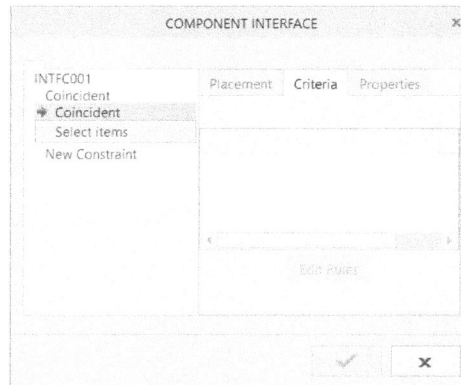

COMPONENT INTERFACE

INTFC001
  Coincident
→ Coincident
  Select items
  New Constraint

Placement   Criteria   Properties

Edit Rules

✓   ✗

Enables you to assign conditions to help you select assembly references.

Figure 2–8

To assemble the component manually, click ⬒.

When you assemble a component that has a predefined interface, the *Component Placement* tab opens as shown in Figure 2–9. The tab lists the interfaces that have been defined in the component.

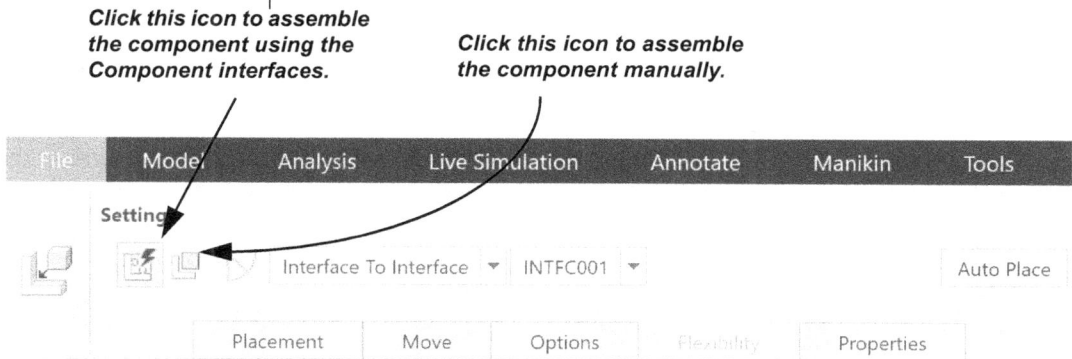

Click this icon to assemble the component using the Component interfaces.

Click this icon to assemble the component manually.

File	Model	Analysis	Live Simulation	Annotate	Manikin	Tools

Setting

Interface To Interface ▼ INTFC001 ▼   Auto Place

Placement   Move   Options   Flexibility   Properties

Figure 2–9

4. To assemble the component using an interface, select the appropriate assembly references.

Auto Place

If you click **Auto Place** in the *Component Placement* tab, the component can be placed by selecting a point on the model in the area of the required placement. If the appropriate references are available in the selected area, the component is placed automatically. If several reference options are in that area, the Auto Place dialog box opens. Use this dialog box to select the appropriate reference to use, as shown in Figure 2–10.

The number of references listed in the Auto Place dialog box varies, based on the references available in the selected location.

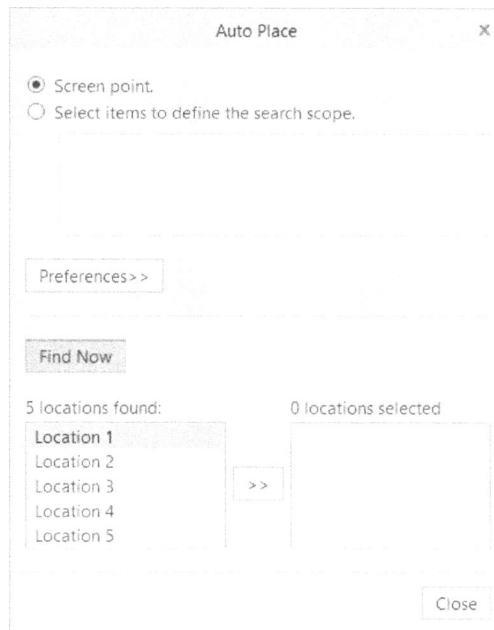

Auto Place   ✕

◉ Screen point.
◯ Select items to define the search scope.

Preferences>>

Find Now

5 locations found: 0 locations selected

Location 1
Location 2
Location 3   >>
Location 4
Location 5

Close

Figure 2–10

2.4 Flexible Components

Flexible components are identified in the Model Tree using 🗒 for components and 🗒 for assemblies.

Flexible components enable you to display a component in different geometric representations, while still reporting it in the Bill of Materials report. For example, **spring.prt** (model shown in Figure 2–11) has been assembled three times. Two of the three components are flexible, and identified by 🗒 in the Model Tree. The spring was varied for the flexible components by changing the length and pitch dimensions.

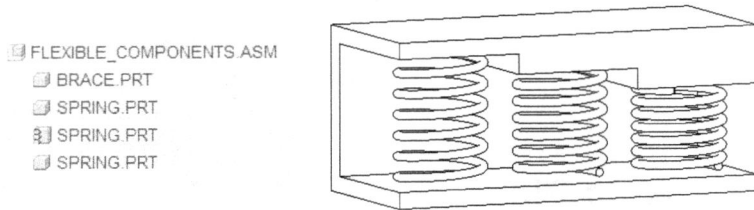

🗒 FLEXIBLE_COMPONENTS.ASM
   🗒 BRACE.PRT
   🗒 SPRING.PRT
   🗒 SPRING.PRT
   🗒 SPRING.PRT

Figure 2–11

How To: Create a Flexible Component

1. To assemble a flexible component into an assembly, you can use any of the following techniques:
   - Components can be made flexible in Part mode by selecting **File>Prepare>Model Properties**. The Model Properties dialog box opens. Select **change** next to *Flexible*, as shown at the top in Figure 2–12. The Flexibility dialog box opens, as shown at the bottom in Figure 2–12.

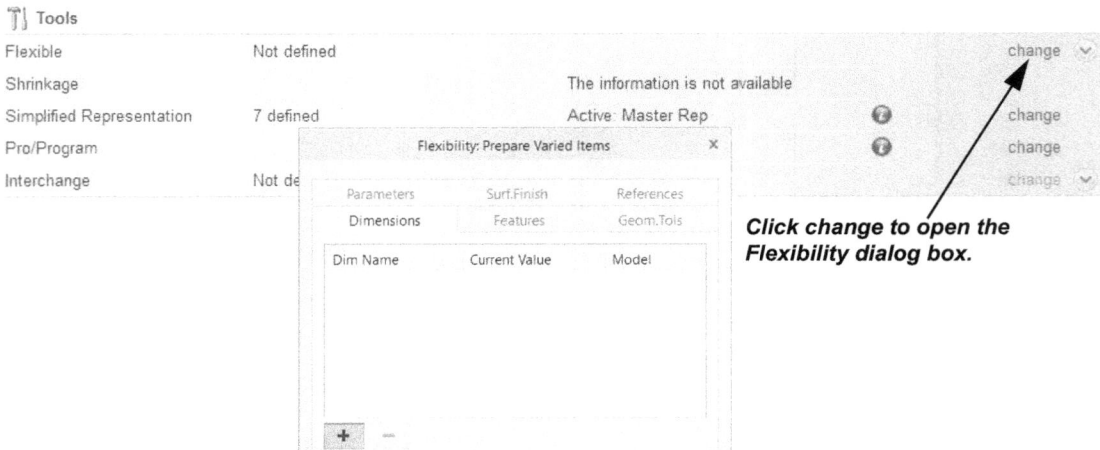

🗒 Tools

Flexible	Not defined			change ∨
Shrinkage		The information is not available		
Simplified Representation	7 defined	Active: Master Rep	🛈	change
Pro/Program			🛈	change
Interchange	Not de			change ∨

Flexibility: Prepare Varied Items   ✕

Parameters	Surf.Finish	References
Dimensions	Features	Geom.Tols

Dim Name	Current Value	Model

➕ ➖

Click change to open the Flexibility dialog box.

Figure 2–12

- Components can be made flexible while they are being assembled by expanding ⬚ (Assemble) in the *Model* tab and select **Flexible**.
- Components can be made flexible after the component has been placed in the assembly by right-clicking and selecting **Make Flexible**.

2. Regardless of the method used to create a flexible component, the Varied Items dialog box opens, as shown in Figure 2–13. The sub-window options at the top of the dialog box only display in Assembly mode.

Subassemblies can also be made flexible. In this situation, an additional Components tab is available in the Varied Items dialog box.

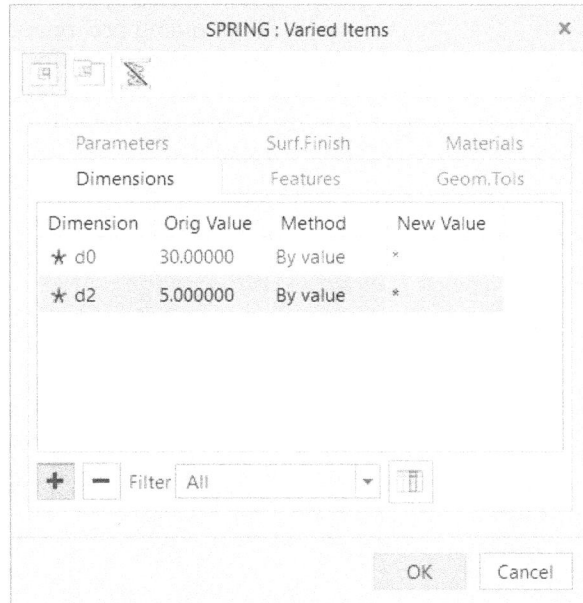

Figure 2–13

You can vary any of the following items to create a flexible component:

- Dimensions and Dimension Tolerances

- Features

- Components (for flexible subassemblies)

- Geometric Tolerances

- Parameters

- Surface Finishes

- Materials

Using flexible components increases the assembly file size by approximately the size of the flexible model file. This should be a consideration when applying flexibility to complex models.

Tabs corresponding to each of these items are available in the Varied Items dialog box. By adding items and defining new values in the Varied Items dialog box, you can generate different flexible representations. If flexibility was predefined in the part model, you can edit its definition in the assembly to make changes.

3. To complete the creation of a flexible component in Part mode, click **OK**. When this component is used in an assembly, you are prompted to confirm whether you want to use it for flexible component definition. If so, click **Yes** in the Confirm dialog box, as shown in Figure 2–14. The Varied Items dialog box opens after you confirm, enabling you to enter a new value for any of the varied items.

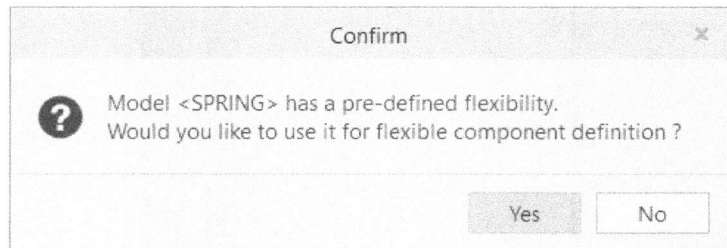

Figure 2–14

4. To complete the creation of a flexible component in Assembly mode, click **OK** to parametrically place the component in the assembly.

When you right-click on a component that has been made flexible, you can access the **Varied Items** command (as shown in Figure 2–15), which enables you to open the Varied Items dialog box to define or redefine the varied items.

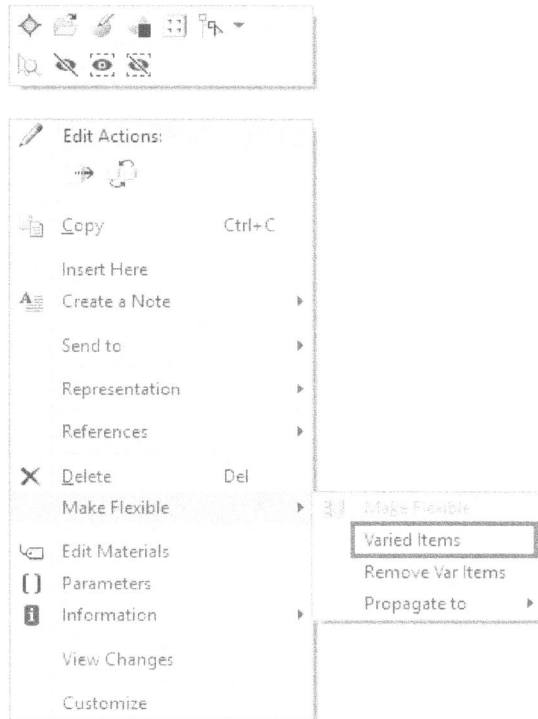

Figure 2–15

2.5 Copy and Paste

In many cases, components are duplicated in the assembly using the same component constraints, with small variations in the references or offset values. Using the **Copy** and **Paste** functionality, Creo Parametric enables you to copy a component and make the required modifications to its placement.

How To: Copy an Existing Component

1. To copy an existing component in an assembly, select the component, and click ⬚ (Copy).

2. Click ⬚ (Paste) to display the *Component Placement* tab, as shown in Figure 2–16. Creo Parametric retains the existing component reference for each constraint that was used to place the component originally, and prompts you to select new references.

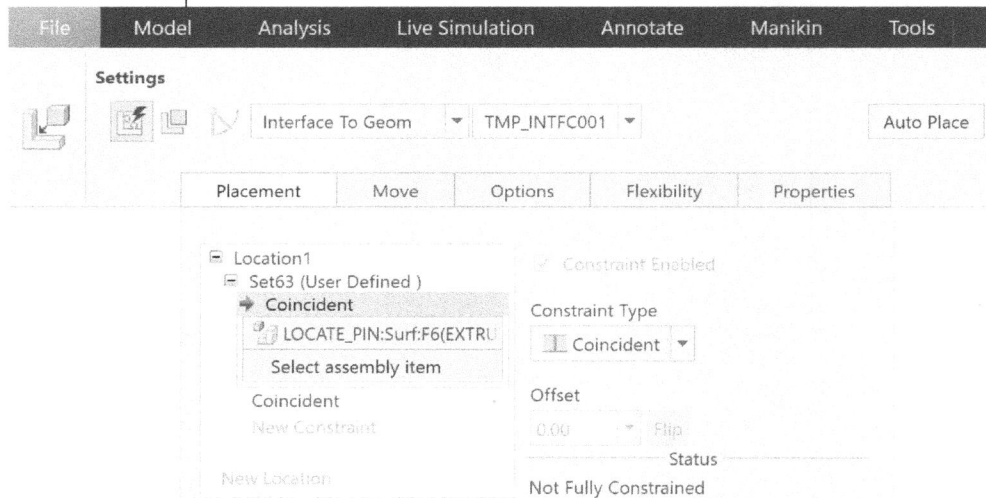

| File | Model | Analysis | Live Simulation | Annotate | Manikin | Tools |

Settings

| Interface To Geom | ▼ | TMP_INTFC001 | ▼ | Auto Place |

| Placement | Move | Options | Flexibility | Properties |

```
⊟ Location1
   ⊟ Set63 (User Defined )
      ➔ Coincident
         ⬚ LOCATE_PIN:Surf:F6(EXTRL
         Select assembly item
      Coincident
      New Constraint

   New Location
```

☑ Constraint Enabled

Constraint Type
Ⅱ Coincident ▼

Offset
0.00 ▼ Flip
─────────── Status ───────────
Not Fully Constrained

Figure 2–16

3. Click ✓ (OK) to complete the component placement.

Paste Special

To maintain greater control over the dependency of the copied feature, you can expand ⬓ (Paste) and select ⬓ (Paste Special) to paste the selected component in an assembly. The Paste Special dialog box opens, as shown in Figure 2–17.

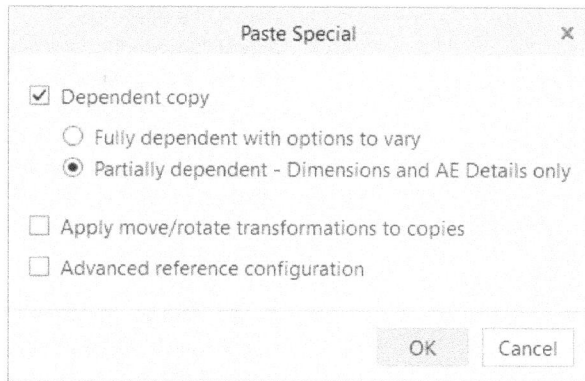

Figure 2–17

The various **Paste Special** options available are described as follows:

Option		Description
Dependent Copy		
	Fully dependent with options to vary	Creates copies of the original feature that are fully dependent on all of its attributes, elements, and parameters, but enables you to vary the dependency of dimensions, annotations, parameters, sketches, and references.
	Dimensions and annotation element details only	Creates copies of the original feature that are dependent on the dimensions, the sketch, or both, or on the annotation elements of the original feature. This is the default **Dependent copy** option.
Apply move/rotate transformations to copies		Moves the copy by translation, rotation, or both. You can create a fully dependent moved copy of a feature. This option is not available when pasting features across models.
Advanced reference configuration		Pastes the copied features using the original or new references in the same model or across models. Lists references of the original feature and enables you to retain these references or replace them with new references in the pasted feature.

Practice 2a

Repeating Components

Practice Objectives

- Use the **Repeat** command to quickly add the same component multiple times in the assembly.
- Repeat component constraints.
- Use assembly revision tools.
- Use a reference pattern to assemble components.

In this practice, you will assemble a number of components into the **air_entry** assembly. To assemble the components, you will use both **Repeat** and **Pattern** to quickly duplicate the instances in the assembly.

- The **Repeat** option is used to duplicate the series of constraints used to assemble the first component. The benefit is that you can then edit the definition of any repeated component, and make the required changes. Each component is shown as a separate component in the Model Tree (e.g., **locate_pin.prt**).

- Duplicating components with the **Pattern** option enables you to take advantage of previous patterns that are referenced to place the first instance of the component. Each component is a member of the pattern in the Model Tree (e.g., **chamfer_stud.prt**). The completed assembly displays as shown in Figure 2–18.

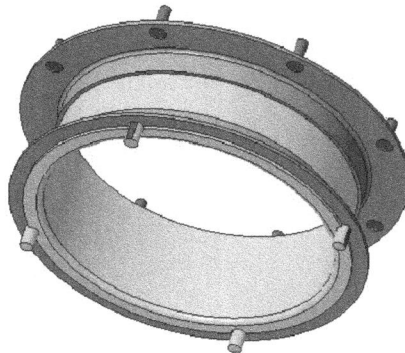

Figure 2–18

Task 1 - Open an assembly file.

1. Set the current working directory to the *Repeat_Component* folder.

2. Open **air_entry.asm**.

3. Set the model display as follows:

- ✗⁄ᵪ *(Datum Display Filters)*: All Off
- ⟫ *(Spin Center)*: Off
- ⌧ *(Display Style)*: ⬜ (Shading With Edges)

4. Assemble **locate_pin.prt** using the following constraints:

- Use coincident to constrain the surface of **locate_pin.prt**, as shown in Figure 2–19, with the surface of the **air_entry_fore_flange.prt**, shown in Figure 2–20.

3D Dragger is toggled off for clarity.

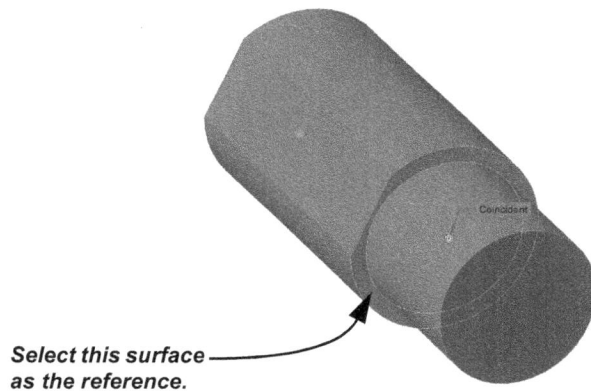

Select this surface as the reference.

Figure 2–19

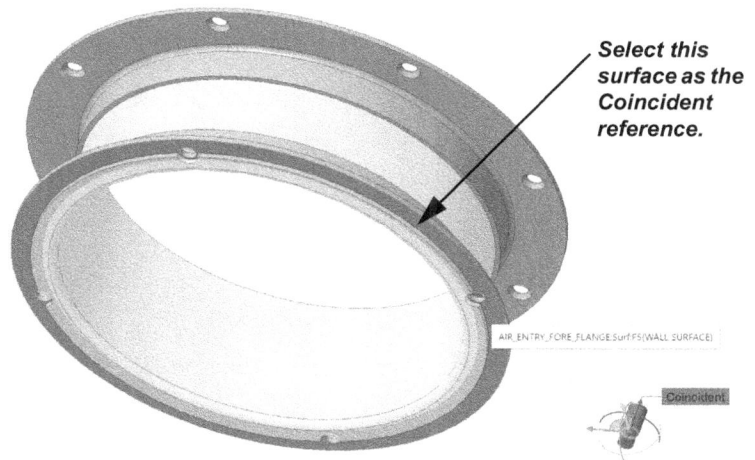

Select this surface as the Coincident reference.

AIR_ENTRY_FORE_FLANGE:Surf:F5(WALL SURFACE)

Figure 2–20

3D Dragger is toggled off for clarity.

- Use coincident to assemble the component using the references shown in Figure 2–21.

Select these cylindrical surfaces as references for the Coincident constraint.

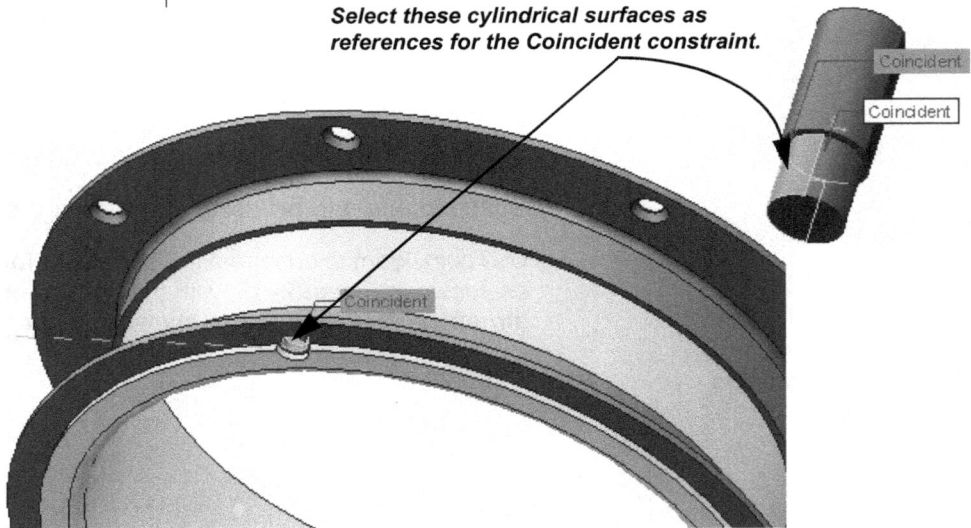

Figure 2–21

- The **locate_pin.prt** displays as shown in Figure 2–22.

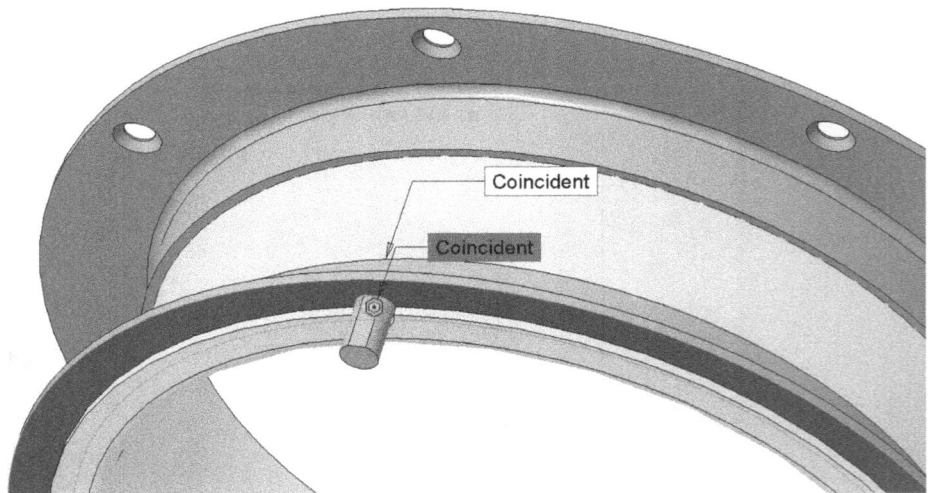

Figure 2–22

5. Right-click and clear the **Assumptions** option.

Design Considerations

Once the **Assumptions** option (**Allow Assumptions** in the *Placement* panel) has been cleared, the placement status for the component is **Partially Constrained**. This is because **locate_pin.prt** can still rotate in the hole. If **Assumptions** is enabled, Creo Parametric automatically constrains the pin to prevent this type of rotational motion.

6. Right-click and select **New Constraint**.

7. In the Constraint Type drop-down list, select **Parallel**, as shown in Figure 2–23.

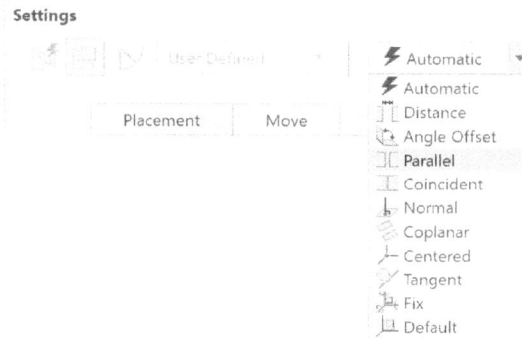

Figure 2–23

8. Select the planar surface of **locate_pin.prt** and select **ASM_TOP** from the Model Tree as the references for the Parallel constraint, as shown in Figure 2–24.

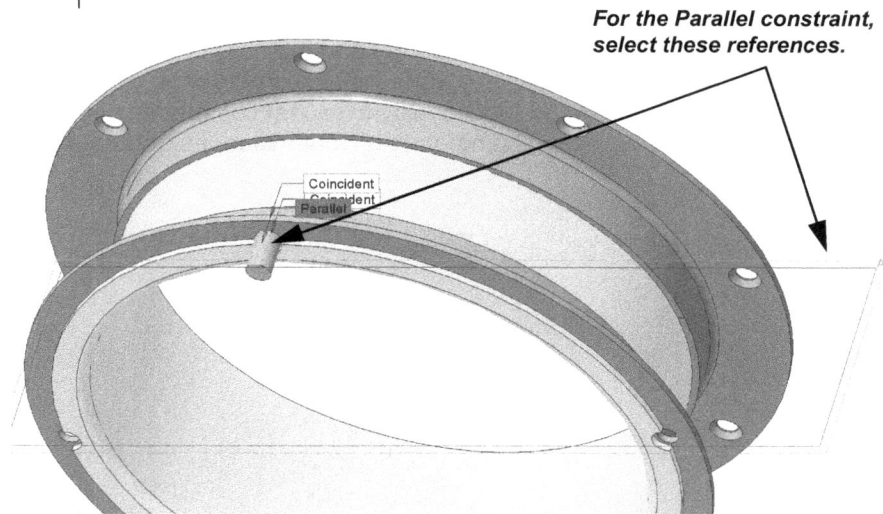

For the Parallel constraint, select these references.

Figure 2–24

9. The component should be fully constrained. Click ✔ (OK).

10. Toggle off the datum plane display. The assembly displays as shown in Figure 2–25.

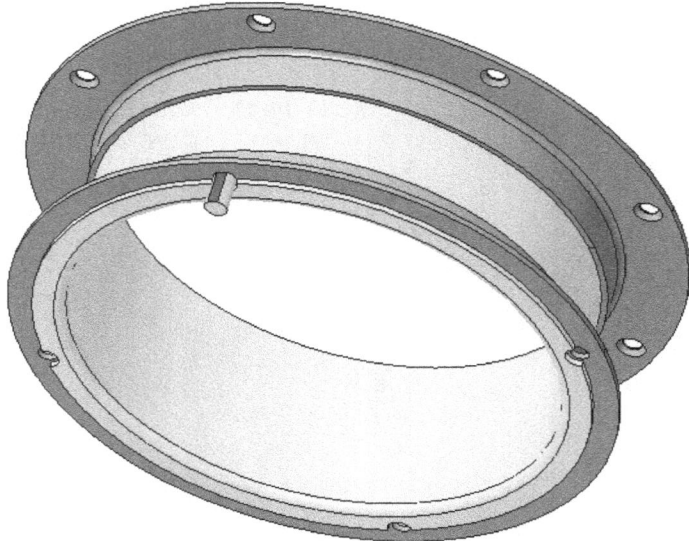

Figure 2–25

Task 2 - Repeat the constraints of a component.

Design Considerations

In this task, you will use the constraint types and references that are used to parametrically constrain **locate_pin.prt** to assemble three more instances of **locate_pin.prt**. You will use the **Repeat** functionality to repeat constraints and references that are common to all four instances of **locate_pin.prt**.

1. Select **locate_pin.prt** in the Model Tree, then right-click and select ↺ (Repeat), as shown in Figure 2–26.

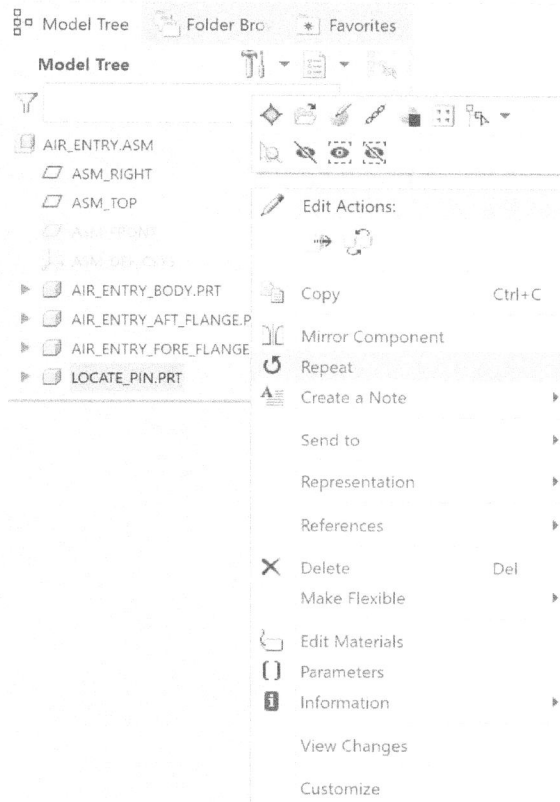

Figure 2–26

2. Select the second Coincident constraint in the *Variable Assembly Refs* area and click **Add**, as shown in Figure 2–27.

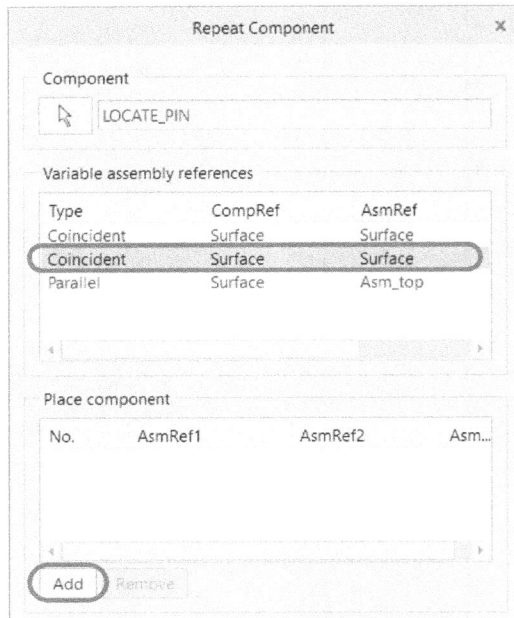

Figure 2–27

3. Select the surface of the hole shown in Figure 2–28 as the new reference for the Coincident constraint.

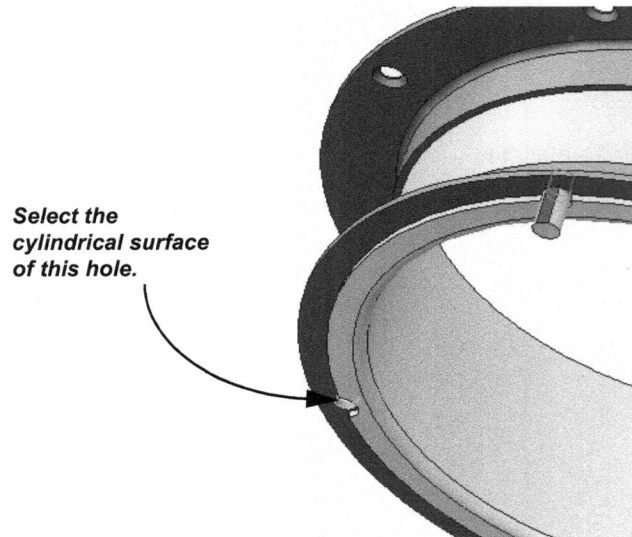

Select the cylindrical surface of this hole.

Figure 2–28

4. Select the inside surface of the two remaining holes. The model displays and the dialog box opens, as shown in Figure 2–29.

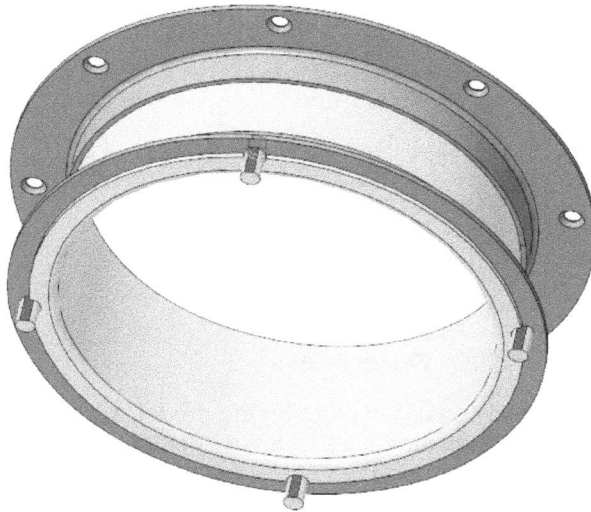

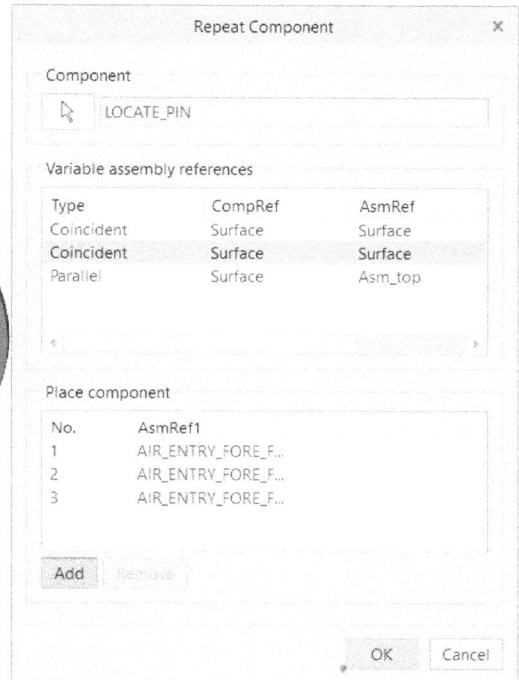

Figure 2–29

5. Click **OK** to complete the repeat constraint process.

Task 3 - Use revision tools to finalize the component placement.

1. Select the second last instance of **locate_pin.prt** in the Model Tree and select ![Edit Definition icon] (Edit Definition) in the mini toolbar, as shown in Figure 2–30.

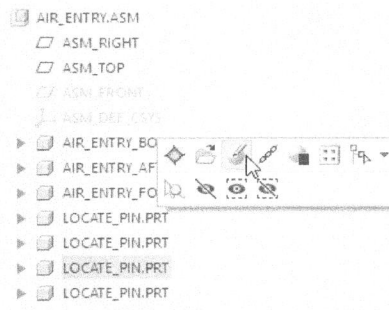

Figure 2–30

2. Select the Parallel constraint label on the model, right-click, and select **Flip Constraint**. This flips the orientation direction of the dark blue planar surface to face the outside of the assembly, as shown in Figure 2–31.

The dark blue planar surface is now oriented to face the outside.

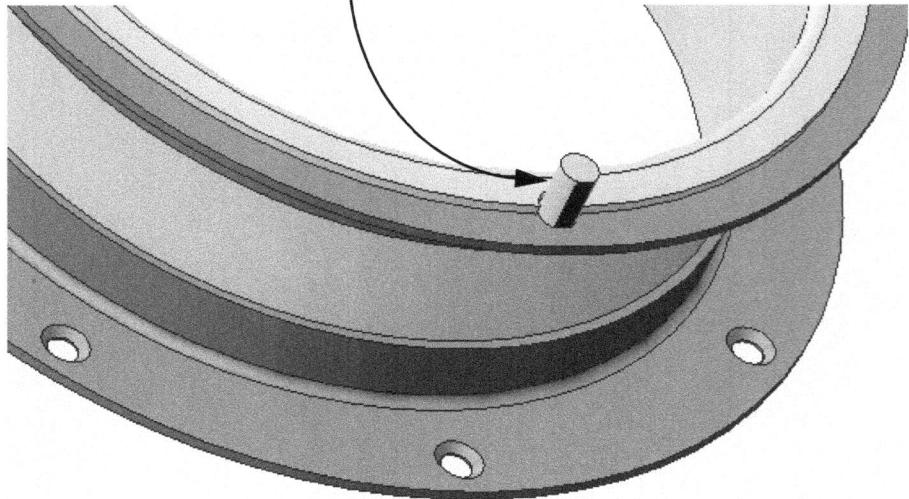

Figure 2–31

3. Edit the definition of the two remaining **locate_pin.prt** parts so that the dark blue planar surfaces are oriented to face the outside of the assembly, as shown in Figure 2–32.

Use **ASM_RIGHT** as the assembly reference for the Parallel constraint.

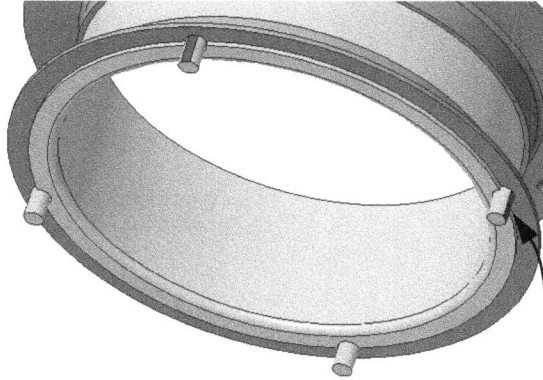

The dark blue planar surfaces of the locate_pin parts should be oriented to face the outside of the assembly.

Figure 2–32

4. Save the assembly.

Task 4 - Use a reference pattern to quickly duplicate a component in the assembly.

---

1. Orient the assembly model to the default orientation as shown in Figure 2–33.

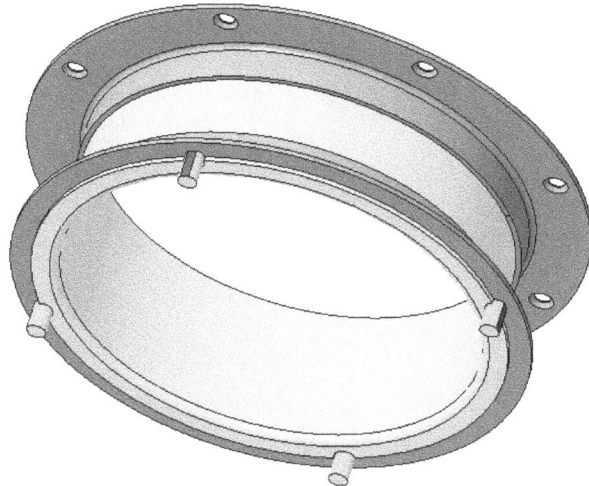

Figure 2–33

Design Considerations

2. Assemble **chamfer_stud.prt** using two Coincident constraints, as shown in Figure 2–34.

Right-click and ensure **Assumptions** is enabled. This can be done because the rotational position of **chamfer_stud.prt** in the hole does not affect the assembly.

3. Complete the component placement. The assembly displays as shown in Figure 2–34.

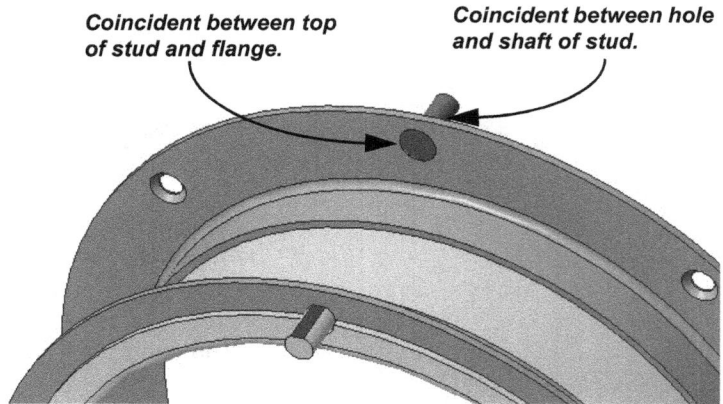

Coincident between top of stud and flange.

Coincident between hole and shaft of stud.

Figure 2–34

4. Select **CHAMFER_STUD.PRT** in the Model Tree and click ⊞ (Pattern) in the mini toolbar, as shown in Figure 2–35.

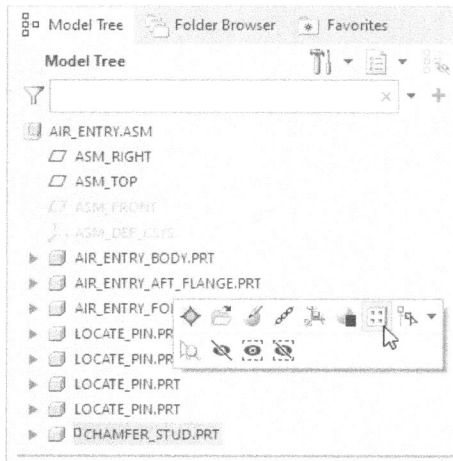

Figure 2–35

Design Considerations

The system recognizes that **chamfer_stud.prt** has been assembled using references of the part-level patterned geometry (i.e., the holes in the **air_entry_aft_flange**). The *Pattern* dashboard displays **Reference**, as shown in Figure 2–36.

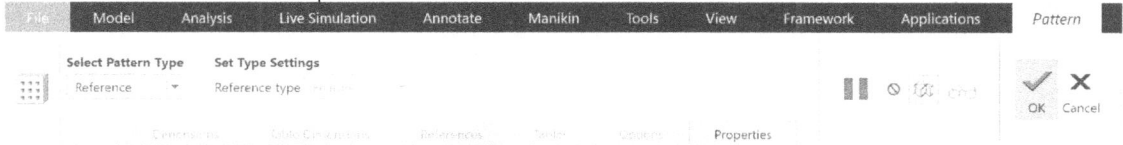

Figure 2–36

5. Click ✓ (OK) to complete the reference pattern. The completed assembly displays as shown in Figure 2–37.

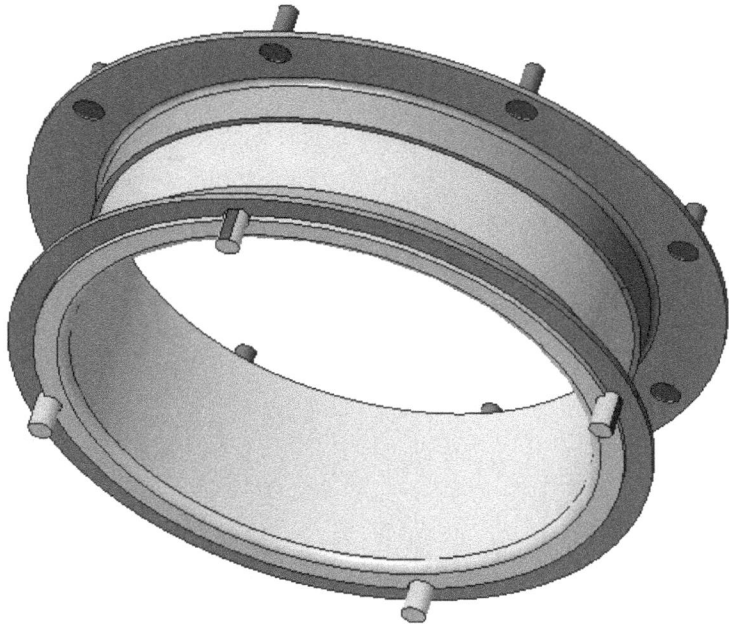

Figure 2–37

6. Save the assembly.

7. Close the window and erase all of the files from memory.

Practice 2b | Using Component Interfaces

Practice Objectives

- Use the component interface to predefine the constraints and references.
- Place the component using the Component Interface command and select assembly references.
- Use the component interface to predefine the constraints and references for a family table member and place the component in the assembly using auto place.

In this practice, you will assemble the various stages of a turbine compressor rotor. The turbine stages are generated from a family table. You will define the component interfaces for the generic part to enable efficient assembly of multiple parts. The completed assembly displays as shown in Figure 2–38.

Figure 2–38

Task 1 - Create an assembly.

1. Set the working directory to the *Component_Interface* folder.

2. Create a new assembly using the default template and set the *Name* to **Rotor**.

3. Set the model display as follows:

   - ⁖ *(Datum Display Filters)*: ⟋ₒ (Axis Display) only

   - ⋙ *(Spin Center)*: Off

   - ⬜ *(Display Style)*: ⬛ (Shading With Edges)

4. Assemble **impeller.prt** using the **Default** constraint.

5. Save the assembly.

Task 2 - Create component interfaces.

1. Open **bolt_tie.prt**.

2. Click ▣ (Component Interface) in the *Model* tab. The Component Interface dialog box opens, as shown in Figure 2–39.

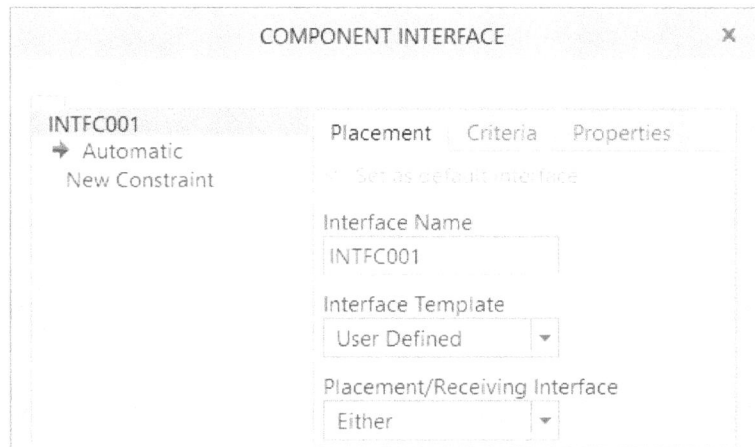

COMPONENT INTERFACE   ✕

INTFC001
→ Automatic
New Constraint

Placement   Criteria   Properties

Set as default interface

Interface Name
INTFC001

Interface Template
User Defined   ▼

Placement/Receiving Interface
Either   ▼

Figure 2–39

3. Set the interface *Name* to **BOLT_TIE**, as shown in Figure 2–40.

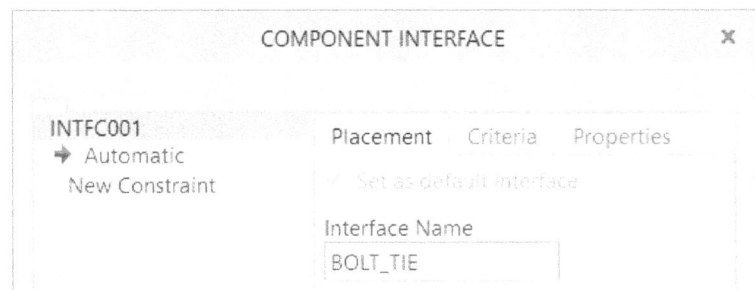

COMPONENT INTERFACE   ✕

INTFC001
→ Automatic
New Constraint

Placement   Criteria   Properties

Set as default interface

Interface Name
BOLT_TIE

Figure 2–40

4. Select the surface shown in Figure 2–41. The automatic *Constraint Type* changes automatically to **Coincident**.

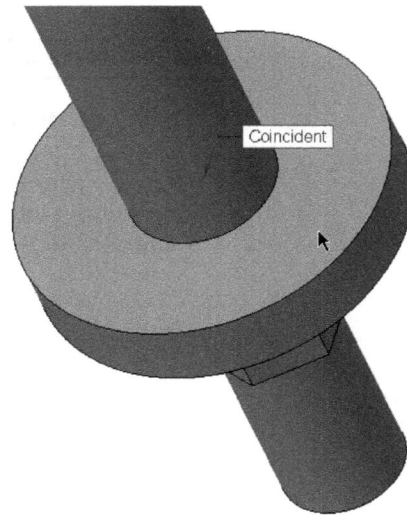

Figure 2–41

5. Click **New Constraint** and set the second *Constraint Type* to **Coincident**, as shown in Figure 2–42.

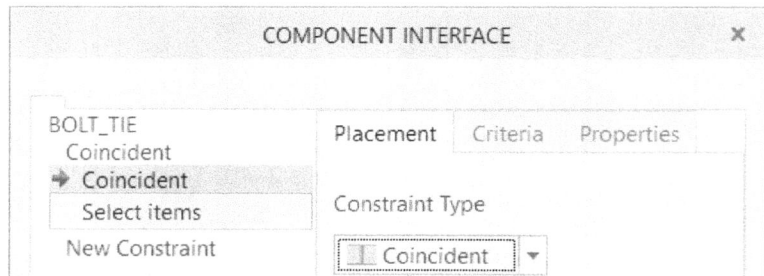

Figure 2–42

6. Select the axis **A_2** that runs through the model, as the *Component Reference* for the constraint.

7. Click ✓ (OK) to complete the set up of the component interfaces. The **Interfaces** branch displays under **Footer**, as shown in Figure 2–43.

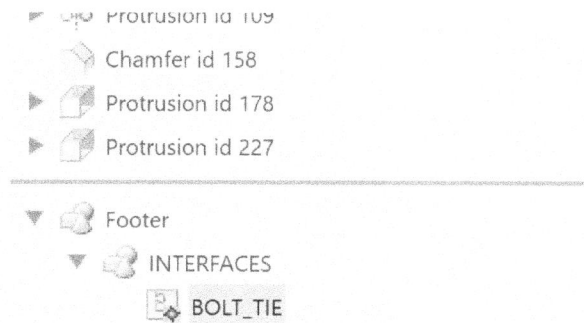

▶ ⊙⊦⊙ Protrusion id 109

⬙ Chamfer id 158

▶ ⬙ Protrusion id 178

▶ ⬙ Protrusion id 227

▼ ⬙ Footer

   ▼ ⬙ INTERFACES

      ⬙ BOLT_TIE

Figure 2–43

8. Save the part file.

Task 3 - Assemble a component using interfaces.

1. Switch to the ROTOR.ASM window.

2. Assemble **bolt_tie.prt**. The **BOLT_TIE** interface is automatically selected in the *Component Placement* dashboard, as shown in Figure 2–44.

| File | Model | Analysis | Live Simulation | Annotate | Manikin | Tools |

Settings

Interface To Geom ▼ BOLT_TIE ▼   Auto Place

Placement   Move   Options   Flexibility   Properties

Figure 2–44

3. Rotate the model and select the planar surface shown in Figure 2–45. This is the corresponding assembly reference for the first Coincident constraint defined in the component interface.

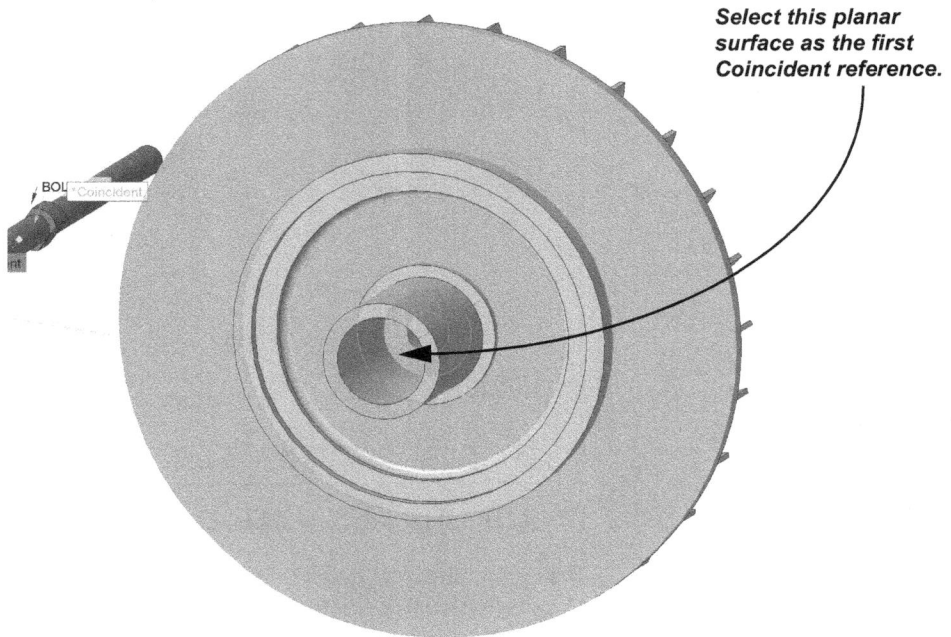

Select this planar surface as the first Coincident reference.

Figure 2–45

4. Select the **A_2 axis** running through the center of the impeller part as the assembly reference for the Coincident constraint, as shown in Figure 2–46.

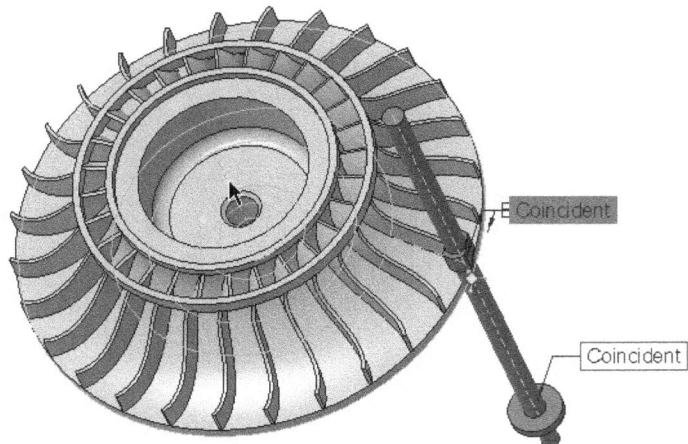

Figure 2–46

5. Allow assumptions and click ✓ (OK) to complete the placement of the **BOLT_TIE** part. The assembly displays as shown in Figure 2–47.

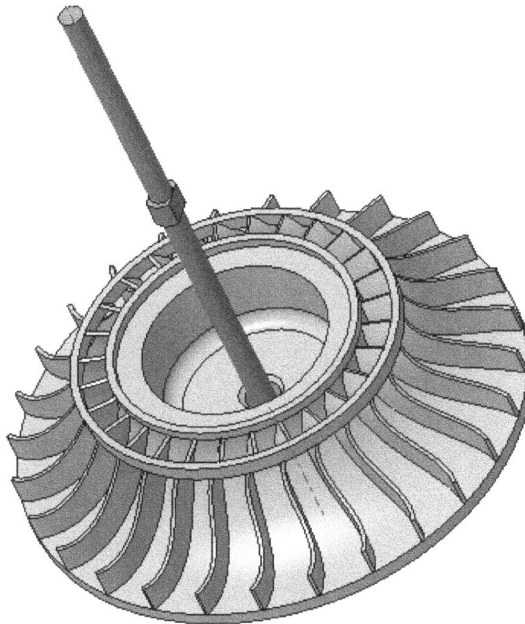

Figure 2–47

6. Save the assembly.

Task 4 - Define component interfaces for family table parts.

1. Open **second_third_stage.prt**.

2. In the Select Instance dialog box, select **The generic** and click **Open**, as shown in Figure 2–48.

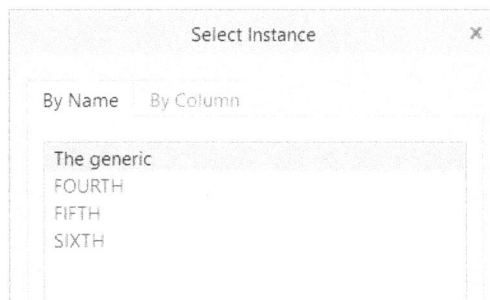

Figure 2–48

3. The part model displays as shown in Figure 2–49.

Figure 2–49

4. Click ⬚ (Component Interface) in the *Model* tab.

5. Set the interface *Name* to **ROTOR_BLADES**.

6. Select the surface shown in Figure 2–50 as the Coincident reference.

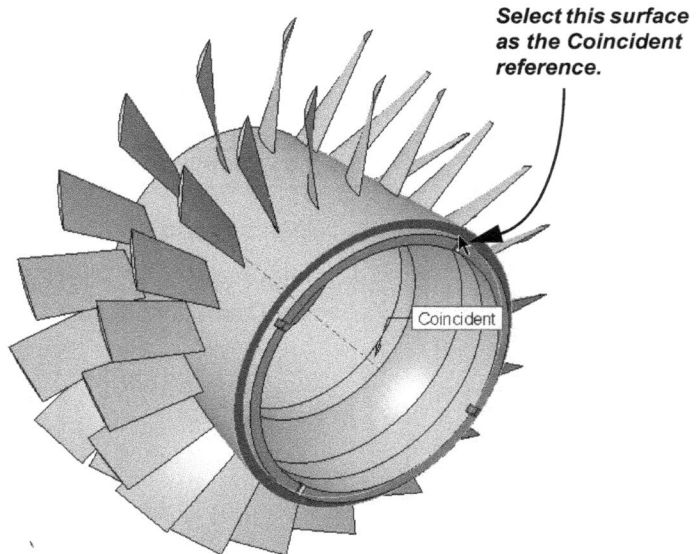

Select this surface as the Coincident reference.

Coincident

Figure 2–50

7. Add a second Coincident constraint and select the axis **A_4** as the reference. The Component Interface dialog box opens, as shown in Figure 2–51.

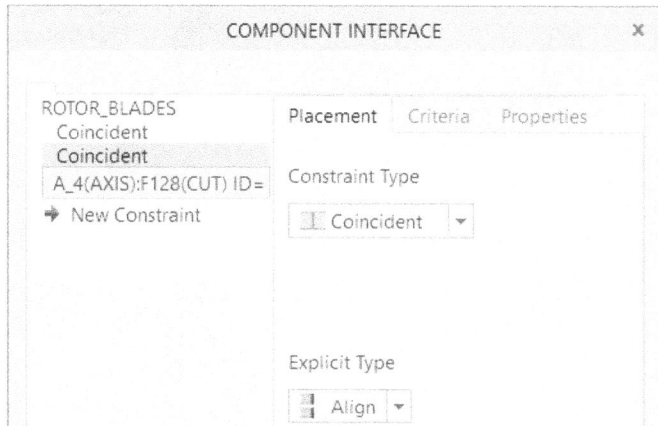

Figure 2–51

8. Complete the interface definition and save the model.

Task 5 - Assemble family table components with interface.

1. Switch to the **ROTOR.ASM** window.

2. Assemble **second_third_stage.prt**.

3. In the Select Instance dialog box, double-click on **SIXTH**.

4. **ROTOR_BLADES** is automatically selected as the interface to use to assemble this instance.

5. Select the surface shown in Figure 2–52 as the Coincident reference.

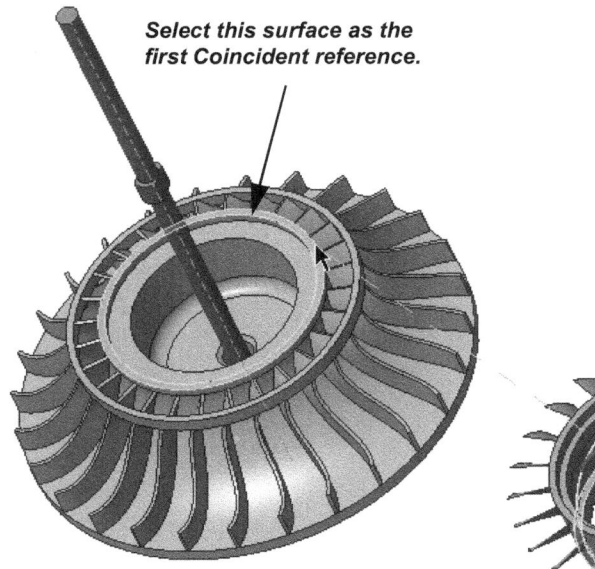

Select this surface as the first Coincident reference.

Figure 2–52

6. Select axis **A_2** on **bolt_tie.prt** as the Coincident reference and click ✓ (OK). The assembly displays as shown in Figure 2–53.

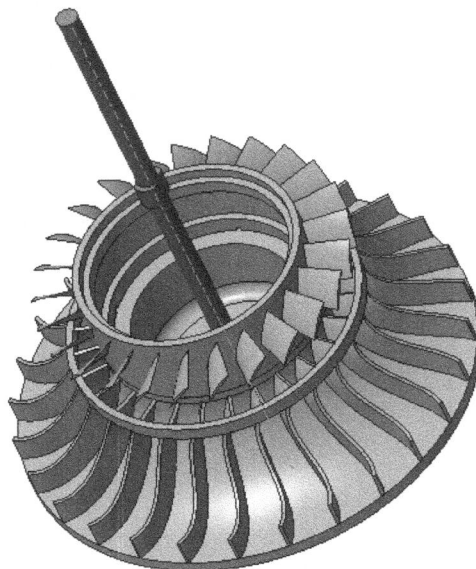

Figure 2–53

Task 6 - Assemble components using Auto Place.

1. Assemble **second_third_stage.prt**.

2. In the Select Instance dialog box, double-click on **FIFTH**.

3. Select **ROTOR_BLADES** and click **Auto Place**, as shown in Figure 2–54.

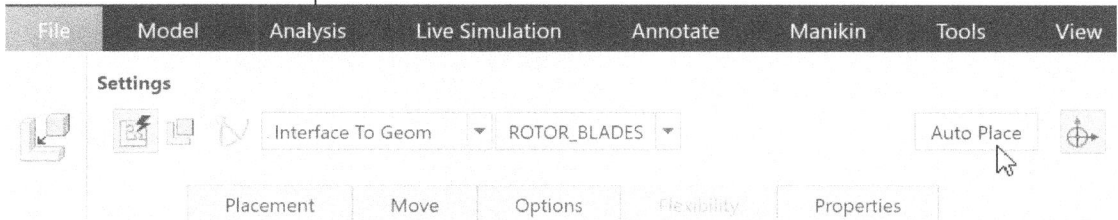

Figure 2–54

4. The Auto Place dialog box opens, as shown in Figure 2–55.

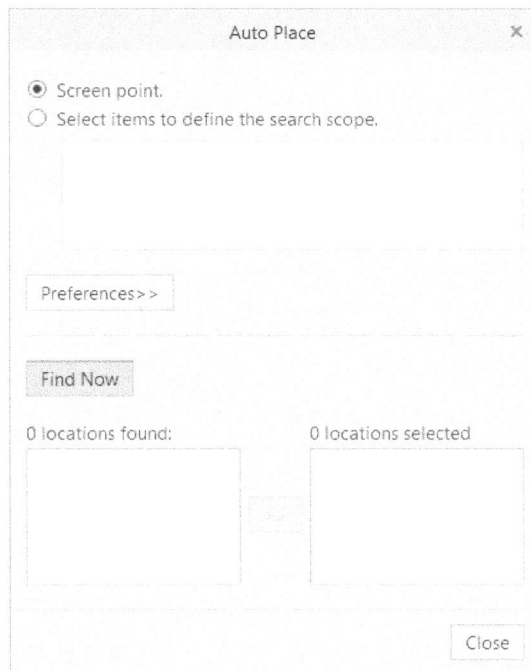

Figure 2–55

5. Select anywhere near the planar surface shown in Figure 2–56.

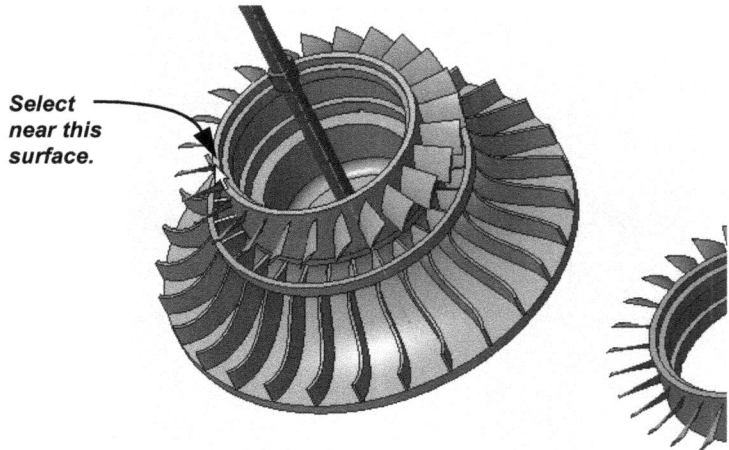

Note that since you are simply clicking a point in space, the surface will not highlight.

Select near this surface.

Figure 2–56

Design Considerations

Creo Parametric calculates possible references based on the location you selected. The Auto Place dialog box returns five possible positions as shown in Figure 2–57, due to the *Max Position* value.

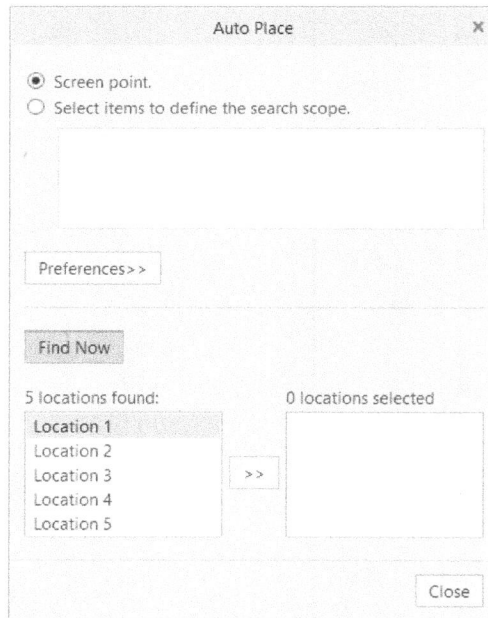

Figure 2–57

6. Select each of the possible positions. Accept the position shown in Figure 2–58. The surface is coincident to the surface of the **SIXTH** part (the top position). Select the correct **Location #**, click ➤➤ (Add Item), and click **Close** to complete the auto placement. The fully constrained component displays as shown in Figure 2–58.

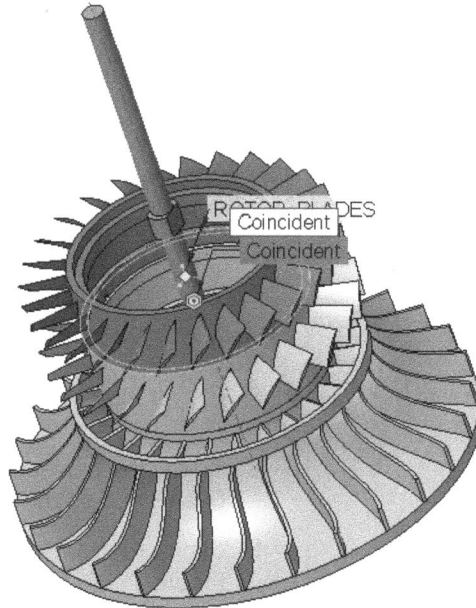

Figure 2–58

7. Click ✓ (OK).

8. Assemble **second_third_stage.prt**.

9. In the Select Instance dialog box, double-click on **FOURTH**.

10. Click **Auto Place** in the dashboard.

11. Select near the location shown in Figure 2–59.

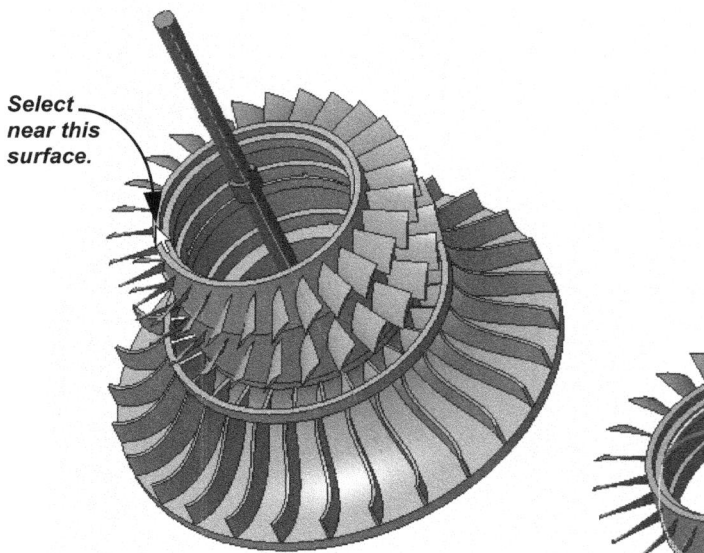

Select near this surface.

Figure 2–59

12. Select the correct **Location #**, click ⤢ (Add Item), and click **Close** to complete the auto placement.

13. Click ✓ (OK). The assembly displays as shown in Figure 2–60.

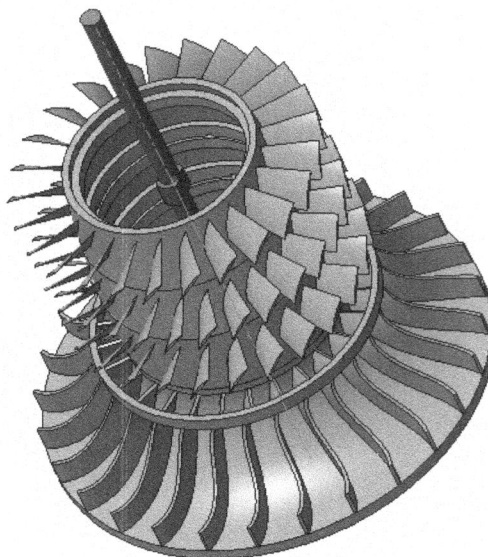

Figure 2–60

14. Assemble **second_third_stage.prt**.

15. Double-click on **The generic**.

16. Click **Auto Place** in the dashboard.

17. Select near the location shown in Figure 2–61.

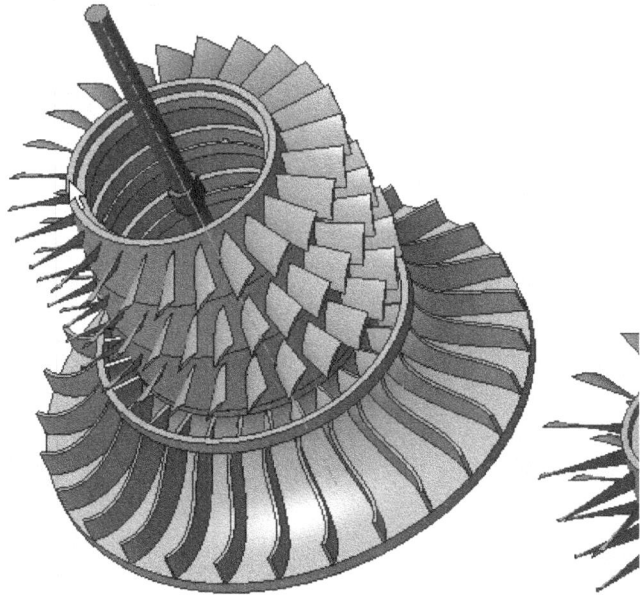

Figure 2–61

18. Select the correct **Location #**, click ≫ (Add Item), and click **Close** to complete the auto placement.

19. Click ✓ (OK).

20. Rotate the assembly so it displays as shown in Figure 2–62.

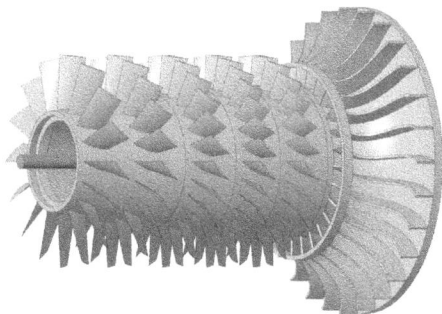

Figure 2–62

Design Considerations

By defining component interfaces, the efficiency of the component placement can be dramatically increased. If many components are to be assembled, the **Auto Place** option can increase efficiency even further. When using **Auto Place**, the system considers the component interface references relative to a selected assembly reference and then generates the possible placement options.

21. Assemble **first_stage.prt** using manual constraints. The completed assembly displays as shown in Figure 2–63.

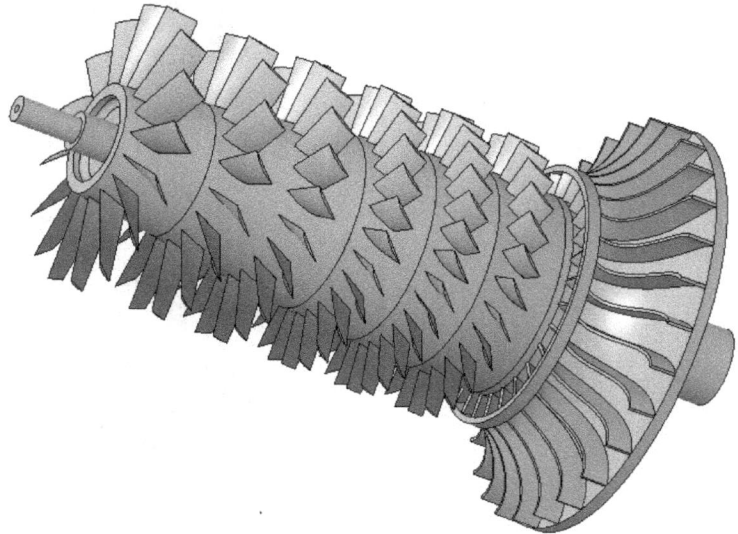

Figure 2–63

22. Save the assembly and erase all of the files from memory.

Practice 2c

Using Flexible Components

Practice Objectives

- Assemble a component using the **Make Flexible** command to change the geometry.
- Define the component to be flexible and then assemble the component.

In this practice, you will assemble flexible variations of a spring, as shown in Figure 2–64. The spring is one model that is varied as required to fit appropriately into the assembly.

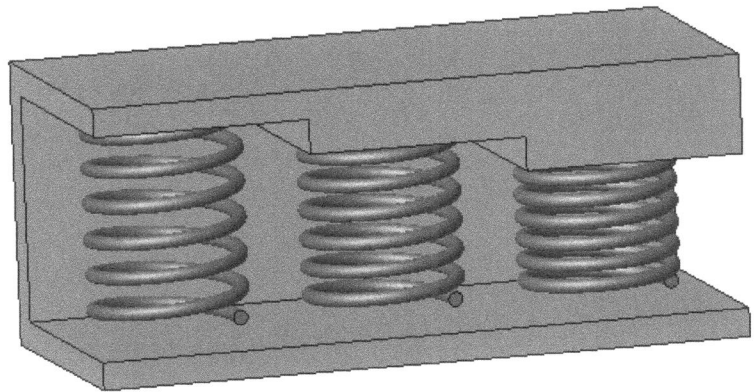

Figure 2–64

Task 1 - Open an assembly file.

1. Set the working directory to the *Flexible_Components* folder.

2. Open **testing_fixture.asm**. The first spring (non-flexible) has been assembled for you.

3. Set the model display as follows:

   - *(Datum Display Filters)*: (Csys Display) Only

   - *(Spin Center)*: Off

   - *(Display Style)*: (Shading With Edges)

Task 2 - Assemble another instance of the spring.

1. If the Materials node is not available, select
   (Settings)>**Tree Filters** and enable **Materials**.

2. In the Model Tree, expand the **Materials** node.

3. Note that three materials are stored with the assembly.

4. In the Model Tree, select **SPRING.PRT**.

5. Right-click and select ↺ (Repeat).

6. In the Repeat Component dialog box, select the **Coincident** assembly reference, as shown in Figure 2–65.

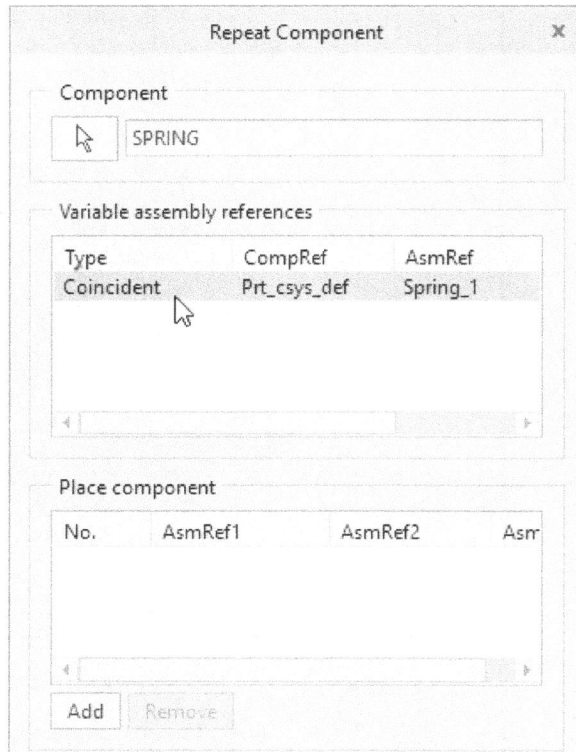

Figure 2–65

7. Click **Add** and select the **SPRING_2** coordinate system.

8. Click **OK**.

9. In the In-graphics toolbar, expand ▦ (Saved Orientations) and select **FRONT**. The assembly displays as shown in Figure 2–66.

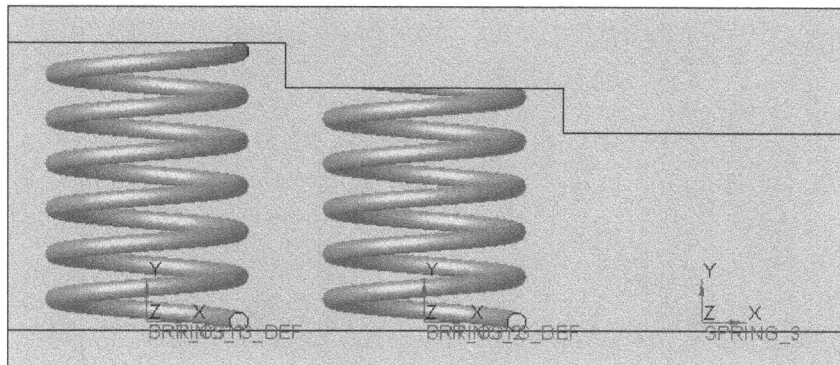

Figure 2–66

Task 3 - Make the spring just assembled a flexible component.

1. In the Model Tree, select the second instance of **SPRING.PRT**, right-click, and select **Make Flexible>Make Flexible**, as shown in Figure 2–67.

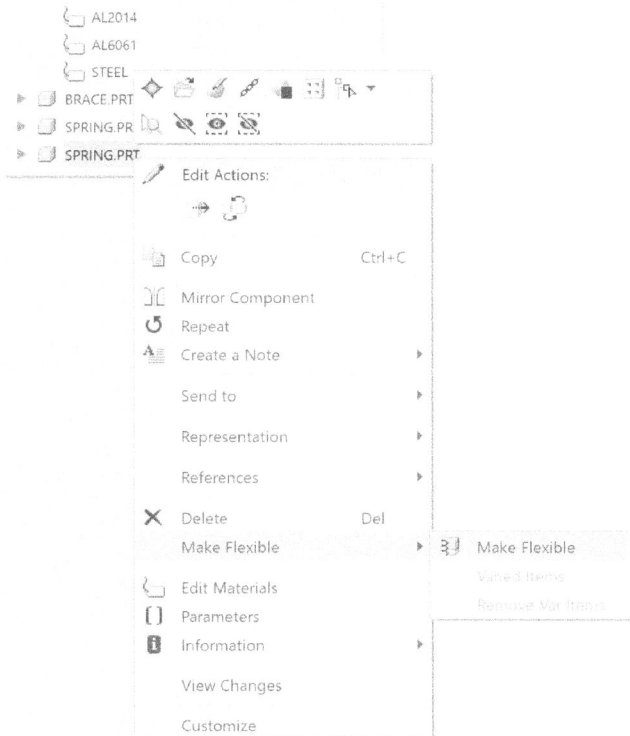

Figure 2–67

2. The Varied Items dialog box opens, as shown in Figure 2–68.

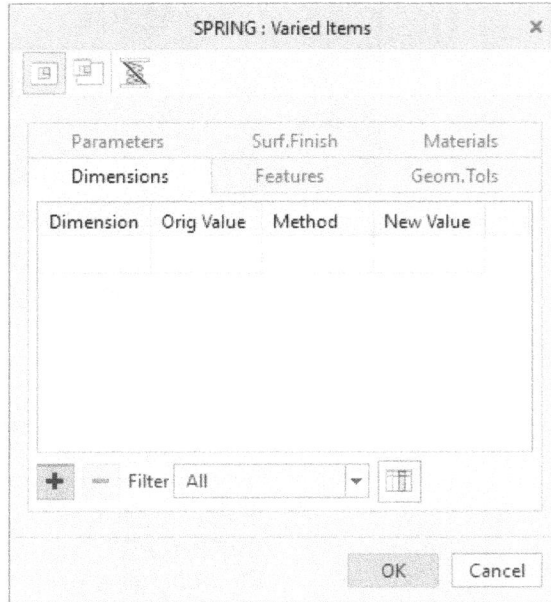

Figure 2–68

3. Select the spring model that has just been added to the assembly.

4. In the Menu Manager, select **Profile** and then **Done**.

Note that the dimensions do not show in the dialog box until you middle-click.

5. Press and hold <Ctrl> and select the **30.00** and PITCH **5.00** dimensions.

6. Click the middle mouse button to add the selected dimensions to the *Dimensions* tab in the Varied Items dialog box, as shown in Figure 2–69.

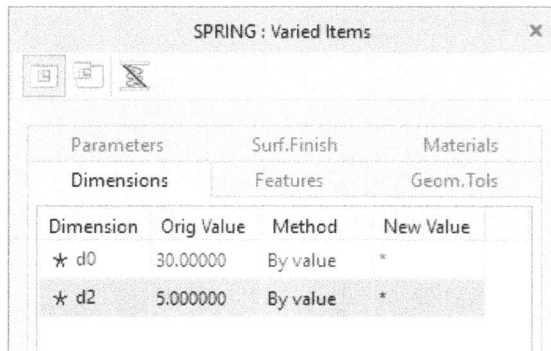

Figure 2–69

7. Select the **d0** cell in the *New Value* column and set the varied length value to **25**.

8. Select the **d2** cell in the *New Value* column and set the varied pitch value to **4**.

9. In the Varied Items dialog box, select the *Materials* tab.

10. Click ✚ (Add Materials).

11. In the *New Material* column, select **AL2014**.

12. Click **OK**. The *Component Placement* dashboard is now active.

13. Click ✓ (OK). The assembly displays similar to that shown in Figure 2–70. The icon that displays in the Model Tree indicates that the spring is a flexible component.

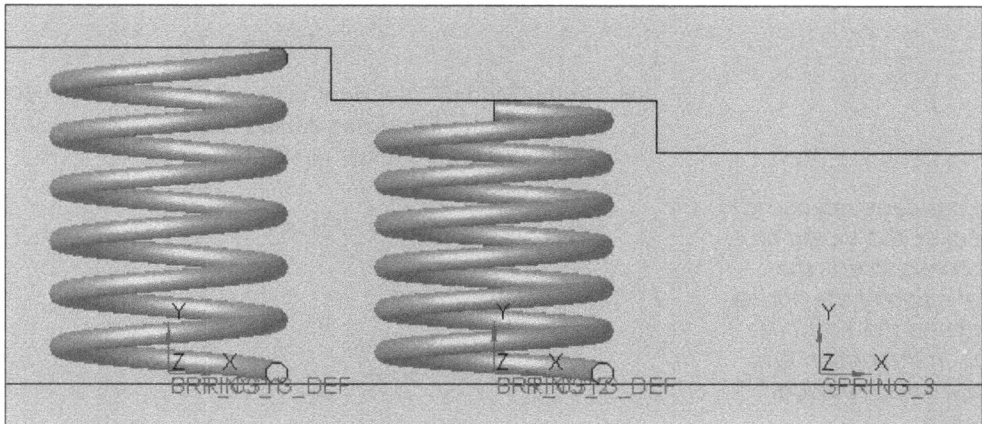

Figure 2–70

Task 4 - Repeat the assembly of the second spring.

1. In the Model Tree, select the second instance of **SPRING.PRT**, then right-click and select ↺ (Repeat).

2. In the Repeat Component dialog box, select the **Coincident** assembly reference.

3. Click **Add** and select coordinate system **SPRING_3**.

4. Click **OK** to complete the component placement.

5. Note that since you repeated the second instance of the spring, the icon in the Model Tree indicates that it is flexible, as shown in Figure 2–71.

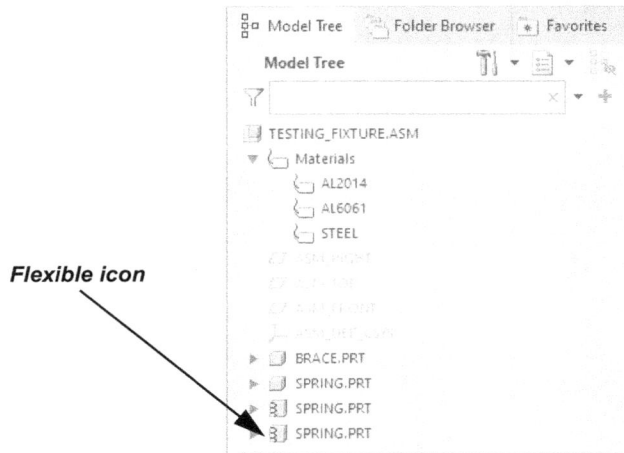

Flexible icon

Figure 2–71

6. In the Model Tree, right-click on the third **SPRING.PRT** and select **Make Flexible>Varied Items**. The Varied Items dialog box displays as shown in Figure 2–72.

In previous releases, to access the dialog box, you had to edit the definition of the spring, expand the Flexibility tab in the ribbon and then select Varied Items.

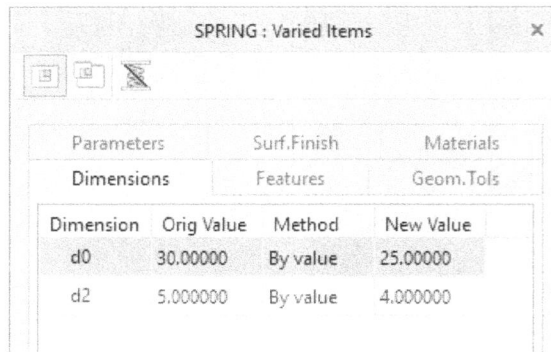

Figure 2–72

7. Select the **d0** cell in the *New Value* column and set the varied length value to **20**.

8. Select the **d2** cell in the *New Value* column and set the varied pitch value to **3**.

9. In the Varied Items dialog box, select the *Materials* tab.

10. In the *New Material* column, select **AL6061**.

11. Click **OK** to display the Component Placement dialog box to parametrically place the component.

12. In the In-graphics toolbar, disable ⌁ (Csys Display). The spring displays similar to that shown in Figure 2–73. The icon that displays in the Model Tree indicates that the spring is a flexible component.

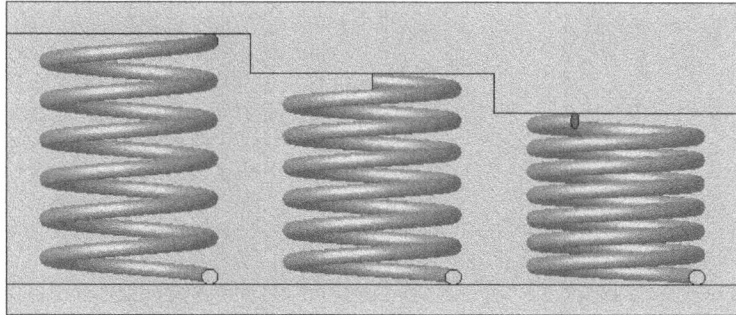

Figure 2–73

13. In the Model Tree, expand the node for each **SPRING.PRT** instance, as shown in Figure 2–74.

Note that the first spring was previously assigned the material STEEL. The next two instances have STEEL available in the models, but are assigned AL2014 and AL6061.

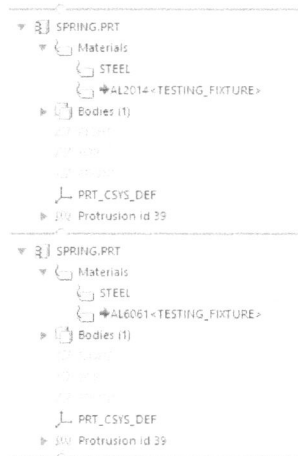

Figure 2–74

14. Close the model and erase it from memory.

Practice 2d | Copy and Paste

Practice Objectives

- Copy and paste component constraints.
- Paste special component constraints.

In this practice, you will assemble a number of components into an assembly using both the **Paste** and **Paste Special** commands. The **Paste** command is used to copy the first component. Using this command, you can quickly redefine the placement of the pasted components in the assembly, while still reusing the original component references. You will also use the **Paste Special** command, which provides greater flexibility over the dependency of the pasted component. The completed assembly displays as shown in Figure 2–75.

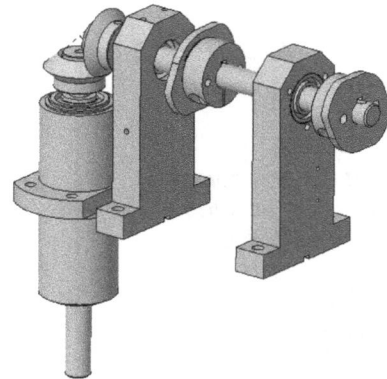

Figure 2–75

Task 1 - Open an assembly file.

1. Set the current working directory to the *Assembly_Copy_Paste* folder.

2. Open **copy_and_paste.asm**.

3. Set the model display as follows:

- *(Datum Display Filters)*: All Off

- *(Spin Center)*: Off

- *(Display Style)*: (Shading With Edges)

- *(Annotation Display)*: Off

Task 2 - Copy na200-9_26_1.prt as a new component.

1. In the Model Tree, click ⏣ ▾ (Settings)>**Tree Filters** and disable **Suppressed objects**.

2. In the Model Tree, select **na200-9_26_1.prt** and click ▢ (Copy) in the *Model* tab.

3. Click ▢ (Paste) in the *Model* tab. A copy of **na200-9_26_1.prt** is inserted into the assembly at the same location as original component.

   Creo Parametric retains the existing component reference for each constraint that was used to place the component. The *Component Placement* dashboard displays and prompts you to select new assembly references.

4. In the dashboard, expand the Placement panel and change the *Distance* constraint to **Coincident**.

5. Select the surface of **na200-9_24_1.prt** as the new assembly reference for the Coincident constraint, as shown in Figure 2–76.

Select this planar surface for the reference.

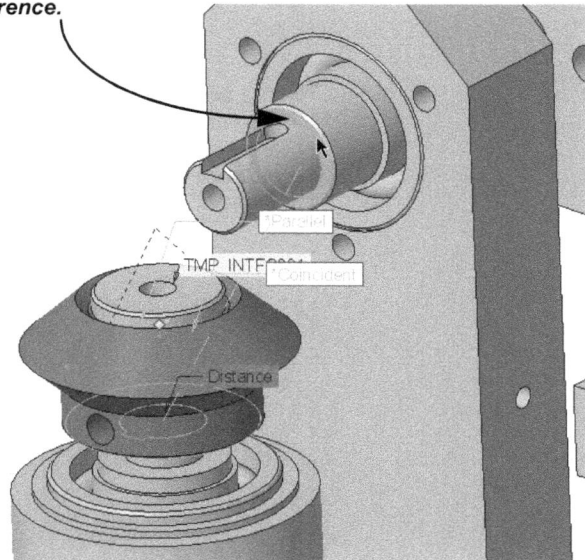

Figure 2–76

6. Select the surface of **na200-9_22_1.prt** as the new assembly reference for the second Coincident constraint, as shown in Figure 2–77.

Select this cylindrical surface for the reference.

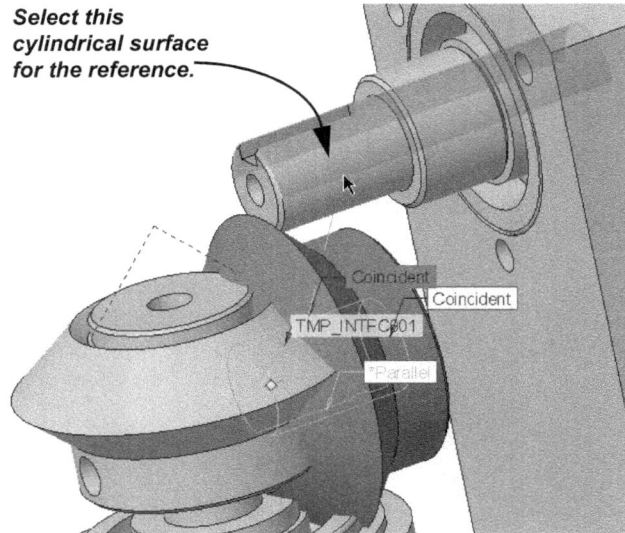

Figure 2–77

7. Select the surface of **na200-9_22_1.prt** as the new reference for the Parallel constraint, as shown in Figure 2–78.

The side face of the two keyway cuts are Parallel.

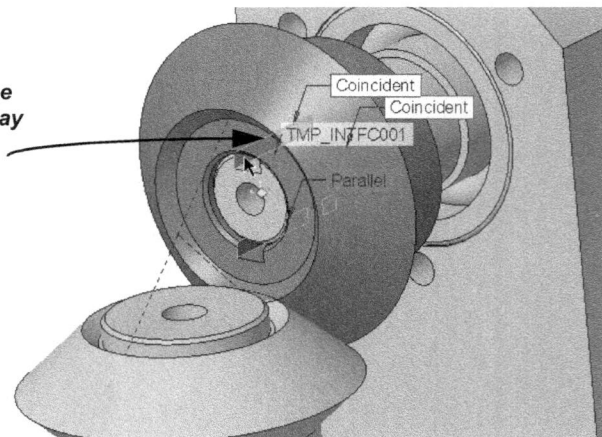

Figure 2–78

8. In the Placement panel, if required, click **Flip** to flip the Parallel constraint so that the keyway cuts line up.

9. With the copied component now fully defined, click ✓ (OK) to close the *Component Placement* dashboard and confirm the new placement.

Task 3 - Copy na200-9_25_1.prt as a new component.

1. In the Model Tree, select **na200-9_25_1.prt** and click
   ▯ (Copy).

2. Click ▯ (Paste). A copy of **na200-9_25_1.prt** is inserted into the assembly in the same location as the original component.

3. Select the surface of **na200-9_26_1.prt** as the new assembly reference for the Coincident constraint, as shown in Figure 2–79.

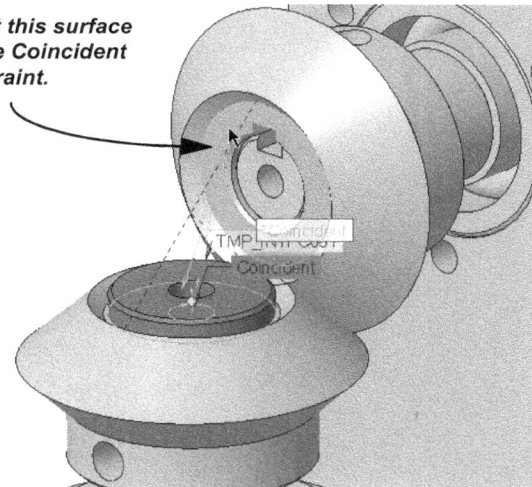

Figure 2–79

4. Select the surface of **na200-9_26_1.prt** as the new assembly reference for the second Coincident constraint, as shown in Figure 2–80.

Select the cylindrical surface of the shaft as the Coincident reference.

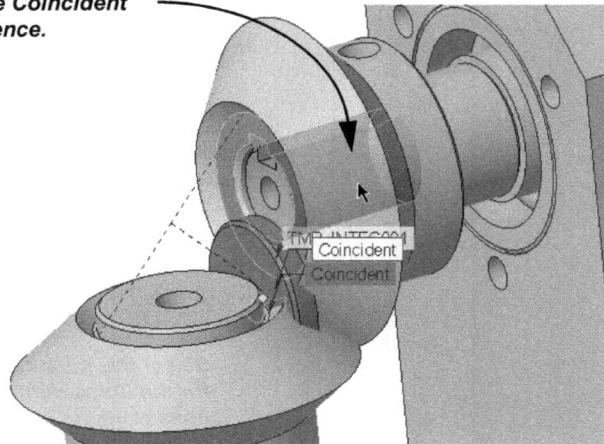

Figure 2–80

5. Click ✔ (OK) to close the tab and confirm the new placement.

Task 4 - Copy na200-9_27_1.prt with the Paste Special option.

---

1. In the Model Tree, select **na200-9_27_1.prt**, right-click and select ▣ (Copy).

2. Right-click and select ▣ (Paste Special). The Paste Special dialog box opens. Select the **Fully dependent with options to vary** option shown in Figure 2–81 to create a dependent copy with the same constraints as the original.

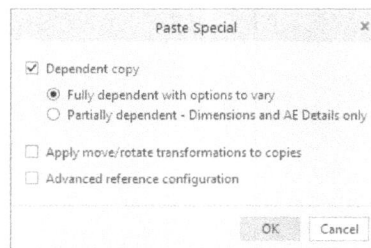

Figure 2–81

---

3. Click **OK**. A copy of **na200-9_27_1.prt** is inserted at the same location as the original component.

4. Select the copied component and select ⟷ (Edit Dimensions) in the mini toolbar.

5. Double-click on the **26.00** offset dimension. Click **Yes** in the Warning dialog box that opens.

6. Change the dimension to **120**, as shown in Figure 2–82.

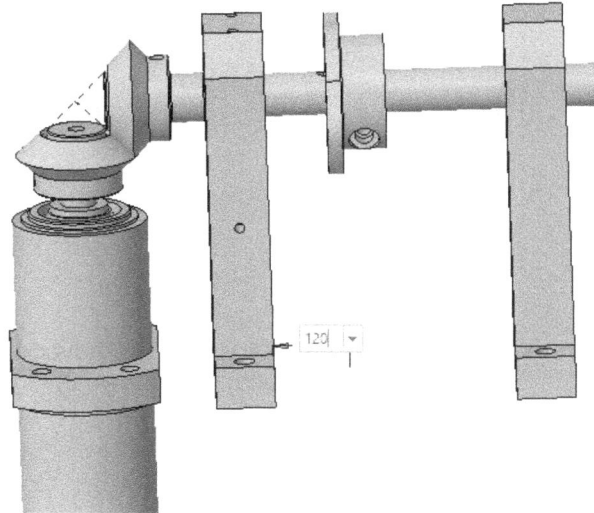

Figure 2–82

7. Regenerate the assembly, as shown in Figure 2–83.

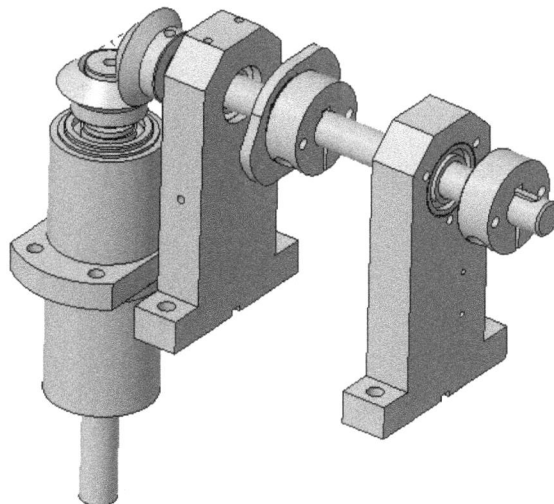

Figure 2–83

Task 5 - Copy na200-9_30_1.prt as a new component.

1. Select **na200-9_30_1.prt**, right-click and select ▧ (Copy).

2. Right-click and select ▧ (Paste Special).

3. In the Paste Special dialog box that opens, select **Advanced reference configuration**, as shown in Figure 2–84.

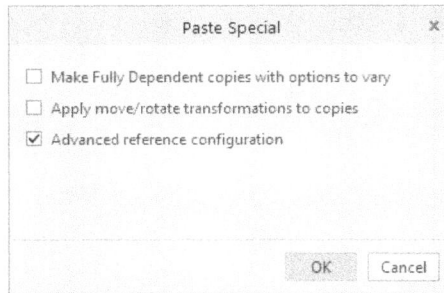

Figure 2–84

4. Click **OK**. The Advanced Reference Configuration dialog box opens as shown in Figure 2–85.

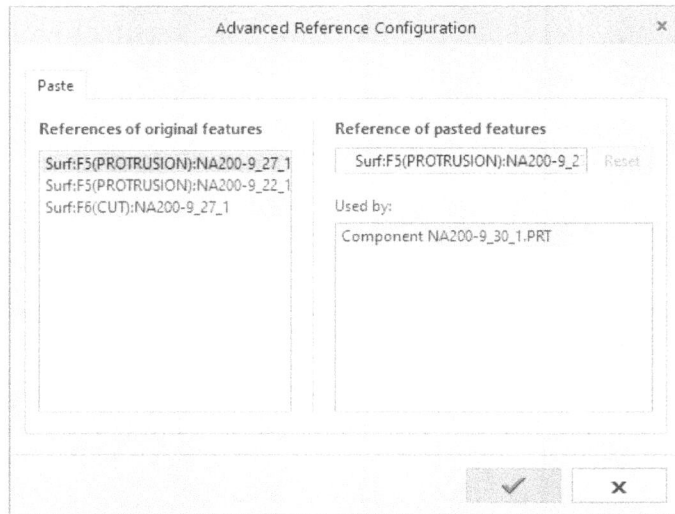

Figure 2–85

5. Select the surface of **na200-9_27_1.prt** as the new assembly reference for the first constraint, as shown in Figure 2–86.

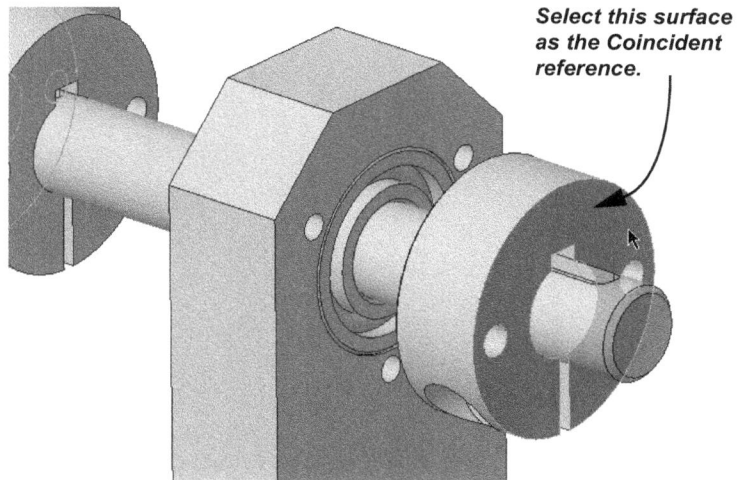

Select this surface as the Coincident reference.

Figure 2–86

6. Select the second row of the *References of original features* field. The old assembly reference can be reused. Do not change the reference for this constraint.

7. Select the third row of the *References of original features* field. Select the surface of **na200-9_27_1.prt** as the new reference for the Parallel constraint, as shown in Figure 2–87.

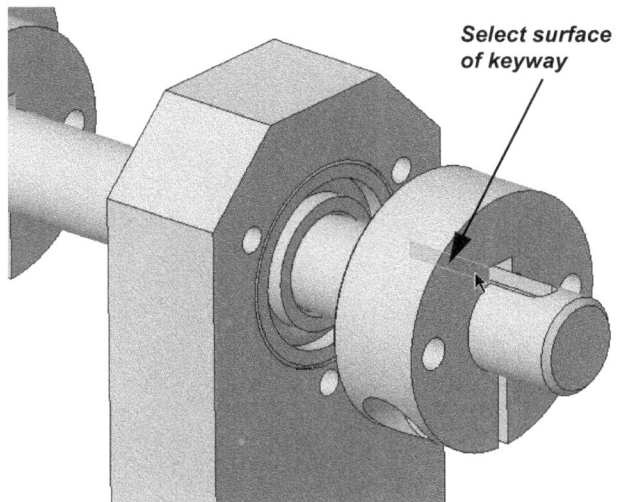

Select surface of keyway

Figure 2–87

8. Confirm the model displays as shown in Figure 2–88.

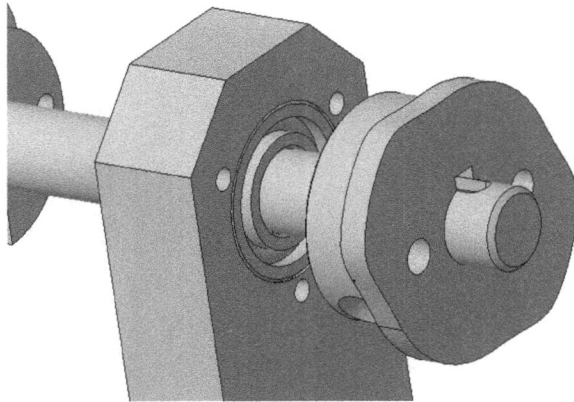

Figure 2–88

9. Click ✓ (OK) to complete this assembly.

10. In the Model Tree, click 🗍 ˅ (Settings)>**Tree Filters** and enable **Suppressed objects**.

11. Save the model and erase it from memory.

Chapter Review Questions

1. Flexible components enable you to display a component in different geometric representations, and reports each configuration as new in the Bill of Materials report.

   a. True

   b. False

2. To assemble a flexible component into an assembly, you can use which of the following techniques? (Select all that apply.)

   a. Select **File>Prepare>Model Properties**. The Model Properties dialog box opens. Select **change**.

   b. Expand ⌐ (Assemble) in the *Model* tab and select **Flexible**.

   c. Components can be made flexible after the component has been placed in the assembly by right-clicking and selecting **Make Flexible**.

   d. Click ⊟ (Component Interface) and select **Flexible** in the *Component Interface* tab.

3. A component containing a Component Interface can be placed by selecting a point on the model in the area of the required placement using **Auto Place**.

   a. True

   b. False

4. Components must already be in an assembly to use the **Paste Special** command.

   a. True

   b. False

5. If a component interface exists for a component that is added to an assembly you cannot manually assemble the component.

   a. True

   b. False

6. Which option enables you to duplicate components in the assembly using the same assembly constraints with small variations in the references or offset values?
    a. Repeat
    b. Component Interface
    c. Reference Pattern
    d. Copy and Paste

Answers: 1.b, 2.abc, 3.a, 4.b, 5.b, 6.a

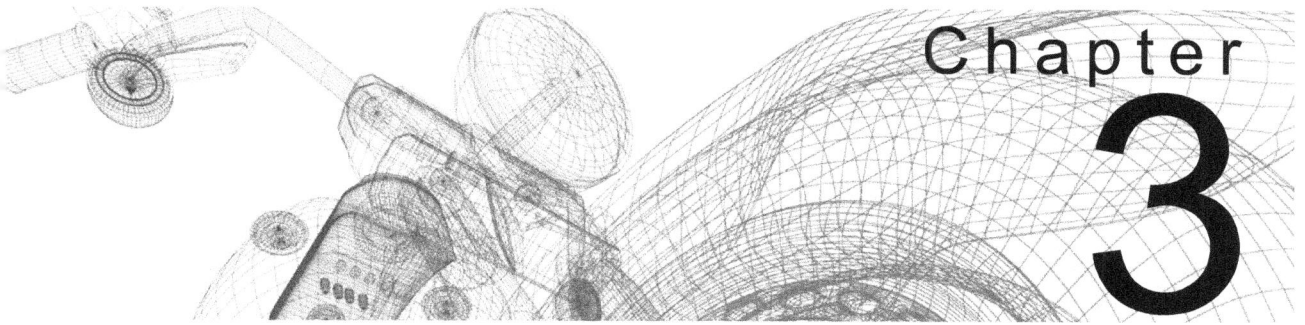

Chapter

3

Assembly Management

Your efficiency in working in Assembly mode is often determined by your use of assembly management techniques. The techniques used to control the display of components and features not only simplify the visual display, but also decrease retrieval and refresh times. Familiarity with component operations, such as Restructure, can also increase overall efficiency when making substantial changes to an assembly's structure.

Learning Objectives in This Chapter

- Review the process of creating a layer and adding components or features to the layer.
- Learn how the system reacts to adding part-level features to an assembly layer.
- Learn to set the display status for the layer to Hide, Unhide, or Isolate and save the layer status.
- Remove a feature temporarily from being included as part of the model geometry and regeneration sequence using the **Suppress** command.
- Move components in the assembly using the **Restructure** command or by dragging and dropping the items in the Model Tree.

3.1 Layers in Assembly Mode

Layers enable you to organize model items (e.g., solid features, datum features, and components) in an assembly, so that display operations can be performed on the items collectively. A layer can contain any number of features and components, and an item can exist on more than one layer. For example, several datum features can be placed together on a layer, which is then blanked so that those datums are not displayed. All of the other datum features remain visible.

How To: Create a Layer

All models created using the default Creo Parametric templates contain default layers. These layers include surfaces and datum features (e.g., planes, axes, curves, points, and coordinate systems) that are added to the model.

1. Layer information is located in the Layer Tree. Click ⊜ (Layers) in the *View* tab or expand ▤ ▾ (Show) in the Model Tree and select **Layer Tree**. The Layer Tree replaces the Model Tree, as shown in Figure 3–1.

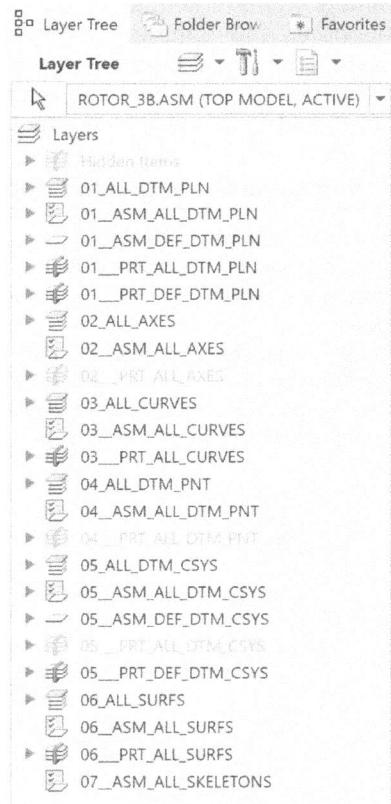

Figure 3–1

2. To create a new layer, right-click anywhere in the Layer Tree and select **New Layer**. The Layer Properties dialog box opens, as shown in Figure 3–2.

Layer names can be numeric or alphanumeric, with a maximum of 31 characters. Names cannot consist of special characters (i.e., !, %, or &) or spaces. If a space is required, you can use an underscore (_).

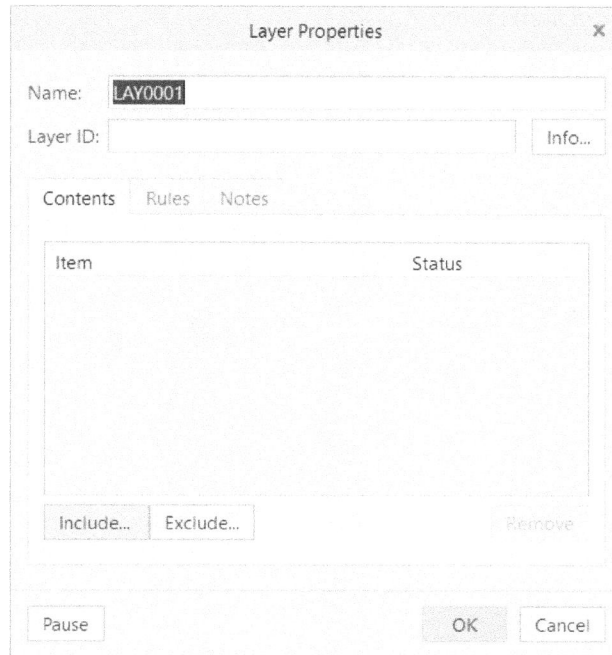

Figure 3–2

The default name of a new layer is **LAY000#**, where # represents the number of layers that are created in the model. For example, the first layer that is created in the model is called **LAY0001** by default. It is recommended that you replace this name with one that describes the contents of the layer.

You can use the selection filter at the bottom of the main window to help select the correct item on the model.

3. Select features or components in the Model Tree or directly on the model to populate the layer. The Layer Properties dialog box opens, as shown in Figure 3–3, listing all of the selected items.

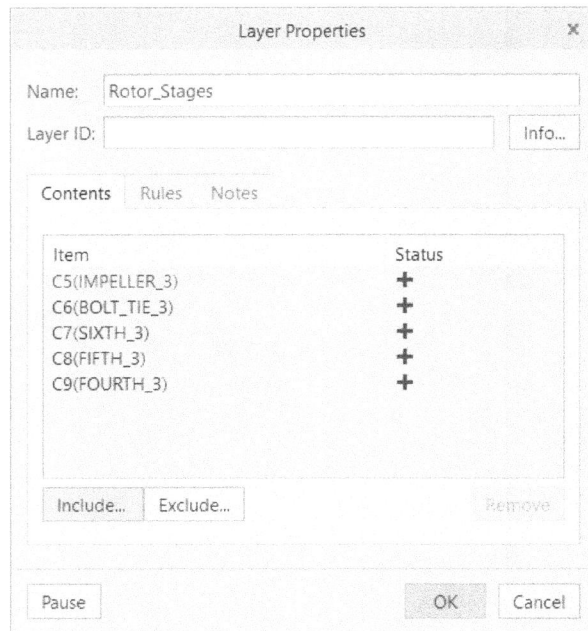

Figure 3–3

Items are listed under the *Contents* tab. You can include, exclude, remove, and pause items in a layer as follows:

- Click **Include** to add items to the layer. Once added, the status updates to display ✛ .

- Click **Exclude** to exclude an item from the layer without actually removing it. Excluded items display ▬ in the *Status* column.

- To remove an item from the layer, select it in the *Contents* tab in the dialog box and click **Remove**.

- Click **Pause** to pause the selection of items without closing the Layer Properties dialog box. This tool is useful if you want to review features before adding them to the layer.

4. Once you finish adding items to a layer, click **OK**.

Add Part Level Features to a Layer

If you add part features to a layer created at the assembly level, the system prompts you to create a new layer at the part level, as shown on the left in Figure 3–4. If a layer already exists in the part with the same name as the assembly layer, the system prompts you to add the item to the part layer, as shown on the right in Figure 3–4.

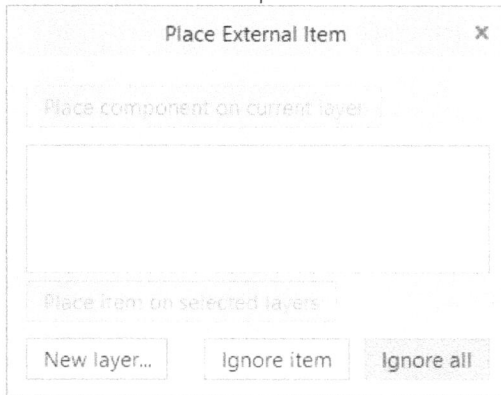

This dialog box opens if the selected items from the assembly do not already exist in a part layer.

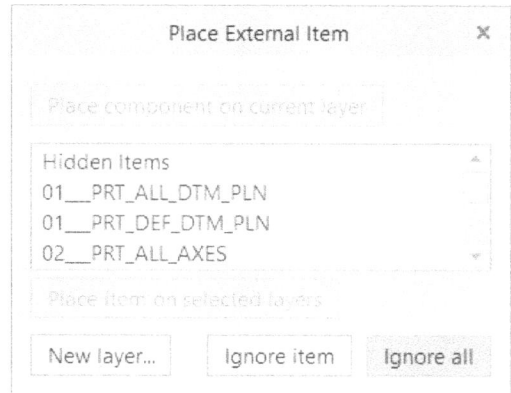

This dialog box opens if the selected items from the assembly already exist in a part layer.

Figure 3–4

Assembly-level layers can control the display of part-level layers with the same name.

For example, the Layer Tree shown in Figure 3–5 has an assembly level layer called **DATUMS**. This layer includes datums from both the assembly level and part level. Since datums from **9002_RH.prt** were added to the assembly level layer, the DATUMS layer is also created in the **9002_RH.prt** model.

Figure 3–5

Display Status

The display status of an assembly layer can include the following settings:

- **Hide:** To set a Hide status, select the layer in the Layer Tree, right-click and select **Hide**.

- **Show:** The Show status is the default display status for all new layers. Once a layer has been hidden, you can display it by right-clicking and selecting **Show**.

- **Isolate:** The Isolate status enables you to display the layers that have their status set to Isolate and all non-isolated layers as hidden. To set the display status of a layer to Isolate, click ≋ ▾ (Layer)>**Isolate**.

- **Hidden Line:** The Hidden Line status enables you to display components in accordance with the Environment settings for hidden-line display. Other items on the hidden layers are not affected. The Environment settings are described as follows:
  - Wireframe = Shown
  - Hidden Line = Hidden Line
  - No Hidden Line = Blanked
  - Shading = Shown

  To set the display status of a layer to **Hidden**, click ≋ ▾ (Layer)>**Hidden Line**.

Layer Info

To view the current display status of a layer, right-click and select **Layer Info** or click ≋ ⋎ (Layer)>**Layer info**. The Information Window for the selected layer opens, as shown in Figure 3–6.

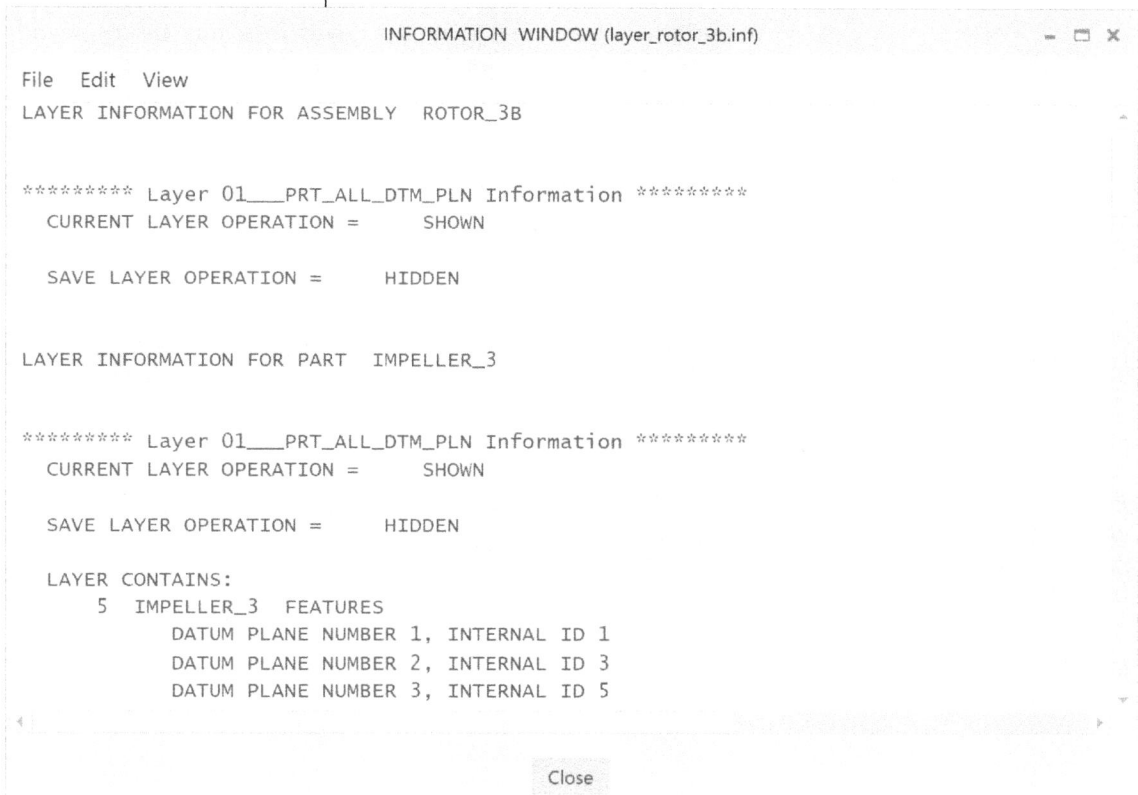

```
INFORMATION WINDOW (layer_rotor_3b.inf)          – ☐ ✕

File   Edit   View
LAYER INFORMATION FOR ASSEMBLY   ROTOR_3B


********* Layer 01___PRT_ALL_DTM_PLN Information *********
  CURRENT LAYER OPERATION =      SHOWN

  SAVE LAYER OPERATION =      HIDDEN


LAYER INFORMATION FOR PART   IMPELLER_3


********* Layer 01___PRT_ALL_DTM_PLN Information *********
  CURRENT LAYER OPERATION =      SHOWN

  SAVE LAYER OPERATION =      HIDDEN

  LAYER CONTAINS:
     5  IMPELLER_3  FEATURES
           DATUM PLANE NUMBER 1, INTERNAL ID 1
           DATUM PLANE NUMBER 2, INTERNAL ID 3
           DATUM PLANE NUMBER 3, INTERNAL ID 5
```

Close

Figure 3–6

The following two lines in the Information Window identify the layer's display status:

- Current Layer Operation

- Save Layer Operation

The Current Layer Operation line identifies the display status of the layer in the current session of Creo Parametric. The Save Layer Operation line identifies the saved status of the layer. The model always opens using the saved display status for each layer.

Save Status

To save the display status for all of the layers in the model, right-click and select **Save Status**. To reset the layer display status to that which was previously saved, right-click and select **Reset Status**.

To perform actions on a layer, the Layer Tree must be displayed. You can make the following modifications on a layer using the Layer Tree:

- Add items to a layer.
- Remove items from a layer.
- Delete a layer.
- Copy and paste items between layers.

Editing Layers

The Layer Tree is displayed to perform actions on a layer. All of the editing options are available using ≋ ▾ (Layer) in the Layer Tree, or by right-clicking. The options for both methods are shown in Figure 3–7.

Items from one layer can be copied and pasted to another layer using the options in ≋ ▾ (Layer), or using the shortcut menu.

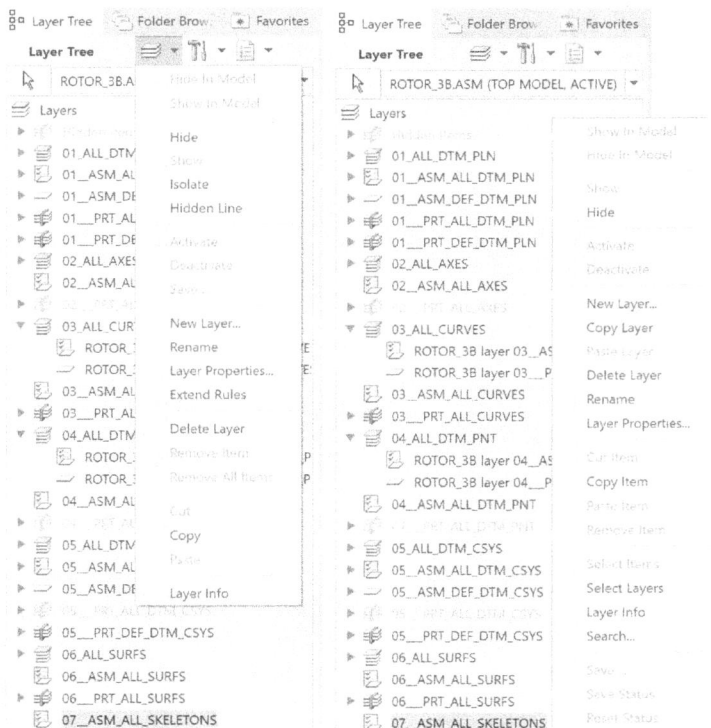

Figure 3–7

To redefine the items in a layer, expand ⬚ ▾ (Layer) and select **Layer Properties**, or right-click and select **Layer Properties**. The Layer Properties dialog box opens with its original settings.

Default Layers

You can create additional default layers that display automatically in the Layer Tree once a particular type of item has been added to the model. For example, if you want to automatically place threaded features as they are created on their own layer, set the **def_layer** configuration option to **layer_thread_feat THREADS**, where **THREADS** is the name of the layer. A complete list of the default layers can be found in the Creo Parametric Help system.

3.2 Suppress and Resume

Suppressed features and components are temporarily removed from the display and the regeneration sequence. This simplifies the appearance of the model and decreases the amount of time it takes to regenerate. For example, if a component is suppressed and the assembly is saved, that component is not opened into session the next time the assembly is opened. This can save considerable time when retrieving large assemblies. The cut shown on the left in Figure 3–8 is selected to be suppressed. Consequently, the cut is removed from the Model Tree and the regeneration sequence, as shown in the right in Figure 3–8.

The cut feature is suppressed

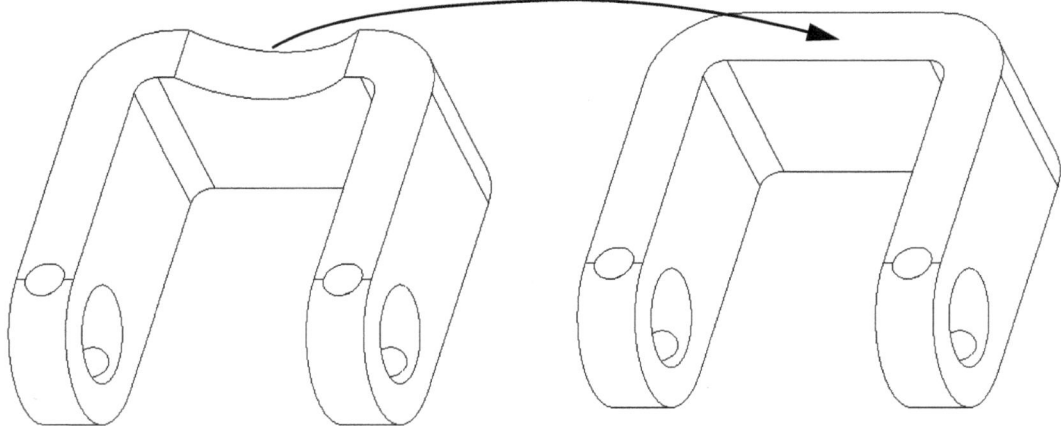

Figure 3–8

How To: Suppress Features or Components

1. Select the feature or component to be suppressed from the Model Tree or directly on the model. Careful consideration must be taken with regard to parent/child relationships. By default, all of the children are suppressed with their parents.

2. To suppress an item, select it and click ▮ (Suppress) in the mini toolbar, or select **Operations>Suppress>Suppress** in the *Model* tab. When suppressing a feature or component with children, all of the children are also selected and the Suppress dialog box opens, as shown in Figure 3–9.

All of the suppressed settings are saved when the model is explicitly saved to the disk.

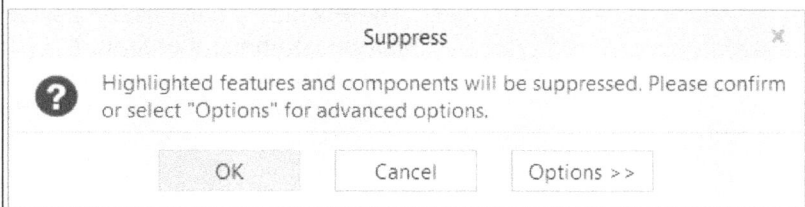

Figure 3–9

3. Click **OK** to confirm the suppression of the feature or component and all of its children, or click **Cancel** to cancel the operation. For advanced options on controlling children, click **Options>>**. The Children Handling dialog box opens, as shown in Figure 3–10.

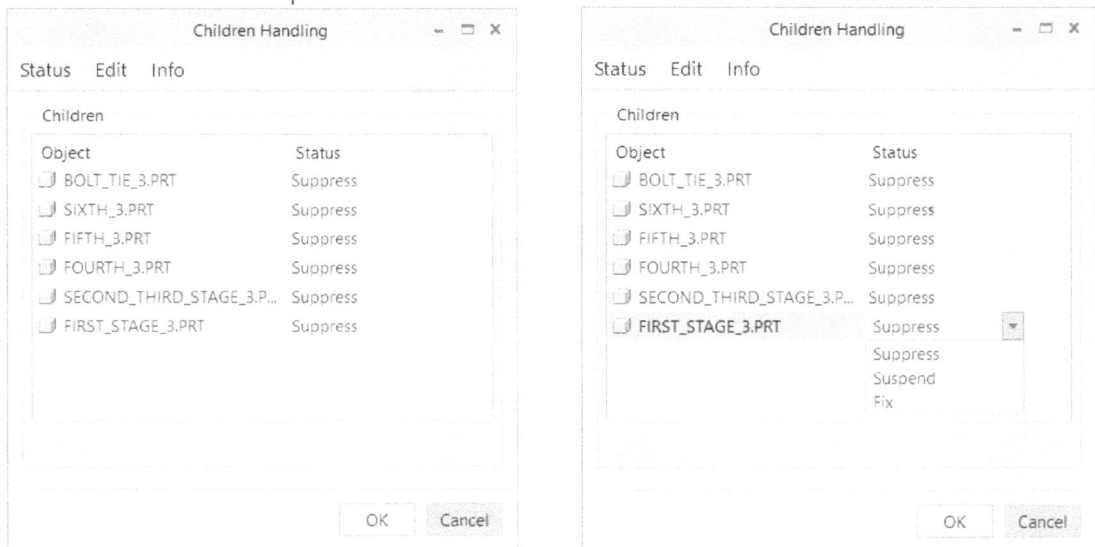

Figure 3–10

You can set the status of any of the children to **Suppress**, **Suspend**, or **Fix**.

- The **Suppress** status suppresses the child with the parent. The status is set to **Suppress** by default.

- The **Suspend** status temporarily removes the parent/child relationship, which enables you to edit the feature or component separately. Suspending does not suppress the child, but the child cannot be regenerated with its parent missing. If you attempt to regenerate the model, it fails and an Information Window opens, indicating that the parent of the feature/component is missing.

- The **Fix** status can also be assigned when suppressing a parent component or feature. Fixing enables you to lock the item in its current location so that you can continue working in the assembly. A Fixed item displays as shown in Figure 3–11.

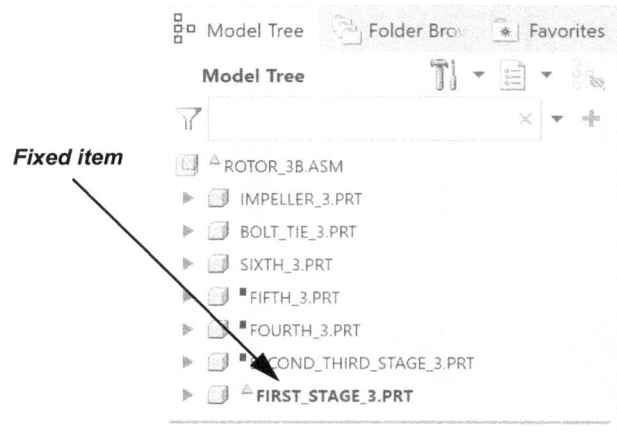

Figure 3–11

Suppressed items can be restored to the display by selecting **Operations>Resume>Resume**. The following options are available to resume previously suppressed items:

- Resume

- Resume Last Set

- Resume All

If the suppressed feature/component is displayed in the Model

Tree, you can resume it by selecting it and clicking ⇒ (Resume) in the mini toolbar. A selected item can also be resumed by selecting **Operations>Resume>Resume** in the *Model* tab.

To hide or show suppressed features/components in the Model Tree, click 🔧 ▾ (Settings) in the Model Tree, select **Tree Filters** and toggle **Suppressed objects** in the *Display* section in the Model Tree Items dialog box.

Suppressed items are marked with a black square in the Model Tree, as shown in Figure 3–12.

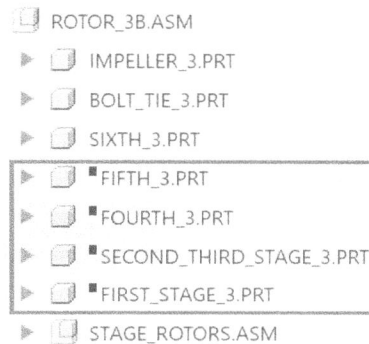

Resuming individual items by clicking

🔹 *(Resume) can cause failures if the resumed feature/ component references items that are still suppressed.*

ROTOR_3B.ASM
 ▷ ◻ IMPELLER_3.PRT
 ▷ ◻ BOLT_TIE_3.PRT
 ▷ ◻ SIXTH_3.PRT
 ▷ ◻ ■FIFTH_3.PRT
 ▷ ◻ ■FOURTH_3.PRT
 ▷ ◻ ■SECOND_THIRD_STAGE_3.PRT
 ▷ ◻ ■FIRST_STAGE_3.PRT
 ▷ ◻ STAGE_ROTORS.ASM

Four components are suppressed in this assembly.

Figure 3–12

The **Resume Last Set** option restores the last set of suppressed objects, while the **Resume All** option restores all of the features/ components that are currently suppressed in the model.

3.3 Restructure

Restructuring enables you to move components from one assembly to another while remaining in a top-level assembly. Components can be restructured from a top-level assembly into a subassembly or from a subassembly to a higher level assembly. The Model Trees shown in Figure 3–13 have components that were restructured from the top-level assembly into a subassembly.

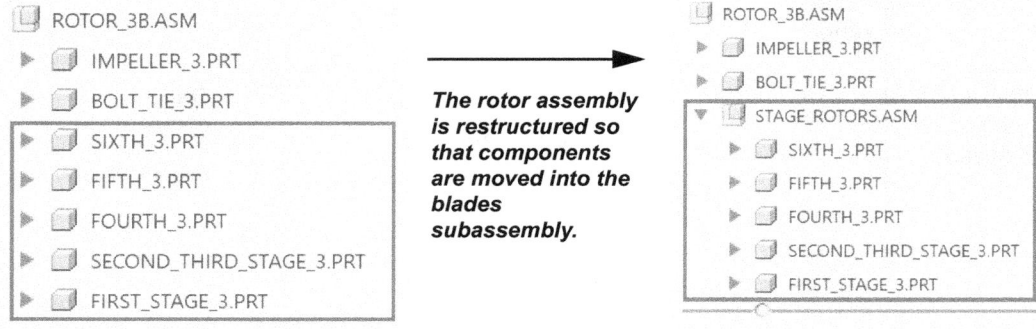

ROTOR_3B.ASM
▶ IMPELLER_3.PRT
▶ BOLT_TIE_3.PRT
▶ SIXTH_3.PRT
▶ FIFTH_3.PRT
▶ FOURTH_3.PRT
▶ SECOND_THIRD_STAGE_3.PRT
▶ FIRST_STAGE_3.PRT

→

The rotor assembly is restructured so that components are moved into the blades subassembly.

ROTOR_3B.ASM
▶ IMPELLER_3.PRT
▶ BOLT_TIE_3.PRT
▼ STAGE_ROTORS.ASM
   ▶ SIXTH_3.PRT
   ▶ FIFTH_3.PRT
   ▶ FOURTH_3.PRT
   ▶ SECOND_THIRD_STAGE_3.PRT
   ▶ FIRST_STAGE_3.PRT

Figure 3–13

Remember to consider any parent/child relationships that can result when you move from a top-level assembly into a subassembly. References to the original top-level assembly are missing if the subassembly is opened into a session on its own, which means you must redefine the references to fix the failure.

How To: Restructure Components

1. To begin restructuring, select **Component>Restructure** in the *Model* tab. The Restructure dialog box opens as shown in Figure 3–14. This helps identify which components are being moved.

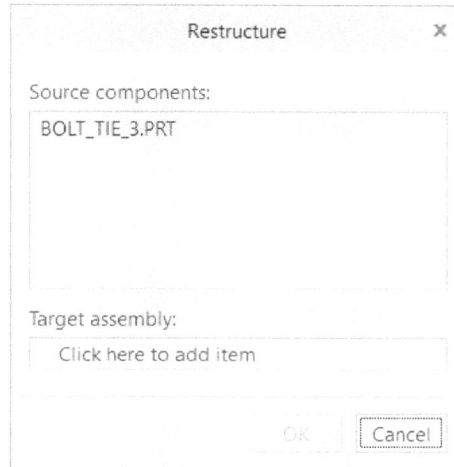

Figure 3–14

2. Once the Restructure dialog box opens, you can select one or more components to move. Components can be selected in the Model Tree or directly on the model.

3. In the Restructure dialog box, click in the *Target assembly* field and select the target assembly in the Model Tree or on the model. The Model Tree updates to display the selected component as part of the target subassembly, or in the main assembly if moving a component out of a subassembly.

   - Parent-child relationships can impact your ability to use the restructure tool. You cannot restructure a parent component such that it would regenerate after a child component.

4. In many cases, a restructured subassembly fails when it is opened without the top-level assembly being in session. This failure occurs because the placement references were established in the top-level when the component was originally assembled. These references might be missing from the moved component when the subassembly is opened on its own. To resolve the failure, you must redefine the component placement references or fix the component in the subassembly.

Note that in addition to the previous method, you can also drag and drop components into the required subassembly to restructure, as shown in Figure 3–15.

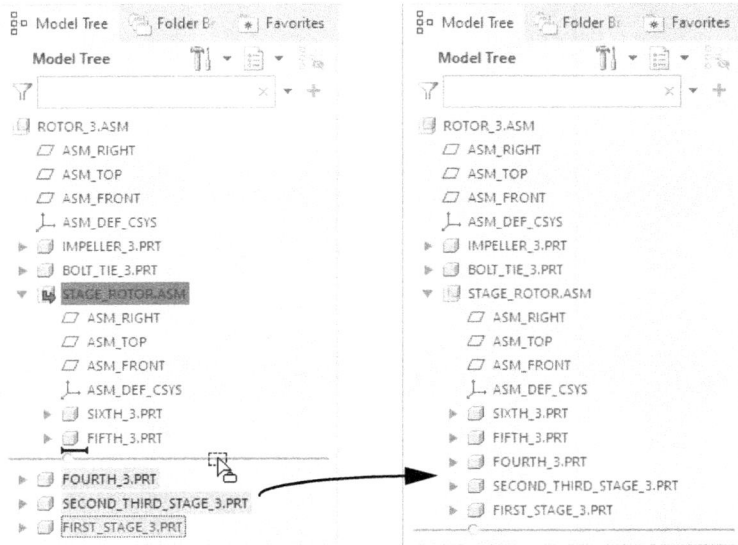

Figure 3–15

3.4 Move to New Subassembly

The Restructure tool enables you to move components from the top level assembly to existing subassemblies. The limitation is that the target assembly must already be in the top-level assembly.

You can create a new subassembly on the fly and move a component to it by right-clicking the component and selecting ⇢ (Move to New Subassembly), as shown in Figure 3–16.

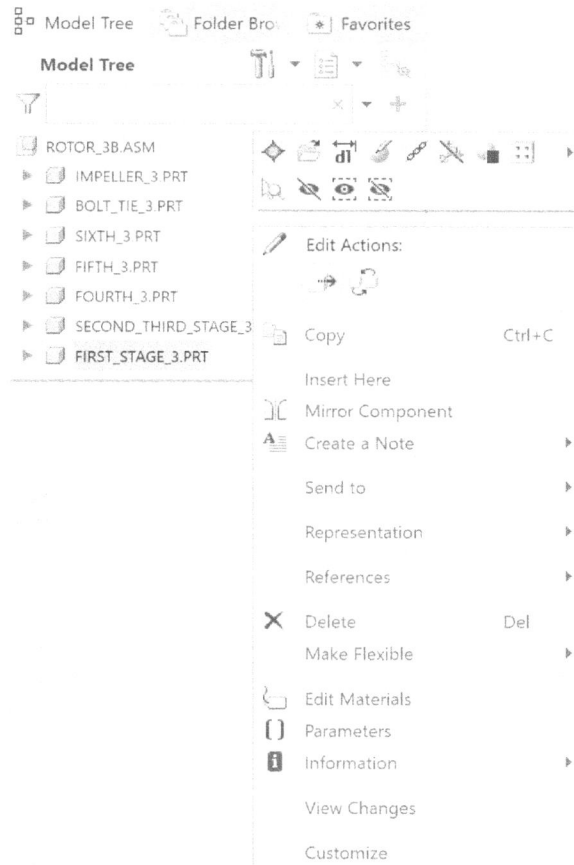

Figure 3–16

The Create Component dialog opens, as shown in Figure 3–17.

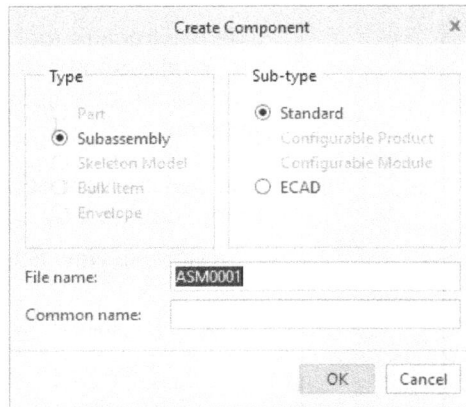

Figure 3–17

Edit the name and click **OK**. The Creation Options dialog box opens, as shown in Figure 3–18.

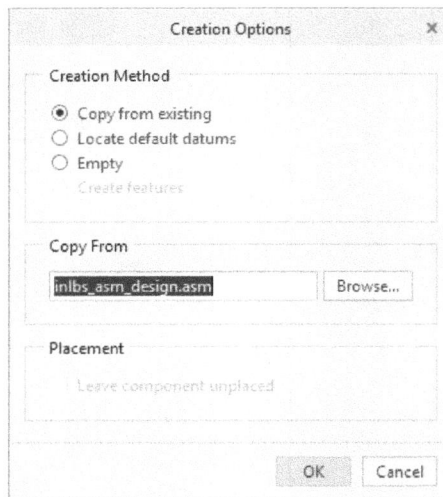

Figure 3–18

In the Creation Options dialog box, select the creation options for the new subassembly, such as copying from an existing file or template, locate a set of default datums, and so on.

Assemble the new subassembly, and the selected component will be moved into it. You can then restructure any other components.

Practice 3a | Working with Layers

Practice Objectives

- Manage the display of datum features using layers.
- Manage the display of components using suppression.
- Use a layer to select components to be suppressed.
- Resume suppressed items.

In this practice, you will manage the feature and component display using both layers and suppression. Once you complete the practice you will understand the difference between layers and suppression, and their implications on model regeneration.

Task 1 - Open an assembly file.

1. Set the working directory to the *Assembly_Layers* folder.

2. Open **rotor_3.asm**.

3. Set the model display as follows:

   - ⅔ *(Datum Display Filters)*: All On

   - ⅔ *(Spin Center)*: Off

   - ⅃ *(Display Style)*: ⬚ (Shading With Edges)

   The assembly should display as shown in Figure 3–19.

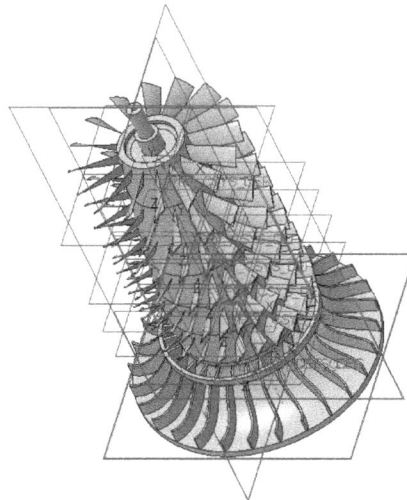

Figure 3–19

Task 2 - Manage the feature display using layers.

1. In the Model Tree, click ▤ ▼ (Show)>**Layer Tree** to activate the Layer Tree.

2. Select **01_ALL_DTM_PLN** in the Layer Tree, right-click, and select **Hide**, as shown in Figure 3–20.

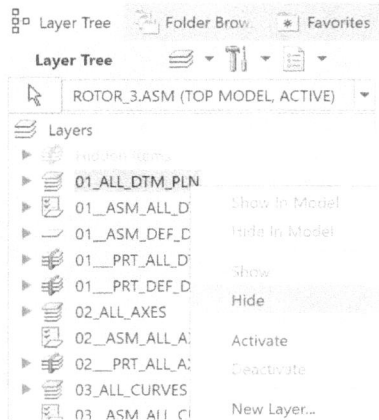

Figure 3–20

3. In the In-graphics toolbar, click ◿ (Repaint) to redraw the current view. The assembly displays as shown in Figure 3–21.

Only the datum planes at the assembly level have been hidden. This is because the assembly is the active model.

Figure 3–21

4. Right-click on **01__PRT_ALL_DTM_PLN** and select **Hide** to hide all of the part datum planes, as shown in Figure 3–22.

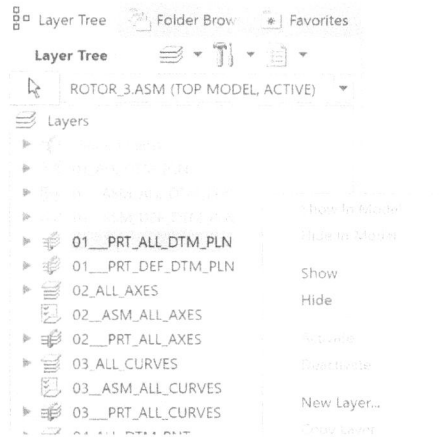

Figure 3–22

5. Repaint the screen. The assembly displays as shown in Figure 3–23.

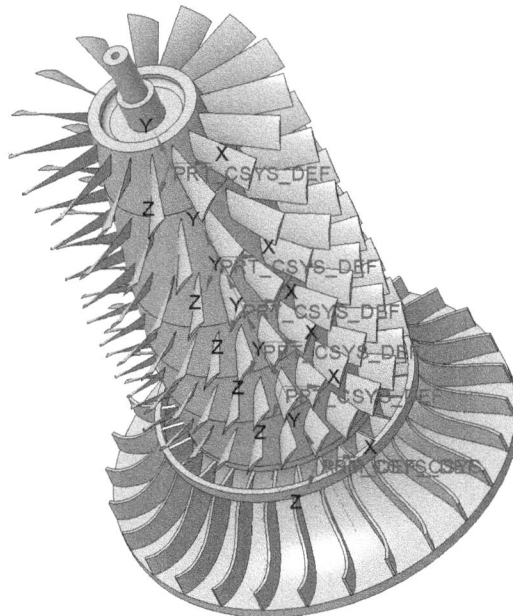

Figure 3–23

6. Hide the following default layers at the part level:

- Datum axis (**02___PRT_ALL_AXES**)
- Datum points (**04___PRT_ALL_DTM_PNT**)
- Datum coordinate systems
  (**05___PRT_ALL_DTM_CSYS**)

7. Repaint the screen. The assembly displays as shown in Figure 3–24. The assembly coordinate system should remain on screen because you have only hidden features at the part level.

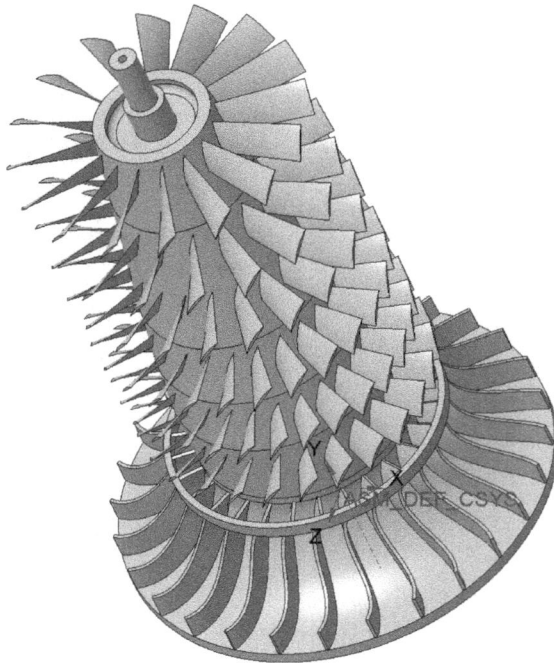

Figure 3–24

Task 3 - Create a layer.

1. Place the cursor in the Layer Tree, right-click, and select **New Layer**.

2. Set the *Name* of the new layer to **rotor_stages**, as shown in Figure 3–25. Do not press <Enter>.

*If you press <Enter> after you enter the layer name, the Layer Properties dialog box closes. To re-open it, select the layer in the Layer Tree, right-click, and select **Layer Properties**.*

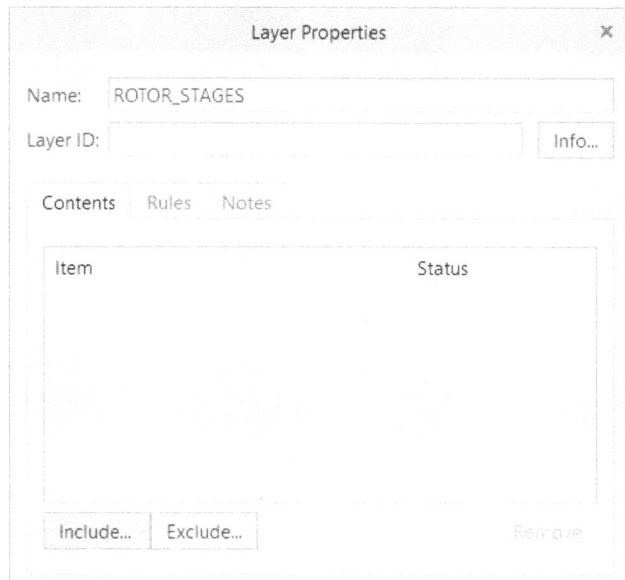

Figure 3–25

3. Show the Model Tree and select all five rotor parts. The Layer Properties dialog box opens, as shown in Figure 3–26.

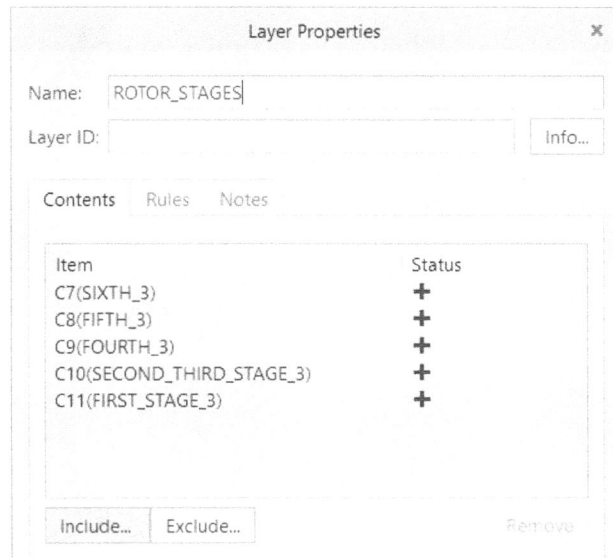

Figure 3–26

4. Click **OK** to complete the creation of the new layer.

5. Show the Layer Tree. The new layer has been added to the bottom of the Layer Tree list, as shown in Figure 3–27.

    04_ASM_ALL_DTM_PNT
▶ 04__PRT_ALL_DTM_PNT
▶ 05_ALL_DTM_CSYS
▶ 05_ASM_ALL_DTM_CSYS
▶ 05_ASM_DEF_DTM_CSYS
▶ 05__PRT_ALL_DTM_CSYS
▶ 05__PRT_DEF_DTM_CSYS
▶ 06_ALL_SURFS
    06_ASM_ALL_SURFS
▶ 06__PRT_ALL_SURFS
    07_ASM_ALL_SKELETONS
▶ ROTOR_STAGES

Figure 3–27

6. Hide the new **ROTOR_STAGES** layer and repaint the screen. The components on that layer are now hidden, as shown in Figure 3–28.

Figure 3–28

Design Considerations

Hidden components still regenerate, although they are hidden. Therefore, hiding components visually simplifies the assembly, but does not reduce regeneration time.

7. **Show** the **ROTOR_STAGES** layer and repaint the screen.

Task 4 - Suppress components by layer.

---

1. Select the **ROTOR_STAGES** layer in the Layer Tree, right-click, and select **Select Items**.

2. Move the cursor into the main window, right-click and select ▪ (Suppress) in the mini toolbar.

3. Click **OK** in the Suppress dialog box.

4. Show the Model Tree, as shown in Figure 3–29.

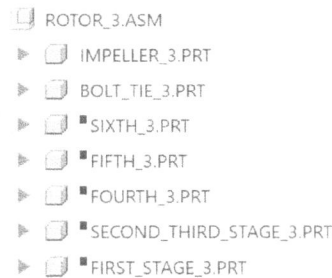

Figure 3–29

Design Considerations

The components that have been suppressed are no longer visible and do not regenerate. Suppression can be used to reduce the regeneration time of a large assembly. By default, Creo Parametric will display suppressed items in the Model Tree; this setting can be changed. If suppressed objects are not displayed, complete the following three steps.

5. Click ⊤ ˅ (Settings)>**Tree Filters**.

6. Ensure that **Suppressed objects** is selected, as shown in Figure 3–30.

   - It is recommended to always have this option selected so that you are aware of any suppressed objects.

7. Click **OK**.

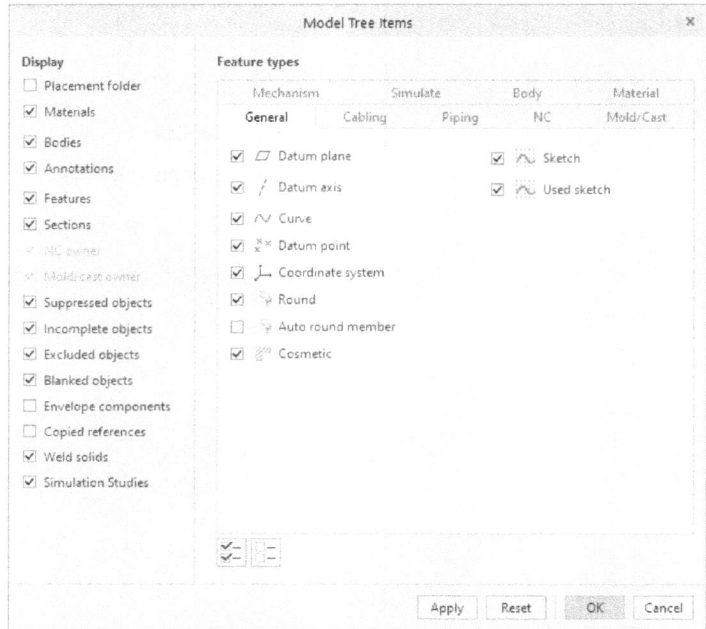

Figure 3–30

You can also select
Operations>Resume>
Resume All *in the*
Model tab.

8. Select all of the suppressed components and click
   (Resume) in the mini toolbar, as shown in Figure 3–31.

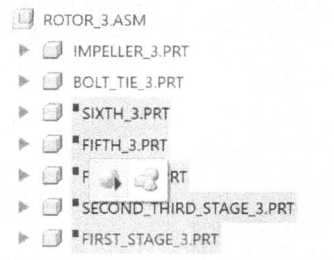

Figure 3–31

Task 5 - Suppress a component with children.

1. Select **SIXTH_3.PRT** in the Model Tree and click
   ◼ (Suppress) in the mini toolbar. The Suppress dialog box
   opens, as shown in Figure 3–32.

Figure 3–32

Design Considerations

When suppressing components, parent/child relationships must
be considered. The **sixth_3.prt** is a parent to all of the stage
rotors due to constraint references. Options are available to
control the suppression status of affected components.

2. Click **Options**. The Children Handling dialog box opens, as
   shown in Figure 3–33. It lists all of the affected components.

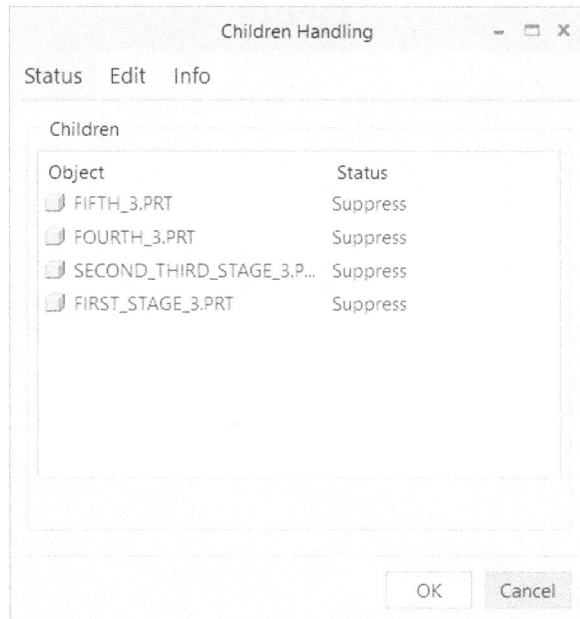

Figure 3–33

3. Use the **Status** menu to change the status of
   FIRST_STAGE_3.PRT to **Fix**, as shown in Figure 3–34.

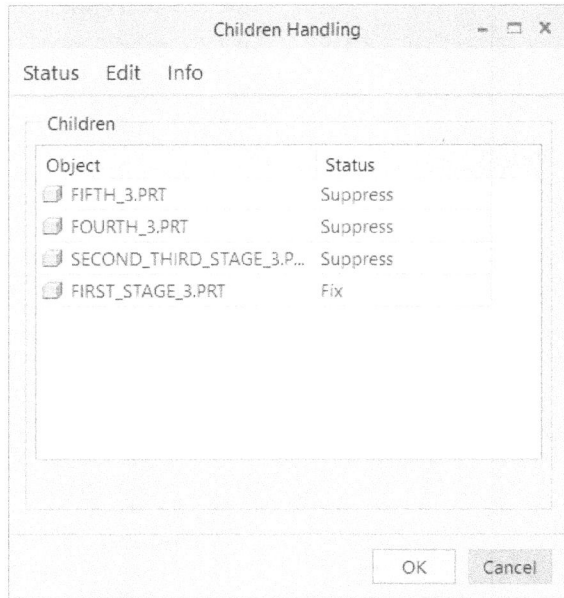

| Children Handling | — ☐ ✕ |

Status   Edit   Info

Children

Object	Status
FIFTH_3.PRT	Suppress
FOURTH_3.PRT	Suppress
SECOND_THIRD_STAGE_3.P...	Suppress
FIRST_STAGE_3.PRT	Fix

OK   Cancel

Figure 3–34

4. Click **OK**. The assembly displays as shown in Figure 3–35.

Figure 3–35

- The Model Tree displays as shown in Figure 3–36.

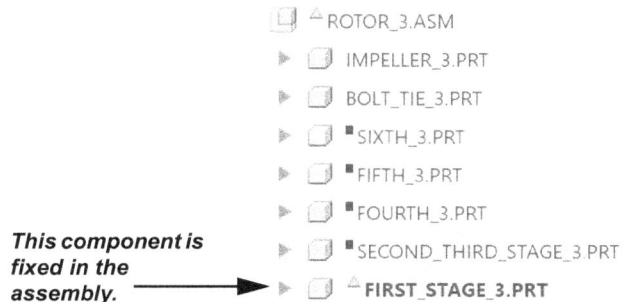

△ ROTOR_3.ASM
▷ ☐ IMPELLER_3.PRT
▷ ☐ BOLT_TIE_3.PRT
▷ ☐ ■ SIXTH_3.PRT
▷ ☐ ■ FIFTH_3.PRT
▷ ☐ ■ FOURTH_3.PRT
▷ ☐ ■ SECOND_THIRD_STAGE_3.PRT

This component is fixed in the assembly. ⟶ ▷ ☐ △ **FIRST_STAGE_3.PRT**

Figure 3–36

Design Considerations

Through handling children, you have frozen **first_stage_3.prt**. This part is visible, but its position in the assembly does not regenerate.

The Fixed status temporarily removes the parent/child relationship, which enables you to edit the feature or component separately. Suspending does not suppress the child. However, the child cannot be regenerated with its parent missing.

5. Resume all of the suppressed components.

6. Save the assembly and erase all files from memory.

Practice 3b | Assembly Restructure

Practice Objectives

- Move a component from the main assembly into a subassembly on the fly.
- Restructure several components.
- Assign new references to the restructured components.
- Move components in the assembly by dragging and dropping the items into a subassembly.

In this practice, you will restructure the **rotor_3b** assembly, which requires restructuring due to a design change. The current assembly structure is shown in Figure 3–37. A design change requires that all of the stage rotors be in a separate subassembly called **stage_rotors**, as shown in Figure 3–38.

Figure 3–37

Figure 3–38

Once the components have been moved, you must redefine the assembly references because the original references were made to the rotor_3b assembly.

Task 1 - Create a subassembly and move a component to it on the fly.

1. Set the working directory to the *Restructure* folder.

2. Open **rotor_3b.asm**.

3. Set the model display as follows:

   - ⅍ *(Datum Display Filters)*: All On
   - ⋗ *(Spin Center)*: Off
   - ⬛ *(Display Style)*: ▱ (Shading With Edges)

4. In the Model Tree, select **SIXTH_3.PRT**.

5. Right-click and select ⤳ (Move to New Subassembly).

6. In the Create Component dialog box, set the *File Name* to **stage_rotors** and click **OK**.

7. In the Creation Options dialog box, accept the default template listed in the *Copy From* field, as shown in Figure 3–39.

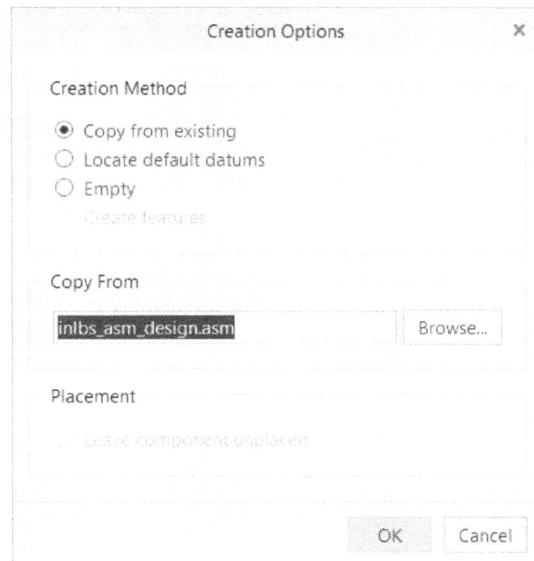

Figure 3–39

8. Click **OK**.

9. In the *Component Placement* dashboard, select **Default** from the Constraint Type drop-down list and click ✓ (OK).

10. In the Model Tree, expand **STAGE_ROTORS.ASM** and note that **SIXTH_3.PRT** is now a component in it, as shown in Figure 3–40.

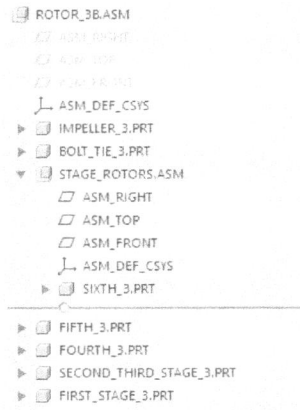

ROTOR_3B.ASM
  ASM_RIGHT
  ASM_TOP
  ASM_FRONT
  ⌐ ASM_DEF_CSYS
▶ ⬚ IMPELLER_3.PRT
▶ ⬚ BOLT_TIE_3.PRT
▼ ⬚ STAGE_ROTORS.ASM
    ⬚ ASM_RIGHT
    ⬚ ASM_TOP
    ⬚ ASM_FRONT
    ⌐ ASM_DEF_CSYS
  ▶ ⬚ SIXTH_3.PRT
▶ ⬚ FIFTH_3.PRT
▶ ⬚ FOURTH_3.PRT
▶ ⬚ SECOND_THIRD_STAGE_3.PRT
▶ ⬚ FIRST_STAGE_3.PRT

Figure 3–40

Task 2 - Restructure the assembly.

1. In the Model Tree, select **FIFTH_3.PRT**.

2. In the *Model* tab, select **Component>Restructure** and note that **FIFTH_3.PRT** is added to the *Source components* field in the Restructure dialog box.

3. Select the *Target Assembly* field in the Restructure dialog box and select **STAGE_ROTORS.ASM** as the target, as shown in Figure 3–41.

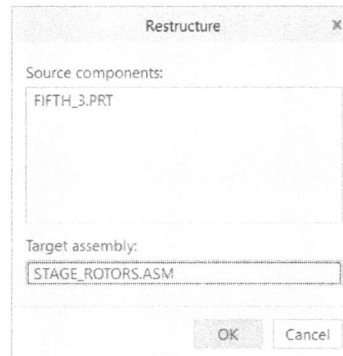

Restructure

Source components:

FIFTH_3.PRT

Target assembly:

STAGE_ROTORS.ASM

OK   Cancel

Figure 3–41

4. Click **OK**. The moved component is now part of the **stage_rotors** assembly, as shown in Figure 3–42.

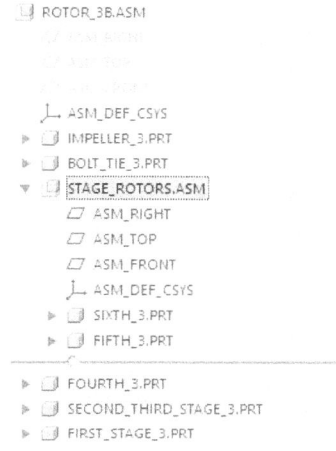

Figure 3–42

Task 3 - Use the drag-and-drop method to restructure the remaining rotor stages.

---

1. Select **FOURTH_3.PRT** in the Model Tree.

2. Press and hold <Shift> and select **FIRST_STAGE_3.PRT**. Drag and drop the parts directly onto the **STAGE_ROTORS.ASM** assembly, as shown in Figure 3–43.

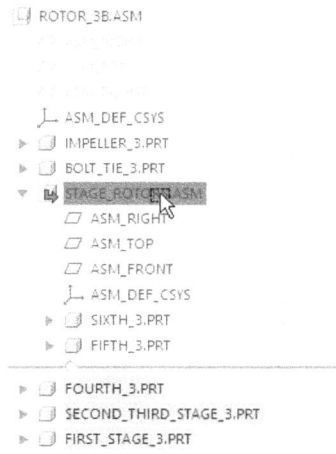

Figure 3–43

3. The components are now part of the **STAGE_ROTORS.ASM** assembly, as shown in Figure 3–44.

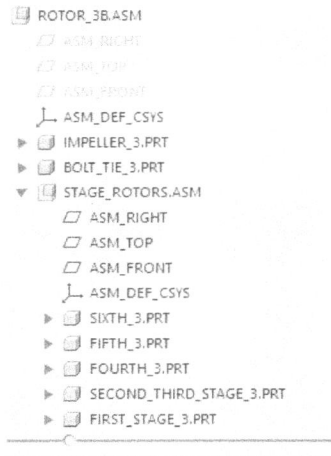

ROTOR_3B.ASM
　　ASM_RIGHT
　　ASM_TOP
　　ASM_FRONT
　　ASM_DEF_CSYS
▶ IMPELLER_3.PRT
▶ BOLT_TIE_3.PRT
▼ STAGE_ROTORS.ASM
　　ASM_RIGHT
　　ASM_TOP
　　ASM_FRONT
　　ASM_DEF_CSYS
▶ SIXTH_3.PRT
▶ FIFTH_3.PRT
▶ FOURTH_3.PRT
▶ SECOND_THIRD_STAGE_3.PRT
▶ FIRST_STAGE_3.PRT

Figure 3–44

4. Save the assembly.

___

Task 4 - Finalize the restructuring of the assembly.

___

1. Select **STAGE_ROTORS.ASM** in the Model Tree and click
   📁 (Open) in the mini toolbar.

**Design
Considerations**

You have successfully restructured the assembly. However, the assembly references for the rotor stages still reference the **rotor_3b** assembly. In this task, you will use revision tools to correct this problem.

2. Select **SIXTH_3.PRT** and click 🖌 (Edit Definition) in the mini toolbar. A warning message opens, as shown in Figure 3–45.

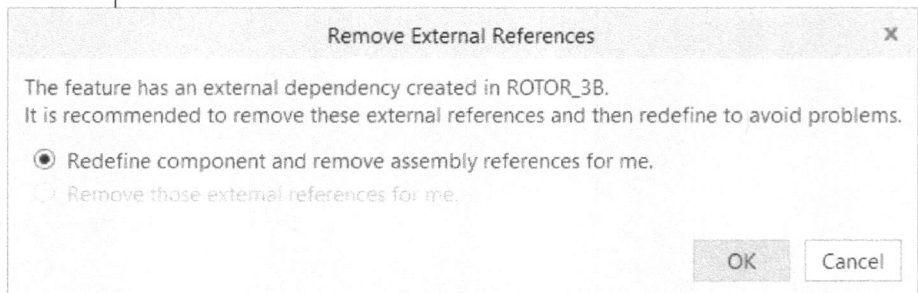

Remove External References   ✕

The feature has an external dependency created in ROTOR_3B.
It is recommended to remove these external references and then redefine to avoid problems.

◉ Redefine component and remove assembly references for me.
○ Remove those external references for me.

OK   Cancel

Figure 3–45

3. Click **OK** in the Warning dialog box. This removes the **rotor_3b** assembly references.

4. The *Component Placement* dashboard opens, enabling you to select appropriate assembly references for **sixth_3.prt**.

5. Select **ASM_TOP** as the assembly reference for the first Coincident constraint.

6. In the *Component Placement* dashboard, expand ▦ (Datum) and select ╱ (Axis), as shown in Figure 3–46.

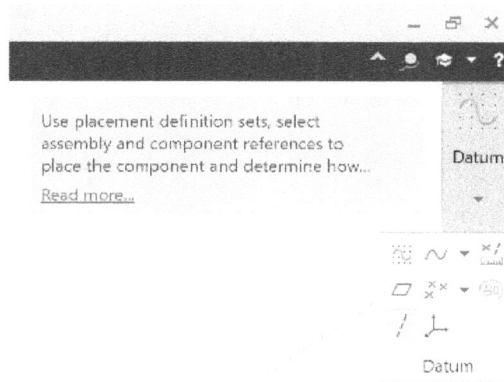

Figure 3–46

7. Select **ASM_RIGHT**, press and hold <Ctrl> and select **ASM_FRONT**.

8. Click **OK** in the Datum Axis dialog box.

9. Click ▶ (Resume).

*This constrains the axis **SIXTH_3.PRT** to the axis you just created.*

10. Click ✓ (OK). The assembly displays as shown in Figure 3–47.

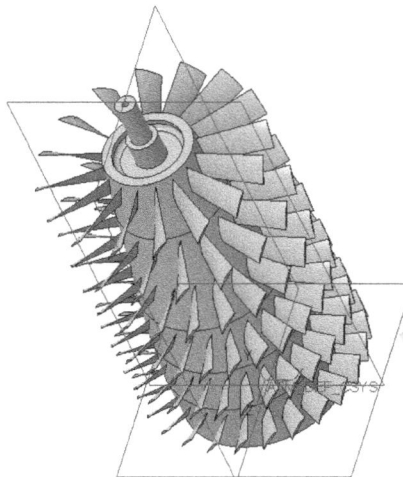

Figure 3–47

11. Switch to the **ROTOR_3B.ASM** window. The assembly displays as shown in Figure 3–48.

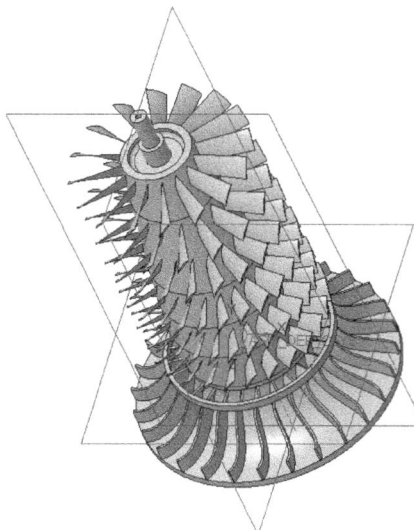

Figure 3–48

12. Save the assembly, close all open models, and erase them from memory.

Chapter Review Questions

1. If you add part features to a layer created at the assembly level, the system prompts you to create a new layer at the part level.

   a. True

   b. False

2. Parent/child relationships do not affect the children of suppressed parents.

   a. True

   b. False

3. Which of the following statements is true regarding suppressing a part or feature in an assembly?

   a. When you suppress a part or feature, it is displayed in the Model Tree with ■ next to its name.

   b. When you suppress a part or feature, it continues to regenerate.

   c. When you suppress a part or feature, solid geometry remains visible.

   d. When you suppress a feature, only datum features that are associated with it are suppressed.

4. Which part(s) shown in Figure 3–49 are suppressed?

Figure 3–49

   a. FIFTH_3.PRT, FOURTH_3.PRT, SECOND_THIRD_STAGE_3.PRT

   b. FIRST_STAGE_3.PRT

   c. SIXTH_3.PRT, FIFTH_3.PRT, FOURTH_3.PRT, SECOND_THIRD_STAGE_3.PRT, FIRST_STAGE_3.PRT

   d. IMPELLER_3.PRT

5. Which part(s) shown in Figure 3–50 are fixed?

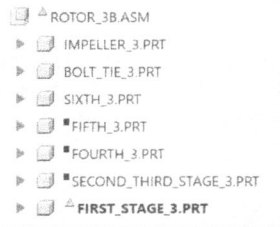

ROTOR_3B.ASM
▶ IMPELLER_3.PRT
▶ BOLT_TIE_3.PRT
▶ SIXTH_3.PRT
▶ ∎FIFTH_3.PRT
▶ ∎FOURTH_3.PRT
▶ ∎SECOND_THIRD_STAGE_3.PRT
▶ FIRST_STAGE_3.PRT

Figure 3–50

a. FIFTH_3.PRT, FOURTH_3.PRT, SECOND_THIRD_STAGE_3.PRT

b. FIRST_STAGE_3.PRT

c. SIXTH_3.PRT, FIFTH_3.PRT, FOURTH_3.PRT, SECOND_THIRD_STAGE_3.PRT, FIRST_STAGE_3.PRT

d. IMPELLER_3.PRT

6. How do you set the display of suppressed components on and off in the Model Tree?

a. Expand 🔽 ▾**>Tree Filters** and select **Suppressed objects**.

b. Expand 🔽 ▾**>Tree Columns** and select **Suppressed objects**.

c. Expand 📄 ▾**>Tree Filters** and select **Suppressed objects**.

d. Expand 📄 ▾**>Tree Columns** and select **Suppressed objects**.

7. Which of the following statements are true regarding adding a part to a layer and hiding it? (Select all that apply.)

a. When you add a part to a layer and hide it, it remains in the Model Tree.

b. When you add a part to a layer and hide it, it continues to regenerate.

c. When you add a part to a layer and hide it, solid geometry remains visible.

d. When you add a part to a layer and hide it, the solid geometry disappears.

8. Which of the following settings are valid display statuses for a layer? (Select all that apply.)
    a. Hide
    b. Show
    c. Isolate
    d. Activate
9. Which of the following statements are true regarding restructuring components in an assembly? (Select all that apply.)
    a. Restructuring enables you to drag and drop components.
    b. When restructuring, components can be moved from a subassembly into the top level assembly.
    c. Assembly references for components that are restructured into another subassembly need to be checked or changed.
    d. You can restructure by selecting **Component> Restructure**.

Answers: 1.a, 2.b, 3.a, 4.a, 5.b, 6.a, 7.abd, 8.abc, 9.abcd

Chapter 4

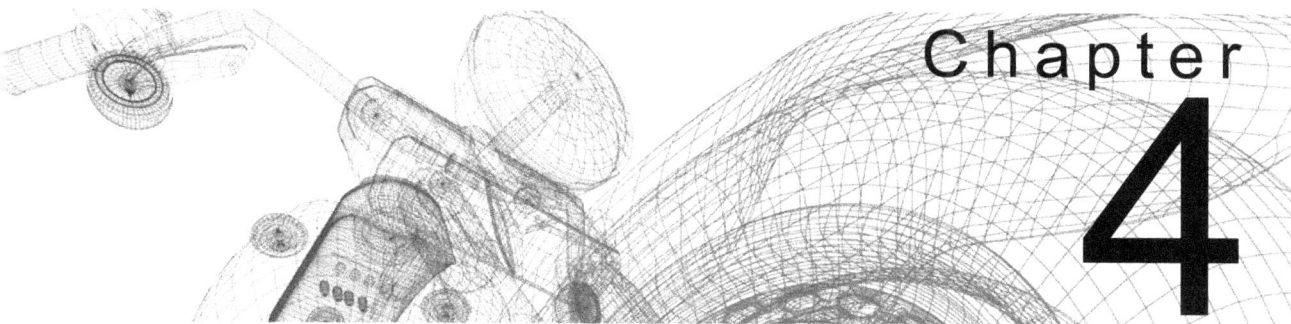

Assembly Family Tables

An assembly family table enables you to quickly and easily create variations in your design. Family tables can be used to create similar assemblies instead of manually recreating similar assemblies multiple times.

Learning Objectives in This Chapter

- Create a family table by adding columns and instances to vary in the table.
- Use the **Patternize** option to create additional family table instances with varying values for selected columns.
- Verify existing instances in a pattern table to ensure that the instance can be created.
- Open an existing instance in a pattern table.
- Note the different results when a dimension is modified, components are added, or components are removed between the generic assembly and an instance assembly.

4.1 Creating Assembly Family Tables

Family tables are created and stored in a model. A family table can be as simple as representing the design variations in an assembly, or it can be used to create similar assemblies.

A family table can be created for any assembly by adding items such as dimensions, parameters, components, or features to its family table. Once the items have been added, variations of the model can be created. These variations are known as instances. An example of an assembly family table is shown in Figure 4–1.

			d118 PITCH	p212 VANES	d97 ROTATE_ANGLE	d257
Type	Instance Name	Common Name				
	STATOR_BAND		20.00	7	22.00	0.26
	STATOR_25		25.00	13	17.00	0.25
	STATOR_30		30.00	14	18.00	0.24
	STATOR_35		35.00	16	17.00	0.23
	STATOR_40		40.00	18	16.00	0.21
	STATOR_45		45.00	15	19.00	0.20

Figure 4–1

How To: Create an Assembly Family Table

1. A family table is created in the original (generic) model. To open the family table editor, click ▦ (Family Table) in the Model Intent group of the *Model* tab or *Tools* tab. The Family Table dialog box opens as shown in Figure 4–2.

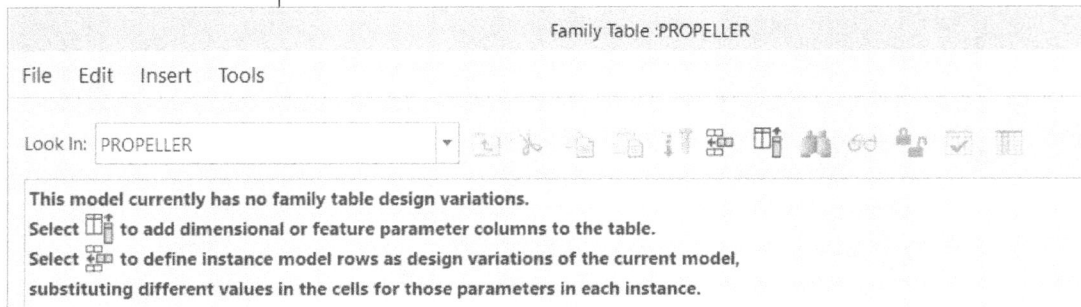

Family Table :PROPELLER

File   Edit   Insert   Tools

Look In: PROPELLER

This model currently has no family table design variations.
Select ▦ to add dimensional or feature parameter columns to the table.
Select ▦ to define instance model rows as design variations of the current model,
substituting different values in the cells for those parameters in each instance.

Figure 4–2

When you select
Parameters*, the
Parameter dialog box
opens. Parameters can
be selected in this
dialog box.*

2. Begin creating the family table by adding any items that are going to vary in the instances. Remember the design intent of the model when selecting items to add to a family table. Consider which design variations are required and can be created.

3. To start adding items to the family table, click ⬚ (Add Column). The Family Items dialog box opens.

   Items such as assembly dimensions and features, components, parameters, groups, and pattern tables can all be added to the table. Select the type of item you want to add in the *Add Item* area in the dialog box and select the item from the model or in the Model Tree. Items are added as columns in the family table. The order in which the items are selected is the order in which they are displayed in the family table.

   For example, the fastener assembly shown in Figure 4–3 has several versions.

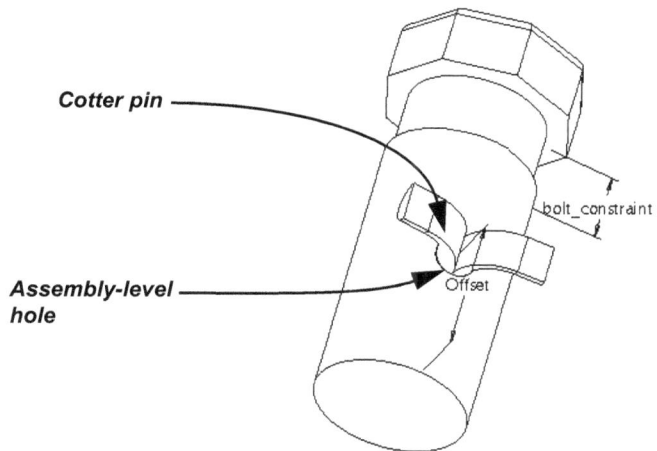

Figure 4–3

Depending on where the assembly is used, it might need a cotter pin, straight pin, or no pin at all. The offset distance of the bolt from the holder also varies. Therefore, the offset distance of the pin hole must be changed when the bolt offset distance changes. These items all need to be added to the family table. The required family table items listed in the Family Items dialog box are shown in Figure 4–4.

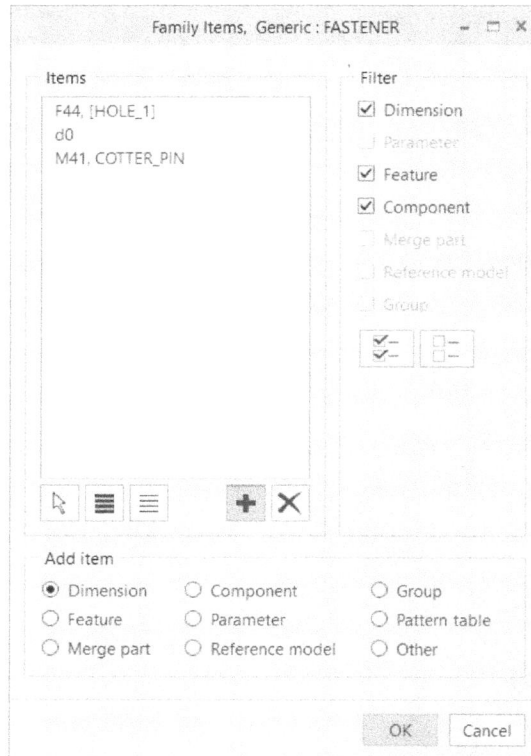

Figure 4–4

4. Once you finish adding the items to include in the family table, click **OK** to return to the Family Table dialog box.
5. The rows of the table represent the unique instances of the generic assembly.

   Instances can be added by editing the family table or patterning an existing instance (see Step 4). To add instances, click ⊞ (Add Instance) in the Family Table dialog box. Each added row represents one instance. The five instances added to the family table are shown in Figure 4–5.

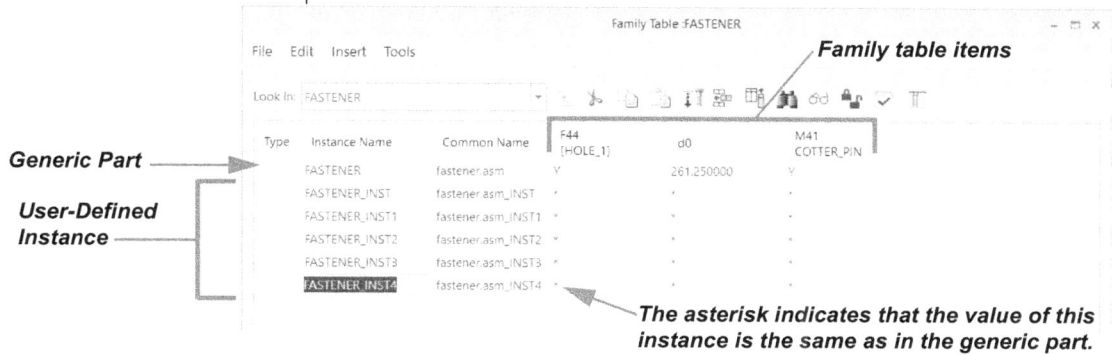

Figure 4–5

6. Once columns and rows have been added to the table, you can change the values for each item to suit the requirements for a specific instance.

Before any changes are made, the instances have an asterisk (*) in the cells of each column. This indicates that the value used in the instance is the same as that of the generic. An asterisk is also used in cells where an actual value is unnecessary (i.e., if the dimension is controlling a component that is suppressed).

7. Every instance can be used as the generic for its own family table. This results in multi-level family tables (i.e., nested family tables). Multi-level family tables can be used to manage large data sets.

For example, the fastener's family table shown in Figure 4–6 has five instances. If each instance has six hole diameters, the table would require thirty rows of data. Creating separate family tables for each instance makes data management easier. The 🗀 icon in the *Type* column for **CONFIG2** indicates that it has its own family table.

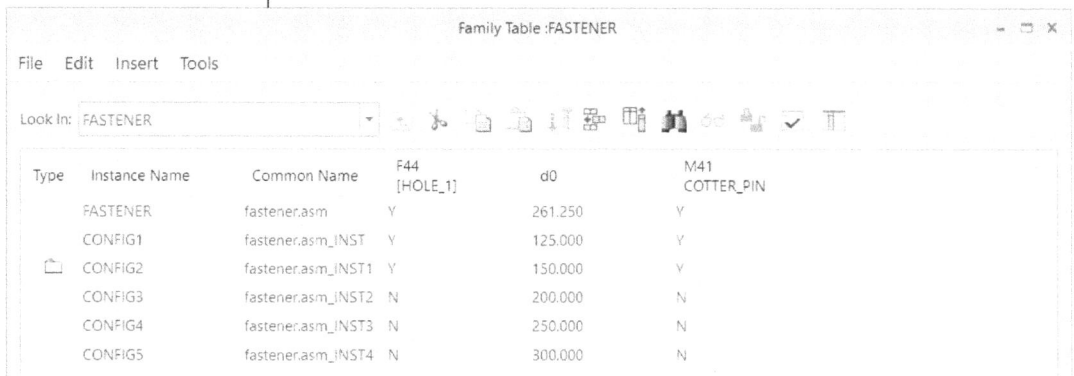

Figure 4–6

8. A model must successfully regenerate to open an instance.

   To verify that the instances are valid, click ☑ (Verify) in the Family Table dialog box. The Family Tree dialog box opens, which enables you to select individual instances or regenerate all of the instances in the family table. The regeneration status of each instance displays in the *Verify status* column in the dialog box. The regeneration status is also written to a file called **<model_name>.tst**.

9. The Family Tree dialog box, after the instances have been verified, is shown in Figure 4–7. Instance **CONFIG2_INST** has failed regeneration. The instance values must be adjusted so that the model can regenerate and the instance can be opened.

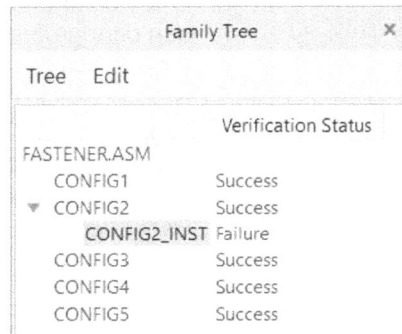

Figure 4–7

By default, if an instance index file exists, all of the instances are displayed in the Open dialog box when opening the generic model.

10. The family table information, including each instance, is stored with the generic assembly file. When opening the assembly, you are prompted to open the generic or one of the instances, as shown in Figure 4–8. You can also open **By Column** and make a selection based on a parameter value.

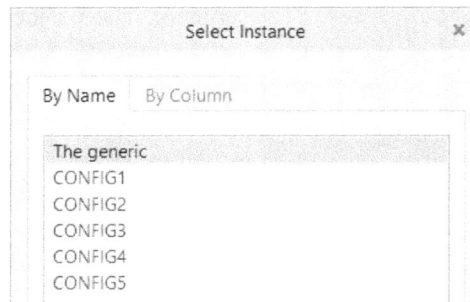

Figure 4–8

11. An instance can also be opened directly from the generic by clicking ▢ (Family Table). Select the instance in the Family Table dialog box and click **Open**.

Component Manipulation

A component that is added to a family table can be suppressed or replaced with instances. It can be replaced with another component that belongs in its family table or by an interchange group. Place the new component in the assembly instance by entering the instance or model name. In Figure 4–9, the generic component **COTTER_PIN** is replaced with its family table instance PIN in instance **CONFIG2**.

Suppress a component in an instance by entering **N** in the appropriate cell. For example, the instances **CONFIG3**, **CONFIG4**, and **CONFIG5** all have the **cotter_pin** part and Assembly Feature Hole suppressed, as shown in Figure 4–9.

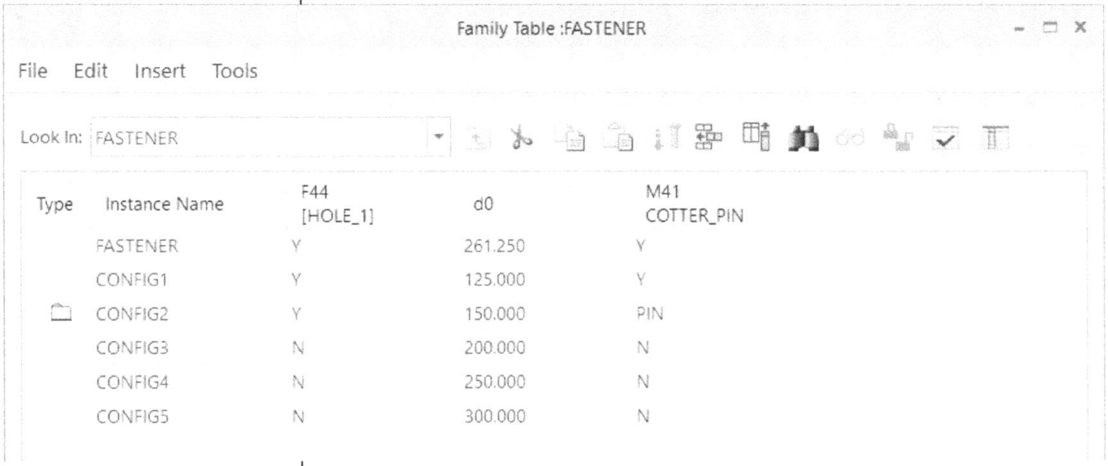

Family Table :FASTENER — □ ✕

File   Edit   Insert   Tools

Look In: FASTENER

Type	Instance Name	F44 [HOLE_1]	d0	M41 COTTER_PIN
	FASTENER	Y	261.250	Y
	CONFIG1	Y	125.000	Y
🗀	CONFIG2	Y	150.000	PIN
	CONFIG3	N	200.000	N
	CONFIG4	N	250.000	N
	CONFIG5	N	300.000	N

Figure 4–9

Pattern

Once an instance has been created, you can pattern it to create additional instances with varying values for selected items (e.g., parameters or dimensions).

How To: Pattern an Instance

1. Click ⬍⬍ (Patternize). The Patternize Instance dialog box opens as shown in Figure 4–10.

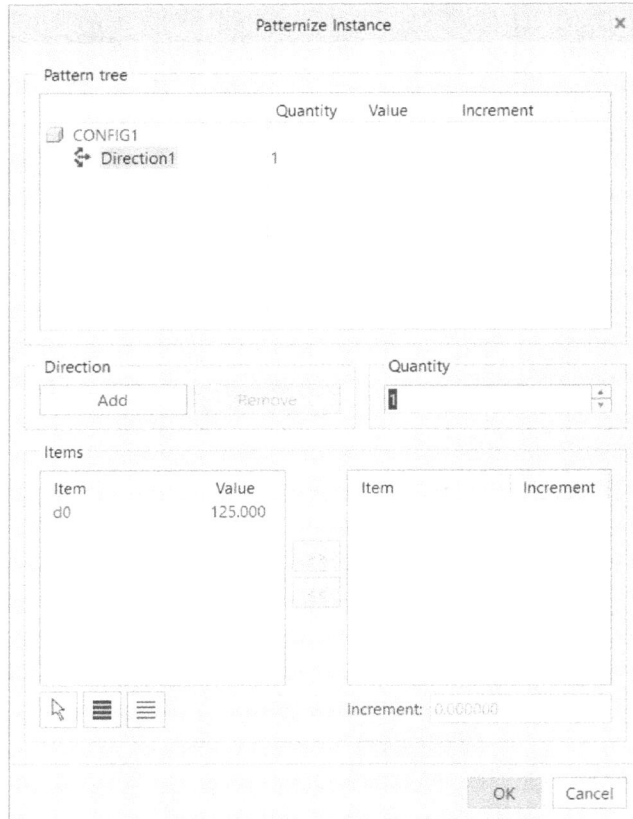

Figure 4–10

2. Enter the number of instances required in the *Quantity* field.
3. In the *Items* area at the bottom of the dialog box, use

   ≫ (Add Item) to move the items that you want to vary from the left side to the right side.

4. Enter an incremental value in the *Increment* field for each varying item. A positive value indicates an increasing increment and a negative value indicates a decreasing increment.

The dialog box shown in Figure 4–11 is set to create five instances. The offset value decreases by 1.

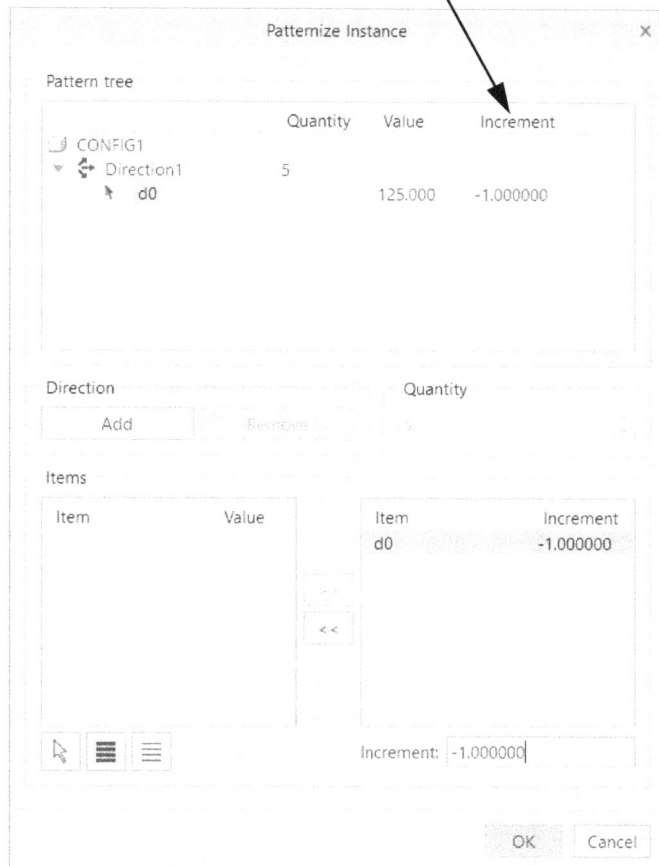

Figure 4–11

5. Click **OK** to complete the patterned instance. The family table populates automatically.

Controlling Lower Level Items

For the dimension to update in the part when it is changed at the assembly level, you must add it to a family table at the part level. Otherwise, the dimension does not update when the parameter driving the dimension is changed at the assembly level.

For an item to be added to an assembly family table, it must exist in the assembly. An entire subassembly is considered to be one component at the top-level. To add individual components of a subassembly, a family table must be created in the subassembly. Instances of this subassembly can then be added to the top-level family table.

Similarly, dimensions or parameters controlling features in a component cannot be added to a family table because the item is in the part. To control items that belong to the component level, a relation must be created at the assembly level. This relation equates an assembly-level parameter to the component level dimension or parameter. This assembly parameter can then be added to the family table. Changing the assembly parameter in the family table causes the relation to change the component level dimension or parameter.

Instance Index

The instance index file (stored in the current working directory as **<current_directory_name>.idx**) enables you to open instances by name from the Open dialog box. The instance index file contains cross-references for all of the Creo Parametric files with family tables in that directory. Once you have verified the instances and saved the generic model file, an instance index file is automatically created or updated to include the newly saved generic assembly and its instances. You can also manually create or update the instance index file by selecting **File> Manage Session>Update Index**.

To remove instances from the display when opening the file, you can set the **menu_show_instances** config.pro option to **No**.

4.2 Modifying Family Tables

Models are constantly modified to reach the final design. The following examples describe how to manage changes to a generic model that contains family table instances. The component and dimensions shown in Figure 4–12 are used as family table items.

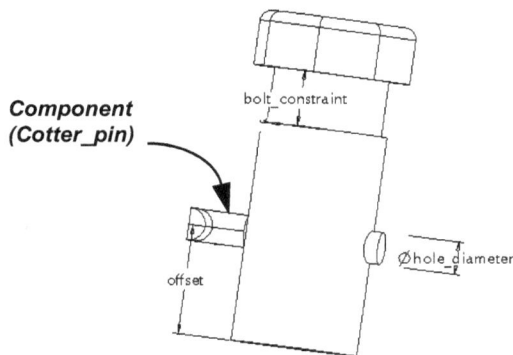

Figure 4–12

To modify a dimension in an instance, open the instance and change the value using the standard modification techniques, or use the family table editor by selecting the cell and entering a new value. Any modifications made to an instance are also updated in the family table editor. An example is shown in Figure 4–13.

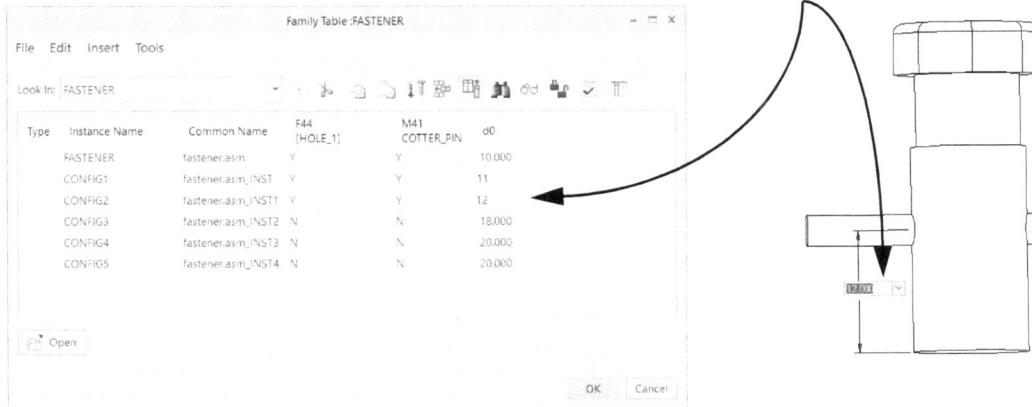

Figure 4–13

Modifying Non-family Tables

Any modifications to items that do not belong to the family table can be changed in the generic or in an instance, as shown in Figure 4–14. These changes are reflected in the generic and all of its instances.

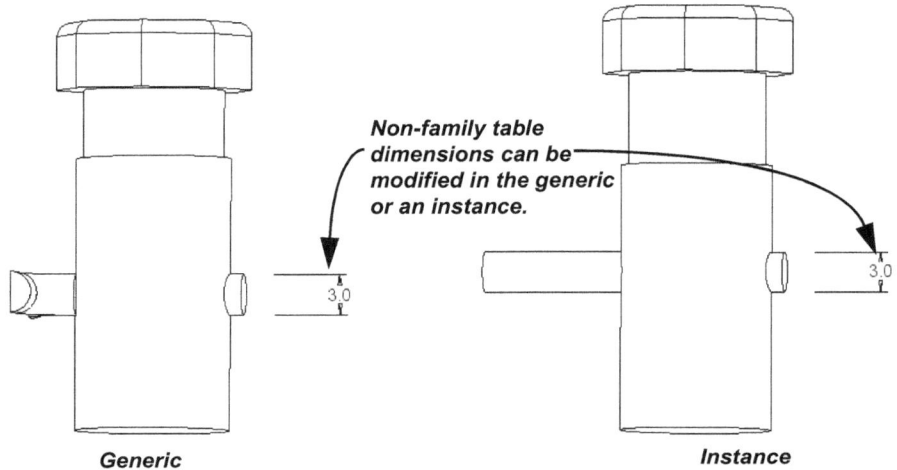

Non-family table dimensions can be modified in the generic or an instance.

Generic

Instance

Figure 4–14

Adding Components to the Generic Model

Adding a component to the generic is reflected in the generic and all of its instances, as shown in Figure 4–15. The feature is not added to the family table.

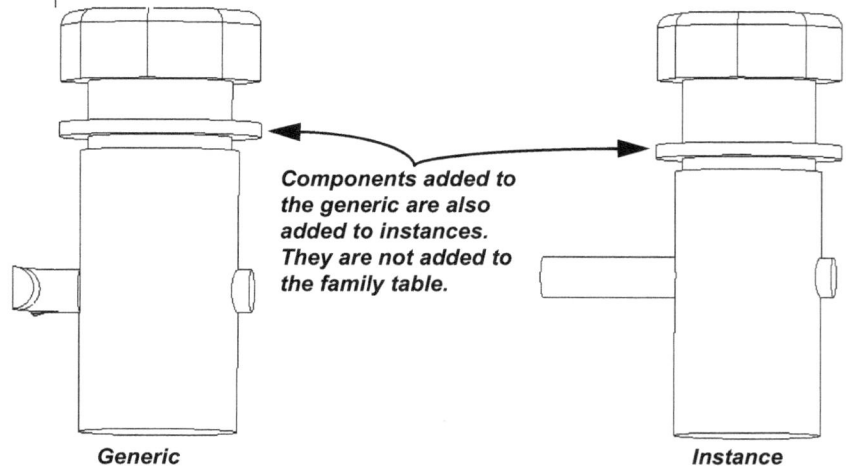

Components added to the generic are also added to instances. They are not added to the family table.

Generic

Instance

Figure 4–15

Adding Components to an Instance

Adding a component to an instance creates an additional column in the family table. The generic is permanently marked as **N** to prevent the component from displaying in the generic model. By default, all of the instances are assigned with an asterisk (*) to maintain the same status as the generic. However, this can be modified in the family table editor. Components added to an instance are not added to the generic, as shown in Figure 4–16.

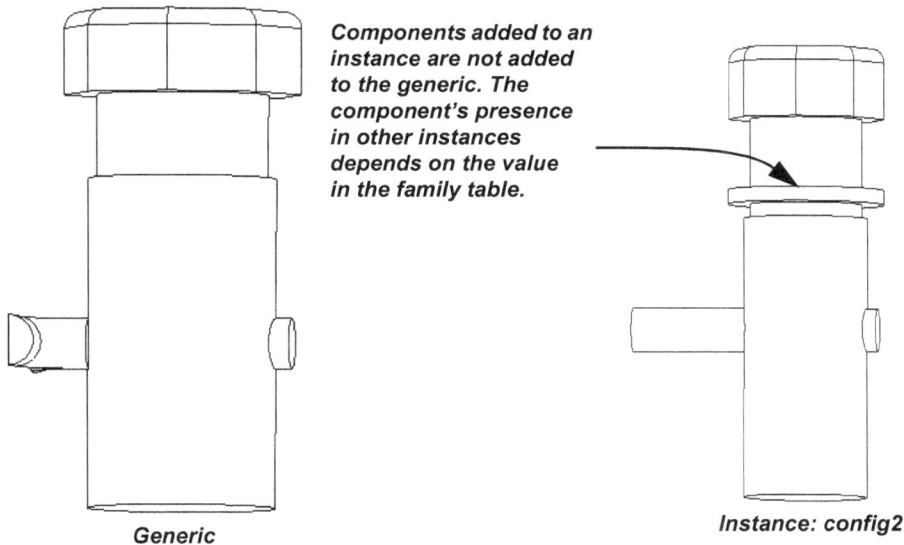

Components added to an instance are not added to the generic. The component's presence in other instances depends on the value in the family table.

Generic

Instance: config2

Type	Instance Name	Common Name	F44 [HOLE_1]	M41 COTTER_PIN	d0	M86 WASHER
	FASTENER	fastener.asm	Y	Y	10.000	N
	CONFIG1	fastener.asm_INST	Y	Y	11.000	*
	CONFIG2	fastener.asm_INST1	Y	Y	12.000	Y
	CONFIG3	fastener.asm_INST2	N	N	18.000	*
	CONFIG4	fastener.asm_INST3	N	N	20.000	*
	CONFIG5	fastener.asm_INST4	N	N	20.000	*

Figure 4–16

Deleting Components from an Instance

If a component is deleted from an instance, the following scenarios can occur:

- If the component exists in the family table, the value of the instance changes to **N**.

- If the component does not exist in the family table, the item is added to the family table and the value changes to **N**. The generic is assigned the value of **Y** and all of the other instances are assigned as * to maintain the same status as the generic.

An example is shown in Figure 4–17.

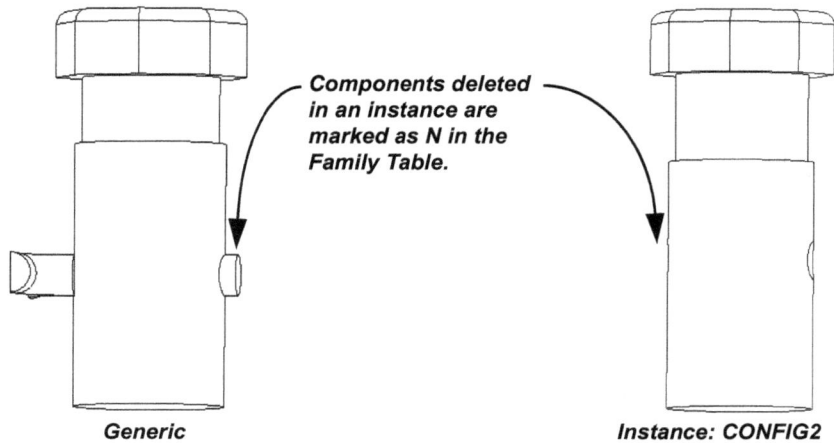

Components deleted in an instance are marked as N in the Family Table.

Generic   Instance: CONFIG2

Type	Instance Name	Common Name	F44 [HOLE_1]	d0	M41 COTTER_PIN
	FASTENER	fastener.asm	Y	10.000	Y
	CONFIG1	fastener.asm_INST	Y	11.000	*
	CONFIG2	fastener.asm_INST1	Y	12.000	N
	CONFIG3	fastener.asm_INST2	N	18.000	*
	CONFIG4	fastener.asm_INST3	N	20.000	*
	CONFIG5	fastener.asm_INST4	N	20.000	*

Family Table :FASTENER

File   Edit   Insert   Tools

Look In: FASTENER

Figure 4–17

Deleting Components from the Generic

If a component is deleted from the generic, it is deleted from all of the instances. If the item is a family table item, the column is removed from the table, as shown in Figure 4–18.

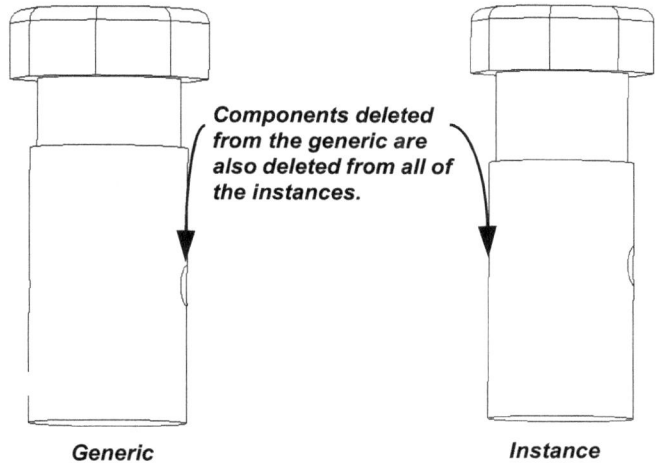

Components deleted from the generic are also deleted from all of the instances.

Generic   *Instance*

Figure 4–18

Practice 4a

Assembly Family Tables

Practice Objective

- Create an assembly family table.

In this practice, you will assemble the compressor's **stator_blade** to the **stator_band** using the Coordinate System constraint. Once assembled, you will create a family table and pattern the blades in the generic. The final generic model is shown in Figure 4–19.

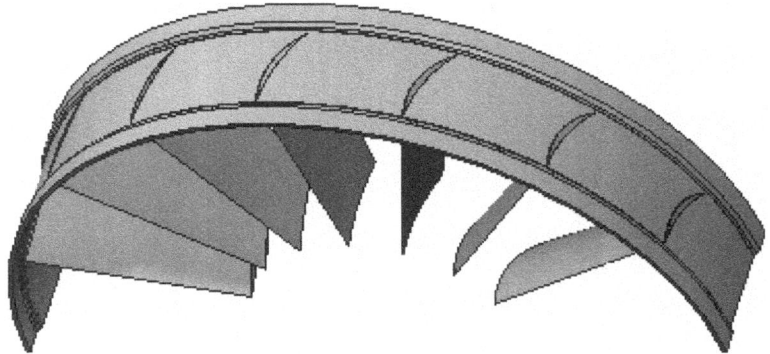

Figure 4–19

Task 1 - Open a part file.

1. Set the working directory to the *Assembly_Fam_Tab* folder.

2. Open **stator_blade.prt**.

3. The Select Instance dialog box opens, indicating that the part has family table instances. Select **The generic** and click **Open**.

4. Set the model display as follows:

   - ⁺⁄⊹ *(Datum Display Filters)*: All Off

   - ⅜ *(Spin Center)*: Off

   - ⌐ *(Display Style)*: ⬚ (Shading With Edges)

You can also click

⬚ *(Family Table) in the Tools tab.*

5. Select **Model Intent>Family Table** in the *Model* tab. The family table displays, as shown in Figure 4–20. The table rows represent variations of the generic part with the **ANGLE** and **BLADE_HEIGHT** parameter values specified in the columns.

ANGLE parameter

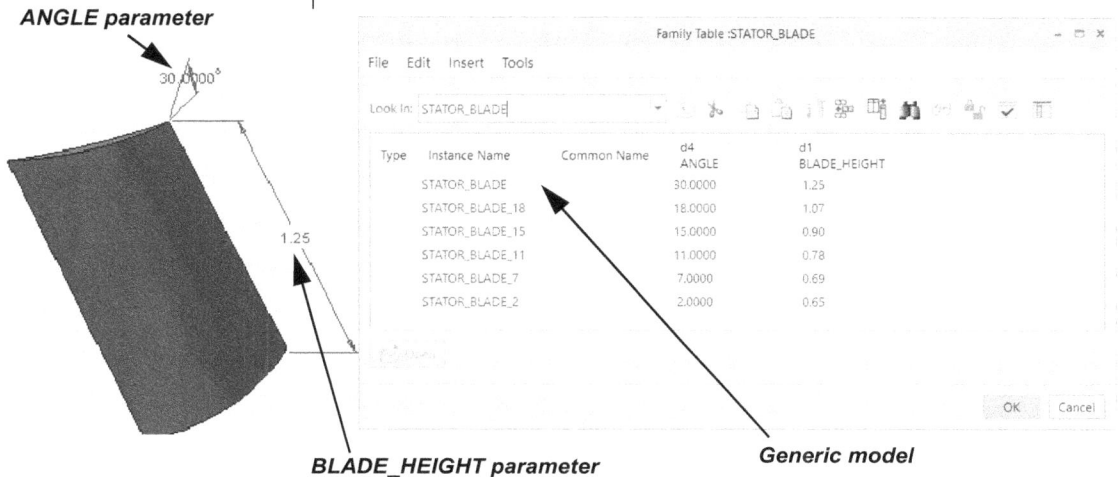

BLADE_HEIGHT parameter

Generic model

Figure 4–20

6. Click ✓ (Verify) to open the Family Tree dialog box. All of the family instances have been successfully verified, as shown in Figure 4–21.

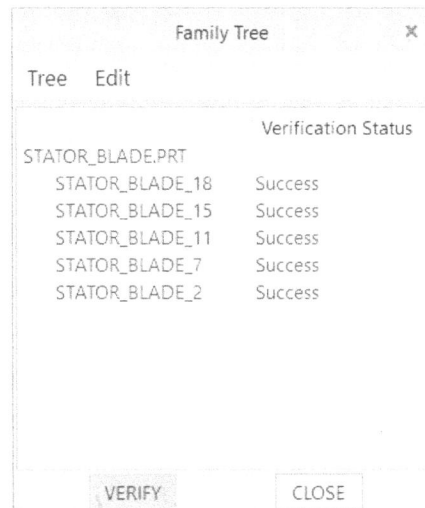

Figure 4–21

7. Close the Family Tree dialog box.

8. Select the instance with an *Angle* of **18** (**STATOR_BLADE_18**) and click ◌ (Preview) to preview it.

9. Preview the instance with an *Angle* of **2**.

10. Click **OK** to close the family table dialog box.

11. Close the window. These instances are used later in a top-level assembly.

Task 2 - Open the band part.

1. Open **stator_band.prt**.

2. The Select Instance dialog box opens, indicating that the part has family table instances. Open **The generic**. The band part displays as shown in Figure 4–22.

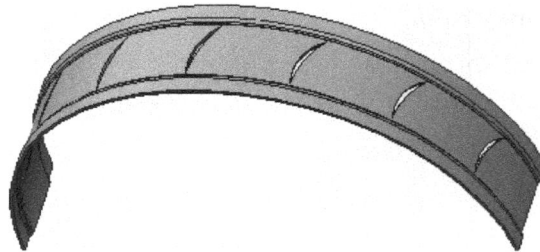

Figure 4–22

3. Select **Model Intent>Family Table** in the *Model* tab. The family table for the band part displays, as shown in Figure 4–23.

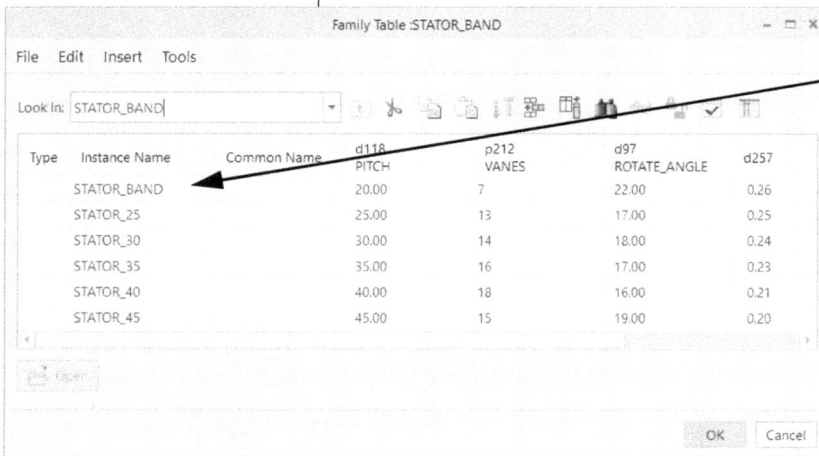

Type	Instance Name	Common Name	d118 PITCH	p212 VANES	d97 ROTATE_ANGLE	d257
	STATOR_BAND		20.00	7	22.00	0.26
	STATOR_25		25.00	13	17.00	0.25
	STATOR_30		30.00	14	18.00	0.24
	STATOR_35		35.00	16	17.00	0.23
	STATOR_40		40.00	18	16.00	0.21
	STATOR_45		45.00	15	19.00	0.20

Generic model

The last two columns in the family table are dimensions that ensure that the stator_band cuts are a constant size as they are projected from its sketch plane to the band.

Figure 4–23

- An explanation of the band part is shown in Figure 4–24.

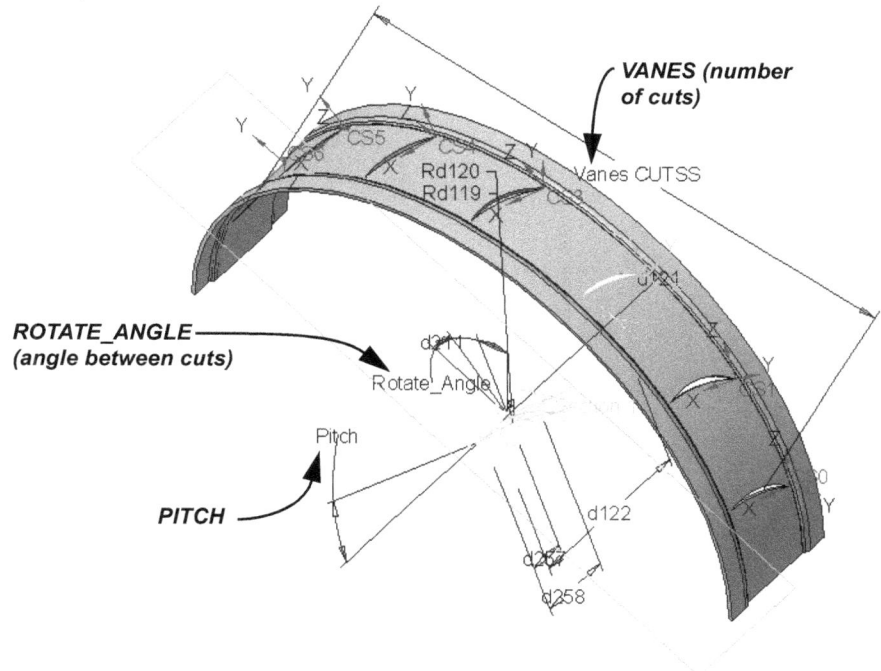

Figure 4–24

4. Click ☑ (Verify) to open the Family Tree dialog box. All of the family instances have been successfully verified for this part as well. Close the dialog box.

5. Preview each instance using ♂ (Preview).

6. Click **OK** to close the family table.

7. Close the window. These instances are used later in the practice in a top-level assembly.

Task 3 - Create a new assembly.

1. Create a new assembly using the default template and set the *Name* to **stator**.

2. Assemble the generic instance of the **stator_band.prt** part in the default location using the **Default** constraint type. The model displays as shown in Figure 4–25.

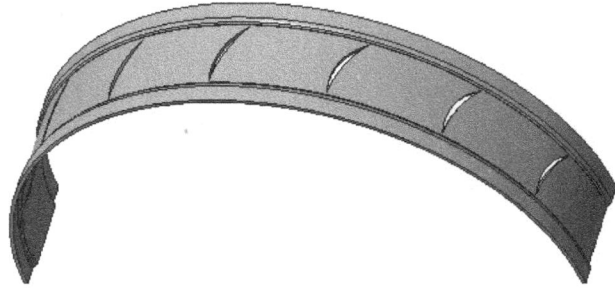

Figure 4–25

Task 4 - Assemble the stator_blade component.

1. Assemble the generic instance of the **stator_blade.prt** part.

2. In the In-graphics toolbar, enable ⌇ (Csys Display).

3. Assemble using a Coincident constraint and select **CS0** in both the **stator_band** and **stator_blade**. The assembly displays as shown in Figure 4–26.

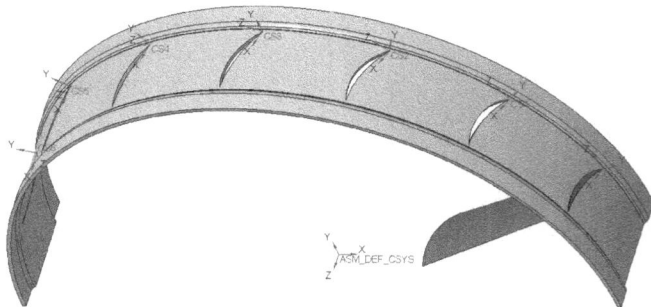

Figure 4–26

4. In the In-graphics toolbar, disable ⌇ (Csys Display).

Task 5 - Create an assembly family table.

1. In the *Model* tab, click ▦ (Family Table).

2. Click ▦ (Add Column) to open the Family Items dialog box to add items.

3. Select **Component** in the Family Items dialog box and select **stator_band.prt** and **stator_blade.prt** in the Model Tree. The Family Items dialog box displays as shown in Figure 4–27.

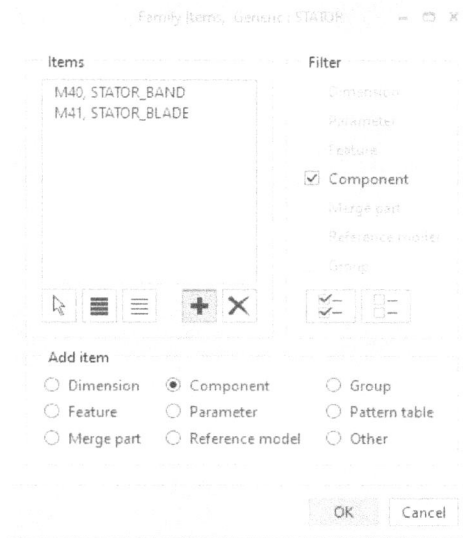

Figure 4–27

4. Click **OK**. The Family Table dialog box opens.

5. Click (Add Instance) in the Family Table dialog box to add an instance to the table.

6. Edit the family table instance information, as shown in Figure 4–28.

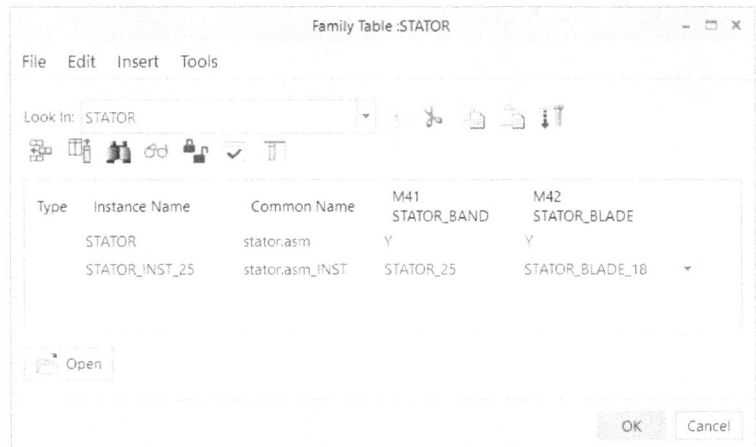

Figure 4–28

Task 6 - Use Patternize to add additional instances.

1. Select the **STATOR_INST_25** instance and click ↓⫠ (Patternize).

2. In the Patternize Instance dialog box, set the *Quantity* to **4** and click **OK**.

3. The Family Table dialog box updates, as shown in Figure 4–29.

   - Note: The **Patternize** option is a quick way to create multiple instances, without manually adding them.

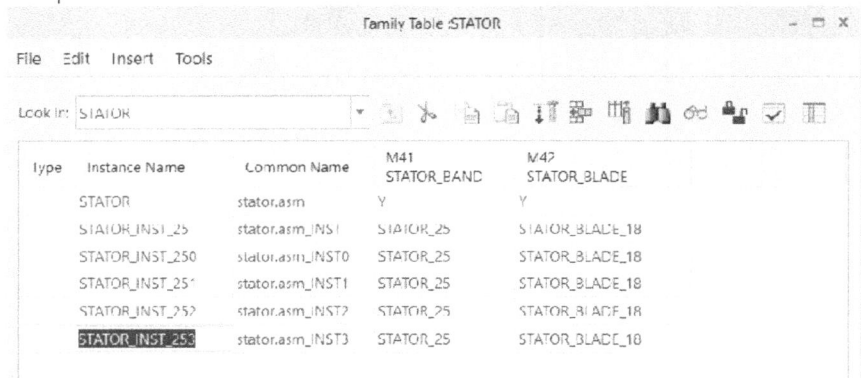

Type	Instance Name	Common Name	M41 STATOR_BAND	M42 STATOR_BLADE
	STATOR	stator.asm	Y	Y
	STATOR_INST_25	stator.asm_INST	STATOR_25	STATOR_BLADE_18
	STATOR_INST_250	stator.asm_INST0	STATOR_25	STATOR_BLADE_18
	STATOR_INST_251	stator.asm_INST1	STATOR_25	STATOR_BLADE_18
	STATOR_INST_252	stator.asm_INST2	STATOR_25	STATOR_BLADE_18
	STATOR_INST_253	stator.asm_INST3	STATOR_25	STATOR_BLADE_18

Figure 4–29

4. Edit the family table instance information, as shown in Figure 4–30.

   - Check the column headers and ensure you type the instance names in the correct column. The columns were added in the order in which you selected them.

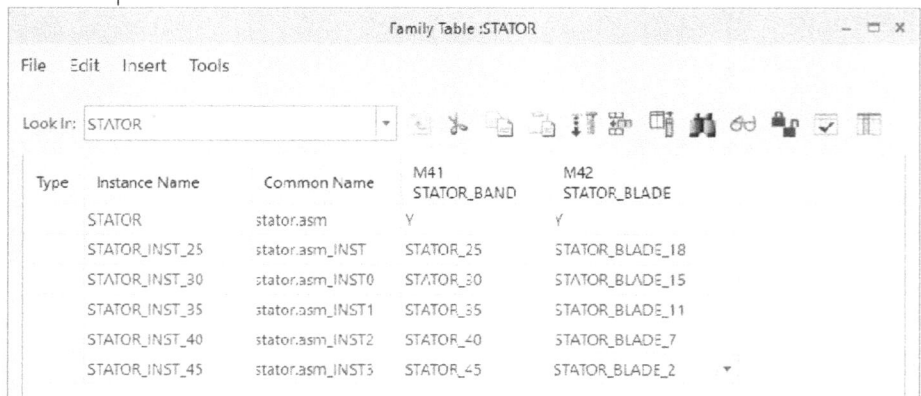

Type	Instance Name	Common Name	M41 STATOR_BAND	M42 STATOR_BLADE
	STATOR	stator.asm	Y	Y
	STATOR_INST_25	stator.asm_INST	STATOR_25	STATOR_BLADE_18
	STATOR_INST_30	stator.asm_INST0	STATOR_30	STATOR_BLADE_15
	STATOR_INST_35	stator.asm_INST1	STATOR_35	STATOR_BLADE_11
	STATOR_INST_40	stator.asm_INST2	STATOR_40	STATOR_BLADE_7
	STATOR_INST_45	stator.asm_INST3	STATOR_45	STATOR_BLADE_2

Figure 4–30

5. Click ☑ (Verify) to open the Family Tree dialog box.

6. Click **VERIFY** to verify the family table instances.

7. Close the dialog box once all of the instances have been successfully verified.

8. Preview a few of the instances.

9. Click **OK** in the Family Table dialog box.

10. Save the assembly.

Task 7 - Pattern the blade component along the band.

---

1. Select the **stator_blade** and click ⊞ (Pattern) in the mini toolbar to create a reference pattern of the blade.

2. Click ✔ (OK) to complete the pattern. The model displays as shown in Figure 4–31.

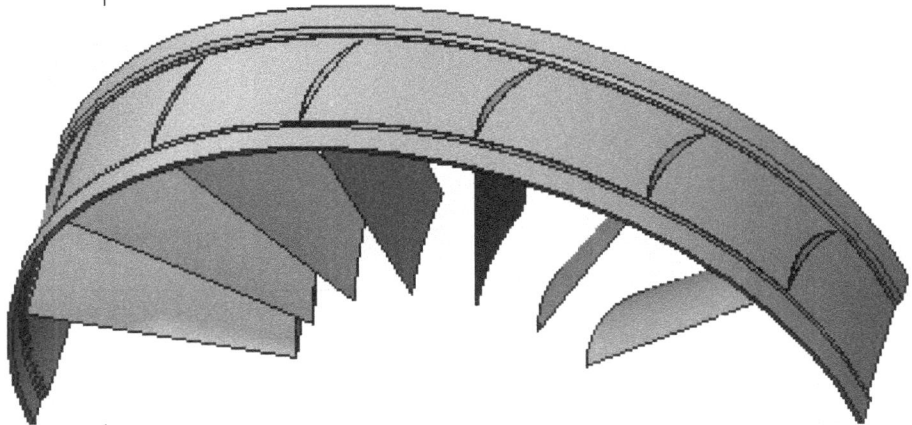

Figure 4–31

3. Click ☐ (Family Table) in the *Model* tab.
4. Preview a few of the instances. Note that **STATOR_BLADE** is patterned in the instances.
5. Save the assembly and erase from memory.

Practice 4b

(Optional) Model Plane

Practice Objectives

- Create an assembly family table.
- Exclude a component in an instance.
- Include a component in only one instance.

In this practice, you will create a family table for a model plane assembly. You will create four types of kits: Ready To Fly (All components), Almost ready (without battery, propeller, and engine), Only carbon parts (only specially shaped parts without the battery, propeller, engine, servos, receiver, and speed controller), and Special (with the special power unit). The final generic model (Ready To Fly) is shown in Figure 4–32.

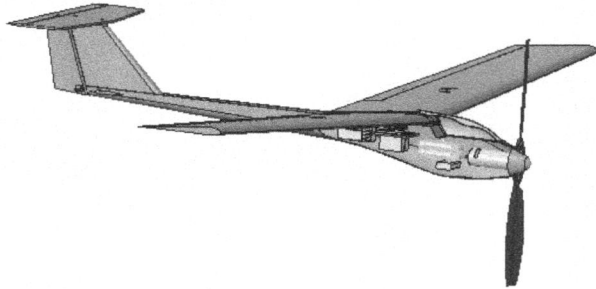

Figure 4–32

Task 1 - Create an assembly family table in the fuselage subassembly.

In the next two tasks, you will create family tables in subassemblies that are part of the top-level model plane assembly. These subassembly tables are referenced in the top-level assembly to create the final model plane options.

1. Set the working directory to the *Model_Plane* folder.

2. Open **assembly_fuselage.asm**.

3. Set the model display as follows:

- *(Datum Display Filters)*: All Off

- *(Spin Center)*: Off

- *(Display Style)*: (Shading With Edges)

4. Click ⬚ (Family Table) in the *Model* tab.

5. Click ⬚ (Add Column) to open the Family Items dialog box.

6. Select **Component** in the Family Items dialog box.

7. Select **SERVO.PRT** and **OTOC_180<SERVO>.PRT** in the Model Tree. The Family Items dialog box opens, as shown in Figure 4–33.

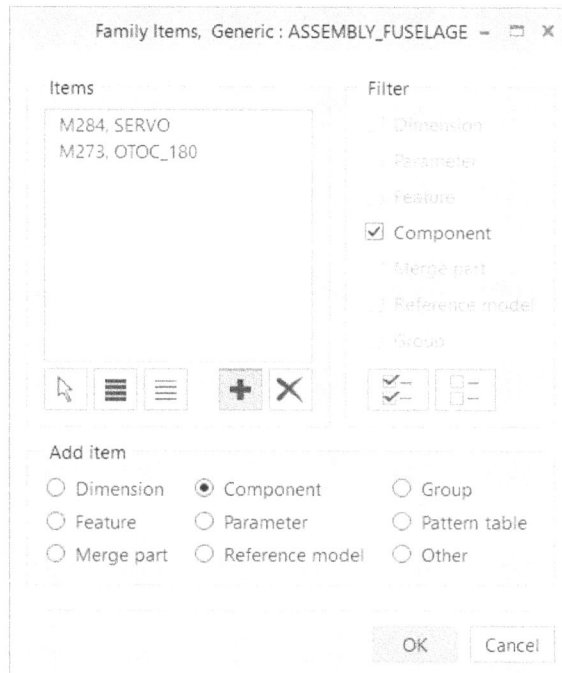

Figure 4–33

8. Click **OK**. The Family Table dialog box opens, as shown in Figure 4–34.

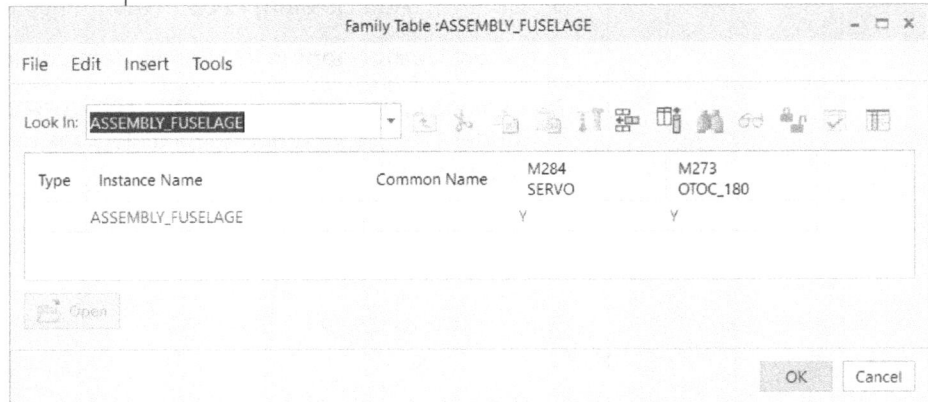

Figure 4–34

Each row added to the table represents one instance.

9. Click 🔳 (Add Instance) in the Family Table dialog box and add an instance to the table.

10. Edit the family table instance information, as shown in Figure 4–35.

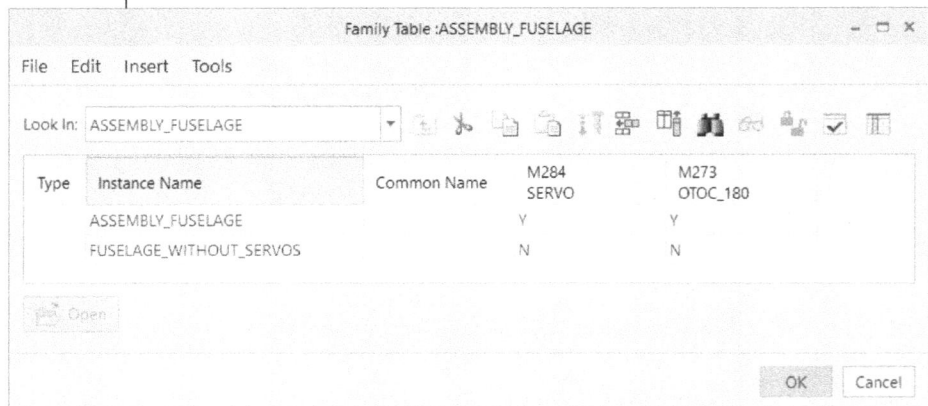

Figure 4–35

11. Click ✓ (Verify) to open the Family Tree dialog box.

12. Click **VERIFY** to verify the family instances. Close the dialog box once all of the instances have been successfully verified.

*If prompted to verify the instances in an unregenerated generic, click **Confirm**.*

13. Preview the **FUSELAGE_WITHOUT_SERVOS** instance. Once finished, click **OK** in the Family Table dialog box.

14. Save the assembly. The model displays as shown in Figure 4–36.

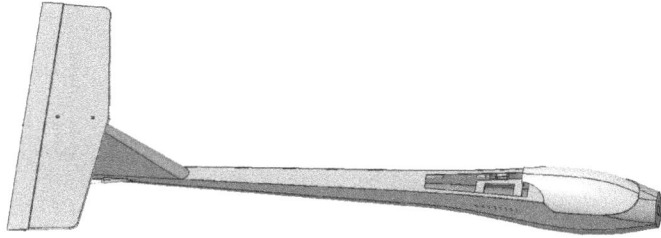

Figure 4–36

Task 2 - Create an assembly family table in the wing subassembly.

---

1. Open **wing.asm**.

2. Click ⬚ (Family Table).

3. Click ⬚↑ (Add Column) to open the Family Items dialog box. Select **Component** in the Family Items dialog box and select **SERVO_MALE.PRT** and **SERVO_L1.PRT** in the Model Tree. The Family Items dialog box displays, as shown in Figure 4–37.

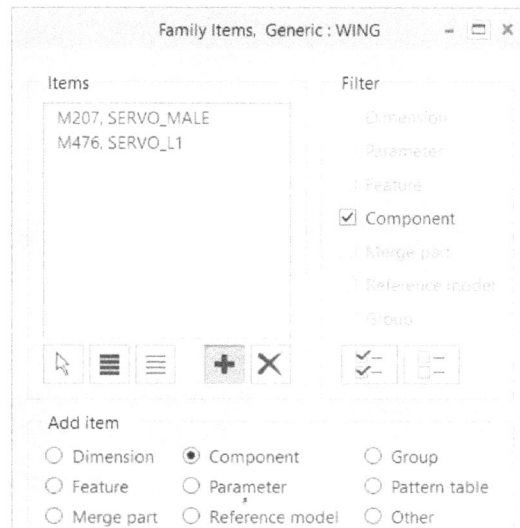

Figure 4–37

4. Click **OK**. The Family Table dialog box opens, as shown in Figure 4–38.

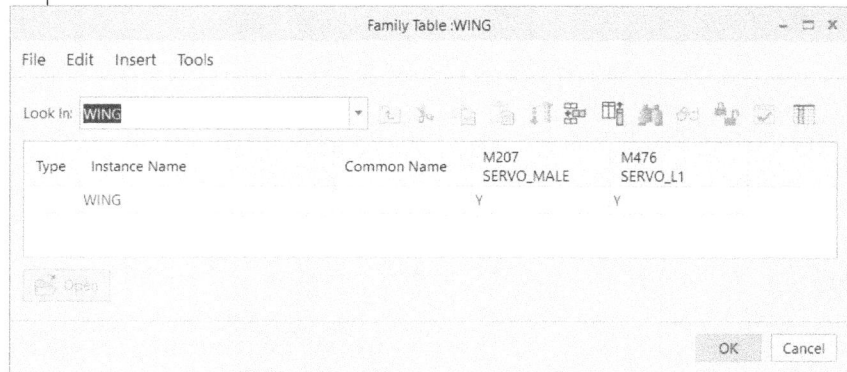

Figure 4–38

5. Click 🔳 (Add Instance) in the Family Table dialog box and add an instance to the table.

6. Edit the family table instance information, as shown in Figure 4–39.

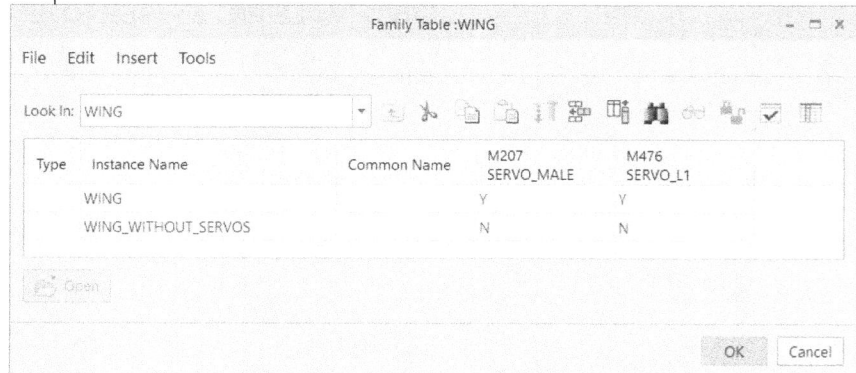

Figure 4–39

7. Click ☑ (Verify) to open the Family Tree dialog box.

8. Click **VERIFY** to verify the family instances. Close the dialog box once all of the instances have been successfully verified.

If prompted to verify the instances in an unregenerated generic, click Confirm.

9. Preview the **WING_WITHOUT_SERVOS** instance. Once finished, click **OK** in the Family Table dialog box.

10. Save the assembly.

Task 3 - Create a top assembly family table.

Now that the subassembly family tables have been defined, they can be referenced in the top-level assembly to create the final product types.

1. Open **assembly_bel.asm**.

2. Click ☐ (Family Table).

3. Click ⊞⫯ (Add Column) to open the Family Items dialog box.

4. Select **Component** in the Family Items dialog box and select the **ASSEMBLY_FUSELAGE.ASM, WING.ASM, PROPELLER.ASM, MOTOR_PREVOD.PRT, RECEIVER.PRT, BATTERY.PRT**, and **SPEED_CONTROLLER.PRT** in the Model Tree. The Family Items dialog box opens as shown in Figure 4–40.

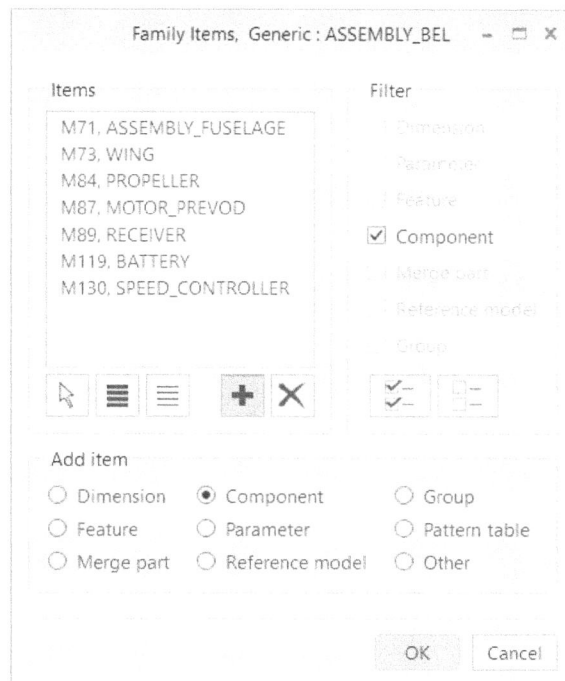

Figure 4–40

5. Click **OK**. The Family Table dialog box opens, as shown in Figure 4–41.

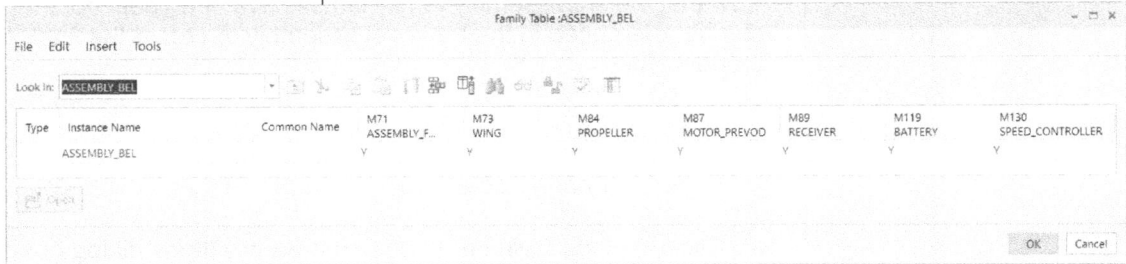

Figure 4–41

Each row added to the table represents one instance.

6. Click 🔳 (Add Instance) in the Family Table dialog box to add three instances to the table.

7. Edit the family table instance information as shown in Figure 4–42.

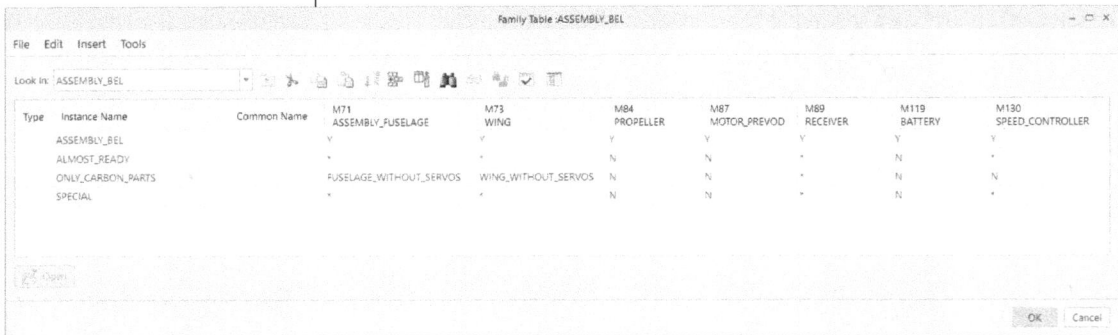

Figure 4–42

8. Click ☑ (Verify) to open the Family Tree dialog box.

If prompted to verify the instances in an unregenerated generic, click Confirm.

9. Click **VERIFY** to verify the family instances.

10. Close the dialog box once all of the instances have been successfully verified.

11. Preview the three new instances. **Assembly_BEL** and **Almost Ready** display as shown in Figure 4–43.

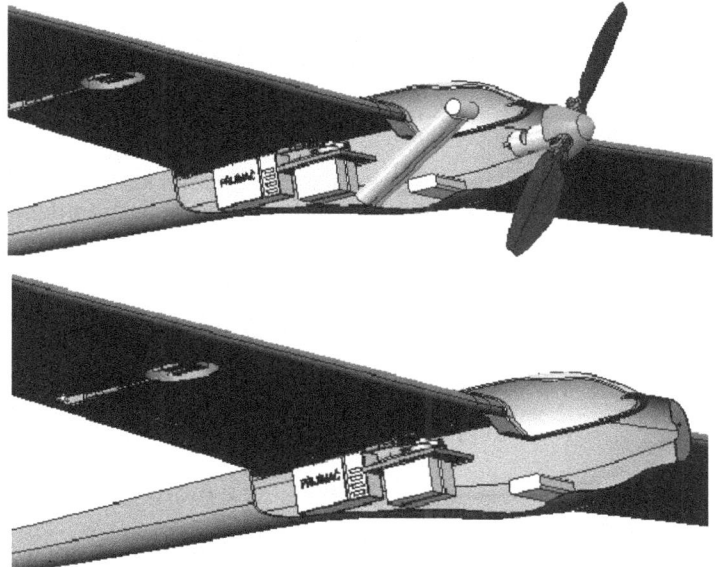

Figure 4–43

Only carbon parts and **Special** display as shown in Figure 4–44. The Only carbon parts instance does not have the power unit.

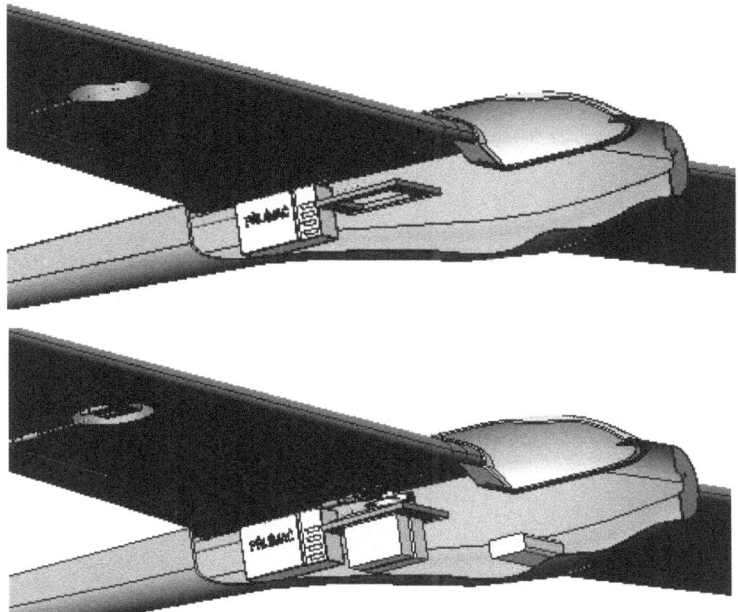

Figure 4–44

12. Once finished, close the Family Table dialog box.

13. Save the assembly and close all open models.

Task 4 - Assemble three components only to the Special instance.

In this task, you will add several additional components that only exist in the Special instance of the plane. You will then review the family table and note the effect that these added components have on both the Special instance and the other family table instances.

1. Open **assembly_bel.asm**.

2. The Select Instance dialog box opens, indicating that the part has family table instances. Select the **Special** instance and click **Open**.

3. Assemble **motor_prevod_big.prt**.

4. In the Model Tree, click 🗊 ▾ (Settings)>**Tree Filters**.

5. Under **Features** enable all datum features and click **OK**.

6. Assemble the component using two Coincident constraints and select the appropriate surfaces, as shown in Figure 4–45, in both **motor_prevod_big.prt** and **assembly_bel.asm**.

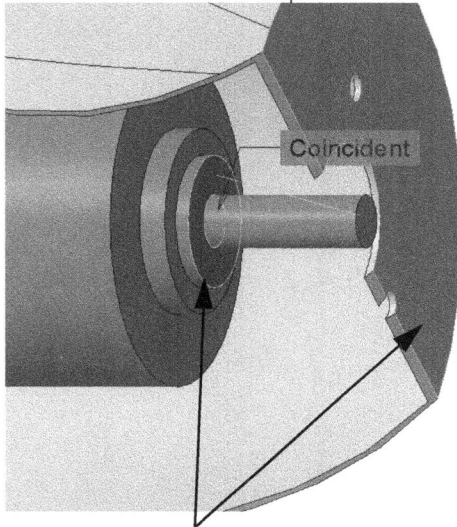

Use the Coincident constraint for the surface on motor_prevod_big.prt with the surface on assembly_bel.asm (hidden in the image).

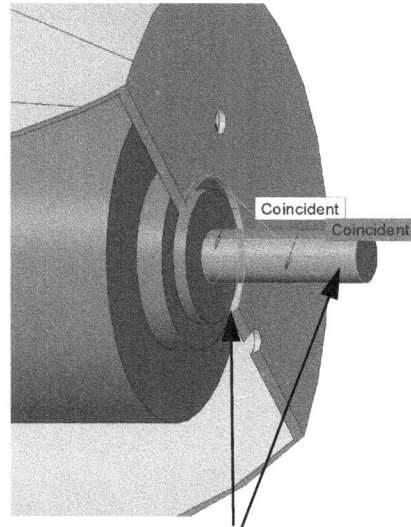

Use the Coincident constraint for the surface on motor_prevod_big.prt with the surface on the assembly_bel.asm.

Figure 4–45

7. The assembled component updates as shown in Figure 4–46.

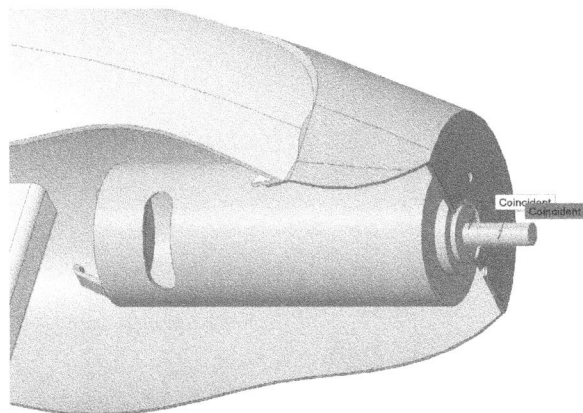

Figure 4–46

8. Assemble **propeller_big.asm**.

9. Assemble the component using two Coincident constraints and select the appropriate surfaces in both **propeller_big.asm** and **assembly_bel.asm**, as shown in Figure 4–47.

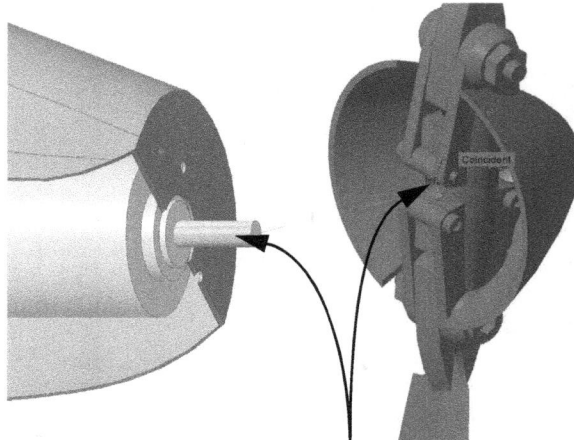

Use the Coincident constraint for the cylindrical surface on propeller_big.asm with the cylindrical surface on assembly_bel.asm.

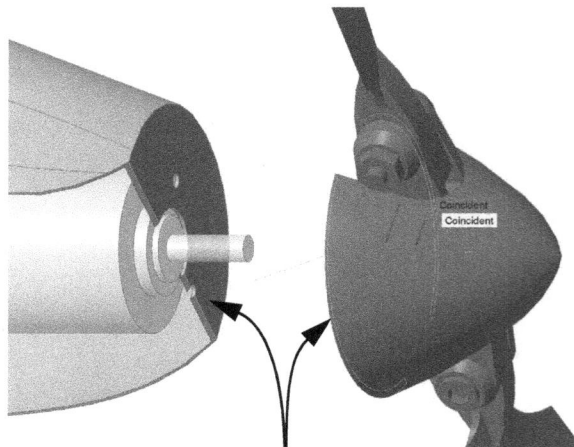

Use the Coincident constraint for the surface on propeller_big.asm with the thin surface on assembly_bel.asm (hidden in the image).

Figure 4–47

10. The assembled component updates as shown in Figure 4–48.

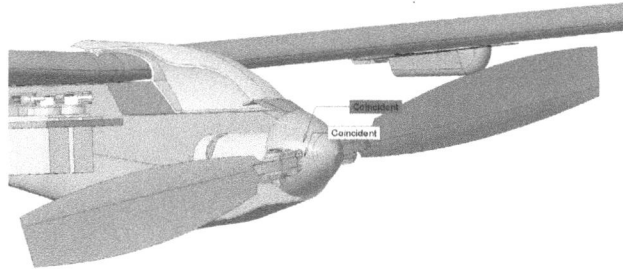

Figure 4–48

11. Assemble **battery_big.prt**.

12. Assemble the component using a Coincident constraint. Select **DTM2** in **battery_big.prt** and **ADTM3** in **assembly_bel.asm**, as shown in Figure 4–49.

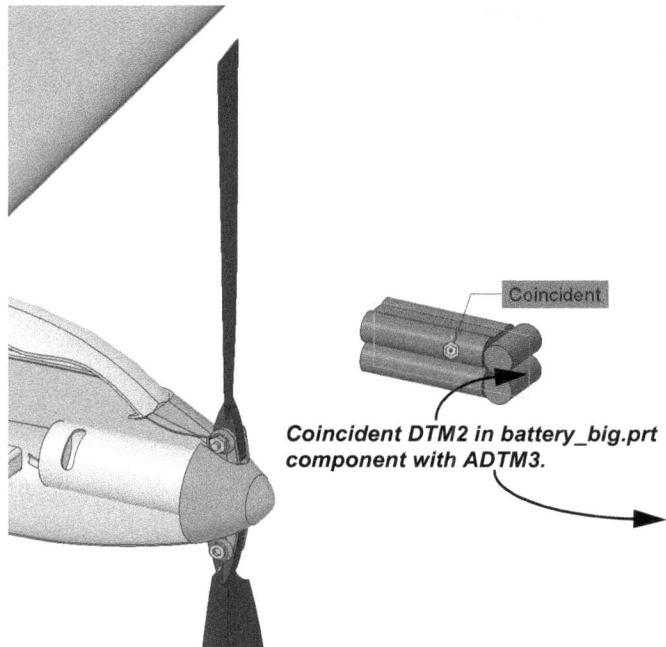

Coincident DTM2 in battery_big.prt component with ADTM3.

Figure 4–49

13. Add a **Distance** constraint type. Select **DTM6** in **battery_big.prt** and **ADTM2** in **assembly_bel.asm**. Apply an *Offset* of **-35**, as shown in Figure 4–50.

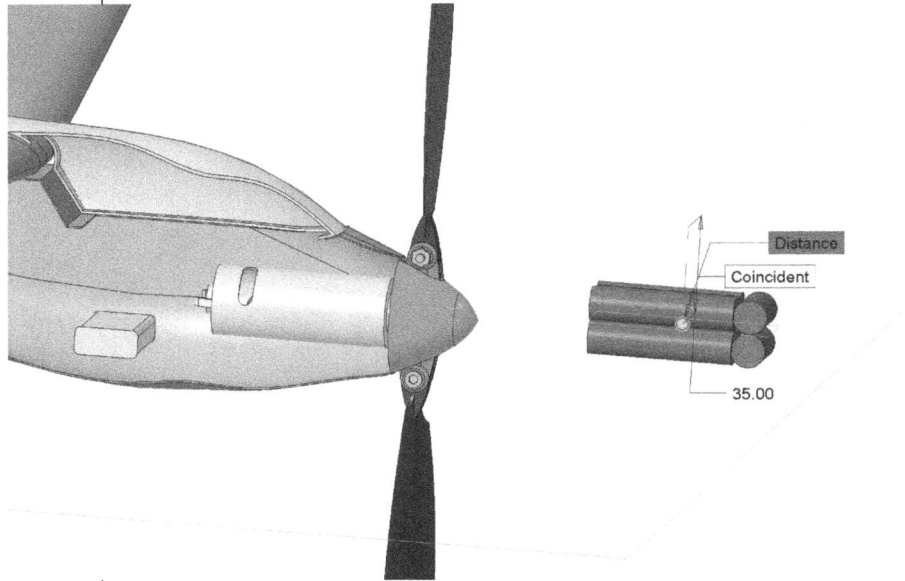

Figure 4–50

14. Add a **Distance** constraint type for the third constraint. Select **DTM1** in **battery_big.prt** and **ADTM1** in **assembly_bel.asm**. Apply an *Offset* of **510**. The assembly displays as shown in Figure 4–51.

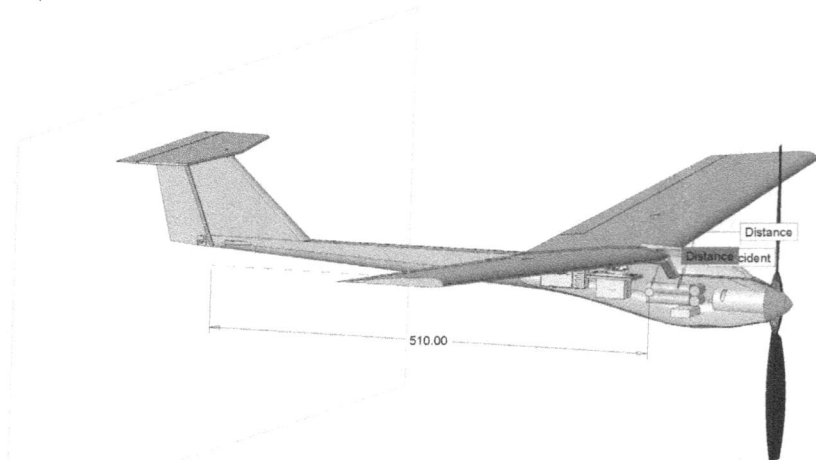

Figure 4–51

15. The Special instance displays as shown in Figure 4–52.

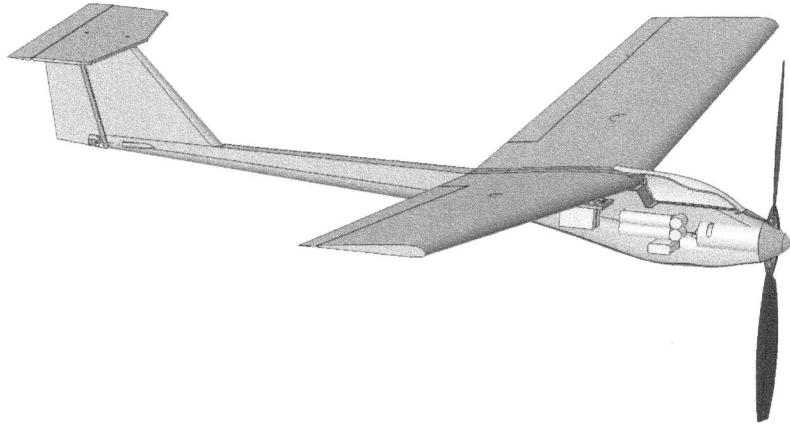

Figure 4–52

Task 5 - Review family table of the top assembly.

1. Open the generic instance of **assembly_bel.asm**.

2. Click ☐ (Family Table) in the *Model* tab.

3. Review the family table instance information, as shown in Figure 4–53.

   There are three new columns. The Special instance has all three parameters defined as **Yes**. All other instances are set to **No** (i.e., the generic and other instance are without changes).

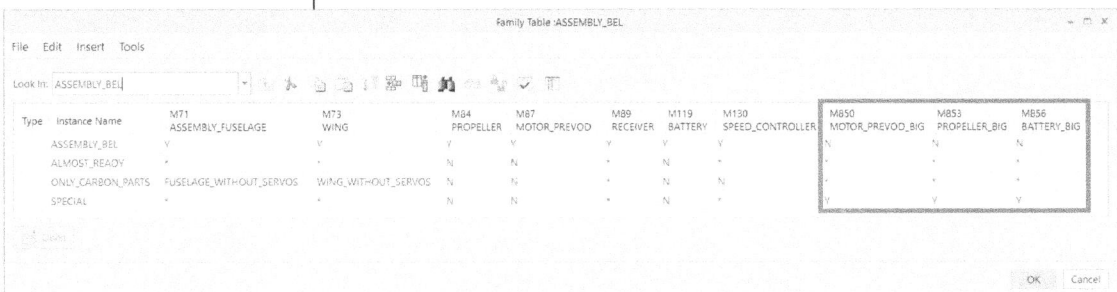

Figure 4–53

4. Save the assembly and erase it from memory.

Chapter Review Questions

1. A family table can be created for any assembly by adding which of the following types of items? (Select all that apply.)

   a. Dimensions

   b. Groups

   c. Parameters

   d. Features

   e. Components

2. Which icon is used to patternize and create additional instances with varying values for selected items?

   a.

   b.

   c.

   d.

3. Which symbol or icon indicates multi-level family tables or nested family tables?

   a. Y

   b. There is no icon or symbol.

   c. *

   d.

4. Any modifications to items that do not belong to the family table cannot be modified in an instance.

   a. True

   b. False

5. Adding a new component to the generic results in which of the following?

   a. Creates an additional column in the family table.

   b. Only adds the new component to the generic.

   c. Adds the new component to the generic and is reflected in all of the instances.

   d. Cannot add a new component to the generic.

6. Adding a new component to an instance results in which of the following?

    a. Creates an additional column in the family table.

    b. Only adds the new component to the generic and that instance.

    c. Adds the new component to the generic and is reflected in all of the instances.

    d. Cannot add a new component to an instance.

7. If a component is deleted from an instance, which of the following scenarios might occur? (Select all that apply.)

    a. If the component exists in the family table, the value of the instance is changed to **N**.

    b. If the component does not exist in the family table, the item is added to the family table and the value is changed to **N**. The generic is assigned the value of **Y** and all of the other instances are assigned as * to maintain the same status as the generic.

    c. Cannot delete a component to an instance.

    d. The component is removed from the family table.

8. If a component is deleted from the generic, which of the following scenarios might occur?

    a. If the item is a family table item, the value of the generic is changed to **N**.

    b. Cannot delete a component in the generic.

    c. The component is removed from the generic.

    d. If the item is a family table item, the column is removed from the table.

Answers: 1.abcde, 2.c, 3.d, 4.b, 5.c, 6.a, 7.ab, 8.a

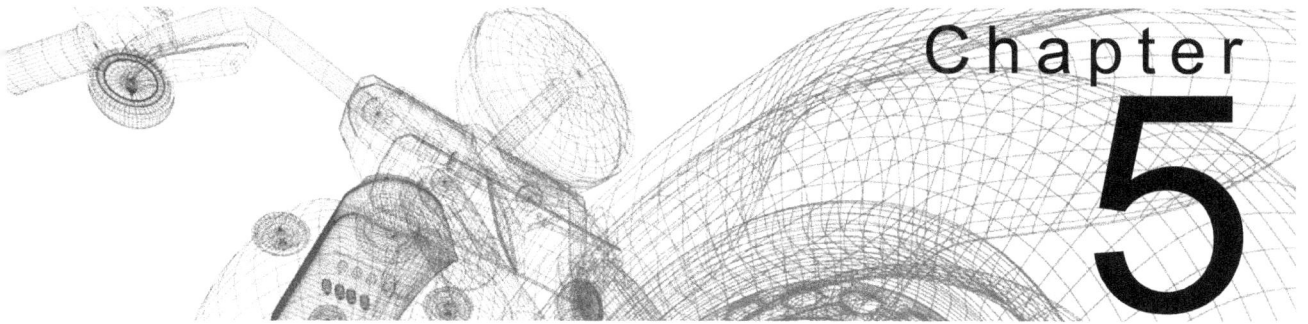

View Manager

Creo Parametric offers tools that can be used to make large assemblies more manageable. You can simplify an assembly to ease display resources and regeneration times by using simplified representations. Component styles can also be defined to simplify the display of an assembly.

Learning Objectives in This Chapter

- Learn how to create and use the display styles for components in an assembly for multiple purposes.
- Use simplified representations to control how components are displayed and when they are opened to improve efficiency.
- Learn the advantages and disadvantages of the different types of system-defined simplified representations available in an assembly.
- Learn to create user-defined simplified representations to help reduce regeneration times for large assemblies.
- Learn to open a simplified representation without having to open the top-level assembly.

5.1 Component Display Styles

*The global display settings can be set using the tools in the In-graphics toolbar, the Display Style icons in the View tab, or the configuration option **entity_display** in the Creo Parametric dialog box.*

By default, all of the components in an assembly are displayed according to the global display setting. The choice of setting can affect the display refresh rates for large assemblies. The six display types and how they affect the display are described as follows:

Option	Icon	Description
Shaded With Edges		Shades all of the model surfaces with highlighted edges. Performance depends on the hardware's graphics capabilities.
Shaded With Reflections		Shades all of the model surfaces and adds reflections. Performance depends on the hardware's graphics capabilities.
Wireframe		Reduces the display refresh rates in situations, such as when the model is reoriented or regenerated.
Shaded		Shades all of the model surfaces. Performance highly depends on the hardware's graphics capabilities.
Hidden Line		Facilitates better visualization of the model by displaying hidden lines in a different color. This option can take more time to refresh large, detailed models.
No Hidden		Facilitates better visualization of the model by not displaying hidden lines. This option can take even more time to refresh large, detailed models.

Instead of using the same display setting for all of the components in an assembly, you can specify display styles for individual components as shown in Figure 5–1.

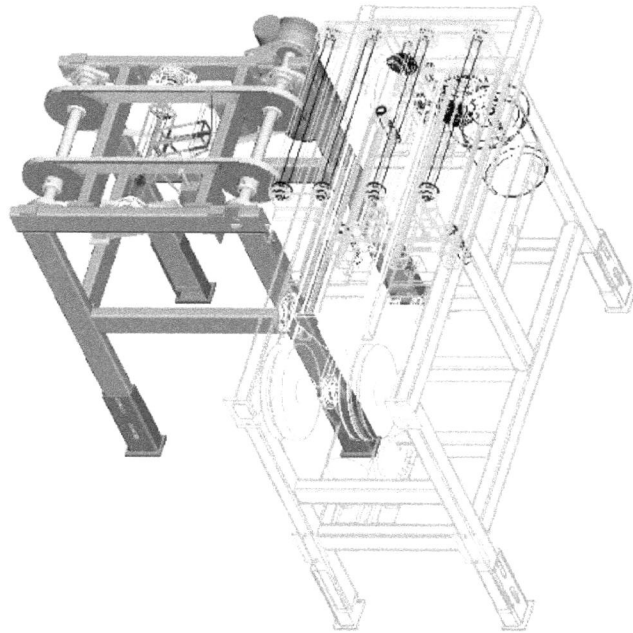

Figure 5–1

Display styles are defined using the View Manager. To open the View Manager, click (View Manager) in the In-graphics toolbar or click (Manage Views) in the *View* tab. In the View Manager dialog box, select the *Style* tab, as shown in Figure 5–2.

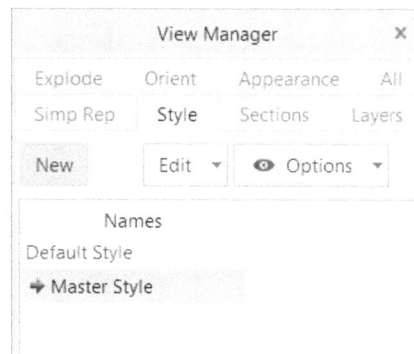

Figure 5–2

To create a display style, click **New**. Enter a name for the style and press <Enter>. The EDIT dialog box opens, as shown in Figure 5–3. You can select the components to blank, or select the *Show* tab and select the display method, as shown in Figure 5–4.

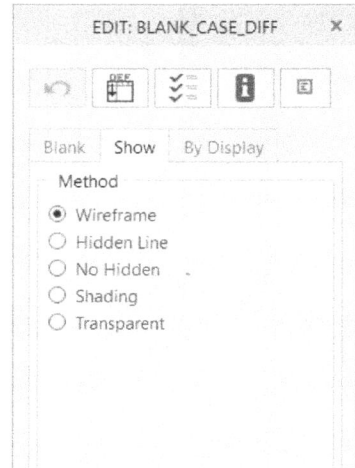

Note that you do not have to make any selections in the EDIT dialog box to continue.

➜ *indicates the active display setting.*

Figure 5–3   **Figure 5–4**

Once finished in the EDIT dialog box, click **OK**. The View Manager displays as shown in Figure 5–5.

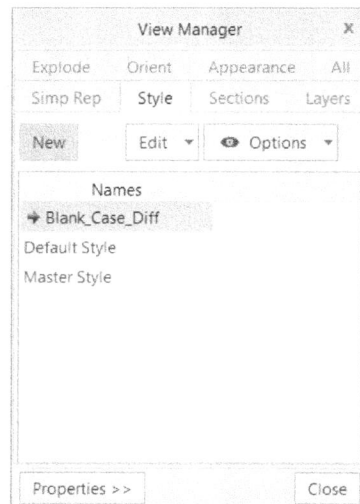

Figure 5–5

To define the display setting for selected components, click **Properties**. Select a component in the Model Tree and select the required display setting in the top row of icons in the *Style* tab. Similar to the global display settings, you can assign the following display settings to a component:

- ⬜ (Shaded With Edges)
- ⬜ (Wireframe)
- ⬜ (Transparent)
- ⬜ (No Hidden)

- ⬜ (Shaded With Reflection)
- ⬜ (Shaded)
- ⬜ (Hidden line)

Components can be set as transparent in assemblies so that you can display the interior components more clearly, as shown in Figure 5–6. The **style_state_transparency** configuration option sets the level of transparency for components. The value can range from 0 to 100.

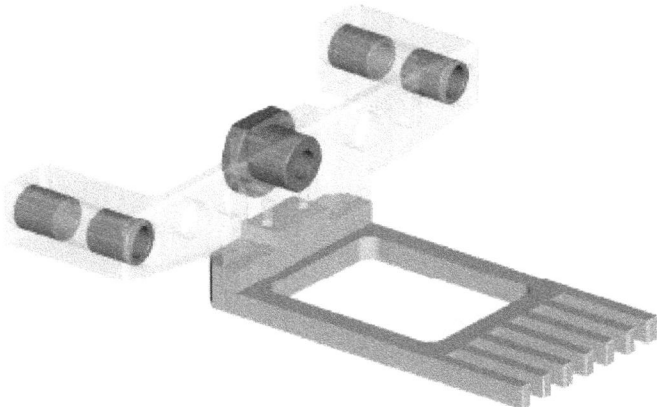

Figure 5–6

In addition, you can use ✎ (Blank) to blank a component or 🔲 (Activate From Selected) to assign the display style from a selected component.

For example, when a component with a defined style is assembled into a top-level assembly, you can use its user-defined style in the top-level assembly. The component and its display setting status are displayed in the View Manager, as shown in Figure 5–7.

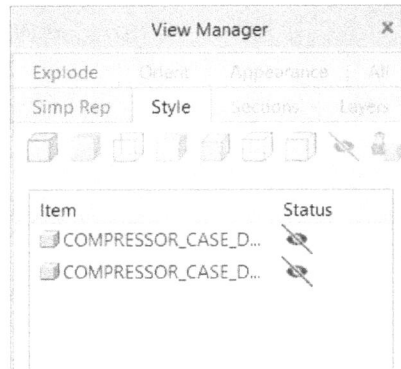

Figure 5–7

Continue selecting components and assigning display settings as required.

To display a component's style in the Model Tree, click **Options>Add Column**. *To remove the column, select* **Remove Column**.

Once you have defined the display settings for the components, click **List** to return to the list of display styles. The current style that was defined has a plus (+) symbol next to its name, as shown in Figure 5–8.

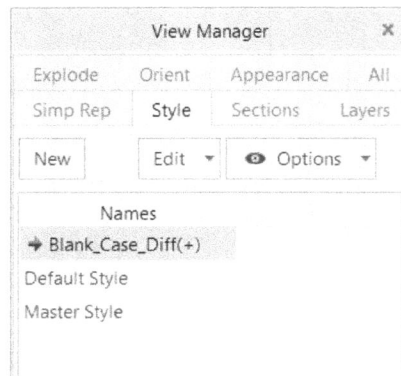

Figure 5–8

The plus (+) symbol indicates that the style has been modified. Click **Edit>Save** and click **OK** to save the style. Click **Close** to complete the display style. The assembly shown in Figure 5–9 displays the **Wireframe_Housing** style where the **grip_housing** component has been set to wireframe and all of the other components in the assembly maintain the current display style (i.e., shaded). You can easily identify that a style state is displayed because its name is listed in the main working window next to the model.

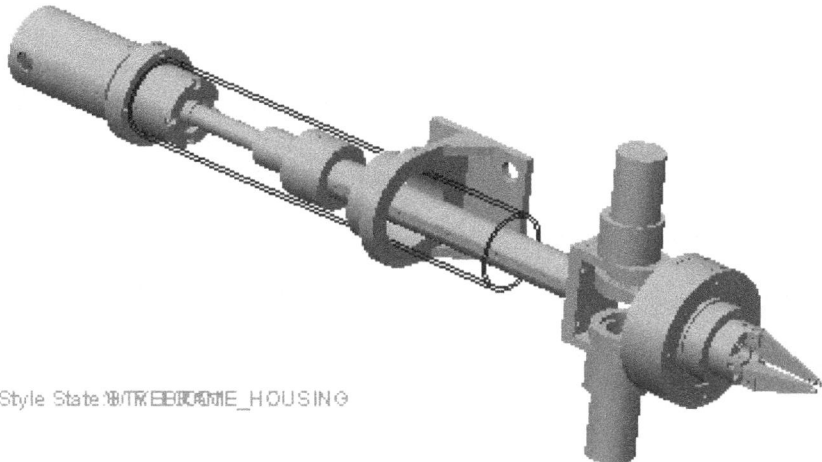

Style State WIREFRAME_HOUSING

Figure 5–9

To make changes to an existing display style, open the View Manager, select the display style, and click **Properties** to redefine the style's display settings. You can also set the temporary display styles of selected components by selecting **Display Style** in the *Model* tab.

Temporary display styles can be used to quickly control the display of components without having to use the View Manager. A temporary display style is not saved with the model unless you open the View Manager and create a new style.

Appearance States

You can define different appearance states for your model using the *Appearance* tab in the View Manager dialog box, as shown in Figure 5–10. You can define and switch between different color combinations for your designs.

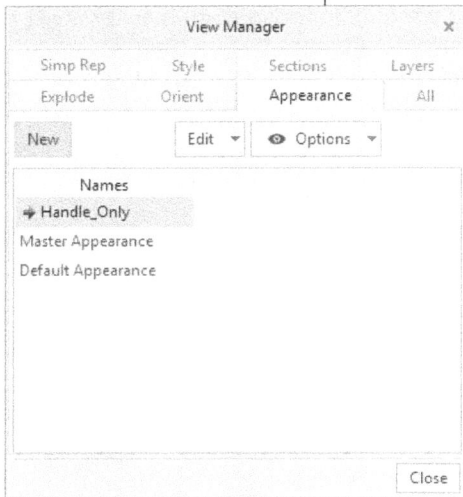

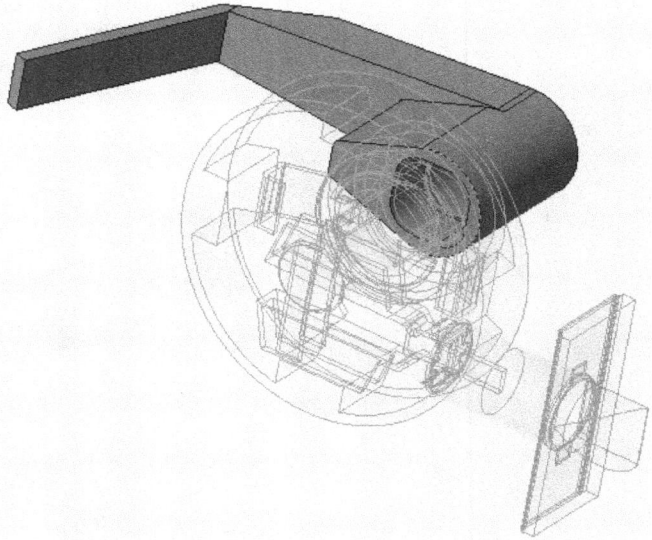

Figure 5–10

Apply appearances to surface, features, or components in your model. In the *Appearance* tab of the View Manager, click **New** and enter a name. You can repeat this for as many different combinations of colors, textures, etc. that you require. This enables you to quickly change the appearance for various use cases.

5.2 Simplified Representations

Simplified representations (simplified reps) are used to improve retrieval, display, and regeneration times, which significantly increases efficiency while working with assemblies. They are used to control which components (parts or subassemblies) of an assembly are opened and how they are displayed. The model shown on the left in Figure 5–11 is a complete assembly. The model shown on the right is the simplified version. When the assembly simplified rep is opened, only those components in the rep are opened, the other components are not brought into the session.

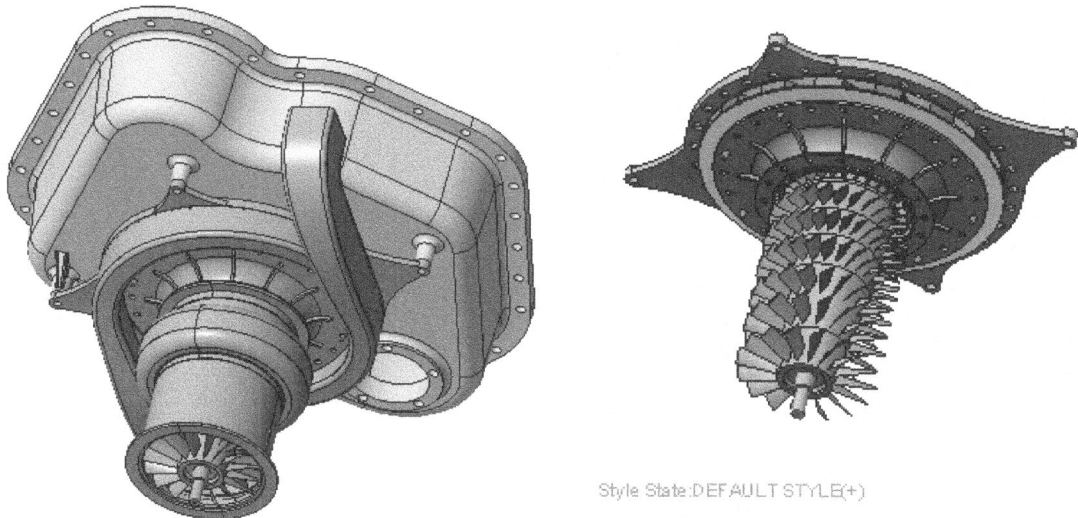

Style State:DEFAULT STYLE(+)

The top-level assembly has been simplified to remove components.

Figure 5–11

You can represent your model using system-defined simplified representations or a user-defined simplified representation.

5.3 Automatic Representations

Previous releases of Creo Parametric enabled you to create several different types of Simplified representations, such as Graphics representations, Geometry representations, Boundary Box representations, etc. As of Creo Parametric 4.0, all of the representation types are obsolete and are replaced with a single Automatic representation, as shown in Figure 5–12.

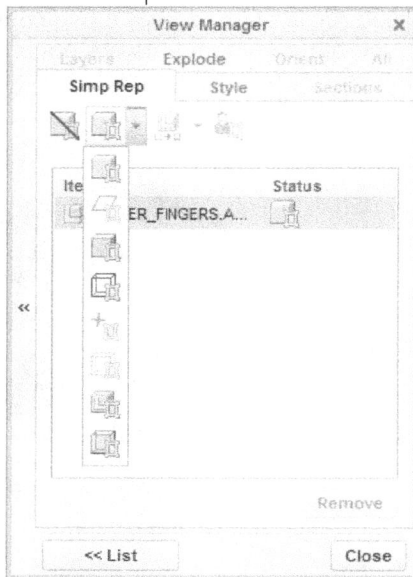

Previous releases   *Creo 4.0+*

Figure 5–12

The Automatic representation retrieves the assembly geometry as light-weight surfaces to retrieve your assembly as fast as possible. Some operations such as taking measurements can be conducted on the light-weight geometry, or you can bring the full models into session to conduct more extensive operations such as adding assembly features.

Note that only assembly components included in the representation are retrieved in an Automatic representation, whereas all other components remain excluded.

You can control the handling of simplified representations from previous releases using the configuration option *hide_pre_creo4_reps*:

- **yes:** Hides all simplified representations created in Creo Parametric 3.0 and earlier, except for **Exclude** simplified representations. By default, when opening an assembly, it opens as an Automatic representation.

- **no:** Maintains all simplified representations for Creo 3.0 and earlier.

- **maintain_master:** (Default) Hides all simplified representations for Creo 3.0 and earlier, except for **Master** and **Exclude** simplified representations.

5.4 Additional System-Defined Simplified Representations

In addition to the Automatic representation, assemblies have other system-defined simplified representations that are created automatically. These can be used to simplify the display and speed up the retrieval process of large assemblies.

System-defined simplified representations are enabled in the View Manager. Open the View Manager and select the *Simp Rep* tab. The View Manager displays as shown in Figure 5–13.

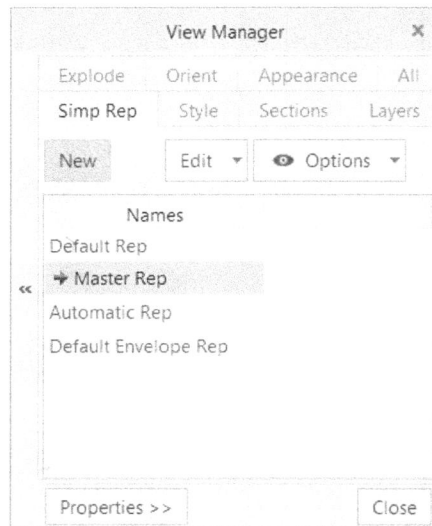

Figure 5–13

Double-click on a system-defined representation in the View Manager to enable it.

- **Default Representation:** Enables you to set a representation that automatically opens when the model is opened. By default, this representation is identical to the **Master Representation**. You do not actually see any difference in the model display until you redefine the **Default Representation** and manipulate the components.

- **Master Representation:** The representation that is used by default if customized simplified representations are not created. It opens the full assembly into session, including all of the components. All of the simplified representations are based on the master representation. Any assembly actions or modifications applied to a simplified representation are also applied to the master representation.

- **Default Envelope Representation:** Substitutes selected components with the default envelope representation. An envelope is a part that represents the geometry of any number of components in an assembly. It enables you to simplify the model by substituting complex geometry with a simple envelope feature (i.e., extrude or revolve). If there is no default envelope, the system opens the dialog box to create one.

5.5 User-Defined Simplified Representations

You can create user-defined simplified representations in an assembly to simplify the display and help ease the regeneration times of working with large assemblies.

To delete a simplified representation, click **Edit>Remove** *or right-click and select* **Remove**.

User-defined simplified representations are created using the View Manager. Open the View Manager and select the *Simp Rep* tab. Click **New** in the *Simp Rep* area in the View Manager. Enter a name for the simplified rep and press <Enter>. The Edit dialog box opens, which enables you to quickly exclude components. Click **OK** to close the dialog box. The new representation is now active, as indicated by ⇥ .

You can select components for a simplified representation manually using the Model Tree, selecting directly on the model, or using defined rules.

Manual Selection

Use one of the following two methods to modify the representation settings by manually selecting components.

Method 1

Use the Edit dialog box by clicking **Edit** and selecting **Edit Definition**. The dialog box opens as shown in Figure 5–14.

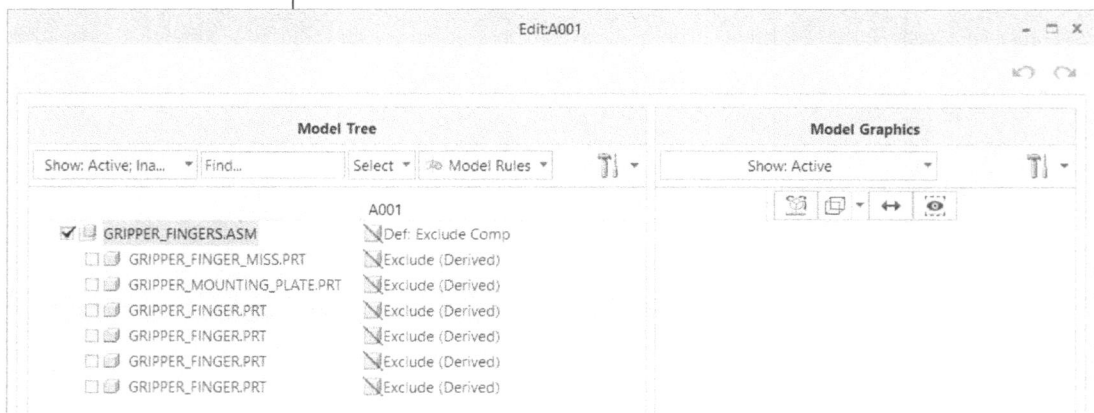

Figure 5–14

When creating a new simplified representation, components are excluded by default and the Default Simp Rep rule changes from *Master Rep* to **Exclude**. This eliminates the unnecessary retrieval of large data into the Creo Parametric session. This is useful when you are managing large assemblies. You can change the status of the top-level assembly using the flyout menu, as shown in Figure 5–15.

Figure 5–15

Assign representation settings using the options in the drop-down list as shown in Figure 5–16, or select the check box to switch between **Master Rep** and **Exclude**. The view window updates to reflect the changes.

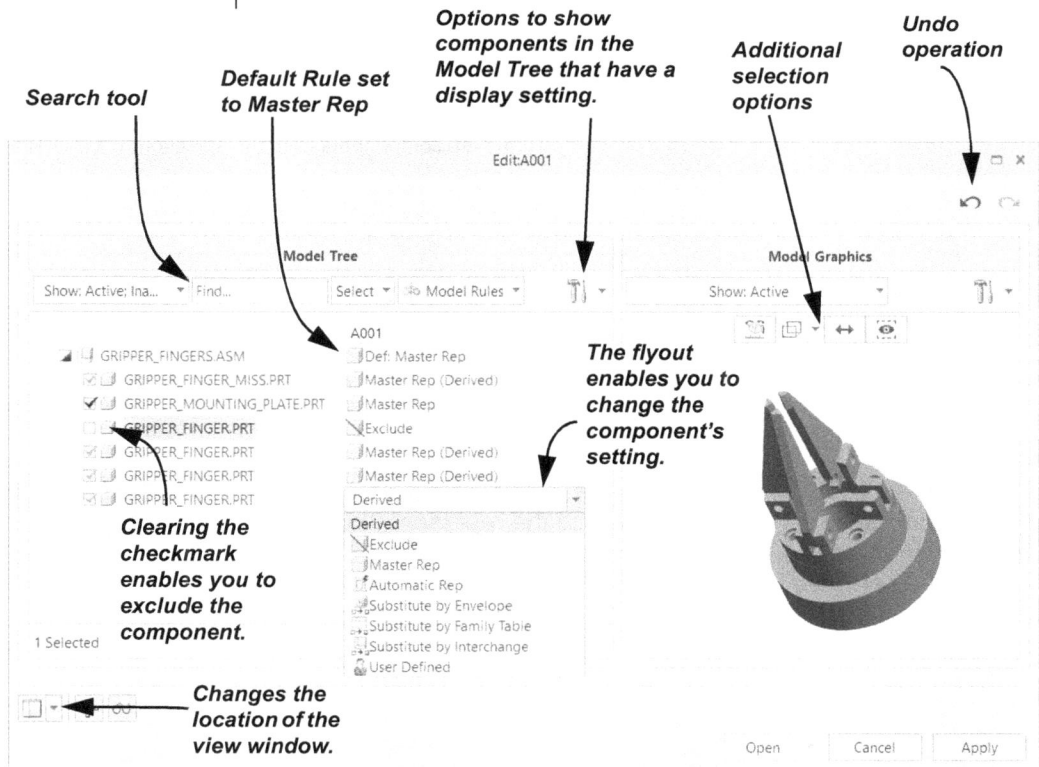

Figure 5–16

The Show: Active, Inactive drop-down list enables you to specify what is displayed. For example, you can remove the components that are inactive to simplify the amount of components listed in the column. The two components that were excluded from the simplified representation have been removed from the column as shown in Figure 5–17.

Clear the Inactive option and the two excluded components are removed from the column.

Figure 5–17

Additional options in the View window in the Edit dialog box are described as follows:

Icon	Description
	Removes components from the selection by geometric size.
	Removes internal components from the selection.
	Removes external components from the selection.
	Inverts the selection of displayed objects.
	Includes only the selected components and excludes all of the others.

Click **OK** to close the dialog box. The Model Tree adds a column to indicate the representation of the components.

A component's representation setting can also be assigned by selecting the component, right-clicking, and selecting Set Representation to.

Method 2

Select the simplified rep in the View Manger dialog box and click **Properties**. The View Manager opens. The default rule when creating a new simplified representation is **Master Representation**, as shown in Figure 5–18.

Select from these options to change the representation settings.

The status of the master assembly indicates the default rule that is being used. This icon indicates that the default rule is Master Representation.

Select arrows to open a preview window.

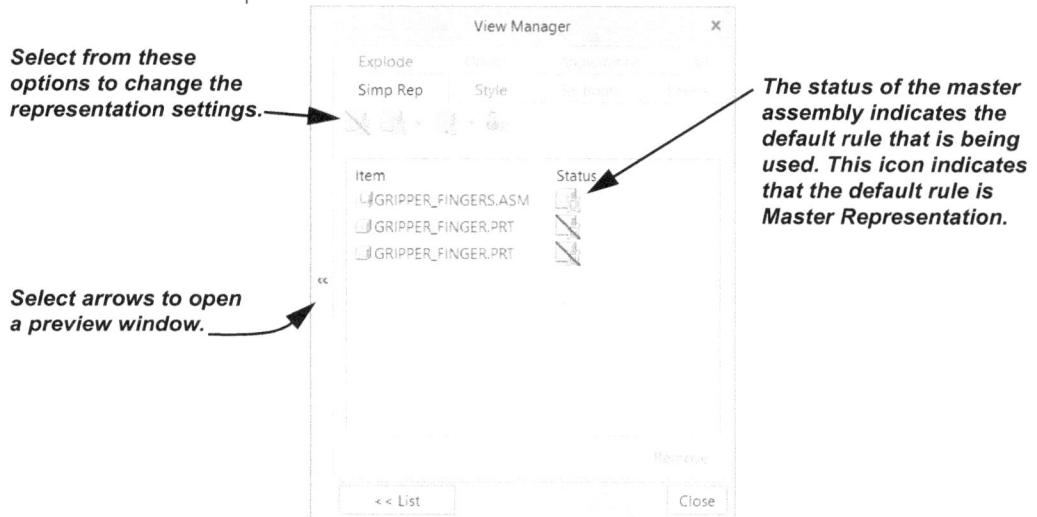

Figure 5–18

Select components in the model or Model Tree and assign representation settings using the options in the drop-down list as shown in Figure 5–19.

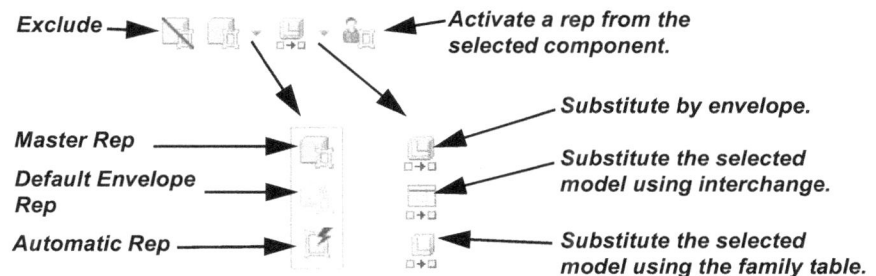

Exclude

Activate a rep from the selected component.

Master Rep

Default Envelope Rep

Automatic Rep

Substitute by envelope.

Substitute the selected model using interchange.

Substitute the selected model using the family table.

Figure 5–19

Click **List** to return to the listing of the simplified reps.

*To display the simp rep settings in the Model Tree, click **Options** in the Listings page and select **Add Column**.*

The settings and their icons for each method are described as follows:

Option	Icon	Description
Exclude		Selected components of the master representation are excluded as members of the simplified representation.
Master Rep		Selected components of the master representation are included as members of the simplified representation.
User Defined		Substitutes a user-defined simplified representation from a selected component.
Automatic Rep		Selected components of the master representation are included as Automatic.
Default Envelope Representation		Substitutes the selected components with the default envelope representation.

The current representation (⭢) is temporarily modified with the new settings and displayed with a plus (+) symbol appended to the end of its name. For example, **No_Engine** (+) indicates that the **No_Engine** representation was displayed and that is has been modified.

To save the changes to the simplified rep, click **Edit>Save** and click **OK**.

You might need to make changes to the simplified representation once it has been created. Use either of the following techniques to redefine the representation settings:

- Click **Properties** and use the technique that was used in Method 2.
- Click **Edit>Edit Definition** and use the technique that was used in Method 1.
- Right-click on a simplified representation, click **Edit Definition**, and use the techniques that was used in Method 1.

5.6 Opening Simplified Representations

One of the main purposes of a simplified representation is to improve retrieval times when working with large assemblies. By directly opening a simplified rep instead of the master rep, only the required components are opened into session. To open a simplified rep you can select the **Open Representation**, **Open Automatic**, or **Open Subset** options in the File Open dialog box. You can also set the **open_simplified_rep_by_default** configuration option to determine how the model is opened. **No** is the default option and opens the **Master Rep**. If set to **Yes**, the Open Rep dialog box opens, enabling you to select a representation.

Use the Default Rep to eliminate the use of selecting **Open Representation**, **Open Subset**, or using the **open_simplified_rep_by_default** configuration file option.

Open Representation

Click 📂 (Open), select the assembly in the File Open dialog box, expand **Open**, and select **Open Representation**. The Open Rep dialog box opens as shown in Figure 5–20, enabling you to select the representation that you want to open.

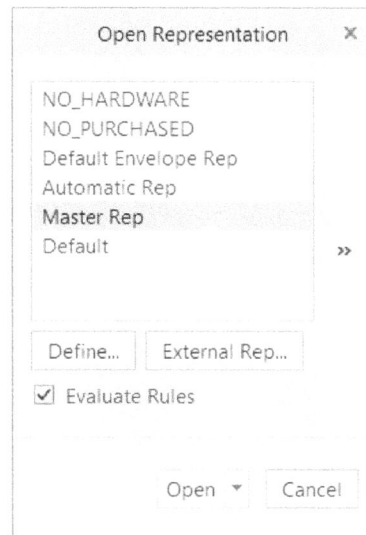

Figure 5–20

You can easily define and edit simplified representations without loading models into memory. Using the dynamic preview, you can display the preview and add or remove the components easily from a simplified representation, as shown in Figure 5–21.

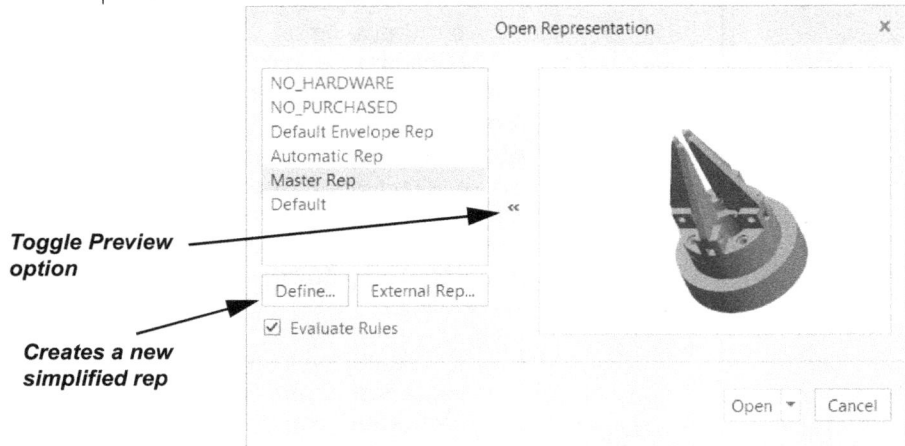

Toggle Preview option

Creates a new simplified rep

Figure 5–21

Open Automatic

Click (Open), select the assembly in the File Open dialog box, expand **Open**, and then select **Open Automatic**. The Automatic representation of the assembly will open.

Open Subset

Click ⌷ (Open), select the assembly in the File Open dialog box, and click **Open Subset**. The Retrieval Customization dialog box opens as shown in Figure 5–22. It is similar to the Edit dialog box.

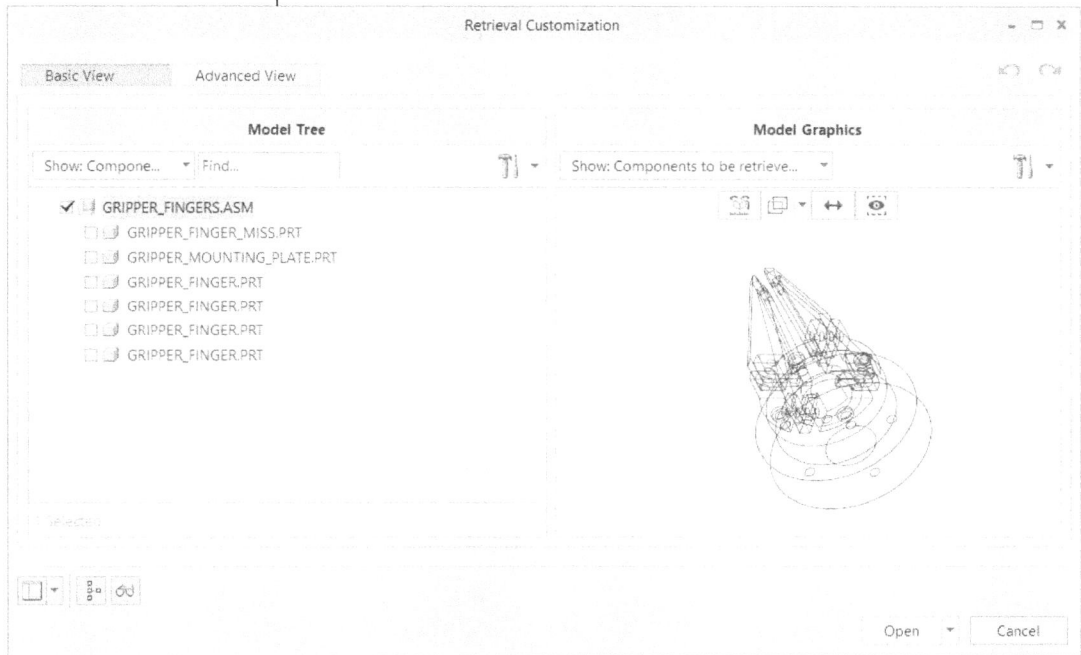

Figure 5–22

Practice 5a

Using Component Display Styles

Practice Objectives

- Set the display style of an assembly and of a subassembly.
- Set the default display style.

In this practice, you will create display styles to customize how the model is displayed. You will create styles in the top-level assembly and in subassemblies so that their styles are passed back to the top-level assembly. In addition, you will customize the default style to control the style that is used when the model is opened. The model shown on the left in Figure 5–23 is the complete top-level assembly and the model on the right is one of the display styles that you will create.

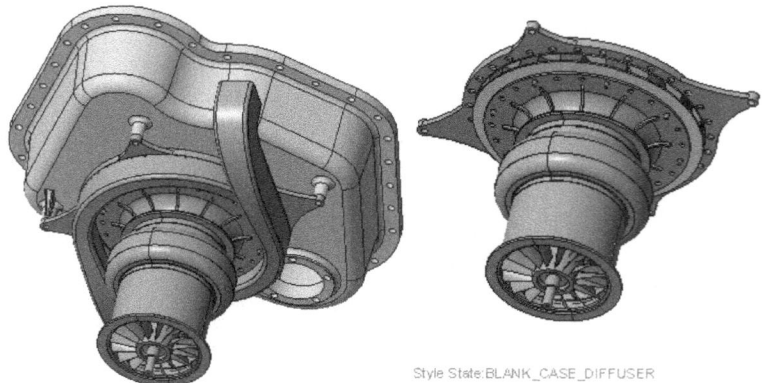

Style State:BLANK_CASE_DIFFUSER

Figure 5–23

Task 1 - Open an assembly file.

1. Change your working directory to the *Component_Display_Styles* folder.

2. Open **turbine.asm**.

3. Set the model display as follows:

- *(Datum Display Filters)*: All Off
- *(Spin Center)*: Off
- *(Display Style)*: (Shading With Edges)

You can also click
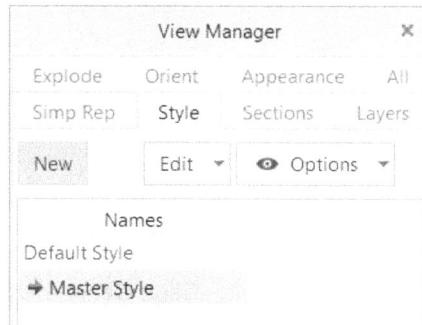 *(Manage Views) in the Model tab.*

4. In the In-graphics toolbar, click 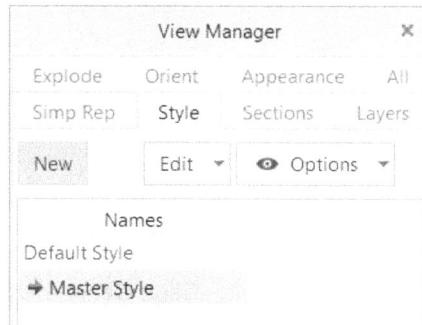 (View Manager) to open the View Manager.

5. Select the *Style* tab, as shown in Figure 5–24.

Figure 5–24

Task 2 - Create a user-defined view style.

---

1. Click **New**.

2. Enter **Blank_Case_Diffuser**, as shown in Figure 5–25.

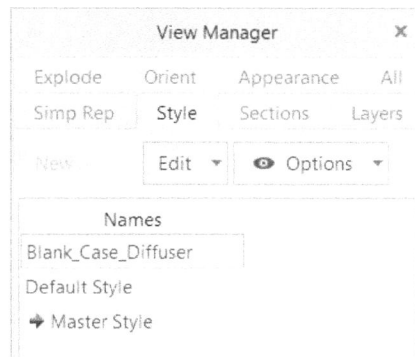

Figure 5–25

3. Press <Enter>.

4. Hold <Ctrl> and select **GEAR_CASE.PRT** and **DIFFUSER.PRT** in the Model Tree, as shown in Figure 5–26.

EDIT: BLANK_CASE_DIFFUSER

TURBINE.ASM
▶ GEAR_CASE.PRT   Blank
▶ AFT_COVER.PRT
▶ VANE.ASM
▶ DIFFUSER.PRT   Blank
▶ ROTOR.ASM
▶ IMPELLER_COVER.PRT
▶ COMP_CASE.ASM

Figure 5–26

5. Click **OK** in the EDIT dialog box.

6. Click **Properties** in the View Manager dialog box.

7. The *Item* and *Status* columns display in the View Manager dialog box, as shown in Figure 5–27.

View Manager   ✕

Explode   Orient   Appearance   All
Simp Rep   Style   Sections   Layers

Item   Status
GEAR_CASE.PRT
DIFFUSER.PRT

Figure 5–27

8. Click **List**.

9. Click **Close**. The assembly view style displays as shown in Figure 5–28.

*The model continues to display the **BLANK_CASE_DIFFU SER** display style. This is because it is the active style, as indicated by ✦ .*

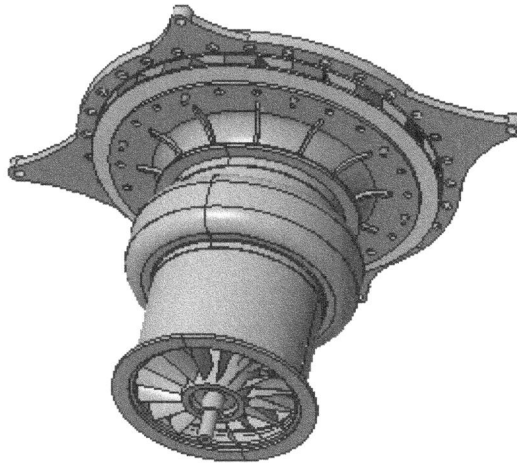

Style State:BLANK_CASE_DIFFUSER

Figure 5–28

Task 3 - Activate the Default Style and modify its settings.

Design Considerations

The Default Style is the view style that is displayed when the assembly is opened. By default, it includes all of the components and uses the global display setting for the current session for all of the components. In this task, you will edit the default style so that when the model is opened, it automatically displays a custom style.

1. Open the View Manager. The **Blank_Case_Diffuser** is still the active style. Double-click on **Default Style** to activate it. This style contains all of the components, and they all use the global display setting for the current session, as shown in Figure 5–29.

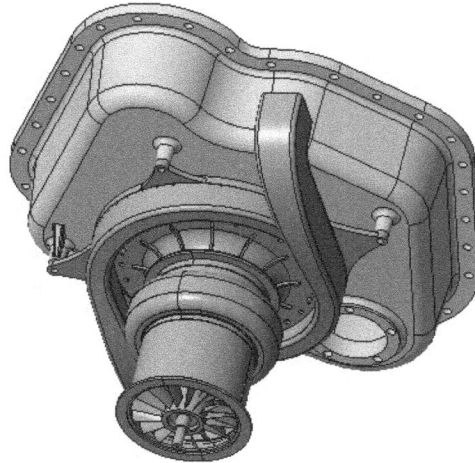

Style State:DEFAULT STYLE

Figure 5–29

2. Click **Properties**.

3. Select the three components shown in Figure 5–30 and remove them from the display by clicking ✎ (Blank). The model displays as shown in Figure 5–30.

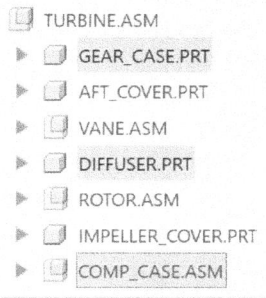

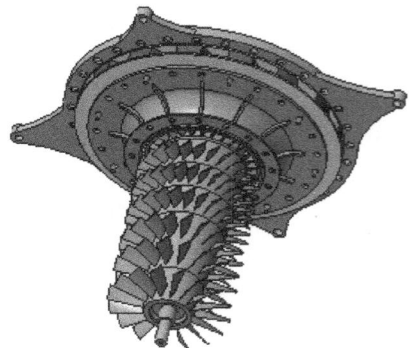

Style State:DEFAULT STYLE(+)

Figure 5–30

4. Click **List**.

5. Click **Edit>Save** and click **OK** to save the style. The warning shown in Figure 5–31 displays.

Update Default State	×

You are about to update the default display style state. This will affect what the model looks like upon retrieval. Do you wish to continue?

Update Default	Cancel

Figure 5–31

6. Click **Update Default**.

7. Close the View Manager.

8. Regenerate the assembly.

9. Save the assembly.

10. Close the window and erase it from memory.

Task 4 - Open the assembly.

1. Open **turbine.asm**. The model displays as shown in Figure 5–32.

Design Considerations

The assembly opens and is displayed in the default style that you just customized, as shown in Figure 5–32. Now that you have changed the default state, the state is displayed each time this assembly is opened. However, the file retrieval time has not been reduced. Setting a view state only simplifies the visual display of an assembly. File retrieval and regeneration time are not affected.

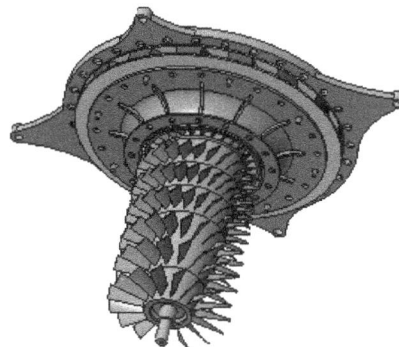

Style State:DEFAULT STYLE

Figure 5–32

Task 5 - Use a display style of a subassembly in the top-level assembly.

1. Open **comp_case.asm** using the Model Tree. The assembly displays as shown in Figure 5–33.

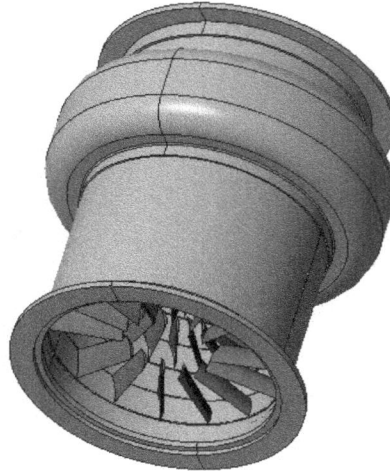

Figure 5–33

2. Use the View Manager to create a display style called **NO_HIDDEN**.

3. In the EDIT dialog box, click the *Show* tab.

4. Select **No Hidden** in the Method area as shown in Figure 5–34.

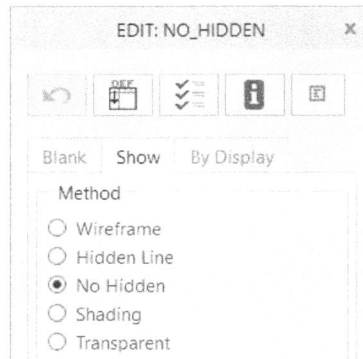

Figure 5–34

5. In the Model Tree, select all of the components in the assembly, then click **OK** in the EDIT dialog box.

6. Save the display style and close the View Manager. The assembly displays as shown in Figure 5–35.

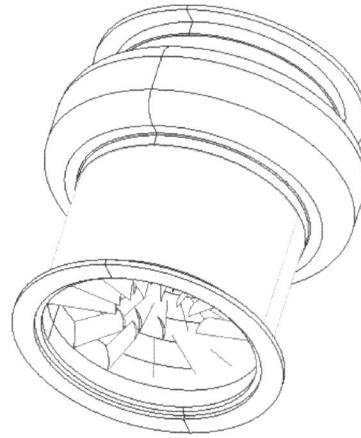

Style State:NO_HIDDEN

Figure 5–35

7. Save the assembly and close the window. The TURBINE window should now be active.

Task 6 - Create a view state by copying an existing state.

1. Open the View Manager.

2. Select the **Blank_Case_Diffuser** state, right-click, and select **Copy**, as shown in Figure 5–36.

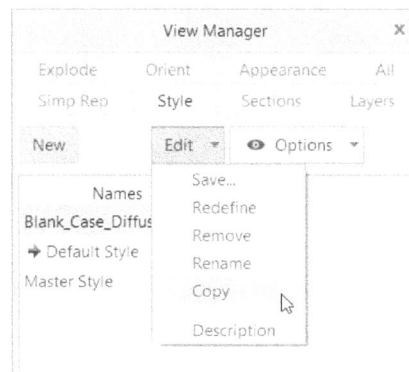

Figure 5–36

3. Enter **Comp_Case_No_Hidden** in the *Copy to* field, as shown in Figure 5–37.

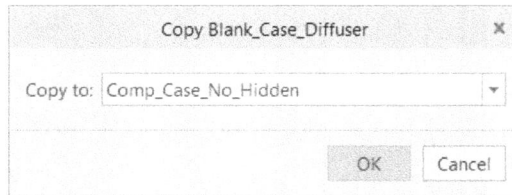

Copy Blank_Case_Diffuser	✕
Copy to: Comp_Case_No_Hidden	▼
	OK Cancel

Figure 5–37

4. Click **OK**.

5. Activate **Blank_Case_Diffuser** and click **Properties**.

6. Select **COMP_CASE.ASM** in the Model Tree and click 🔒 (Activate From Selected) to assign a style from the subassembly level.

7. In the SELECT DISPLAY STYLE dialog box, select **NO_HIDDEN** and click **OK**. The View Manager updates as shown in Figure 5–38.

View Manager	✕
Explode Orient Appearance All	
Simp Rep Style Sections Layers	

Item	Status
GEAR_CASE.PRT	⊘
DIFFUSER.PRT	⊘
COMP_CASE.ASM	🔒 NO_HIDDEN

Figure 5–38

8. Click **List** and save the **Blank_Case_Diffuser**.

9. Close the View Manager. The assembly displays as shown in Figure 5–39.

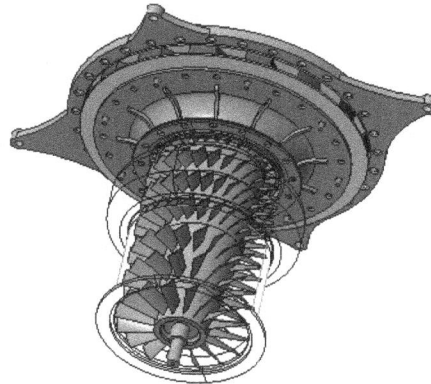

Style State:BLANK_CASE_DIFFUSER

Figure 5–39

Task 7 - Edit the default style.

1. Open the View Manager.

Design Considerations

By customizing the default style, each time you open the assembly it displays with this display style. This might only be required while you are working on a specific aspect of the assembly. To return the style to display all of the components, such as the master style when opened, you must remove all of the customization from this style. It can be further customized at a later date, if required.

2. Double-click on **Default Style** and click **Properties**.

3. Select all three items as shown in Figure 5–40, and click **Remove**.

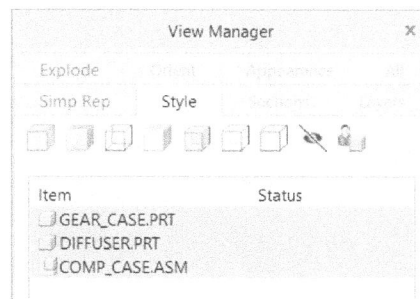

Figure 5–40

4. Save the default style. Click **Update Default** to complete the save.

5. Set **Master Style** to be the active view style and close the View Manager.

6. Save the assembly and erase all files from memory.

Practice 5b

Simplified Representations

Practice Objectives

- Create and open simplified representations.
- Set the default simplified representation.

In this practice, you will create simplified representations that remove components from the display. In addition, you will learn how to open these user-defined representations so that the removed components are not brought into session. The model shown on the left in Figure 5–41 is the complete top-level assembly and the model shown on the right is one of the simplified representations that you will create.

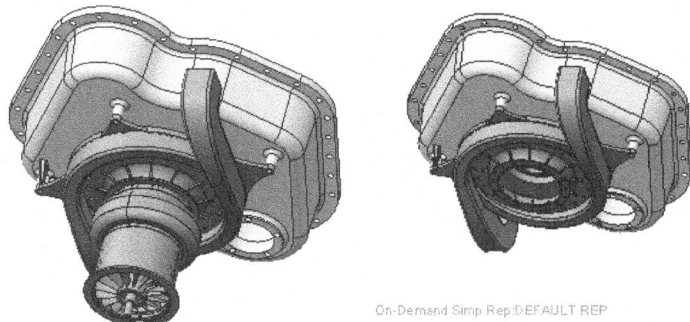

On-Demand Simp Rep:DEFAULT REP

Figure 5–41

Task 1 - Open the View Manager.

1. Change your working directory to the *Simplified_Representations* folder.

2. Open **turbine.asm**.

3. Set the model display as follows:

  - $\overset{\times\angle}{\not{\triangleright}}$ *(Datum Display Filters)*: All Off

  - ⤳ *(Spin Center)*: Off

  - ⬛ *(Display Style)*: ⬜ (Shading With Edges)

4. In the In-graphics toolbar, click 📷 (View Manager) to open the View Manager.

5. Select the *Simp Rep* tab. The View Manager updates as shown in Figure 5–42.

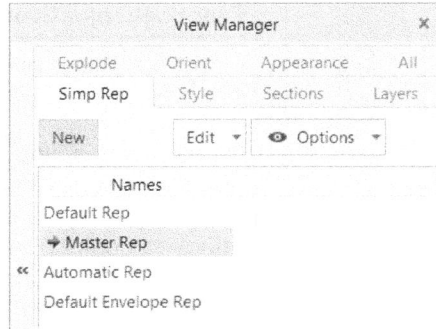

Figure 5–42

6. Click **New**, set the new simplified representation *Name* to **No_Case_Diffuser**, and press <Enter>.

7. The Edit dialog box opens as shown in Figure 5–43.

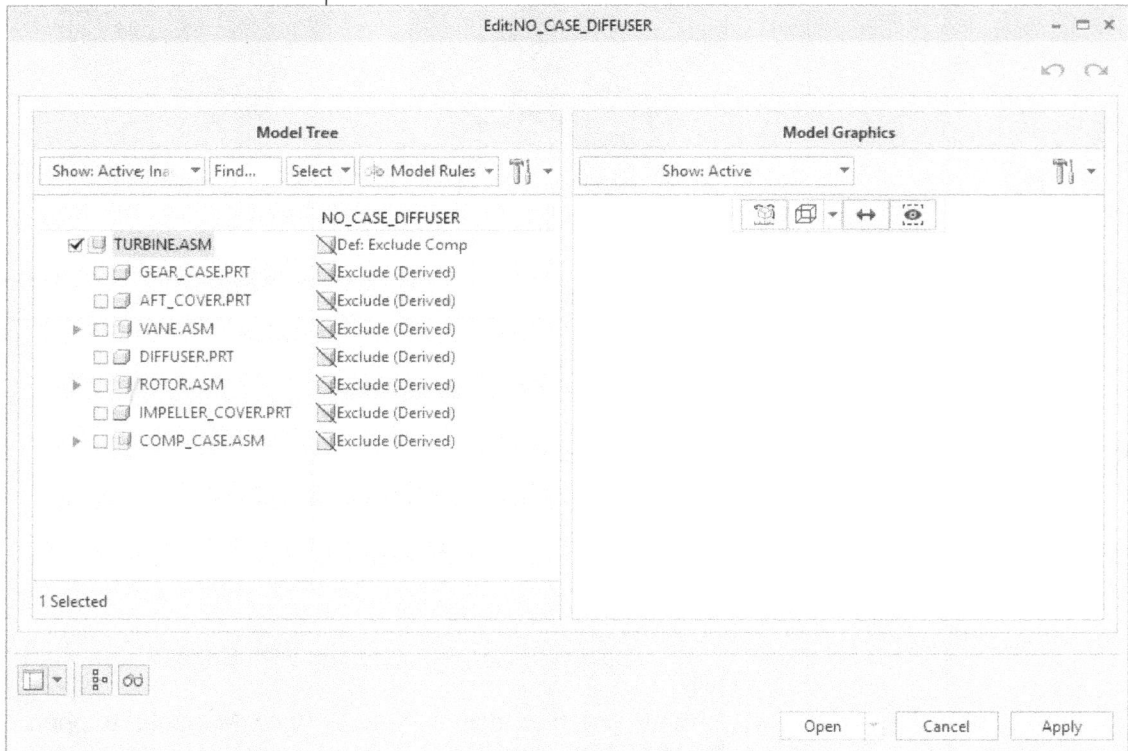

Figure 5–43

8. Select **Def: Exclude Comp** next to **TURBINE.ASM** and select **Master Rep** in the drop-down list, as shown in Figure 5–44. This changes the default rule to Master Representation.

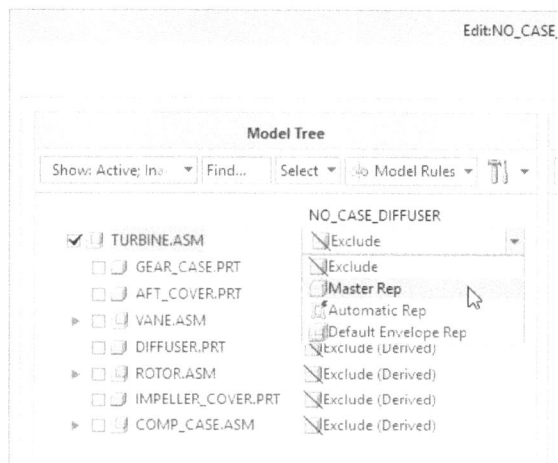

Figure 5–44

9. Click twice on the check box next to **GEAR_CASE.PRT** and **DIFFUSER.PRT** to clear the selection and change *Master Rep (Derived)* to **Exclude** as shown Figure 5–45. The column indicates the components that have been excluded in this representation (you may need to include **Inactive Components** in the **Show: Active; Inactive** menu in the upper left to display the rows for the excluded components).

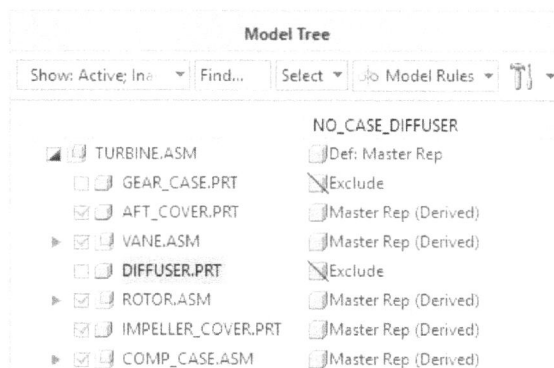

Figure 5–45

10. Click **Open**.

11. Turn on Feature display in the Model Tree, if required.

12. The assembly and the Model Tree display as shown in Figure 5–46.

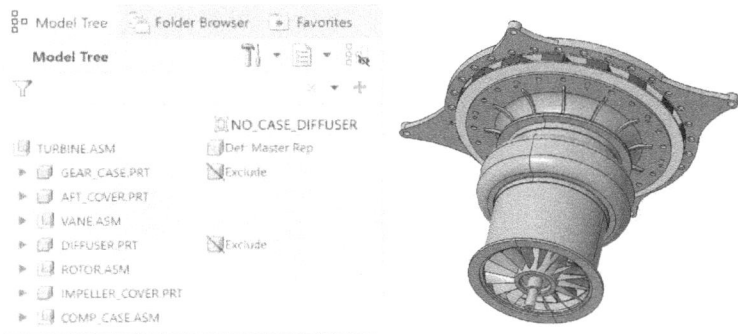

Figure 5–46

Design Considerations

When you create a simplified rep that excludes components or a display style that excludes components, the display of the model displays in the same way. However, using a simplified rep reduces system resources and retrieval and regeneration times. A view state does not reduce system resources.

Task 2 - Edit an existing simplified representation.

1. Select **No_Case_Diffuser**, and click **Edit>Edit Definition**. The Edit dialog box opens as shown in Figure 5–47.

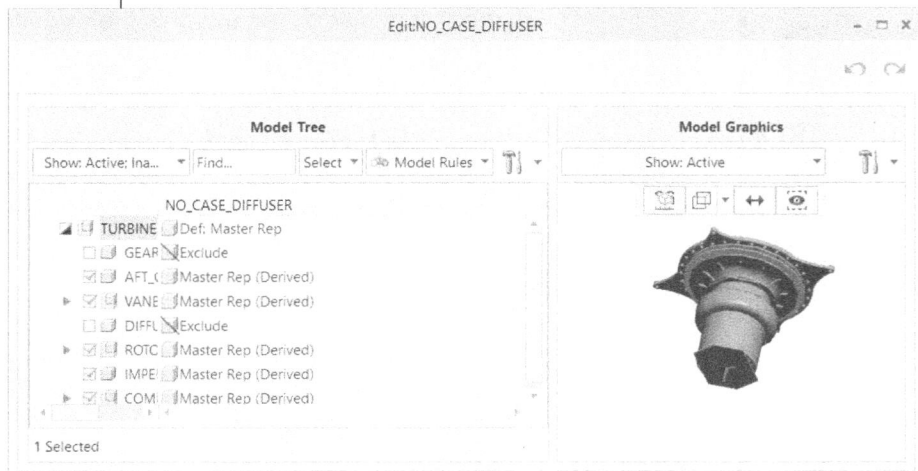

Figure 5–47

2. Clear the checkmarks next to **VANE.ASM** and **ROTOR.ASM**, as shown in Figure 5–48. The column indicates that the components have been excluded in this representation.

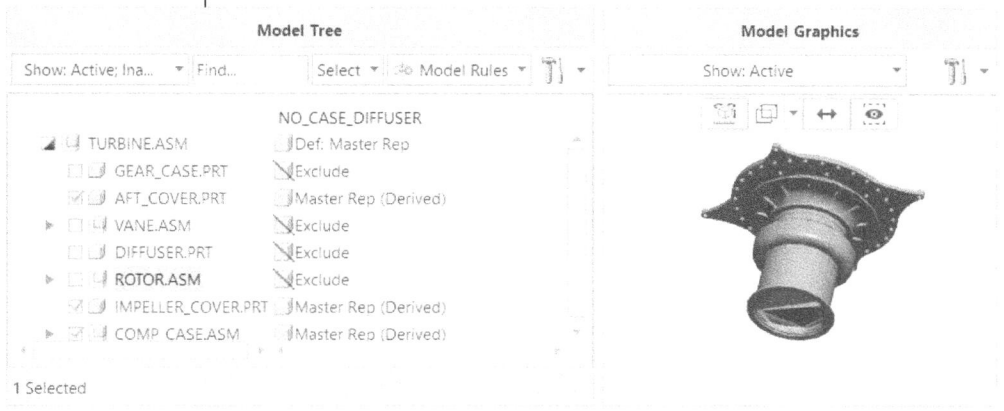

Figure 5–48

3. Click **Open** to complete the redefinition of the **No_Case_Diffuser** representation. The assembly displays as shown in Figure 5–49.

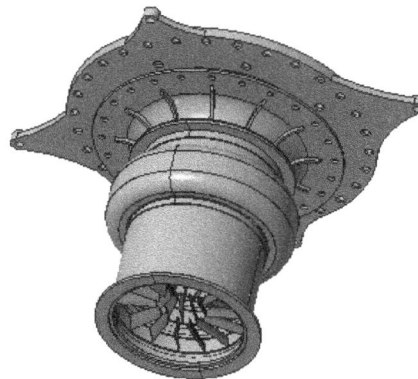

On-Demand Simp Rep.NO_CASE_DIFFUSER

Figure 5–49

4. Close the View Manager.

5. Save the assembly.

6. Close the window and erase all of the files from memory.

Task 3 - Open a simplified representations of an assembly.

1. In the *Home* tab, click ☐ (Open).

2. Select **turbine.asm**, expand **Open**, and select **Open Representation**, as shown in Figure 5–50.

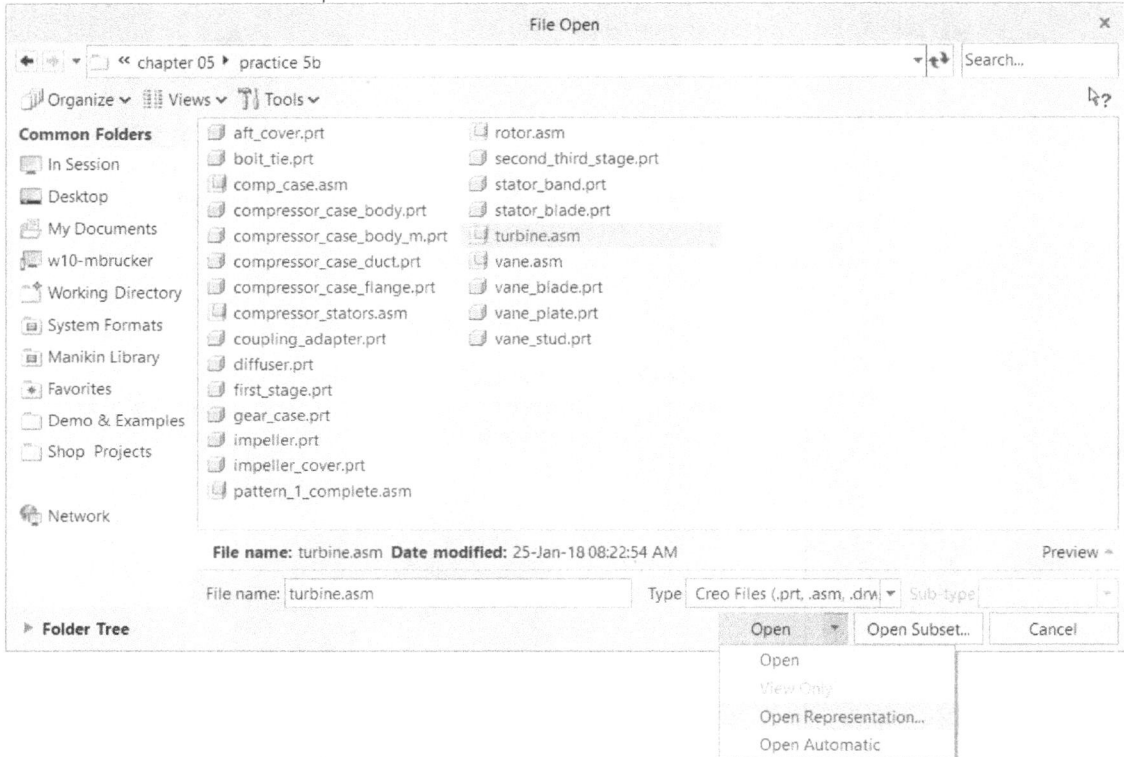

Figure 5–50

3. Select **NO_CASE_DIFFUSER** in the Open Rep dialog box, as shown in Figure 5–51.

Figure 5–51

4. Click **Open**.

Design Considerations

The assembly opens according to the selected simplified representation, as shown in Figure 5–52. The file retrieval time has decreased.

On-Demand Simp Rep:NO_CASE_DIFFUSER

Figure 5–52

Design Considerations

Task 4 - Review the files that are in memory.

1. Select **File>Manage Session>Object List**.

The information window lists all of the components that have been loaded into memory, as shown in Figure 5–53. The excluded components, such as **gear_case.prt**, **diffuser.prt**, and **vane.asm** are not listed, but are listed in the Model Tree. A simplified representation only loads the required data, which reduces the file retrieval and regeneration time.

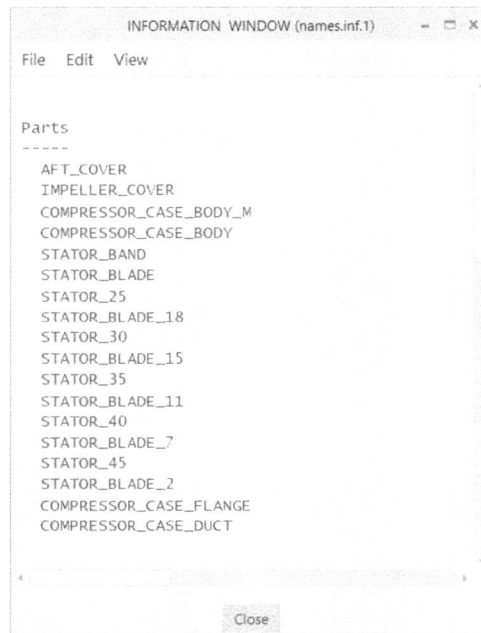

```
INFORMATION  WINDOW (names.inf.1)       −  □  ×

File   Edit   View


Parts
- - - - -
   AFT_COVER
   IMPELLER_COVER
   COMPRESSOR_CASE_BODY_M
   COMPRESSOR_CASE_BODY
   STATOR_BAND
   STATOR_BLADE
   STATOR_25
   STATOR_BLADE_18
   STATOR_30
   STATOR_BLADE_15
   STATOR_35
   STATOR_BLADE_11
   STATOR_40
   STATOR_BLADE_7
   STATOR_45
   STATOR_BLADE_2
   COMPRESSOR_CASE_FLANGE
   COMPRESSOR_CASE_DUCT

                    Close
```

Figure 5–53

Task 5 - Erase memory and open without representation.

1. Close the Information Window.

2. Close the window and erase all of the files from memory.

3. Open the Master Rep for **turbine.asm** (do not use Open Rep).

4. Select **File>Manage Session>Object List** and view all of the files that have been loaded into memory. **Gear_case.prt**, **diffuser.prt**, and **vane.asm** are now listed.

Task 6 - Set the default representation.

1. Open the View Manager.

Design Considerations

Customizing the Default Rep is good practice when working with large resource-intensive assemblies. By starting work using a customized Default Representation, only the required components are brought into session each time the assembly is opened. If at any time you need to work with another rep or the Master Rep, you can use the View Manager to activate another rep. Any missing components are automatically brought into session.

2. Double-click on **Default Rep** to make it the active representation.

3. Customize the Default Rep to exclude the three memory intensive assemblies:
   - **vane.asm**
   - **rotor.asm**
   - **comp_case.asm**

   The Edit dialog box displays as shown in Figure 5–54.

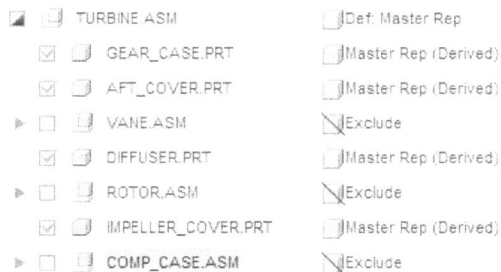

	TURBINE ASM	Def: Master Rep
	GEAR_CASE.PRT	Master Rep (Derived)
	AFT_COVER.PRT	Master Rep (Derived)
▶	VANE.ASM	Exclude
	DIFFUSER.PRT	Master Rep (Derived)
▶	ROTOR.ASM	Exclude
	IMPELLER_COVER.PRT	Master Rep (Derived)
▶	COMP_CASE.ASM	Exclude

Figure 5–54

4. Save the changes that you have made to the Default Rep. The model displays as shown in Figure 5–55.

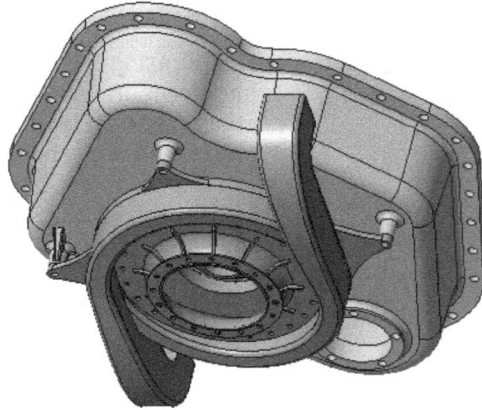

On-Demand Simp Rep.DEFAULT REP

Figure 5–55

5. Close the View Manager.

6. Save the assembly.

7. Close the window and erase all of the files from memory.

8. Open the Default Rep for **turbine.asm** (without using Open Rep).

9. The model loads very quickly and is displayed in the **DEFAULT REP** state.

10. Close the assembly and erase it from memory.

Practice 5c

Automatic Simplified Representations

Practice Objectives

- Apply materials to components in the assembly.
- Review the simplified representations in the assembly.
- Review the Automatic Rep.

In this practice, you will work with a motor assembly and investigate some of the assembly updates, including applying materials and simplified representations.

Task 1 - Open the aft_engine_section model.

1. Set the working directory to *Automatic_Simplified_Rep*.

2. Open **aft_engine_section.asm**.

3. Set the model display as follows:

   - ⁺⁄⁴ *(Datum Display Filters)*: None

   - ⊱ *(Spin Center)*: Off

   - ⬜ *(Display Style)*: ⬜ (Shading With Edges)

   The model displays as shown in Figure 5–56.

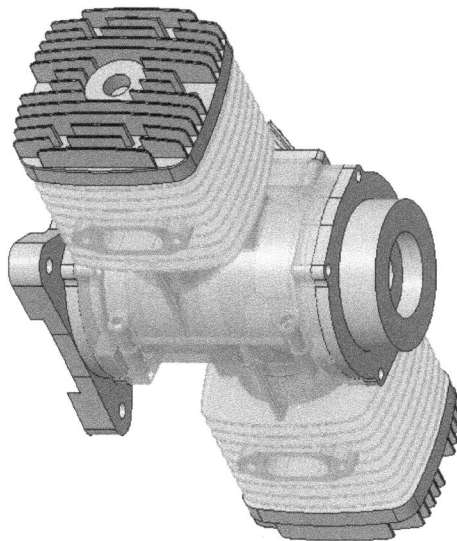

Figure 5–56

Task 2 - Apply an aluminum material to the block part.

1. In the Model Tree, select **BLOCK.PRT** and click 🗁 (Open) from the mini toolbar.

2. Click **File>Prepare>Model Properties**.

3. In the Model Properties dialog box, click **change** in the *Material* field, as shown in Figure 5–57.

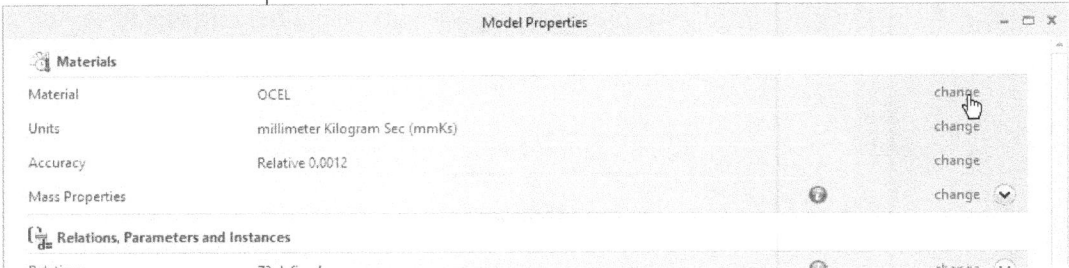

Figure 5–57

4. The Materials dialog box displays, as shown in Figure 5–58.

Note that a Material Preview displays in the Materials dialog box, listing the material properties. You can toggle the preview on and off using

∞ (Show/Hide Material Preview).

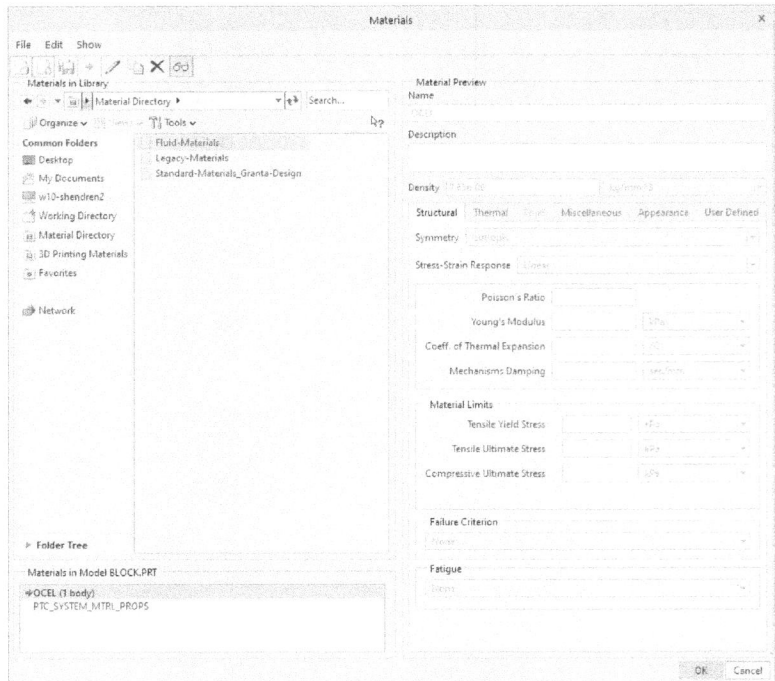

Figure 5–58

5. Double-click on **Legacy-Materials** to open the folder.

6. Double-click on **al2014.mtl**. Note that it is not assigned to the model but rather it is added to the list of materials available in the model, as shown in Figure 5–59.

The custom material OCEL is the still assigned to the model.

steel.mtl
tially.mtl
tipure.mtl
tungsten.mtl

Mat

Com

Fail

Folder Tree

Materials in Model BLOCK.PRT

Fati

OCEL (1 body)
  PTC_SYSTEM_MTRL_PROPS
  AL2014

Figure 5–59

7. Click **OK**.

8. In the Model Properties dialog box, click **Close**.

9. In the Model Tree, expand the **Materials** node, as show in Figure 5–60.

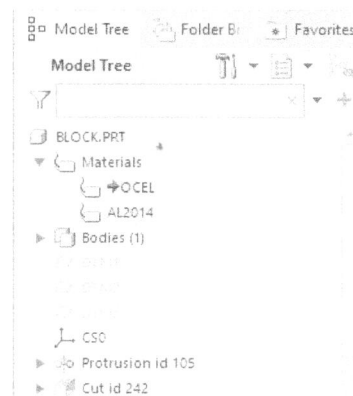

Model Tree   Folder B   Favorites

Model Tree

BLOCK.PRT
▼ Materials
    OCEL
    AL2014
▶ Bodies (1)

CSO
▶ Protrusion id 105
▶ Cut id 242

Figure 5–60

10. Right-click on **AL2014** and select **Set as Master**. Note the warning that displays, as shown in Figure 5–61.

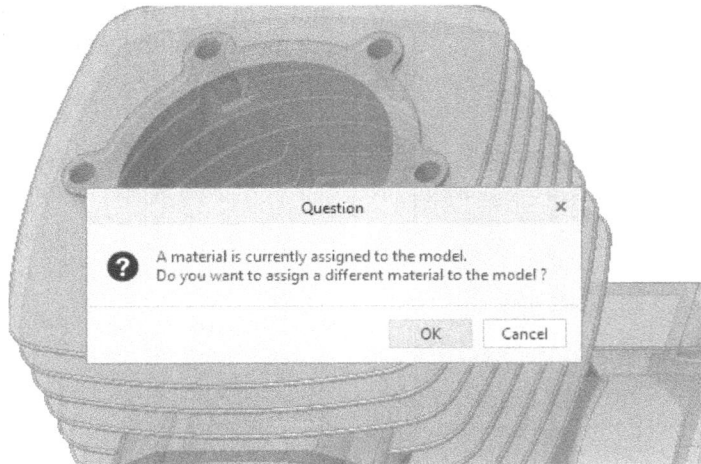

Figure 5–61

11. Click **OK**.

12. Right-click on **AL2014** and select **Info**. The browser window displays the material parameters, as shown in Figure 5–62.

Relations and Parameters : BLOCK

PART NAME : BLOCK

Relation Table

Relation	Parameter	New Value

Local Parameters

Symbolic constant	Current value	TYPE	SOURCE	ACCESS	DESIGNATED	DESCRIPTION	RESTRICTED	UNIT
PTC_MATERIAL_DESCRIPTION	---	String	Material	Full	NO		---	---
TEMPERATURE	0.000000e+00	Real Number	Material	Full	NO		---	F
PTC_INITIAL_BEND_Y_FACTOR	5.000000e-01	Real Number	Material	Full	NO		YES	---
PTC_BEND_TABLE	---	String	Material	Full	NO		---	---
PTC_MATERIAL_TYPE	9	Integer	Material	Locked	NO		---	---
PTC_FAILURE_CRITERION_TYPE	NONE	String	Material	Locked	NO		YES	---
PTC_FATIGUE_TYPE	NONE	String	Material	Locked	NO		YES	---
PTC_MATERIAL_SUB_TYPE	LINEAR	String	Material	Locked	NO		YES	---
PTC_YOUNG_MODULUS	7.308443e+07	Real Number	Material	Full	NO		YES	kPa
PTC_POISSON_RATIO	3.300000e-01	Real Number	Material	Full	NO		YES	---
PTC_THERMAL_EXPANSION_COEF	2.304000e-05	Real Number	Material	Full	NO		YES	/C
PTC_SPECIFIC_HEAT	9.637529e+08	Real Number	Material	Full	NO		YES	mm^2/(sec^2 C)
PTC_THERMAL_CONDUCTIVITY	1.921632e+05	Real Number	Material	Full	NO		YES	mm kg /(sec^3 C)
PTC_MASS_DENSITY	2.793554e-06	Real Number	Material	Full	NO		YES	kg/mm^3
PTC_XHATCH_FILE	AL2014	String	Material	Full	NO		---	---

Figure 5–62

13. Right-click on **AL2014** and click **Delete**.

14. In the Warning dialog box, click **OK**.

15. Right-click on the **Materials** node and select **Edit Materials**, as shown in Figure 5–63.

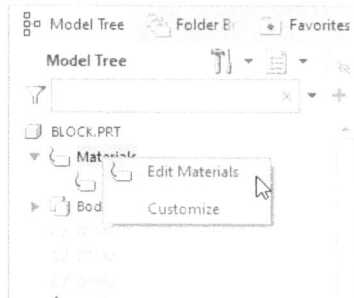

Figure 5–63

16. In the Materials dialog box, double-click on **Legacy-Materials** to open the folder.

17. Double-click on **al6061.mtl**.

18. In the *Materials in Model BLOCK.PRT* area, right-click on **AL6061** and select **Set as Master**, as shown in Figure 5–64.

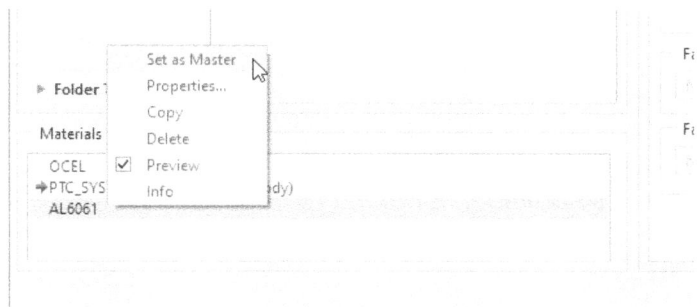

Figure 5–64

19. Click **OK** in the Materials dialog box. Note that the material is assigned as shown in Figure 5–65.

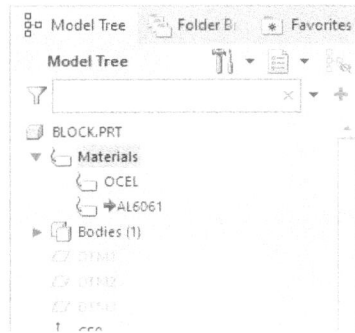

Figure 5–65

20. Close the part window and return to the assembly.

Task 3 - Investigate the simplified representations in the assembly.

Design Consideration

The assembly was created in a previous release of Creo Parametric. In this task, you will investigate how legacy simplified representations are handled.

1. In the In-graphics toolbar, select (View Manager).

2. In the View Manager, select the *Simp Rep* tab, as shown in Figure 5–66.

Note that only four representations are visible in the View Manager.

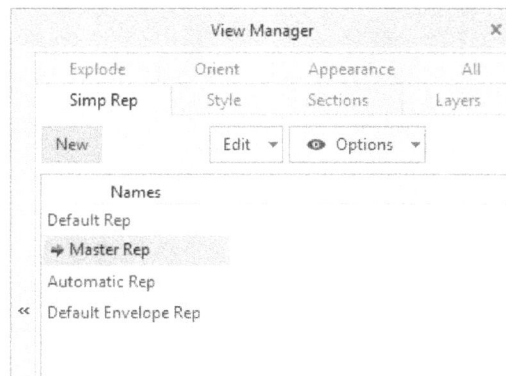

Figure 5–66

3. Close the View Manager.

4. Click **File>Options>Configuration Editor**.

5. In the Creo Parametric Options dialog box, click **Add** and type **hide**. Note that the *Option name* automatically fills in with **hide_pre_creo4_reps** and the default *Option value* is **maintain_master**, as shown in Figure 5–67.

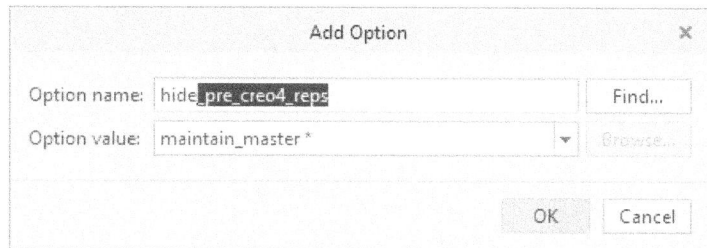

Figure 5–67

6. In the Option value drop-down list, select **no**.

7. Click **OK**.

8. Click **OK** in the Creo Parametric Options dialog box.

9. When prompted to save the settings in the configuration file, click **No**.

10. In the In-graphics toolbar, select (View Manager). Note that the list updates to include the representations made before the release of Creo Parametric 4.0, as shown in Figure 5–68.

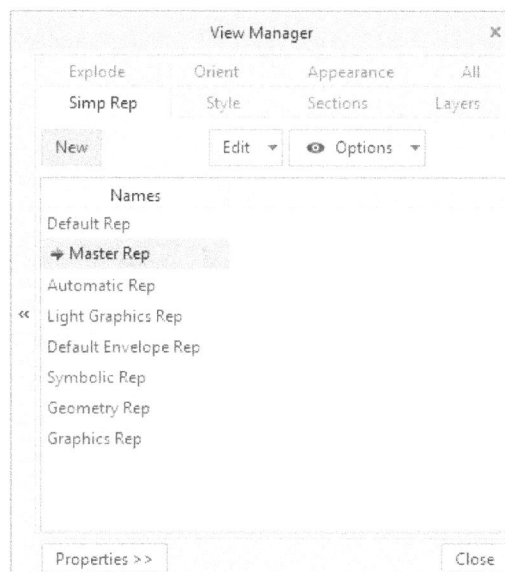

Figure 5–68

11. Close the View Manager.

12. Click **File>Options>Configuration Editor**.

13. In the Creo Parametric Options dialog box, in the Show drop-down list, select **Current Session**.

14. Beside **hide_pre_creo4_reps**, click in the *Value* field and select **maintain_master***, as shown in Figure 5–69.

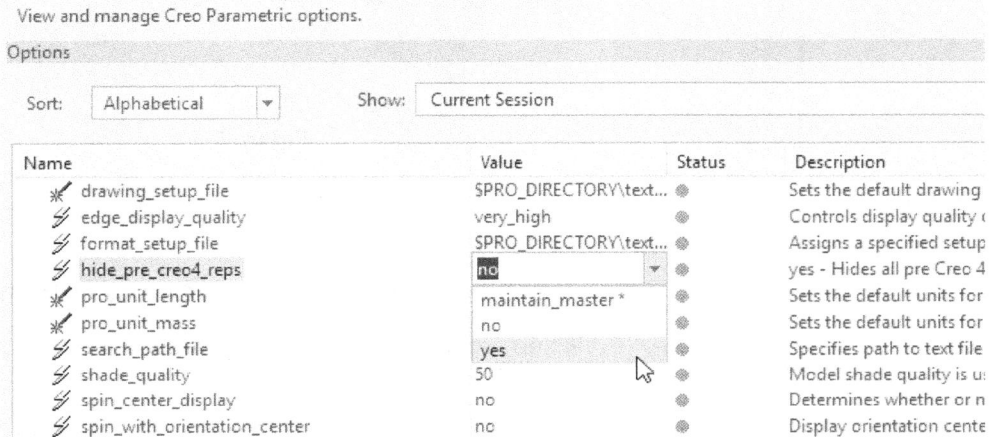

View and manage Creo Parametric options.

Options

Sort:	Alphabetical	⌄	Show:	Current Session		

Name	Value	Status	Description
drawing_setup_file	$PRO_DIRECTORY\text... ⊛		Sets the default drawing
edge_display_quality	very_high	⊛	Controls display quality (
format_setup_file	$PRO_DIRECTORY\text... ⊛		Assigns a specified setup
hide_pre_creo4_reps	no	⌄ ⊛	yes - Hides all pre Creo 4
pro_unit_length	maintain_master *	⊛	Sets the default units for
pro_unit_mass	no	⊛	Sets the default units for
search_path_file	yes	⊛	Specifies path to text file
shade_quality	50	⊛	Model shade quality is u:
spin_center_display	no	⊛	Determines whether or n
spin_with_orientation_center	no	⊛	Display orientation cente

Figure 5–69

15. Click **OK**, then click **No** when prompted to save the configuration file.

16. In the Quick Access toolbar, click ⌗ (Close) to close the window.

17. In the *Home* tab, click 🗑 (Erase Not Displayed).

18. Click **OK**.

Task 4 - Investigate the Automatic Representation.

---

1. In the *Home* tab, click 📂 (Open).

2. Select **aft_engine_section.asm** and select **Open Automatic**, as shown in Figure 5–70.

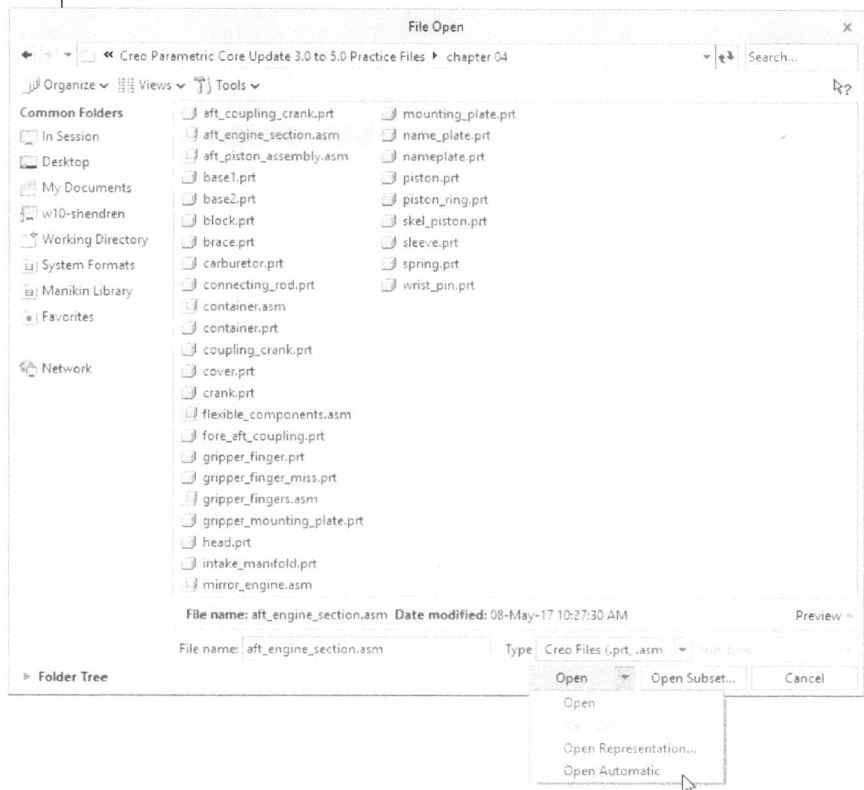

Figure 5–70

3. The assembly opens, as shown in Figure 5–71.

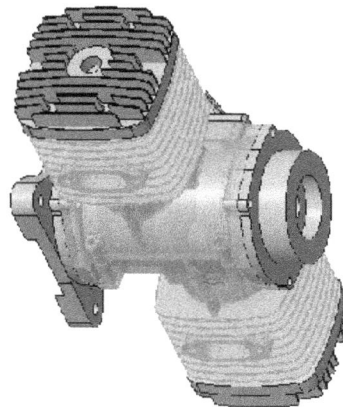

Figure 5–71

4. Hover the cursor over several surfaces of the assembly and note that the surfaces are indicated as Light Surfaces, as shown in Figure 5–72.

The light surfaces allow certain surface-based actions such as measuring. The light surfaces allow the full assembly to be visible, without having to retrieve the full solid geometry into session.

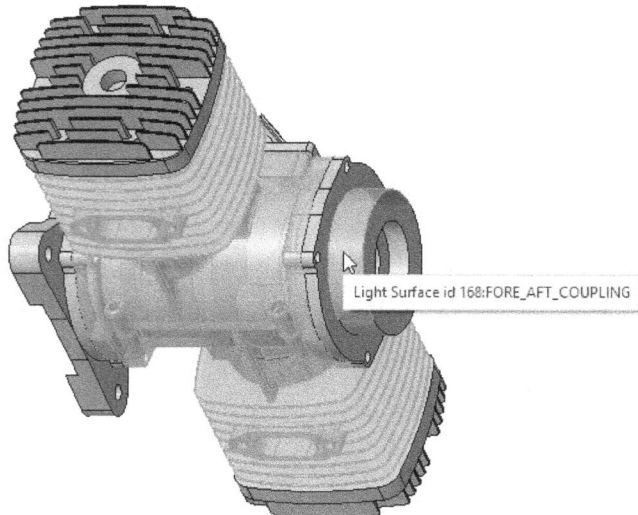

Light Surface id 168:FORE_AFT_COUPLING

Figure 5–72

5. In the In-graphics toolbar, select 📷 (View Manager).

6. In the View Manager, click **Properties**, and the dialog box displays as shown in Figure 5–73.

Figure 5–73

7. Hold <Ctrl>, and in the model or Model Tree, select both instances of **HEAD.PRT**.

8. In the View Manager, click ⬚ (Exclude) to remove the components from the representation.

9. Hold <Ctrl>, and in the model or Model Tree, select both instances of **BLOCK.PRT**.

10. In the View Manager, click 🖼 (Master Representation).

11. Click **Close** in the View Manager dialog box. The Model Tree updates to indicate the representation status, as shown in Figure 5–74.

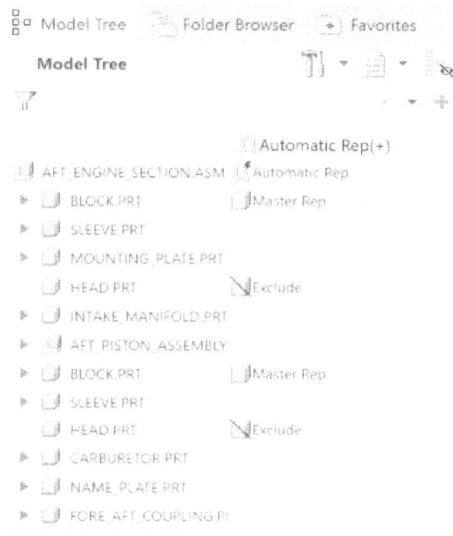

Figure 5–74

12. Hover the cursor over the surface of the block part shown in Figure 5–75.

The surface is no longer a light surface due to the representation being set to Master Rep. This results in the object being fully retrieved into session.

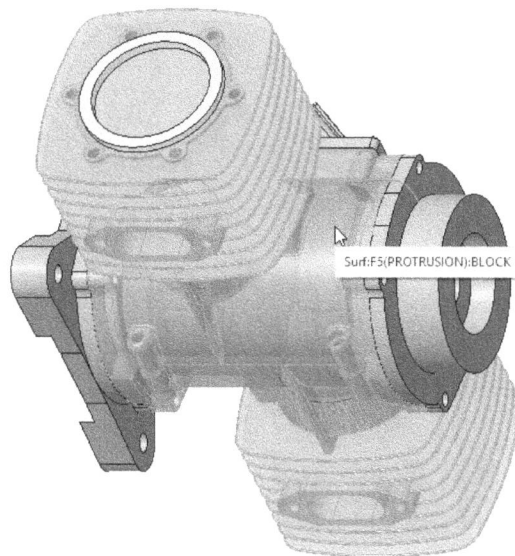

Figure 5–75

13. Select the surface shown in Figure 5–76 and select
    (Retrieve) from the mini toolbar.

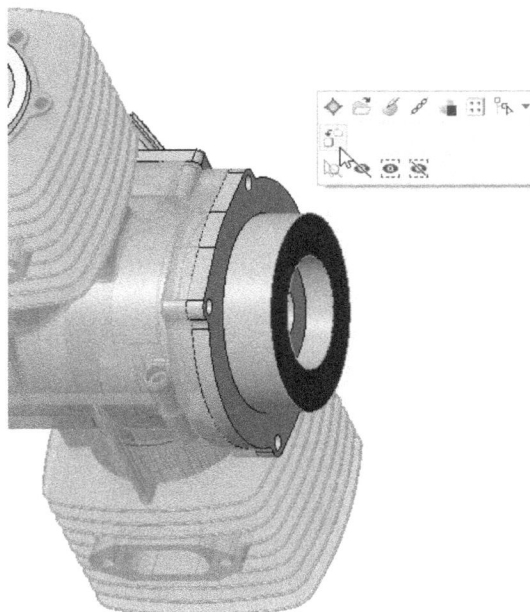

Figure 5–76

14. Hover the cursor over the surface of **for_aft_coupling.prt**
    shown in Figure 5–77 and note that it is no longer a light
    surface.

The component was retrieved into session, so it is now the solid model.

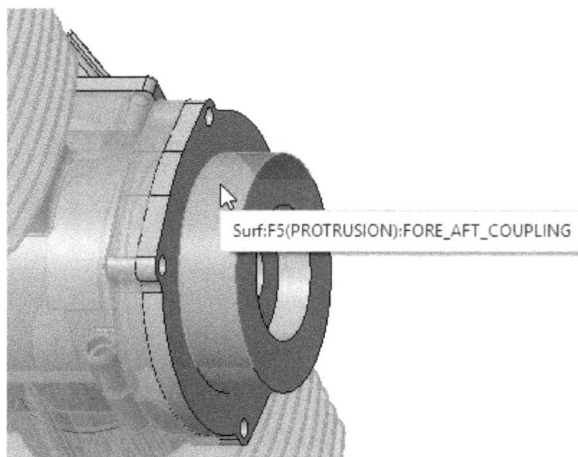

Surf:F5(PROTRUSION):FORE_AFT_COUPLING

Figure 5–77

The automatic representation retrieves the components with no solid geometry, allowing the assembly to be retrieved quickly. When you manually retrieve a component, the retrieval applies only to the current session.

- Note that manually retrieving the component into session does not impact the simplified representation, as shown in Figure 5–78.

Figure 5–78

15. Close and erase all files.

Practice 5d

(Optional) Define a Simplified Rep Without Loading the Model

Practice Objective

- Create a simplified rep before loading the assembly.

In this practice, you will create a simplified representation without opening the assembly and load a part that needs to be viewed. The model shown in Figure 5–79 is the complete top-level assembly.

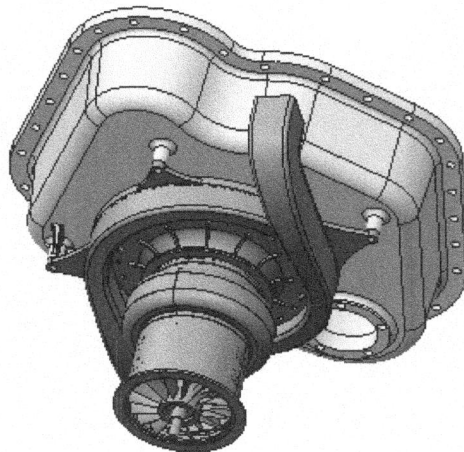

Figure 5–79

Task 1 - Create a simplified rep with no parts.

1. Change your working directory to the *Rep_Without_Loading* folder.

2. Click 📂 (Open) in the *Home* tab.

3. Select **turbine.asm**, expand **Open**, and select **Open Representation**. The Open Rep dialog box opens, as shown in Figure 5–80.

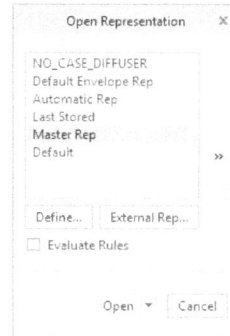

Open Representation   X

NO_CASE_DIFFUSER
Default Envelope Rep
Automatic Rep
Last Stored
Master Rep
Default   »

Define...   External Rep...
☐ Evaluate Rules

Open ▼   Cancel

Figure 5–80

4. Click **Define**, edit the new simplified rep *Name* to **No_Parts**, and press <Enter>.

5. In the Edit dialog box, leave the default rule as **Exclude Comp**, as shown in Figure 5–81.

This excludes all of the parts from the assembly, which enables you to open the assembly more quickly. Use this simplified rep when you only need to work with a small number of components in a large assembly.

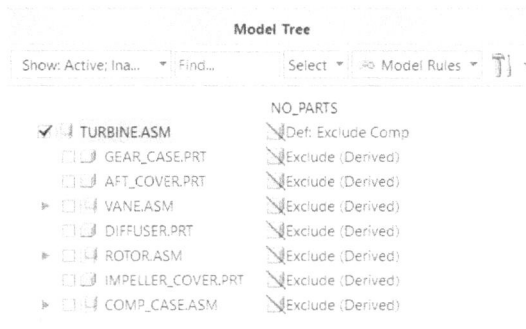

Model Tree

Show: Active; Ina... ▼ Find...   Select ▼ ⊶ Model Rules ▼ 🗍 ▼

                 NO_PARTS
✓ ☑ TURBINE.ASM   ↘Def: Exclude Comp
   ☐ GEAR_CASE.PRT   ↘Exclude (Derived)
   ☐ AFT_COVER.PRT   ↘Exclude (Derived)
▸ ☐ VANE.ASM   ↘Exclude (Derived)
   ☐ DIFFUSER.PRT   ↘Exclude (Derived)
▸ ☐ ROTOR.ASM   ↘Exclude (Derived)
   ☐ IMPELLER_COVER.PRT   ↘Exclude (Derived)
▸ ☐ COMP_CASE.ASM   ↘Exclude (Derived)

Figure 5–81

6. Click **Open** to close the Edit dialog box.

7. Set the model display as follows:

- ⚓ *(Datum Display Filters)*: All Off

- ⤙ *(Spin Center)*: Off

- ⬚ *(Display Style)*: ⬚ (Shading With Edges)
- Model Tree: Show Features

You can also select ***Automatic Rep*** *in the drop-down list in the NO_PARTS column in the Model Tree.*

Task 2 - Open two parts in automatic rep to view.

1. Select **AFT_COVER.PRT** and **VANE.ASM** in the Model Tree.

2. Right-click and select **Representation>Automatic**, as shown in Figure 5–82. **AFT_COVER.PRT** and **VANE.ASM** open in the assembly.

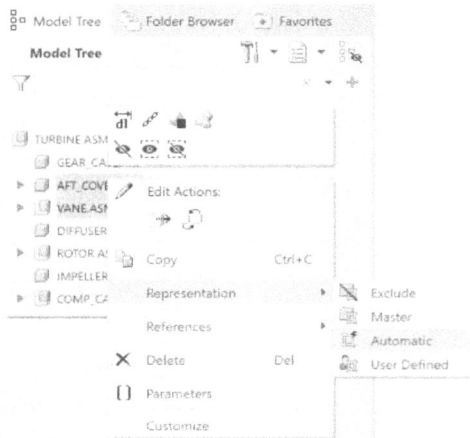

Figure 5–82

- The model displays as shown in Figure 5–83.

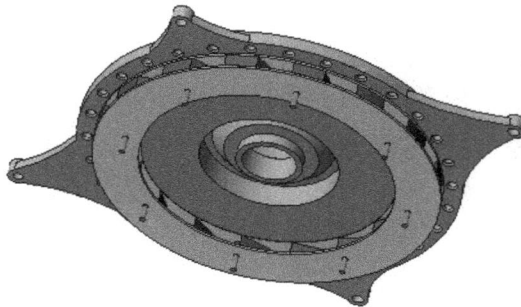

On-Demand Simp Rep:NO_PARTS(+)

Figure 5–83

3. Erase the assembly without saving.

Chapter Review Questions

1. Which of the following statements are true regarding simplified representations? (Select all that apply.)

   a. Improve retrieval time.

   b. Improve regeneration times.

   c. Increase efficiency while working with large assemblies.

   d. They control which components of an assembly are opened and how they are displayed.

2. The **Open Subset** option can only be used to open existing simplified representations.

   a. True

   b. False

3. The Automatic representation retrieves the minimum required data and is used to retrieve your assembly as fast as possible.

   a. True

   b. False

4. Which option enables you to create a simplified representation without opening the assembly? (Select all that apply.)

   a. Select **Open Representation** in the File dialog box.

   b. Click **Open Subset...** in the File dialog box.

   c. Click **Open** in the File dialog box.

   d. Click ⬚ in the Quick Access toolbar.

5. In the *Style* tab, components can be set as **Transparent** in assemblies so you can display the interior components more clearly.

   a. True

   b. False

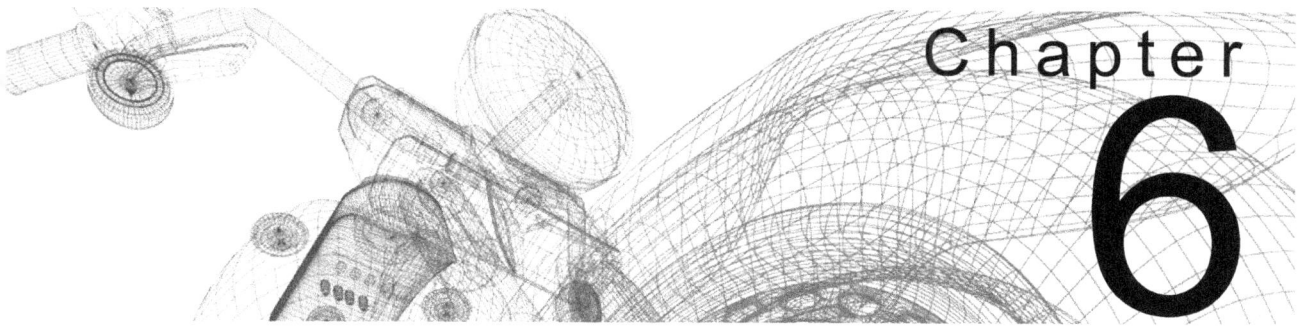

Chapter
6

Advanced View Manager

You can define zones that divide an assembly into geometrical work regions or envelopes to represent complete geometry. Both zones and envelopes are used in conjunction with simplified representations to simplify large assemblies.

Learning Objectives in This Chapter

- Use names, types, zones, etc. to create rules and define new simplified representations.
- Learn to use external simplified representations of a master assembly to create multiple versions of the assembly.
- Use simplified representations to control how components are displayed and when they are opened to improve efficiency when working with assembly files.
- Learn to create envelopes that can represent the selected geometry and simplify the assembly.
- Learn to substitute the envelope to represent the selected geometry using simplified representations.

6.1 Advanced Simplified Reps

You can select components for a simplified representation using manual selection or defined rules.

Definition Rules

Definition rules enable you to assign a rule for defining the representation settings for a simplified rep. A rule consists of an action and a condition. If the condition is met, the action (e.g., exclude) is assigned to the component.

How To: Define Representation Settings Using a Definition Rule

1. Click **Edit>Edit Definition**. The Edit dialog box opens, displaying the **Model Rules**, **Show: Active, Inactive**, **Options**, and various view buttons.
2. Click **Model Rules>Edit Rules**, as shown in Figure 6–1.

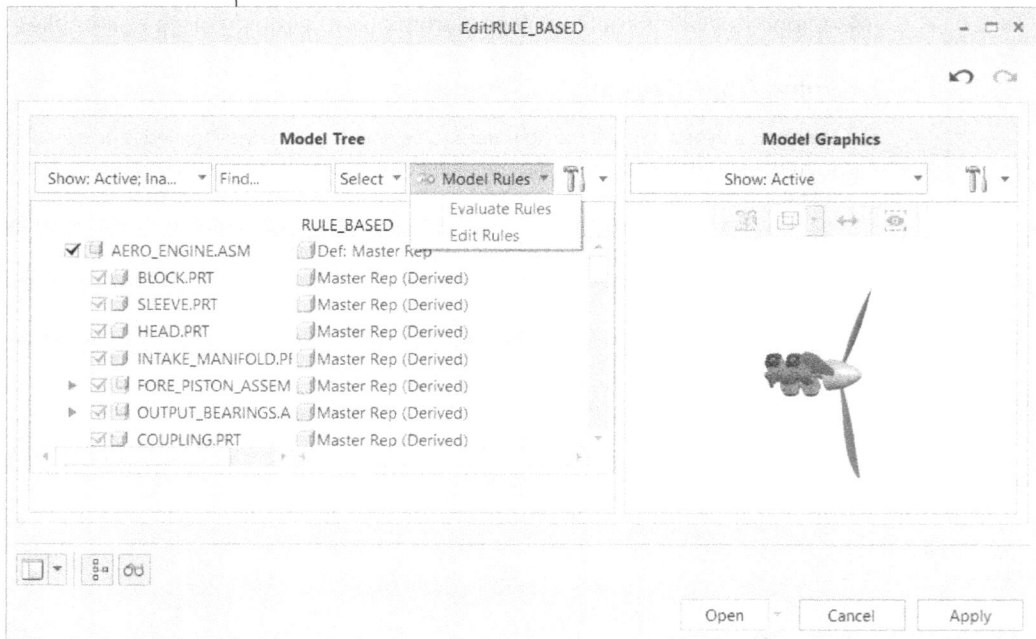

Figure 6–1

3. A dialog box opens, enabling you to define the rule actions.

4. Click ✚ (Add Condition) to add a new condition. The dialog box opens as shown in Figure 6–2. Define the **Rep Action** using the Rep Action drop-down list.

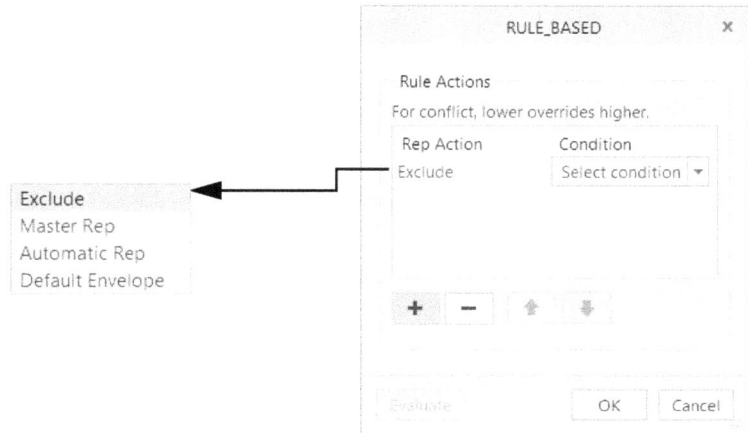

Figure 6–2

5. To define the condition for the rule, right-click in the *Condition* field and select **New**. Enter a name for the condition. The Rule Editor dialog box opens as shown in Figure 6–3, enabling you to set the conditions.

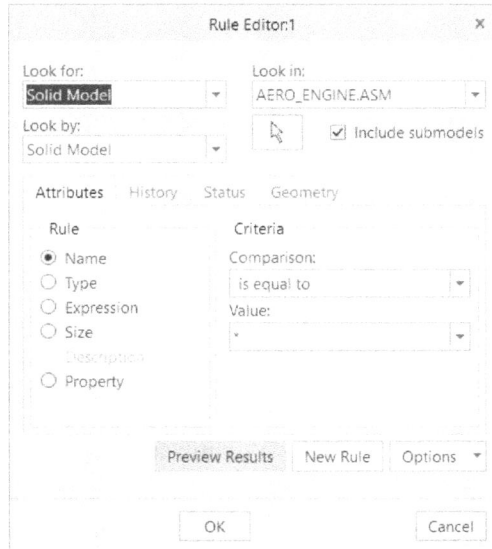

Figure 6–3

6. Define the comparison criteria using the Rule Editor to find the components to which the Rep Action should be applied. Click **Preview Results** to display the results of the rule. For example, the results of one that was set to find all of the assemblies in the top-level assembly are shown in Figure 6–4. The system has selected all of the components that meet this criteria.

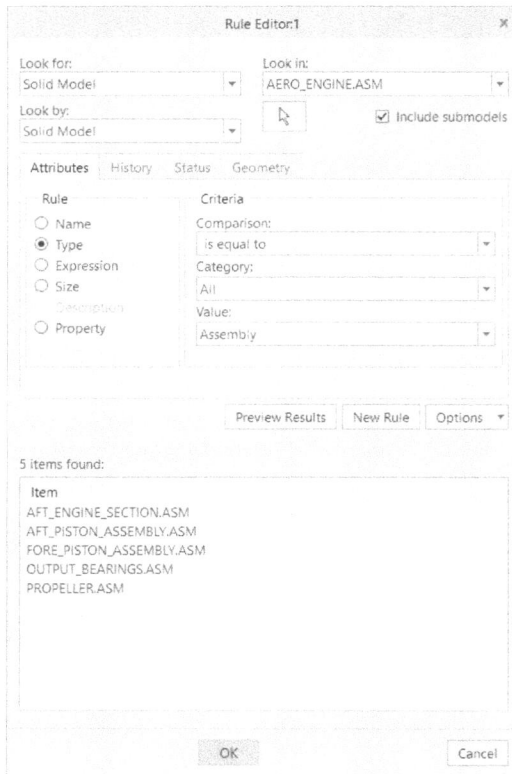

Figure 6–4

7. Click **OK** and **Evaluate**. The Model Tree updates to exclude the components that met the defined condition.
8. Click **OK** to close the dialog box.
9. Click **OK** in the Edit dialog box to return to the listing of simplified reps.

External Simplified Representations

External simplified reps are representations of a master assembly, which are stored as separate assembly models. They enable you to create multiple versions of an assembly, enabling multiple users to work on it simultaneously. All of the components included in an external simplified rep are the same as those in the master assembly.

How To: Create an External Simplified Rep

1. Select **File>New>Assembly** and select **External simplified representation** in the *Sub-type* area in the New dialog box. Select the master assembly in the Open dialog box. The Edit dialog box opens as shown in Figure 6–5, enabling you to define the representation.

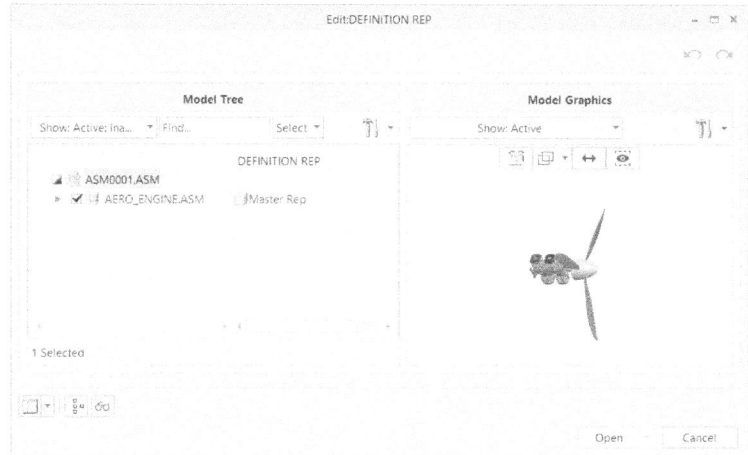

Figure 6–5

2. Another method to create an external simplified representation is to open the View Manager. Select the representation that you want to copy and click **Edit>Copy as External**. Enter the name of the new external simplified representation in the dialog box that opens, as shown in Figure 6–6.

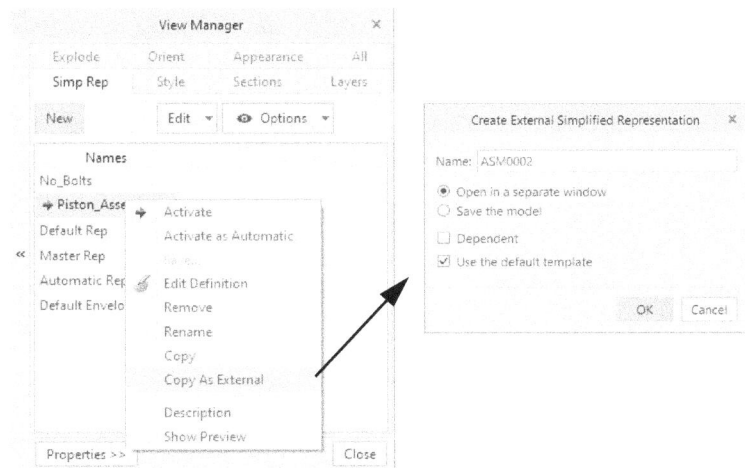

Figure 6–6

3. A third method is to open the assembly and activate the required simplified rep. Select **File>Save As>Save a Copy**. Enter a new name for the assembly and select **External Simplified Representation (*.asm)** in the Type drop-down list, as shown in Figure 6–7.

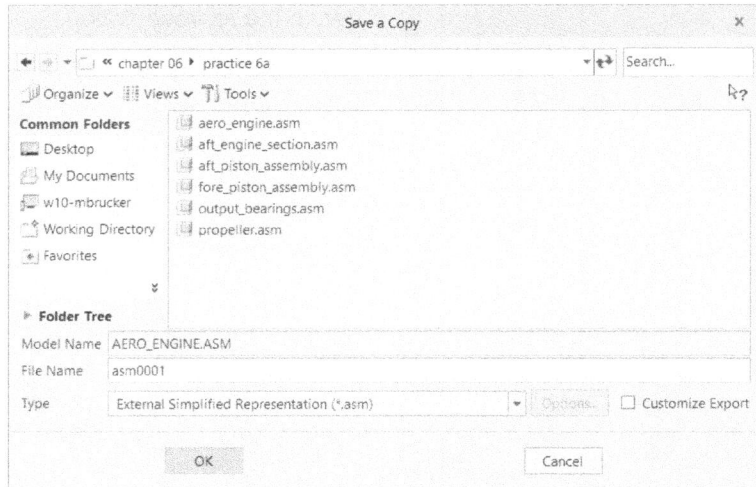

Figure 6–7

4. The following are rules and information about external simplified representations:

- When working in the external simplified rep, only components contained in the simplified rep and the top-level assembly need to be in session. The top-level assembly is required to define the placement for the components that have been included.

- All of the changes made to the components of an external simplified rep are automatically reflected in the master assembly.

- You cannot assemble components into the external simplified rep.

- Components that are added to the master rep are excluded from the external simplified rep.

- Component and feature operations are permitted on components that are included in an external simplified representation. However, assembly-level features cannot be created in the external simplified representation.

6.2 Zones

Zones enable you to divide a large assembly into geometric work regions that can be used to define a condition for rule-driven simplified representations. Zones are defined by selecting the area to one side of a datum plane, in a closed surface, in an area using a coordinate system, or within a specified radius. A component is considered to be a member of a zone if the component lies entirely within or is intersected by the zone. Any combination of multiple references can be combined to create a zone.

How To: Create a Zone to Define a Condition for Rule-driven Simplified Representations

1. Use any of the following methods to open the View Manager and create a zone:

   • Click (View Manager) in the In-graphics toolbar and select the *Sections* tab.

   • Click (Manage Views) in the *View* tab and select the *Sections* tab.

   • Expand (Manage Views) and select **Zone**.

   The View Manager or Zone opens, as shown in Figure 6–8.

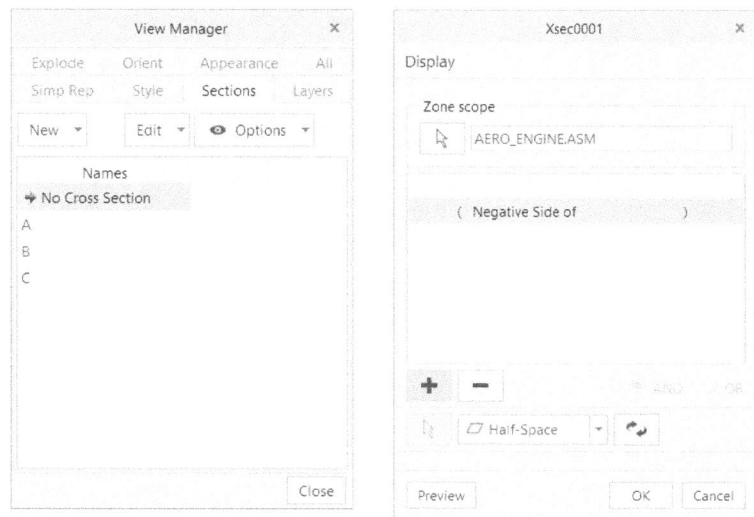

Click (View Manager) in the In-graphics toolbar and select the Sections tab.

Click (Manage Views) and select Zone.

Figure 6–8

2. Click **New>Zone** (if required), enter a name, and press
   <Enter>. The Zone dialog box opens (as shown in
   Figure 6–9) to define the zones in the model.

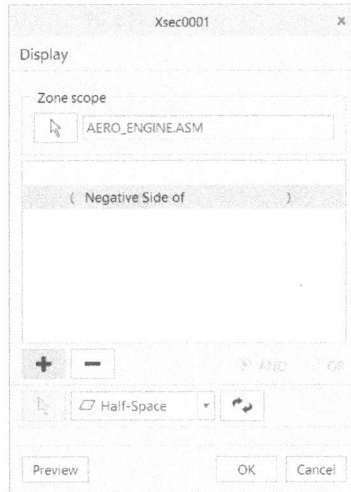

Figure 6–9

3. Zones can be defined based on planar surfaces, closed
   surfaces, or within a specified distance from an entity. These
   options are selected in the menu at the bottom of the dialog
   box. They are described as follows:

Option	Description
Half-Space	Enables you to create a zone on one side of a datum plane or planar surface.

Inside-Outside	Enables you to create a zone inside or outside a closed surface quilt.

Radial Distance From	Enables you to create a zone consisting of components in a specific area. The area can be specified by selecting a point on the assembly and entering a radial distance.
	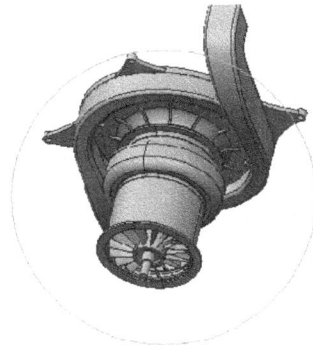
Offset CSYS	Enables you to create a zone consisting of components in a specific area. The area can be specified by selecting or creating a coordinate system and entering the X, Y, and Z offsets.
	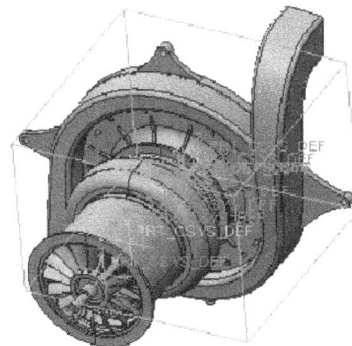

4. Click ✚ (Add Reference) to continue adding references to define the zone. You can combine multiple conditions with different reference types to complete the zone. References can be made to any level of the current assembly.

5. To remove a zone condition, click ━ (Remove Reference). Once the zone has been defined, click **OK** to close the dialog box.

The editing options can also be accessed by selecting the zone and right-clicking.

6. You can expand **Edit** in the Model Sectioning dialog box and use the options to remove, redefine, copy, rename, and insert a description for an existing zone.

7. Select the *Simp Rep* tab in the View Manager and select an existing simplified rep or create a new one. Click **Edit> Edit Definition**, and click **Model Rules>Edit Rules** at the top of the Edit dialog box. Create a rule so that the condition selects all of the geometry that exists in the zone that was defined, as shown in Figure 6–10.

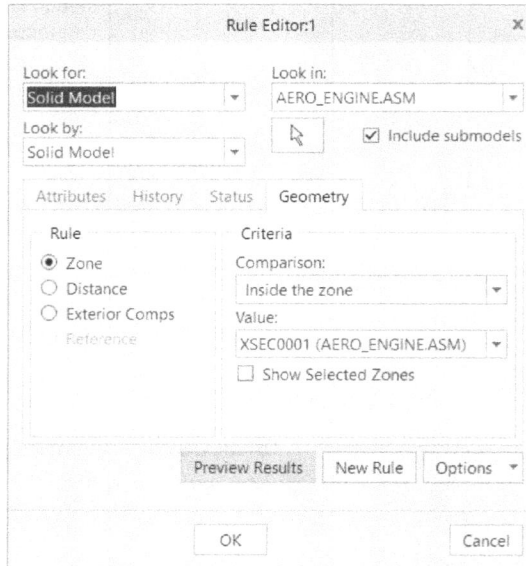

Figure 6–10

6.3 Envelopes

An envelope is a part that represents the geometry of any number of components in an assembly. It can be used to simplify the model by substituting complex geometry with a simple envelope feature (i.e., extrude or revolve). The model shown on the left in Figure 6–11. An envelope was created and substituted to simplify the blades of the fan as shown on the right.

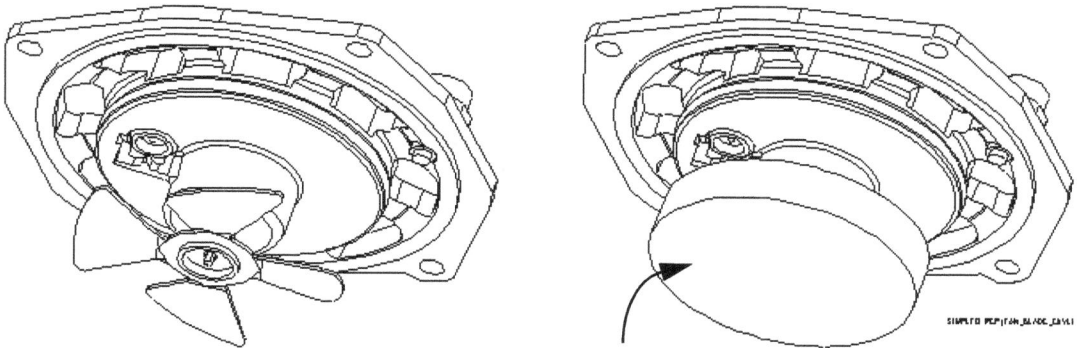

Envelope component substituted for the blade components in the fan.

Figure 6–11

How To: Create an Envelope and Substitute It into a Simplified Representation

1. To create an envelope, use one of the following methods:
   - In the Model Display group of the *Model* tab, expand (Manage Views) and select **Envelope Manager**.
   - Click (Create) and select **Envelope**.

2. The dialog boxes open, as shown in Figure 6–12.

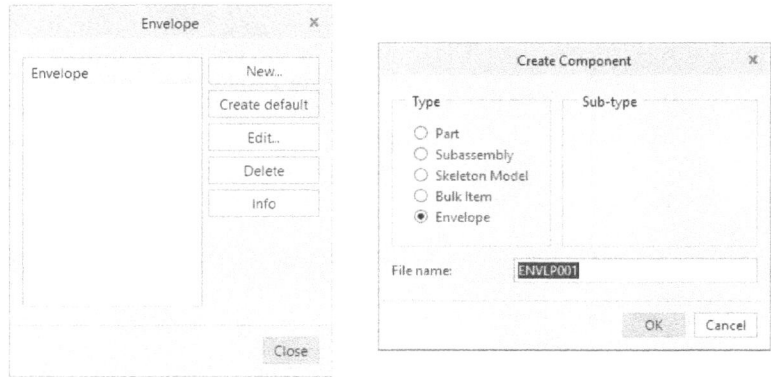

Expand 📷 *(Manage Views)*
and select Envelope Manager

Click 🔧 *(Create) and select*
Envelope

Figure 6–12

3. Click **New**, enter a name, and press <Enter>. The Envelope Definition dialog box opens, as shown in Figure 6–13.

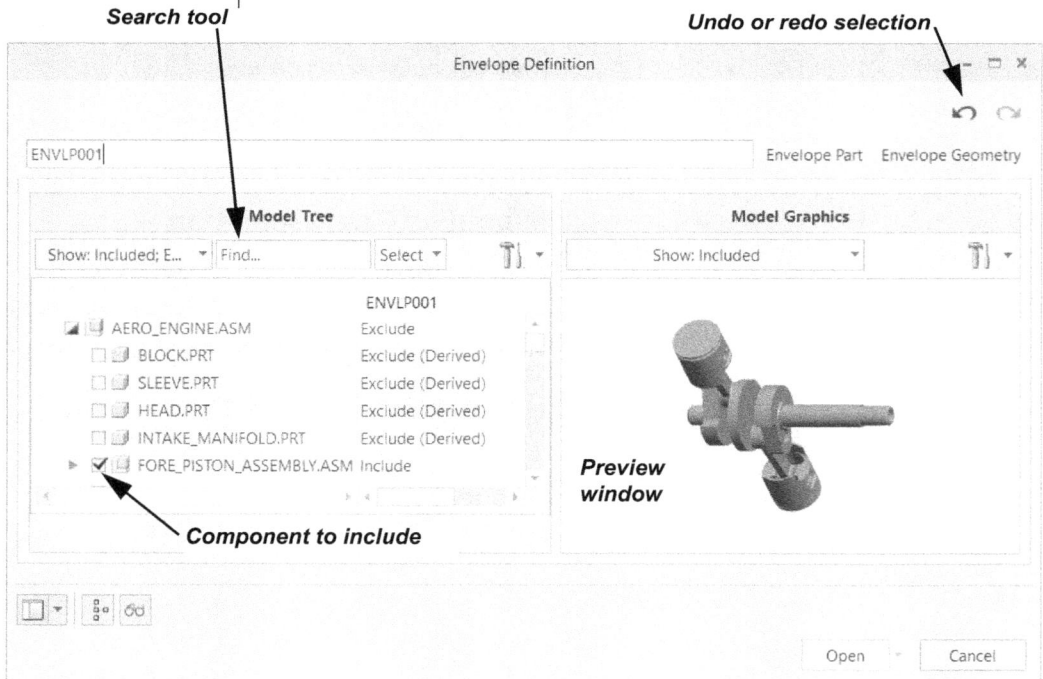

Figure 6–13

Multiple components can be selected to be represented by the envelope.

4. To select the component(s) to include in the envelope, you can do the following:
   - Place a checkmark next to the component or assembly, as shown in Figure 6–14.
   - Select the components in the graphics window by selecting **Select>Select in main window**.
   - Select components using a zone by selecting **Select> Advance Search** to open a Search dialog box, as shown in Figure 6–14.

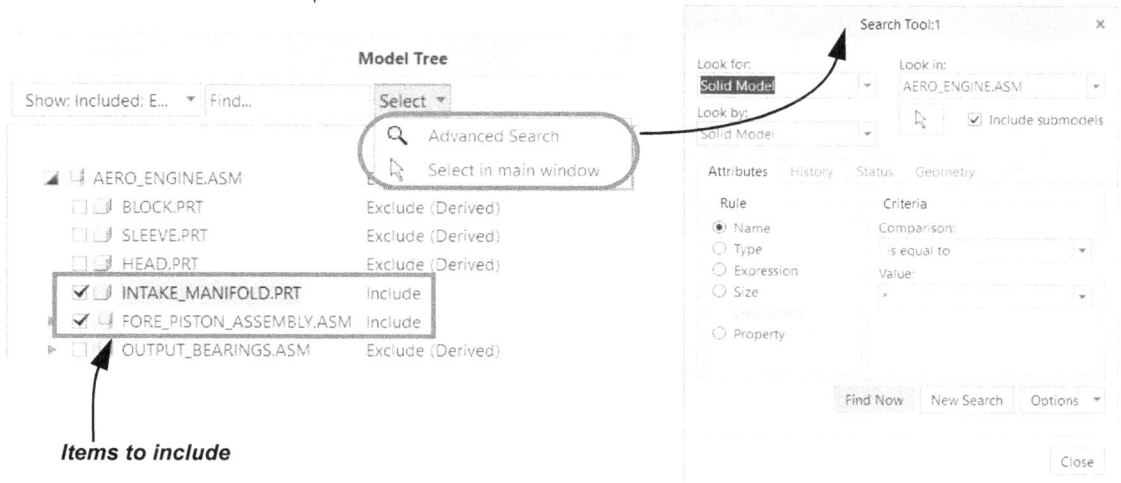

Items to include

Figure 6–14

5. Click **Envelope Part**. To begin the definition of the envelope model, you must define the method of creating the model using the Envelope Method dialog box shown in Figure 6–15.

Figure 6–15

The available options are described as follows:

Option	Description
Create Envelope Part	Enables you to create a new envelope part to represent the selected components. You must further define the creation options if this option is selected, as with creating parts in Assembly mode (i.e., **Copy From Existing**, **Locate Default Datums**, **Empty**, and **Create features**).
Select Existing Assembly Component	Enables you to use an existing component in the assembly as the envelope for selected components.
Surface Subset Shrinkwrap	Enables you to create a surface subset Shrinkwrap as the envelope for selected components.
Faceted Solid Shrinkwrap	Enables you to create a faceted solid Shrinkwrap as the envelope for selected components.
All Solid Surfaces Subset Shrinkwrap	Enables you to create a faceted solid Shrinkwrap as the envelope for selected components using **Copy From Existing** or **Empty**.

Once the creation method has been defined, click **Envelope Geometry** to create the geometry used to represent the selected model using the standard feature creation options in the

Envelope Geometry tab. Click ✓ (Done) once the geometry has been created.

The Envelope is stored as a part file with a .PRT extension. You can only use envelopes in the assembly in which they were created.

6. Click (Manage Views) and select an existing simplified
rep, or create a new one in the View Manager dialog box.
Click **Edit>Edit Definition**, and select **Substitute by
Envelope** in the flyout option, as shown in Figure 6–16.

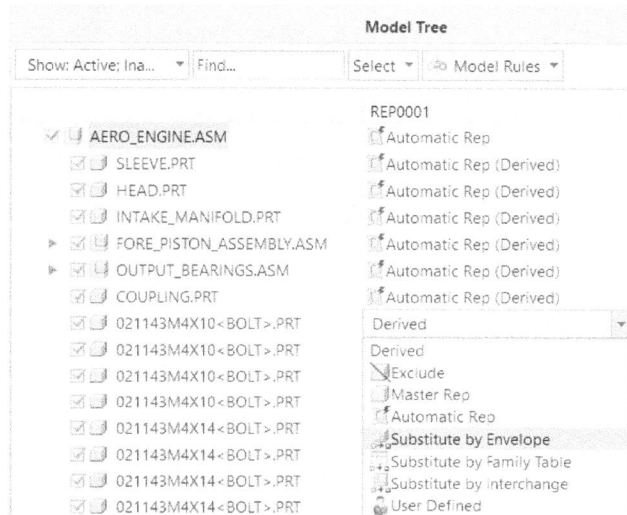

Figure 6–16

You can also select the component or assembly, right-click, and
select **Substitute>Envelope**, as shown in Figure 6–17.

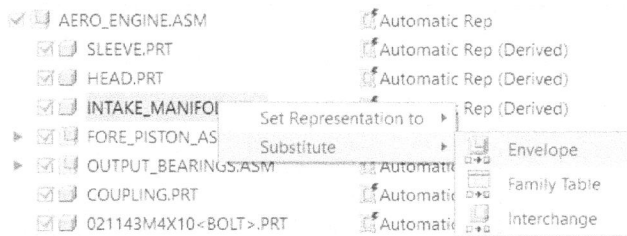

Figure 6–17

Practice 6a

Rule-Based Simplified Reps

Practice Objectives

- Create a simplified representation using rules.
- Select components using the Search tool.
- Create an external representation.

In this practice, you will select the components for the simplified reps using rules and the **Search** tool. Both methods enable you to efficiently select multiple components that are similarly named or contain other common information. To complete the practice, you will create an external simplified rep that separates components in the rep into its own assembly file. The model shown on the left in Figure 6–18 is the complete top-level assembly and the model shown on the right is one of the simplified reps that you will create.

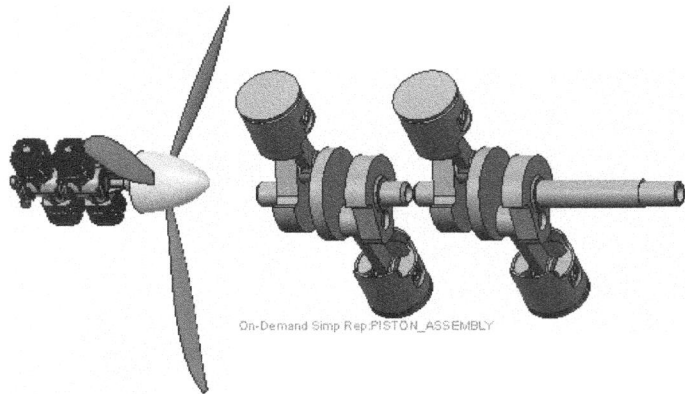

On-Demand Simp Rep:PISTON_ASSEMBLY

Figure 6–18

Task 1 - Create a simplified representation that selects components based on a defined rule.

1. Change the working directory to the *Rule_Based_Reps* folder.

2. Open **aero_engine.asm**.

3. Set the model display as follows:

   - ⌖ *(Datum Display Filters)*: All Off

   - ⊱ *(Spin Center)*: Off

   - ◻ *(Display Style)*: ▭ (Shading With Edges)

---

4. Create a new simplified representation and set the *Name* to **No_Bolts**. The Edit dialog box opens, displaying the default rule as **Exclude**.

5. Change the default rule to **Master Rep**, as shown in Figure 6–19.

*This will place a checkmark next to each item and change Exclude to **Master Rep** for each component.*

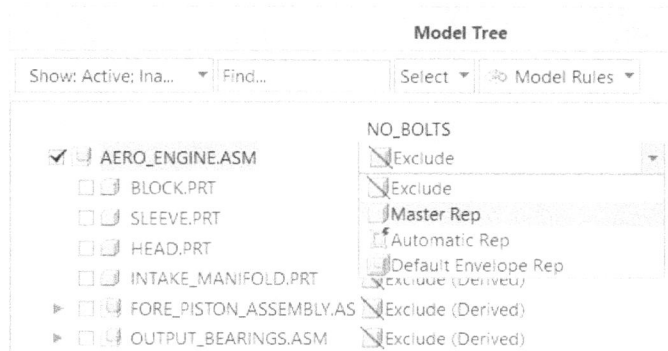

Figure 6–19

6. Click **Model Rules>Edit Rules**. A dialog box opens, enabling you to define the rule actions, as shown in Figure 6–20.

Figure 6–20

*You might need to right-click in the dialog box and select **New** twice to open the Rule Editor dialog box.*

7. Click ✚ (Add Condition) to add a new condition.

8. Maintain the default Rep Action **Exclude** option.

9. Right-click on the *Condition* field in the dialog box and select **New**, as shown in Figure 6–21.

Figure 6–21

10. Set the *Name* to **M4_Comp** as and press <Enter> to open the Rule Editor.

11. Customize the Rule Editor settings to search for solid models that have the characters **M4** in their name, as shown in Figure 6–22.

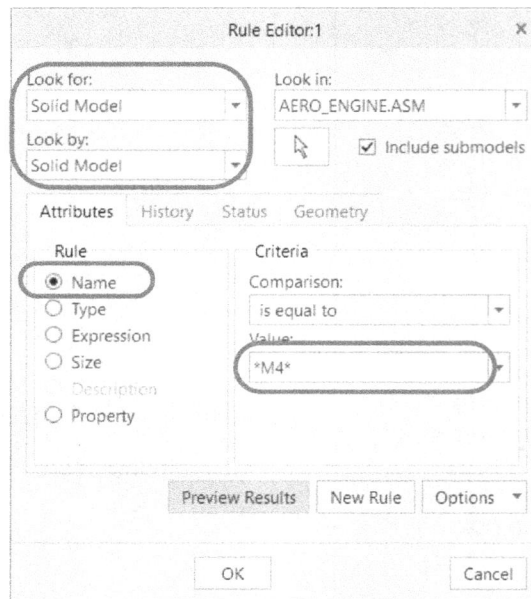

Figure 6–22

12. Click **Options>Build Query**, if required.

13. Click **Preview Results** to review the results of the rule. The system reports that 55 items have been found, as shown in Figure 6–23.

55 items found:

Item
021143M4X8.PRT
021143M4X8.PRT
021143M4X8.PRT
021143M4X8.PRT
021143M4X8.PRT
021143M4X8.PRT
021143M4X8.PRT
021143M4X8.PRT
021143M4X10.PRT
021143M4X10.PRT

Figure 6–23

14. Click **Add New** to add the rule.

15. Click **OK** in the Rule Editor dialog box. The NO_BOLTS dialog box displays as shown in Figure 6–24.

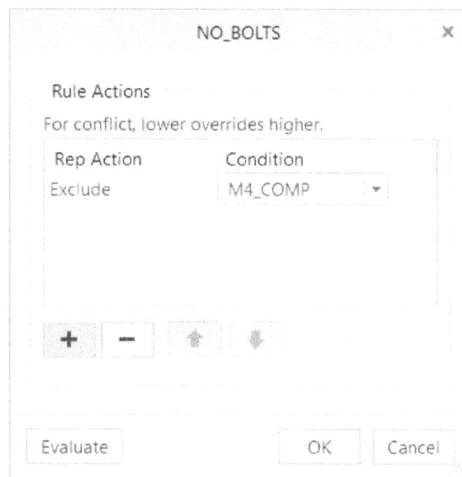

Figure 6–24

16. Click **Evaluate** and **OK**. All of the components with M4 in the name have been excluded.

17. Click **Apply** to update the *Model Graphics* area of the Edit dialog box, which displays as shown in Figure 6–25.

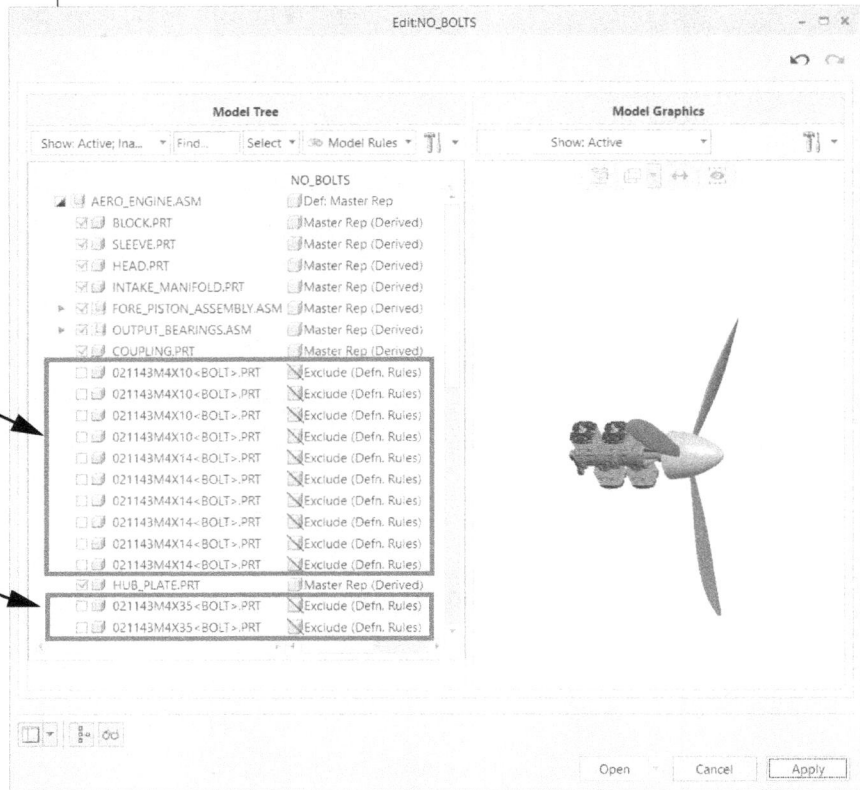

These components have been cleared and removed.

Figure 6–25

18. Click **Open** to close the Edit dialog box.

19. Zoom in on the updated assembly, as shown in Figure 6–26. Note that all of the bolts have been removed.

Figure 6–26

20. Activate the **Master Rep** of the model.

Task 2 - Create a representation with the default rule set to Exclude.

1. Create a new simplified rep, set the *Name* to **Only_Pistons**, and press <Enter>.

Design Considerations

Aero_engine.asm has a status of **Def: Exclude Comp**. This means that unless otherwise set, all of the components are excluded.

In this task, you will keep the default rule. All of the components are removed from the rep and you must select the components to include. The Edit dialog box displays as shown in Figure 6–27. All of the components are removed from the display.

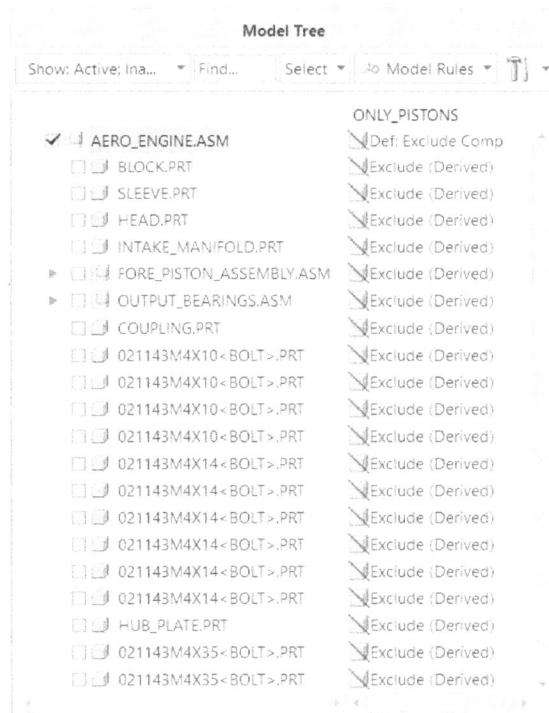

Model Tree

Show: Active; Ina... ▼ Find...   Select ▼ ⁴⁰ Model Rules ▼ T̅ ▼

	ONLY_PISTONS
✓ AERO_ENGINE.ASM	Def: Exclude Comp
BLOCK.PRT	Exclude (Derived)
SLEEVE.PRT	Exclude (Derived)
HEAD.PRT	Exclude (Derived)
INTAKE_MANIFOLD.PRT	Exclude (Derived)
▶ FORE_PISTON_ASSEMBLY.ASM	Exclude (Derived)
▶ OUTPUT_BEARINGS.ASM	Exclude (Derived)
COUPLING.PRT	Exclude (Derived)
021143M4X10<BOLT>.PRT	Exclude (Derived)
021143M4X10<BOLT>.PRT	Exclude (Derived)
021143M4X10<BOLT>.PRT	Exclude (Derived)
021143M4X10<BOLT>.PRT	Exclude (Derived)
021143M4X14<BOLT>.PRT	Exclude (Derived)
021143M4X14<BOLT>.PRT	Exclude (Derived)
021143M4X14<BOLT>.PRT	Exclude (Derived)
021143M4X14<BOLT>.PRT	Exclude (Derived)
021143M4X14<BOLT>.PRT	Exclude (Derived)
HUB_PLATE.PRT	Exclude (Derived)
021143M4X35<BOLT>.PRT	Exclude (Derived)
021143M4X35<BOLT>.PRT	Exclude (Derived)

Figure 6–27

2. Click **Select>Advanced Search** to search for all of the parts with **piston** in their names.

- *Look for:* **Solid Model**
- *Rule:* **Name**
- *Value:* ***piston***

3. Click **Find Now**. The system reports that ten items have been found, as shown in Figure 6–28.

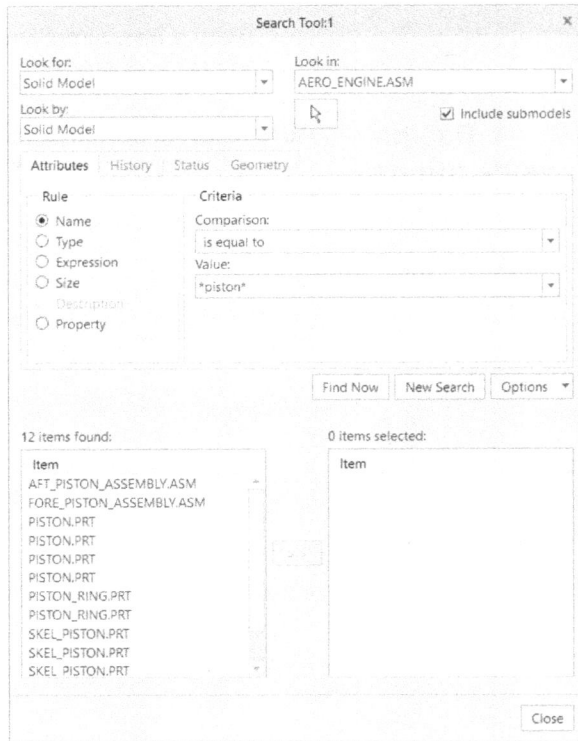

Figure 6–28

4. Select six items (4 **PISTON.PRT** and 2 **PISTON_RING.PRT**. Do not select any **skel_piston.prt** items) and move them to the selected list using ≫ (Add Item). The Search Tool updates as shown in Figure 6–29.

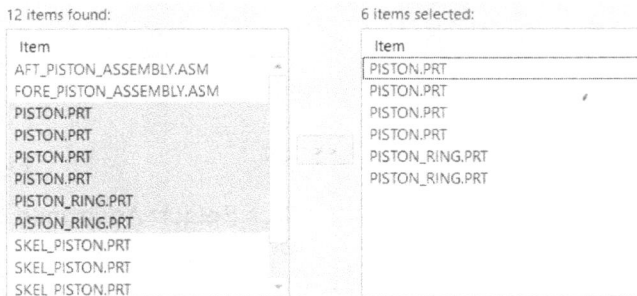

Figure 6–29

5. **Close** the Search tool. All six items are now selected.

6. Right-click on one of the selected items and select **Set Representation to>Master**, as shown in Figure 6–30.

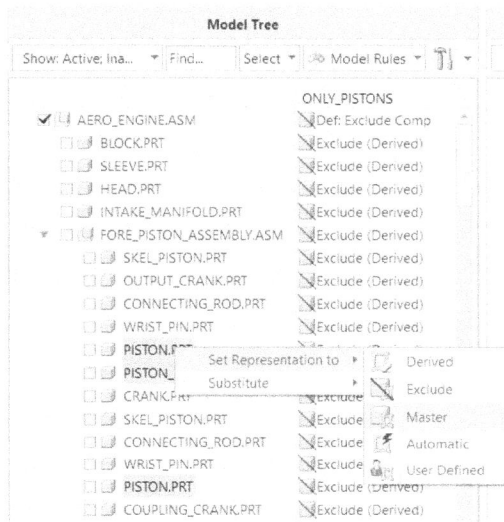

Figure 6–30

- This sets the display of these components to **Master Rep**. The Edit dialog box and model display, as shown in Figure 6–31.

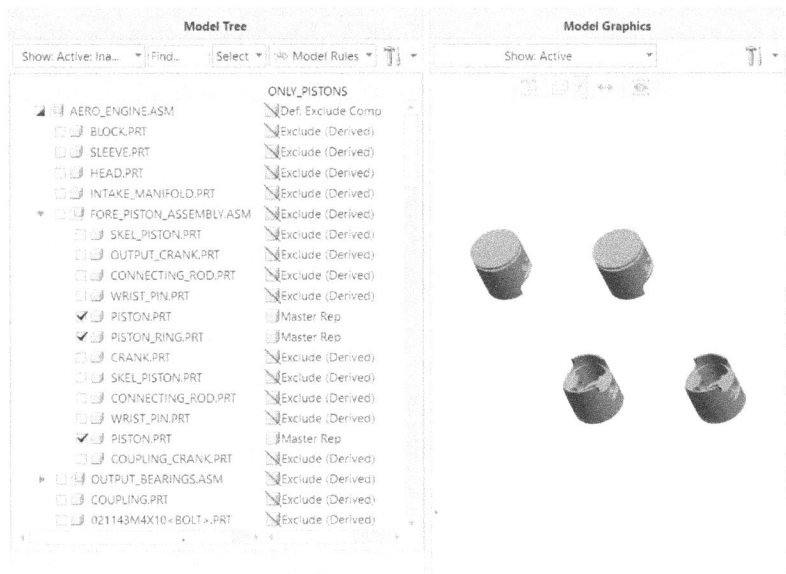

Figure 6–31

7. Click **Open**.

Design Considerations

Note that the Model Tree reports that the top-level assembly is excluded and any models that have *piston* in their name have been set to the master representation setting, as shown in Figure 6–32.

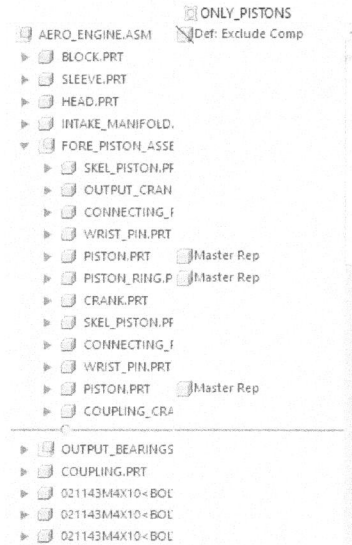

Figure 6–32

Task 3 - Redefine a rule-based simplified representation.

1. Ensure that the **Only_Pistons** representation is active.

2. Right-click and select **Rename** to change the *Name* of the representation to **Piston_Assembly**, as shown in Figure 6–33.

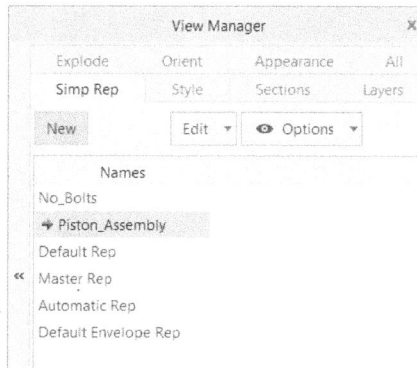

Figure 6–33

---

3. Click **Edit>Edit Definition** to redefine the **Piston_Assembly** representation. The Edit dialog box opens as shown in Figure 6–34. Expand the **FORE_PISTON_ ASSEMBLY.ASM**.

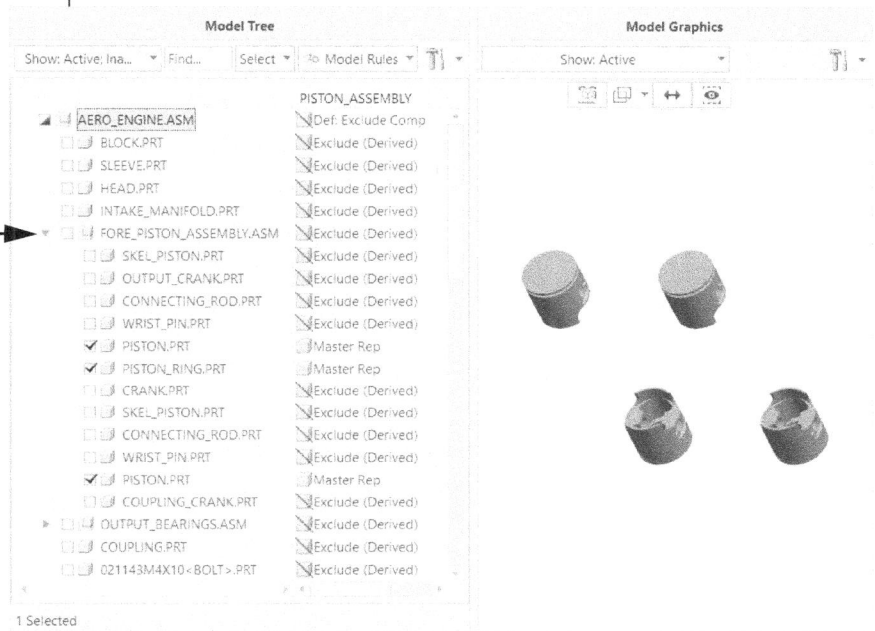

Expand the assembly

Figure 6–34

4. Click **Model Rules>Edit Rules**. The **PISTON_ASSEMBLY** dialog box opens, as shown in Figure 6–35.

Figure 6–35

5. Click ✚ (Add Condition). Use the Rep Action drop-down list to change the *Rep Action* to **Master Rep**, as shown in Figure 6–36.

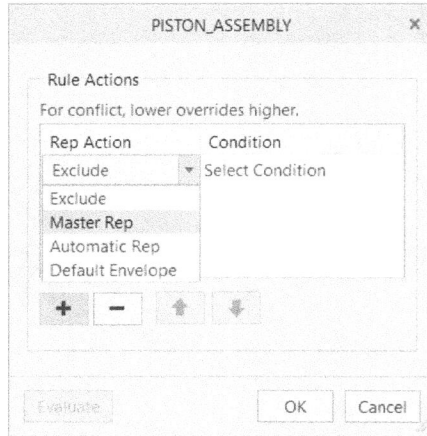

Figure 6–36

6. Right-click in the *Condition* field and select **New**.

7. Set the *Name* to **Piston_Assem** and press <Enter>.

8. In the Rule Editor dialog box, set the *Criteria Value* to ***PISTON_ASSEM***, as shown in Figure 6–37.

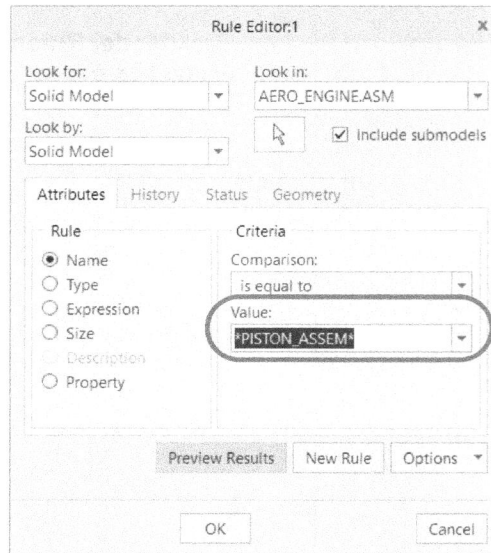

Figure 6–37

9. Click **Options>Build Query**, if required.

10. Click **Add New**. The *Query Builder* area updates as shown in Figure 6–38.

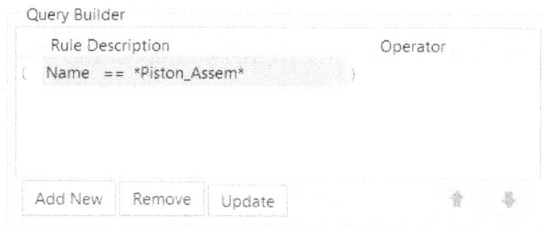

Figure 6–38

11. Click **Preview Results** and select both items in the Items Found results, as shown in Figure 6–39.

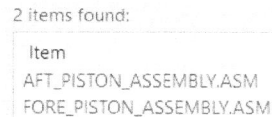

Figure 6–39

12. Click **OK**.

13. Click **Evaluate** and **OK** in the PISTON_ASSEMBLY dialog box.

14. Click **Apply**.

15. Click **Open** to close the Edit dialog box.

16. The updated assembly displays as shown in Figure 6–40.

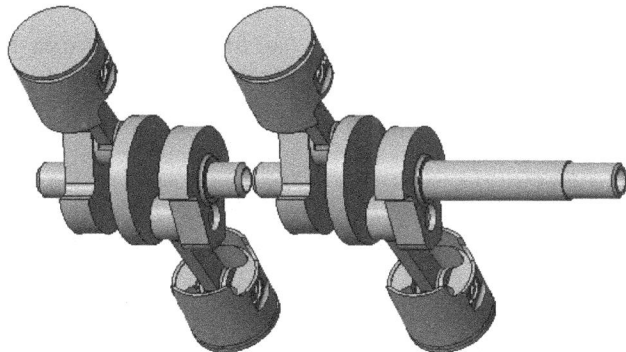

Figure 6–40

Design Considerations

Once a simplified representation has been created, it can be copied as an external representation. This method is very useful when you are working in a concurrent engineering environment. A great benefit of this method is that you do not need to consider the top-level assembly structure. The system takes components at any level (any components that are part of the selected representation) and externalizes them. In the next task, you will externalize the **Piston_Assembly** representation and save it as a new assembly. This assembly can then be sent to a design team responsible for changing these components.

Task 4 - Create an external representation.

1. In the View Manager, select **Piston_Assembly**, right-click and select **Copy As External**, as shown in Figure 6–41.

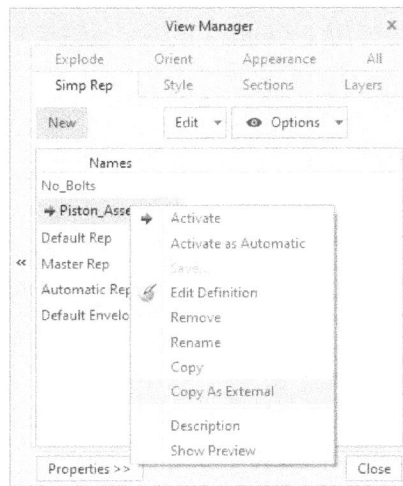

Figure 6–41

2. Set the *Name* to **Aero_Piston_Assem** and select **Save the model**, as shown in Figure 6–42.

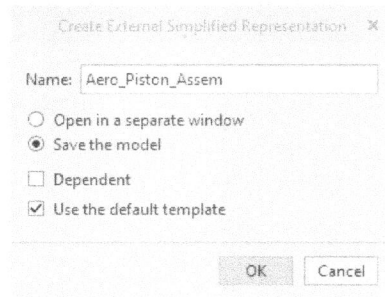

Figure 6–42

3. Click **OK**. It could take a few moments for the system to generate the assembly.

4. Close the View Manager.

5. Save the assembly and erase it from memory.

Task 5 - Open the assembly created from an external representation.

1. Open **aero_piston_assem.asm**.

Design Considerations

The assembly created from an external simplified representation displays as shown in Figure 6–43. Only the components required for this external simplified representation have been brought into session. The text in the display and the symbol of the assembly in the Model Tree 🖼 also indicate that it is an external representation.

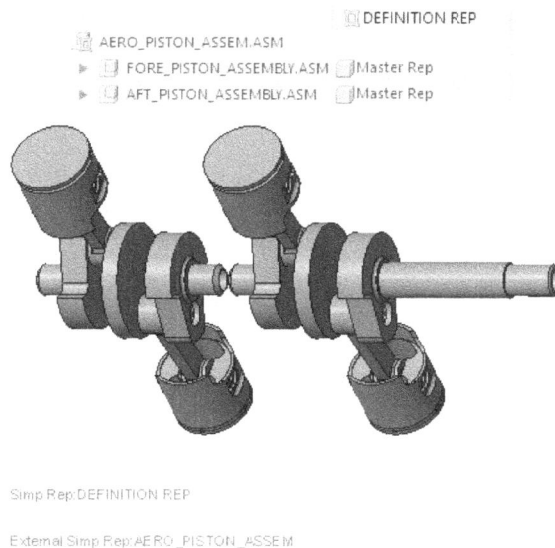

Figure 6–43

2. Close the AERO_PISTON_ASSEM window and erase it from memory.

Practice 6b | Zone-Based Simplified Reps

Practice Objectives

- Create a zone.
- Use a zone rule to define a simplified representation.

In this practice, you will create a zone that defines an area of the assembly. Once the zone has been created, you will use it to create a rule-based simplified rep. By creating the simplified rep using a rule, any changes made to the zone can be updated to reflect the changes in the simplified rep. You will use the **areo_engine** assembly to begin the practice and create a zone that enables you to create the simplified rep shown in Figure 6–44.

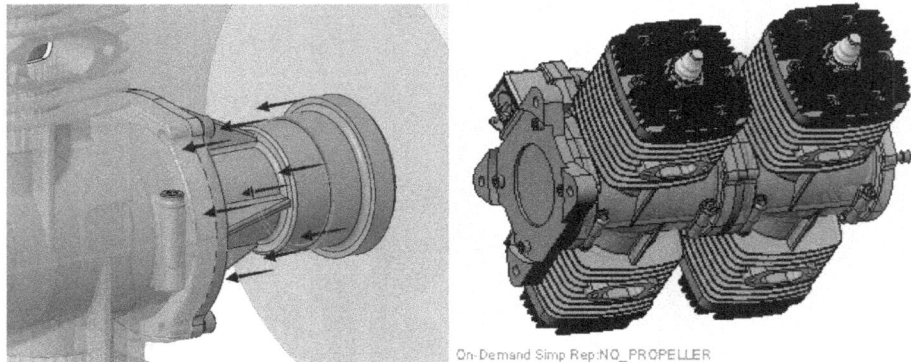

On-Demand Simp Rep:NO_PROPELLER

The simplified rep is created using the zone shown on the left. All of the components in the direction of the arrows are displayed as shown on the right.

Figure 6–44

Task 1 - Create a zone.

1. Change the working directory to the *Zone_Based_Reps* folder.

2. Open the Master Rep of **aero_engine.asm**.

3. Set the model display as follows:

- ⁺⁄⊹. *(Datum Display Filters)*: All Off

- ⋟ *(Spin Center)*: Off

- ⬜. *(Display Style)*: ⬜ (Shading With Edges)

4. In the *View* tab, expand 🗇 (Section) and select **Zone**.

5. The Zone dialog box opens as shown in Figure 6–45.

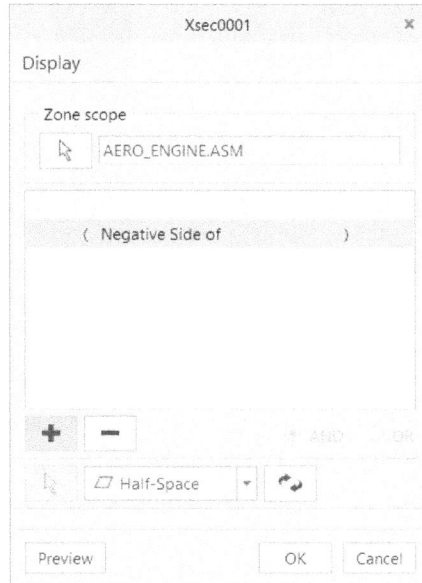

Figure 6–45

6. Rotate the model, zoom in to the area shown in Figure 6–46, and select the planar surface of **coupling.prt**.

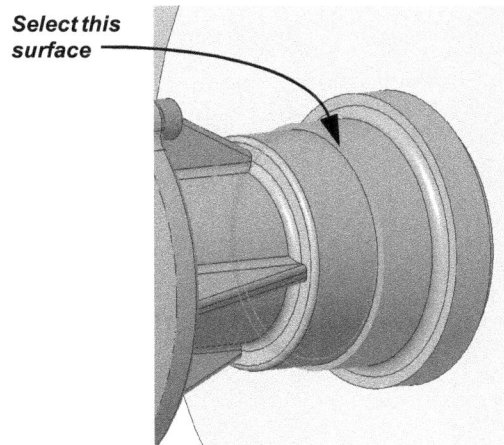

Figure 6–46

7. Arrows display as shown in Figure 6–47, indicating the direction that the zone will be created. Reverse the arrow direction to match the figure, if required.

The arrow direction can be reversed by clicking

↻ *(Change Orientation), if required.*

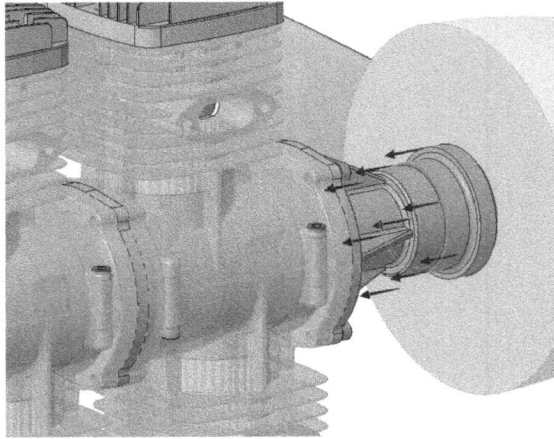

Figure 6–47

8. Select **Display>Zone Only**, as shown in Figure 6–48.

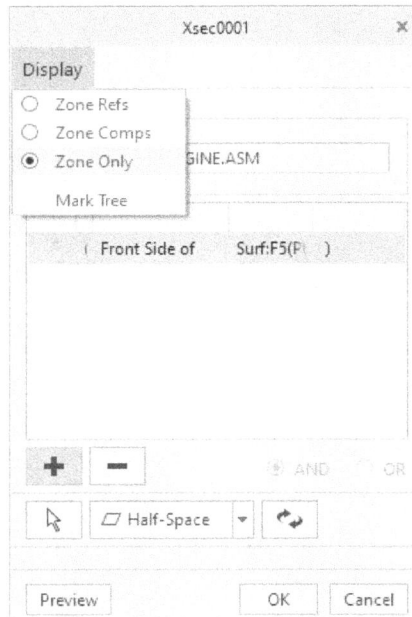

Figure 6–48

Design Considerations

The assembly displays as shown in Figure 6–49. The **Zone Only** display option in the drop-down list enables you to visually check which components are included in the zone.

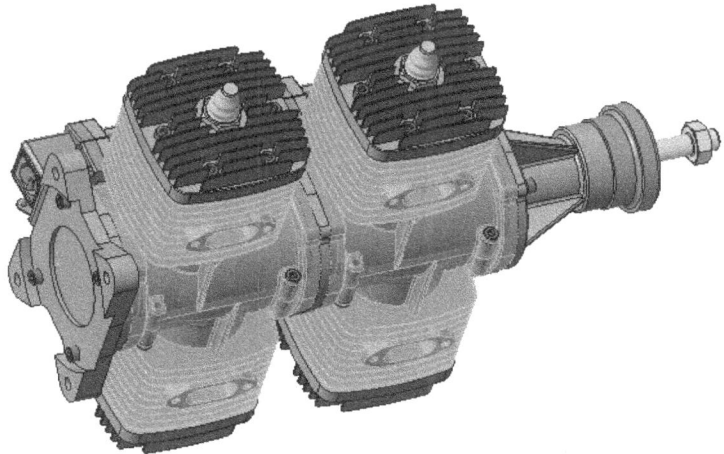

Figure 6–49

9. Click **OK** to complete the zone creation.

10. Scroll to the bottom of the Model Tree and expand the **Footer** node to display the new zone.

11. Right-click the zone in the Model Tree click **Rename**. Edit the *Name* to **Propeller**.

Task 2 - Create a simplified representation using the zone.

---

1. Open the View Manager and create a new simplified rep with the *Name* of **Propeller**. In the Edit dialog box, change the default rule to **Master Rep**.

2. Click **Model Rules>Edit Rules.**

3. Click ✚ (Add Condition).

4. Leave the *Rep Action* as **Exclude**.

5. Right-click in the *Condition* field and select **New**.

6. Edit the name to **Prop_Zone** and press <Enter>.

7. In the Rule Editor dialog box, click **Options** and enable **Build Query**, if required.

8. Select the *Geometry* tab and **Zone** as the rule. Click **Preview Results**.

9. Click **Add New** to create the rule. The Rule Editor dialog box updates as shown in Figure 6–50.

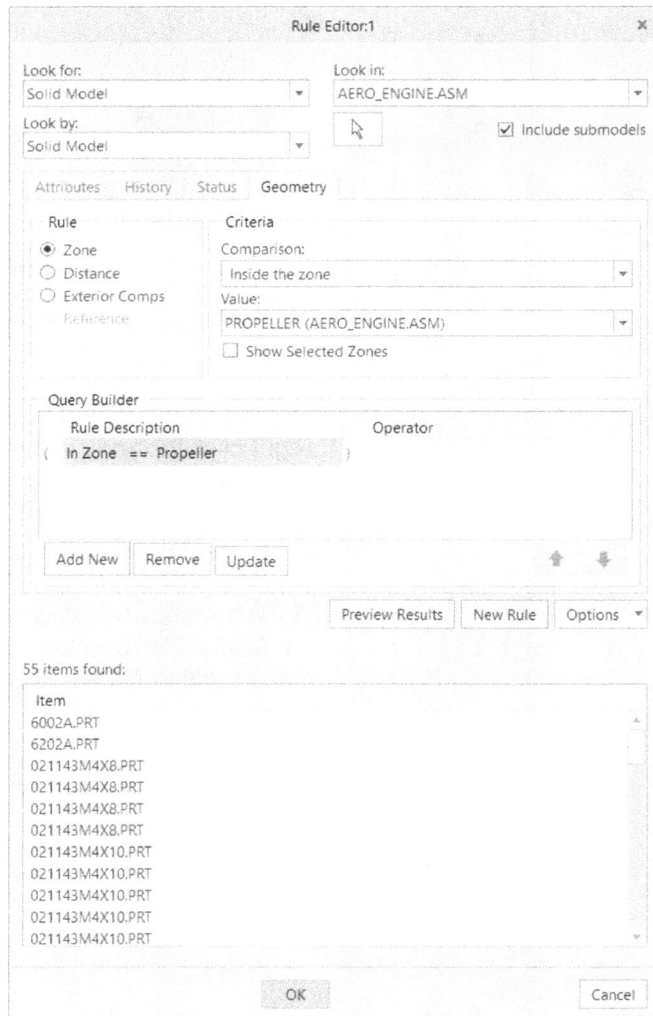

Figure 6–50

10. Click **OK** in the Rule Editor dialog box.

11. Click **Evaluate** and click **OK** in the Rule Action dialog box. The Edit dialog box opens, as shown in Figure 6–51.

Figure 6–51

12. Click **Apply** and **Open**.

13. Close the View Manager. The assembly displays as shown in Figure 6–52.

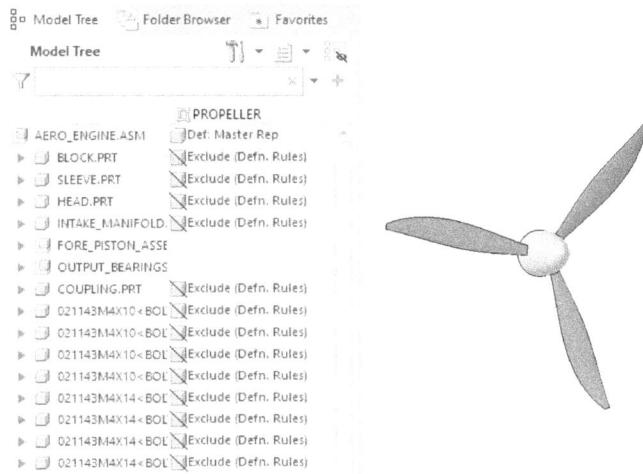

Figure 6–52

14. Save the assembly.

Task 3 - Edit a zone-based simplified representation.

Design Considerations

You can also use the View Manager to redefine the zone.

A simplified representation that is defined using a zone rule is also driven by the zone. In this task, you will redefine the zone to change the Propeller representation.

1. Click on the **PROPELLER** zone in the Model Tree and select 🖌 (Edit Definition) in the mini toolbar.

2. Select the reference in the dialog box, as shown in Figure 6–53.

Select this reference

Zone scope

AERO_ENGINE.ASM

Front Side of   Surf:F5(P   )

Half-Space

Preview   OK   Cancel

Figure 6–53

3. Click ↻ (Change Orientation) to reverse the direction of the Propeller zone. The directional arrows point toward the Propeller, as shown in Figure 6–54.

Figure 6–54

4. Select **OK**.

5. If it is not already open, open the View Manager dialog box and select the *Simp Rep* tab. Right-click on **Propeller** and select **Rename**. Rename the **Propeller** simplified representation to **No_Propeller**, as shown in Figure 6–55.

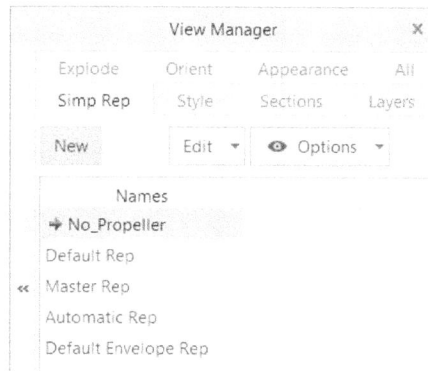

Figure 6–55

6. Click **Edit>Save** and click **OK** in the Save Display Elements dialog box.

7. Right-click on **No_Propeller** and select **Edit Definition**. To update the simplified representation, click **Model Rules>Evaluate Rules**. Click **OK**. The assembly displays as shown in Figure 6–56.

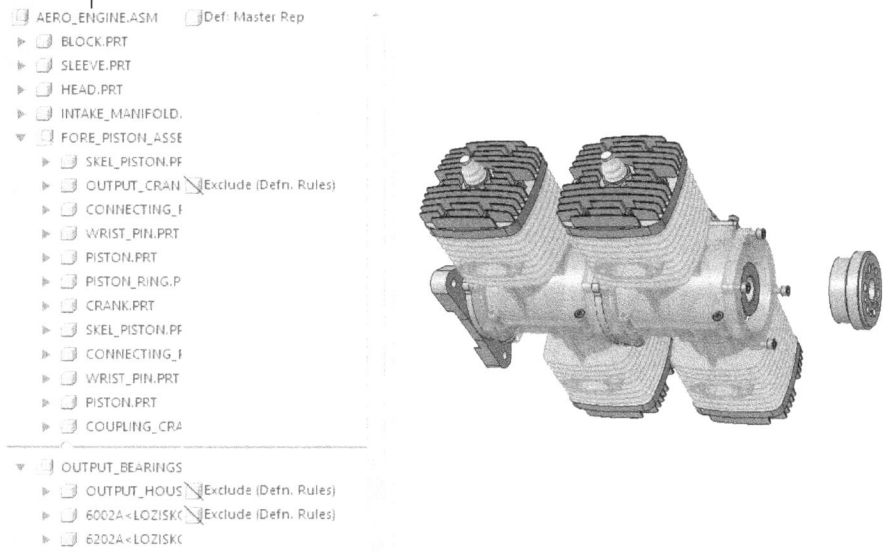

Figure 6–56

8. Save the assembly and erase it from memory.

Practice 6c

(Optional) Substitute by Envelope

Practice Objectives

- Create an envelope part.
- Create a simplified representation that substitutes an assembly with an envelope part.

In this practice, you will create an envelope to represent the geometry for the Propeller assembly. Once the envelope has been created, you will use it to create a rule-based simplified rep. You will use **areo_engine.asm** to begin the practice and create a zone that enables you to create the simplified rep shown in Figure 6–57.

On-Demand Smp Rep PROP_ENVELOPE

Figure 6–57

Task 1 - Create an envelope.

1. Change the working directory to the *Substitute_Envelope* folder.

2. Open the Master Rep of **aero_engine.asm**.

3. Set the model display as follows:

- ⚊ *(Datum Display Filters)*: All Off
- ⚊ *(Spin Center)*: Off
- ⚊ *(Display Style)*: ⬜ (Shading With Edges)

4. Open the View Manager.

5. Double-click on **Automatic Rep** to make it active. The assembly displays as shown in Figure 6–58.

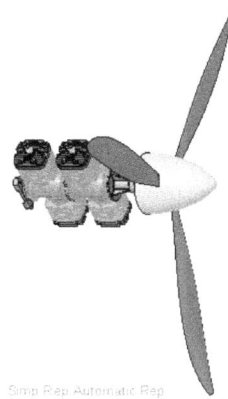

Simp Rep Automatic Rep

Figure 6–58

6. Close the View Manager.

7. In the *View* tab, expand ⚊ (Manage Views) and select **Envelope Manager**. The Envelope Manager dialog box opens, as shown in Figure 6–59.

Figure 6–59

8. Click **New**.

9. In the Envelope Definition dialog box, edit the *Name* to **Prop_Envlp**, as shown in Figure 6–60.

Enter name →

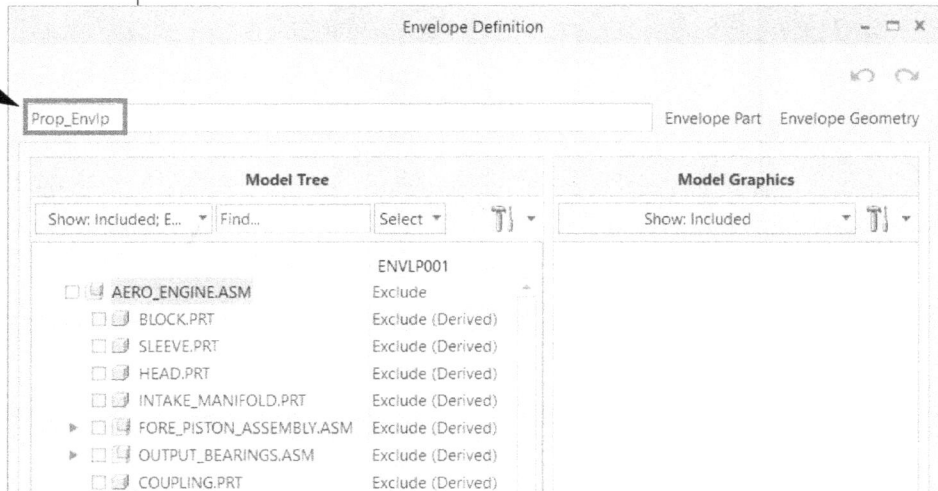

Figure 6–60

10. Place a checkmark next to **propeller.asm** in the Edit dialog box, as shown in Figure 6–61.

You might have to click more than once to place a checkmark next to the assembly.

Figure 6–61

11. The *Model Graphics* area in the Envelope Definition dialog box displays **PROPELLER.ASM**.

12. Click **Envelope Part**, as shown in Figure 6–62.

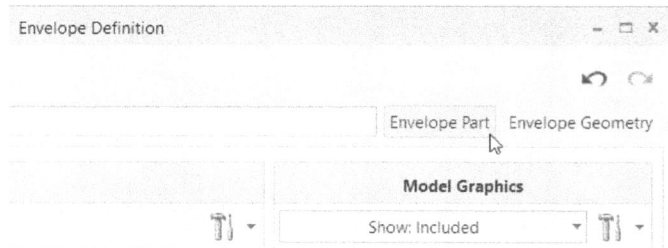

Figure 6–62

13. Set the new envelope part *Name* to **Prop_Envlp**, as shown in Figure 6–63.

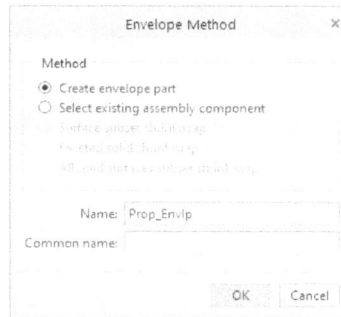

Figure 6–63

14. Click **OK**.

15. Browse to and select **start_part.prt** from the current working directory, as shown in Figure 6–64.

Figure 6–64

16. Click **OK**.

17. Set the *Constraint Type* to **Default** and click ✔ (OK).

Task 2 - Define envelope geometry.

Design Considerations

At this point in the process, you have created a new part file and assembled it into the top-level assembly. This part file only contains the default datum features that are standard in the default template. You must now create solid geometry that defines the envelope geometry. You will use a **Revolve** feature to define the envelope geometry. Once this envelope has been created, it is used in a simplified rep.

1. In the Envelope Definition dialog box, click **Envelope Geometry**.The system sets **PROP_ENVLP.prt** to be active and activates the *Envelope Geometry* dashboard.

2. Click ⛴ ▾ (Settings)**>Tree Filters**.

3. Check **Envelope components** and click **OK**. The Model Tree displays, as shown in Figure 6–65.

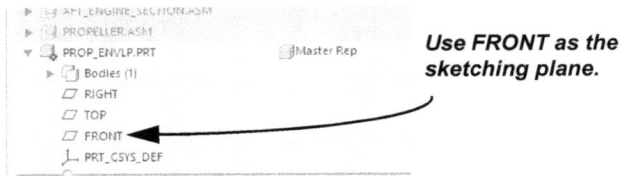

Figure 6–65

4. Click ⏣ (Revolve) in the *Envelope Geometry* dashboard.

5. Select datum plane **FRONT** in **prop_envlp.prt** as the sketching plane and begin sketching. If necessary, click ⬚ (Sketch View).

6. Use ⦙ (Centerline) to sketch a centerline on the horizontal reference and then sketch the section shown in Figure 6–66. For this practice, exact dimensions are not required. Ensure that the sketched geometry is outside the existing propeller assembly.

Dimensions removed from display for clarity. Exact dimensions are not required.

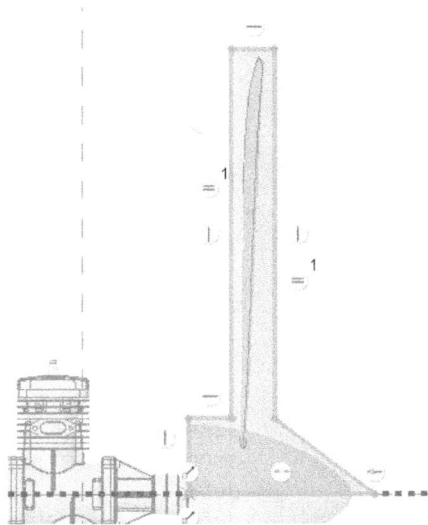

Figure 6–66

7. Click ✓ (OK) to complete the sketch.

8. Click ✓ (OK) to complete the revolve.

9. Click ✓ (Done) to close the *Envelope Geometry* dashboard.

10. Click **Open** in the Envelope Definition dialog box.

11. Close the Envelope dialog box.

Design Considerations

Prop_envlp.prt has been saved to the working directory. The assembly displays as shown in Figure 6–67. The envelope part is listed in the Model Tree because the tree filter Enveloped Components was activated in a previous step.

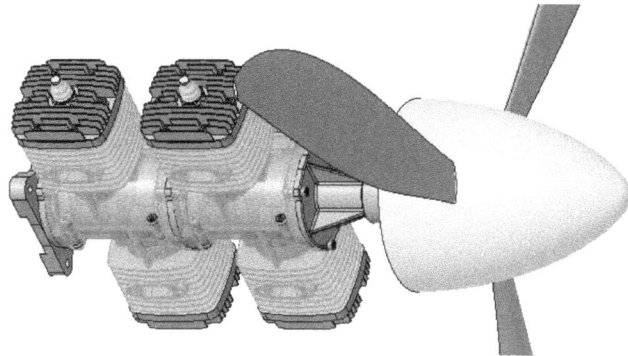

Figure 6–67

Task 3 - Substitute an envelope for an assembly.

---

*Click **No** if prompted to save the modified Geometry Rep.*

1. Create a simplified representation and set the *Name* to **Prop_Envelope**.

2. Change the default rule to **Master Rep**.

3. Select the **PROPELLER.ASM**. Right-click and select **Substitute>Envelope**, as shown in Figure 6–68.

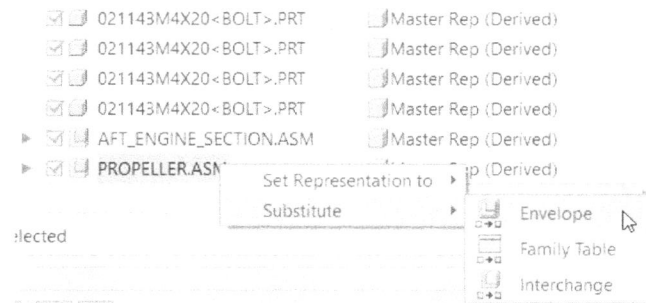

Figure 6–68

---

4. Select **PROP_ENV** and click **OK**.

5. Click **Open** in the Edit dialog box.

Design Considerations

The envelope part displays as shown in Figure 6–69. Envelope substitution is a technique that reduces regeneration time (the simple revolve part regenerates more quickly than the propeller assembly), while still visually maintaining the component(s) space claim.

On-Demand Simp Rep PROP_ENVELOPE

Figure 6–69

6. Close the View Manager.

7. Save the assembly.

8. Close the window and erase it from memory.

Chapter Review Questions

1. Which of the following statements are true regarding an external simplified representation? (Select all that apply.)

    a. Stored as a separate assembly model.

    b. Enables multiple versions of an assembly to be stored.

    c. Enables multiple users to work on the external representations simultaneously.

    d. All of the components included in the external simplified representation are the same as those in the master assembly.

2. The **Open Subset** option can only be used to open existing simplified representations.

    a. True

    b. False

3. To create an envelope, you can use which of the following methods? (Select all that apply.)

    a. Expand in the *View* or *Model* tab and select **Envelope Manager**.

    b. Expand and select **Envelope Manager**.

    c. Click and select **Envelope**.

    d. Select **Operations>Envelope**.

4. Which of the following options enables you to define a work area of the assembly? You can then create a simplified representation that selects components based on a defined rule that uses that defined area.

    a. Zone

    b. Envelope

    c. Section

    d. Plane

5. Only one plane or surface can be selected to create a zone.

   a. True

   b. False

6. Multiple components can be included in an envelope.

   a. True

   b. False

Interchange Assemblies

Interchange is a sub-type of a Creo Parametric assembly. Interchange assemblies enable you to substitute components in an assembly with functionally similar components to simplify an existing model.

Learning Objectives in This Chapter

- Learn how to create an interchange assembly by assembling functional components and assigning reference tags.
- Learn to replace a component in the assembly with a functional component from an interchange assembly.
- Create an interchange assembly and assemble functional components.
- Learn to assemble or create a simplified component into the interchange assembly and specify the additional options.
- Learn to replace a component in the assembly with a simplified component from an interchange assembly.
- Learn to replace a complex model with a shrinkwrap model to increase the performance when working with large or complex assemblies.
- Learn the advantages of using interchange assemblies through examples.

7.1 Functional Components

Using an interchange assembly, components can quickly be replaced in design assemblies without the need to constrain the replacing component again. This reduces the requirement for multiple assemblies. Additionally, reference tags eliminate the need for references when replacing components.

How To: Create a Functional Interchange Assembly to Replace Components in an Assembly

1. In the Quick Access toolbar, click ☐ (New) to create an interchange assembly. Set the *Type* to **Assembly** and the *Sub-type* to **Interchange**.
2. To complete the creation, enter a *Name* for the interchange assembly, as shown in Figure 7–1. Click **OK**.

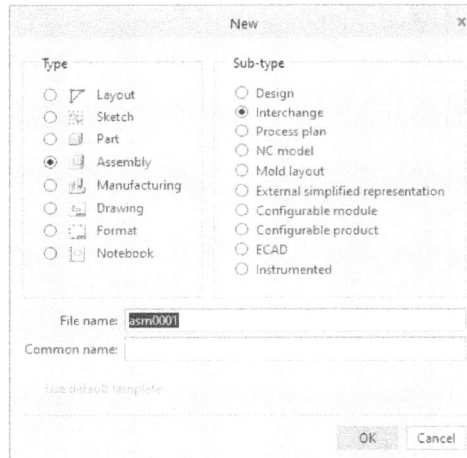

Figure 7–1

3. To assemble the first component in a functional interchange assembly, click ⬓ (Functional) in the *Model* tab.
4. Once all of the functional components have been added to the assembly, you must specify the reference tags. Assigning reference tags enables automatic placement when components are replaced with other members of the interchange assembly.

5. To specify references, click ⌐ (Reference Tag) in the *Model* tab. The Reference Tags dialog box opens, as shown in Figure 7–2.

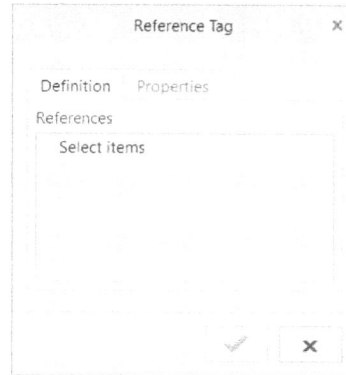

Figure 7–2

6. Select the common references. For example, an axis can be selected on both parts, as shown in Figure 7–3.

Figure 7–3

7. Enter a name for the reference, as shown in Figure 7–4.

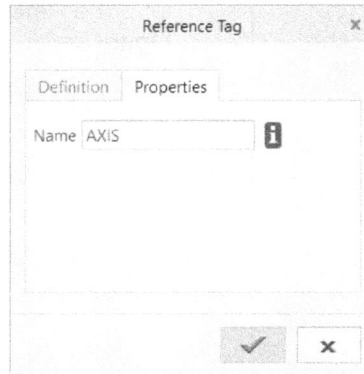

Figure 7–4

8. Once the reference tags have been defined, save the interchange assembly and close the window.

9. Once you have created an interchange assembly, you can replace members of the assembly with other functional components in the interchange assembly. To replace components, select a component in the assembly, right-click, and select 🔁 (Replace Component). The Replace dialog box opens as shown in Figure 7–5.

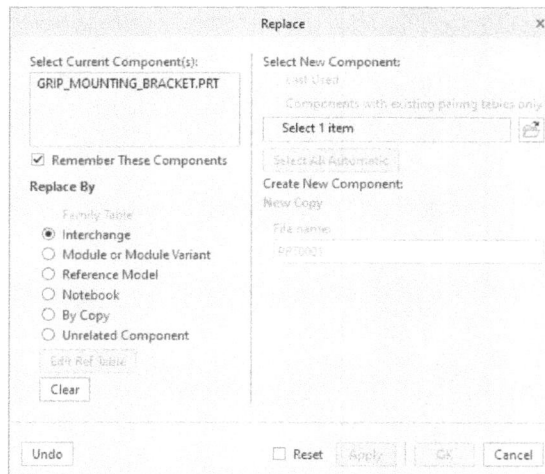

Figure 7–5

10. Select **Interchange** in the *Replace By* area and click ☝. The Family Tree dialog box opens, similar to that shown in Figure 7–6.

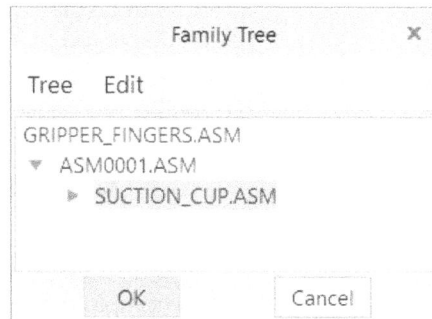

Figure 7–6

11. All of the interchange assemblies associated with the components display in the Family Tree list. Expand the assemblies and select the component to be substituted. Click **OK** to complete the placement.

7.2 Simplified Components

A simplified component is a component (part or assembly) that is created to display different information, or used to simplify the detail displayed in a part or assembly.

How To: Create an Interchange Assembly that Substitutes Components with a Simplified Component

1. To create an interchange assembly, click ⬜ (New). Set the *Type* to **Assembly** and the *Sub-type* to **Interchange**.
2. To complete the creation, enter a name for the interchange assembly and click **OK**.
3. To assemble the first component in a simplify interchange assembly, click (Functional) in the *Model* tab and select the component to be replaced in the Open dialog box. The component is automatically placed in the assembly and considered a functional component. The first functional component and the Model Tree are shown in Figure 7–7.

SIMPLE_GRIP.ASM
▶ GRIPPER_FINGERS.ASM

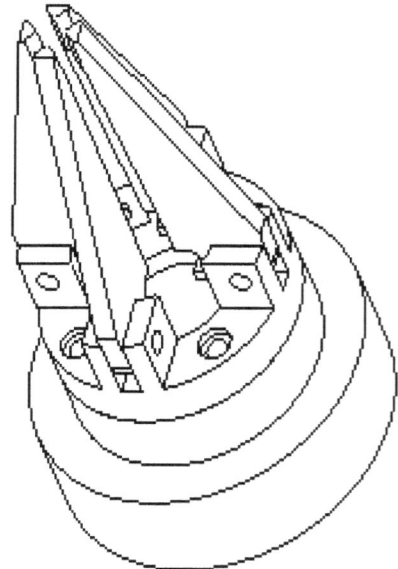

Figure 7–7

4. You can define the method of creation and the type of interchange component, and you can either assemble or create a simplified model.

Assemble

To assemble the first simplified component, click ⬚ (Simplify) in the *Model* tab.

To assemble a component, click **Placement**. Use the *Component Placement* dashboard to constrain the simplify component to the functional component, as shown in Figure 7–8.

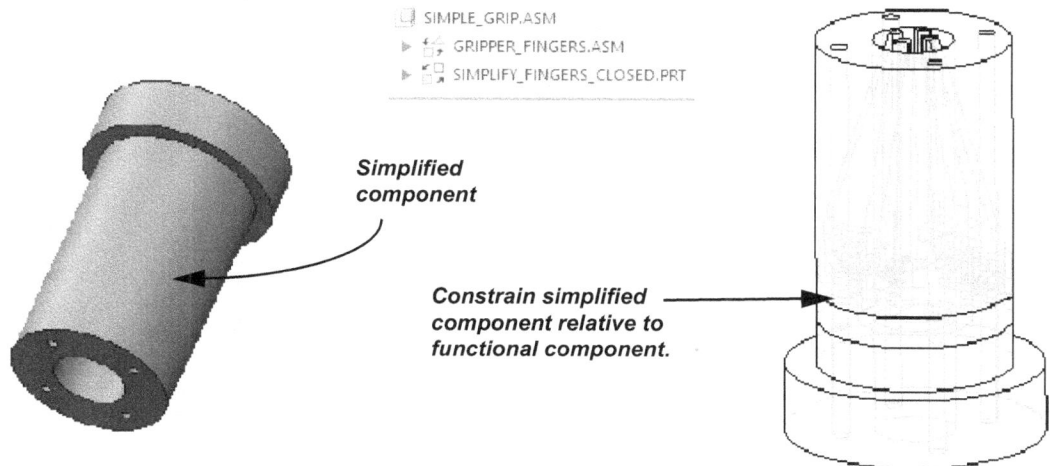

Simplified component

Constrain simplified component relative to functional component.

Figure 7–8

The assembly constraints and references that are used are important. The simplified component is substituted based on its location relative to the functional component. To complete the component placement, click **OK**.

Create

To create a simplified component, click ⬚ (Create) in the *Model* tab and use the standard Component Create and Creation Options dialog boxes to define the part. The new part displays in the Model Tree and you are prompted to constrain it relative to the functional component. If the new component was created using the **Empty** option, you are not prompted to constrain it.

Placement enables you to return to the Component Placement dialog box to redefine the placement constraints.

5. By default, the first simplified component is automatically associated with the first functional component, as shown in Figure 7–9. Click **OK** to close the Simplify Component dialog box.

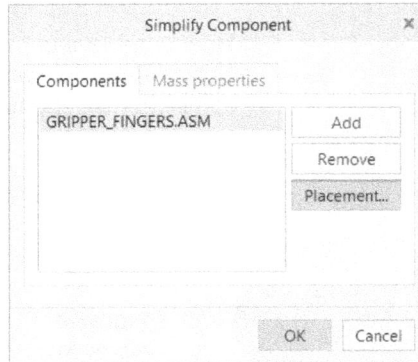

Figure 7–9

The *Mass Properties* tab in the Simplify Component dialog box enables you to define how the mass properties should be handled once a component has been substituted with a simplified one. The options are shown in Figure 7–10.

By default, mass properties are based on the original model if it is in session. Otherwise, it is based on the functional component.

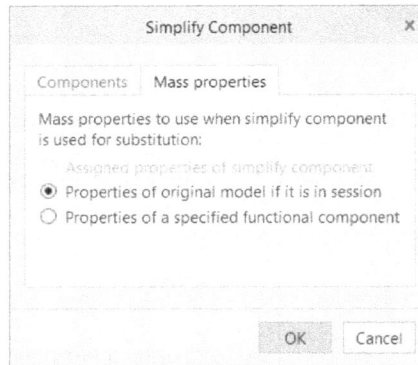

Figure 7–10

6. To assemble additional functional components, click
   (Functional). Package the component by clicking ✔ (OK) in the Component Placement dialog box.

A second functional component assembled in the interchange assembly is shown in Figure 7–11.

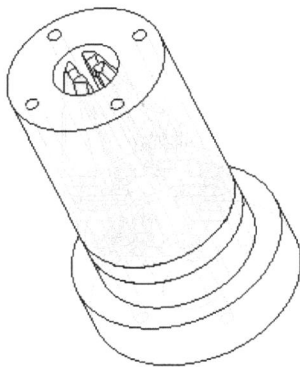

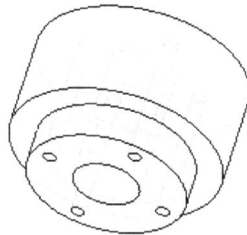

SIMPLE_GRIP.ASM
▶ GRIPPER_FINGERS.ASM
▼ SIMPLIFY_FINGERS_CLOSED.PRT
    ▶ Simplify for GRIPPER_FINGERS.ASM
▶ MOUNT_PLATE.PRT

Figure 7–11

7. To assemble additional simplified components, click

   (Simplify) and select an existing component or create a

   new one by clicking (Create).

To place the simplified component, use the Component placement dialog box to constrain it relative to a functional component. Additionally, you must select a functional component with which to associate it. If only one functional component exists in the interchange assembly, it is selected by default. Otherwise, you must manually select the functional component. If the Simplify Component dialog box is empty when it opens, as shown in Figure 7–12, it indicates that there are multiple functional components and that you must select one.

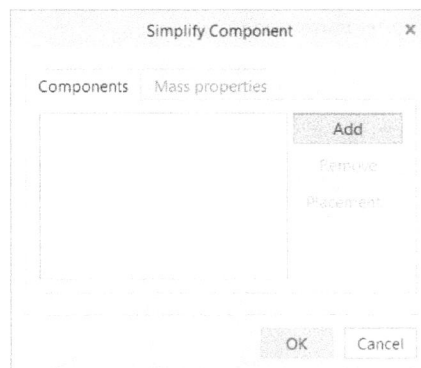

Figure 7–12

A single simplified component can be associated with multiple functional components. To assign it, select the simplified component in the Model Tree and select **Edit Definition** in the drop-down list. Click **Add** in the Simplify Component dialog box and select the additional functional component. The simplified component is copied automatically and you are prompted to assign the constraints. An example of a simplified component associated with multiple functional components is shown in Figure 7–13.

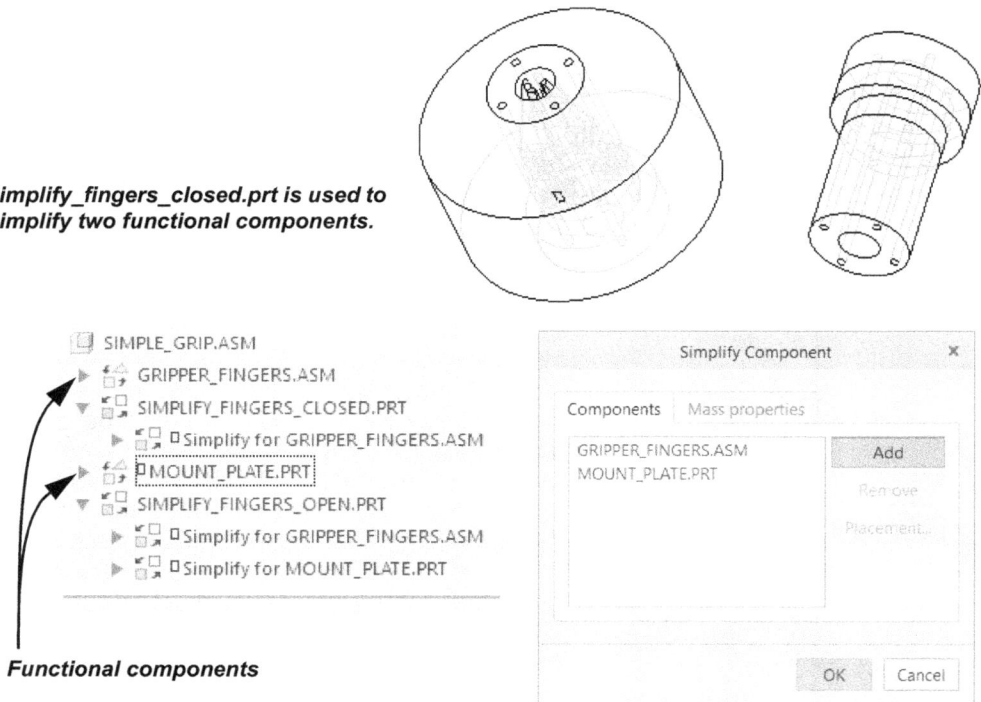

simplify_fingers_closed.prt is used to simplify two functional components.

Functional components

Figure 7–13

8. To complete the interchange assembly, close all of the dialog boxes, save the assembly, and close the window.

9. To substitute the simplified component, click ⚙ (View Manager) and select an existing simplified representation. Alternatively, create a new one in the View Manager. Click **Edit>Edit Definition**. The Component Chooser dialog box opens. Set the status of the component that you want to substitute and select **Substitute by Interchange**, as shown in Figure 7–14.

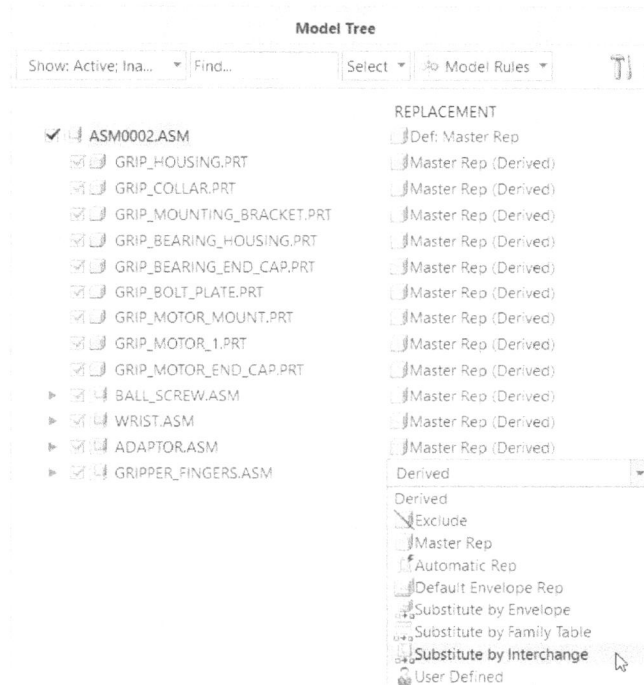

Model Tree

| Show: Active; Ina... ▼ | Find... | | Select ▼ | Model Rules ▼ | | ⊤ | ▼ |

	REPLACEMENT
✓ ☐ ASM0002.ASM	☐ Def: Master Rep
☑ ☐ GRIP_HOUSING.PRT	☐ Master Rep (Derived)
☑ ☐ GRIP_COLLAR.PRT	☐ Master Rep (Derived)
☑ ☐ GRIP_MOUNTING_BRACKET.PRT	☐ Master Rep (Derived)
☑ ☐ GRIP_BEARING_HOUSING.PRT	☐ Master Rep (Derived)
☑ ☐ GRIP_BEARING_END_CAP.PRT	☐ Master Rep (Derived)
☑ ☐ GRIP_BOLT_PLATE.PRT	☐ Master Rep (Derived)
☑ ☐ GRIP_MOTOR_MOUNT.PRT	☐ Master Rep (Derived)
☑ ☐ GRIP_MOTOR_1.PRT	☐ Master Rep (Derived)
☑ ☐ GRIP_MOTOR_END_CAP.PRT	☐ Master Rep (Derived)
▶ ☑ ☐ BALL_SCREW.ASM	☐ Master Rep (Derived)
▶ ☑ ☐ WRIST.ASM	☐ Master Rep (Derived)
▶ ☑ ☐ ADAPTOR.ASM	☐ Master Rep (Derived)
▶ ☑ ☐ GRIPPER_FINGERS.ASM	Derived ▼

Derived
⊠ Exclude
☐ Master Rep
☐ Automatic Rep
☐ Default Envelope Rep
☐ Substitute by Envelope
☐ Substitute by Family Table
☐ Substitute by Interchange   ⟵
☐ User Defined

Figure 7–14

10. Select the simplified component and click **OK**. The Component Chooser dialog box indicates that the model was substituted with the simplified component. Click **OK** to close the Component Chooser dialog box. Complete the simplified representation. An assembly where a subassembly is substituted by a simplified component is shown in Figure 7–15.

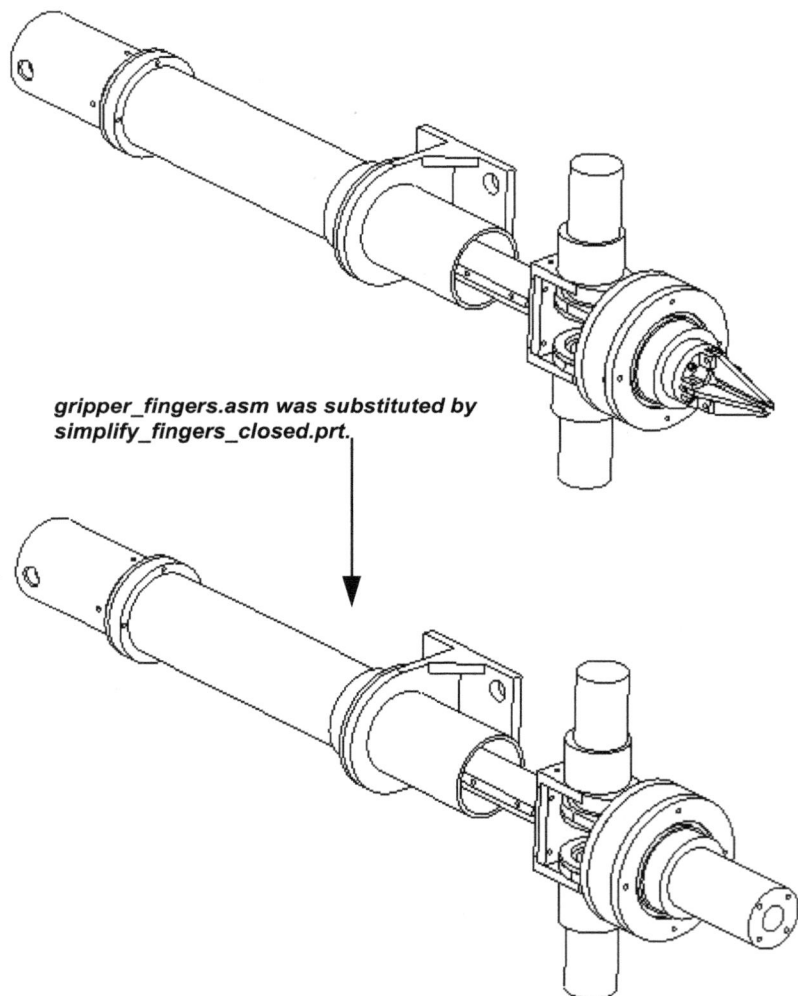

gripper_fingers.asm was substituted by simplify_fingers_closed.prt.

Figure 7–15

7.3 Simplifying Using Shrinkwrap Features

Replacing a complex model with a Shrinkwrap feature enables you to work more efficiently with complex assemblies. Shrinkwrap features can be used to simplify a complex model using either of the following techniques:

- Replace

- Simplified Representation Substitution

Shrinkwrap features and interchange assemblies must already exist for these operations.

Replace

To replace a component using a Shrinkwrap feature, select the component in the Model Tree, right-click and select 🔁 (Replace Component). The Replace dialog box opens as shown in Figure 7–16.

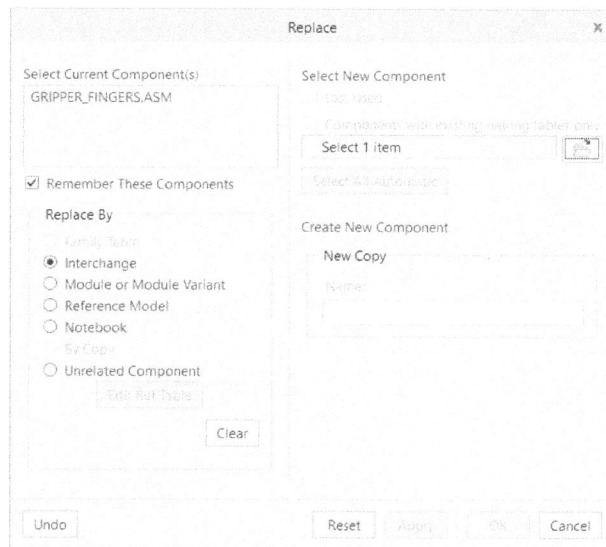

Figure 7–16

You can also replace using the **Interchange** or **Reference Model** options.

Simplified Representation Substitution

When an interchange assembly exists with a component and its Shrinkwrap, the Shrinkwrap can be substituted into an assembly.

7.4 Case Studies

Example 1 shows the practical advantage of using functional components in assemblies. Examples 2 and 3 show the practical advantage of using simplified components.

Example 1

Consider the parts shown in Figure 7–17 and Figure 7–18. These parts are nozzles that can be assembled to the hose attachment of a vacuum cleaner. The two nozzles are functionally similar and therefore an interchange assembly can be created. The reference tags that enable these two components to be automatically constrained in an assembly are Axis and Surface (their references are shown).

Surface ref = hidden surface
Axis ref = A_1

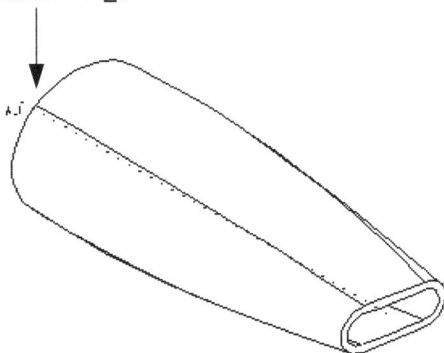

Figure 7–17

Surface ref = hidden surface
Axis ref = A_1

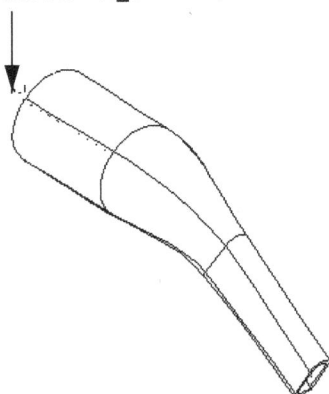

Figure 7–18

In the assembly shown in Figure 7–19, the straight nozzle was assembled to **attachment.prt**. In Figure 7–20, the straight nozzle was replaced by the curved nozzle using **Replace**.

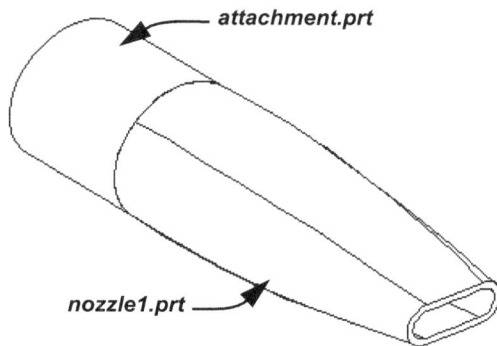

attachment.prt

nozzle1.prt

Figure 7–19

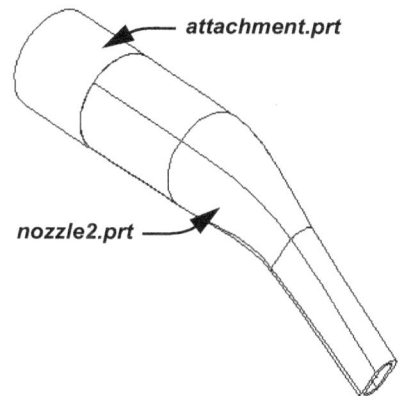

attachment.prt

nozzle2.prt

Figure 7–20

Example 2

Consider the component shown in Figure 7–21. The simplified component in Figure 7–22 can be added to the interchange assembly so that it can be used to simplify the part. By doing so, a downstream assembly can substitute the simpler part for the more detailed part to help reduce regeneration and display times.

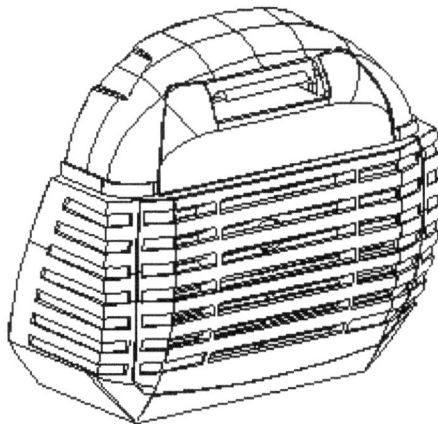

Figure 7–21

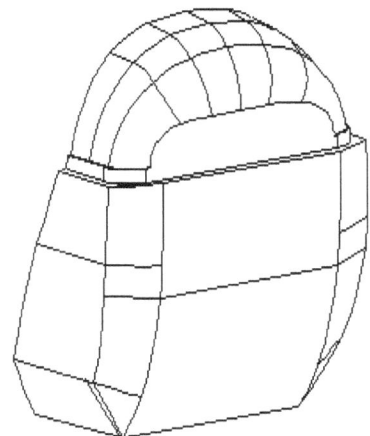

Figure 7–22

Example 3

Assemblies often have space requirements for their components. Using concept parts, you can define the size of each of the assembly's components without designing the specifics. According to the required size, the component can be designed within the specifications. Consider the assembly shown in Figure 7–23. The rotor component in this assembly was designed to fit in an enclosure.

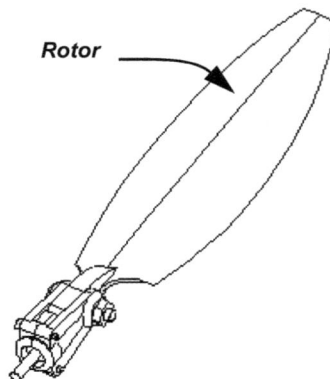

Figure 7–23

The original assembly was assembled, as shown in Figure 7–24. The **rotor_concept_part** defined the size.

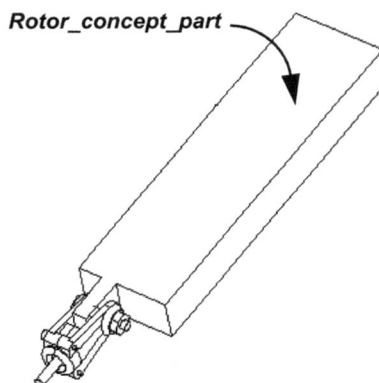

Figure 7–24

Multiple parts or assemblies can be assembled into an interchange assembly.

Once all of the concept parts have been assembled, you can obtain a better overview of the design requirements. In the example shown in Figure 7–24, the rotor component was built to fit inside the **rotor_concept_part** component.

Concept components can be replaced in the assembly using a simplified component in an interchange assembly or by manually replacing the components.

Practice 7a

Functional Interchange Assemblies I

Practice Objectives

- Create a simplify interchange assembly for parts.
- Create a Shrinkwrap component.
- Replace a component using the interchange assembly.

In this practice, you will open **robot_arm.asm** and create an interchange assembly of the functional components. You will also replace the functionally similar component in **robot_arm.asm**. The model shown in Figure 7–25 is an assembly with a replaced bracket.

An interchange assembly is created for this component.

The interchange assembly contains the two bracket components that can be interchanged.

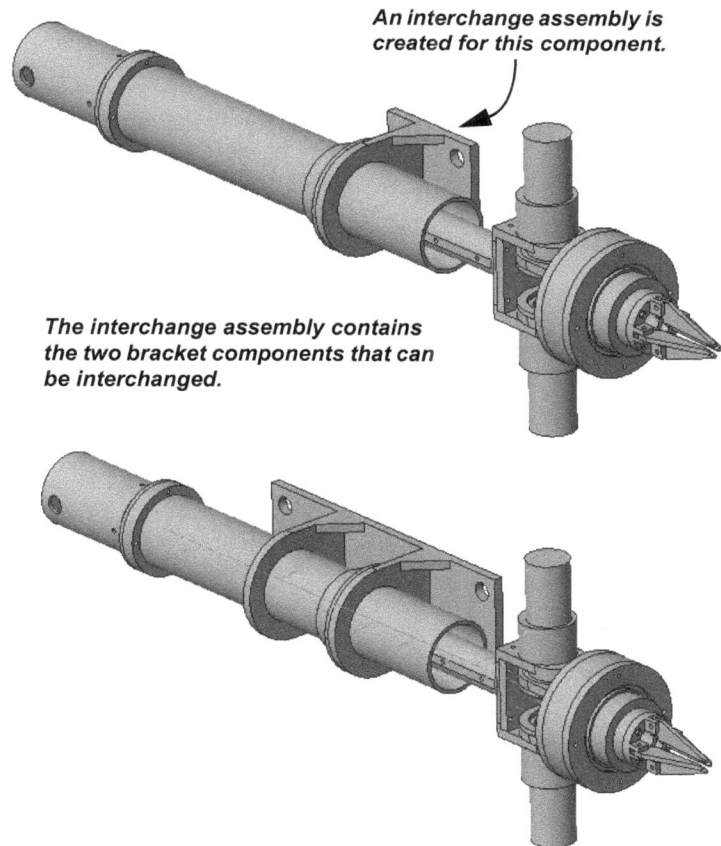

Figure 7–25

Task 1 - Investigate how the mounting bracket was assembled.

1. Change the working directory to the *Functional_Interchange* folder.

2. Open **robot_arm.asm**.

3. Set the model display as follows:

   - ⚒ *(Datum Display Filters)*: ⟋ₒ (Axis Display) Only

   - ⤳ *(Spin Center)*: Off

   - ⬜ *(Display Style)*: ▱ (Shading With Edges)

4. Select **grip_mounting_bracket.prt** in the Model Tree and click ✎ (Edit Definition) in the mini toolbar.

5. Select the Placement panel.

6. Select the first Coincident constraint. The two aligning axes (**A_1** of the **GRIP_HOUSING** and **A_1** of the **GRIP_MOUNTING_BRACKET**) highlight in the main window, as shown in Figure 7–26.

7. Select the second Coincident constraint. The two surfaces highlight in the main window, as shown in Figure 7–26.

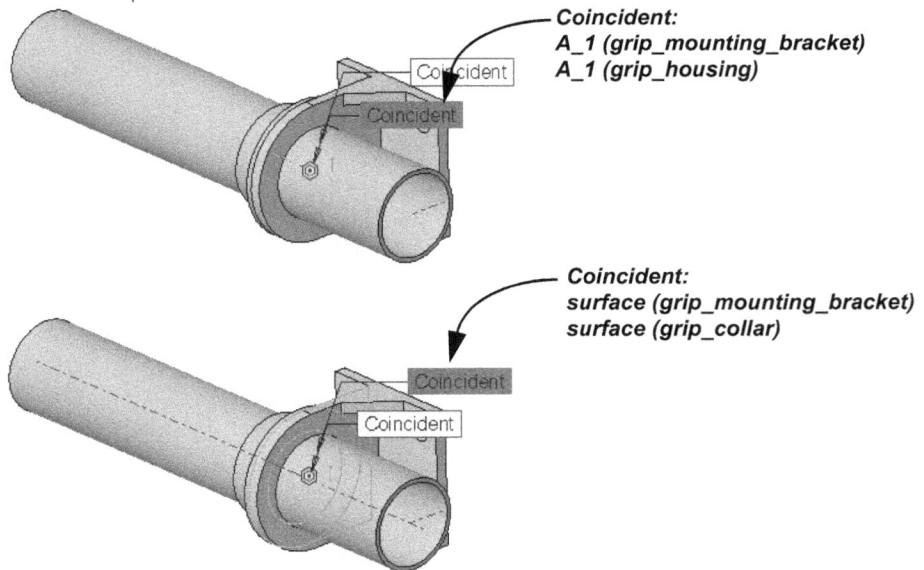

Coincident:
A_1 (grip_mounting_bracket)
A_1 (grip_housing)

Coincident:
surface (grip_mounting_bracket)
surface (grip_collar)

Figure 7–26

8. Click ✕ (Cancel) to close the *Component Placement* dashboard.

Task 2 - Open an alternate mounting bracket.prt.

1. Open **GRIP_MOUNTING_BRACKET2.PRT**.

Design Considerations

This component is functionally equivalent to the mounting bracket that is currently assembled in **ROBOT_ARM.ASM**. The part displays as shown in Figure 7–27. The intent of the assembly is to be able to replace the two brackets, depending on the design requirements. This is accomplished using an interchange assembly.

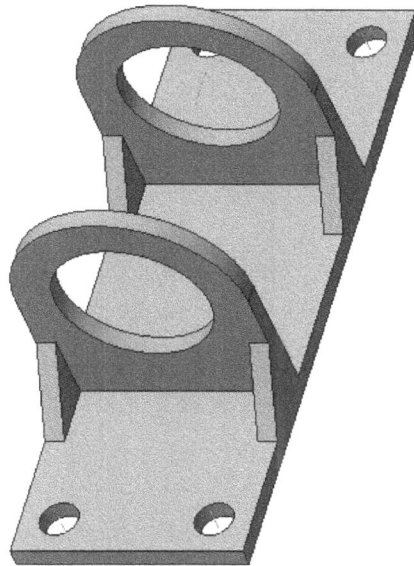

Figure 7–27

2. Close the window.

Task 3 - Create an interchange group.

1. In the Quick Access toolbar, click ☐ (New). The New dialog box opens.

2. Set the following:

    - *Type:* **Assembly**
    - *Sub-type:* **Interchange**
    - *File name:* **BRACKETS**

3. Click **OK** and click ⛭ (Functional) in the *Model* tab.

4. Double-click on **grip_mounting_bracket.prt**. The part displays. No constraints are required for this operation.

5. Click ⛭ (Functional).

6. Double-click on **grip_mounting_bracket2**. The *Component Placement* tab opens.

7. Click ✔ (OK) in the *Component Placement* dashboard to package the component.

The **grip_mounting_bracket2** component should now be packaged in the assembly, as shown in Figure 7–28.

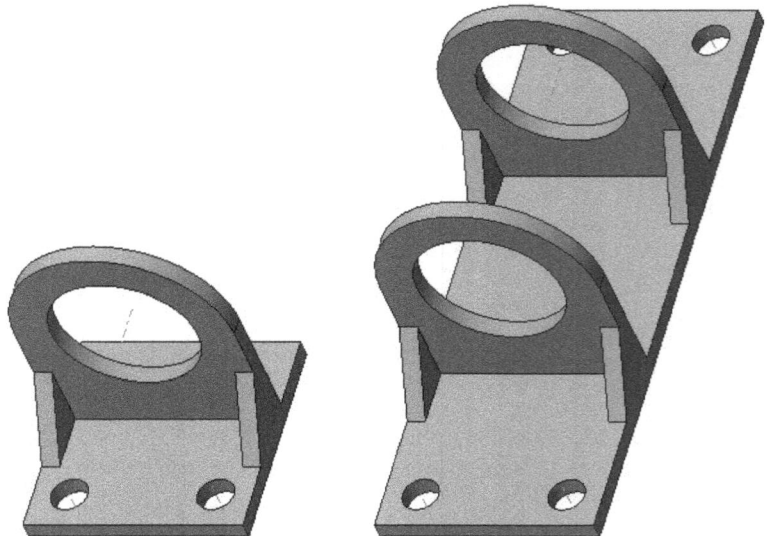

Figure 7–28

Task 4 - Assign tags for automatic assembly.

1. Click ⌐ (Reference Tag). The Reference Tag dialog box opens as shown in Figure 7–29.

Figure 7–29

2. While pressing <Ctrl>, select **axis A_1** in the **grip_mounting_bracket** component, and select **axis A_1** in the **grip_mounting_bracket2** component, as shown in Figure 7–30.

Select axis A_1 in the grip_mounting_bracket2 component.

Select axis A_1 in the grip_mounting_bracket component.

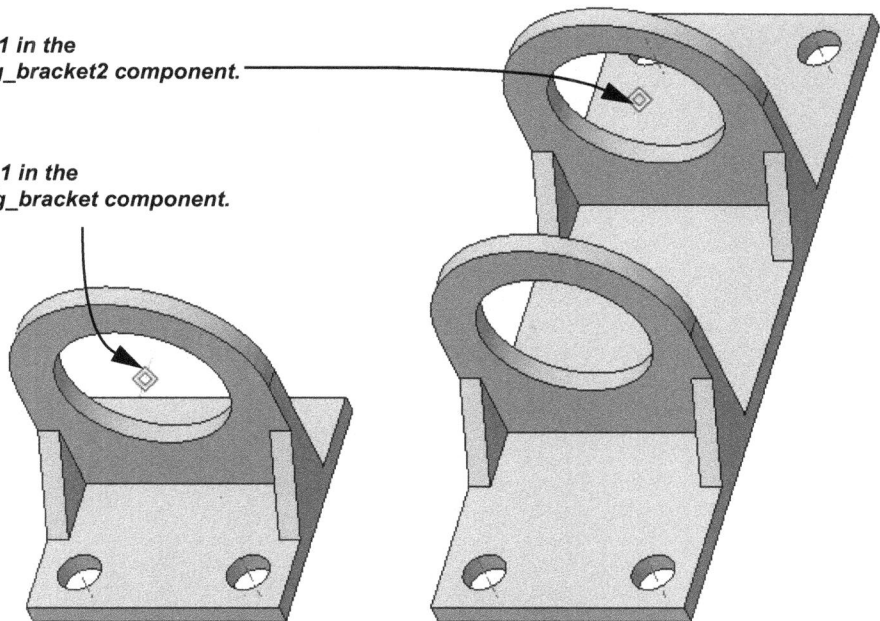

Figure 7–30

- The references are listed in the Reference Tag dialog box, as shown in Figure 7–31.

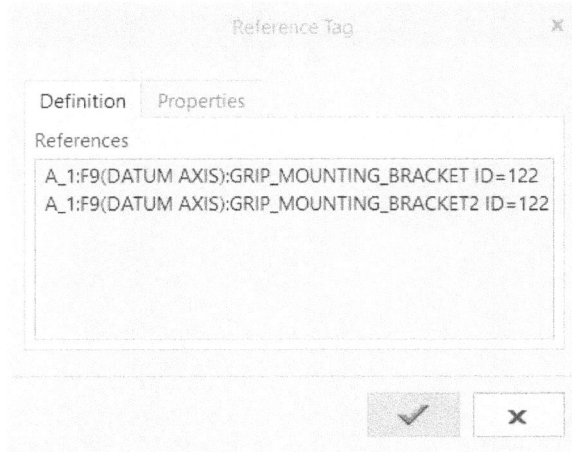

Figure 7–31

3. In the *Properties* tab, set the reference tag *Name* to **AXIS**, as shown in Figure 7–32.

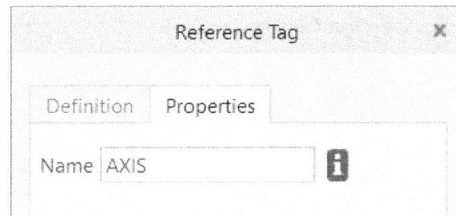

Figure 7–32

4. Click ✓ (OK).

5. Create another reference tag that describes the references used to assemble the mounting bracket to the **grip_collar**, as shown in Figure 7–33. Select the two hidden surfaces while holding <Ctrl>.

Select the back hidden surface in the grip_mounting_bracket2 component.

Select the back hidden surface in the grip_mounting_bracket component.

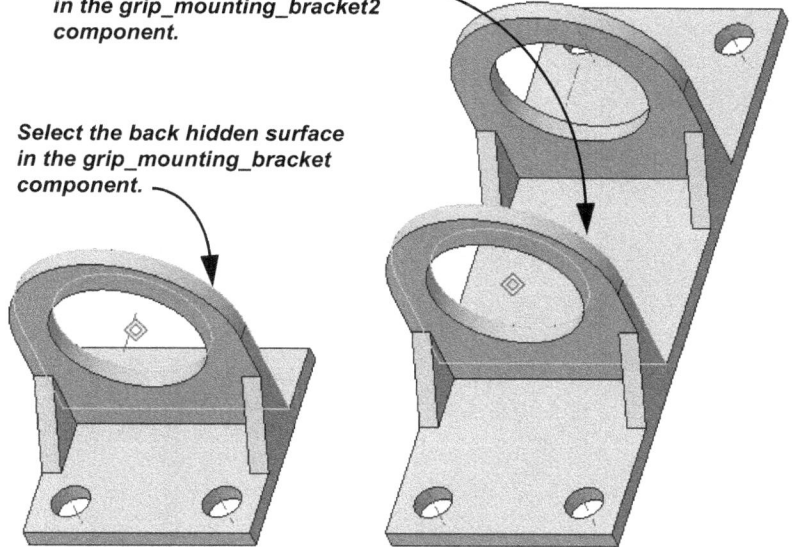

Figure 7–33

6. Set the reference tag *Name* to **SURFACES**.

7. Click ✓ (OK).

8. Save the interchange assembly and close the window.

Task 5 - Replace brackets in the assembly.

1. The **ROBOT_ARM** window should still be open.

2. Select **GRIP_MOUNTING_BRACKET.PRT** in the Model Tree, right-click, and select (Replace Component). The Replace Component dialog box opens, as shown in Figure 7–34.

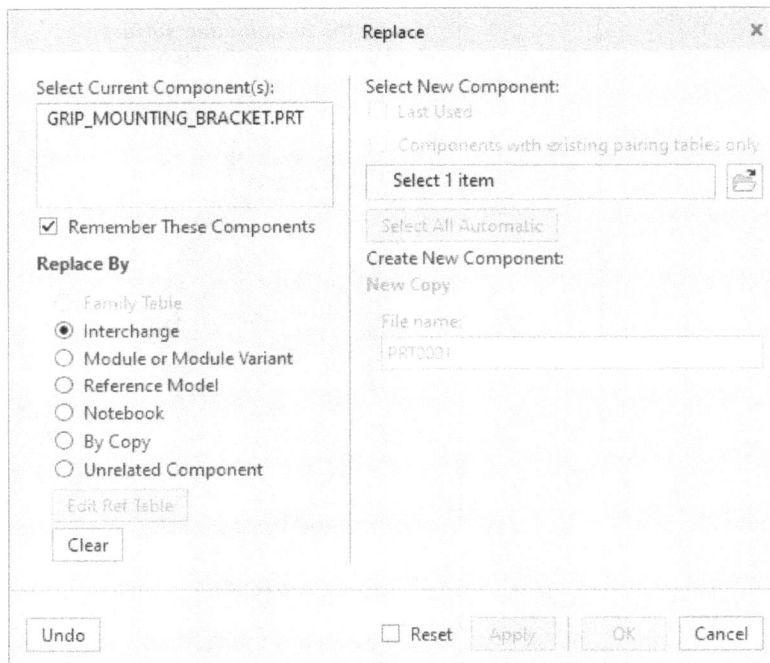

Figure 7–34

3. In the Replace dialog box, in the *Replace By* area, ensure that the **Interchange** option is selected.

4. Click 🖼. The Family Tree dialog box opens as shown in Figure 7–35.

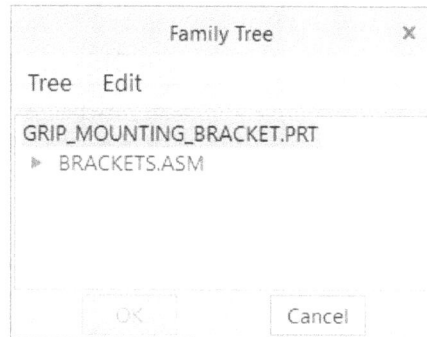

Figure 7–35

5. Expand the **BRACKETS.ASM** interchange assembly, select **GRIP_MOUNTING_BRACKET2.PRT** in the list, and click **OK**.

6. Click **OK** in the Replace dialog box to replace the components. The assembly displays as shown in Figure 7–36.

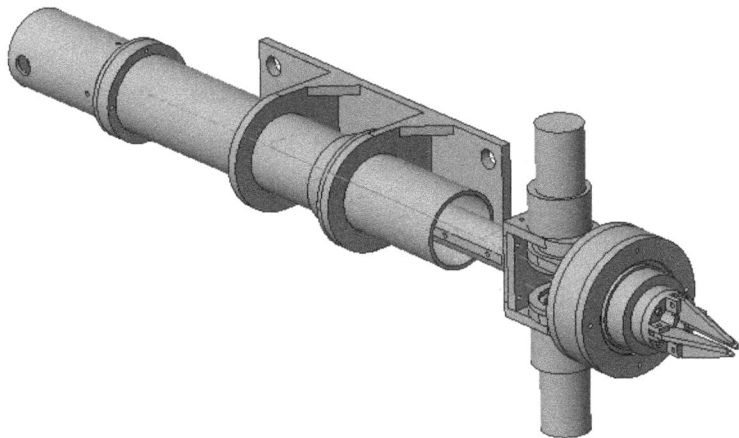

Figure 7–36

7. Save the assembly and erase it from memory.

Practice 7b

Functional Interchange Assemblies II

Practice Objectives

- Create interchange assemblies for parts.
- Create reference tags.
- Replace a part using interchange assemblies.

In this practice, you will open **robot_arm.asm** and create a shrinkwrap of the **gripper_fingers** assembly. You will then create a simplify interchange assembly using the shrinkwrap.

Task 1 - Open the assembly.

1. Change the working directory to the *Simplify_Interchange* folder.

2. Open **robot_arm.asm**.

3. Set the model display as follows:

   - ⸽⸽ *(Datum Display Filters)*: None

   - ⸾ *(Spin Center)*: Off

   - ▢ *(Display Style)*: ▢ (Shading With Edges)

4. In the Model Tree, select **GRIPPER_FINGERS.ASM**, and then click ▣ (Open).

Task 2 - Create a shrinkwrap of the gripper_fingers subassembly.

1. Click **File>Save As>Save a Copy**.

2. From the Type drop-down list, select **Shrinkwrap**, as shown in Figure 7–37.

	Optegra Vis (*.gbf)
	Medusa (*.asc)
	XPatch (*.facet)
▶ Folder Tree	**Shrinkwrap**
	Motion Envlp
File name	ACIS File (*.sat)
	CATIA V4 Model (*.model)
New file name	Parasolid (*.x_t)
Type	Assembly (*.asm)

OK   Can

Figure 7–37

3. Edit the *Name* to **gripper_fingers_shrink** and click **OK**.

4. Leave the default options in the Create Shrinkwrap dialog box, as shown in Figure 7–38.

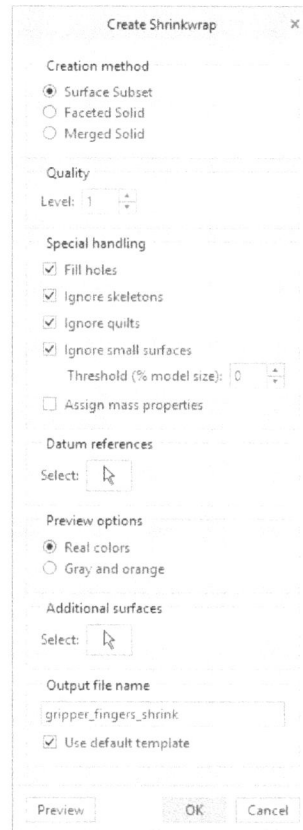

Create Shrinkwrap   ×

Creation method
◉ Surface Subset
◯ Faceted Solid
◯ Merged Solid

Quality
Level: 1

Special handling
☑ Fill holes
☑ Ignore skeletons
☑ Ignore quilts
☑ Ignore small surfaces
    Threshold (% model size): 0
☐ Assign mass properties

Datum references
Select:

Preview options
◉ Real colors
◯ Gray and orange

Additional surfaces
Select:

Output file name
gripper_fingers_shrink
☑ Use default template

Preview   OK   Cancel

Figure 7–38

The message area in the lower left of the Creo Parametric window should read **GRIPPER_FINGERS_S HRINK has been saved***.*

5. Click **OK**.

6. Click **Cancel** in the Create Shrinkwrap dialog box.

7. Close the GRIPPER_FINGERS window to return to the **ROBOT_ARM** assembly.

Task 3 - Create an interchange assembly.

1. In the Quick Access toolbar, click ☐ (New). The New dialog box opens.

2. Set the following:
   - *Type:* **Assembly**
   - *Sub-type:* **Interchange**
   - *Name:* **SIMPLE_GRIP**

3. Click **OK**.

4. Click ⛭ (Functional) in the *Model* tab.

5. Double-click on **gripper_fingers.asm** The assembly displays. No constraints are required for this operation.

6. Click ⛭ (Simplify).

7. Double-click on **gripper_fingers_shrink.prt**. The *Component Placement* dashboard opens.

8. Set the *Constraint Type* to **Default**.

9. Click ✓ (OK) in the *Component Placement* dashboard to package the component.

10. The components sit on top of one another, as shown in Figure 7–39.

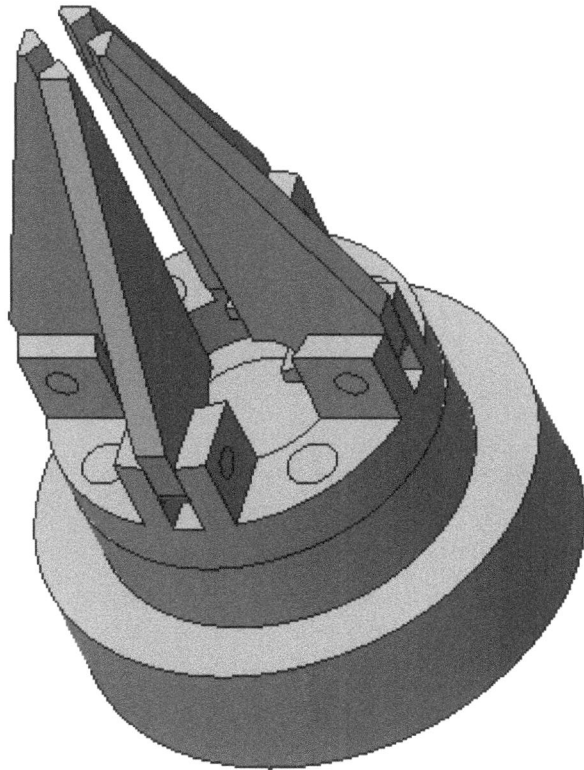

Figure 7–39

11. Click **OK**.

12. Click ⌐⌐ (Simplify).

13. Double-click on **simplify_fingers_closed.prt**. The *Component Placement* dashboard opens.

14. Expand the objects in the Model Tree to expose the datum features, as shown in Figure 7–40.

    SIMPLE_GRIP.ASM
    ▼ GRIPPER_FINGERS.ASM
           ADTM1
           ADTM2
           ADTM3
          ▶ GRIPPER_FINGER_MISS.PRT
          ▶ GRIPPER_MOUNTING_PLATE.PRT
          ▶ GRIPPER_FINGER.PRT
          ▶ GRIPPER_FINGER.PRT
          ▶ GRIPPER_FINGER.PRT
          ▶ GRIPPER_FINGER.PRT
    ▶ GRIPPER_FINGERS_SW.PRT
    ▼ SIMPLIFY_FINGERS_CLOSED.PRT
        ▼ Simplify for GRIPPER_FINGERS.ASM
           DTM1
           DTM2
           DTM3
          ▶ Protrusion id 7
          ▶ Protrusion id 22
           Hole id 41
          ▶ Pattern (Hole)
    ▶ Simplify for GRIPPER_FINGERS.ASM

Figure 7–40

15. Set the *Constraint Type* to **Coincident** and select **ADTM2** and **DTM3**.

16. Click (Change Constraint Orientation) to flip the orientation of the cylinder.

17. Right-click and select **New Constraint**.

18. Select **ADTM1** and **DTM1** and set the *Constraint Type* to **Coincident**.

19. Select **ADTM3** and **DTM2** and set the *Constraint Type* to **Coincident**.

20. Click (OK) in the *Component Placement* dashboard to package the component.

21. The components sit on top of one another, as shown in Figure 7–41.

Figure 7–41

22. Click **OK**.

23. Save the interchange assembly and close the window.

Task 4 - Replace the GRIPPER_FINGERS assembly with simplified versions.

---

1. The **ROBOT_ARM** window should still be open.

2. In the In-graphics toolbar, click (View Manager).

3. Select the *Simp Rep* tab.

4. Click **New**.

5. Edit the *Name* to **Simple_Grip** and press <Enter>.

6. Click on the checkmark next to **ROBOT_ARM.ASM**, which selects all objects to be included, as shown in Figure 7–42.

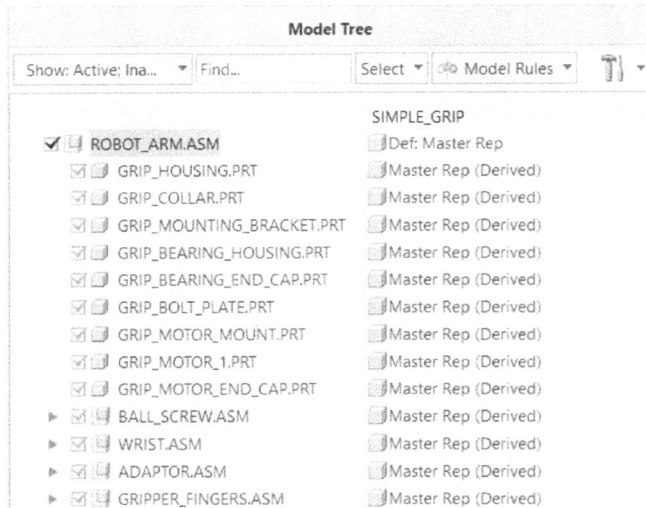

Figure 7–42

7. Select in the *SIMPLE_GRIP* column next to **GRIPPER_FINGERS.ASM** and select **Substitute by Interchange**, as shown in Figure 7–43.

Figure 7–43

8. Select **SIMPLIFY_FINGERS_CLOSED.PRT** in the Family Tree dialog box, as shown in Figure 7–44.

Figure 7–44

9. Click **OK** in the Family Tree dialog box.

10. Click **Open** in the Edit dialog box. The model updates as shown in Figure 7–45.

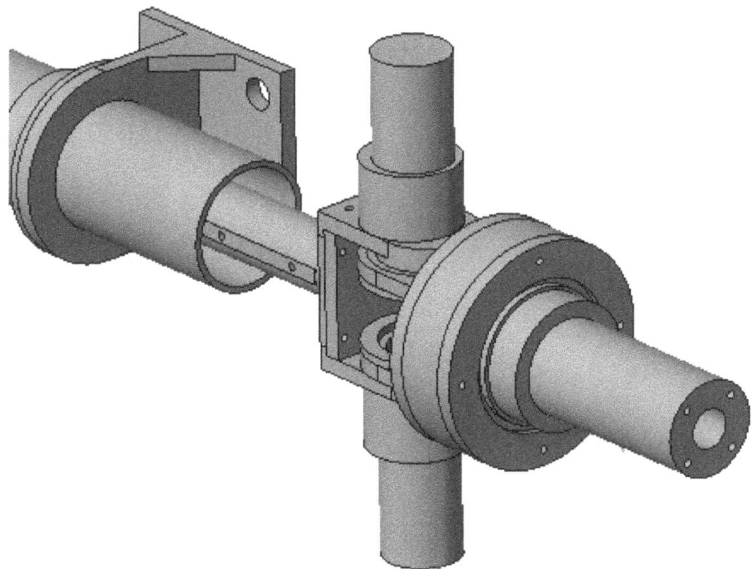

Figure 7–45

11. With **Simple_Grip** still selected in the View Manager, click **Edit>Edit Definition**.

12. Select in the *SIMPLE_GRIP* column next to **GRIPPER_FINGERS.ASM** and select **Substitute by Interchange**,

13. Select **GRIPPERS_FINGERS_SHRINK.PRT** in the Family Tree dialog box

14. Click **OK** in the Family Tree dialog box to replace the components.

15. Click **Open** to finish editing the simplified representation. The assembly displays as shown in Figure 7–46.

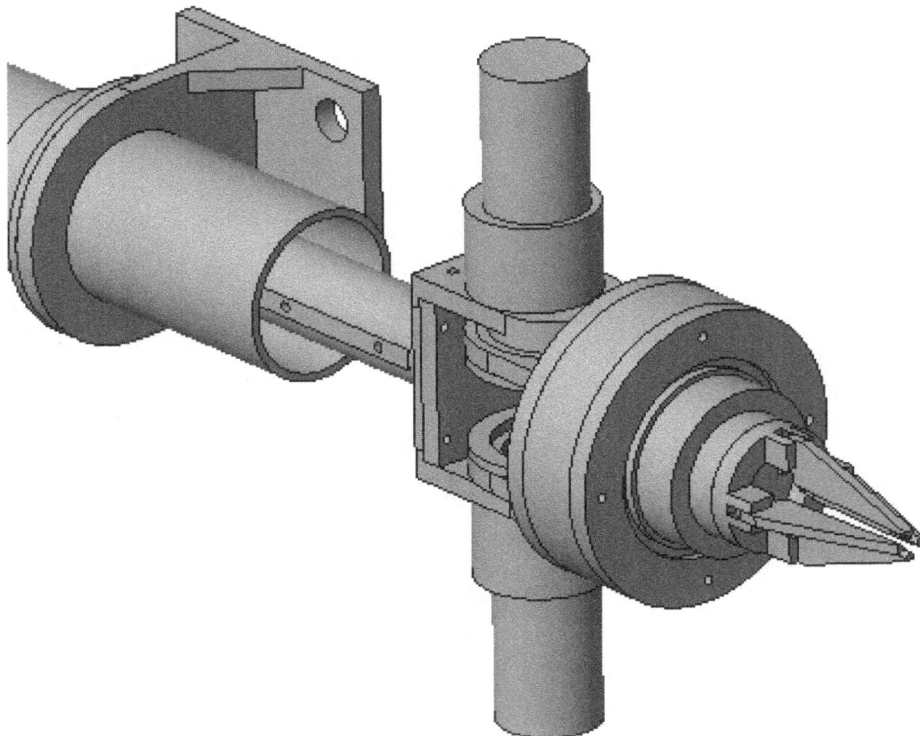

Figure 7–46

16. Close the View Manager, save the assembly, and erase it from memory.

Chapter Review Questions

1. Using Interchange Assemblies, components can quickly be replaced in design assemblies without the need to constrain the replacing component again.

   a. True

   b. False

2. Assigning reference tags enables automatic placement when components are replaced with other members of the interchange assembly.

   a. True

   b. False

3. A simplify component in an interchange assembly is assembled using reference tags.

   a. True

   b. False

4. What is the difference between a *Functional* interchange assembly and a *Simplify* interchange assembly?

   a. Functional replaces a component with a less detailed version while Simplify replaces a component that has a different use.

   b. Simplify replaces a component with a less detailed version while Functional replaces a component that has a different use.

   c. Simplify creates a Shrinkwrap of the assembly.

Answers: 1.a, 2.a, 3.b, 4.b

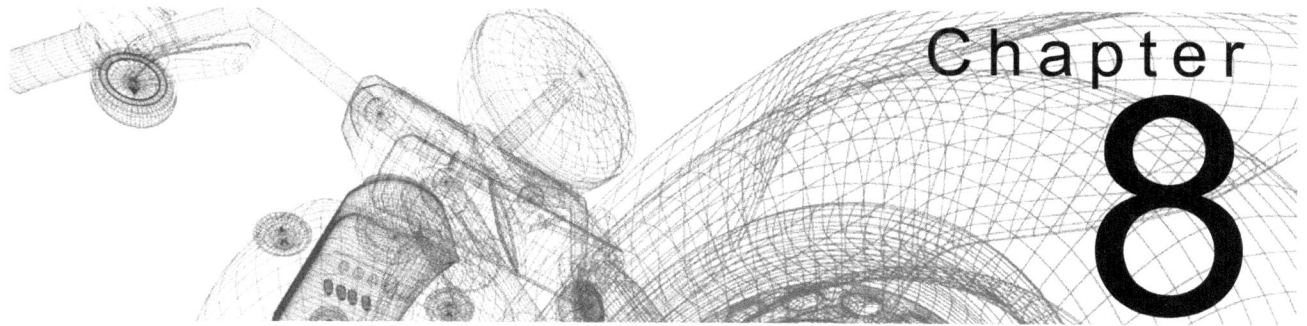

Skeleton Models

Skeleton techniques are used in Assembly mode to create an underlying structure for assembly models. They generally consist of datum and surface features to which assembly components are constrained and geometry can be created.

Learning Objectives in This Chapter

- Discover how the skeleton model can be used to help avoid unwanted parent/child relationships, incorporate motion, and create spatial claims for conceptual parts.
- Learn how to create skeleton models using sketches, curves, datum features, and surface geometry.
- Review the properties of a skeleton model.
- Understand how motion skeletons can be used to define motion in an assembly.
- Learn how to create motion and body skeletons.
- Learn how to copy applicable geometry and connections from the motion skeleton into the various body skeletons.

8.1 Skeleton Models

A skeleton model acts as a 3D layout of an assembly and facilitates a top-down design strategy. The skeletal structure is defined by creating part-level datum, surface, and solid features in the skeleton model.

A skeleton model can be used to control parent/child relationships, incorporate motion, define spatial claims, and create geometry. By default, only a single skeleton can exist in an assembly. Subassemblies can also contain a skeleton. However, it must be created in the subassembly.

Parent/Child Relationships

By assembling to a skeleton instead of referencing other components, the likelihood of creating unwanted parent/child relationships between components is reduced. Using this technique makes operations, such as suppressing, deleting, and interchanging components, easier because fewer dependency relationships exist between the components.

Consider suppressing components as you are selecting your assembly references to ensure that references are only established with the skeleton model.

In the example shown in Figure 8–1, the component is being assembled to datum features in a skeleton model. Additional components are assembled that only reference the skeleton, so that no parent/child relationships are established between components.

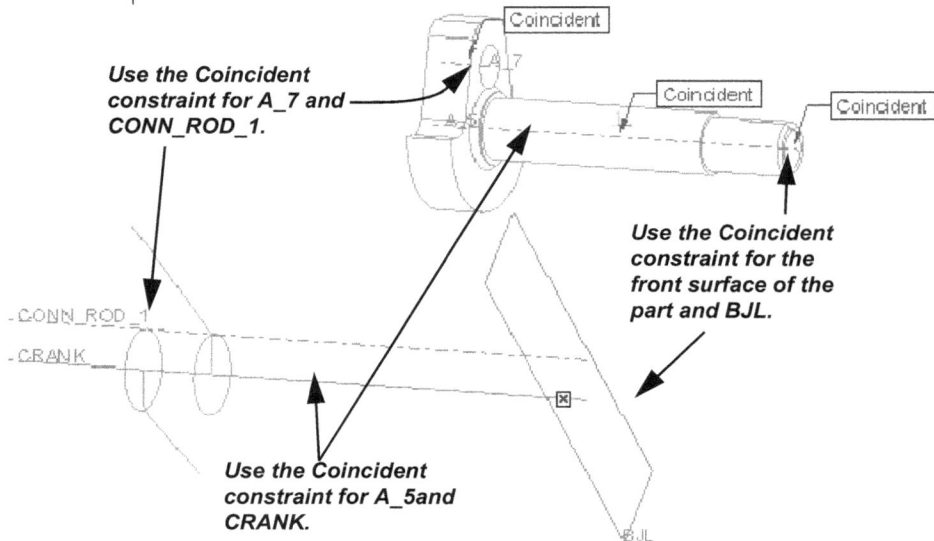

Figure 8–1

Incorporating Motion

When creating the skeleton, the capacity for motion can be incorporated into the design using dimensioning and construction techniques. You can simulate motion by modifying the skeleton model dimensions in the assembly instead of modifying the components or assembly constraints.

In the example shown in Figure 8–2, the assembly is created by assembling components to the features in the skeleton model. Changes made to the angular dimension value affect the position of components in the top-level assembly. This is because the linear entity in the skeleton was used as a reference when assembling the components.

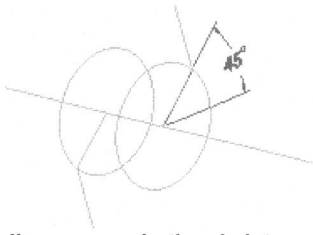

The linear curve in the skeleton was dimensioned using an angular value.

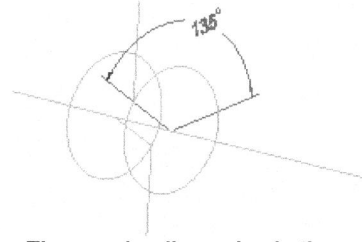

The angular dimension in the skeleton can be modified.

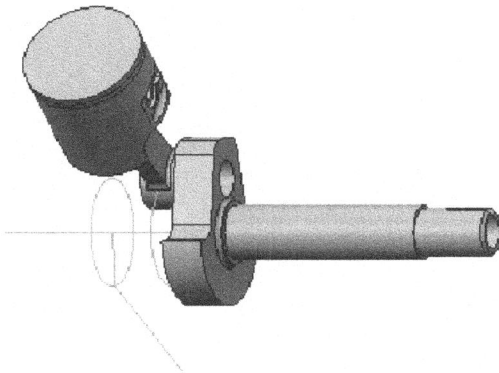

The components in the assembly were assembled referencing the skeleton.

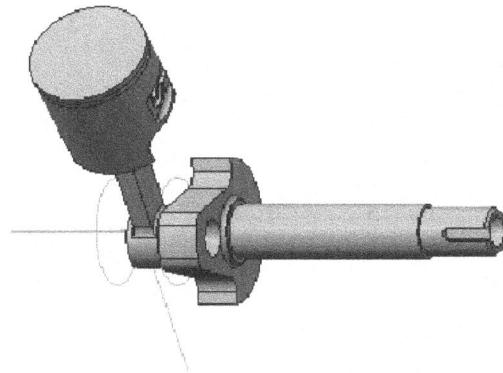

The new dimension value affects the component's positions in the assembly, simulating rotational motion.

Figure 8–2

Spatial Claims

A skeleton can be used to create conceptual parts that define regions of an assembly, called *spatial claims*. These regions represent the volume to be occupied or avoided by components that have yet to be created. The skeleton model representing the volume of these regions can then be referenced during the construction of these components, to ensure that they fall in the location and volume limitations.

For example, the skeleton model shown at the top of Figure 8–3 represents the base and electrical components for a power assembly. Neither of these subassemblies has yet been designed. However, their size is accounted for when the top-level assembly is created, as shown at the bottom of Figure 8–3.

This surface feature is created in the skeleton to represent the electrical subassembly.

This surface feature is created in the skeleton to represent the base. subassembly.

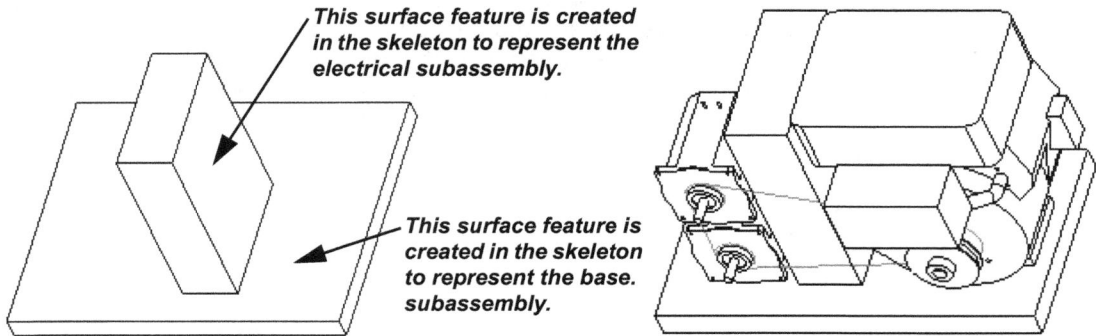

Figure 8–3

8.2 Geometry Creation

The process of creating geometry from the skeleton model is covered in more detail in Chapter 9: Designing in Context, but this section provides a brief overview.

In a top-down design environment, component geometry can be created in the context of the assembly. The benefit of this technique is that references can be made between components to create the required geometry. However, as the number of references increase, they can become difficult to organize and control. In this case, creating or copying cross-referenced geometry from the skeleton model creates a centralized location for exchanging information between assembly components. The reference geometry is easily distinguished from the final assembly geometry because it is in a single location.

The solid model shown on the right in Figure 8–4 is created in the assembly, referencing datum points **PNT0** and **PNT1** in the skeleton model, as shown in the sketched section on the left. Additional components can be created in the assembly, referencing the same skeleton.

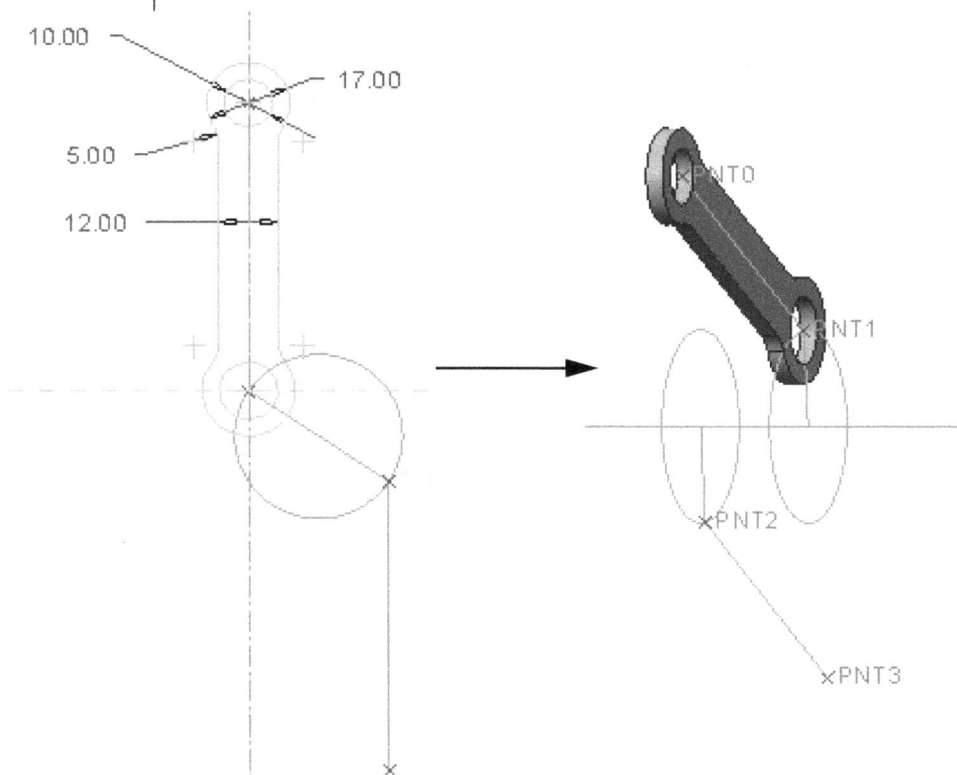

Figure 8–4

To create a skeleton model, click ⊞ (Create) in the *Model* tab. Select **Skeleton Model** in the Component Create dialog box, as shown on the left in Figure 8–5. Enter a name for the skeleton and click **OK**. The Creation Options dialog box opens as shown on the right in Figure 8–5.

- The default skeleton name consists of the parent assembly model name with **skel** appended to it (e.g., **crank_skel.prt**). You can also enter a user-defined name for the skeleton.

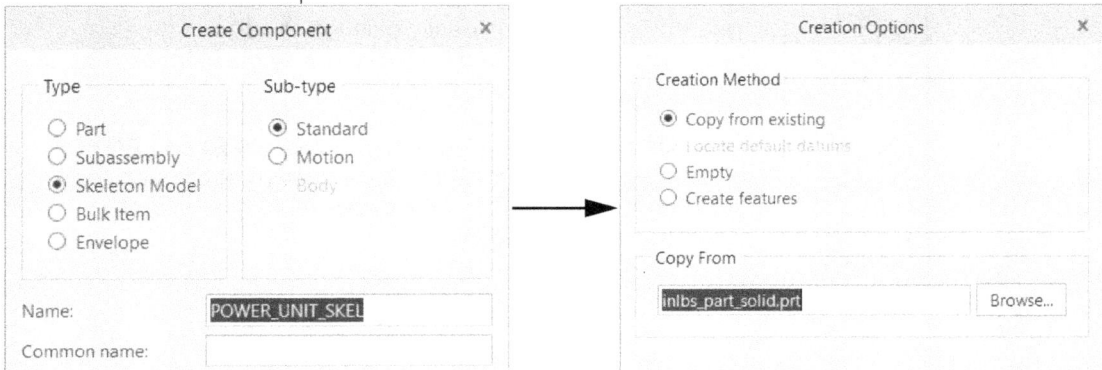

Figure 8–5

Skeleton models can be created using one of the following three options:

- **Copy from existing:** Copies features from an existing model. This option is valuable when the skeleton model is created before the top-level assembly.

- **Empty:** Creates a blank part file in which all of the features, including the default datum planes, must be created.

- **Create features:** Creates a feature in the skeleton model at the assembly level. This option can be used to create the default datum planes for the skeleton model by selecting three perpendicular planes in the assembly to copy into the skeleton.

The skeleton model always exists as the first component in the assembly Model Tree. Even if it is created after other components, the skeleton is placed before the assembly default datum planes and any previously assembled components.

If the assembly contains existing components, an origin to origin constraint is added. This constraint aligns the origin (the point of intersection of the three default datum planes) of the first component to the origin of the skeleton model. This alignment can result in the reorientation of the first component and its children. You can manually redefine the component's placement constraints to correct the orientation. However, you can avoid this situation entirely by creating the skeleton model before assembling any components.

Skeleton models display with a unique icon in the Model Tree to distinguish them from other components. The Model Tree icons for parts, subassemblies, and skeletons are shown in Figure 8–6.

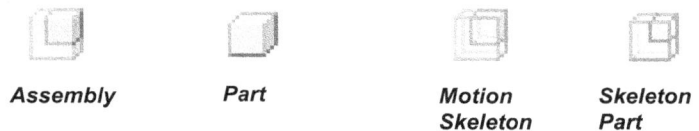

Assembly   *Part*   *Motion Skeleton*   *Skeleton Part*

Figure 8–6

To define the geometry for a skeleton created in the assembly, use either of the following techniques:

• Activate the skeleton and create the geometry within the context of the assembly.

• Open the skeleton in Part mode and create the geometry.

Any type of feature can be added to the skeleton model, including solid and sheet metal features. However, skeleton models should only consist of surface and datum features.

8.3 Skeleton Properties

Skeleton models in Creo Parametric have the following properties:

- By default, only one skeleton model can be created for an assembly. By setting the **multiple_skeletons_allowed** config option to **Yes**, you can have more than one skeleton belonging to an assembly.

- Skeleton models can exist in subassemblies, but must be created at the subassembly level.

- Skeleton models have a default name of **assembly_name_skel.prt**, where **assembly_name** is the name of the parent assembly model. You can use an alternative name if required. If you are creating multiple skeletons, the default name is incremented for each skeleton (**assembly_name_ skel0002.prt**).

- Skeleton models can be created at any time, but they are automatically reordered to display before the first component and feature in the assembly.

- Assembly features, such as cuts and holes, do not intersect skeleton models.

- Skeleton models are not included in the mass property calculations.

- Skeleton models can be filtered out of the assembly bill of material listings.

- The display of skeleton models can be removed from assembly drawings and simplified representations.

- By default, the color of all of the solid and surface geometry in the skeleton is medium blue. This color is controlled by the **skeleton_model_default_color** config option. The color is defined by three values (ranging between 0 and 100), which specify the percentages of red, green, and blue. This option only applies to skeleton models that are created after the config option is set.

8.4 Motion Skeletons

A motions skeleton is a special type of skeleton that can be used to define mechanisms. When discussing motion skeletons, there are actually two distinct skeleton types involved:

- **Motion Skeleton:** Assembly skeleton in which body skeletons are created.

- **Body Skeleton:** Special part-level skeleton created within the context of the Motion Skeleton.

A motion skeleton is an assembly of body skeletons assembled using mechanism connections. Mechanisms are covered in detail in the *Creo Parametric 7.0: Mechanism Design Guide*.

It is important understood that components are assembled with dynamic connections, such as pin, slider, and bearing connections, rather than rigid connections like coincident, offset, and so on.

For example, Figure 8–7 shows a Pin connection.

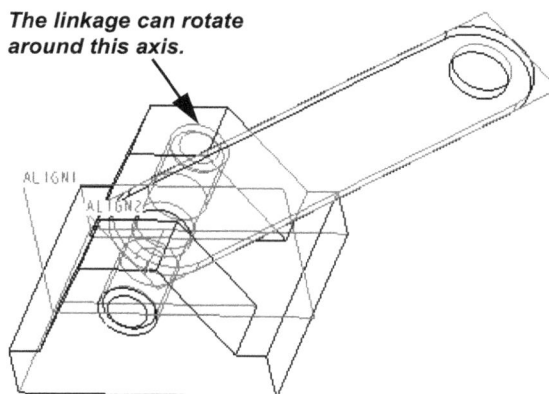

Figure 8–7

Figure 8–8 shows a Slider connection.

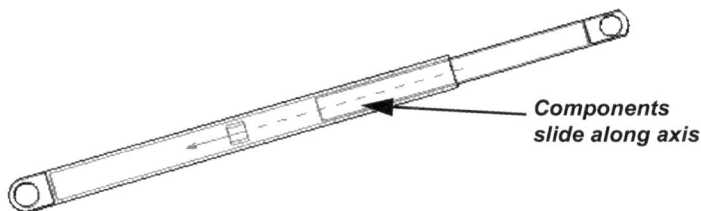

Figure 8–8

Rather than connecting components to one another, they can be connected as to the body skeletons in the Motion Skeleton. In fact, the body skeletons can be used to create the geometry for the components, as shown in Figure 8–9.

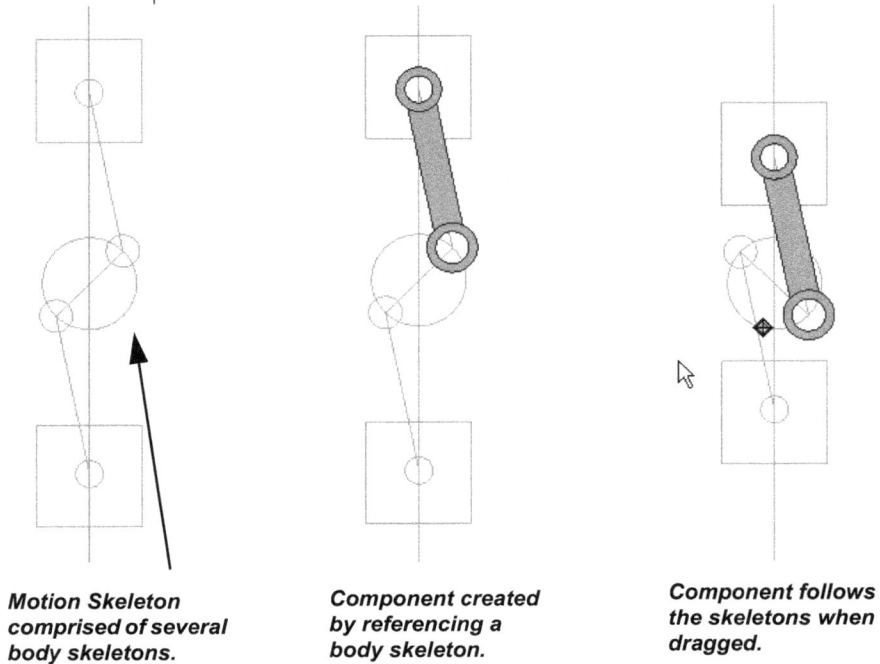

Motion Skeleton comprised of several body skeletons.

Component created by referencing a body skeleton.

Component follows the skeletons when dragged.

Figure 8–9

To create a motion skeleton, create or open an assembly, then click ⬚ (Create) in the *Model* tab. The New Component dialog box opens. Set the *Type* to **Skeleton Model** and the *Sub-type* to **Motion**, as shown in Figure 8–10.

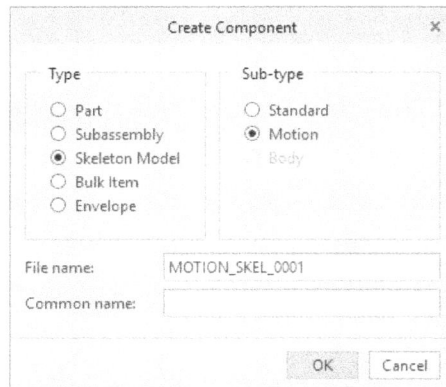

Figure 8–10

Enter the name and click **OK**. It is good practice to use a common naming convention for skeletons, to easily find them in the model. In this course, you will append the names with **_SKEL**.

The Creation Options dialog box opens. You can use a default template for the motion skeleton by selecting **Copy from existing** and selecting the template to copy from.

The motion skeleton does not require any assembly references, and is added as an assembly, as shown in Figure 8–11.

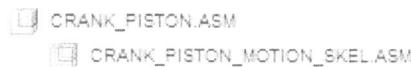

CRANK_PISTON.ASM
CRANK_PISTON_MOTION_SKEL.ASM

Figure 8–11

The skeleton geometry is added directly to the motion skeleton assembly. You can either right-click on the motion skeleton assembly and select **Activate** to work in the context of the top-level assembly, or right-click and select **Open** to work on the motion skeleton outside of the top-level assembly.

The geometry of the skeleton will include sketched entities representing a ground body, mechanism bodies, and joint connections.

- **Ground Body:** Any components that do not move.

- **Mechanism Body:** Any components in the assembly that move.

- **Joint Connections:** The following joints can be defined:

Pin Connection	Defined at the intersection of entities or circle centers.
Ball or Cylinder Connections	Can be selected wherever a Pin connection is defined.
Bearing Connection	Defined where a line meets another line, other than at an endpoint.
Slot Connection	Defined where a line endpoint intersects an arc or circle.
Slider Connection	Defined where a line lies on another line.

For each body, you can create a body skeleton. A body skeleton is created in the Motion Skeleton dialog box by clicking

 (Create) and selecting **Body** in the Create Component dialog box, as shown in Figure 8–12.

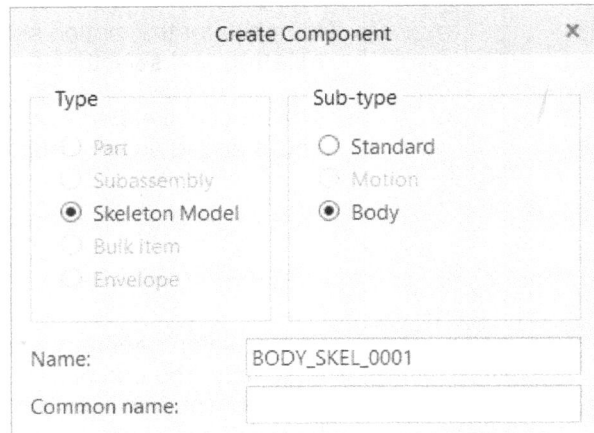

Figure 8–12

You can use a default template or create an **Empty** component. The BODY DEFINITION dialog box opens, as shown in Figure 8–13.

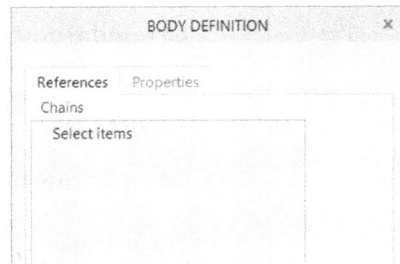

Figure 8–13

You then select the sketched entities you want to include in the body skeleton, from the motion skeleton, and it is copied into the body skeleton in the form of a Copy Geometry feature.

Geometry defined in the motion skeleton can only be used in one body skeleton, so you need to ensure that you sketch all of the entities required. For example, the geometry shown in Figure 8–14 will be used to control a journal bearing, a connecting rod, and a piston. In order to accomplish that, multiple circles are sketched on top of one another, so that when a circle is selected for one body skeleton, there is another circle is available for the next body skeleton.

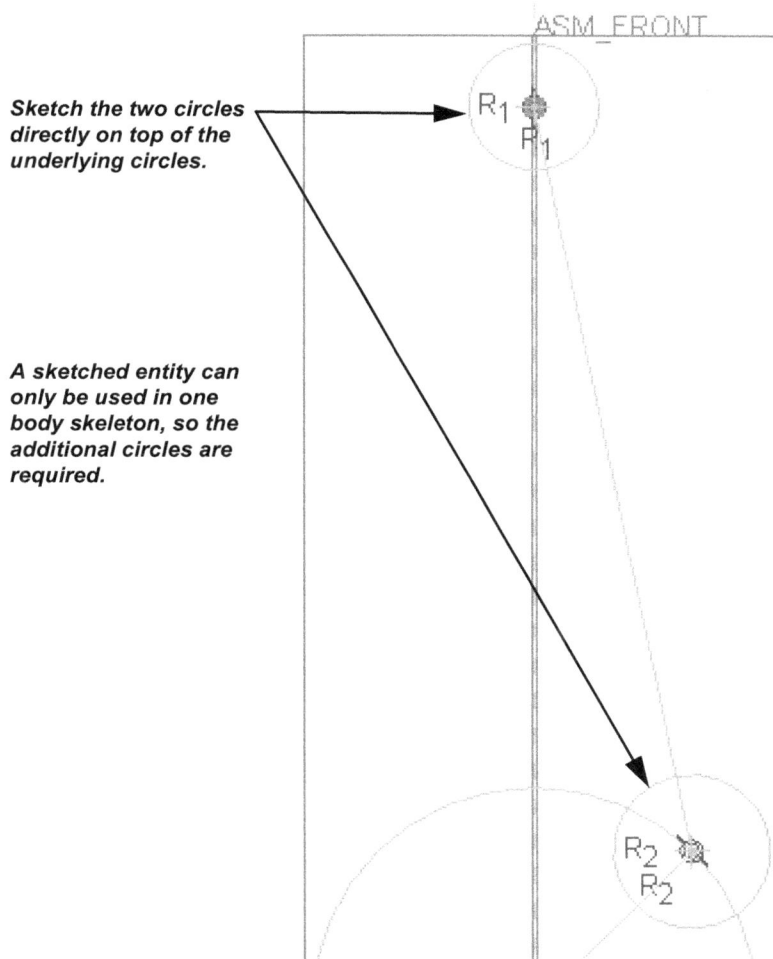

Sketch the two circles directly on top of the underlying circles.

A sketched entity can only be used in one body skeleton, so the additional circles are required.

Figure 8–14

The selected entities are listed in the BODY DEFINITION dialog box, as shown in Figure 8–15.

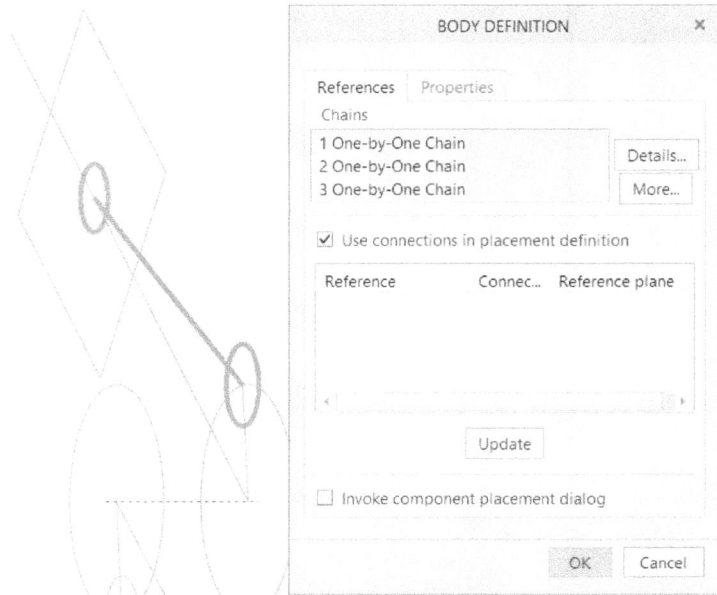

Figure 8–15

If you click **Update**, the system evaluates the sketched entities and updates the list with potential connections based on the geometry, as shown in Figure 8–16.

*Some connections, such as **Pin**, have a drop-down from which you can select other connections such as **Cylinder** or **Ball**.*

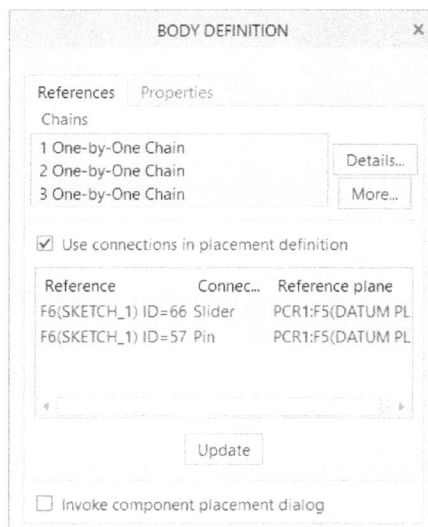

Figure 8–16

You can select any number of the possible connections to keep or remove. To remove them, right-click in the *Reference* column and select **Remove**. Generally, you will want to leave one connection to avoid ambiguity.

Once you click **OK**, the geometry and connections are copied into the body skeleton.

You can verify the motion of the assembly by clicking 🖑 (Drag Components) and selecting any sketched geometry, Move the cursor to view the range of motion.

Practice 8a	# Creating a Skeleton Part

Practice Objectives

- Create a skeleton for assembly layout.
- Create a space claim.

In this practice, you will create an assembly that contains a skeleton. The skeleton model is created with non-solid features, and helps in capturing information at the top level of an assembly so that it can be used to assemble or create additional geometry. The skeleton that you will create must capture the design intent of the location of a tank model and the centerline and location of a pipe part. In addition, no components can extend beyond the sides of the tank. The skeleton model that you will create in this practice is shown in Figure 8–17.

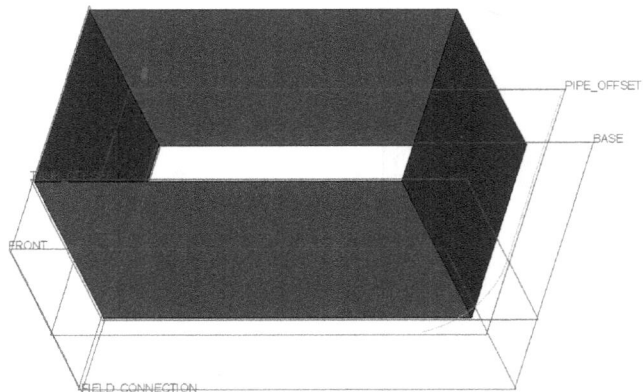

Figure 8–17

This skeleton model is also used in a future practice to create and assemble components, as shown in Figure 8–18.

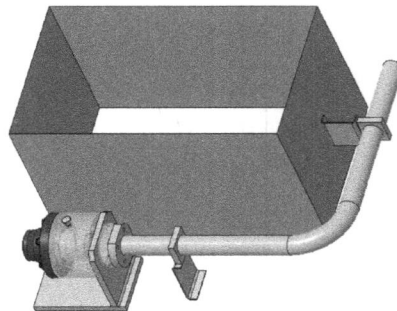

Figure 8–18

Task 1 - Create an assembly.

1. Change the working directory to the *Skeleton_Part* folder.

2. Create a new assembly using the default template and edit the *File name* to **power_unit**.

3. Set the model display as follows:

   - ⅍ *(Datum Display Filters)*: All On

   - ⅊ *(Spin Center)*: Off

   - ⌐ *(Display Style)*: ⬜ (Shading With Edges)

4. Select **ASM_DEF_CSYS** and click ⬥ (Hide) in the mini toolbar, as shown in Figure 8–19.

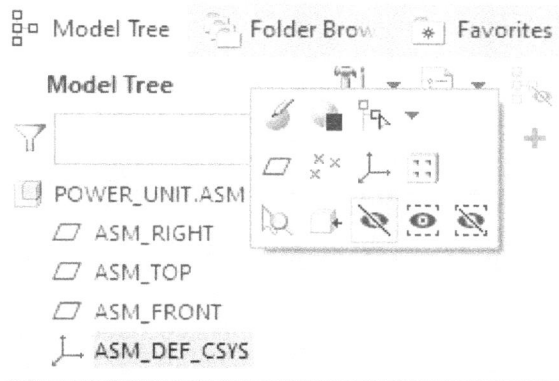

Figure 8–19

5. Save the assembly.

Task 2 - Create a skeleton model.

1. Click 🖳 (Create) and select **Skeleton Model** as the component *Type*, as shown in Figure 8–20.

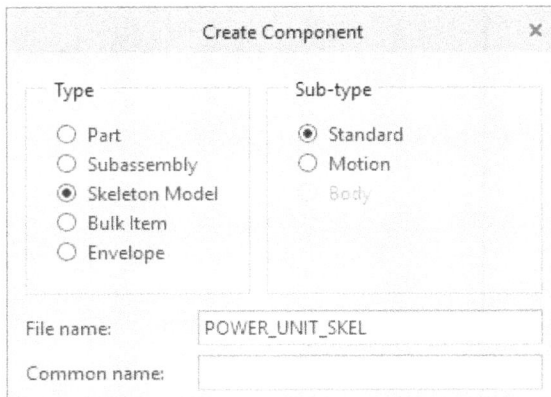

Figure 8–20

Design Considerations

The system provides a default name for the skeleton model, which includes the name of the assembly and the suffix **SKEL**. It is recommended that you use this naming convention because it promotes consistency for all of the skeleton models.

2. Click **OK**. Select **Copy From Existing** and then browse to and select **start_part.prt** in the working directory, as shown in Figure 8–21.

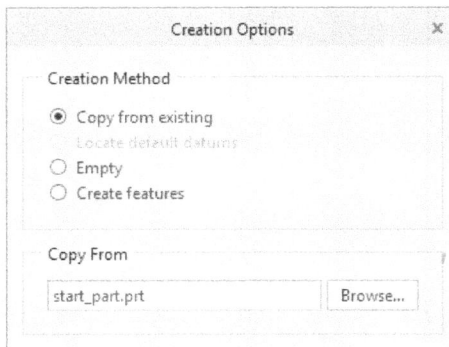

Figure 8–21

Design Considerations

A start part is a part file that holds company-specific datum features and parameters that are included with the creation of a new part. Using start parts for model creation ensures consistency between all of the new parts.

3. Click **OK** to complete the creation of the skeleton. The skeleton model displays at the origin of the assembly, as shown in Figure 8–22.

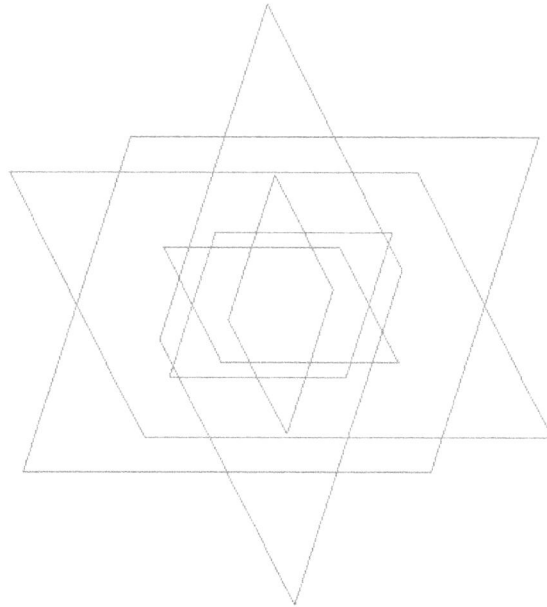

Figure 8–22

The skeleton model does not need to be constrained. In the Model Tree it is listed as the first item, before the default datum planes and coordinate system.

Task 3 - Add information to the skeleton model.

1. In the Model Tree, click on **POWER_UNIT_SKEL.PRT** and click 📂 (Open) in the mini toolbar.

2. Rename datum plane *RIGHT* to **FIELD_CONNECTION** and datum plane *TOP* to **BASE**, as shown in Figure 8–23.

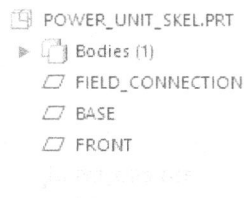

    🗐 POWER_UNIT_SKEL.PRT
    ▶ 🗂 Bodies (1)
       ◻ FIELD_CONNECTION
       ◻ BASE
       ◻ FRONT

Figure 8–23

3. Select the *View* tab and enable ⬦ (Plane Tag Display).

4. Select the *Model* tab.

5. Create a datum plane using the following parameters:

   - *Reference:* datum plane **FRONT**
   - *Offset Translation*: **- 8.0**

6. Use the *Properties* tab to set the new datum plane *Name* to **TANK_OFFSET**.

7. Click **OK**. The plane displays as shown in Figure 8–24.

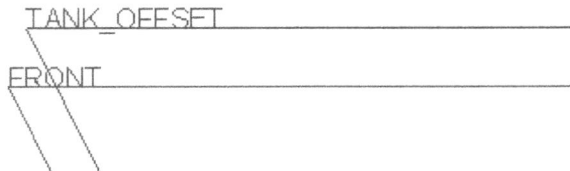

Figure 8–24

Design Considerations

At this point in the design of the skeleton model, you have added some information to the model, giving datum planes meaningful names that are associated with their purpose in the skeleton. The development of a skeleton model is an iterative process. Information is added as soon as it is available, and can continue to be added and/or removed throughout the design cycle of a product.

Task 4 - Create a space claim for the tank.

The location of the tank is known, but the tank is being designed and supplied by a vendor, and is not yet available. In this task, you will create a space claim for the tank so that the design and positioning of other components can continue.

1. Click ⬦ (Extrude).

2. In the *Extrude* dashboard, click ⬦ (Surface).

3. Select in the background and click ⬦ (Define Internal Sketch).

4. Select datum plane **BASE** as the sketch plane and **TANK_OFFSET** as the orientation plane. Set the orientation plane to face the **Bottom**, as shown in Figure 8–25.

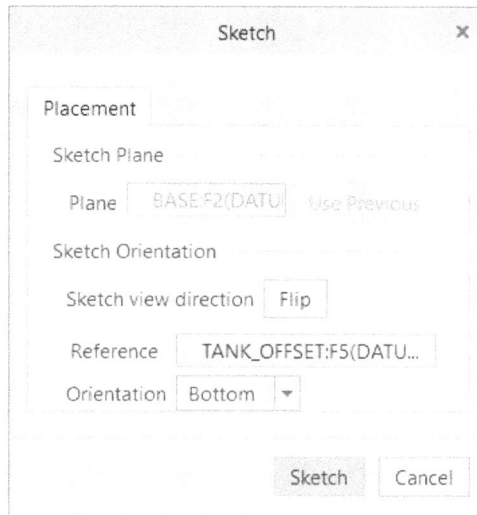

Figure 8–25

5. Sketch a rectangle 35 x 20, as shown in Figure 8–26.

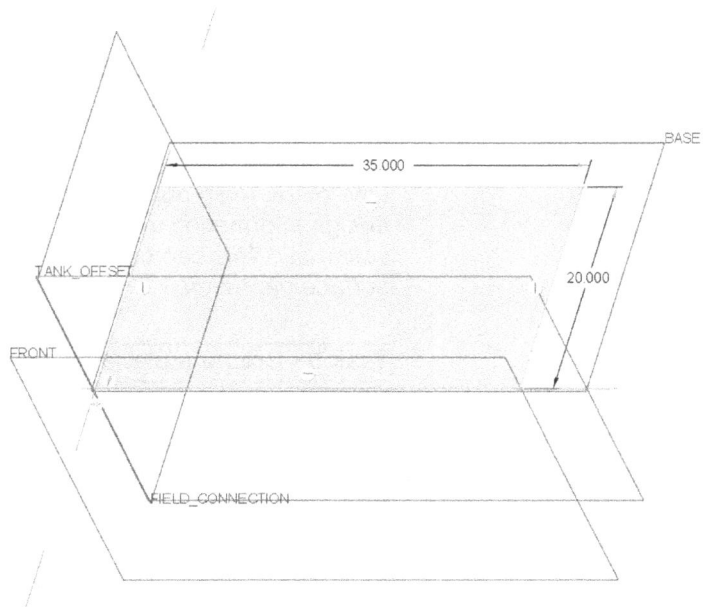

Figure 8–26

6. Click ✓ (OK).

7. Edit the *Depth* to **20**, as shown in Figure 8–27.

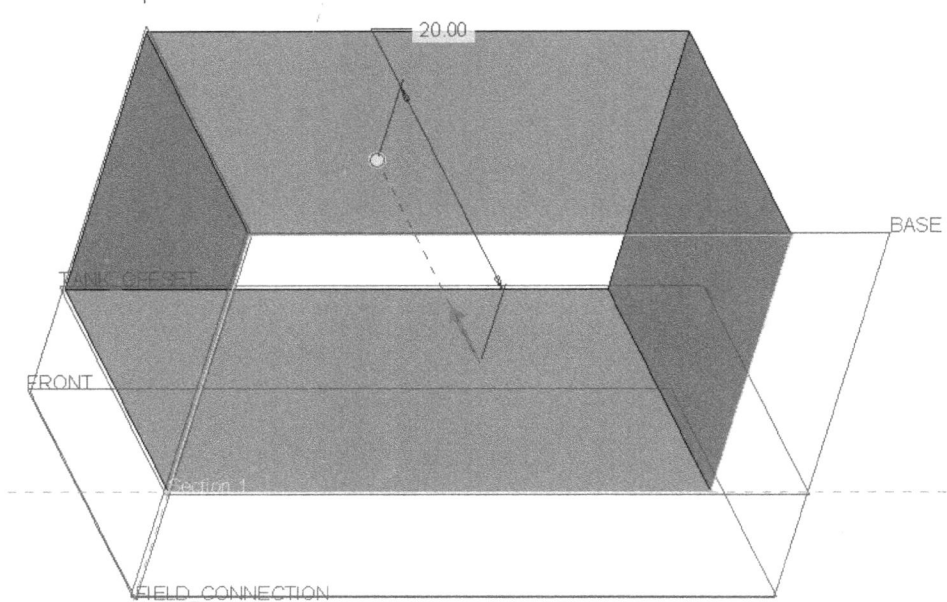

Figure 8–27

8. Click ✓ (OK) to complete the surface.

Design Considerations

Ensure that you have created an extruded surface and not an extruded solid. It is a recommended that skeleton models never hold any solid information that can affect the model mass properties or center of gravity, unless this is otherwise required. One of the main purposes of a skeleton model is to provide design information in one location that can be used to create the assembly. This can be accomplished using datum features and surface geometry.

Task 5 - Create a plane for the pipe.

Design Considerations

Information regarding the positioning of the pipe is known and can be captured in the skeleton model. The design intent of the assembly requires that the pipe be positioned eight units from the base.

1. Create a datum plane with the following settings:

   • *References:* datum plane **BASE**
   • *Offset Translation:* **8.0** (you may need to use a negative value).

2. Edit the new datum plane *Name* to **PIPE_OFFSET**. The
    plane displays as shown in Figure 8–28.

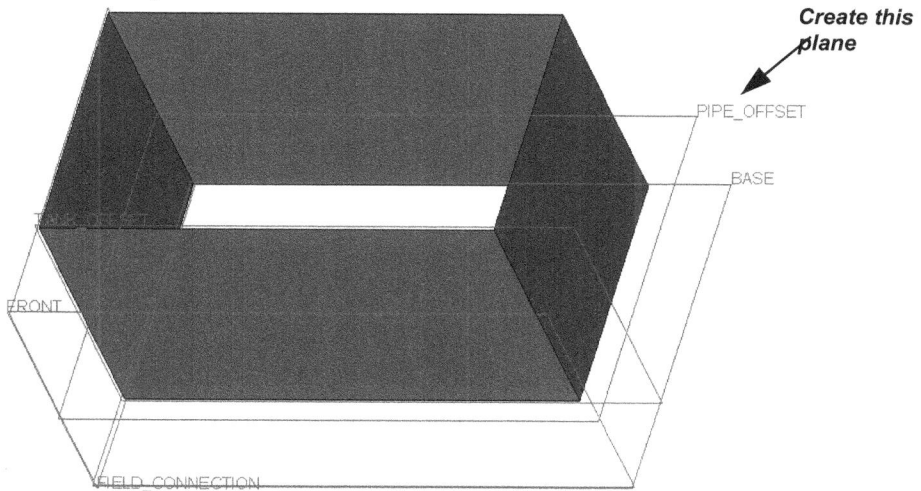

Figure 8–28

Task 6 - Create a path for the pipe.

---

1. Click ▧ (Sketch) to create a sketch. Select datum plane
    PIPE_OFFSET as the sketch plane and **FRONT** as the
    orientation plane. Set the orientation plane to face **Bottom**.

**Design
Considerations**

The design intent of this assembly stipulates that the center line
of the pipe is six units away from the right side of the tank and
eight units away from the front of the tank.

2. In the Setup group of the *Sketch* tab, click ▢ (References), and select the right hand, front and back surfaces of the tank as Sketcher references. Ensure datum plane **FRONT** is also selected as a reference. The selected Sketcher references display as shown in Figure 8–29. Delete the reference to datum plane **FIELD_CONNECTION**, if it was included.

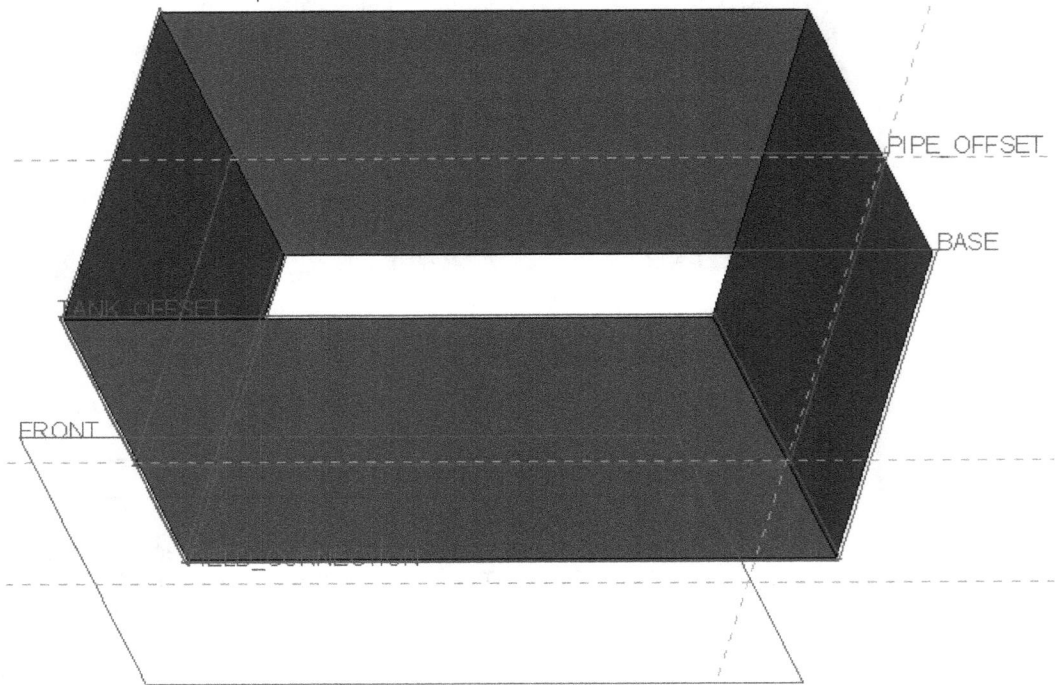

Figure 8–29

3. In the *Sketch* tab, click ▨ (Sketch View).

4. Create the sketch shown in Figure 8–30 using a straight line and an arc.

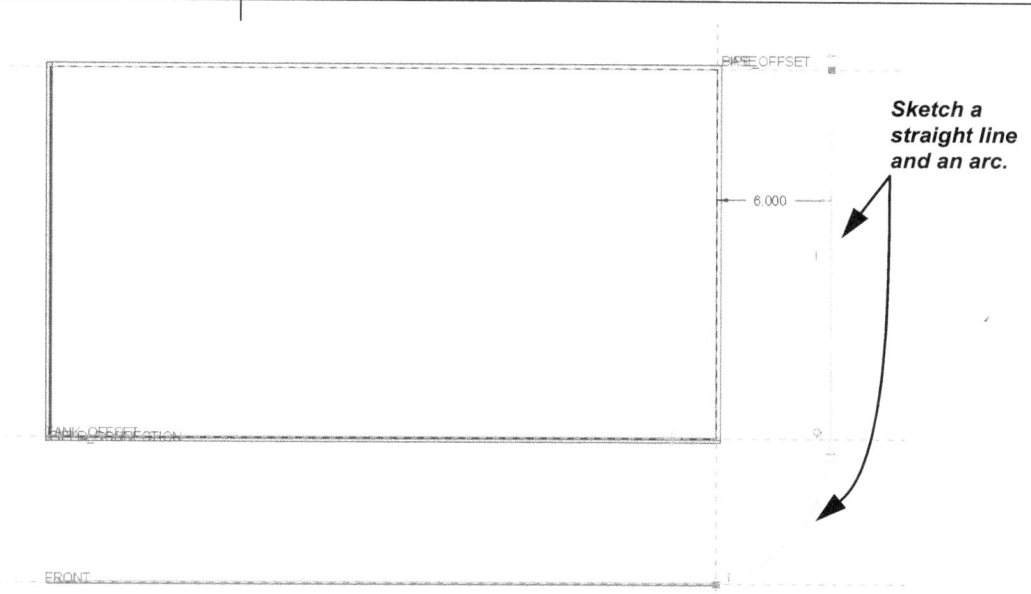

Sketch a straight line and an arc.

PIPE_OFFSET

6.000

TANK_OFFSET

FRONT

Figure 8–30

5. Complete the sketch. The skeleton model displays as shown in Figure 8–31.

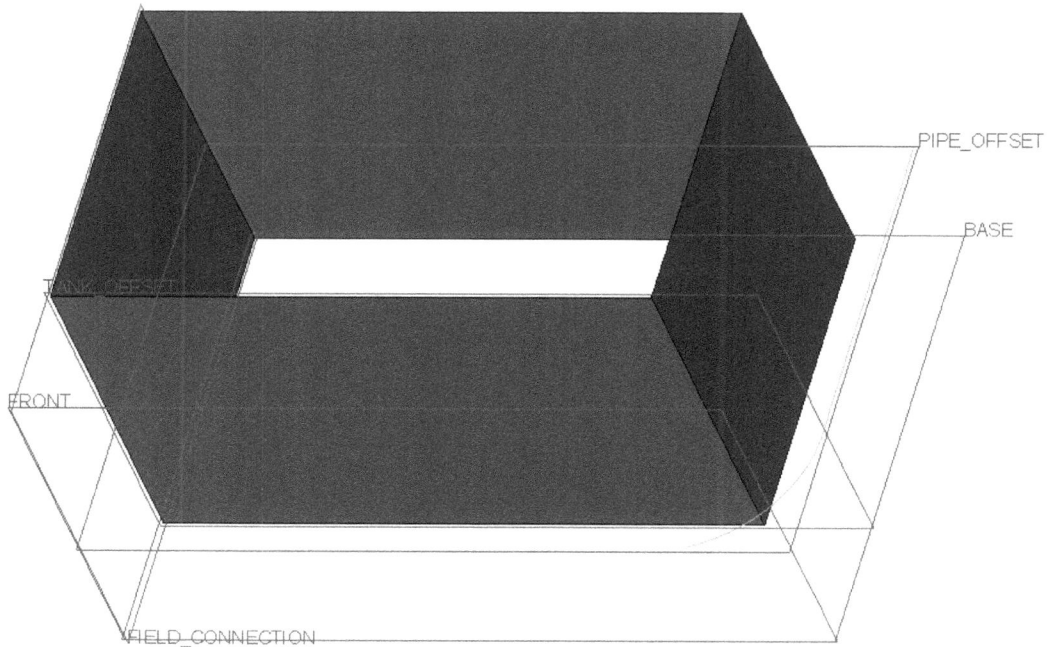

PIPE_OFFSET

BASE

TANK_OFFSET

FRONT

FIELD_CONNECTION

Figure 8–31

Design Considerations

Skeleton modeling is an excellent technique for capturing assembly design intent. A skeleton model enables the definition of component positioning, which results in a 3D layout of an assembly. Space claims can be created to define component areas to stay out of or stay within.

6. Save the skeleton and close the window.

7. In the Model Tree, click ▤ ▾ (Show)>**Layer Tree**.

8. Select **01__ASM_DEF_DTM_PLN**, right-click, and select **Hide**.

9. Right-click and select **Save Status**.

10. Save the assembly and erase it from memory.

Practice 8b | Using Motion Skeletons

Practice Objectives

- Create a motion skeleton.
- Create multiple body skeletons and copy applicable geometry and connections into them.
- Verify appropriate motion in the assembly.

In this practice, you will create a motion skeleton and associated body skeletons for the assembly shown in Figure 8–32 and Figure 8–33. The motion skeleton will be used in upcoming practices to define component geometry. It will also be used to define circular motion for the crankshaft and linear motion for the pistons.

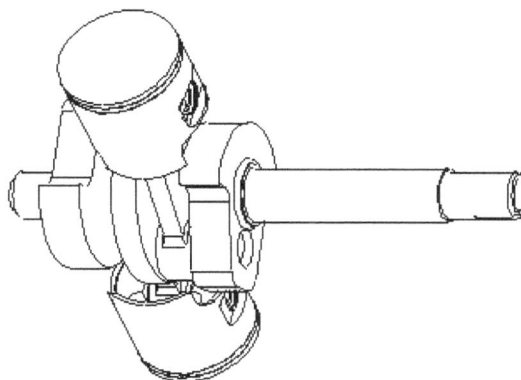

Figure 8–32

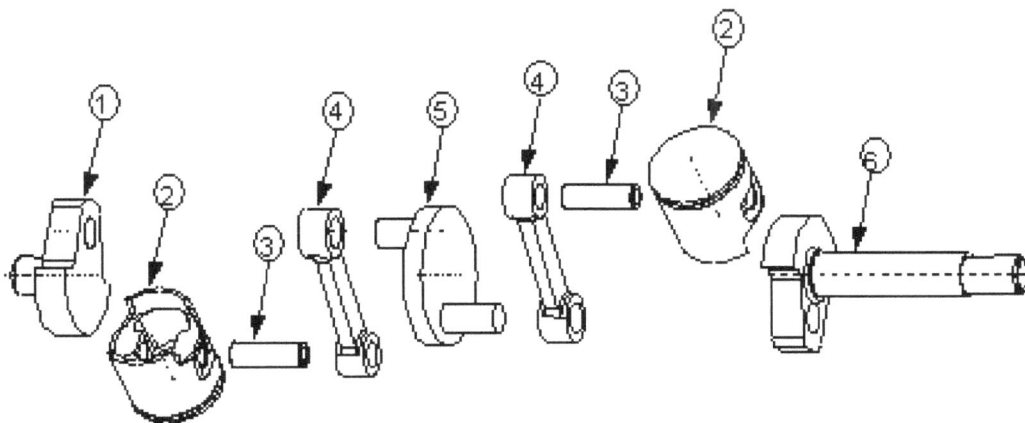

Figure 8–33

The assembly components will include the following:

- bearing_journal_short.prt
- piston.asm
- piston_pin.prt
- connecting_rod.prt
- connecting_rod_journal.prt
- bearing_journal_main.prt

Task 1 - Create the assembly and set up the motion skeleton model.

1. Change your working directory to the *Motion_Skeleton* folder.

2. Create a new assembly using the default template and set the *Name* to **crank_piston**.

3. Set the model display as follows:

   - *(Datum Display Filters)*: (Axis Display) (Point Display) (Plane Display)

   - *(Spin Center)*: Off

   - *(Display Style)*: (Shading With Edges)

4. Ensure (Plane Tag Display) is enabled.

5. Set the length units for the assembly by selecting **File> Prepare>Model Properties**. Select **change** next to *Units*, as shown in Figure 8–34.

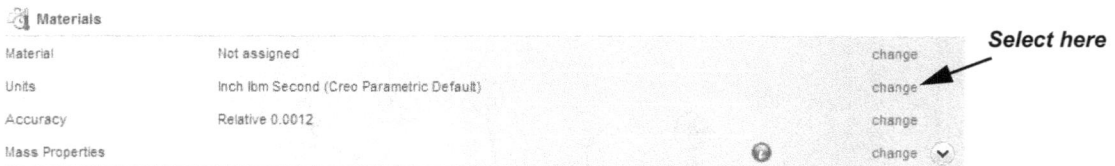

Materials			
Material	Not assigned		change
Units	Inch lbm Second (Creo Parametric Default)		change
Accuracy	Relative 0.0012		change
Mass Properties			change

Select here

Figure 8–34

6. Select **millimeter Newton Second (mmNS)** in the *Systems of Units* area in the Units Manager dialog box. Click **Set** to set the new units.

7. Select **Convert dimensions** in the Changing Model Units dialog box. Click **OK**.

8. Click **Close** in the Units Manager and Model Properties dialog boxes.

9. Click ▣ (Create) to create a new component.

10. Set the *Type* to **Skeleton Model** and the *Sub-type* to **Motion**, in the Component Create dialog box.

11. Edit the file name to **CRANK_PISTON_MOTION_SKEL**, as shown in Figure 8–35.

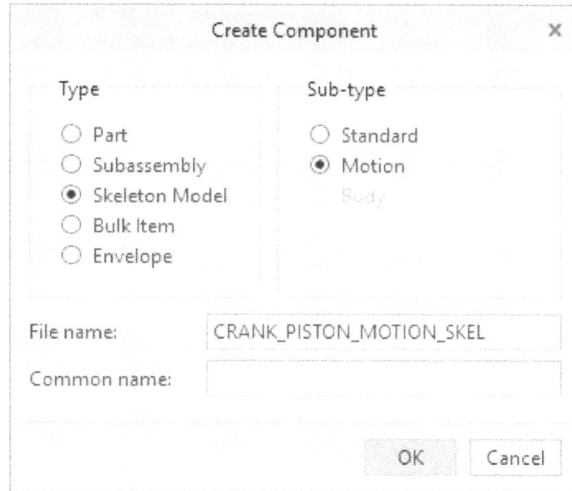

Create Component   ✕

Type
○ Part
○ Subassembly
◉ Skeleton Model
○ Bulk Item
○ Envelope

Sub-type
○ Standard
◉ Motion
  Body

File name: CRANK_PISTON_MOTION_SKEL

Common name:

OK   Cancel

Figure 8–35

12. Click **OK**.

13. In the Creation Options dialog box, click **Browse** and double-click on **start_asm_mmns.asm**.

14. Click **OK**.

Design Considerations

A motion skeleton is an assembly, as shown in Figure 8–36.

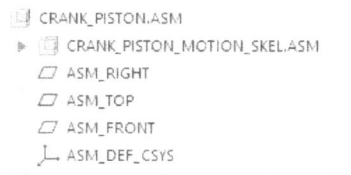

CRANK_PISTON.ASM
▸ CRANK_PISTON_MOTION_SKEL.ASM
    ASM_RIGHT
    ASM_TOP
    ASM_FRONT
    ASM_DEF_CSYS

Figure 8–36

Task 2 - Create datum features for the skeleton.

1. In the Model Tree, click on **CRANK_PISTON_MOTION_ SKEL.ASM** and click 🗁 (Open) in the mini toolbar.

2. The first component in the assembly, **bearing_journal_main.prt**, will be coincident with **ASM_RIGHT** in the skeleton. Rename **ASM_RIGHT** to reflect this alignment. Click twice on **ASM_RIGHT** in the Model Tree and rename the datum plane to **BJL**.

3. Create a datum plane offset from datum plane **BJL**, as shown in Figure 8–37. Use an *Offset* dimension of **107**. This locates the first instances of the **piston**, **piston_pin**, and **connecting_rod** components. Rename this datum plane as **PCR1**.

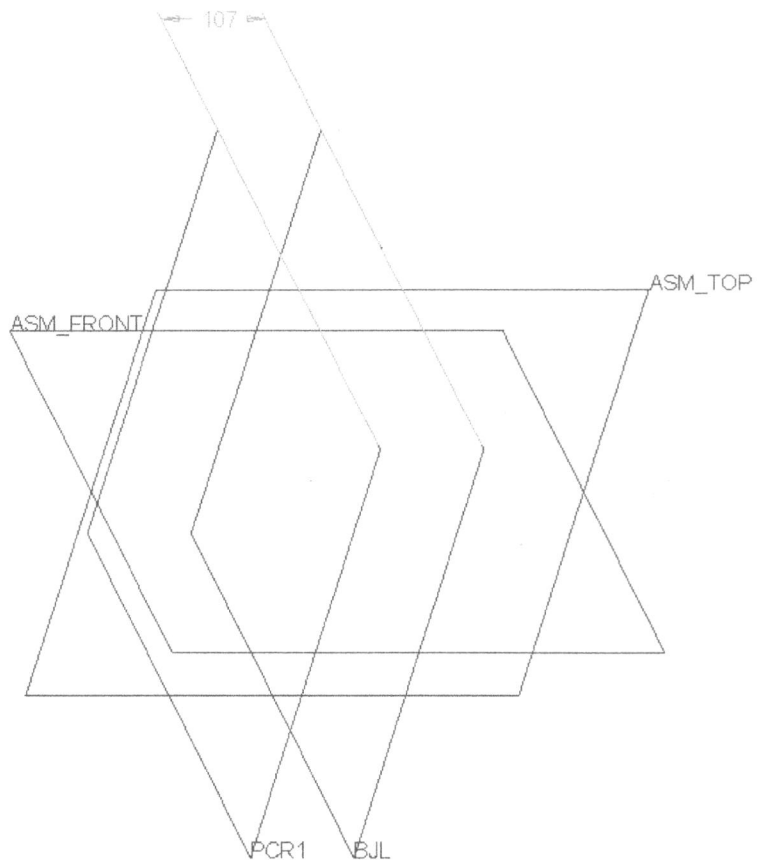

Figure 8–37

Task 3 - Sketch a datum curve on datum plane PCR1 to represent the first piston.

1. Use **PCR1** as the sketching plane and **ASM_TOP** as the Top reference.

Datum entities is toggled off for clarity.

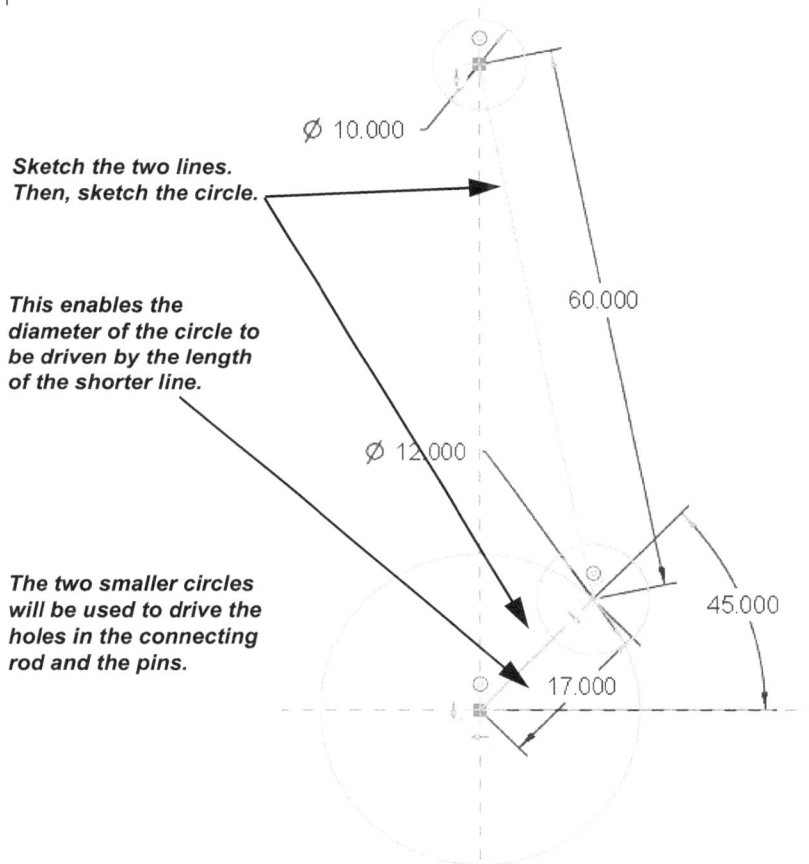

2. Sketch the two line entities first, dimension them as shown in Figure 8–38, and then sketch the circles.

Sketch the two lines.
Then, sketch the circle.

This enables the diameter of the circle to be driven by the length of the shorter line.

The two smaller circles will be used to drive the holes in the connecting rod and the pins.

Ø 10.000

60.000

Ø 12.000

45.000

17.000

Figure 8–38

Datum entities is toggled off for clarity.

3. While still in **Sketch 1**, sketch two additional circles on top of each of the smaller circles, as shown in Figure 8–39.

Sketch the two circles directly on top of the existing circles.

A sketched entity can only be used in one body skeleton, so the additional circles are required.

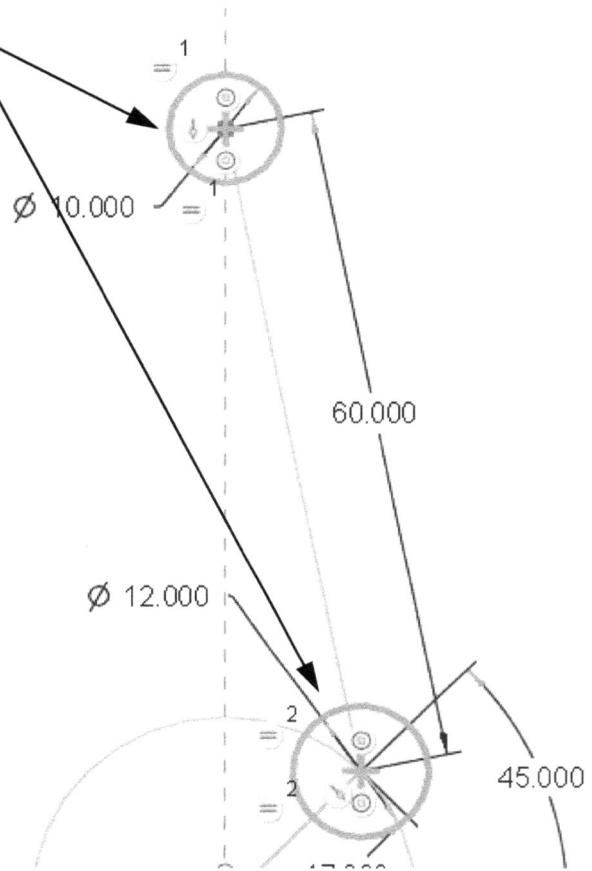

Ø 10.000

Ø 12.000

60.000

45.000

Figure 8–39

4. Sketch the vertical line (in the center of the rectangle) and the rectangle shown in Figure 8–40 to represent the piston.

Datum entities is toggled off for clarity.

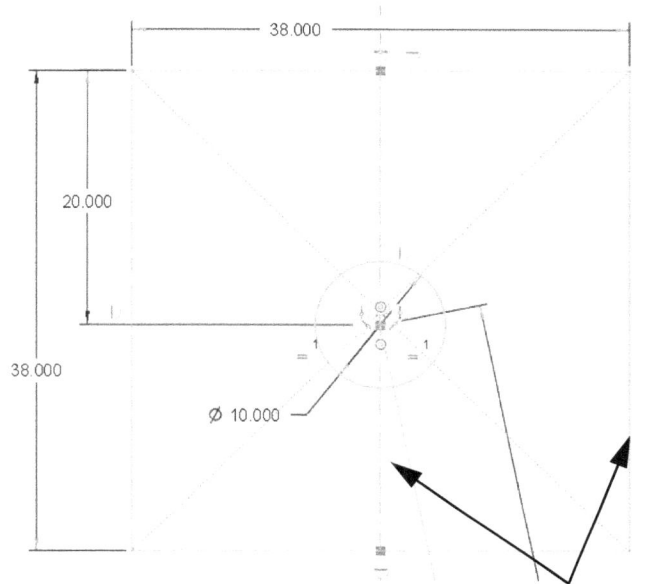

Sketch the rectangle and vertical line.
Figure 8–40

5. Sketch a vertical line 130 long, starting at the center of largest circle, to be used as the ground body, as shown in Figure 8–41.

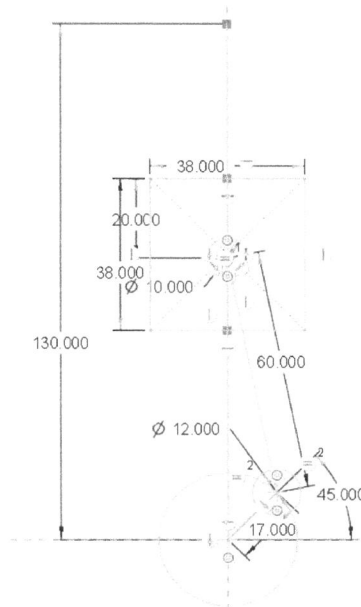

Figure 8–41

6. Complete the sketch.

Design Considerations

The angled line represents the connecting rod length and the large circle represents the path of the rotation or throw of the crank shaft. The smaller circles will be used in an upcoming practice to define geometry on the piston and connecting rods. In the next task, you will change the symbolic value of a dimension. This is done to help identify the dimension for modification or when used in a relation.

Task 4 - Change the symbol of the angular dimension.

1. Select **Sketch 1** and select $\overset{\longleftrightarrow}{\text{d1}}$ (Edit Dimensions) in the mini toolbar.

2. Select the angular dimension and enter **crank_angle** as symbolic name of the dimension in the *Dimension* tab, as shown in Figure 8–42.

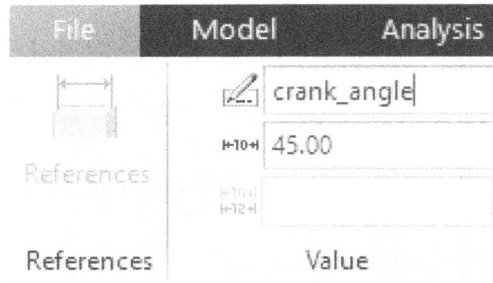

File	Model	Analysis
↦—→	⬩	crank_angle|
	⊢-10-⊣	45.00
References	⊢-20-⊣ ⊢-12-⊣	
References		Value

Figure 8–42

3. In the Model Intent group, click $\overset{15}{\cancel{x}}$ (Switch Dimensions). The symbolic value for the angular dimension displays as shown in Figure 8–43.

Datum entities is toggled off for clarity.

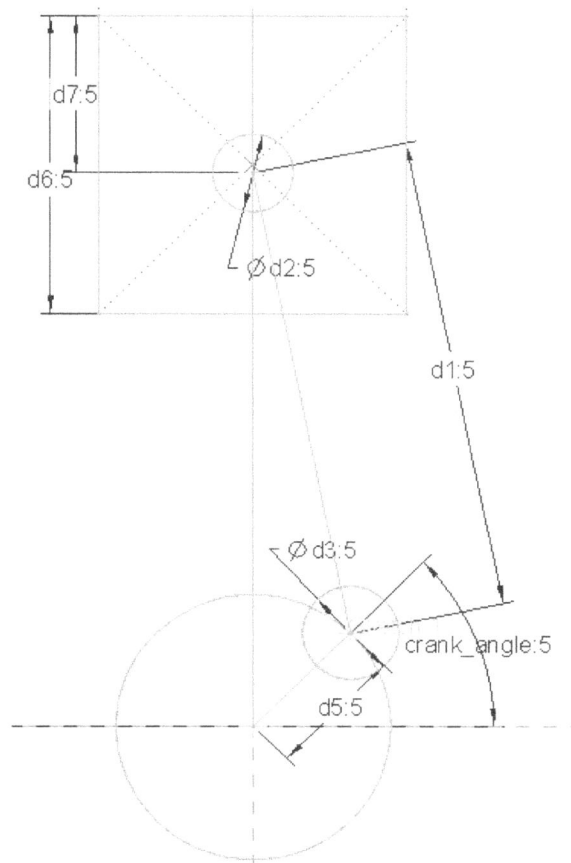

Figure 8–43

4. Click ✎ (Switch Dimensions) to set the dimensions back to numerical form.

Task 5 - Create datum planes.

1. Create a datum plane offset from datum plane **BJL** by a *Distance* of **117**. Note the direction may need to be reversed. Rename the new datum plane as **CRJ** as shown in Figure 8–44. This plane is used to locate the connecting rod journal component.

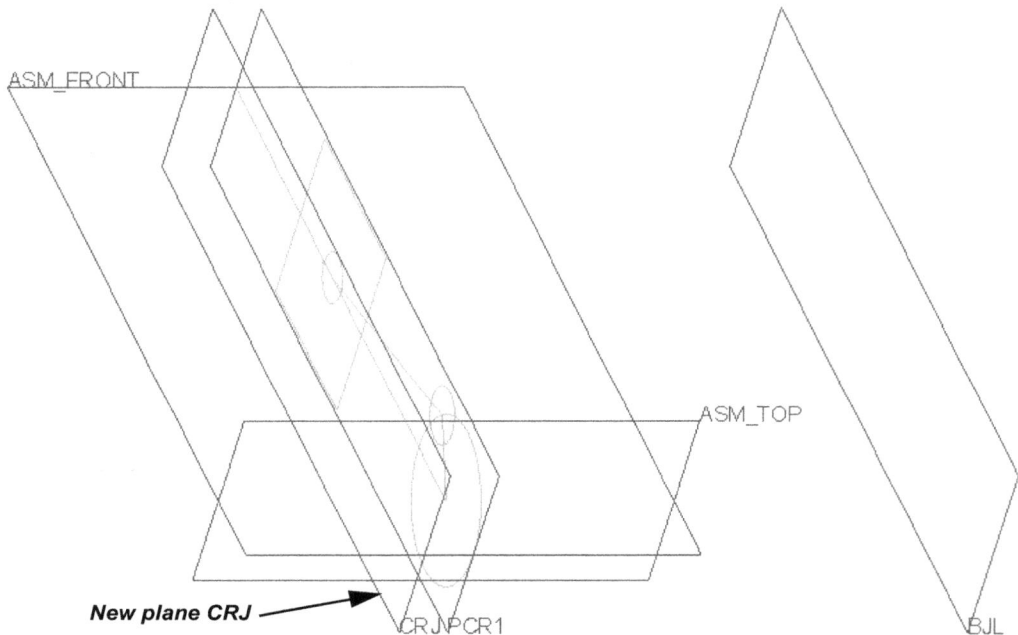

Figure 8–44

2. Create another datum plane offset from datum plane **BJL**. Use an *Offset* dimension of **127**. Note the direction may need to be reversed. This plane locates the second instances of the **piston**, **piston_pin**, and **connecting_rod** components.

3. Rename the datum plane as **PCR2**.

4. Create another datum plane offset from datum plane **BJL**. Use an *Offset* dimension of **163**. Note the direction may need to be reversed. This plane locates the **bearing_journal_short** component.

5. Rename the datum plane to **BJS**. The skeleton model displays as shown in Figure 8–45.

Figure 8–45

Design Considerations

So far, you have created various datum planes to aid in the assembly of components. You have also created sketches that are used as references for the assembly of the connecting rod and piston. In the next task, you will create a sketch that is used for assembly references for the second connecting rod and piston. You will use the entities of the first sketch as Sketcher references for the second sketch.

Task 6 - Create a sketch.

1. Create a sketch using **PCR2** as the sketching plane and **ASM_TOP** as the Top reference.

2. Create a similar sketch as in Task 4, as shown in Figure 8–46. The constraint symbols have been removed in the right hand figure for clarity. There are two of each of the smaller circles.

Note: Datum entities and constraints are toggled off for clarity in the image on the right.

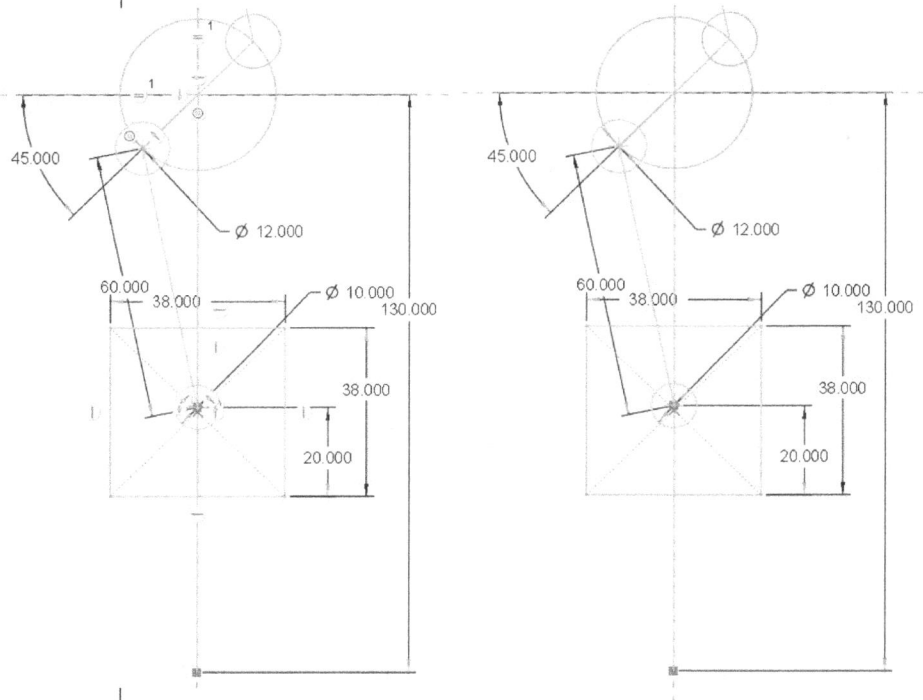

Figure 8–46

- The completed motion skeleton displays as shown in Figure 8–47.

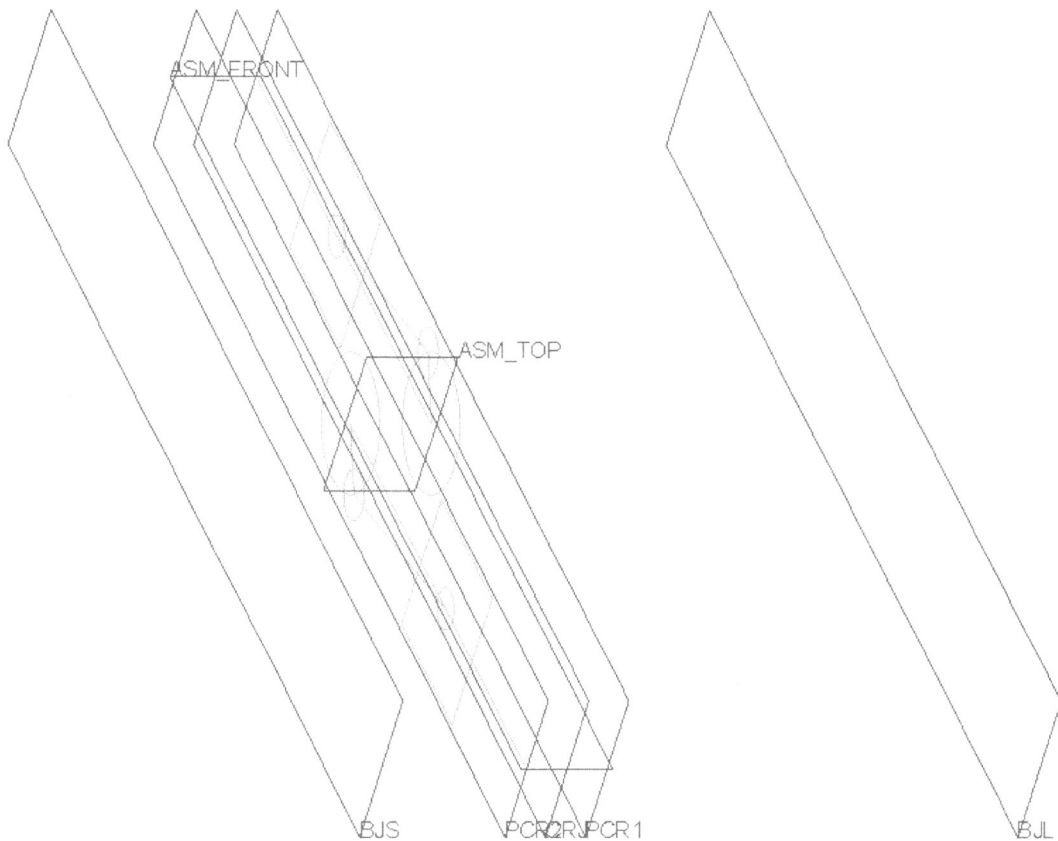

ASM_FRONT

ASM_TOP

BJS   PCR2RJPCR1   BJL

Figure 8–47

3. The motion skeleton is now complete. Save the file.

Task 7 - Create the ground body skeleton.

1. Toggle off the display of datum entities.

2. In the *Model* tab, click ⬚ (Create).

3. Set the *Sub-type* to **Body**.

4. Edit the name to **GROUND_SKEL** and click **OK**.

5. Select **Empty** in the Creation Options dialog box, as shown in Figure 8–48.

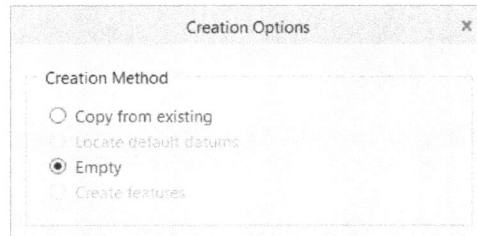

Figure 8–48

6. Click **OK**. The BODY DEFINITION dialog box opens, as shown in Figure 8–49.

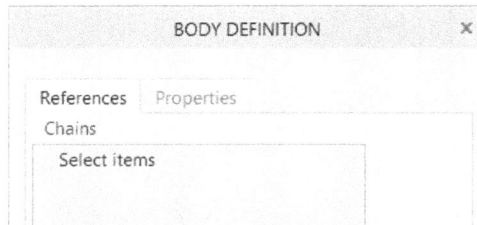

Figure 8–49

7. Use **Pick From List** (or the right-click selection technique) to select the longest line from **Sketch 1** and **Sketch 2**, as shown in Figure 8–50.

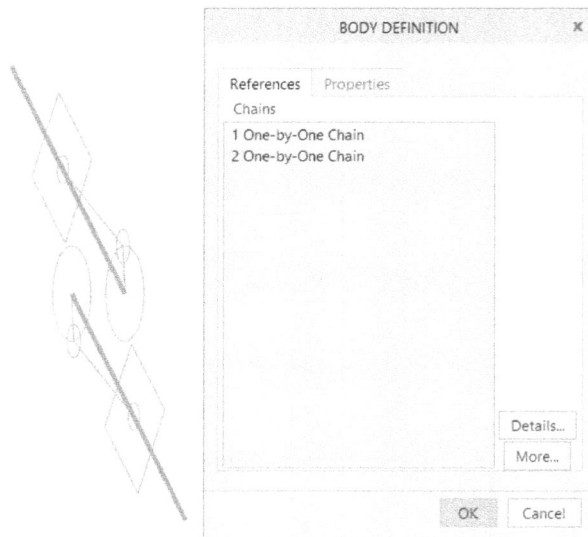

Figure 8–50

8. Click **OK** in the BODY DEFINTION dialog box. The body skeleton is added to the Model Tree, as shown in Figure 8–51.

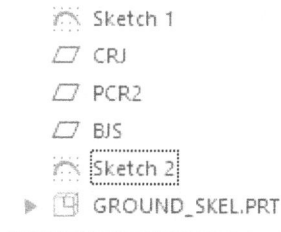

Sketch 1
CRJ
PCR2
BJS
Sketch 2
▶ GROUND_SKEL.PRT

Figure 8–51

Task 8 - Create the CR_JOURNAL_SKEL body skeleton.

---

1. In the *Model* tab, click (Create).

2. Set the *Sub-type* to **Body**.

3. Edit the name to **CR_JOURNAL_SKEL** and click **OK**.

4. In the Creation Options dialog box, select **Empty**.

5. Click **OK**.

6. Select the six curves shown in Figure 8–52. Use **Pick From List** (or the right-click selection technique) to select the angled lines.

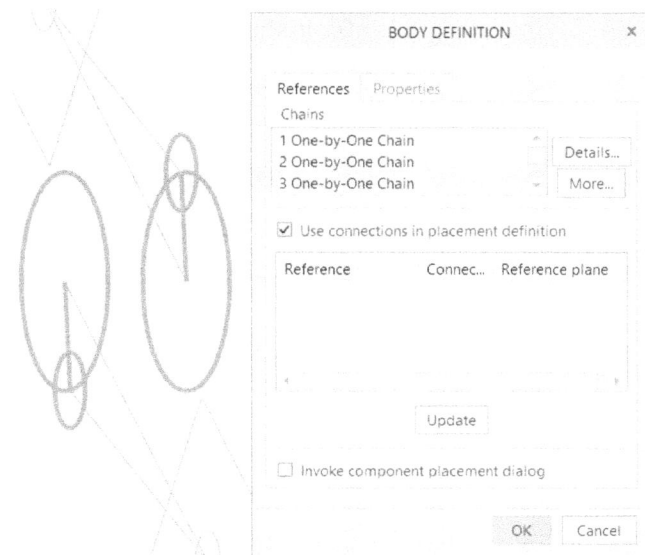

BODY DEFINITION

References   Properties
Chains
1 One-by-One Chain   Details...
2 One-by-One Chain
3 One-by-One Chain   More...

☑ Use connections in placement definition

Reference   Connec... Reference plane

Update

☐ Invoke component placement dialog

OK   Cancel

Figure 8–52

7. Click **Update** to update the BODY DEFINITION dialog box with a list of possible connections, as shown in Figure 8–53.

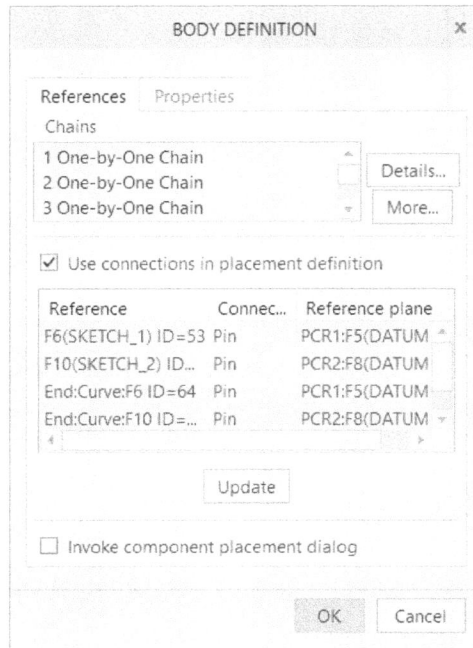

Figure 8–53

8. Select the **F6(SKETCH_1)** and **F10(SKETCH_2)** Pin connections, right-click and select **Remove**.

9. In the BODY DEFINTION dialog box, click **OK**.

Task 9 - Create the CONN_ROD1_SKEL body skeleton.

1. In the *Model* tab, click ⬚ (Create).

2. Set the *Sub-type* to **Body**.

3. Edit the name to **CONN_ROD1_SKEL** and click **OK**.

4. In the Creation Options dialog box, select **Empty**.

5. Click **OK**.

6. Use **Pick From List** (or the right-click selection technique) to select the three curves shown in Figure 8–54.

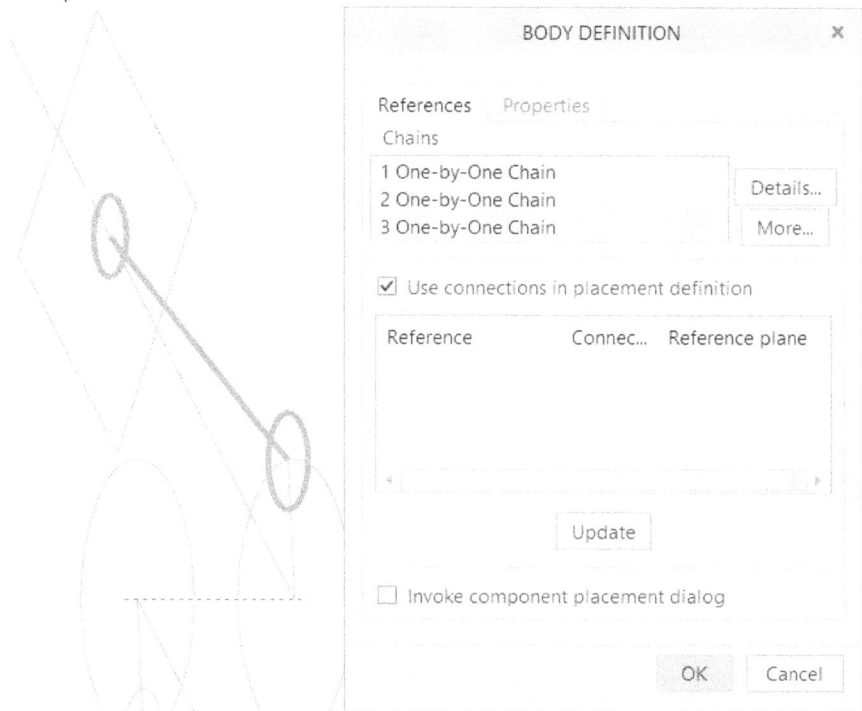

Figure 8–54

7. In the BODY DEFINTION dialog box, click **Update**.

8. Remove all connections except the Pin connection for **F6(SKETCH_1)**.

9. Click **OK**.

Task 10 - Create the PISTON1_SKEL body skeleton.

---

1. In the *Model* tab, click ⬚ (Create).

2. Set the *Sub-type* to **Body**.

3. Edit the name to **PISTON1_SKEL** and click **OK**.

4. In the Creation Options dialog box, select **Empty**.

5. Click **OK**.

6. Select the curves shown in Figure 8–55.

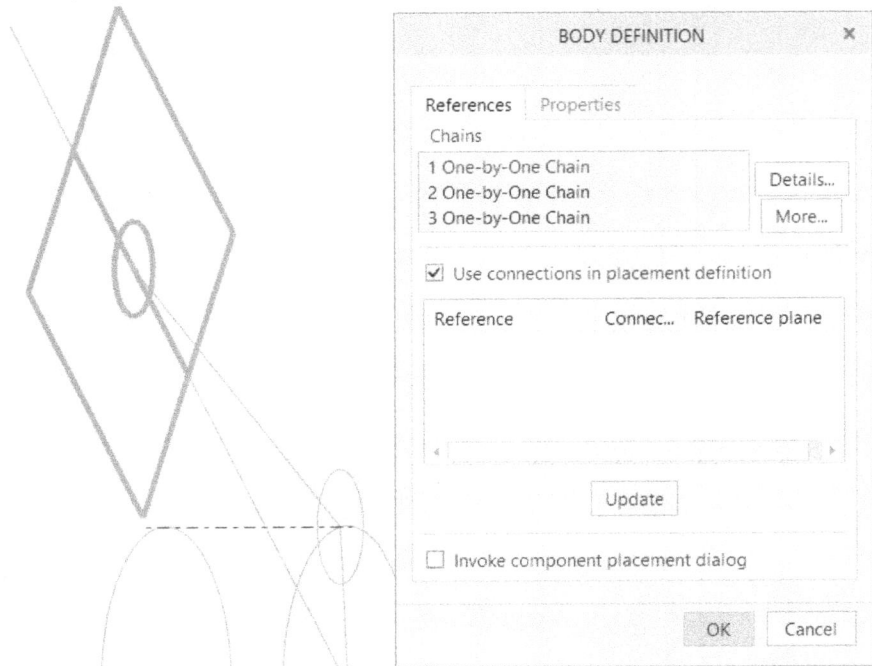

Figure 8–55

7. In the BODY DEFINTION dialog box, click **Update**.

8. Remove all connections except the Pin connection for **F6(SKETCH_1)** and the Slider connection for **F6(SKETCH_1)**.

9. Click **OK**.

Task 11 - Create the CONN_ROD2_SKEL body skeleton.

---

1. In the *Model* tab, click [] (Create).

2. Set the *Sub-type* to **Body**.

3. Edit the name to **CONN_ROD2_SKEL** and click **OK**.

4. In the Creation Options dialog box, select **Empty**.

5. Click **OK**.

6. Use **Pick From List** (or the right-click selection technique) to select the curves shown in Figure 8–56.

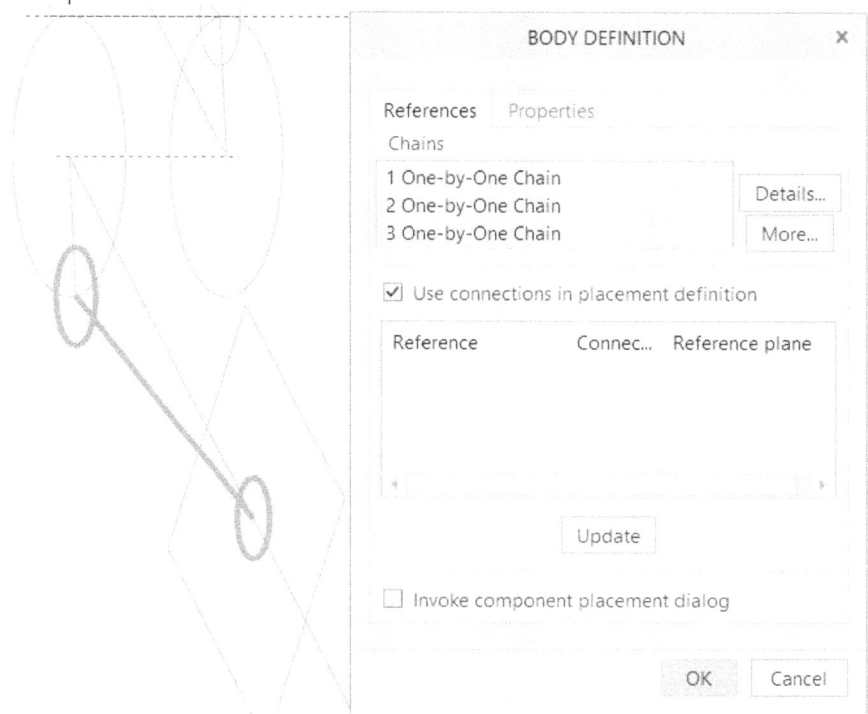

Figure 8–56

7. In the BODY DEFINTION dialog box, click **Update**.

8. Remove all connections except the Pin connection for **F10(SKETCH_2)**.

9. Click **OK**.

Task 12 - Create the PISTON2_SKEL body skeleton.

1. In the *Model* tab, click (Create).

2. Set the *Sub-type* to **Body**.

3. Edit the name to **PISTON2_SKEL** and click **OK**.

4. In the Creation Options dialog box, select **Empty**.

5. Click **OK**.

6. Select the curve shown in Figure 8–57.

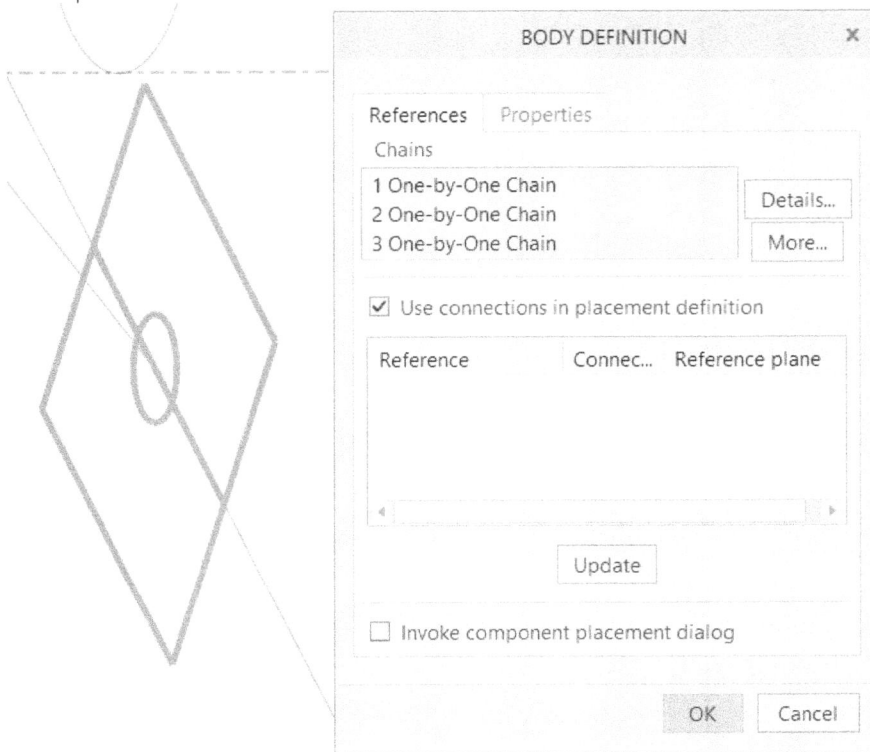

Figure 8–57

7. In the BODY DEFINTION dialog box, click **Update**.

8. Remove all connections except the Slider connection at **F10(SKETCH_2)** and the Pin connection at **F10(SKETCH_2)**.

9. Click **OK**.

Task 13 - Test the motion of the assembly.

1. In the *Model* tab, click ☝ (Drag Components).

2. Click on the circle shown in Figure 8–58.

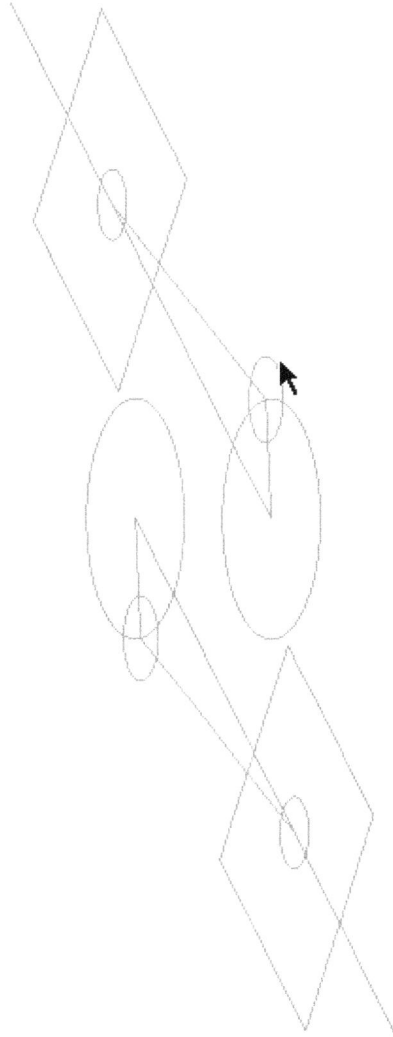

Figure 8–58

3. Without clicking, move the cursor to see the resulting motion, as shown in Figure 8–59.

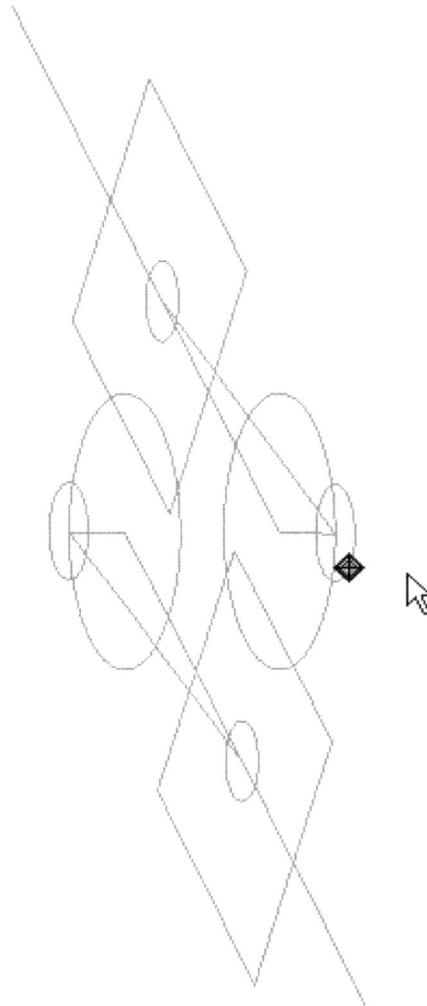

Figure 8–59

4. Right-click to cancel the motion.

5. In the Drag dialog box, click **Close**.

6. Regenerate the motion skeleton.

7. Save **CRANK_PISTON_MOTION_SKEL** then close the window.

8. Save the top-level assembly and erase it from memory.

Practice 8c

(Optional) Adding Components Using Package

Practice Objectives

- Package a subassembly
- Use snap by proximity to package parts

In this practice, you will package an assembly and instances from a part family table. Many components for this assembly have not been designed yet. However, the valve assembly and clamp parts are purchased items and can be added to the assembly. When using top-down design techniques, it is recommended that you include as much information in the top-level assembly as possible. Packaging is used to temporarily position these components. At the end of this practice, the assembly displays as shown in Figure 8–60.

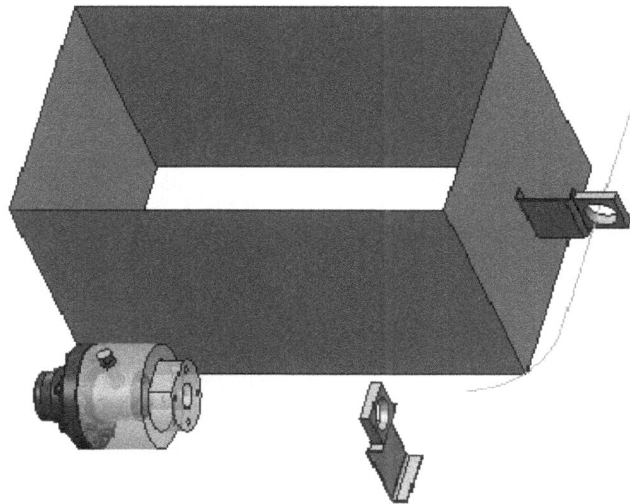

Figure 8–60

Task 1 - Open an assembly file.

1. Change the working directory to the *Package_Components* folder.

2. Open **power_unit.asm**.

3. Set the model display as follows:

- *⚡ (Datum Display Filters)*: All On

- *↣ (Spin Center)*: Off

- *⬛. (Display Style)*: ⬛ (Shading With Edges)

4. Ensure ⬛ (Plane Tag Display) is enabled.

Task 2 - Package a component.

Design Considerations

At this point in the design cycle, you can add all of the available components to the assembly, even if the assembly placement references do not exist. The current power unit assembly design requires a valve assembly that is a purchased item and is available to be assembled. It should be added to the assembly so that its information is captured. Since the assembly references are not known at this time, the component is placed in its approximate position and remains packaged.

As with most practices in this guide, the default ⬛ (In Window) option is used when assembling components.

1. Assemble **valve.asm**. It also displays as shown in Figure 8–61.

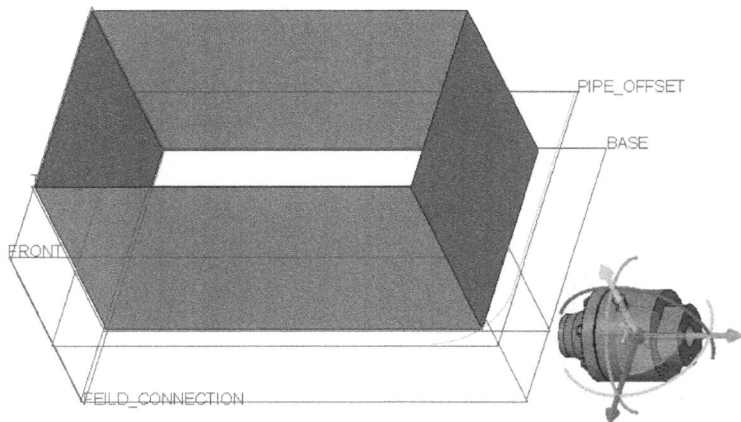

Figure 8–61

You can also press and hold <Ctrl>+<Alt> and hold the right mouse button down to pan the component.

2. Use the **3D Dragger** (red and blue arrows) to drag the component to a position similar to that shown in Figure 8–62.

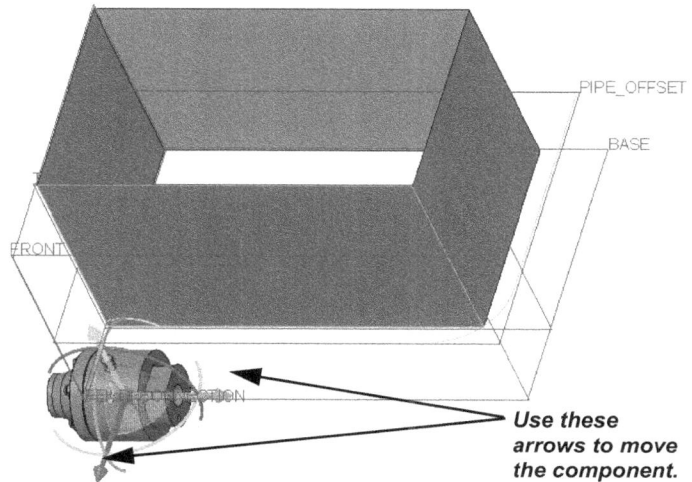

Use these arrows to move the component.

Figure 8–62

3. In the In-graphics toolbar, click (Saved Orientations) and select **FRONT.**

4. Use the **3D Dragger** to drag the component to a position similar to that shown in Figure 8–63.

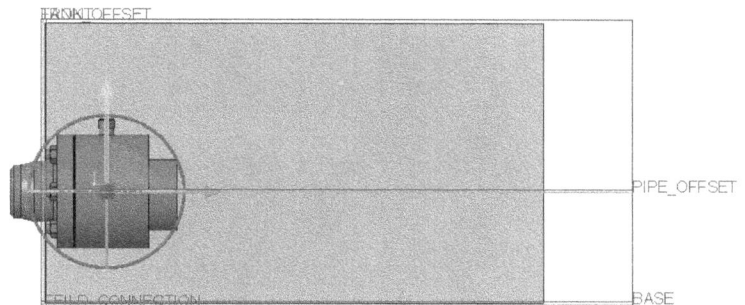

Figure 8–63

5. Click (Saved Orientations) and select **TOP.**

6. Use the **3D Dragger** to drag the component to a position similar to that shown in Figure 8–64.

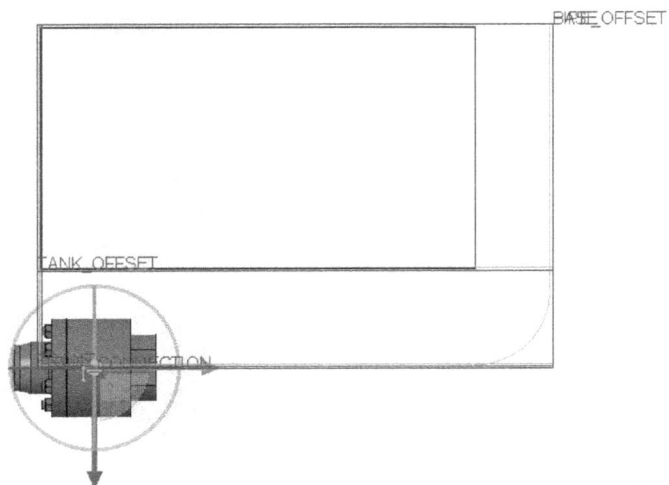

Figure 8–64

7. Press <Ctrl>+<D> to return to default orientation. The assembly displays similar to that shown in Figure 8–65.

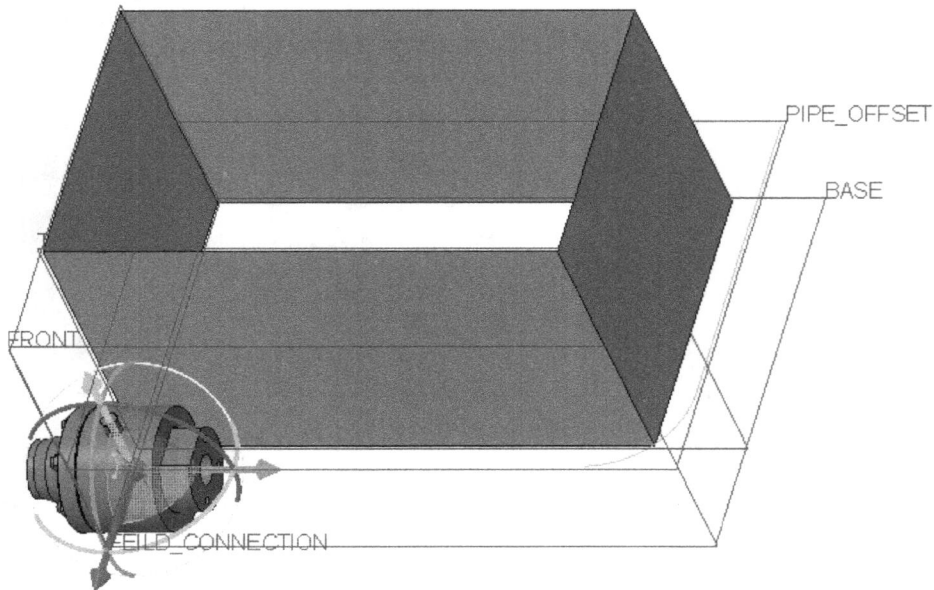

Figure 8–65

8. Click ✓ (OK) to complete the component placement, leaving it as packaged.

9. Save the assembly.

Task 3 - Use Snap by Proximity to package components.

Design Considerations

In the next task, you will package two pipe clamps. The pipe clamps are also purchased items and should be included in the assembly. You also know that one of the clamps will be constrained to the base, and the other constrained to the right side of the tank.

1. Click 🖫 (Assemble) and double-click on **clamp.prt**.

2. Select the instance **<clamp_25_80>** of **clamp.prt** and click **Open**. The assembly updates as shown in Figure 8–66.

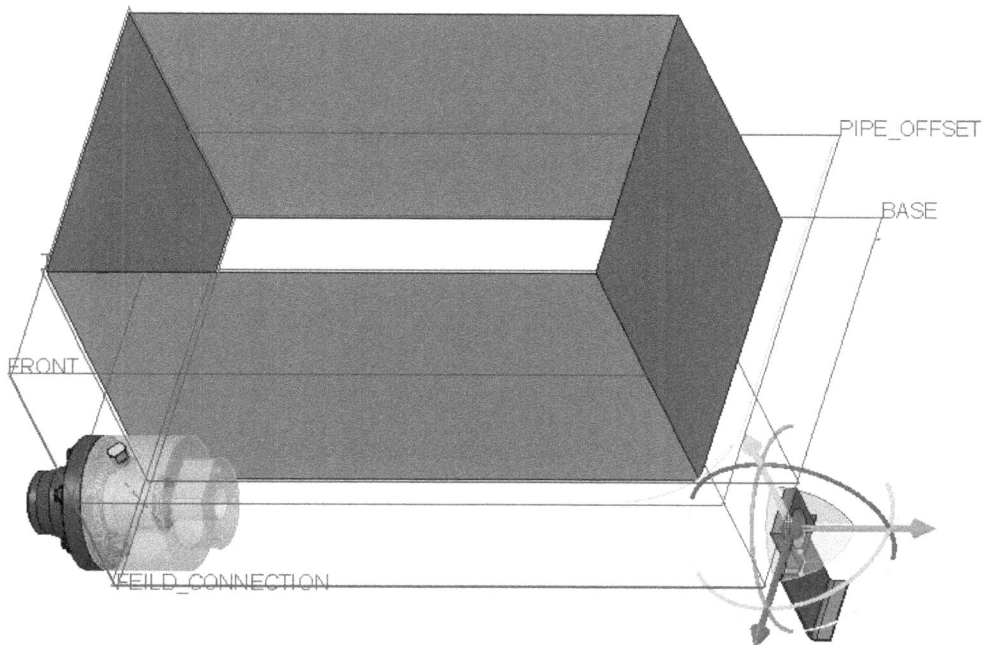

Figure 8–66

3. Select datum plane **BASE** of the skeleton part as the Assembly Reference.

4. Select the bottom surface of the clamp part. The assembly updates as shown in Figure 8–67.

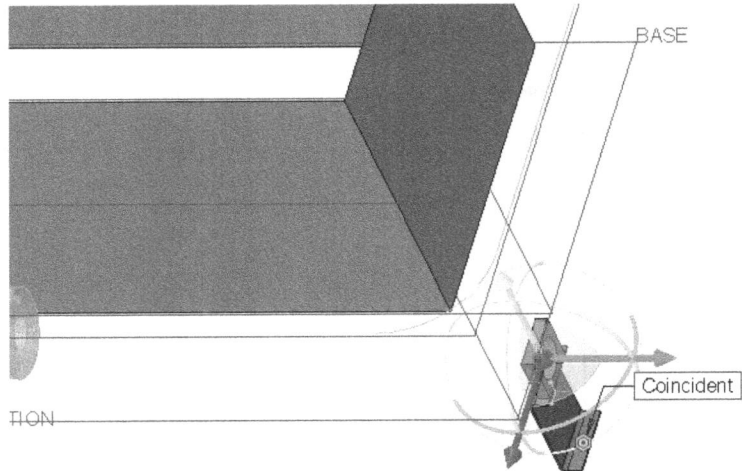

Figure 8–67

5. Use the **3D Dragger** to move the component to the position shown in Figure 8–68.

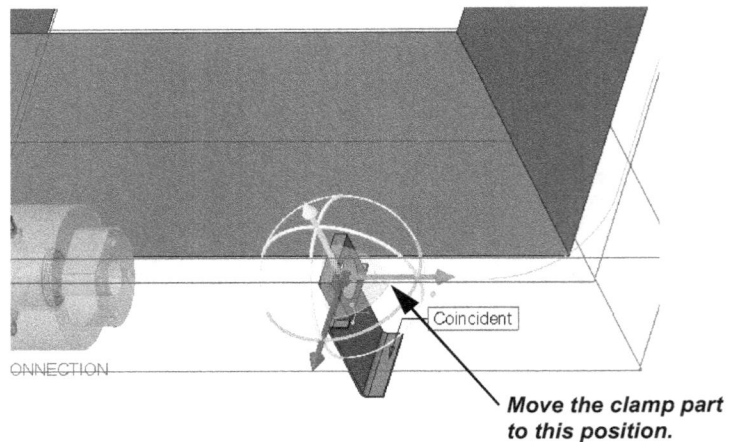

Move the clamp part to this position.

Figure 8–68

6. Click ✓ (OK) to complete the component placement, leaving it as packaged.

7. Assemble instance **<clamp_25_60>** of **clamp.prt**.

You can also use <Ctrl>+<Alt> and the middle mouse button to rotate the component.

8. Use the **3D Dragger** to orient the component to the orientation shown in Figure 8–69.

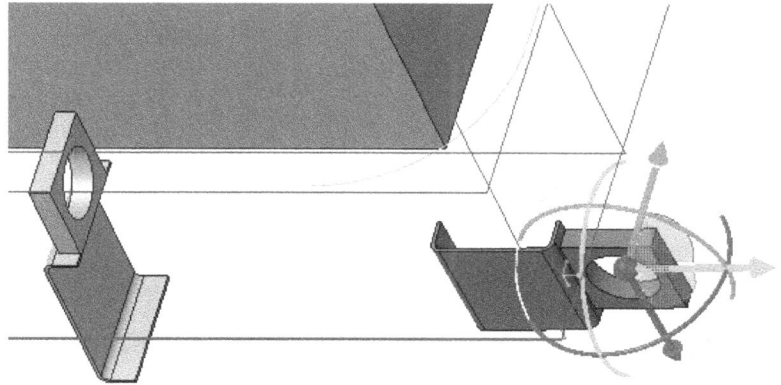

Figure 8–69

9. Add a Coincident constraint between the surface of the skeleton and the bottom surface of the part, as shown in Figure 8–70.

Select this surface of the tank space claim as the assembly reference.

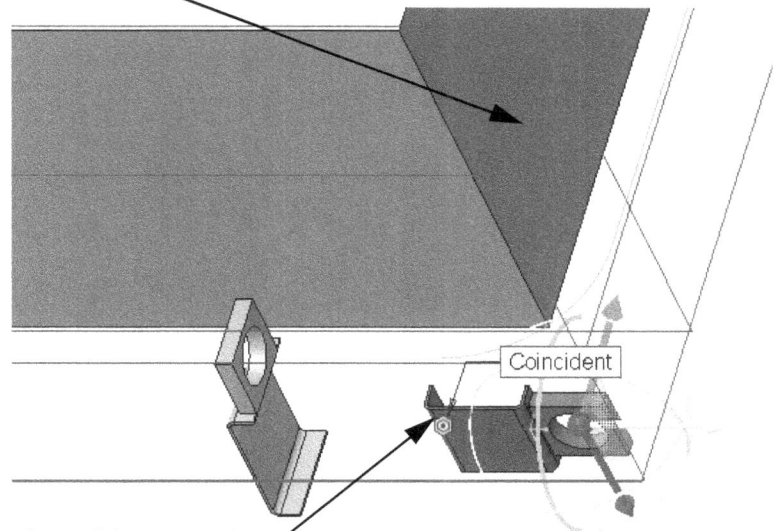

Coincident

Select the bottom surface of the part as the component reference.

Figure 8–70

10. Move the component to the position shown in Figure 8–71. Rotate it as required.

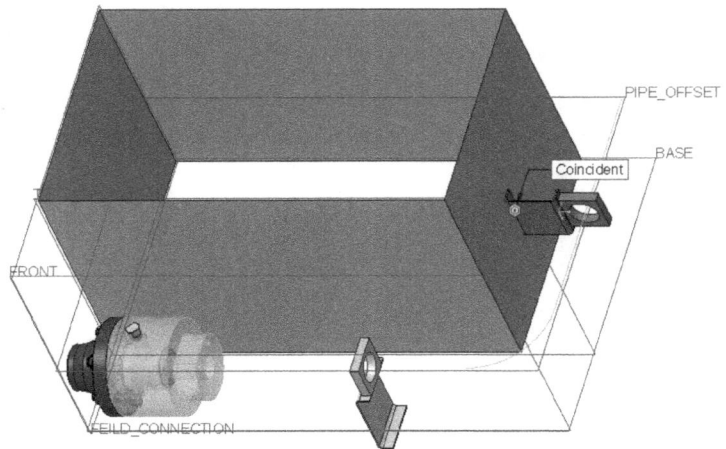

3D Dragger is toggle off for clarity.

Figure 8–71

11. Click ✓ (OK) to complete the component placement, leaving it as packaged.

12. Set the orientation to the default orientation.

13. Turn off the datum feature display, and the assembly and Model Tree display as shown in Figure 8–72.

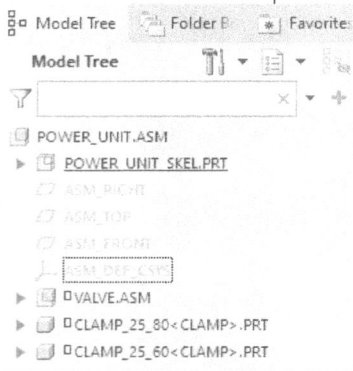

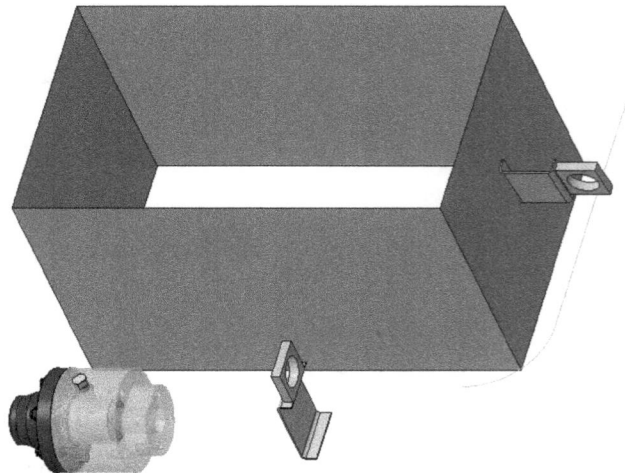

Figure 8–72

14. Save the assembly and erase all of the files from memory.

Design Considerations

A skeleton model provides assembly references in the initial stages of the design and throughout the design cycle. When using the top-down design technique, strive to add information to the assembly as it is made available. As other components are being designed and completed, they should also be added to the assembly. As components are added, they typically need to be redefined and reordered as the design evolves. Packaged components can be finalized as more components are added. Using a skeleton model enables flexibility when making assembly design changes.

Chapter Review Questions

1. Which of the following statements are true regarding a skeleton model? (Select all that apply.)

   a. A skeleton model controls parent/child relationships.

   b. A skeleton model defines spatial claims.

   c. Using this technique makes operations easier, such as suppressing, deleting, and interchanging components.

   d. You can simulate motion by modifying the skeleton model dimensions in the assembly instead of modifying the components.

   e. Creates a centralized location for exchanging information between assembly components.

2. How many skeleton models can be created in an assembly by default.

   a. 1

   b. 2

   c. 3

   d. There is no limit.

3. Skeleton models can be created using which of the following options? (Select all that apply.)

   a. Copy and Paste Special

   b. Copy From Existing

   c. Empty

   d. Create First Feature

4. The skeleton model is always listed as the last part in the assembly.

   a. True

   b. False

5. A Motion Skeleton helps define motion in an assembly and is an assembly consisting of Body Skeletons.

   a. True

   b. False

Answers: 1.abcde, 2.a, 3.bcd, 4.b, 5.a

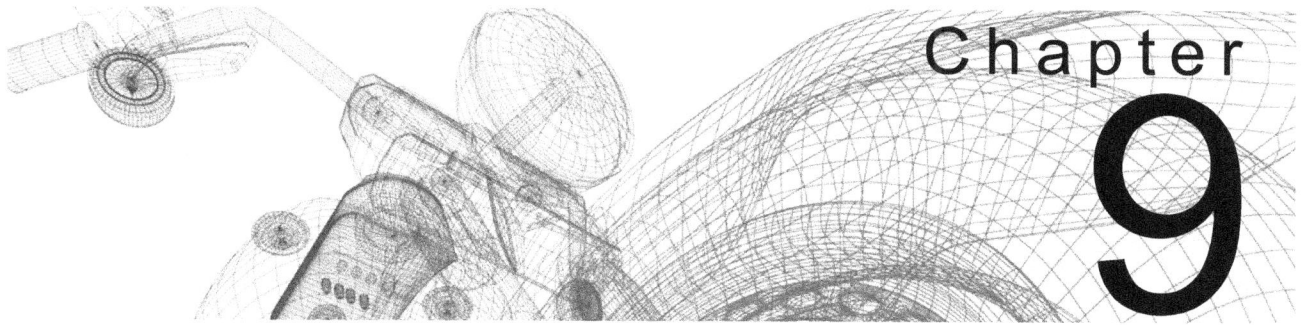

Designing in Context

You can create component parts and features (e.g., holes or cuts) in Assembly mode. In this chapter, you learn how to create features at the assembly level and about the external references that are created as a result.

Learning Objectives in This Chapter

- Learn when external references are created and how to manage the references using global and assembly settings.
- Learn the advantages and how to create parts in an assembly.
- Learn to create features at the assembly level and about the available options.
- Learn to create components from Motion Skeletons.

9.1 External References

When creating parts in Assembly mode, you have the advantage of seeing the geometry of existing components. The existing geometry can be used when creating geometry for the new part. When creating new geometry, external references can be made.

An external reference is any reference that is used to create features of a part that do not belong directly to the part in which the feature is being created. They can be formed with the top-level assembly, subassemblies, or other components. External references should be avoided, but can easily be created in the following situations:

- Selecting the sketching and orientation planes.

- Creating geometry by clicking ⬚ (Project) and ⬓ (Offset), and creating concentric circles and arcs.

- Selecting references for sketching.

- Selecting references for depth options.

Creating external references cannot be avoided in some cases, and you must note how the part reacts. When the assembly is in session, all of the references required to create and display the part are recognized by Creo Parametric and the part functions as expected. If the assembly is not in session and the part is opened on its own, some references are missing and you have limited control over the part. In this case, the modification and redefinition of features might not be possible. Consider the design intent when deciding whether or not to build the part in Assembly mode.

Creo Parametric offers tools that can help you to manage the external references. They enable you to specify the scope of the external references, and how Creo Parametric reacts to invalid reference selections.

9.2 Creating Parts in Assembly

Creating parts in Assembly mode enables you to use other assembly component references and features to create new parts. This creates a parent/child relationship between components, which can greatly enhance your ability to modify the related parts at the same time (i.e., when a parent part is modified, all of the child parts are updated). This consideration is important to your design intent when creating parts in an assembly. An example of a part created in Assembly mode is shown in Figure 9–1.

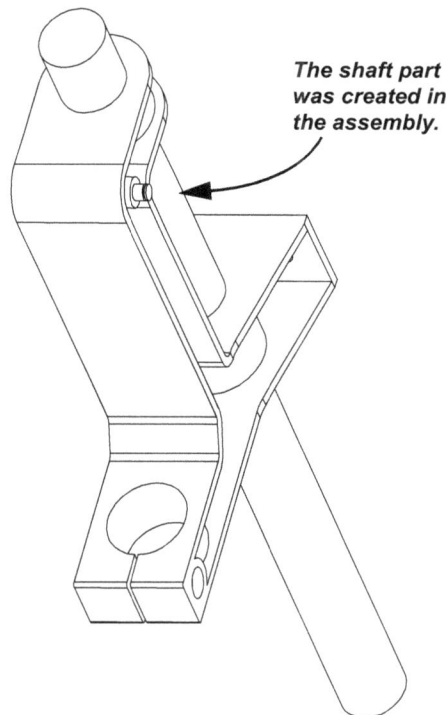

The shaft part was created in the assembly.

Figure 9–1

How To: Create Components in Assembly Mode

1. To create a component in an assembly, click ⬚ (Create) in the *Model* tab. The Create Component dialog box opens as shown in Figure 9–2.

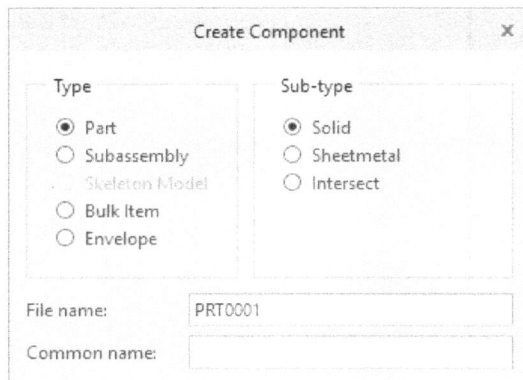

Figure 9–2

*A **Bulk Item** is a part created to represent a non-geometric part that is required in the BOM (e.g., paint).*

2. You can create a **Part**, **Subassembly**, **Skeleton Model**, **Bulk Item**, or **Envelope** in an assembly. The **Bulk Item** and **Envelope** options do not have additional subtypes. The additional options for parts and subassemblies include the following:

Solid	Used to create a solid part.
Sheetmetal	Used to create a sheet metal part.
Intersect	Used to create a part by intersecting two or more parts.
Mirror	Used to create a part or subassembly by mirroring an existing component
Standard	Used to create a standard subassembly or Skeleton part.
Motion	Used to create a motion skeleton assembly.
Body	Used to create body skeletons.

3. Enter a name for the part and click **OK** to create the component.
4. The Creation Options dialog box opens once the component has been created, as shown in Figure 9–3. It enables you to define the creation method for the new component.

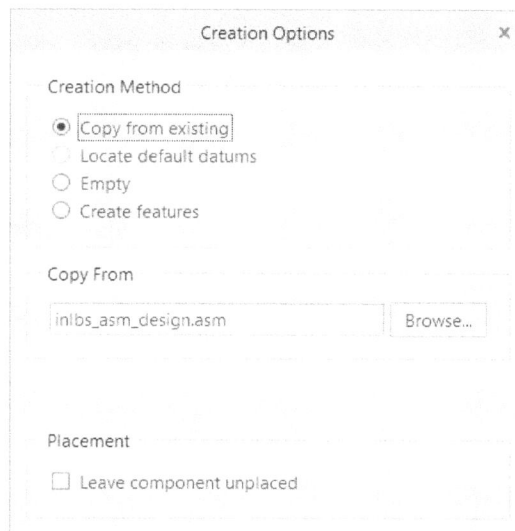

Figure 9–3

The creation options available when creating a component in Assembly mode are described as follows:

Option	Description
Copy from existing (part, subassembly, skeleton model, or bulk item)	Creates a part by copying geometry, parameters, and relations from an existing part. Once the part has been selected and a new name entered, the Component Placement dialog box opens enabling you to place the new component.
Locate default datums (part or subassembly)	Locates datum planes in the new part by referencing existing datum planes in the assembly. No external references are established.
Empty (part, subassembly, skeleton model, or bulk item)	Creates a part without any geometry. The part geometry can be added at any time.
Create features (part, subassembly, or skeleton model)	Creates part geometry without creating datum planes, and uses existing assembly references.

*To activate a component, select it, right-click, and select **Activate**.*

5. Click **OK** to create the component.
6. Once the new component has been created in the assembly, you can activate it in the assembly and create the required geometry or assemble the required components.

- If you are creating geometry or assembling components in a top-level assembly, external references can easily be established. To avoid unwanted external references, consider setting the external reference control. Alternatively, if you do not require references to the top-level assembly, consider opening and working on the new component outside the top-level assembly. All of the geometry creation for parts and component placement options for subassemblies are the same as when created outside a top-level assembly.

Consider the assembly shown in Figure 9–4. The shaft part is created in the assembly so that the diameter of the shaft is the same diameter as the hole in the clamp. If the diameter of the hole in the clamp is changed, the shaft diameter updates accordingly.

To avoid external references when creating this part, delete the constraints and add a dimension for the diameter of the shaft. The diameter of the shaft does not then update if the diameter of the hole is changed.

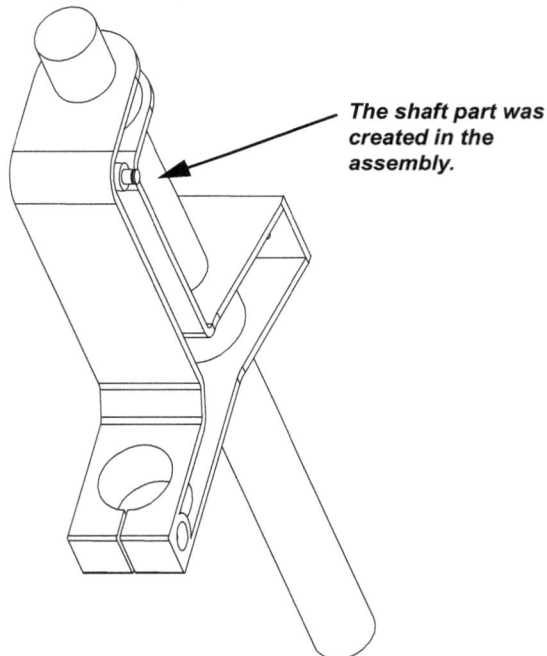

The shaft part was created in the assembly.

Figure 9–4

The part was created by clicking 🔲 (Create) in the *Model* tab. The extrude feature was then created referencing the existing edge of the clamp. An external reference was created as a result.

9.3 Creating Assembly Features

You can create a limited set of features in Assembly mode. Assembly mode features are limited to the following:

- Hole (shown in Figure 9–5)
- Cuts
- Pipe

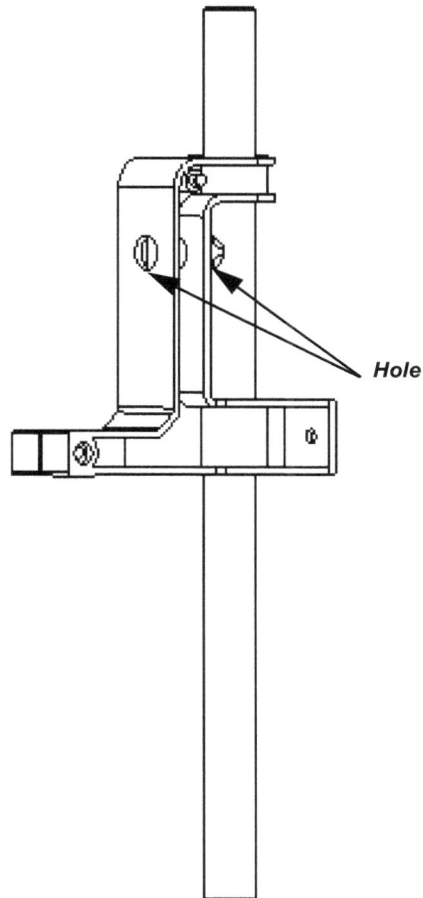

Figure 9–5

When creating features in an assembly, external references can be created in the following situations:

- Selecting the sketching and orientation planes.

- Selecting a placement plane.

- Creating geometry using an edge, offset edge, or concentric circles and arcs.

- Selecting references for sketching.

- Selecting references for depth options.

The reference control and the global reference viewer functionality can also manage external references when creating features in Assembly mode.

How To: Create Assembly Features

1. The feature creation process for assembly features is the same as for creating features in Part mode. To create a feature, select the required command in the *Model* tab. As mentioned above, you can only create holes, cuts, or pipes.
2. The following are differences from Part mode when a cut feature is created in the assembly model:
   - You can only create cuts in Assembly mode.
   - The Intersection panel is added to the dashboard. This panel enables you to select the components that the feature intersects and the level on which the feature is displayed. The dashboard for a cut is shown in Figure 9–6.

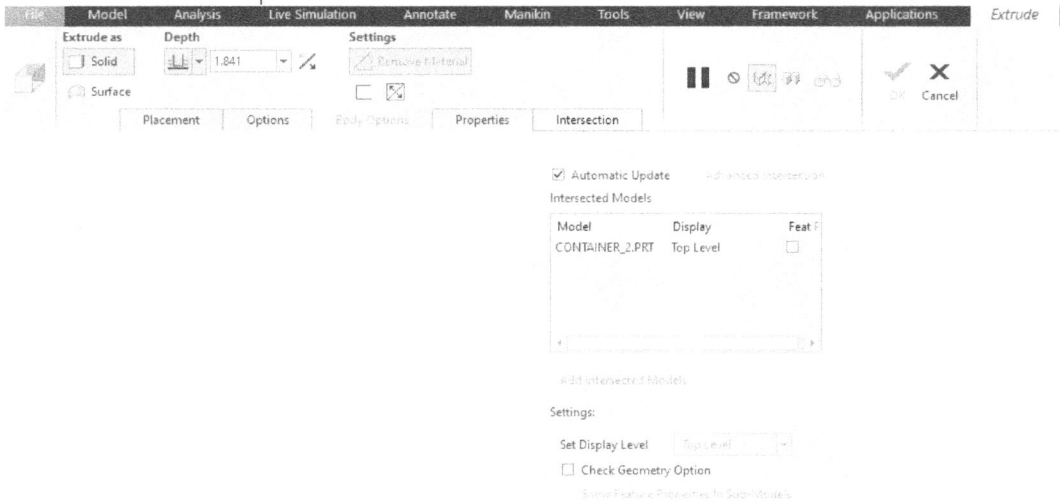

Figure 9–6

By default, features are only visible at the top level of the assembly. Visibility can also be specified to be at the part level, which means assembly features can be seen in the part when it is opened in Part mode. To set visibility at the part level, select **Part Level** in the **Level** menu.

In the advanced intersection environment, you can change the display level by component. Right-click on the component and toggle its display level, as shown in Figure 9–7. The **Check Geometry Option** enables you to create a more stable feature when problem geometry is involved. This is useful when the accuracy level of the assembly components is not the same. Additionally, it increases the regeneration time of the assembly. This option is set for the entire feature and not for individually intersected components.

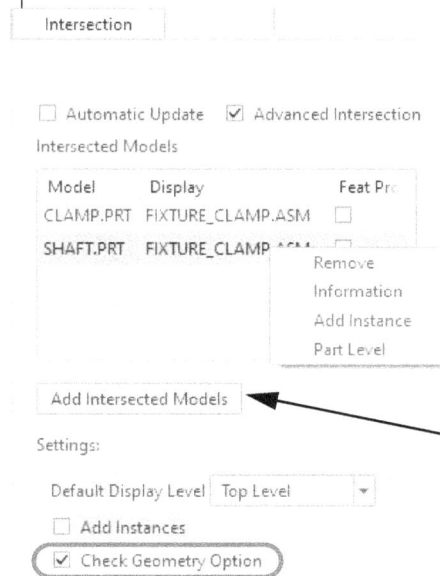

Intersection

☐ Automatic Update   ☑ Advanced Intersection

Intersected Models

Model	Display	Feat Pr
CLAMP.PRT	FIXTURE_CLAMP.ASM	☐
SHAFT.PRT	FIXTURE_CLAMP...	☐

Remove
Information
Add Instance
Part Level

Add Intersected Models

Settings:

Default Display Level Top Level ▼

☐ Add Instances

☑ Check Geometry Option

You can add intersected models with one click. This button is active when Update Automatic is cleared.

Figure 9–7

You can change the display of the feature in the Model Tree. Place a checkmark in the *Feat Props* column to display the intersection as a component feature in the Model Tree, as shown in Figure 9–8. This feature can be edited by right-clicking and selecting an option.

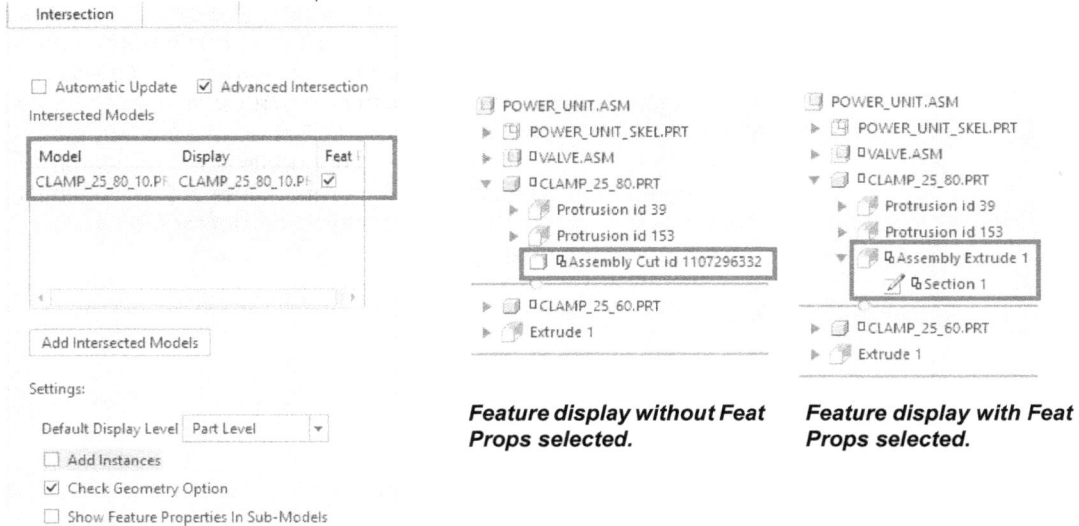

Intersection

☐ Automatic Update   ☑ Advanced Intersection

Intersected Models

Model	Display	Feat
CLAMP_25_80_10.PF	CLAMP_25_80_10.PF	☑

[Add Intersected Models]

Settings:

Default Display Level | Part Level ▾ |

☐ Add Instances
☑ Check Geometry Option
☐ Show Feature Properties In Sub-Models

- POWER_UNIT.ASM
  - ▶ POWER_UNIT_SKEL.PRT
  - ▶ □VALVE.ASM
  - ▼ □CLAMP_25_80.PRT
    - ▶ Protrusion id 39
    - ▶ Protrusion id 153
    - Assembly Cut id 1107296332
  - ▶ □CLAMP_25_60.PRT
  - ▶ Extrude 1

Feature display without Feat Props selected.

- POWER_UNIT.ASM
  - ▶ POWER_UNIT_SKEL.PRT
  - ▶ □VALVE.ASM
  - ▼ □CLAMP_25_80.PRT
    - ▶ Protrusion id 39
    - ▶ Protrusion id 153
    - ▼ Assembly Extrude 1
      - Section 1
  - ▶ □CLAMP_25_60.PRT
  - ▶ Extrude 1

Feature display with Feat Props selected.

Figure 9–8

When the **Add Instances** option is selected, it adds a family table instance of the component that has been selected in the Intersected Models list to the Family table instances list. This option is only available when the display level is set to **Top Level**.

The intersection and visibility levels can be redefined once the feature has been created, by right-clicking and selecting

(Intersect). This option prevents you from having to edit the feature definition and using the tab to set the visibility levels.

The Intersected Components dialog box opens as shown in Figure 9–9 to redefine the intersection and visibility levels.

For some features, the Intersection is defined using the Intersected Components dialog box.

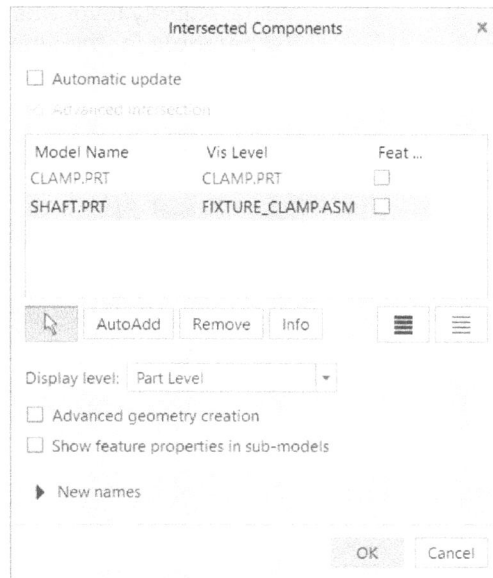

Figure 9–9

In the example shown in Figure 9–10, the assembly Hole feature was added to the assembly. The hole was defined to intersect through both **clamp.prt** and **shaft.prt**.

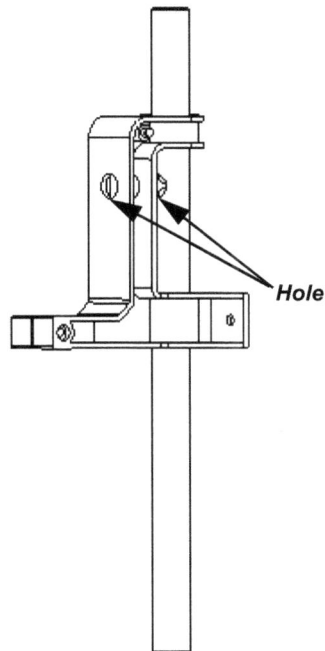

Figure 9–10

The visibility level was specified as **Part** for the clamp and **Assembly** for the shaft. Figure 9–11 shows the two parts in Part mode.

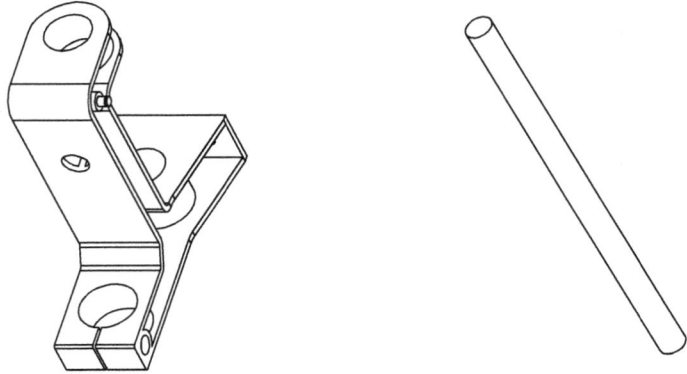

Figure 9–11

9.4 Creating Models from a Motion Skeleton

Solid models can be created from motion skeletons once all body skeletons have been created. You can create a part in the context of the assembly, but rather than selecting references to place the part, you can use **Attach component to body**, as shown in Figure 9–12.

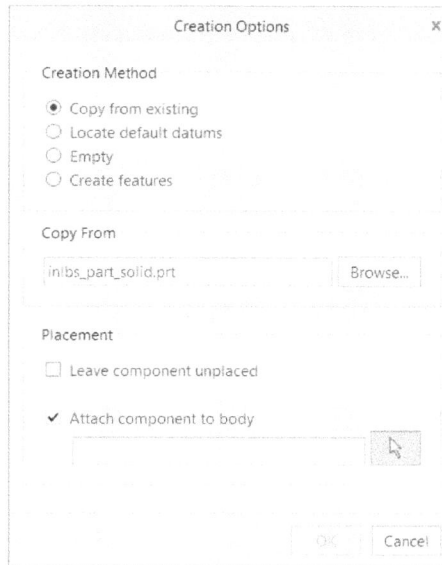

Figure 9–12

Using the Model Tree or direct selection in the model, select the body skeleton you want to reference. When you select the body skeleton, Creo Parametric assembles the new component to the body skeleton, and also copies all of the references from the skeleton to the component, using an **External Merge** feature, as shown in Figure 9–13.

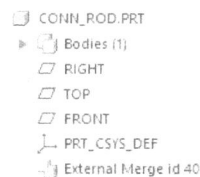

Figure 9–13

Once created, you can activate or open the part, and create geometry that references the skeleton, as shown in Figure 9–14.

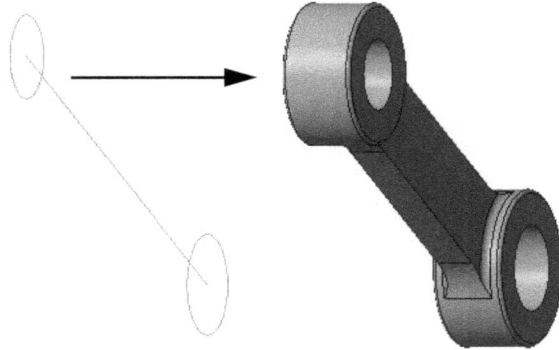

Figure 9–14

The component is then automatically positioned in the top-level assembly, as shown in Figure 9–15.

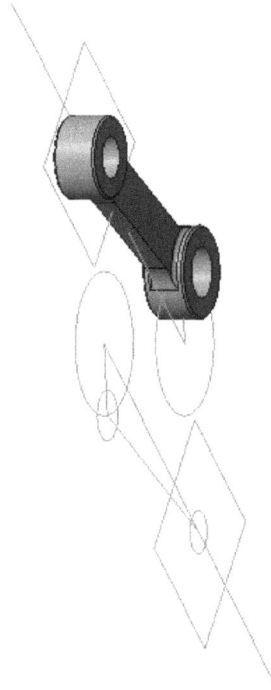

Figure 9–15

The component's motion will be driven by that of the motion skeleton.

Practice 9a

Assembly Features

Practice Objective

- Create an extrude feature at the assembly level and specify the visibility options for the cut feature.

In this practice, you will create an assembly cut and set its visibility at the part level. To begin, you are provided with an assembly that consists of the two plates shown in Figure 9–16.

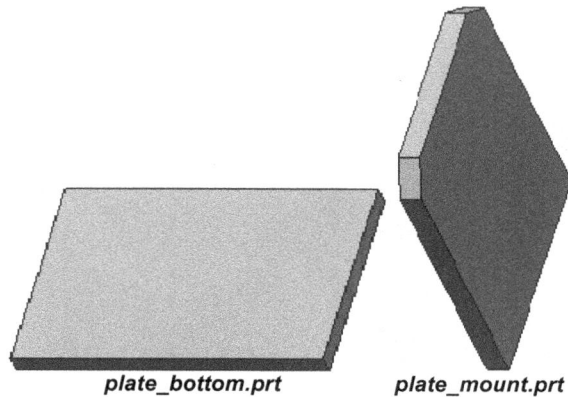

plate_bottom.prt   *plate_mount.prt*

Figure 9–16

Figure 9–17 shows the assembly. It was created by welding the two plates together.

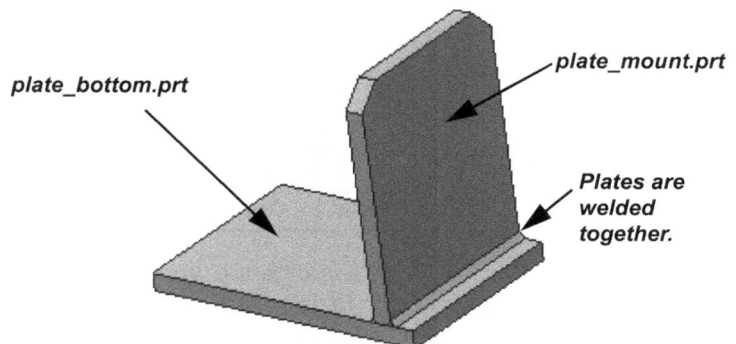

plate_bottom.prt

plate_mount.prt

Plates are welded together.

Figure 9–17

The manufacturing process requires that the two plates are welded together, and that the extruded cut feature is then machined. The machining operation must be relative to the bottom of the weldment. Therefore, the extruded cut cannot be created at the part level. An assembly-level feature is used to capture this intent, as shown in Figure 9–18.

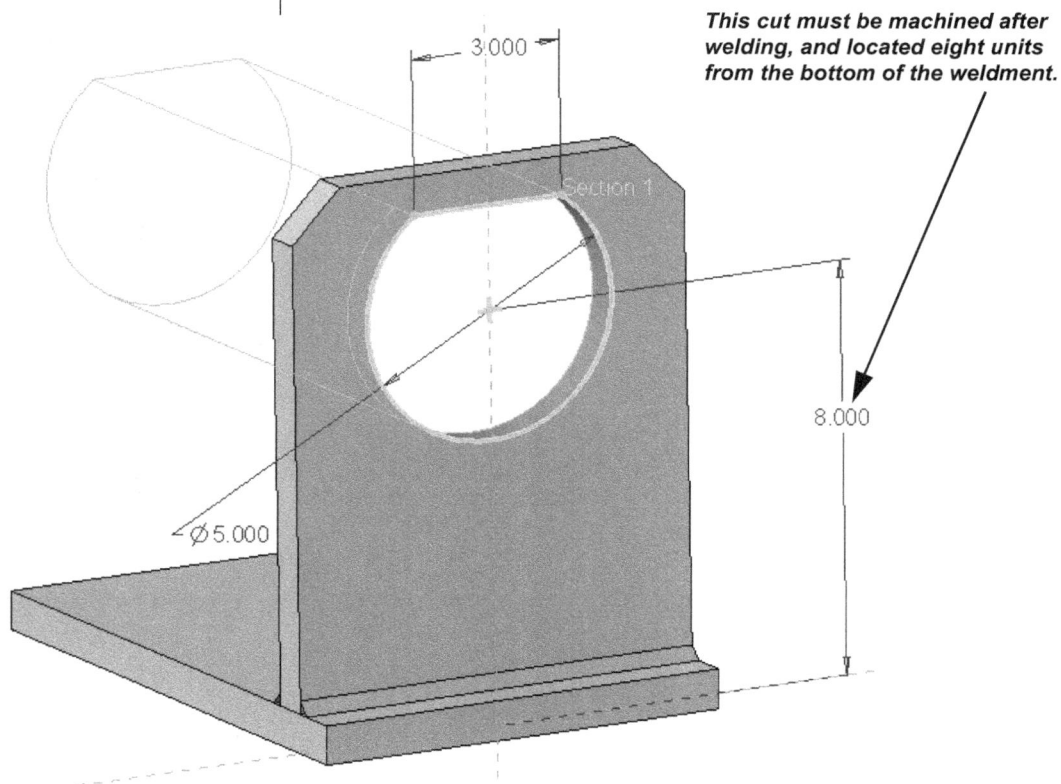

This cut must be machined after welding, and located eight units from the bottom of the weldment.

Figure 9–18

Task 1 - Open an assembly file.

1. Change the working directory to the *Assembly_Features* folder.

2. Open **valve_mount.asm**.

3. Set the model display as follows:

    • (Datum Display Filters): All Off

    • (Spin Center): Off

    • (Display Style): (Shading With Edges)

4. The Model Tree displays as shown in Figure 9–19.

The weld features in this model are defined. Welding features are assembly-level features.

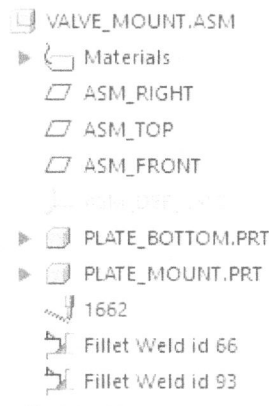

VALVE_MOUNT.ASM
  ▶ Materials
    ASM_RIGHT
    ASM_TOP
    ASM_FRONT
    ASM_DEF_CSYS
  ▶ PLATE_BOTTOM.PRT
  ▶ PLATE_MOUNT.PRT
    1662
    Fillet Weld id 66
    Fillet Weld id 93

Figure 9–19

Task 2 - Create a cut at the assembly level.

1. Click (Extrude) and then select the surface shown in Figure 9–20 as the sketch plane.

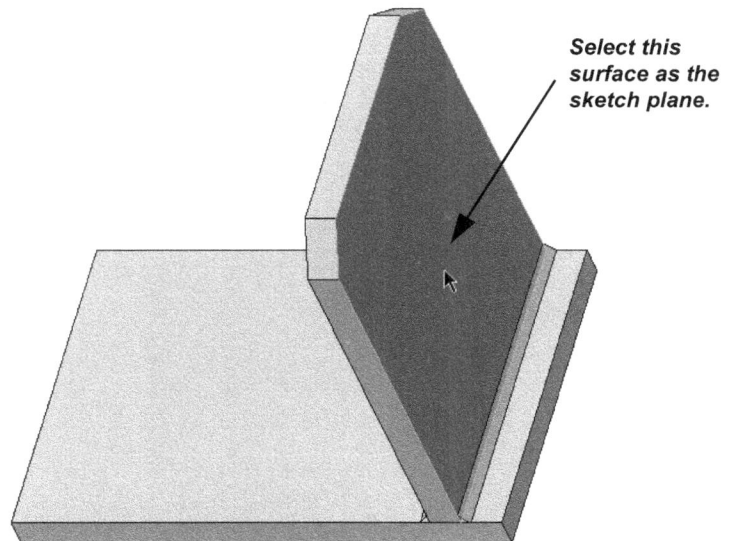

Select this surface as the sketch plane.

Figure 9–20

2. Click (References) in the Setup group in the *Sketch* tab.

3. Select the surface shown in Figure 9–21.

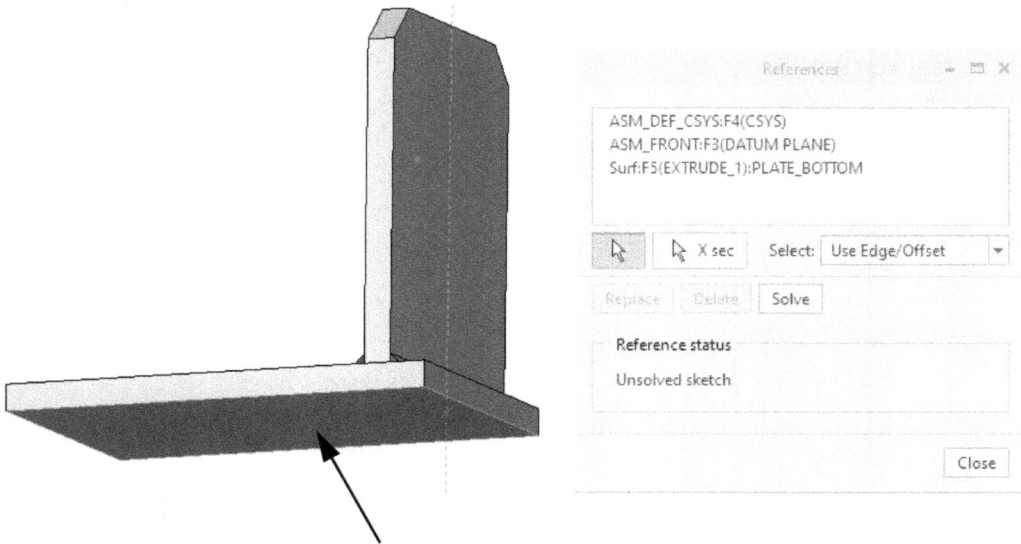

Bottom surface of plate_bottom.prt

Figure 9–21

4. Close the References dialog box and create the sketch shown in Figure 9–22.

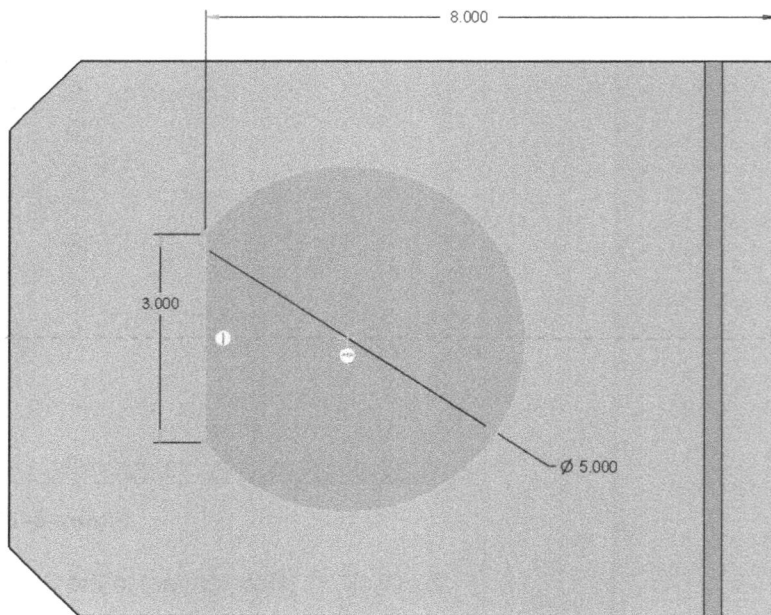

Figure 9–22

5. Click ✓ (OK) and return to default orientation. The assembly displays as shown in Figure 9–23.

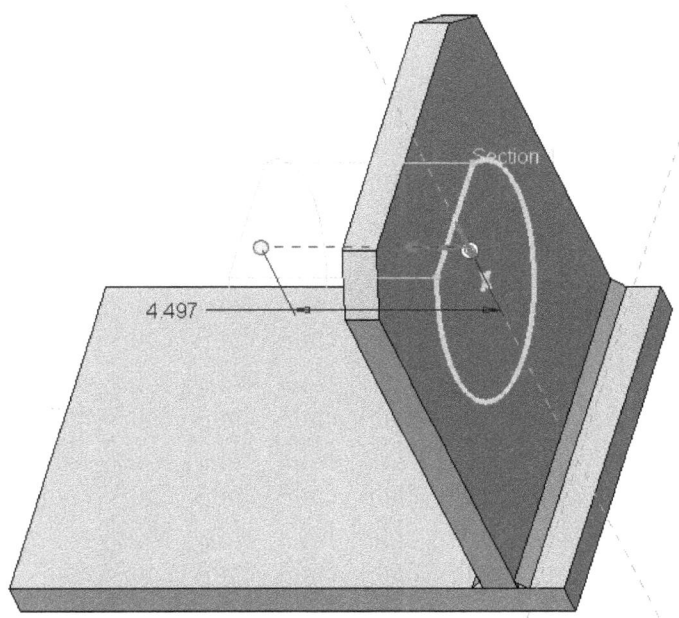

Figure 9–23

6. In the dashboard, select ⊒ ⊑ (Through All) as the *Depth* and click ✓ (OK). The extruded cut feature and Model Tree display as shown in Figure 9–24.

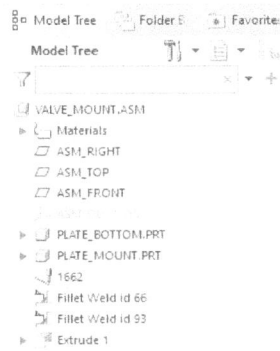

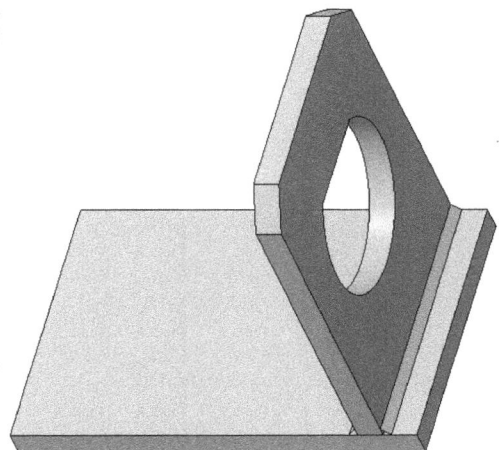

Figure 9–24

7. Save the assembly.

Task 3 - Open the part to review the cut.

1. Select **plate_mount.prt** in the Model Tree and click

   📂 (Open) in the mini toolbar. The part displays as shown
   in Figure 9–25. The extruded cut is not visible in the part.
   The intersect options control the levels at which the
   assembly-level feature is visible. By default, it is set to
   the assembly level.

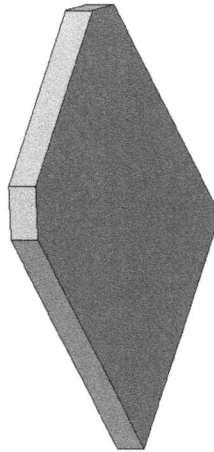

Figure 9–25

2. Switch to the **valve_mount.asm** window.

Task 4 - Set the visibility for an assembly-level feature.

1. Select the assembly-level extruded cut in the Model Tree,
   right-click, and select 🕇 (Intersect), as shown in
   Figure 9–26.

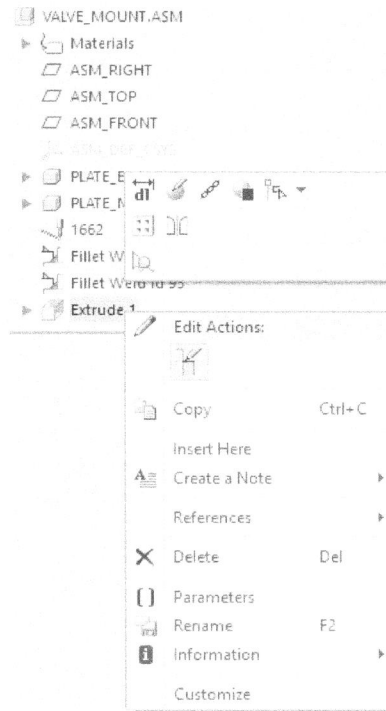

Figure 9–26

Design Considerations

The Intersected Components dialog box opens as shown in Figure 9–27. The **Automatic Update** option has set the *Vis Level* to **Top Level**. When this is done, the assembly-level feature is only displayed in the top-level assembly.

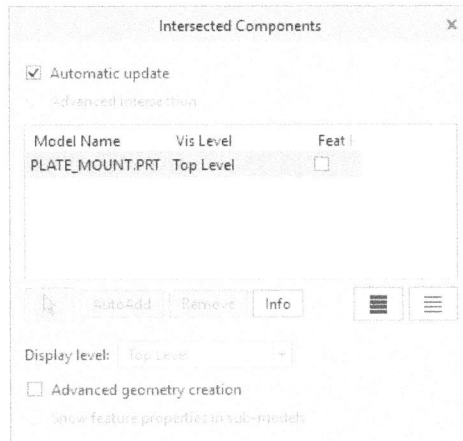

Figure 9–27

2. Make the following changes, as shown in Figure 9–28:

   - Clear the **Automatic Update** option.
   - Set the *Display level* to **Part Level**.

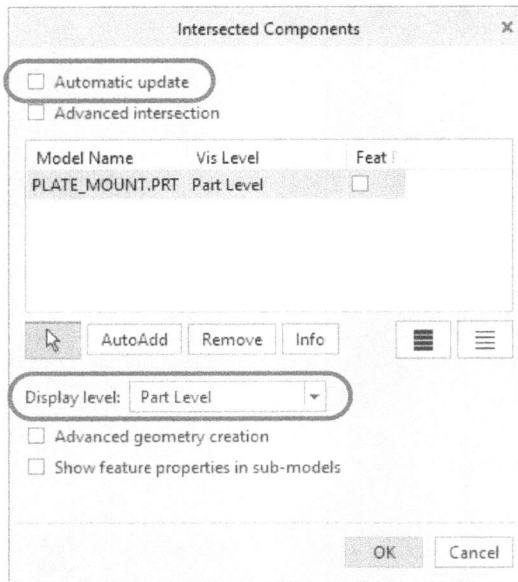

Figure 9–28

3. The *Vis Level* for **PLATE_MOUNT.PRT** model is set to the **Part Level**.

4. Click **OK** to complete the visibility level change.

5. Switch to the PLATE_MOUNT window.

**Design
Considerations**

The part file now displays the assembly-level cut, as shown in Figure 9–29. This is because the intersection level was changed, The feature is also listed in the Model Tree as an assembly cut. Modifications to this feature can only be made at the assembly level. As an alternative to using the Intersected Components dialog box, you can edit the definition of the assembly feature and use the Intersect slide-up panel. The procedure is the same, regardless of the method.

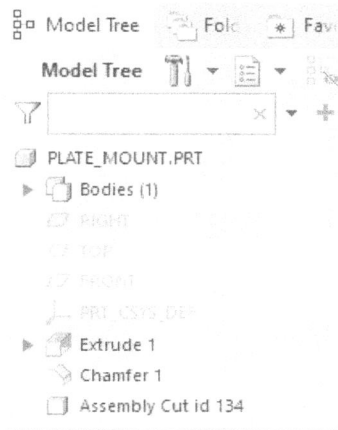

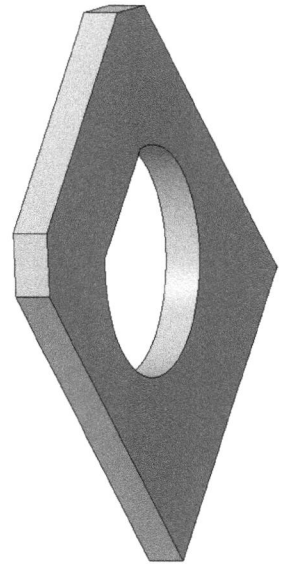

Figure 9–29

6. Close the part window.

7. Save the assembly and erase all of the models from memory.

Practice 9b | Designing in Context

Practice Objective

- Create a part file in the context of an assembly.

In this practice, you will create a part file within the context of an assembly. The final assembly is shown in Figure 9–30.

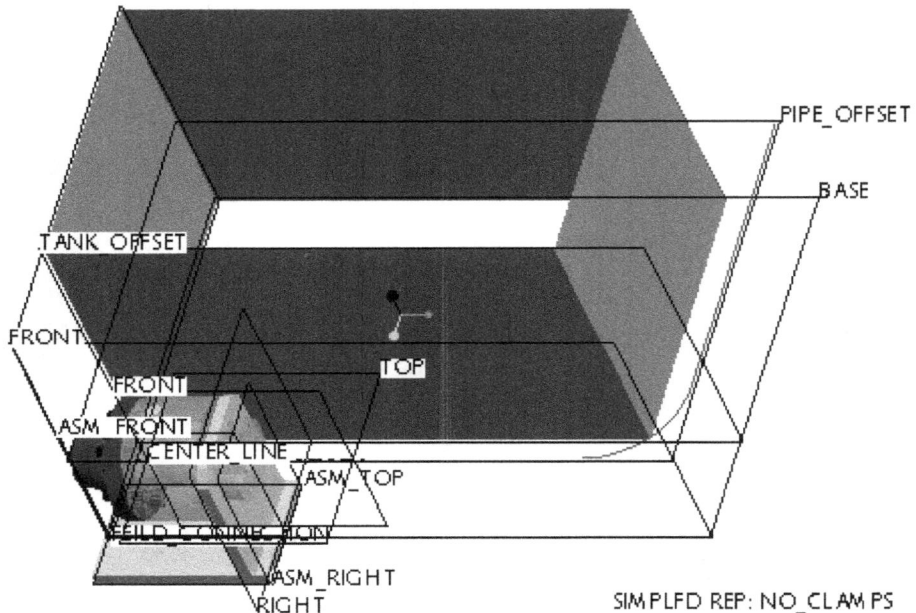

Figure 9–30

Task 1 - Open an assembly file.

1. Change the working directory to the *Designing_In_Context* folder.

2. Open **power_unit_10.asm**.

3. Set the model display as follows:

- *(Datum Display Filters)*: All Off

- *(Spin Center)*: Off

- *(Display Style)*: ☐ (Shading With Edges)

4. If necessary, in the *View* tab, disable ⊡ (Plane Tag Display).

Design Considerations

Including components, such as clamps, is recommended when using top-down design techniques. However, visibility and regeneration time are often compromised. Simplified representations can be used to solve this problem. In this task, you will create a simplified representation that excludes the clamps.

5. Create a simplified representation and set the *Name* to **No_Clamps**.

6. Change the default rule to **Master Rep** and exclude the two clamp parts, as shown in Figure 9–31.

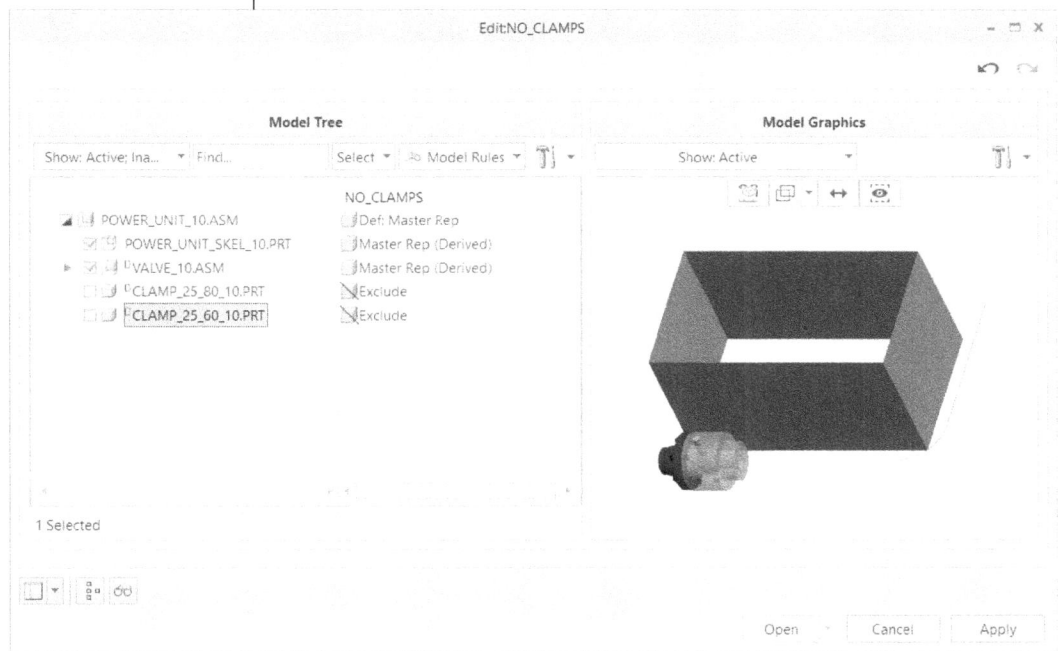

Figure 9–31

7. Click **Open**.

8. Click **Close** in the View Manager. The updated assembly displays without the two clamps.

Task 2 - Assemble valve_mount.asm.

1. Assemble **valve_mount.asm**.

2. Expand **POWER_UNIT_SKEL_10.PRT** and **VALVE_MOUNT.ASM** in the Model Tree, as shown in Figure 9–32.

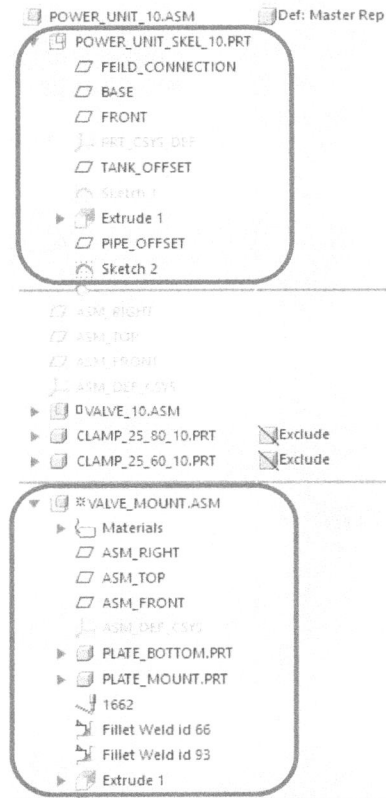

Figure 9–32

3. Use **Coincident** to constrain the following references:

   • *Assembly Reference:* datum plane **BASE**
   • *Component Reference:* datum plane **ASM_TOP**

4. Add a **Coincident** constraint to assemble the following references:

   • *Assembly Reference:* datum plane **FRONT**
   • *Component Reference:* datum plane **ASM_FRONT**

5. Add a third **Coincident** constraint by selecting the two surfaces shown in Figure 9–33.

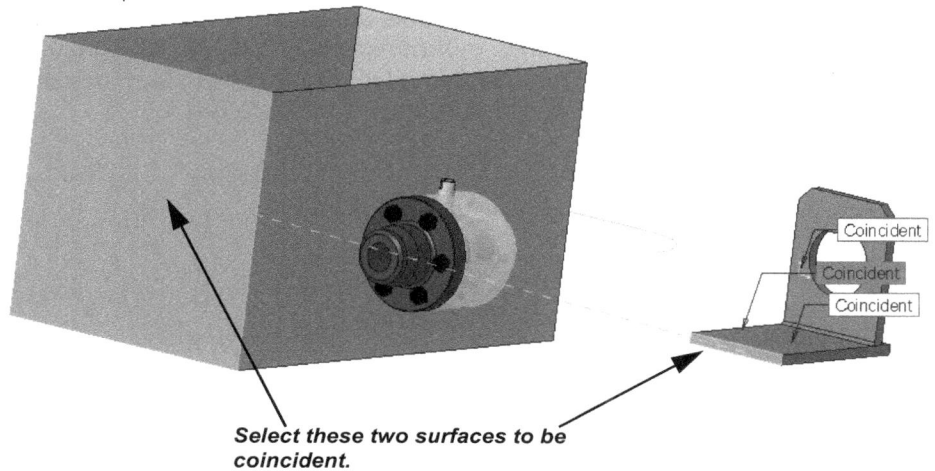

Select these two surfaces to be coincident.

Figure 9–33

6. Complete the component placement. The assembly displays as shown in Figure 9–34.

*The **valve** and **valve_mount** assemblies might intersect because of the packaged placement of the valve assembly. This is expected because the packaged placement was not exact.*

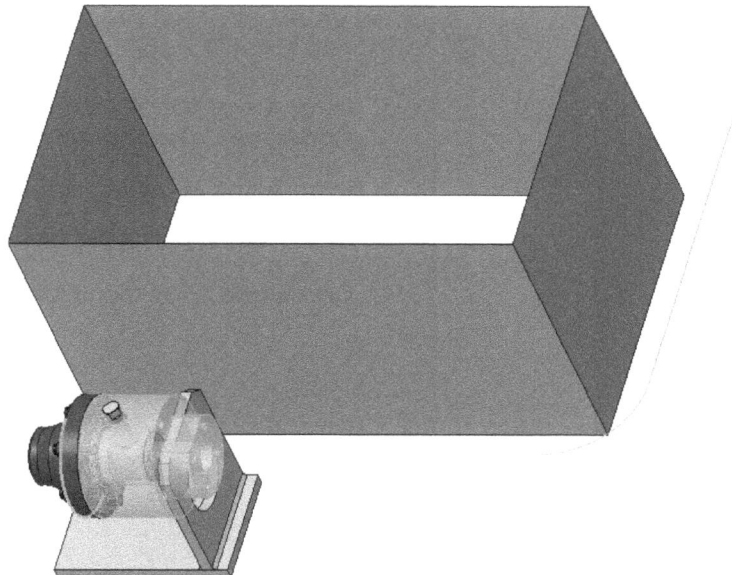

Figure 9–34

Task 3 - Reorder components.

Design Considerations

Since the **valve** assembly needs to be constrained to the **valve_mount** assembly, **VALVE_10.ASM** must be reordered to be after the **valve_mount** assembly. The current Model Tree displays as shown in Figure 9–35.

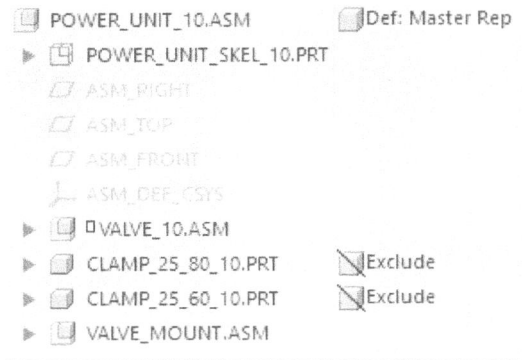

POWER_UNIT_10.ASM   Def: Master Rep
▶ POWER_UNIT_SKEL_10.PRT
    ASM_RIGHT
    ASM_TOP
    ASM_FRONT
    ASM_DEF_CSYS
▶ □VALVE_10.ASM
▶ CLAMP_25_80_10.PRT   Exclude
▶ CLAMP_25_60_10.PRT   Exclude
▶ VALVE_MOUNT.ASM

Figure 9–35

Although you can generally drag and drop to reorder, it is difficult to do in this case, without Creo Parametric attempting to move the **VAVLE_10.ASM** into the **VALVE_MOUNT.ASM**, so you will use the Menu Manager.

1. In the *Model* tab of the ribbon, click **Component> Component Operations**.

2. In the Menu Manager, click **Reorder**.

3. Select **VALVE_10.ASM** from the Model Tree.

4. Click **Done** in the Menu Manager.

5. Click **After** and select **VALVE_MOUNT.ASM** in the Model Tree. **VALVE_10.PRT** is moved to the bottom of the Model Tree, as shown in Figure 9–36.

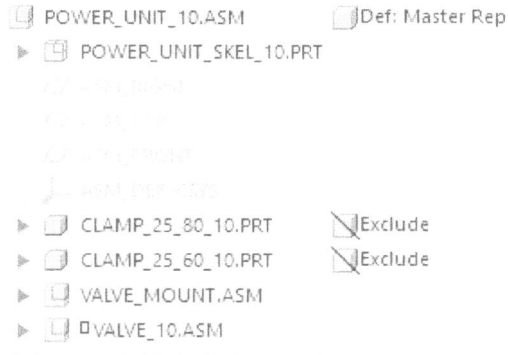

POWER_UNIT_10.ASM   Def: Master Rep
▶ POWER_UNIT_SKEL_10.PRT

▶ CLAMP_25_80_10.PRT   Exclude
▶ CLAMP_25_60_10.PRT   Exclude
▶ VALVE_MOUNT.ASM
▶ VALVE_10.ASM

Figure 9–36

6. Click **Done/Return** in the Menu Manager.

7. Edit the definition of the **valve_10** assembly and drag it to a position similar to the one shown in Figure 9–37.

You can use 3D Dragger to move the component.

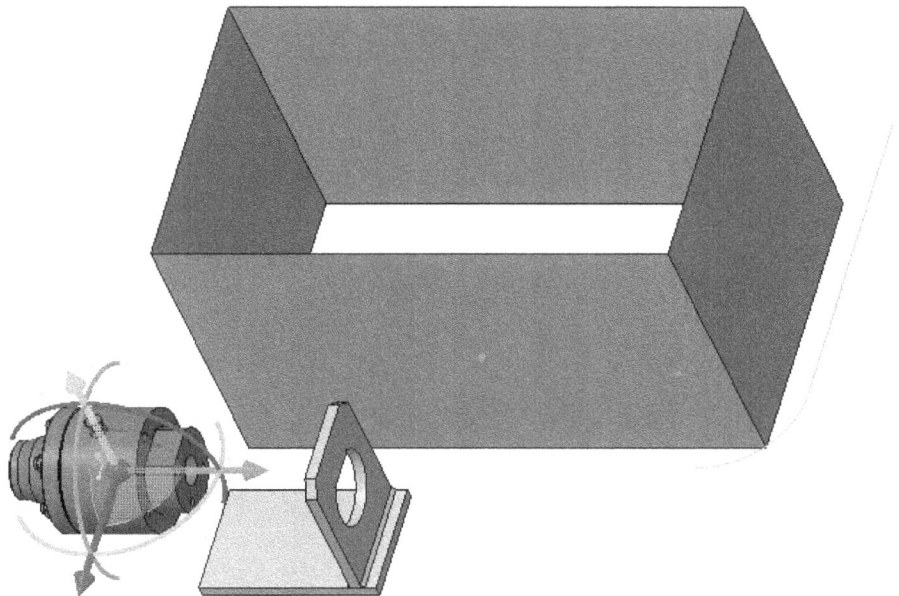

Figure 9–37

8. Use two Coincident constraints and a **Parallel** constraint to fully constrain **VALVE_10.ASM** to **VALVE_MOUNT.ASM**. The fully constrained assembly displays as shown in Figure 9–38.

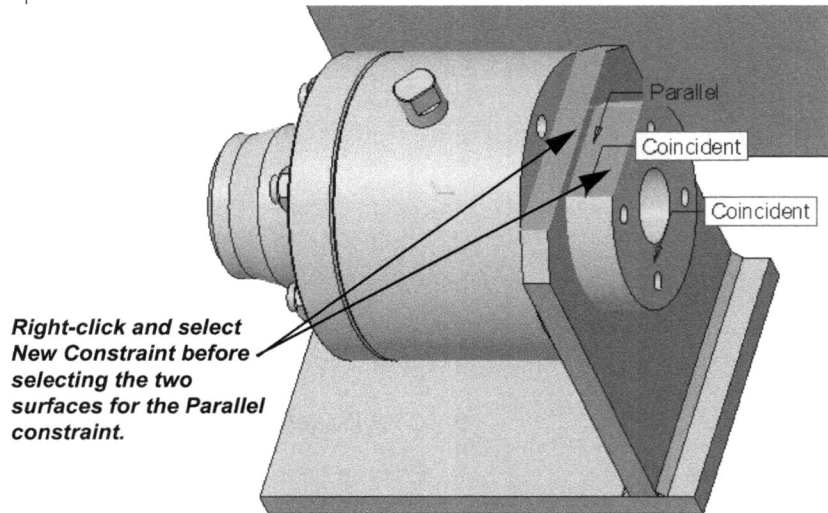

Parallel

Coincident

Coincident

Right-click and select New Constraint before selecting the two surfaces for the Parallel constraint.

Figure 9–38

Task 4 - Create a new part file while in Assembly mode.

1. Click ⬚ (Create). In the Create Component dialog box, select **Part** and then **Solid**. Set the new part *File name* to **pipe**, as shown in Figure 9–39.

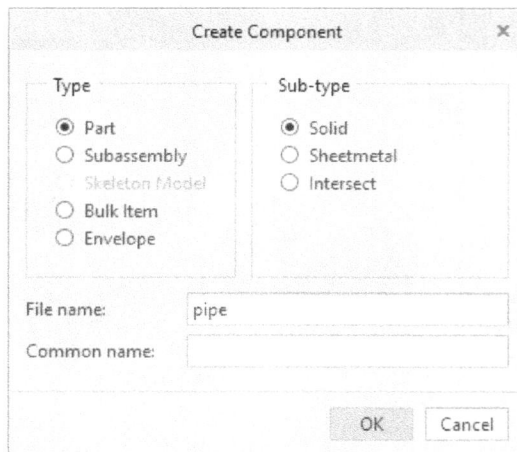

Figure 9–39

2. Click **OK** in the Create Component dialog box.

3. Select the **Copy From Existing** option as the creation method, click **Browse** and select **start_part.prt**, as shown in Figure 9–40.

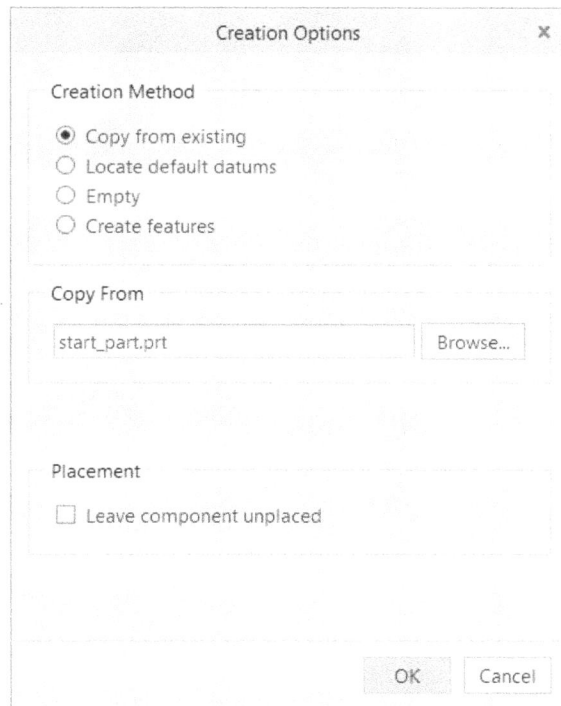

Creation Options   ✕

Creation Method

◉ Copy from existing
○ Locate default datums
○ Empty
○ Create features

Copy From

| start_part.prt | Browse... |

Placement

☐ Leave component unplaced

OK   Cancel

Figure 9–40

4. Click **OK** in the Creation Options dialog box.

5. Click ✔ (OK) in the *Component Placement* tab to leave the component as packaged.

6. Toggle on the datum plane and datum axis display, if they are not visible. The assembly with the new part displays as shown in Figure 9–41.

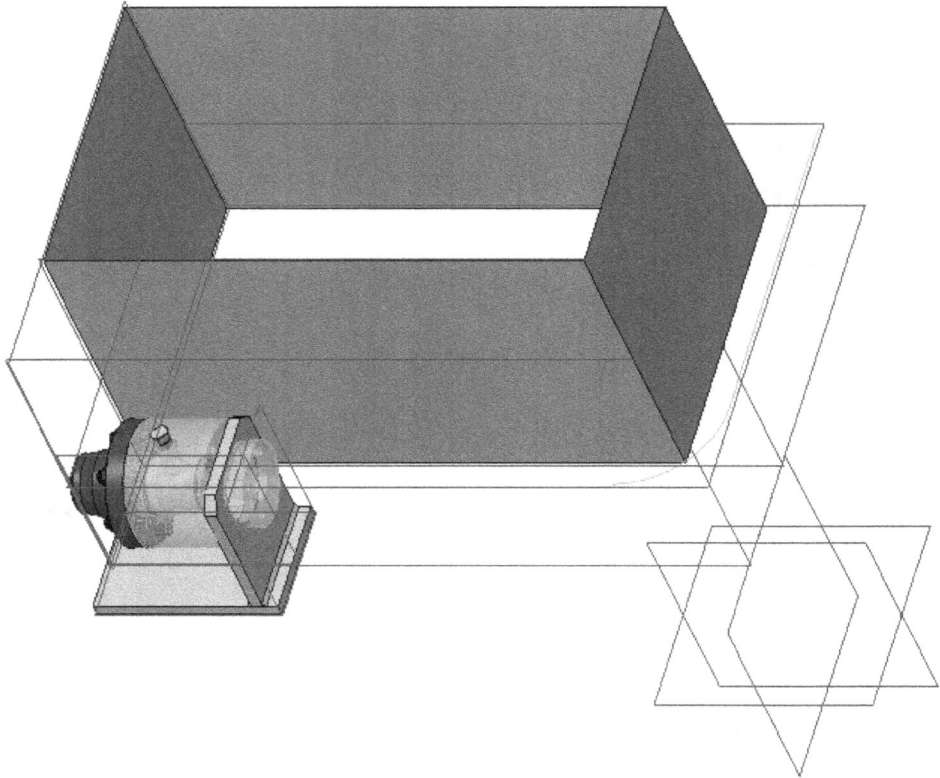

Figure 9–41

Task 5 - Activate the part and create a feature.

1. Select **PIPE.PRT** in the Model Tree and click ◇ (Activate) in the mini toolbar.

2. In the In-graphics toolbar, enable ╱ₒ (Axis Display).

3. Create a datum axis at the intersection of datum planes **TOP** and **FRONT**.

4. Use the *Properties* tab to set the datum axis *Name to* **CENTER_LINE**, as shown in Figure 9–42.

Figure 9–42

5. Click **OK**. The pipe part displays as shown in Figure 9–43.

Figure 9–43

Task 6 - Constrain the pipe part.

Design Considerations

The Pipe part is only packaged in the assembly. In the following steps, you will edit the definition of this component to parametrically place it in the assembly.

1. Activate the top-level assembly.

2. Edit the definition of the pipe's placement. Select the following references from the Model Tree to be coincident:

- *Assembly Reference:* datum plane **PIPE_OFFSET** in the **POWER_UNIT_SKEL_10.PRT**
- *Component Reference:* datum plane **TOP**

3. Add a new constraint. Select the following references to be coincident, as shown in Figure 9–44:

3D Dragger is toggled off for clarity.

- *Assembly Reference:* **Surface of the valve**
- *Component Reference:* datum plane **RIGHT**

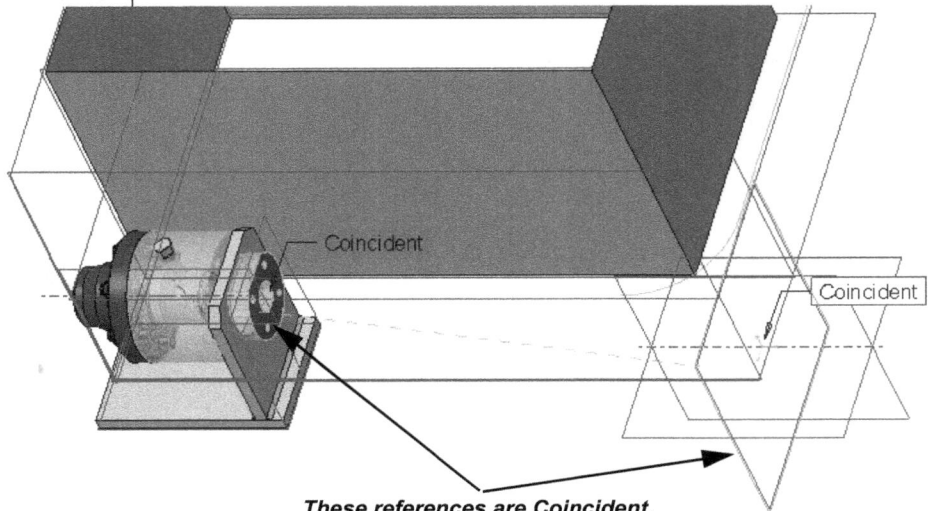

These references are Coincident.

Figure 9–44

4. Add a new constraint. Select the following references to be coincident, as shown in Figure 9–45:

- *Assembly Reference:* datum plane **FRONT** (of Skeleton)
- *Component Reference:* datum plane **FRONT**

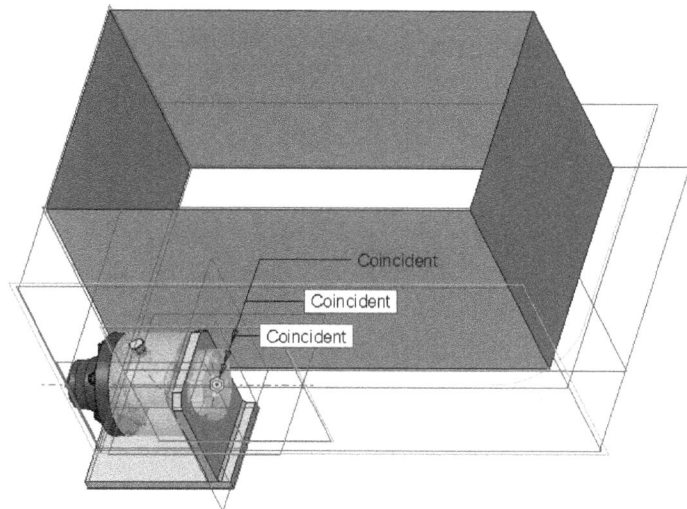

Figure 9–45

5. Complete the placement of the pipe part and toggle off the display of datum entities. The assembly displays as shown in Figure 9–46.

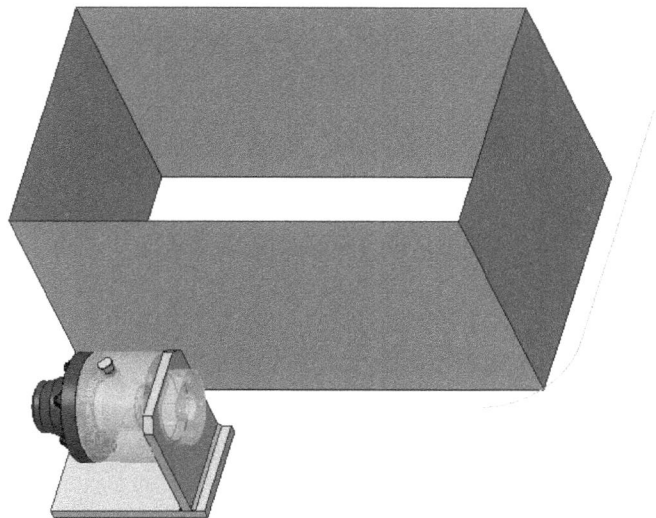

Figure 9–46

6. In the In-graphics toolbar, click 🔯 (View Manager).

7. Double-click the **Master Rep** to activate it and close the View Manager.

Design Considerations

The Model Tree displays as shown in Figure 9–47. **VALVE_MOUNT.ASM**, **VALVE_10.ASM**, and the pipe components are no longer packaged. The clamp parts will be fully placed once the pipe geometry has been created.

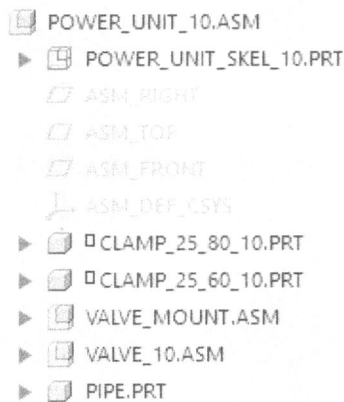

POWER_UNIT_10.ASM
▶ POWER_UNIT_SKEL_10.PRT
　 ASM_RIGHT
　 ASM_TOP
　 ASM_FRONT
　 ASM_DEF_CSYS
▶ □ CLAMP_25_80_10.PRT
▶ □ CLAMP_25_60_10.PRT
▶ VALVE_MOUNT.ASM
▶ VALVE_10.ASM
▶ PIPE.PRT

Figure 9–47

8. Save the assembly and erase it from memory.

Practice 9c

Adding Components to Motion Skeletons

Practice Objective

- Use body skeletons to create components for a mechanism.

In this practice, you will create part files in the context of an assembly using the body skeletons.

Task 1 - Open an assembly file.

1. Change the working directory to the *Components_Motion_Skel* folder.

2. Open **crank_piston.asm**.

3. Set the model display as follows:

   - ⁺⁄₊ *(Datum Display Filters)*: All Off

   - ⋟ *(Spin Center)*: Off

   - ⌐ *(Display Style)*: ☐ (Shading With Edges)

4. Expand **CRANK_PISTON_MOTION_SKEL.ASM** in the Model Tree.

Task 2 - Create the CR_JOURNAL.PRT component.

1. Click ▣ (Create).

2. Set the *Type* to **Part** and the *Sub-type* to **Solid**.

3. Set the *File Name* to **cr_journal** and click **OK**.

4. Click **Browse** and select **start_part_mmns.prt**.

5. Select **Attach component to body**, as shown in Figure 9–48.

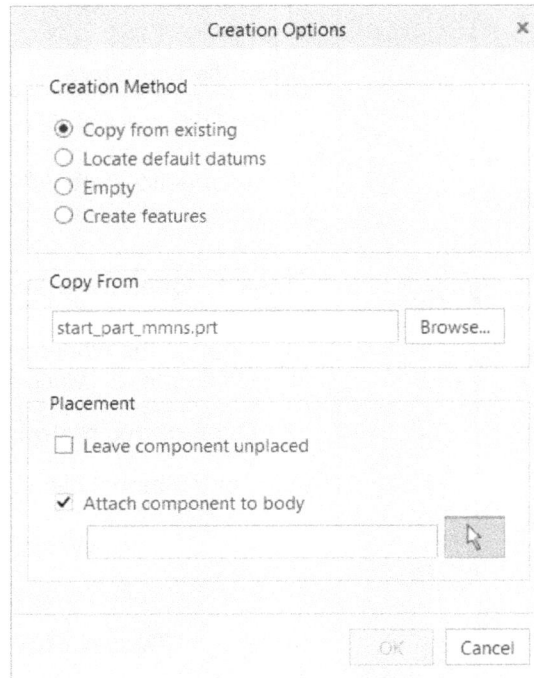

Figure 9–48

6. Select **CR_JOURNAL_SKEL.PRT** in the Model Tree.

7. Click **OK**. The Model Tree updates as shown in Figure 9–49.

To show the tree without datum planes, go to Settings>Tree Filter and uncheck Datum plane.

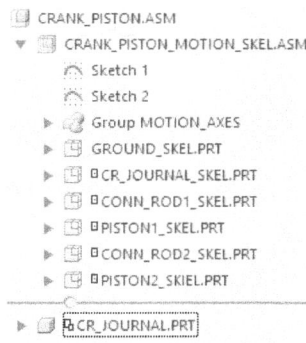

Figure 9–49

8. Select **CR_JOURNAL.PRT** in the Model Tree and select (Open) in the mini toolbar.

9. The skeleton geometry is copied into the part as an **External Merge** feature, as shown in Figure 9–50.

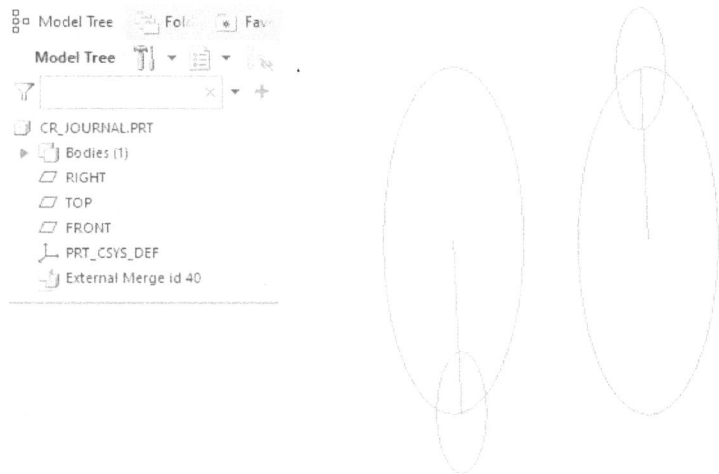

Figure 9–50

10. Save the part and close the CR_JOURNAL window.

Task 3 - Create the CONN_ROD.PRT part.

1. Click ⊞ (Create).

2. Set the *Type* to **Part** and the *Sub-type* to **Solid**.

3. Set the *Name* to **conn_rod** and click **OK**.

4. Click **Browse** and select **start_part_mmns.prt**.

5. Select **Attach component to body** in the Creation Options dialog box.

6. Select **CONN_ROD1_SKEL.PRT** in the Model Tree.

7. Click **OK**. The Model Tree updates as shown in Figure 9–51.

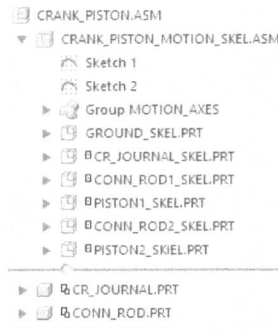

CRANK_PISTON.ASM
▼ CRANK_PISTON_MOTION_SKEL.ASM
    Sketch 1
    Sketch 2
    ▶ Group MOTION_AXES
    ▶ GROUND_SKEL.PRT
    ▶ CR_JOURNAL_SKEL.PRT
    ▶ CONN_ROD1_SKEL.PRT
    ▶ PISTON1_SKEL.PRT
    ▶ CONN_ROD2_SKEL.PRT
    ▶ PISTON2_SKIEL.PRT
▶ CR_JOURNAL.PRT
▶ CONN_ROD.PRT

Figure 9–51

8. Select **CONN_ROD.PRT** in the Model Tree and click (Open) in the mini toolbar.

9. The skeleton geometry is copied into the part as an **External Merge** feature, as shown in Figure 9–52.

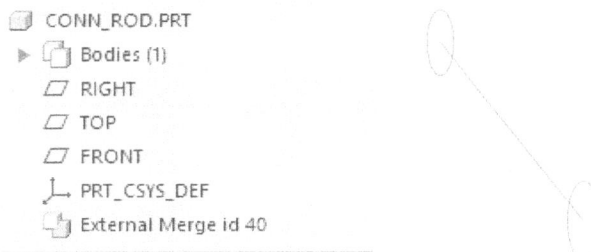

CONN_ROD.PRT
▶ Bodies (1)
    RIGHT
    TOP
    FRONT
    PRT_CSYS_DEF
    External Merge id 40

Figure 9–52

10. Save the part and close the CONN_ROD window.

Task 4 - Create the PISTON.PRT part.

1. Click (Create).

2. Set the *Type* to **Part** and the *Sub-type* to **Solid**.

3. Set the *File Name* to **piston** and click **OK**.

4. Click **Browse** and select **start_part_mmns.prt**.

5. Select **Attach component to body** in the Creation Options dialog box.

6. Select **PISTON1_SKEL.PRT** in the Model Tree.

7. Click **OK**. The Model Tree updates as shown in Figure 9–53.

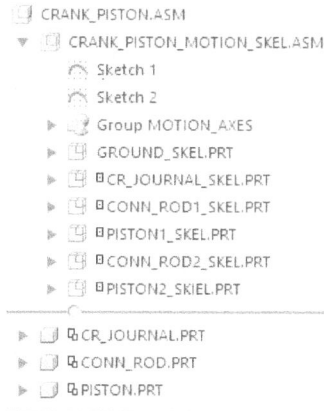

CRANK_PISTON.ASM
  ▼ CRANK_PISTON_MOTION_SKEL.ASM
       Sketch 1
       Sketch 2
    ▶ Group MOTION_AXES
    ▶ GROUND_SKEL.PRT
    ▶ CR_JOURNAL_SKEL.PRT
    ▶ CONN_ROD1_SKEL.PRT
    ▶ PISTON1_SKEL.PRT
    ▶ CONN_ROD2_SKEL.PRT
    ▶ PISTON2_SKIEL.PRT

  ▶ CR_JOURNAL.PRT
  ▶ CONN_ROD.PRT
  ▶ PISTON.PRT

Figure 9–53

8. Select **PISTON.PRT** in the Model Tree, right-click, and select **Open**.

9. The skeleton geometry is copied into the part as an **External Merge** feature, as shown in Figure 9–54.

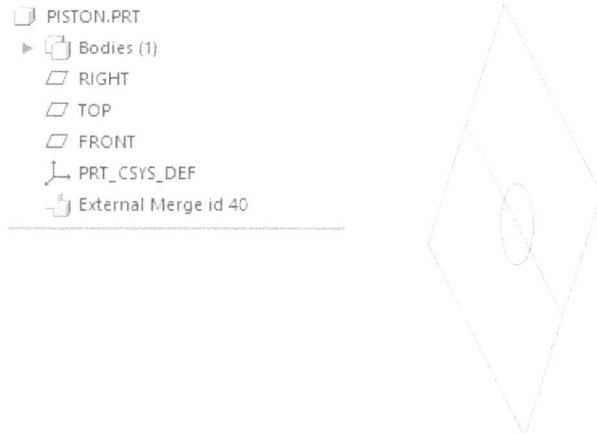

PISTON.PRT
  ▶ Bodies (1)
     RIGHT
     TOP
     FRONT
     PRT_CSYS_DEF
     External Merge id 40

Figure 9–54

10. Save the part and close the PISTON window.

Design Considerations

The components are now ready to add geometry, which will be covered in *Chapter 11: Managing External References*. Note that you did not use the skeletons **conn_rod2_skel** and **piston2_skel** because they will only be used as assembly references.

11. Save the assembly and erase all files from memory.

Chapter Review Questions

1. External references should be avoided, but they can easily be created in which of the following situations? (Select all that apply.)

    a. Selecting the sketching and orientation planes.

    b. Selecting references for sketching.

    c. Selecting depth options.

    d. Creating geometry by clicking ☐ (Project) and ☐ (Offset) and creating concentric circles and arcs.

2. Which of the following statements are true when creating a component at the assembly level? (Select all that apply.)

    a. Enables you to use other assembly component references and features to create new parts.

    b. Can produce a parent/child relationship between components.

    c. Enables you to display the other components and how the part fits in the assembly.

    d. Enables you to decrease the regeneration time.

3. If the assembly is not in session and a part with external references is opened on its own, some references might be missing and you have limited control over the part.

    a. True

    b. False

4. Which of the following items can you create in the assembly? (Select all that apply.)

    a. Parts

    b. Subassemblies

    c. Skeleton models

    d. Bulk items

    e. Envelope

5. You can create a limited set of features in Assembly mode. Which assembly-level features can you create? (Select all that apply.)

   a. Extrude to add material

   b. Pipe

   c. Extrude to remove material

   d. Hole

6. Assembly-level features are only visible at the top level of the assembly.

   a. True

   b. False

Distributing Design Information

Creo Parametric enables you to distribute design information in an assembly using advanced options. These options enable you to share feature information between components of different assemblies, which helps save time. As a result, you can design more efficiently when working with complex assemblies.

Learning Objectives in This Chapter

- Learn how to set up external reference controls for the current assembly and to determine how the assembly reacts to invalid selections.
- Learn how to set up external reference controls globally and the different rules that can be set to control the references.
- Use the Copy Geometry feature to copy geometry from a source model and to create independent or dependent geometry in the target model.
- Create published geometry to control external references when creating geometry in an assembly.
- Learn to copy geometry in a part or assembly using a shrinkwrap feature.
- Learn the advantages and options when creating a shrinkwrap feature.
- Learn to create component geometry that references the skeleton models.

10.1 External Reference Control in Current Assembly

Managing external references in the current assembly enables you to specify both the allowable scope of external references and how the system reacts to invalid selections. The setting is only available for the current assembly.

How To: Control External References for the Current Assembly

1. Select **File>Prepare>Model Properties**. The Model Properties dialog box opens. Select **change** next to the Reference Control, as shown in Figure 10–1.

Click change

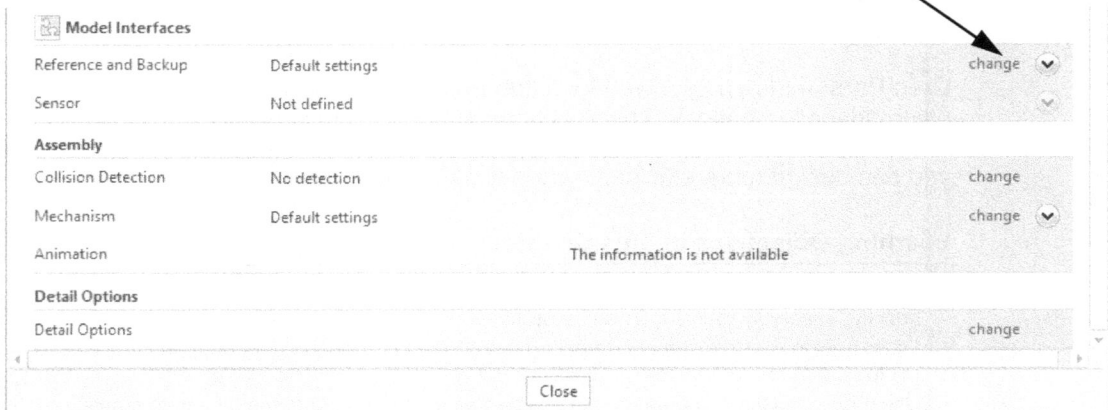

Figure 10–1

You can also select the top-level assembly, right-click, and select **References>Reference Control**. The External Reference Control dialog box opens as shown in Figure 10–2. Use the Look In drop-down list to select the object type (model or component) and the object.

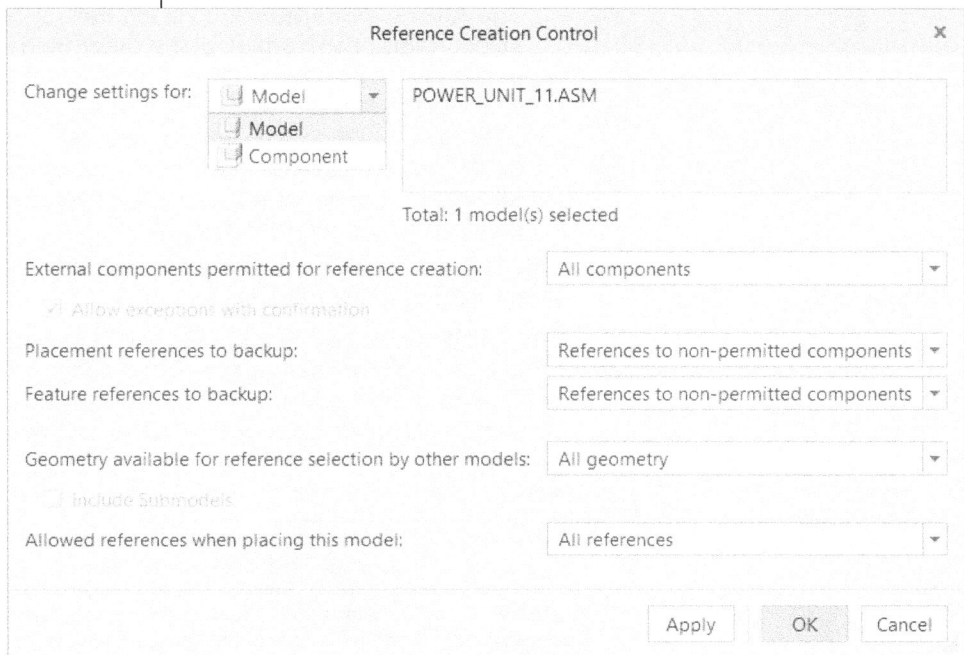

Figure 10–2

2. The External components permitted for reference creation drop-down list enables you to define the scope of components that can be referenced in the current model. The available options are described as follows:

Option	Description
All components	Enables you to select references from any model in the assembly.
Inside Subassembly	Enables you to only select references from the components that belong to the same subassembly.
Skeleton and Layout model	Enables you to only select references from the skeleton or layout model of the subassembly.
None	Prevents you from selecting references from other components.

- The **All components** option is the default option (you can select references from all of the other models in the assembly). It is recommended that you change this option to a more restrictive setting either manually in each assembly, or using the **default_ext_ref_scope** config option. As an added precaution, you can set the **allow_ref_scope_change** config option to **No** to prevent changes to the reference scope.

3. You can specify which geometry in the current model can be referenced by other models.

- The Geometry available for reference selection by other models drop-down list enables you to define which geometry in the current assembly can be referenced for geometry creation. The options are described as follows:

Option	Description
All geometry	Enables you to establish references for all of the geometry in the current model.
Published Geometry	Enables you to restrict references that are made to the model to only published geometry features.
None	Prevents you from establishing any references for the current model.

- The **Allowed references** when placing this model drop-down list enables you to determine whether or not references in the current assembly can be used for component placement. The options are described as follows:

Option	Description
All references	Enables you to use all of the geometry as component constraints.
Interfaces only	Enables you to only use the component interfaces for component constraints.
Default placement only	Only default placement is allowed.

4. Click **OK** to complete the reference control settings for the current assembly. The settings are stored with the model.

10.2 Global External References

Managing external references in each assembly enables you to set individual settings, depending on the assembly and the design intent. Creo Parametric also offers tools to globally set the reference control for all of the assemblies in the current session.

How To: Define the Global External Reference Settings

1. Select **File>Options>Assembly**. The *Reference creation and backup control* area displays in the Creo Parametric Options dialog box, as shown in Figure 10–3.

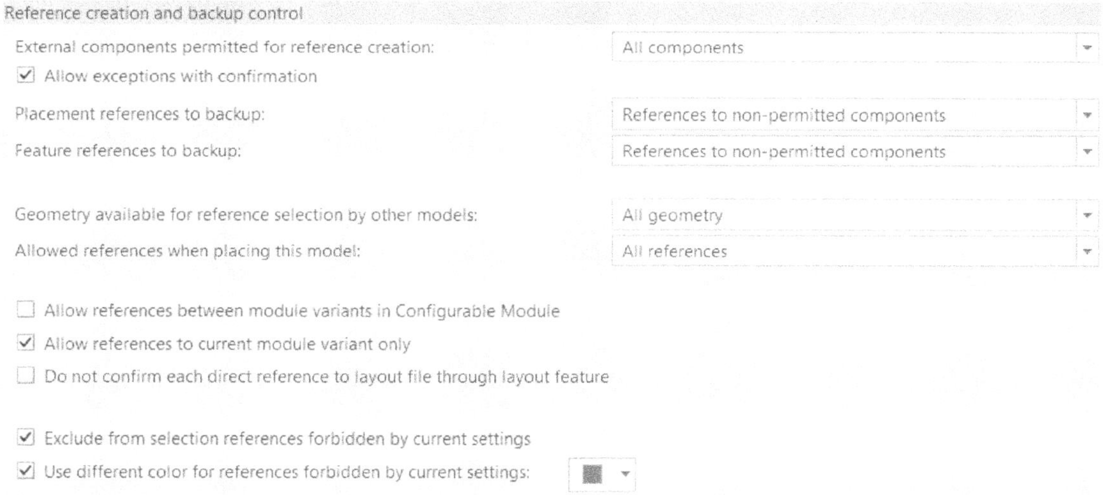

Reference creation and backup control

External components permitted for reference creation:	All components
☑ Allow exceptions with confirmation	
Placement references to backup:	References to non-permitted components
Feature references to backup:	References to non-permitted components
Geometry available for reference selection by other models:	All geometry
Allowed references when placing this model:	All references

☐ Allow references between module variants in Configurable Module
☑ Allow references to current module variant only
☐ Do not confirm each direct reference to layout file through layout feature

☑ Exclude from selection references forbidden by current settings
☑ Use different color for references forbidden by current settings:

Figure 10–3

2. The External components permitted for external reference creation drop-down list contains options that enable you to define the scope of the components that can be referenced, as shown in Figure 10–4.

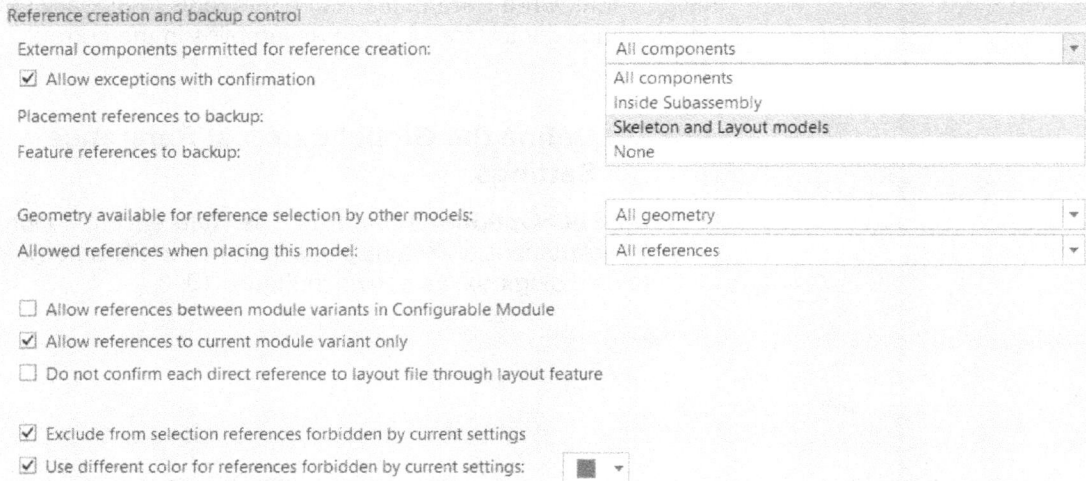

Reference creation and backup control

External components permitted for reference creation:	All components ▼
☑ Allow exceptions with confirmation	All components
	Inside Subassembly
Placement references to backup:	Skeleton and Layout models
Feature references to backup:	None
Geometry available for reference selection by other models:	All geometry ▼
Allowed references when placing this model:	All references ▼

☐ Allow references between module variants in Configurable Module

☑ Allow references to current module variant only

☐ Do not confirm each direct reference to layout file through layout feature

☑ Exclude from selection references forbidden by current settings

☑ Use different color for references forbidden by current settings: ▣ ▼

Figure 10–4

The options are described as follows:

Option	Description
All components	Enables you to make references to any model in the assembly.
Inside Subassembly	Enables you to only make references to the components that belong to the same subassembly.
Skeleton and Layout models	Enables you to only make references to the skeleton model of the subassembly.
None	Prevents you from making references to other components.

The **Geometry available for reference selection by other models** and **Allowed references when assembling this component** options enable you to specify the type of geometry that can be referenced, as shown in Figure 10–5.

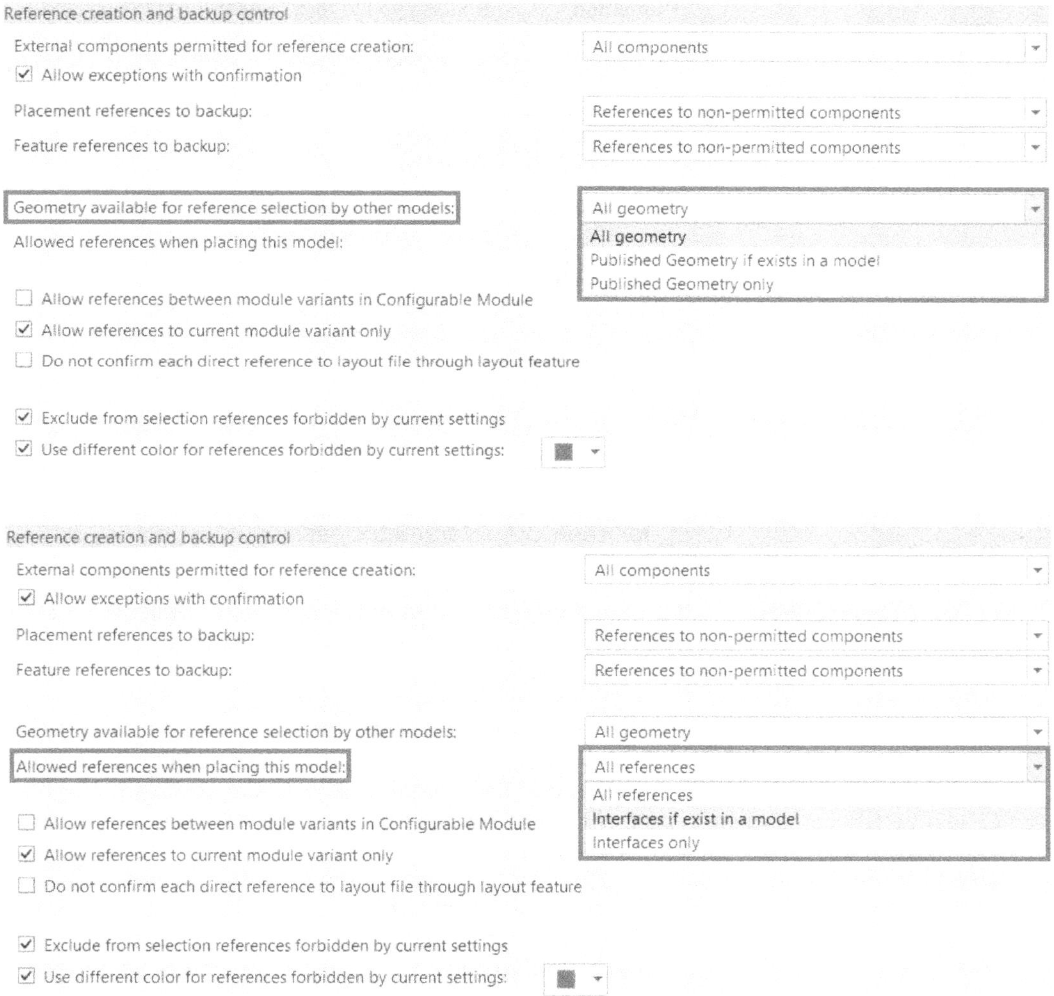

Reference creation and backup control

External components permitted for reference creation: All components
☑ Allow exceptions with confirmation

Placement references to backup: References to non-permitted components

Feature references to backup: References to non-permitted components

Geometry available for reference selection by other models: All geometry

Allowed references when placing this model: **All geometry** / Published Geometry if exists in a model / Published Geometry only

☐ Allow references between module variants in Configurable Module

☑ Allow references to current module variant only

☐ Do not confirm each direct reference to layout file through layout feature

☑ Exclude from selection references forbidden by current settings
☑ Use different color for references forbidden by current settings:

Reference creation and backup control

External components permitted for reference creation: All components
☑ Allow exceptions with confirmation

Placement references to backup: References to non-permitted components

Feature references to backup: References to non-permitted components

Geometry available for reference selection by other models: All geometry

Allowed references when placing this model: All references / **Interfaces if exist in a model** / Interfaces only

☐ Allow references between module variants in Configurable Module

☑ Allow references to current module variant only

☐ Do not confirm each direct reference to layout file through layout feature

☑ Exclude from selection references forbidden by current settings
☑ Use different color for references forbidden by current settings:

Figure 10–5

The options are described as follows:

Option	Description
All geometry	Enables you to make references to all of the geometry.
Published Geometry if exists in a model	Enables you to restrict references to published geometry that currently exists in a model. If none exists in the model, this option enables you to create external references to any geometry.
Published Geometry only	Enables you to restrict references to only published geometry.
All references	Enables you to use all of the geometry as references for the component constraints.
Interfaces if exist in a model	Enables you to only use component interfaces for the component constraints if they exist in the model. If they do not exist, you can select any geometry.
Interfaces only	Enables you to only use component interfaces for component constraints.

3. Click **OK** to complete the global reference control settings for the current session. These settings can be saved or specified for each Creo Parametric session.

Rule Conflicts

If a global reference rule and a component-specific rule are in conflict, the more restrictive rule is applied. Consider the following examples:

- Component A has a reference control set to **None**. The global reference rule for the current session is set to **All geometry**. When component A is assembled, all of the components except for component A can be referenced in the assembly.

- Component A has a reference control set to **All geometry**. The global reference rule for the current session is set to **None**. In this case, no components can be referenced in the assembly.

10.3 Copy Geometry Features

Copy geometry is useful for copying references from a skeleton part into other parts.

The **Copy Geometry** feature passes feature information from a source part into target part(s) while in a top-level assembly. The most common use of **Copy Geometry** is to copy references between parts for further design directly at the part level. You can copy the following references:

* Datum curves

* Datum features

* Surfaces (can only copy from one part)

* Edges (results in the two surfaces next to the edge being copied)

* Publish geometry features

* Vertices

* Copy and external geometry features

When you create features in part models, you are required to select references to locate the feature. As a result, you establish a parent/child relationship between your new feature and the features to which it is dimensioned. This creates a dependency between the parent feature and the child feature, where the child feature cannot be fully defined unless the parent feature is present. Copy geometry also creates an external reference.

Although there are many ways to establish external references between parts, the recommended method of intentionally establishing an external reference is to create a **Copy Geometry** feature. This feature pulls data from the parent model into the child model.

Advantages of using **Copy Geometry** include the following:

* The Copy Geometry feature consolidates all of the feature copy methods into one *super feature*. For example, you can copy planes, axes, points, curves, coordinate systems, and surfaces from a single Copy Geometry feature.

* Using **Copy Geometry** to establish external references helps to standardize your company's approach to data sharing.

- Funneling all of the external references through a Copy Geometry feature consolidates the external references into a few features. This is preferable to having the external references scattered throughout your model.

- The Copy Geometry feature is easily recognizable in the Model Tree. This enables anyone to open the model and immediately recognize that an external reference is present and to know exactly which feature has it.

- The Copy Geometry feature enables more experienced users to determine where external references are required. The model can then be handed off to another designer to construct the geometry around the copied references. The result is a reduced chance that improper external references are created.

- The Copy Geometry feature can be used for task distribution. When working in large design teams, it enables assembly information to be accessible in Part mode.

How To: Create Copy Geometry

1. Create or open an existing assembly. If you are creating the assembly, you must constrain the components so that they are in the required location to create the Copy Geometry feature.
2. To set the reference control, select the top-level assembly in the Model Tree, right-click and select **References> Reference Control**. The External Reference Control dialog box opens as shown in Figure 10–6. Set the reference control options as required to meet your design intent.

Refer to the previous sections for a detailed description on how to set the reference control.

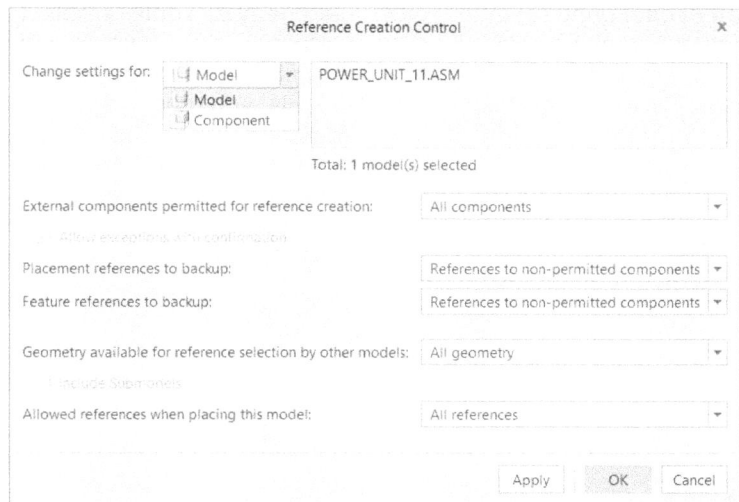

Figure 10–6

3. Activate the component in the Model Tree into which you want to copy the references. Click ⎸┤ (Copy Geometry) in the *Model* tab. The *Copy Geometry* dashboard opens as shown Figure 10–7.

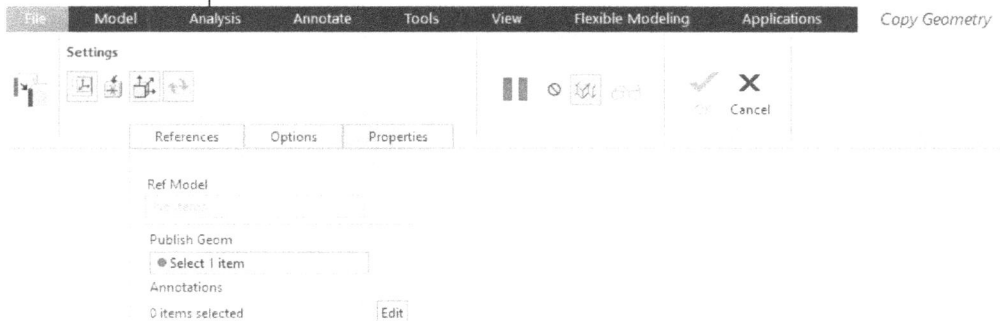

Figure 10–7

*You cannot copy solid features, such as cuts, holes, or protrusions using **Copy Geometry**.*

4. Geometry can only be selected from one part and can include surfaces, edges, curves, published geometry, and other miscellaneous references. To copy geometry from multiple models, you must create multiple Copy Geometry features. To define any of these entities, double-click on the required element and select it on the model. Figure 10–8 shows an assembly with a drive belt that needs to be copied into the belt cover part. Once copied, the geometry is used in Part mode to construct solid features.

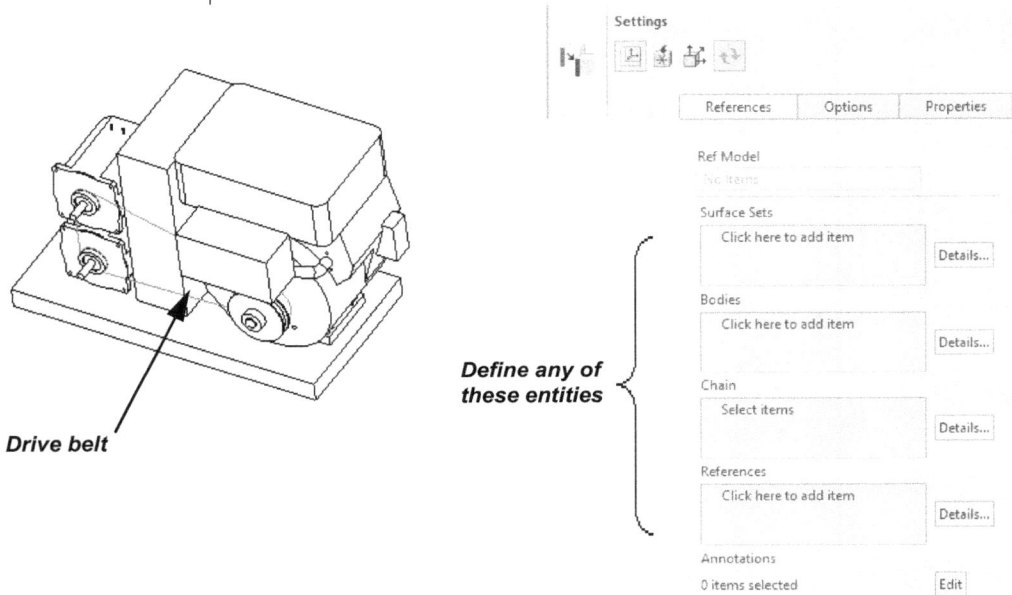

Drive belt

Define any of these entities

Figure 10–8

The options in the References panel in the *Copy Geometry* dashboard are described as follows:

Option	Description
Surface Sets	Enables you to select surfaces to be included in the Copy Geometry feature.
Chain	Enables you to select edges and curves to be included in the Copy Geometry feature.
References	Enables you to select various reference features to be included in the Copy Geometry feature.
Annotations	Enables you to select various annotation features as notes, symbols, surface finishes, geometric tolerances, reference dimensions, and driven dimensions with tolerances to be included in the Copy Geometry feature.

Publish Geom	Enables you to mark features in a model that are to be copied into other parts. It can be used in the following situations:
	• You need to copy the same set of features into multiple parts.
	• You want to group features together to make it easier for others to copy from your model.
	• You want to add features at a later time. If you redefine the Publish Geometry feature and add planes, axes, etc., they are automatically added to any parts that copied the Publish Geometry feature.

5. Set the options to further define the Copy Geometry feature, if required. The *Copy Geometry* dashboard is shown in Figure 10–9.

Figure 10–9

- **Copied Geometry Update**: Enables you to define the copied feature as dependent or independent. If dependent, the copied geometry updates with any changes made to the source component the next time both are in session, or the next time the assembly in which the copied feature was created is in session. To manually update the component, select **Manual Update**.

- ⊞ **(External):** Enables you to convert a Copy Geometry feature into an external Copy Geometry feature.

6. Click ✔ (OK) to complete the Copy Geometry feature. Open the component. The Copy Geometry feature is listed in the Model Tree.

Figure 10–10 shows **belt_cover.prt**, to which features have been copied. The copied references are **drive_belt.prt** and datum plane MOUNT.

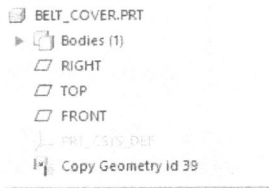

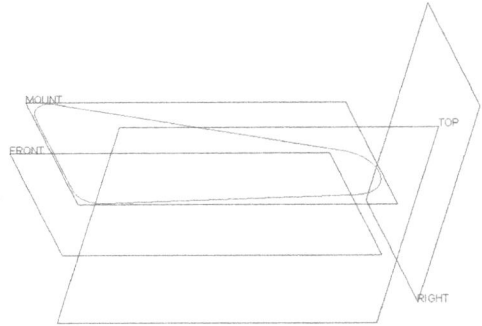

The resulting part is independent of the source entities, which means it can be opened and used as a base for further design.

Figure 10–10

10.4 Publish Geometry Feature

The Publish Geometry feature enables you to mark features in a model that are to be copied into other parts. It can be used in the following situations:

- You need to copy the same set of features into multiple parts.

- You want to group features together to make it easier for others to copy from your model.

- You want to add features at a later time. If you redefine the Publish Geometry feature and add planes, axes, etc., they are automatically added to any parts that copied the Publish Geometry feature, as shown in Figure 10–11.

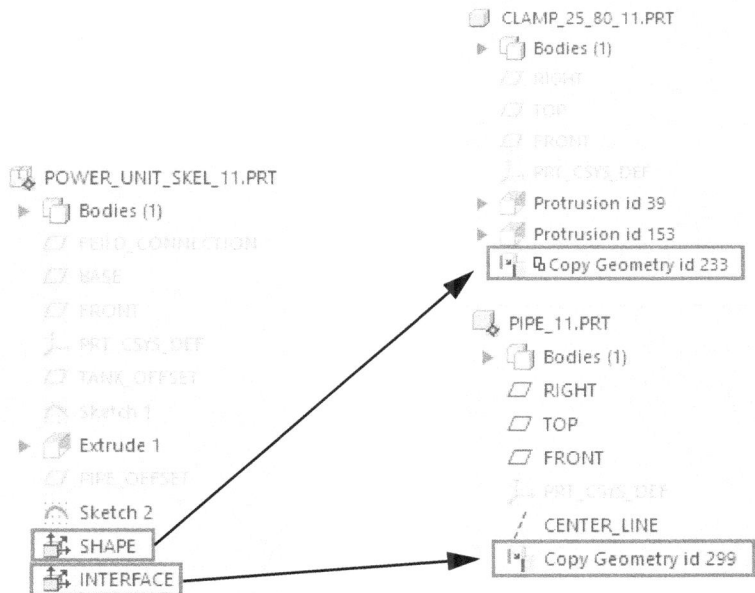

CLAMP_25_80_11.PRT
  ▶ Bodies (1)
    RIGHT
    TOP
    FRONT
    PRT_CSYS_DEF
  ▶ Protrusion id 39
  ▶ Protrusion id 153
    Copy Geometry id 233

POWER_UNIT_SKEL_11.PRT
  ▶ Bodies (1)
    FEED_CONNECTION
    BASE
    FRONT
    PRT_CSYS_DEF
    TANK_OFFSET
    Sketch 1
  ▶ Extrude 1
    PIPE_OFFSET
    Sketch 2
    SHAPE
    INTERFACE

PIPE_11.PRT
  ▶ Bodies (1)
    RIGHT
    TOP
    FRONT
    PRT_CSYS_DEF
    CENTER_LINE
    Copy Geometry id 299

Figure 10–11

How To: Create a Publish Geometry Feature

1. To create a publish geometry feature in a source part, select **Model Intent>Publish Geometry**. You can also click ⌖ (Publish Geometry) in the *Tools* tab. The Publish Geometry dialog box opens, as shown in Figure 10–12.

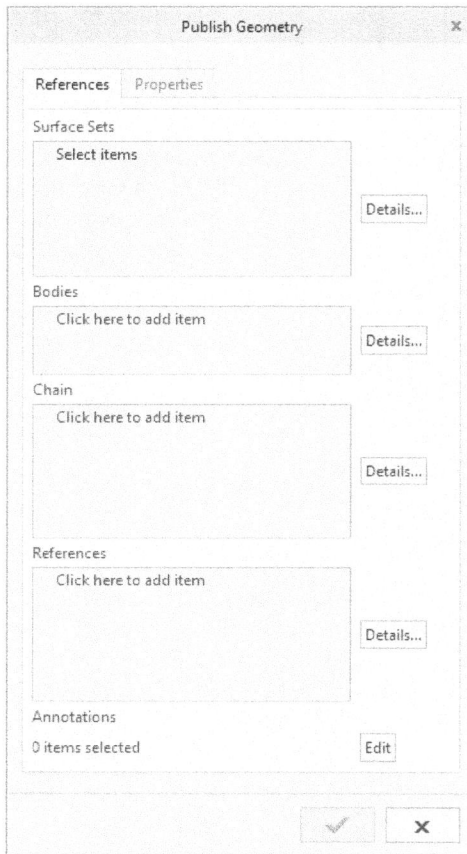

Figure 10–12

2. You can change the name of the Publish Geometry feature to describe the grouping of features. To rename it, double-click on the *Name* element and enter a new name.

3. To select items to be published in the model, use any of the following optional elements in the Published Geometry dialog box:

- Surface Refs
- Chain Refs
- References
- Annotations

Once active, you can select the items to be published.

4. To reference a Publish Geometry feature in a part model, you must have an active assembly that contains both the source and target models. Activate the target model and click

   ⊩ᵢ (Copy Geometry) in the *Model* tab. The *Copy Geometry* dashboard opens, as shown in Figure 10–13.

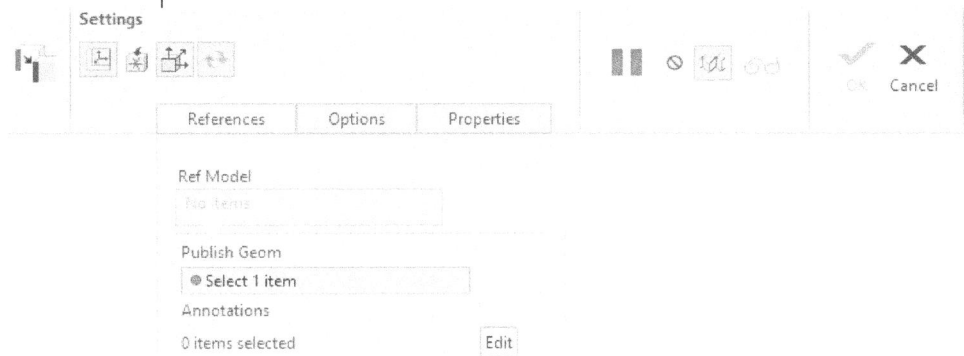

Figure 10–13

To select the Publish Geometry feature for copying, select the published geometry feature in the source model. This option is recommended to ensure that all of the published geometry that was originally captured in the source model is entirely copied into the target, meeting the designer's intent.

10.5 Shrinkwrap Features

Shrinkwrapping is an advanced surface copying technique that copies all of the external surfaces on a part or assembly. The result is a surface quilt that has the shape of the source model and automatically updates if changes are made. A Shrinkwrap feature only includes the external surfaces. Surfaces from interior components are eliminated in a Shrinkwrap feature.

Large Assembly Management

When working with large data sets, you can increase performance by removing unnecessary detail from the display. You can create a Shrinkwrap feature to act as a placeholder for an entire subassembly or a multi-feature model. To accomplish this, you can use simplified representations and interchange assemblies to substitute the Shrinkwrap feature for the detailed component, as shown in Figure 10–14.

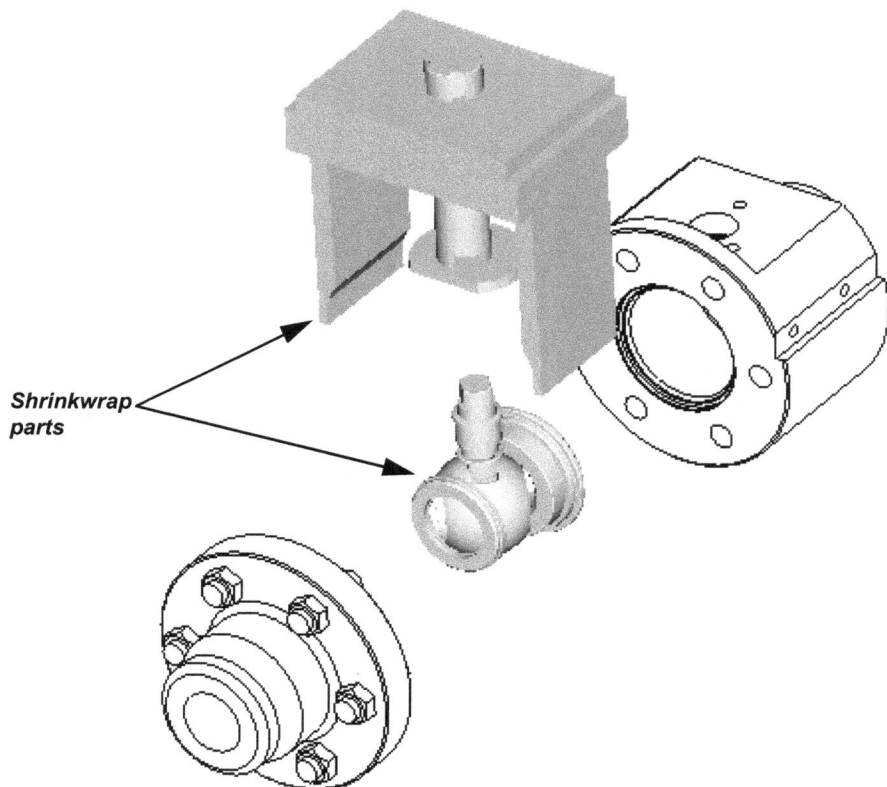

Shrinkwrap parts

Figure 10–14

Incoming Vendor Models

Portions of your design can be modeled by a third party, which you are not required to see. In these cases, all you need for your design is an accurate placeholder for the models. The vendor can provide a shrinkwrap model for you.

Outgoing Models

Alternatively, you might need to send 3D models to another company. You might not want to send the native Creo Parametric file if it contains proprietary design information or an export file (i.e., IGES) that does not update to reflect changes. Using a shrinkwrap model provides the supplier or vendor with an associative Creo Parametric model, as shown in Figure 10–15.

A shrinkwrap model can be customized to remove individual features or components.

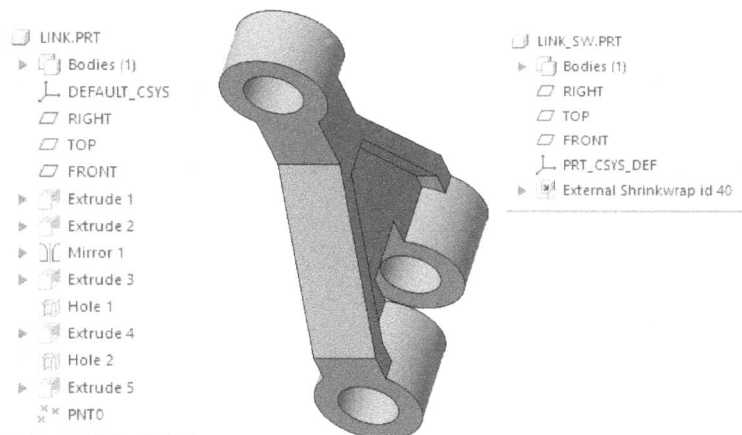

Figure 10–15

Swept Volume Analysis

Sometimes, subassemblies are required to move in your design. A skeleton can be created to accommodate this type of movement by making dimensional changes to increment the assembly through the range of motion. Using the Mechanism module, you can perform interference checks. For example, you can define the joints at the time of assembly and perform a Dynamic interference check.

Shrinkwrap models provide an alternative to swept volume analysis. After creating the shrinkwrap model, you can transform and pattern the surfaces to represent the range of motion. This part can be brought into the assembly and the interference analysis performed. You can develop this model early in the design, knowing that it automatically updates to reflect any changes.

An example of a Swept Volume analysis is shown in Figure 10–16.

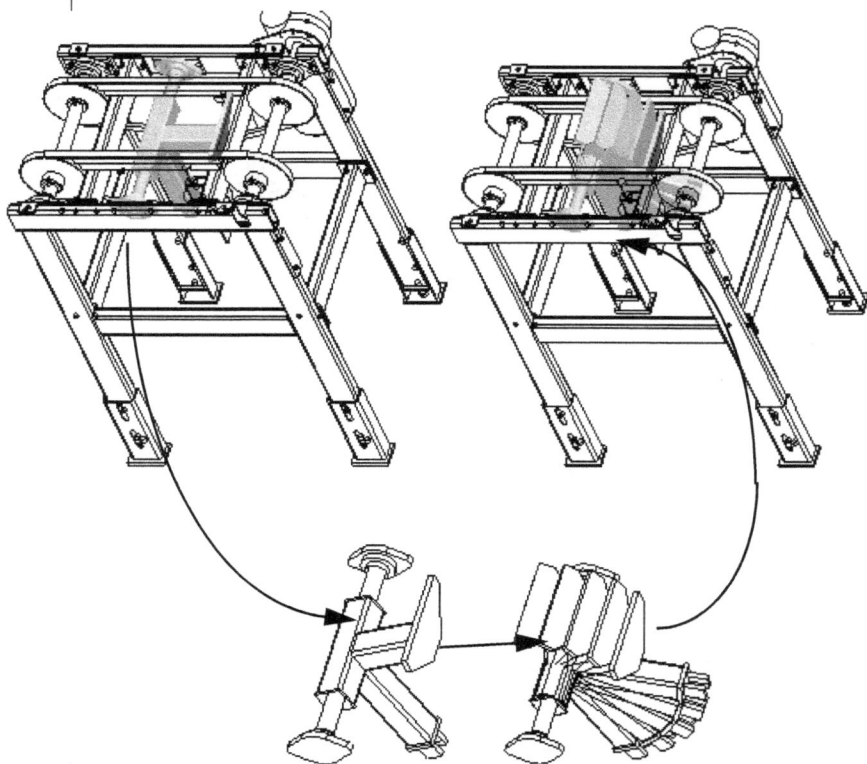

Figure 10–16

How To: Create a Shrinkwrap Feature

1. Create or open an existing assembly. If you are creating the assembly, you must constrain the components so that they are in the required location to create the Shrinkwrap feature.

2. To create a Shrinkwrap feature, click (Shrinkwrap). The *Shrinkwrap* dashboard opens, as shown in Figure 10–17. By default, all of the elements are automatically defined, except those in the Options panel.

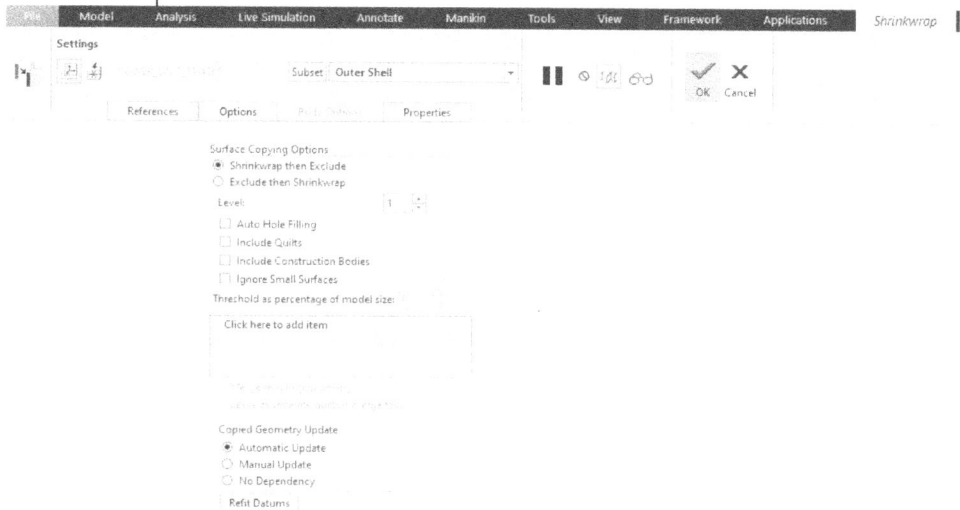

Figure 10–17

You can collect the surface data in three ways, as shown in Figure 10–18.

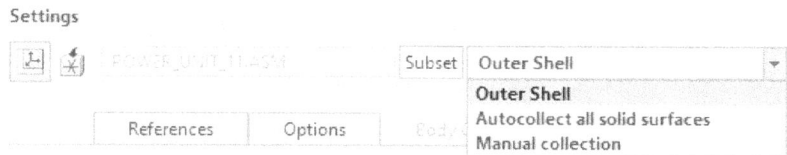

Figure 10–18

By default, all of the outer surfaces of the model are included. You can include or exclude references using the options in the References panel, as shown in Figure 10–19. The following options are available:

- **Always include surfaces:** Select the surfaces that are to be included in the feature.

- **Never include surfaces:** Select the surfaces that are to be excluded in the feature.

- **Chain:** Select wireframe edges and curves that are to be included in the feature.

- **Include Datums:** Select the datums that are to be included in the feature.

References	Options	Body Options

Always include surfaces
Select items
Details...

Never include surfaces
Click here to add item
Details...

Chain
Click here to add item
Details...

Include Datums
Click here to add item
Details...

Annotations
0 items selected   Edit

Figure 10–19

3. The Shrinkwrap Options panel, shown in Figure 10–20, enables you to define the quality and attributes of the shrinkwrap.

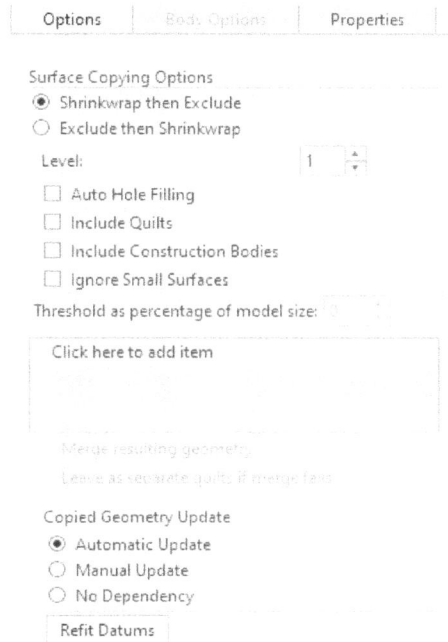

Figure 10–20

- **Shrinkwrap then Exclude** is the default setting. It scans the entire assembly and identifies the external surfaces. However, only the surfaces of the selected components are included in the shrinkwrap.

- **Exclude then Shrinkwrap** only includes selected components in the shrinkwrap.

Quality Level

The **Quality Level** enables you to specify the amount of detail shown in the resulting Shrinkwrap feature. The value ranges between 1 to 10, where 10 is the highest level. At lower settings, details on small surfaces are not collected. At higher settings, the time and processing resources are higher to generate the feature. Since the quality value can be changed at any time, it is recommended that you begin at a low setting and increase as required to suit each model. The model shown in Figure 10–21 is created using a quality level of 1, which leaves gaps in the surface. To create a better model, you can increase the quality.

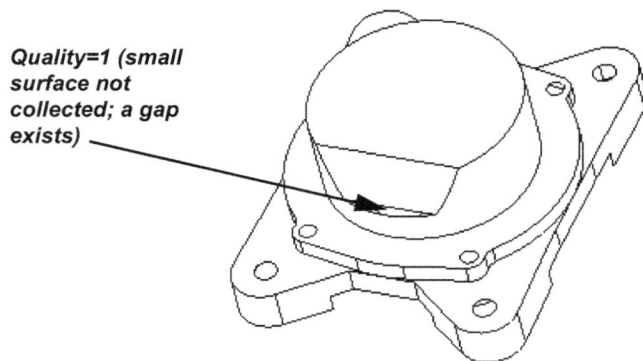

Quality=1 (small surface not collected; a gap exists)

Figure 10–21

Attributes

Holes might not display in a shrinkwrap surface as shown in Figure 10–22. This is because the cylindrical walls might not be included with lower quality settings. Consider using **Auto Hole Filling**.

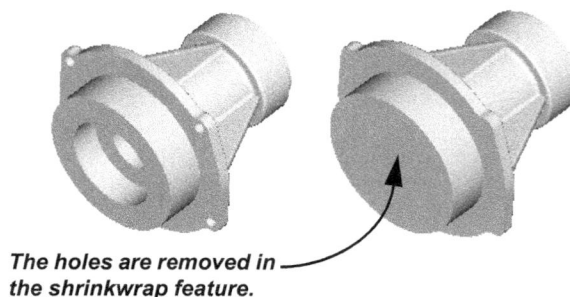

The holes are removed in the shrinkwrap feature.

Figure 10–22

The **Include Quilts** option enables you to include external quilts in the Shrinkwrap feature if the **Quality** and **Ignore Small Surfaces** settings permit it. By enabling **Ignore Small Surfaces** and entering a value, you can exclude surfaces that make up less than X% of the overall volume of the assembly.

The remaining elements in the *Shrinkwrap* dashboard are defined by default, or are optional. Optional elements, are not required to successfully complete the feature.

Option	Description
Subset	Opens the Shrinkwrap Comps dialog box where you can specify which components in the assembly to consider (include) or ignore (exclude) from the Shrinkwrap. By default, all of the components are considered for the Shrinkwrap.
Surface Copying Options	Specifies the method that the system uses to calculate the surfaces to be shrinkwrapped. The default option, **Shrinkwrap then Exclude**, first calculates the surfaces of all models in the assembly, based on the criteria defined in the option. It then includes components that are considered in the Subset element. The **Exclude then Shrinkwrap** option builds the shrinkwrap feature based on selected components only.
References - Surface Sets	Selects additional surfaces that might not have been automatically selected to be included in the Shrinkwrap.
References - Include Datums	Specifies datum features (planes, points, axis, and coordinate systems) to be included in the Shrinkwrap.
External ⬚	Converts the feature to an external Shrinkwrap feature.

4. Click ✔ (OK) in the tab to create the shrinkwrap.

Practice 10a

Designing Parts in Assembly

Practice Objectives

- Set the external reference control.
- Publish part geometry.
- Create copy geometry.
- Create features from copy geometry.

In this practice, you will develop geometry that defines the pipe part. At this point in the design cycle, the pipe part is empty. However, the top-level assembly has enough information to define the pipe geometry and location. The pipe flange references the port of the valve, and the pipe centerline (that has been defined in the skeleton) can be used. This information can be shared down to the pipe part and used to define the pipe flange and pipe geometry. At the end of this practice, the top-level assembly displays as shown in Figure 10–23.

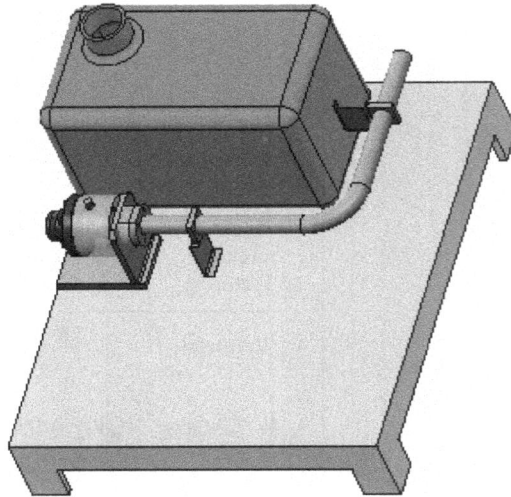

Figure 10–23

Task 1 - Open the top-level assembly.

1. Change the working directory to the *Parts_In_Assembly* folder.

2. Open **power_unit_11.asm**.

3. Set the model display as follows:

   - $\overset{\times}{\nearrow}$ *(Datum Display Filters)*: All Off

   - $\searrow$ *(Spin Center)*: Off

   - $\Box$ *(Display Style)*: $\Box$ (Shading With Edges)

4. Reorder the clamps to the bottom of the component list in the Model Tree. The Model Tree should appear as shown in Figure 10–24.

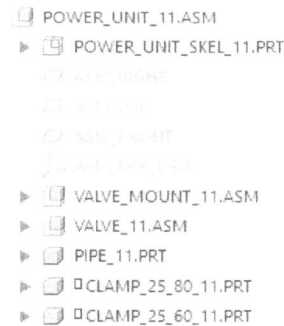

POWER_UNIT_11.ASM
▶ POWER_UNIT_SKEL_11.PRT
    ASM_RIGHT
    ASM_TOP
    ASM_FRONT
    ASM_DEF_CSYS
▶ VALVE_MOUNT_11.ASM
▶ VALVE_11.ASM
▶ PIPE_11.PRT
▶ ⊓CLAMP_25_80_11.PRT
▶ ⊓CLAMP_25_60_11.PRT

Figure 10–24

Task 2 - Publish geometry.

Design Considerations

In this task, you will open a part in a separate window and publish selected geometry from that part. It is recommended that you publish the geometry when you know that you are creating external references, since the reference control can be set to enable only published geometry. Using this method enables all users to quickly determine where external references might exist.

1. Open **BODY_11.PRT** in the **VALVE_11.ASM** assembly, as shown in Figure 10–25.

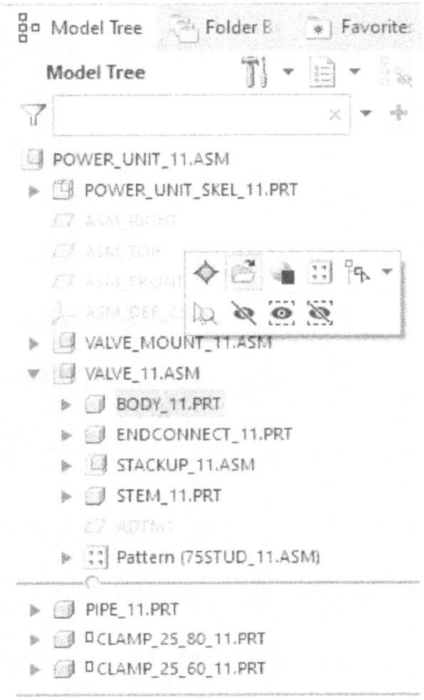

Figure 10–25

You can also select the Tools tab and click

(Publish Geometry).

2. In the *Model* tab, select **Model Intent>Publish Geometry**. The Publish Geometry dialog box opens, as shown in Figure 10–26.

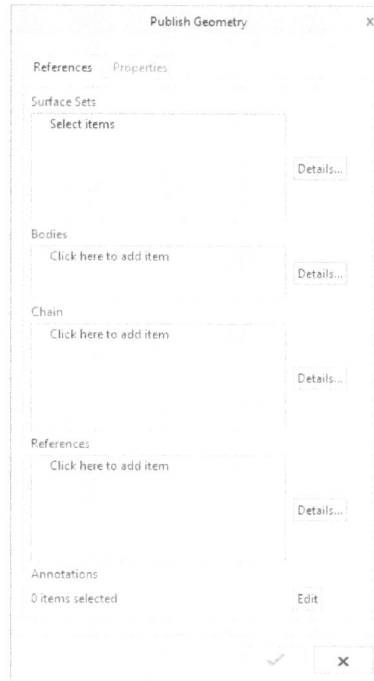

Figure 10–26

3. Select the surface shown in Figure 10–27 to add it to the Surface Sets.

Figure 10–27

4. Use the *Properties* tab to set the feature *Name* to **FLANGE_INTERFACE**, as shown in Figure 10–28.

Figure 10–28

5. Click ✔ (OK) to complete the publish geometry. The feature is listed in the Model Tree, as shown in Figure 10–29.

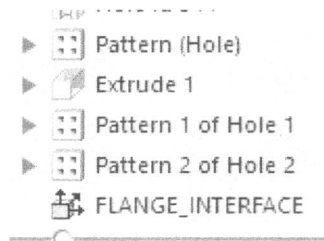

Figure 10–29

This surface has now been published as a selectable surface for later use.

6. Save the model and close the window.

Task 3 - Set the external reference control.

Design Considerations

In this task, you will customize the reference control settings for the current session so that only the published geometry can be selected for external references. In addition, you will customize the settings so that any forbidden geometry is highlighted in red and cannot be selected.

1. Select **File>Options>Assembly**. The External Reference Control options display at the top of the Creo Parametrics dialog box.

2. Select **Published Geometry Only** in the Geometry available for external reference selection by other models drop-down list, as shown in Figure 10–30.

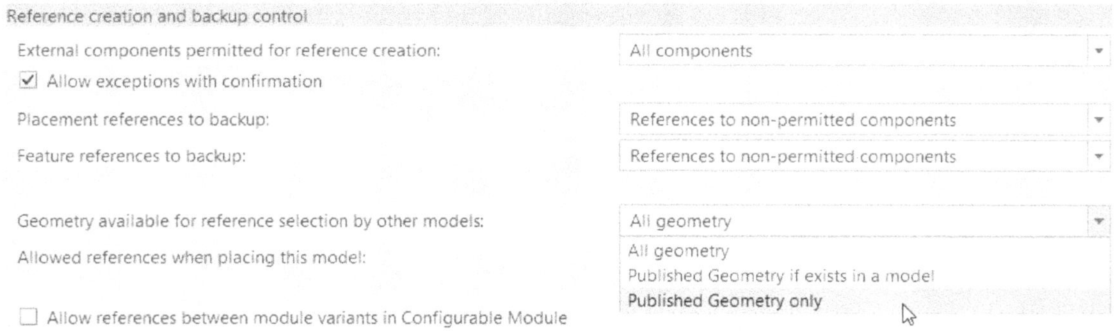

Reference creation and backup control

External components permitted for reference creation:	All components ▼
☑ Allow exceptions with confirmation	
Placement references to backup:	References to non-permitted components ▼
Feature references to backup:	References to non-permitted components ▼
Geometry available for reference selection by other models:	All geometry ▼
Allowed references when placing this model:	All geometry
	Published Geometry if exists in a model
	Published Geometry only
☐ Allow references between module variants in Configurable Module	

Figure 10–30

3. Ensure that *Feature References to backup:* is set to **References to other models**, as shown in Figure 10–31.

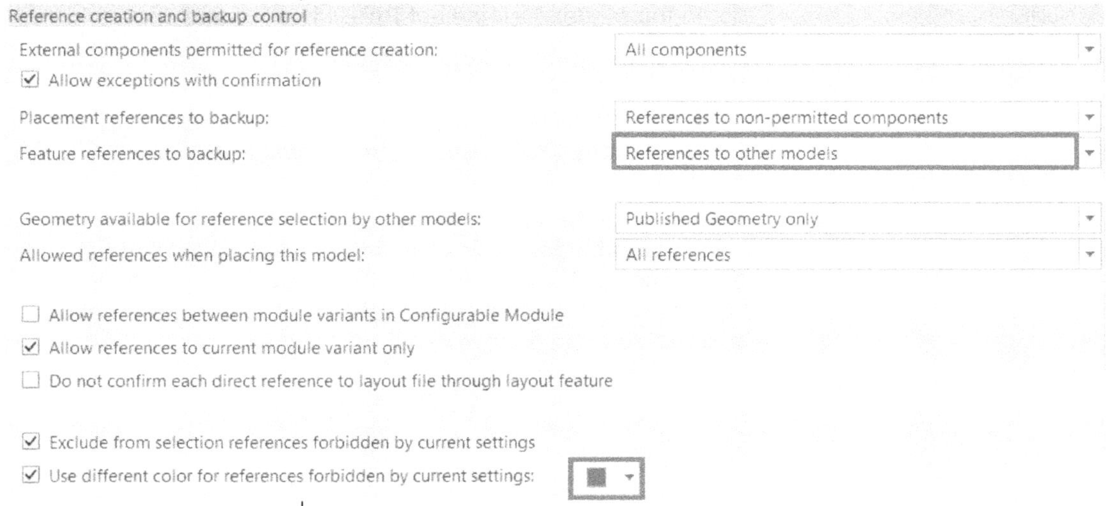

Reference creation and backup control

External components permitted for reference creation:	All components ▼
☑ Allow exceptions with confirmation	
Placement references to backup:	References to non-permitted components ▼
Feature references to backup:	References to other models ▼
Geometry available for reference selection by other models:	Published Geometry only ▼
Allowed references when placing this model:	All references ▼

☐ Allow references between module variants in Configurable Module
☑ Allow references to current module variant only
☐ Do not confirm each direct reference to layout file through layout feature

☑ Exclude from selection references forbidden by current settings
☑ Use different color for references forbidden by current settings: ■ ▼

Figure 10–31

4. Expand ■ ▼ next to the **Use different color for references forbidden by current settings** option.

5. Select the color shown in Figure 10–32 to set the color to orange.

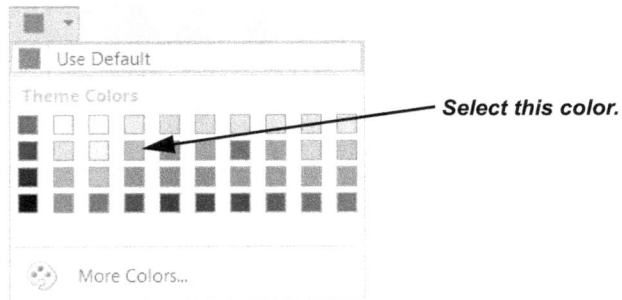

Figure 10–32

6. Click **OK** and click **No**. The reference control settings will only be used for the current session.

Task 4 - Copy geometry into a part.

1. In the Model Tree, select **PIPE_11.PRT** and click ◇ (Activate) in the mini toolbar.

2. In the *Model* tab, in the Get Data group, click ⊡ (Copy Geometry). The *Copy Geometry* dashboard opens.

Design Considerations

Due to the external reference control settings that you have set, all of the forbidden geometry displays in orange. You can only select the published geometry. This methodology ensures that you are only selecting published geometry and not creating external references to unrequired geometry.

3. Display the features in the Model Tree.

4. Expand **BODY_11.PRT** in the **VALVE_11.ASM** assembly, and select the **FLANGE_INTERFACE** publish geometry. This selects the surface shown in Figure 10–33.

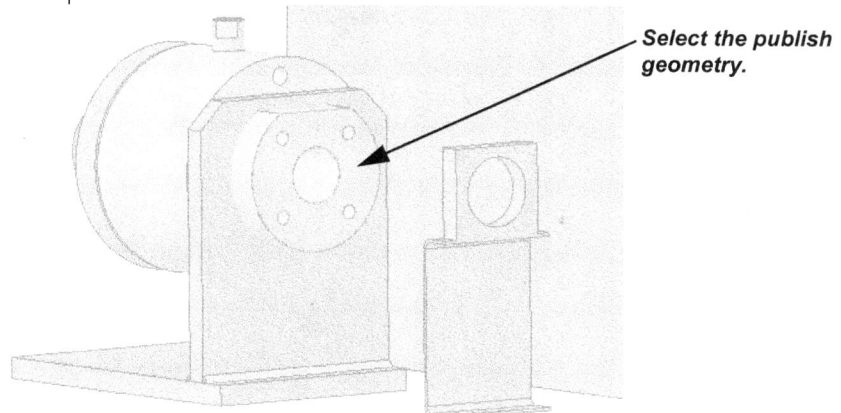

Select the publish geometry.

Figure 10–33

5. Click ✓ (OK) to complete the Copy Geometry feature.

6. Open **PIPE_11.PRT** in a new window. The shared data (copy geometry) displays as shown Figure 10–34.

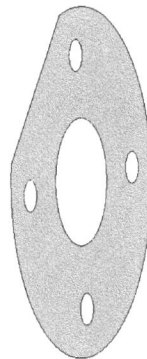

Figure 10–34

7. Switch back to the top-level assembly window.

Design Considerations

Reference control can be changed at any time. In this task, you will change the reference control to enable only elements in the skeleton to be used for external reference selection.

1. Click **File>Options>Assembly**.

2. Select **Skeleton and Layout models** in the External components permitted for reference creation drop-down list, as shown in Figure 10–35.

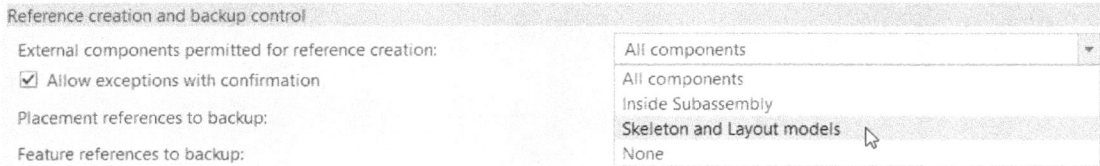

Reference creation and backup control

External components permitted for reference creation:	All components ▼
☑ Allow exceptions with confirmation	All components
	Inside Subassembly
Placement references to backup:	Skeleton and Layout models ↙
Feature references to backup:	None

Figure 10–35

3. Select **All geometry** in the Geometry available for reference selection by other models drop-down list, as shown in Figure 10–36.

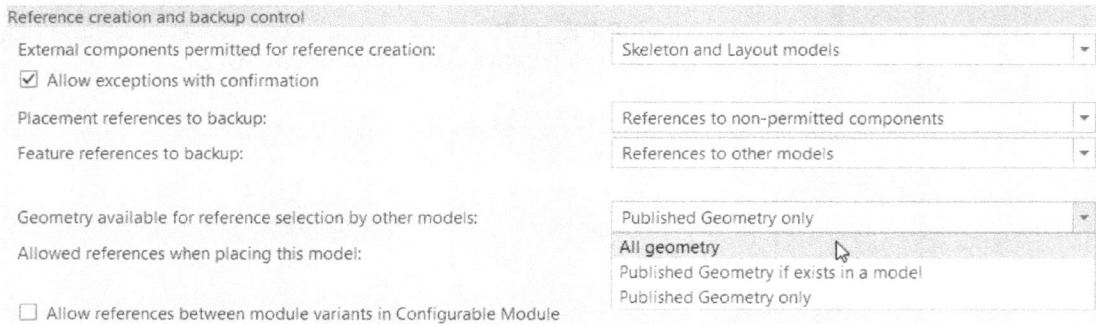

Reference creation and backup control

External components permitted for reference creation:	Skeleton and Layout models ▼
☑ Allow exceptions with confirmation	
Placement references to backup:	References to non-permitted components ▼
Feature references to backup:	References to other models ▼
Geometry available for reference selection by other models:	Published Geometry only ▼
Allowed references when placing this model:	All geometry ↙
	Published Geometry if exists in a model
	Published Geometry only
☐ Allow references between module variants in Configurable Module	

Figure 10–36

4. Click **OK** and click **No**.

5. Make the **PIPE_11.PRT** the active part.

6. Click ⌐ᵢ (Copy Geometry). Click ⛝ (Published Geometry) to clear the **Published Geometry** option.

7. Click the References panel in the *Copy Geometry* dashboard, as shown in Figure 10–37. Select the *Chain* collector to define the curve and chain sets.

Figure 10–37

8. Select the sketched curve of the skeleton, as shown in Figure 10–38.

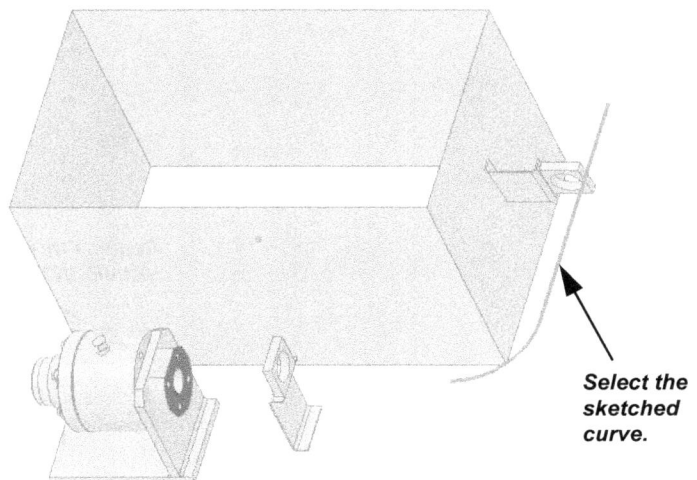

Select the sketched curve.

Figure 10–38

**Design
Considerations**

There are no longer any highlighted orange surfaces that identify prohibited geometry. This is due to the changes made in the external reference control. Any geometry in the skeleton model can now be selected.

9. Click ✓ (OK).

10. Open the **PIPE_11.PRT** window to display the pipe part. The part file displays as shown in Figure 10–39.

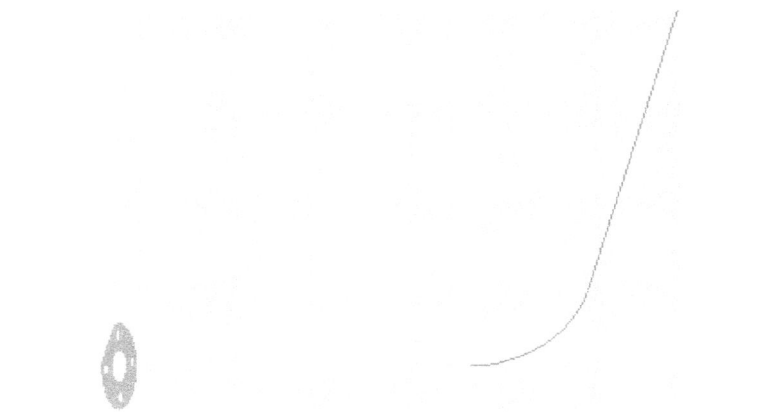

Figure 10–39

11. It is recommended that you rename the copy geometry features with a meaningful name. Rename the copy geometry features, as shown in Figure 10–40.

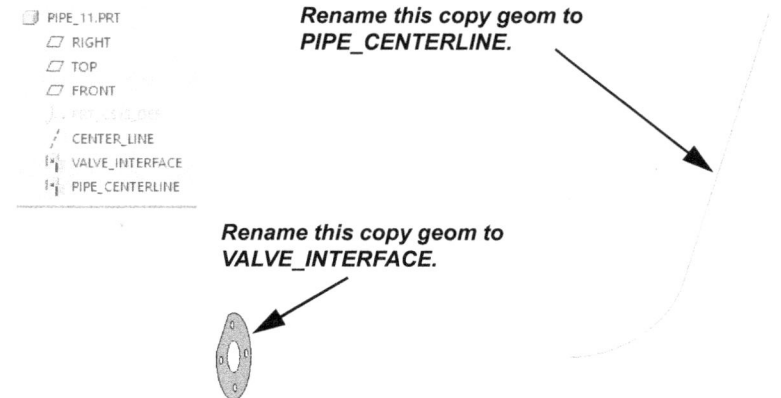

PIPE_11.PRT
   RIGHT
   TOP
   FRONT
   CENTER_LINE
   VALVE_INTERFACE
   PIPE_CENTERLINE

Rename this copy geom to PIPE_CENTERLINE.

Rename this copy geom to VALVE_INTERFACE.

Figure 10–40

12. Save the part.

Task 5 - Create part geometry from shared copied geometry.

1. Click (Extrude).

2. Select in the background and click (Define Internal Sketch).

3. In the Model Tree, select **RIGHT** as the sketching plane and **TOP** as the orientation plane to face the **Top**, as shown in Figure 10–41.

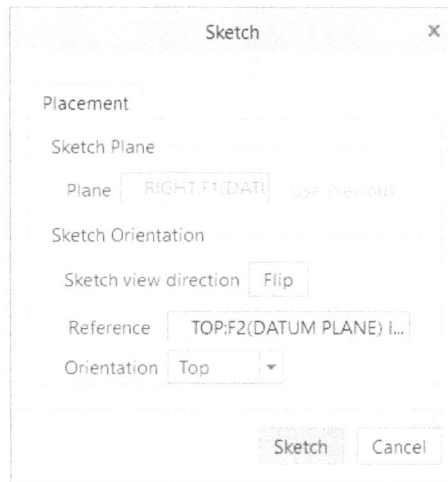

Figure 10–41

4. Click **Sketch**.

Design Considerations

When creating geometry from external references, it is recommended that you use datum planes and features local to the part file as the sketching plane and orientation references. This enables the external references to be broken or easily changed, if required.

5. Click (Sketch View).

6. Click ☐ (Project) and select the edges shown in Figure 10–42. This sketch should not have dimensions.

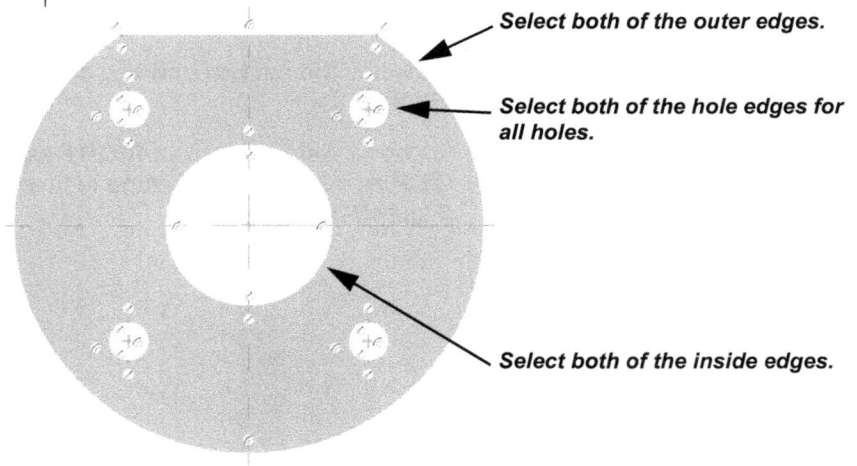

Select both of the outer edges.

Select both of the hole edges for all holes.

Select both of the inside edges.

Figure 10–42

7. Click ✓ (OK).

8. Edit the *Depth* to **1.0**, as shown in Figure 10–43.

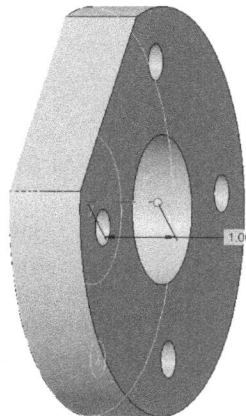

1.00

Figure 10–43

9. Click ✔ (OK).

10. Click ☞ (Sweep) and click ☐ (Create Thin Feature) to create a thin sweep.

11. Expand ⬡ (Datum) on the far right side of the *Sweep* dashboard, and click ⬡ (Sketch) from the *Datum* flyout (as shown in Figure 10–44) to create a trajectory.

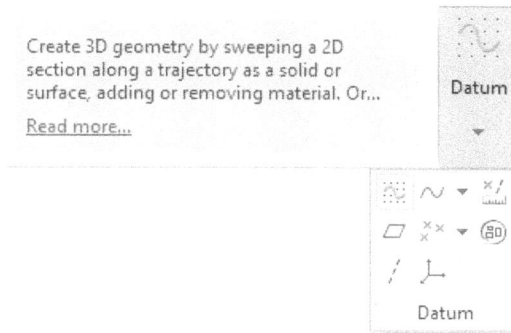

Create 3D geometry by sweeping a 2D section along a trajectory as a solid or surface, adding or removing material. Or...

Read more...

Datum

Figure 10–44

12. Select datum plane **TOP** as the sketching plane and datum plane **RIGHT** as the **Right** orientation plane.

13. Click **Sketch**.

14. Click ⬚ (References).

15. Delete datum plane **RIGHT** as a Sketcher reference and select the surface of the flange as a sketch reference, as shown in Figure 10–45.

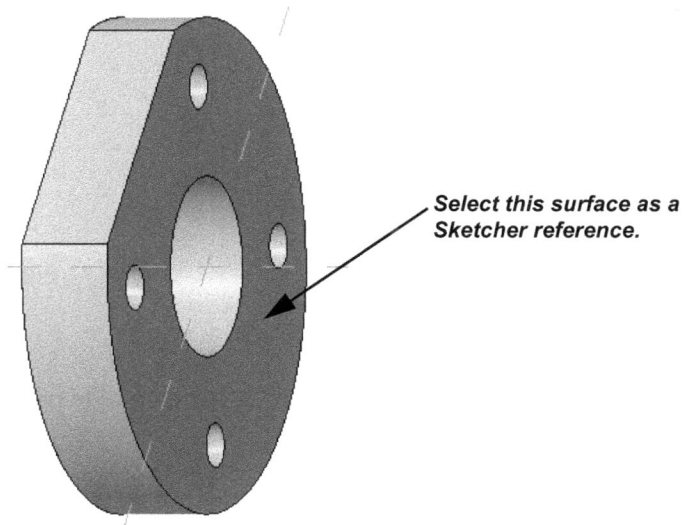

Select this surface as a Sketcher reference.

Figure 10–45

16. Click ▢ (Project) and select both curves of the
    PIPE_CENTERLINE copy geometry, as shown in
    Figure 10–46.

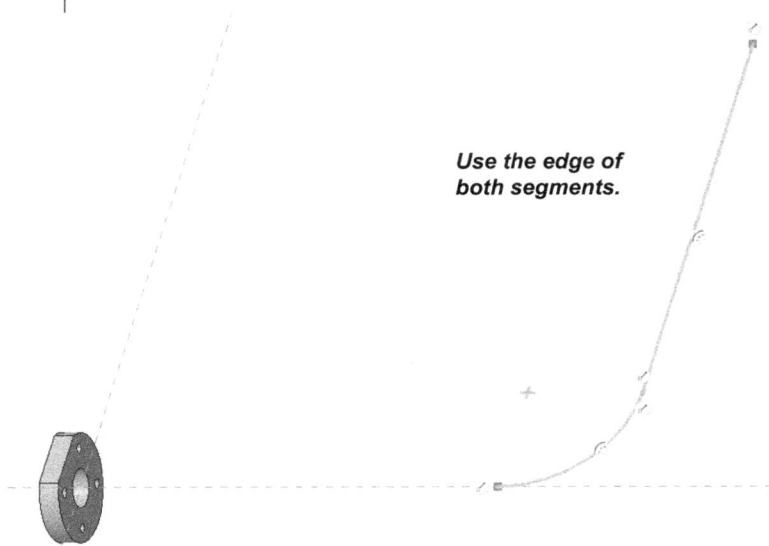

*Use the edge of
both segments.*

Figure 10–46

17. Sketch a line as shown in Figure 10–47. This sketch should
    not have any dimensions.

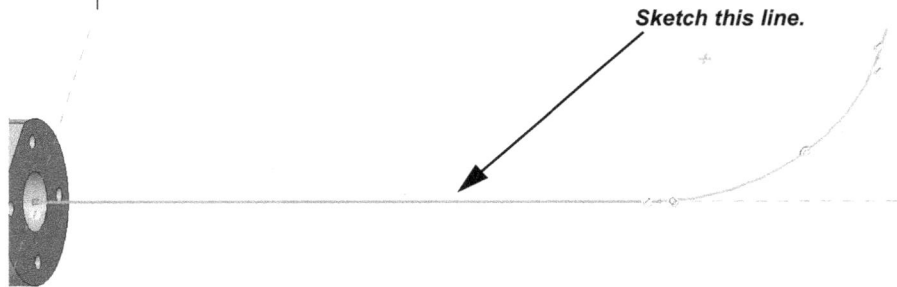

Sketch this line.

Figure 10–47

18. Click ✓ (OK).

19. Click ▶ (Resume) to resume the sweep creation.

If required, click on the arrow to change direction.

20. Verify that the start point is in the location shown in Figure 10–48.

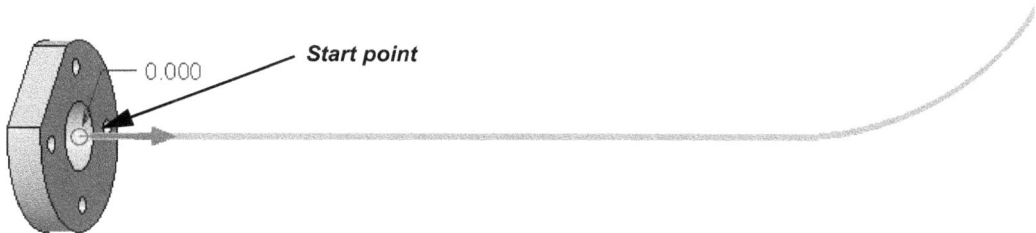
— 0.000   **Start point**

Figure 10–48

21. Click ✐ (Create or Edit Section) to sketch the cross-section.

22. Click ⌖ (Sketch View).

23. Click ⌑ (Project) and select the two edges of the inside diameter of the flange to create the sketch section for the pipe, as shown in Figure 10–49.

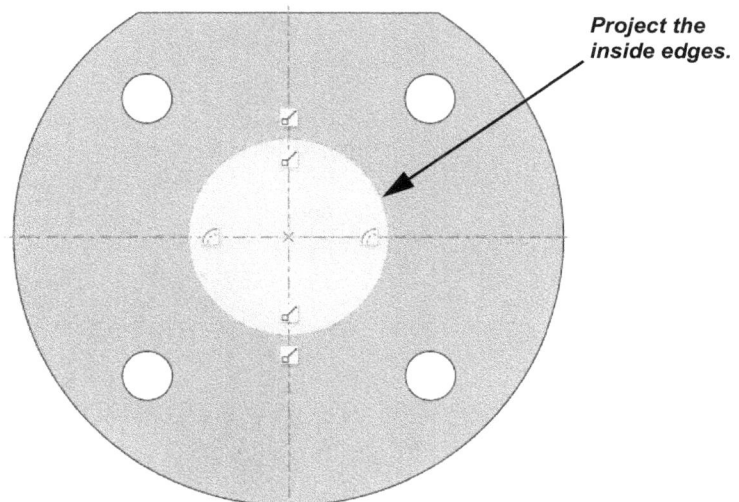
Project the inside edges.

Figure 10–49

24. Click ✓ (OK).

25. Ensure that the geometry is created on the outside of the flange hole, as shown in Figure 10–50. Click ✕ (Change Thickness Direction) if required.

26. Set the *Thickness* to **0.25**.

27. Click ✓ (OK).

28. Set the orientation to the Default Orientation. The pipe part displays as shown in Figure 10–50.

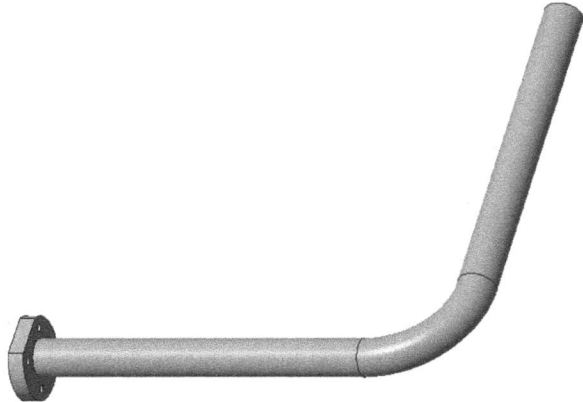

Figure 10–50

29. Save the part and close the window. The pipe displays in the assembly, as shown in Figure 10–51. The clamps interfere with the pipe because they are currently only packaged in the assembly.

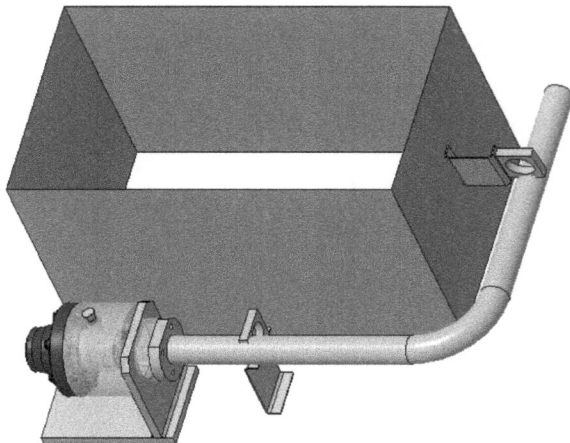

Figure 10–51

Task 6 - Edit the definition of the clamp parts.

1. Edit the definition of both clamp parts so that they reference the pipe part. The pipe part and assembly display similar to that shown in Figure 10–52.

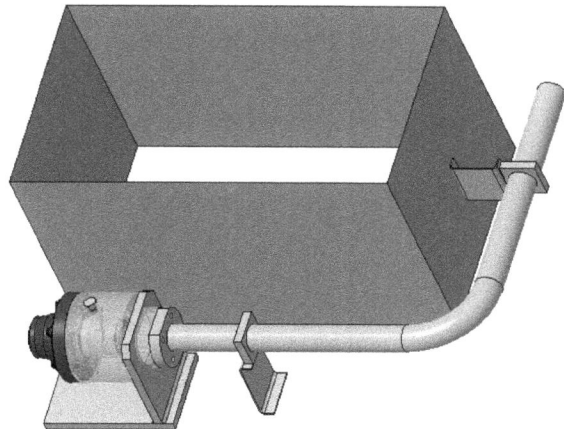

Figure 10–52

2. Save the assembly.

Task 7 - Add components to the top-level assembly.

1. Assemble **base.prt** into the default position. The assembly displays as shown in Figure 10–53.

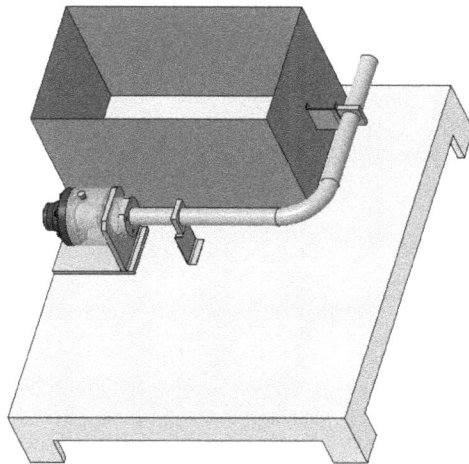

Figure 10–53

2. Assemble **tank.prt** using only assembly references to the skeleton model. The assembly displays as shown in Figure 10–54.

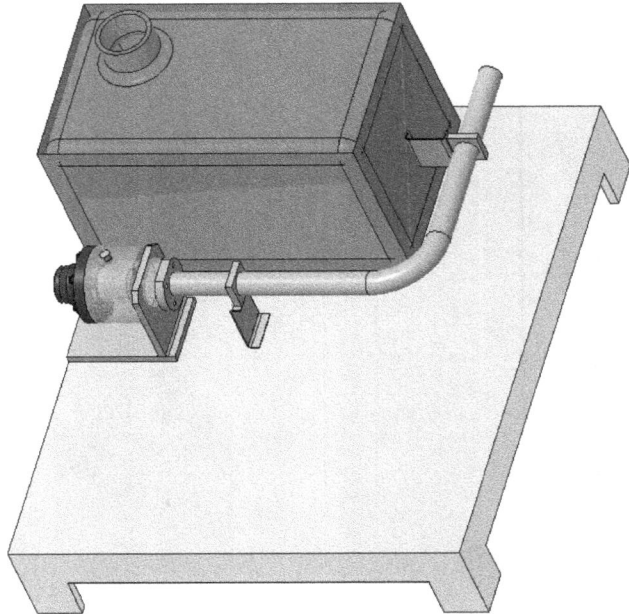

Figure 10–54

3. Reorder the components so that the Model Tree displays as shown in Figure 10–55.

Figure 10–55

4. Hide the skeleton model. The assembly displays as shown in Figure 10–56.

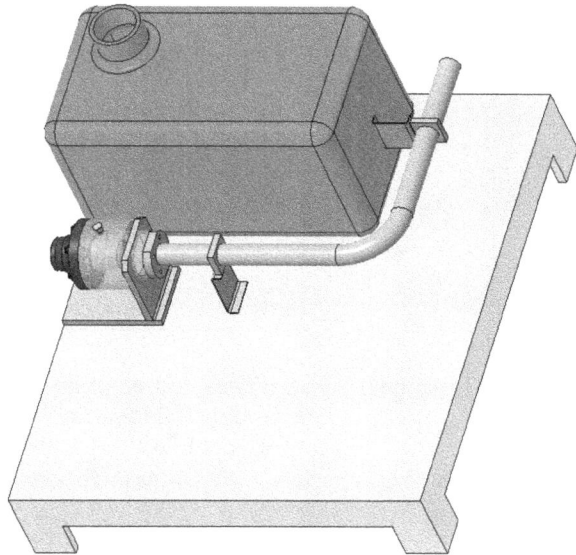

Figure 10–56

5. Save the assembly and erase it from memory.

Practice 10b | Using Shrinkwrap Features

Practice Objective

- Create a Shrinkwrap feature.

In this practice, you are required to send the valve assembly to a contractor who will be designing a handle and handle-locking mechanism. In an effort to send the smallest file and not to disclose any proprietary design information, you will create a Shrinkwrap feature of the valve assembly to be sent.

Task 1 - Create a temporary assembly.

Design Considerations

To distribute this information, you will create a temporary assembly file, assemble the valve assembly into it and create a new part. You will then share the valve information down to the new part using a Shrinkwrap feature.

1. Change the working directory to the *Shrinkwrap_Features* folder.

2. Create an assembly using the default template and set the *File name* to **temp**.

3. Set the model display as follows:

   - *(Datum Display Filters)*: All Off

   - *(Spin Center)*: Off

   - *(Display Style)*: ⬜ (Shading With Edges)

4. Set the external reference control to **All components**.

5. Assemble **valve_11.asm** into the default location, as shown in Figure 10–57.

Figure 10–57

Task 2 - Create a part file while in Assembly mode.

---

1. Create a new part file by clicking ⊞ (Create).

2. Set the new part *File name* to **VALVE_CONTRACTOR** and click **OK**.

3. Use **Copy From Existing** as the creation option.

4. Click **Browse** and select **start_part.prt** as the template from which to copy.

5. Assemble the part in the default location.

Task 3 - Create a shrinkwrap feature.

---

1. Activate **valve_contractor.prt** in the assembly. The Model Tree displays as shown in Figure 10–58.

TEMP.ASM
  ASM_RIGHT
  ASM_TOP
  ASM_FRONT
  ASM_DEF_CSYS
► VALVE_11.ASM
► VALVE_CONTRACTOR.PRT

Figure 10–58

2. Click ▣ (Shrinkwrap) in the *Model* tab.

3. In the Options panel, in the *Shrinkwrap* tab, select **Auto Hole Filling**, as shown in Figure 10–59.

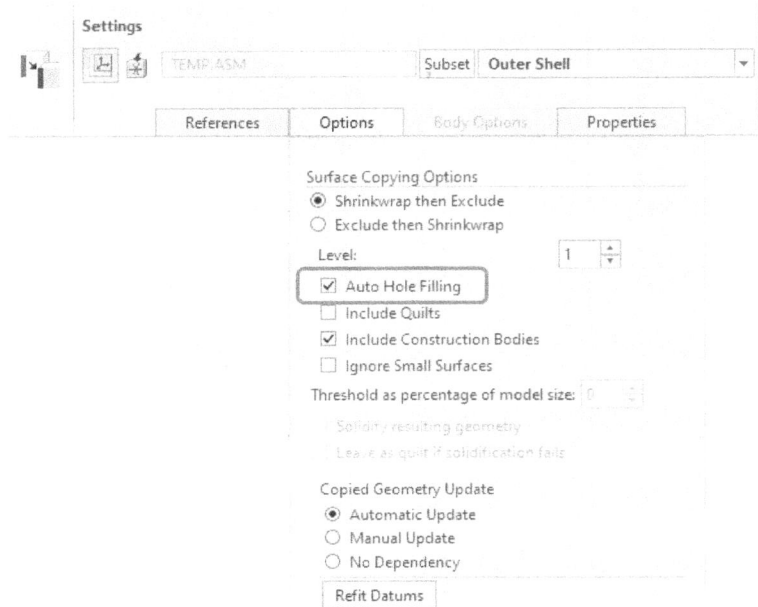

Figure 10–59

4. Click ✓ (OK) to complete the Shrinkwrap feature.

5. Open **VALVE_CONTRACTOR.PRT** in a new window.

Design Considerations

The model is a simple surface representation (shrinkwrap) of the assembly as shown in Figure 10–60. The holes have also been filled (by enabling the **Auto Hole Filling** option). This representation of the valve assembly can now be sent to the contractor without having to provide all of the files or proprietary geometry. A Shrinkwrap feature can also be used to substitute parts or complete assemblies in a top-level assembly to help reduce regeneration time.

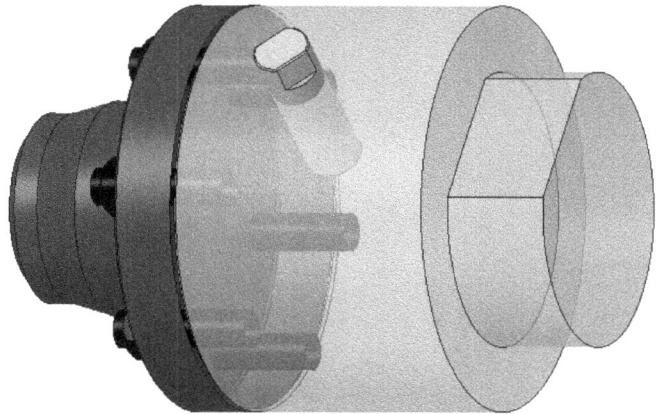

VALVE_CONTRACTOR.PRT
    RIGHT
    TOP
    FRONT
    PRT_CSYS_DEF
  ▶ Shrinkwrap id 41

Figure 10–60

6. Save the part and close the window.

7. Close the **TEMP** assembly without saving and erase it from memory. This assembly is only a temporary file used to create the Shrinkwrap feature.

Practice 10c | Component Geometry from Motion Skeletons

Practice Objective

- Create component geometry using motion skeletons.

In this practice, you will create the geometry for the piston assembly, based on motion skeletons.

Task 1 - Open an assembly.

1. Change the working directory to the *Completing_Motion_Skel* folder.

2. Open **crank_piston.asm**.

3. Set the model display as follows:

   - ⁕ *(Datum Display Filters)*: ▱ (Plane Display) only

   - ⤙ *(Spin Center)*: Off

   - ▱ *(Display Style)*: ▱ (Shading With Edges)

Task 2 - Create geometry for the CR_JOUNRNAL part.

1. Open **CR_JOURNAL.PRT** in a new window. The part displays as shown in Figure 10–61.

Figure 10–61

2. In the Model Tree, click the **External Merge** feature and select ✎ (Edit Definition) in the mini toolbar.

3. Select the References panel in the dashboard, and select **Copy Datums**, as shown in Figure 10–62.

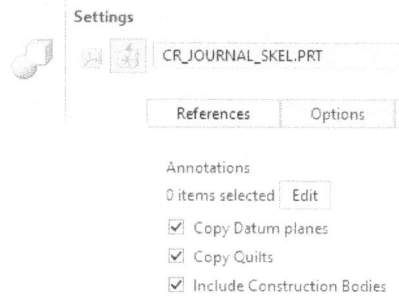

Settings

CR_JOURNAL_SKEL.PRT

References | Options

Annotations

0 items selected | Edit

☑ Copy Datum planes
☑ Copy Quilts
☑ Include Construction Bodies

Figure 10–62

The datums from the skeleton were not automatically copied into the part.

4. Click ✔ (OK).

5. Click (Extrude).

6. On the far right side of the *Extrude* dashboard, expand (Datum) and select ▱ (Plane).

7. Select the plane shown in Figure 10–63.

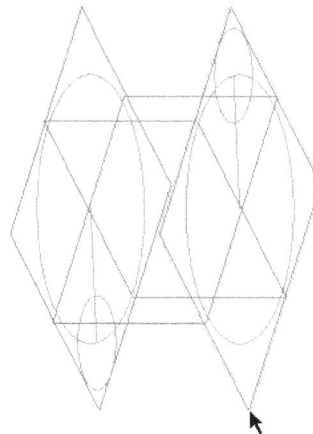

Figure 10–63

8. Select the drag handle and drag the place approximately to the position shown in Figure 10–64.

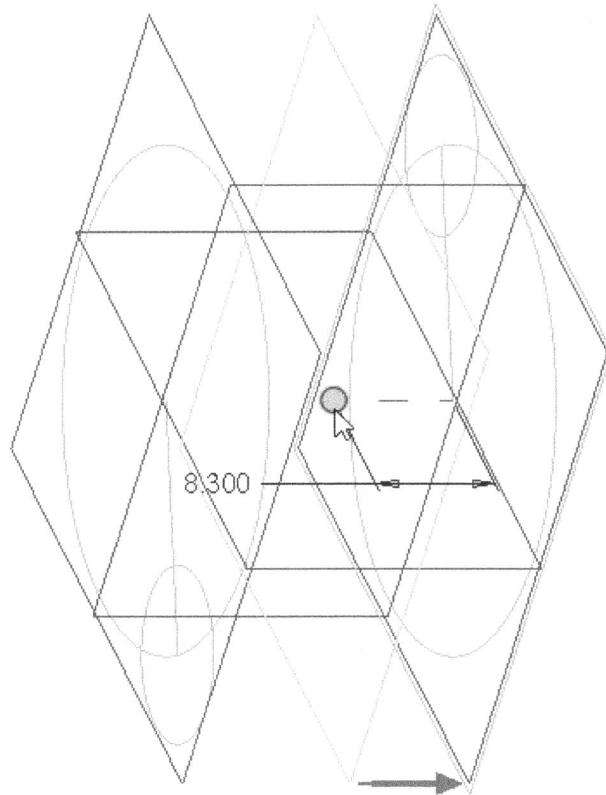

Figure 10–64

9. Edit the *Offset Translation* value to **10** and click **OK**.

10. Click ▶ (Resume) in the dashboard.

11. Click ⌘ (Sketch View).

12. Sketch the circle shown in Figure 10–65.

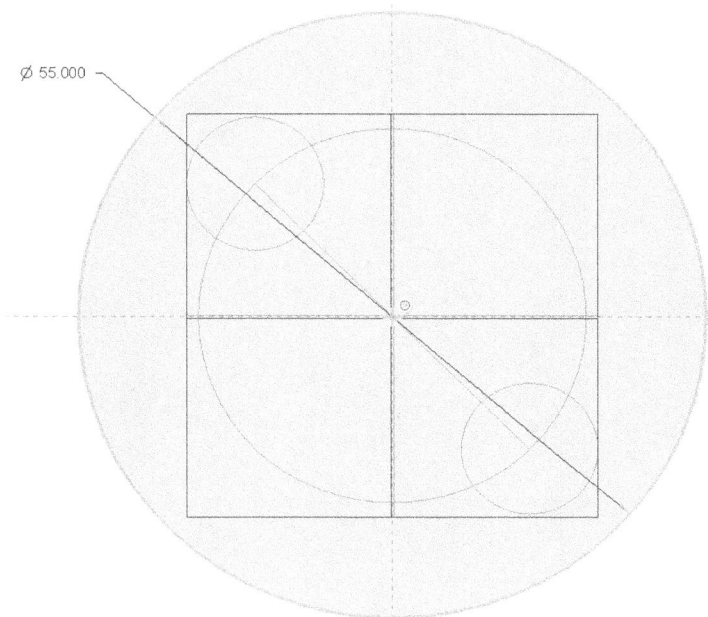

Ø 55.000

Figure 10–65

13. Click ✓ (OK).

14. Set the display to the Default Orientation.

15. Toggle off the display of datum planes.

16. Select ⊟ (Symmetric) for the *Depth* and enter **8**, as shown in Figure 10–66.

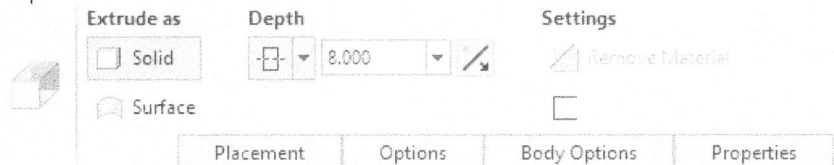

Extrude as	Depth				Settings	
☐ Solid	-⊟-	▼	8.000	▼	⟋	Remove Material
◠ Surface					☐	
	Placement	Options		Body Options	Properties	

Figure 10–66

17. Click ✔ (OK). The model updates as shown in Figure 10–67.

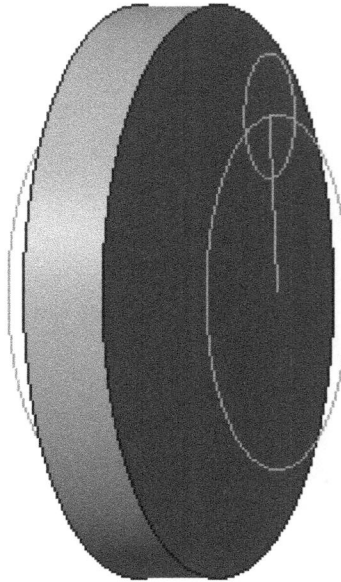

Figure 10–67

18. Click 🗗 (Extrude).

19. Select the surface shown in Figure 10–68.

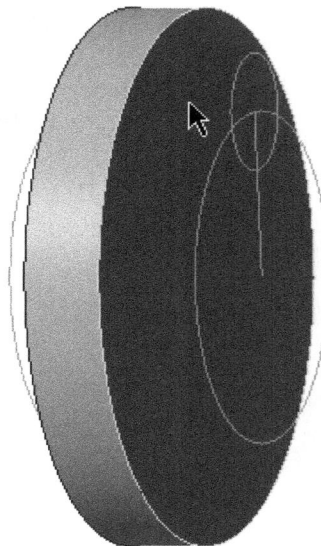

Figure 10–68

20. Click ⬒ (Project) in the *Sketch* tab and select both halves of the small circle, as shown in Figure 10–69.

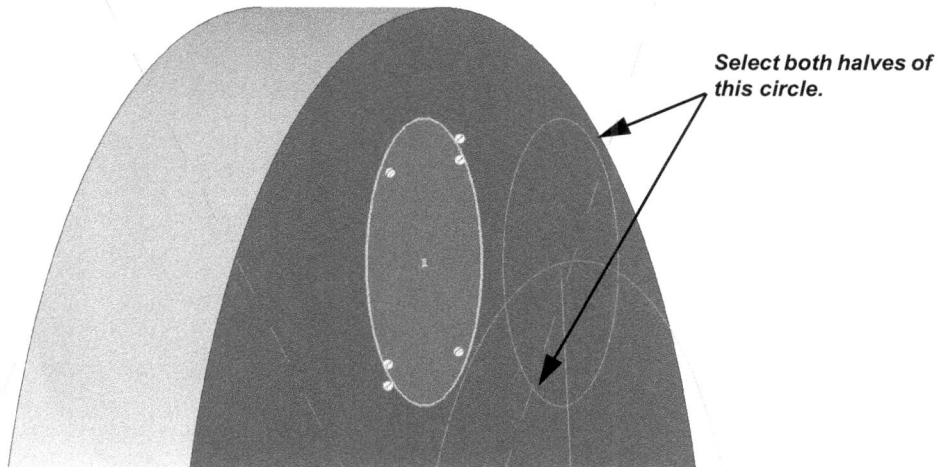

Select both halves of this circle.

Figure 10–69

21. Click ✓ (OK).

22. Edit the *Depth* to **22**.

23. Click ✓ (OK). The model displays as shown in Figure 10–70.

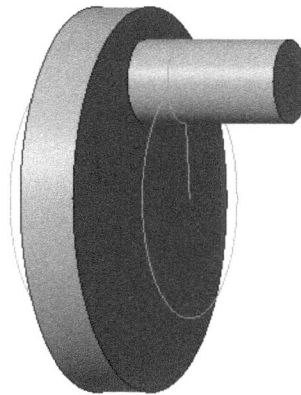

Figure 10–70

24. Rotate the model approximately as shown in Figure 10–71.

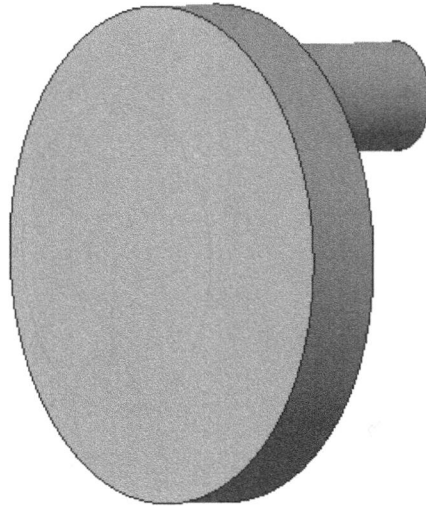

Figure 10–71

25. Click ▱ (Extrude) and select the flat surface of the model.

26. Click ▱ (Project) and select both halves of the small circle.

27. Click ✓ (OK).

28. Edit the *Depth* to **22** and click ✓ (OK). The model displays as shown in Figure 10–72.

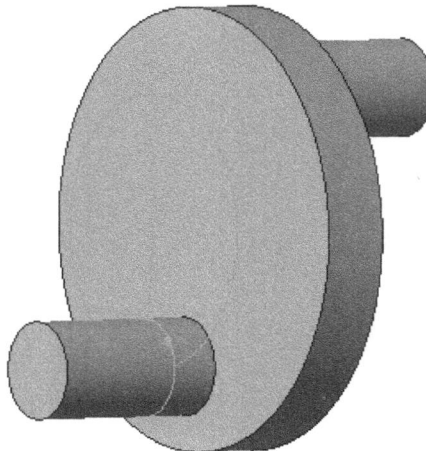

Figure 10–72

29. Save the part and close it. The assembly updates as shown in Figure 10–73.

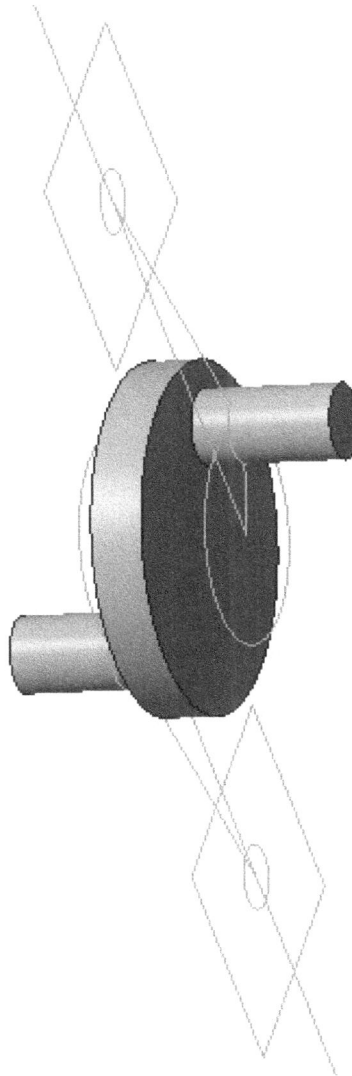

Figure 10–73

Task 3 - Verify the motion.

1. Click 🖑 (Drag Components) in the *Model* tab.

2. Click the location shown in Figure 10–74.

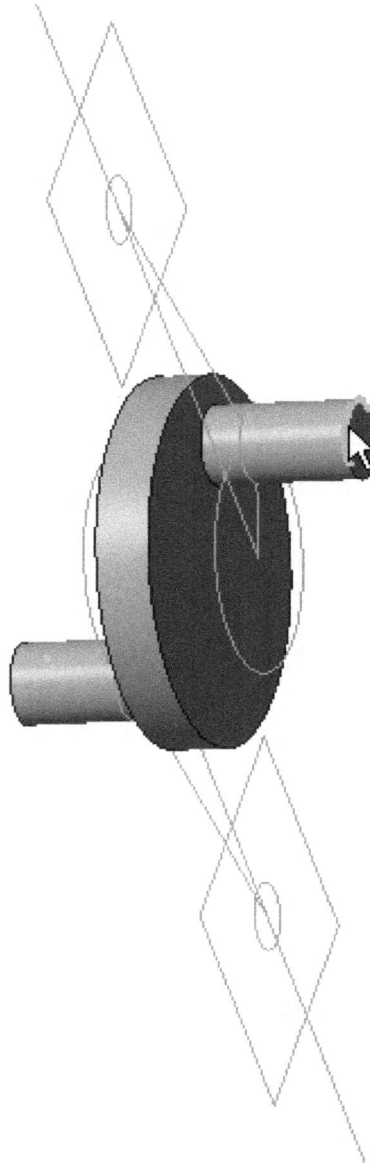

Figure 10–74

3. Move the cursor to view the motion, as shown in Figure 10–75.

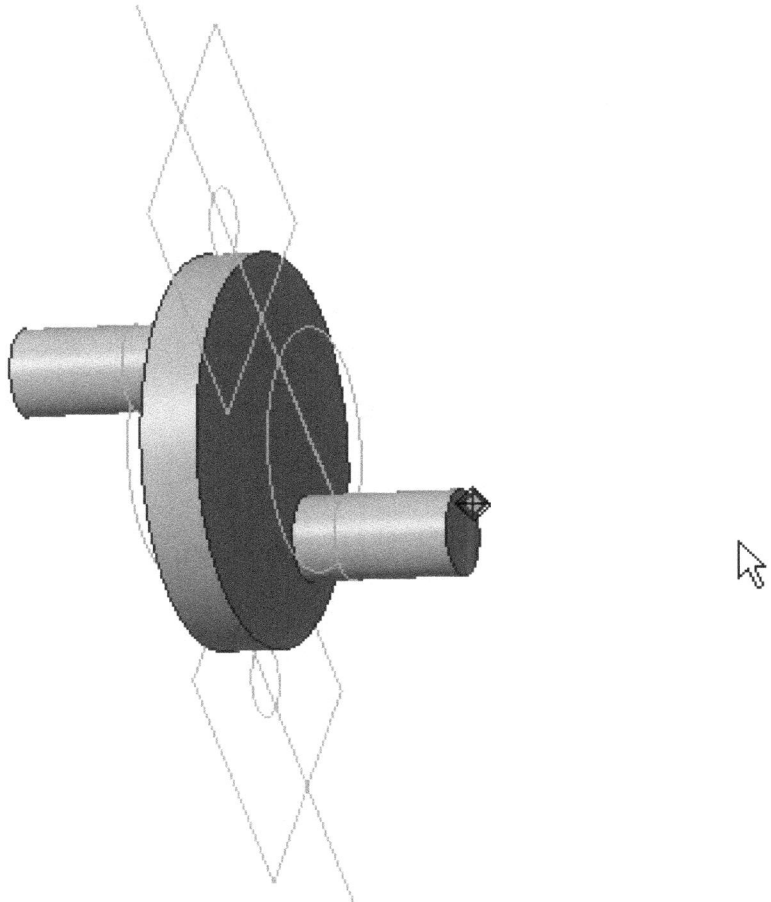

Figure 10–75

4. Right-click to cancel the drag.

___

Task 4 - Create geometry for the connecting rod.

1. Open **CONN_ROD.PRT** in a new window.

2. Select the **External Merge** feature in the Model Tree and click 🖌 (Edit Definition) in the mini toolbar.

3. Select the References panel and enable **Copy Datums**.

4. Click ✓ (OK).

5. Enable the display of datum planes. The model displays as shown in Figure 10–76.

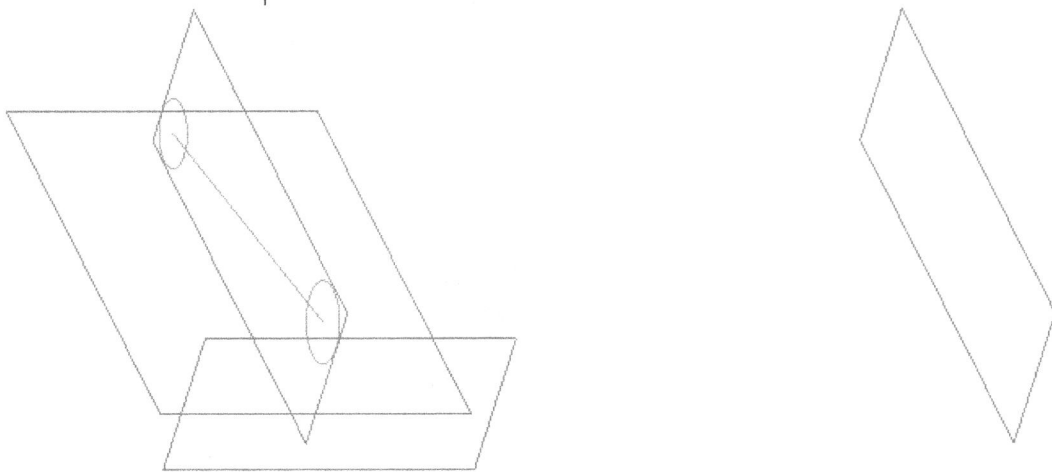

Figure 10–76

6. Click (Extrude).

7. Select the plane running through the circles and line.

8. Click (Sketch View) and the model orients as shown in Figure 10–77.

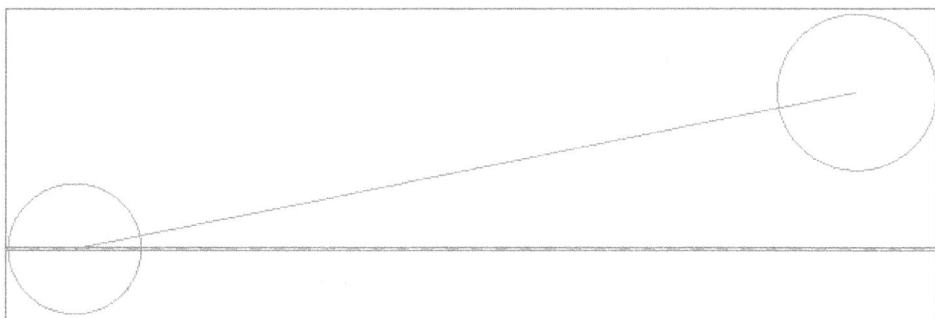

Figure 10–77

9. Create the sketch shown in Figure 10–78 by using

   ☐ (Project) for both halves of the inner circles and creating two new outer circles.

   - Note that the planes are turned off in the image for clarity.

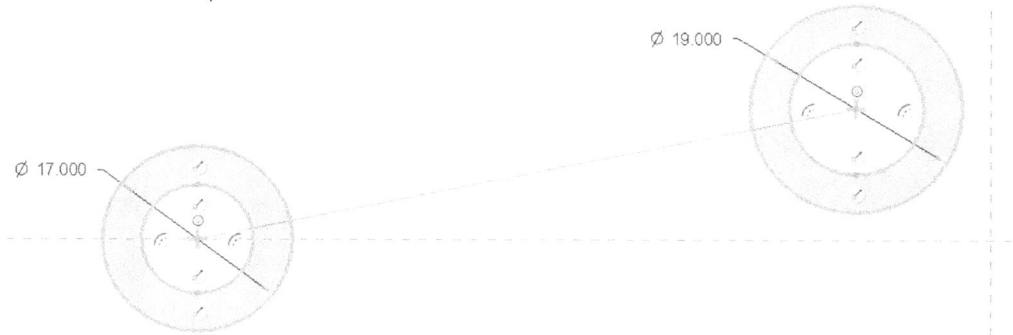

Ø 19.000

Ø 17.000

Figure 10–78

10. Click ✓ (OK).

11. Select ⊡ (Symmetric) for the *Depth* and enter **12**.

12. Click ✓ (OK).

13. Click ☐ (Extrude).

14. Select the plane running through the circles and line.

15. Click ⊡ (Sketch View).

16. Right-click and select **References**.

17. Select the line and two outer circles, as shown in Figure 10–79.

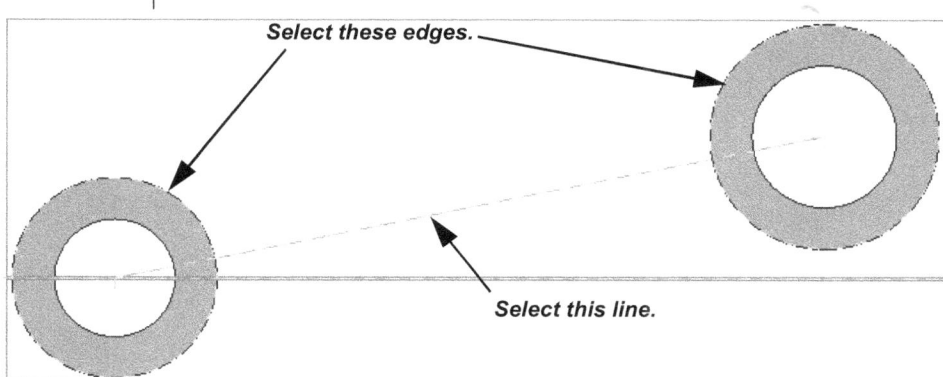

Select these edges.

Select this line.

Figure 10–79

18. Click **Close** in the References dialog box.

19. Sketch a centerline along the line, as shown in Figure 10–80.

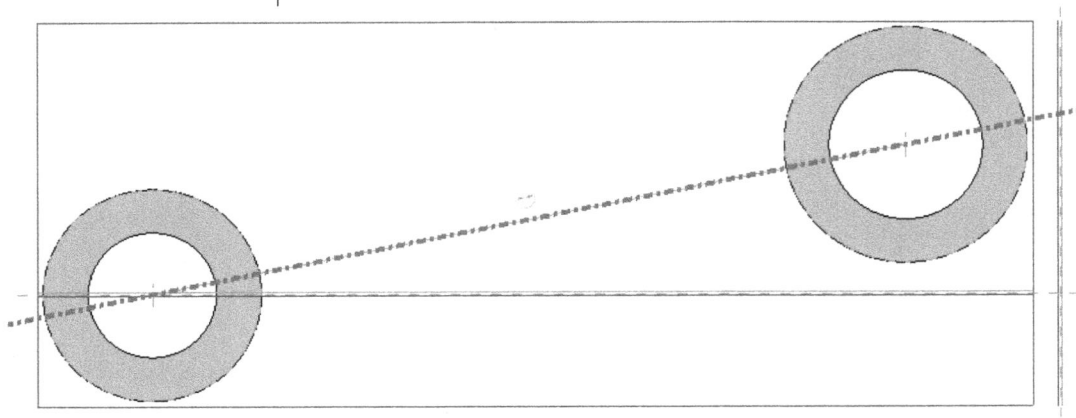

Figure 10–80

20. Create the sketch shown in Figure 10–81. Use ⬜ (Project) to create the circular entities and sketch two parallel lines. Use the lines and ⊢ (Corner) to trim the circular entities.

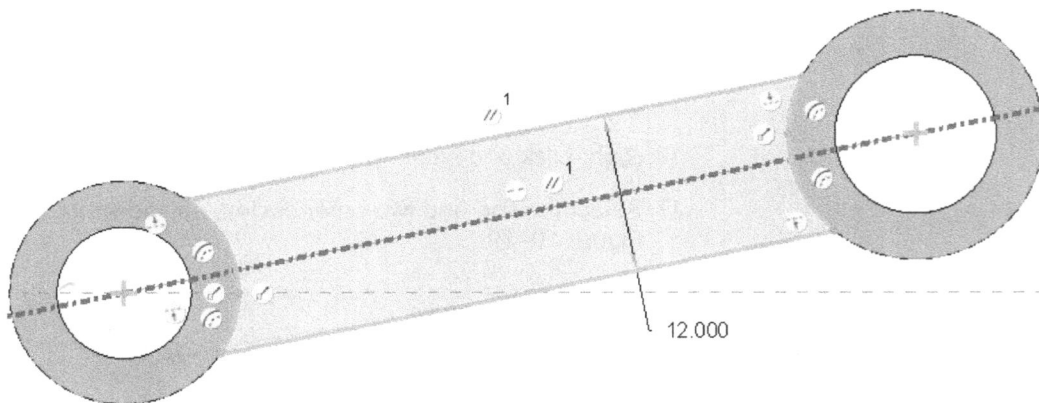

12.000

Figure 10–81

21. Click ✓ (OK).

22. Select ⊟ (Symmetric) for the *Depth* and enter **5**.

23. Click ✔ (OK).

24. Return to Default Orientation. The model displays as shown in Figure 10–82.

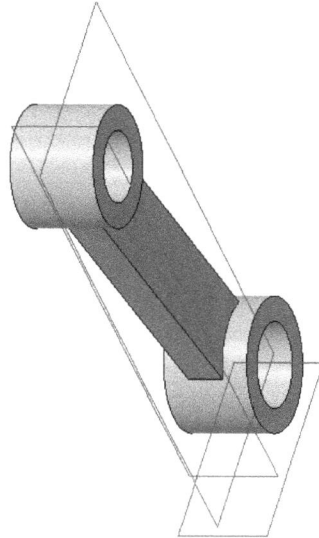

Figure 10–82

25. Save the part and close the window. The assembly displays as shown in Figure 10–83.

Datums turned off for clarity.

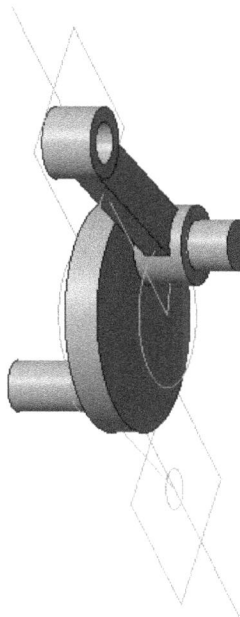

Figure 10–83

Task 5 - Create geometry for the piston.

1. Open **PISTON.PRT** in a new window.

2. Select the **External Merge** feature and click
   ![icon] (Edit Definition) in the mini toolbar.

3. Select the References panel and enable **Copy Datums**.

4. Click ![icon] (OK).

5. Click ![icon] (Revolve).

6. Select the plane the skeleton sketch is on.

7. Click ![icon] (Sketch View), and the model orients as shown in
   Figure 10–84.

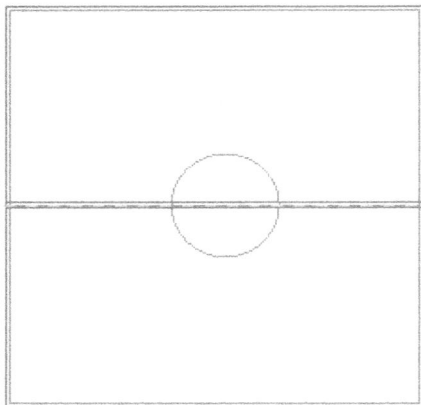

Figure 10–84

8. Disable the display of datum planes.

9. Create the sketch shown in Figure 10–85. Make sure to include the centerline.

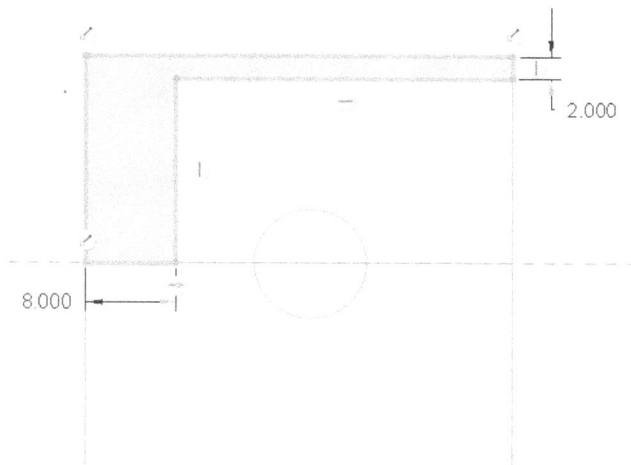

Figure 10–85

10. Click ✓ (OK).

11. Click ✓ (OK)

12. Enable the display of Datum Planes and return to Default Orientation. The model displays as shown in Figure 10–86.

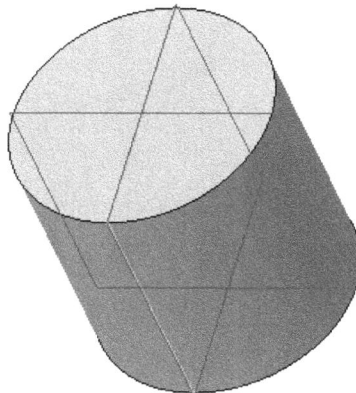

Figure 10–86

13. Click 🗇 (Extrude).

14. Select the same plane as used in the previous feature.

15. Click ⌖ (Sketch View).

16. Set the display to ▢ (Hidden Line).

17. Click ▢ (Project) and select the two halves of the small circle, as shown in Figure 10–87. Note that datums are off for clarity.

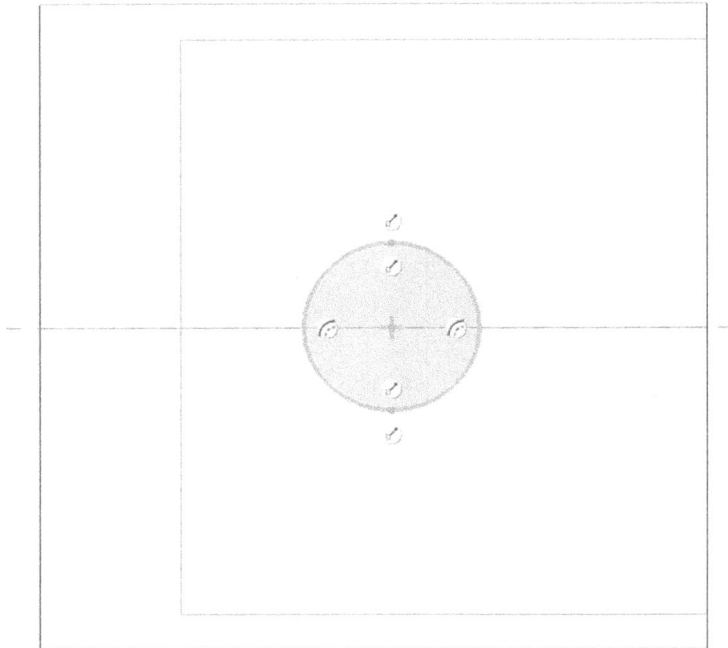

Figure 10–87

18. Click ✓ (OK).

19. Return to the Default Orientation.

20. In the feature **Options**, make Side 1 and Side 2 **Through All**.

21. Right-click and select **Remove Material**.

22. Click ✓ (OK).

23. Set the display to ▢ (Shading With Edges) and the model displays as shown in Figure 10–88.

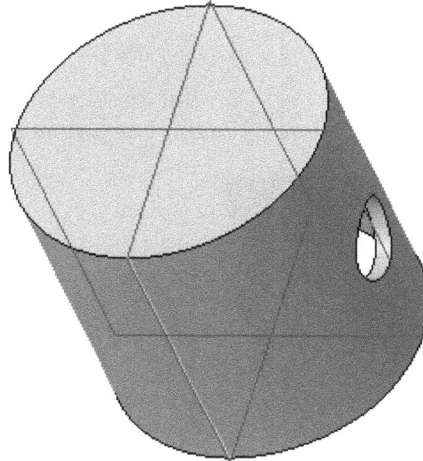

Figure 10–88

24. Save the part and close the window.

25. Toggle off the display of Datum Planes, and the assembly displays as shown in Figure 10–89.

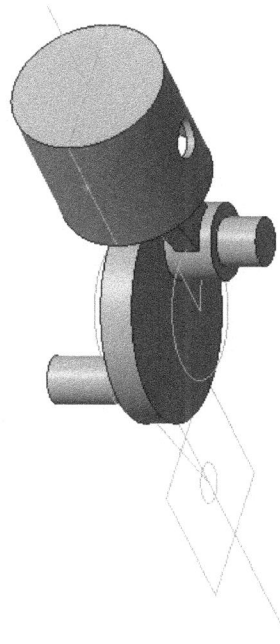

Figure 10–89

Task 6 - Assemble an existing component to the assembly.

1. Enable the display of Datum Axes.

2. ⌐ (Assemble)**bearing_journal_main.prt**.

3. Set the *Constraint Type* to **Coincident** and select the two axes shown in Figure 10–90.

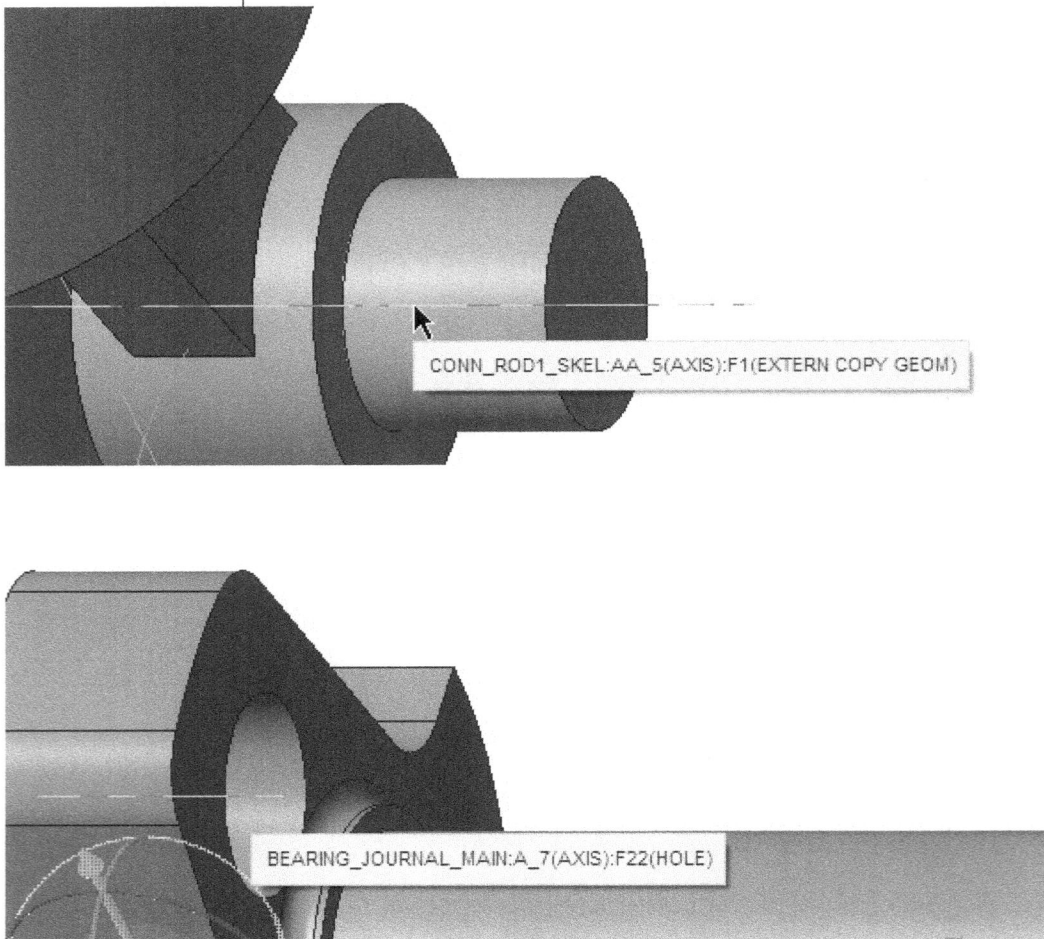

CONN_ROD1_SKEL:AA_5(AXIS):F1(EXTERN COPY GEOM)

BEARING_JOURNAL_MAIN:A_7(AXIS):F22(HOLE)

Figure 10–90

4. Set the *Constraint Type* to **Coincident** and select the two axes shown in Figure 10–91.

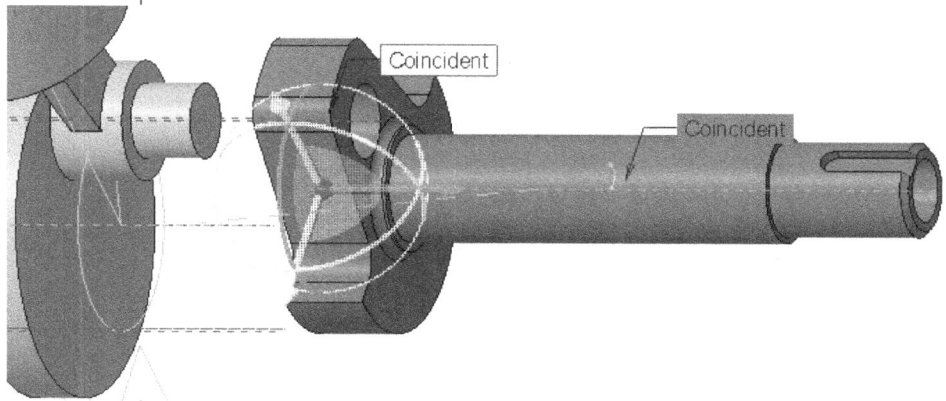

Figure 10–91

5. Select the two surfaces shown in Figure 10–92 as **Coincident** for the final constraint.

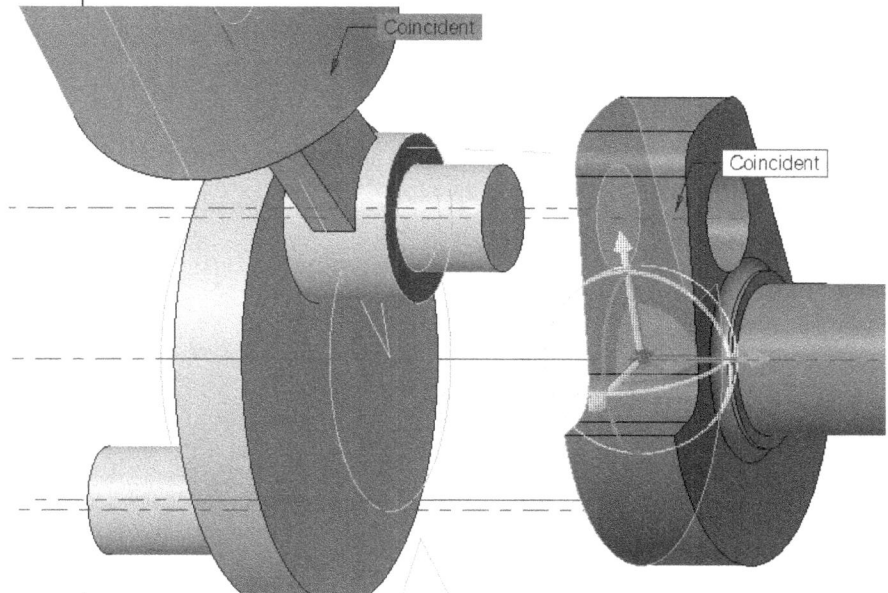

Figure 10–92

6. Click ✔ (OK).

7. Toggle off the display of Datum Axes, and the assembly displays as shown in Figure 10–93.

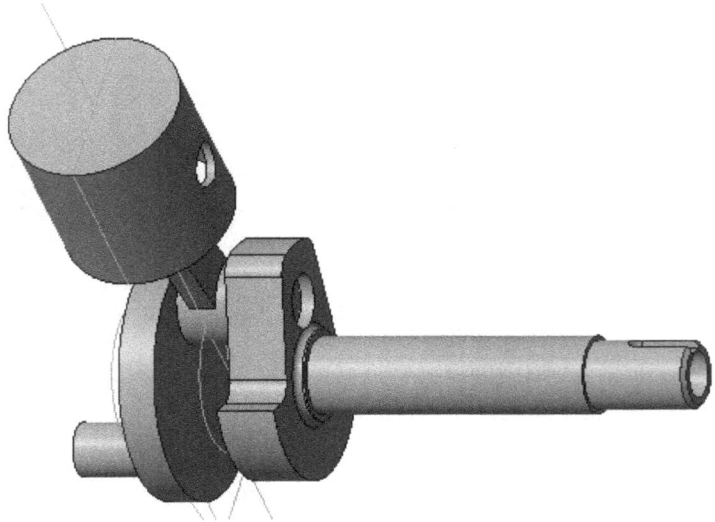

Figure 10–93

Task 7 - Verify the motion of the assembly.

1. Click 🖑 (Drag Components).

2. Click the edge shown in Figure 10–94.

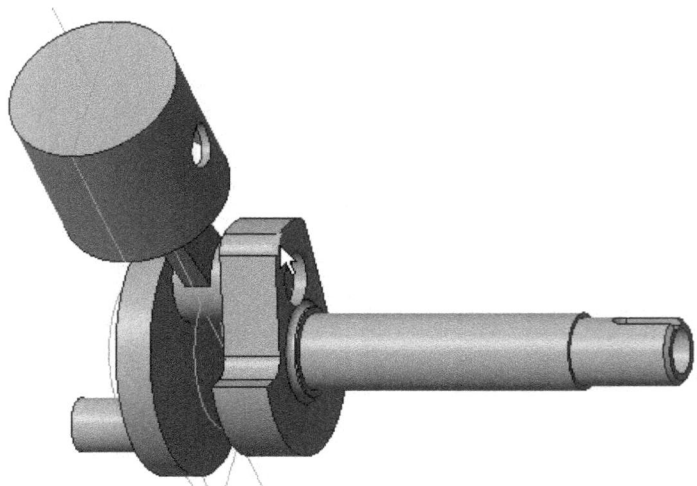

Figure 10–94

3. Move the cursor and note that the components move to follow the skeletons, as shown in Figure 10–95.

Figure 10–95

4. Save the assembly and erase it from memory.

Chapter Review Questions

1. Which option from the external reference control enables you to select references only from the components that belong to the same assembly?

   a. All components

   b. Inside Subassembly

   c. Skeleton and Layout Model

   d. None

2. Which option from the external reference control prevents you from selecting references from other components?

   a. All components

   b. Inside Subassembly

   c. Skeleton and Layout Model

   d. None

3. If a global reference rule and a component-specific rule are in conflict, the more restrictive rule is applied.

   a. True

   b. False

4. Component A has a reference control that is set to **None**. The global reference rule for the current session is set to **All**. What can or cannot be referenced?

   a. When component A is assembled, all of the components except for component A can be referenced in the assembly.

   b. None of the components can be referenced in the assembly.

   c. All of the components can be referenced in the assembly.

5. Component A has a reference control that is set to **All**. The global reference rule for the current session is set to **None**. What can or cannot be referenced?

   a. When component A is assembled, all of the components except for component A can be referenced in the assembly.

   b. No components can be referenced in the assembly.

   c. All components can be referenced in the assembly.

6. The most common use of Copy Geometry is to copy references between parts for further design directly at the part level. Which of the following references can you copy? (Select all that apply.)

   a. Datum curves

   b. Datum features

   c. Publish geometry features

   d. Vertices

   e. Copy and external geometry features

7. What are the advantages of using Copy Geometry? (Select all that apply.)

   a. The Copy Geometry feature consolidates all of the feature copy methods into one super feature.

   b. Using Copy Geometry to establish external references helps to standardize your company's approach to data sharing.

   c. Funneling all of the external references through a Copy Geometry feature consolidates the external references into just a few features.

   d. The Copy Geometry feature does not create external references.

8. Which feature enables you to mark features in a model that are to be copied into other parts?

   a. Copy Geometry

   b. Shrinkwrap

   c. Publish Geometry

9. Which option is an advanced surface copying technique that copies all of the external surfaces on a part or assembly?

   a. Copy Geometry

   b. Shrinkwrap

   c. Publish Geometry

Answers: 1.b, 2.d, 3.a, 4.a, 5.b, 6.abcde, 7.abc, 8.c, 9.b

Managing External References

At some point, you might need to eliminate external references in a model. In situations in which you are not familiar with the model geometry, it is recommended that you investigate the model to gain a complete understanding of the parts and assemblies affected.

Learning Objectives in This Chapter

- Learn to use the appropriate tools to gain information and to check the external references in a part or assembly.
- Learn the techniques to remove unwanted external references.

11.1 Investigating External References

When you need to eliminate external references in a model, you should investigate it to gain a complete understanding of the following:

- Features that have external references.

- Status of the external references. You might want to update them before severing the external reference.

- Parent assembly where the external reference was created. The assembly needs to be in session to update the external references.

- Component and features in the external parent that are referenced in your part.

- Features in the model that are children of the feature with an external reference. When external references are funneled through Copy Geometry features, you need to redefine the children before you can delete the Copy Geometry feature.

With this information, you can determine how much work is required to sever the external references and where to begin. Sometimes, it might seem easier to delete the feature and recreate it, instead of redefining it. However, there might be components in an assembly that are assembled to the feature that you plan to delete. In the long run, it might be easier to save the feature, rather than rebuild it.

There are several methods that can be used to investigate your external references. These include the following:

- Model Tree
- Model Information
- Reference Viewer
- Message window

Model Tree

The Model Tree can be used to investigate external references. The Model Tree lists all of the Copy Geometry and External Copy Geometry features, as shown in Figure 11–1.

NEW_BELT_COVER.PRT
▶ Bodies (1)
▱ RIGHT
▱ TOP
▱ FRONT
PRT_CSYS_DEF

*This feature has an
external reference.*

⊩ Copy Geometry id 39

Figure 11–1

Model Information

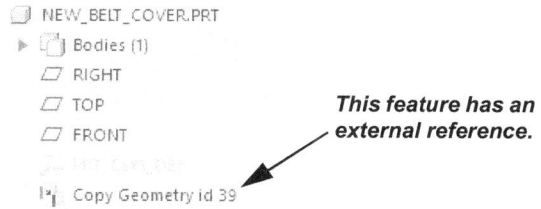

Clicking ▯ (Model Information) in the *Tools* tab or right-clicking the part in the Model Tree and selecting **Information>Model Information** opens an Information window that lists the feature information for each feature in the model. At the end of the file, it summarizes all of the reference assemblies, as shown in Figure 11–2.

Model Info : BELT_COVER

PART NAME :		BELT_COVER				▯
Units:		Length:	Mass:	Force:	Time:	Temperature:
Inch lbm Second (Creo Parametric Default)		in	lbm	in lbm / sec^2	sec	F

Feature List

No.	ID	Name	Type	Actions		Sup Order
1	1	RIGHT	DATUM PLANE	◮	▯	---
2	3	TOP	DATUM PLANE	◮	▯	---
3	5	FRONT	DATUM PLANE	◮	▯	---
4	7	PRT_CSYS_DEF	COORDINATE SYSTEM	◮	▯	---
5	39	---	COPY GEOMETRY	◮	▯	---
6	48	MOUNT-COVER-IF	DATUM PLANE	◮	▯	---
		BASE	PROTRU	◮		
44	487	---	HOLE	◮	▯	---
45	488	---	HOLE	◮	▯	---

REFERENCE ASSEMBLIES:
COMPLETED_POWER_6

Figure 11–2

You can select ⬚ (Feature Information) next to any features in the list to open the Feature info window, as shown in Figure 11–3.

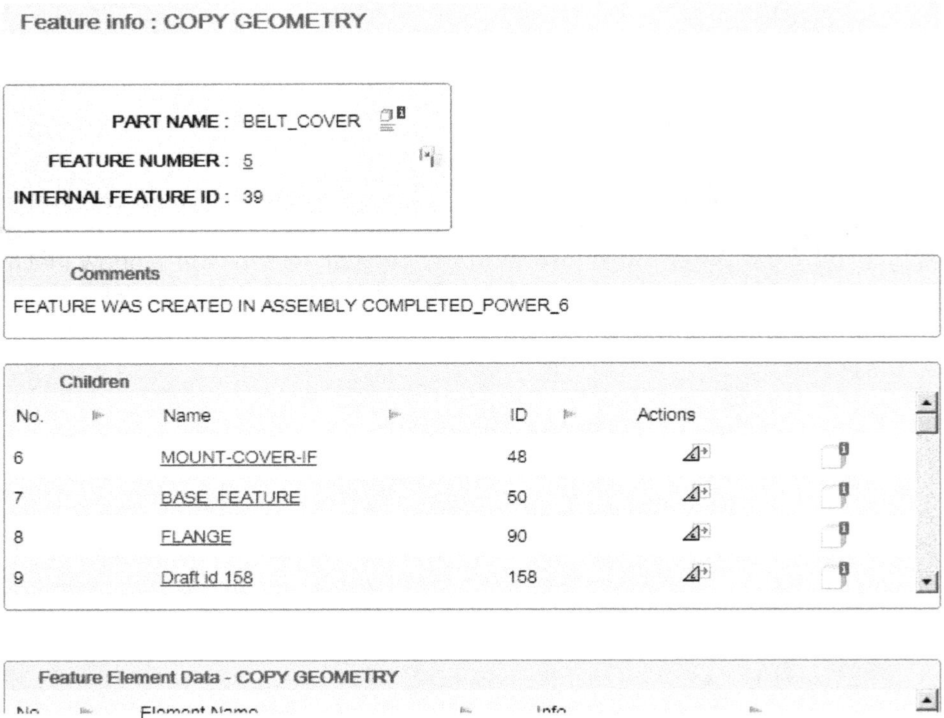

Feature info : COPY GEOMETRY

PART NAME : BELT_COVER

FEATURE NUMBER : <u>5</u>

INTERNAL FEATURE ID : 39

Comments

FEATURE WAS CREATED IN ASSEMBLY COMPLETED_POWER_6

Children

No.	Name	ID	Actions	
6	MOUNT-COVER-IF	48	⬚	⬚
7	BASE_FEATURE	50	⬚	⬚
8	FLANGE	90	⬚	⬚
9	Draft id 158	158	⬚	⬚

Feature Element Data - COPY GEOMETRY

No.	Element Name	Info	

Figure 11–3

To display the information in text format, set the configuration option to **info_output_format text** (HTML is the default).

11.2 Reference Viewer

The Reference Viewer can be used to display the parent/child relationships for selected features in part mode and components in assembly mode. To open it, select the required component, right-click, and select **Information>Reference Viewer**. The Reference Viewer dialog box opens, as shown in Figure 11–4.

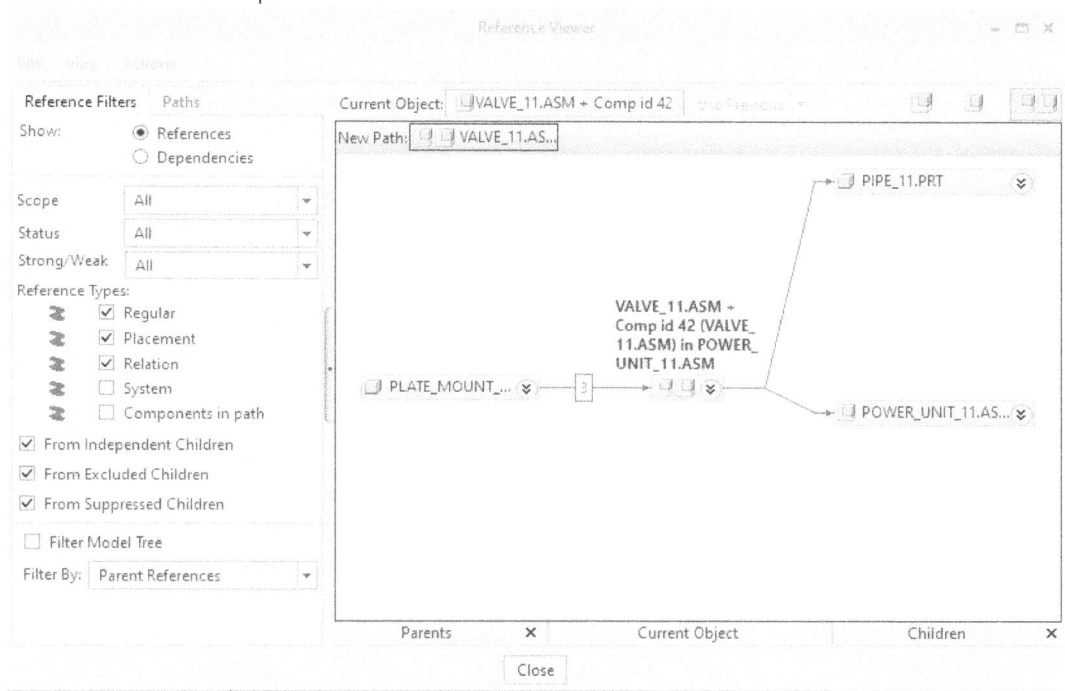

Figure 11–4

An arrow between two objects indicates a reference. When multiple references exist, a number displays on the arrow, indicating the exact number of references.

You can click ⚲ (Zoom To) which will bring into focus a selected feature in the reference viewer. In large assemblies, ⚲ (Zoom To) makes it easier to identify and locate references you are investigating.

Right-click on a reference and select **Display Full Path** to display the full reference path between objects, as shown in Figure 11–5.

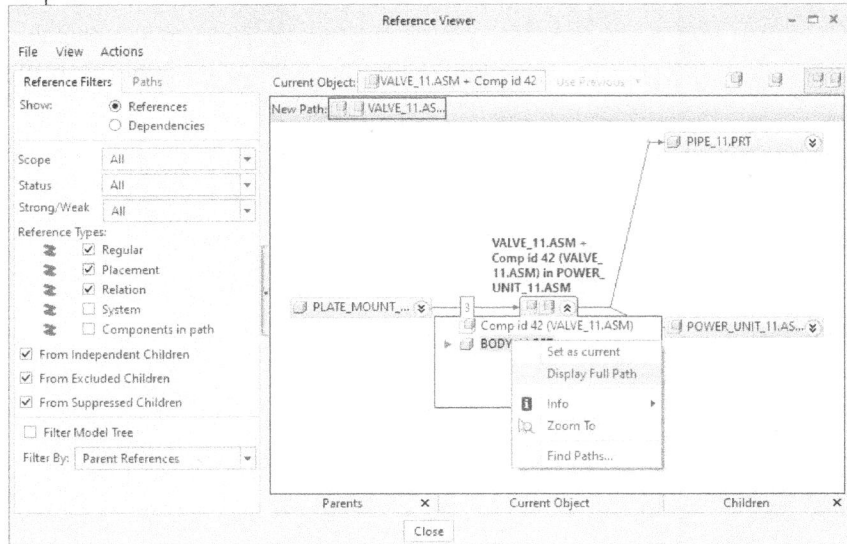

Figure 11–5

The Full Path Display dialog box opens as shown in Figure 11–6.

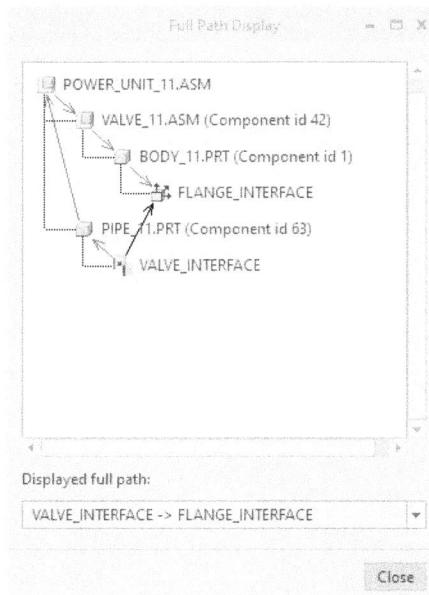

Figure 11–6

You can filter the Reference Viewer to display objects with parents only or objects with children only. To view objects with parents only, select **Parent References** in the Filter By drop-down list as shown in Figure 11–7.

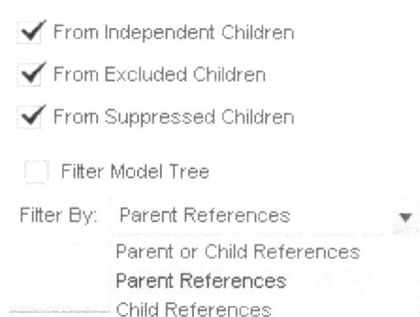

✔ From Independent Children

✔ From Excluded Children

✔ From Suppressed Children

☐ Filter Model Tree

Filter By: Parent References ▼

Parent or Child References
Parent References
Child References

Figure 11–7

Using the Reference Viewer dialog box, you can only delete a reference when Creo Parametric identifies it as an additional reference that can be removed safely. To delete a reference, right-click on it in the Reference Viewer and select **Delete Reference**. You can use this option to delete references to rounds, chamfers, copied geometry, published geometry, annotation features, and through-point datum curves.

Displaying Circular References

You can easily identify circular references in your assemblies using the Reference Viewer.

How To: Review a Circular Reference in an Assembly

1. Open or activate the assembly.

2. Click ⬚ to regenerate the assembly. If circular references exist, the message window displays the number of circular references found and a .CRC file is generated, as shown in Figure 11–8.

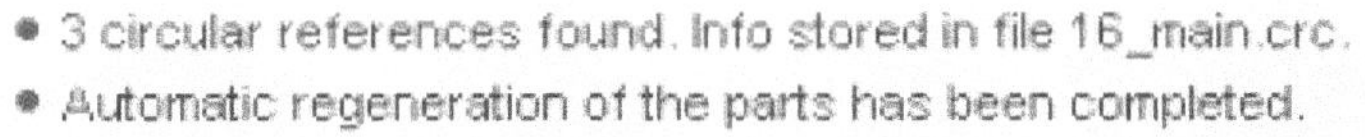

* 3 circular references found. Info stored in file 16_main.crc.
* Automatic regeneration of the parts has been completed.

Figure 11–8

3. Click 🔑 (Reference Viewer) in the *Tools* tab or select the component, right-click, and select **Reference Viewer**. The Reference Viewer dialog box opens, as shown in Figure 11–9.

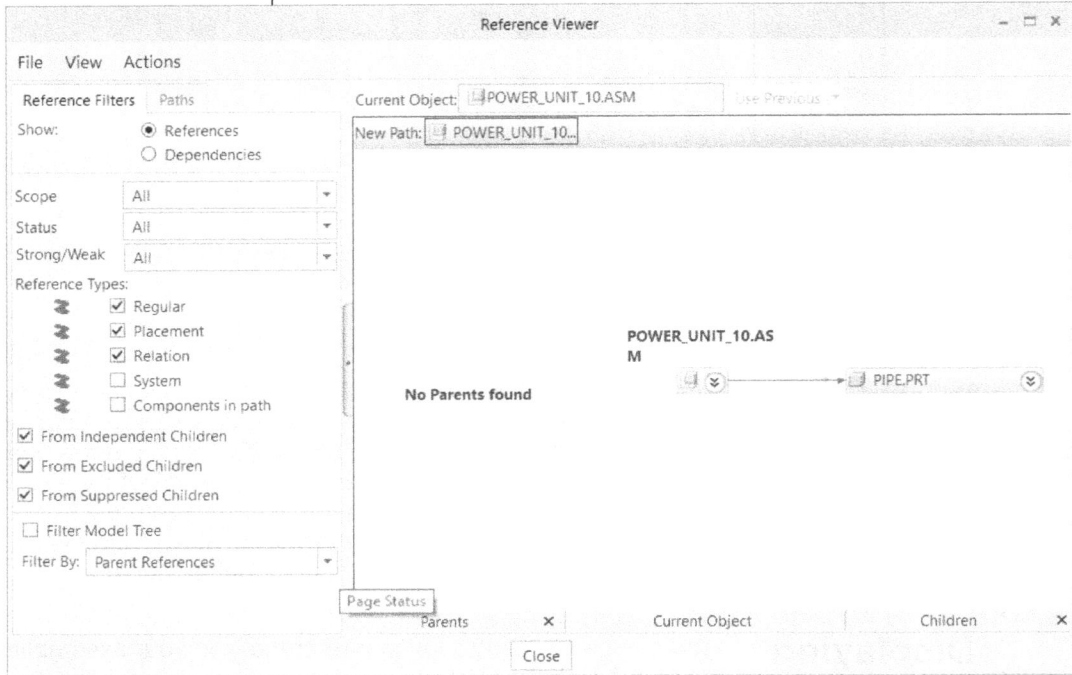

Figure 11–9

4. Select the *Paths* tab and click **Find Circular Paths** to review any circular paths in the model.
5. Select the circular paths to review them. In Figure 11–10, **Circular Path 0** was selected to investigate its circular path.

Displays the circular path. *Displays the current object.*

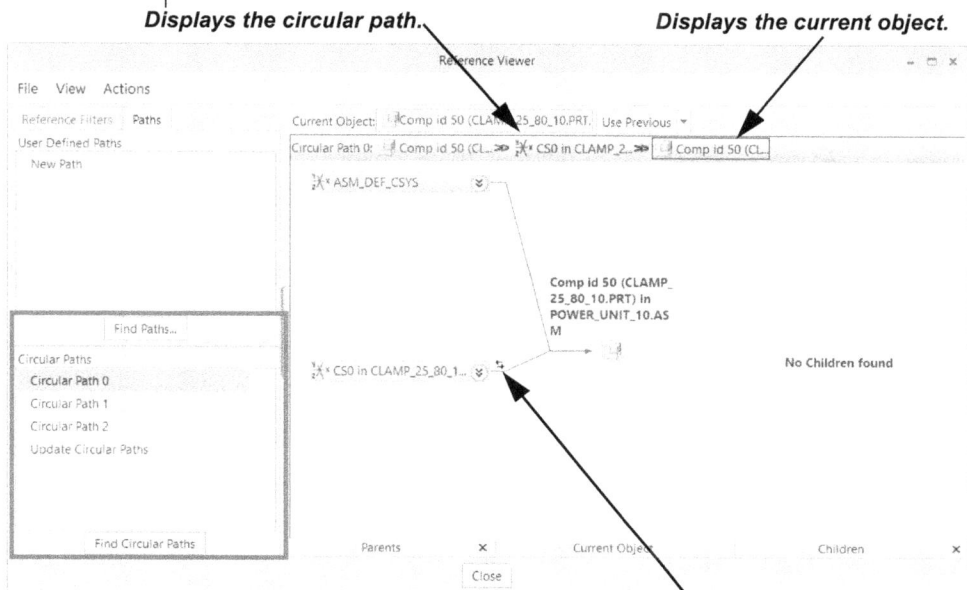

This icon (two arrows) indicates that a circular reference exists.

Figure 11–10

6. Right-click on _____ ⇵, which identifies the circular reference (as shown in Figure 11–11), and select **Display Full Path**. The Full Path Display dialog box opens as shown in Figure 11–11. **CS0** has two paths directed toward it and is the source of the circular reference for the circular path.

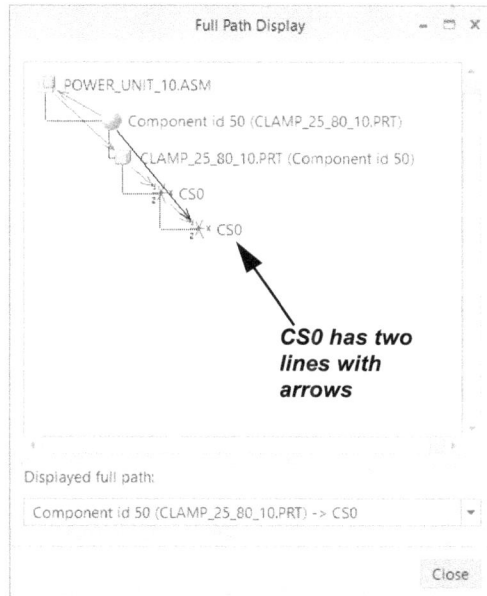

CS0 has two lines with arrows

Figure 11–11

7. You can continue to review any additional circular references, as required.
8. Close the Reference Viewer.

Breaking Dependencies

Additional functionality includes control over the dependency of the components in an assembly context. You can investigate and break/restructure the following:

- Dependencies of reference models to independent Data Sharing features.
- Dependencies of mirrored models to their source models.
- Dependencies of replaced components.
- Dependencies of old assembly cuts.
- Dependencies to layouts.

Checking Memory

To list the parts, assemblies, drawings, layouts, and sections that are in the memory, select **File>Manage Session>Object List**. This can also provide clues about unknown dependencies in your models.

Message Window

Notebook declarations in part and assembly models do not display as external references in the Global Reference Viewer. When the part or assembly is initially opened, the system displays a message prompting you that it is also going to open any layouts associated with the model.

11.3 Severing External References

With a clear understanding of the external references in a model and the parents and children of the features with an external reference, you are now ready to sever any unwanted relationships. This section describes techniques that you can use for certain types of features.

Sketched Features

It is recommended that you never select an external feature as the sketching plane or orientation plane for a sketched feature. Empty datum planes should be assembled into the appropriate location using traditional constraints.

It is acceptable to select external features for the following:

*   Additional Sketcher references.

*   ▭ (Project) and ⌐ (Offset) commands.

*   Concentric circles and arcs.

You can eliminate these by clicking ▭ (References) in the *Sketch* tab and select them in the dialog box, as shown in Figure 11–12. As you select each one, the reference highlights on the screen, enabling you to verify that the correct reference is selected. Clicking **Delete** removes the reference, then the Intent Manager automatically dimensions the sketch to new references that you can add, such as default datum planes.

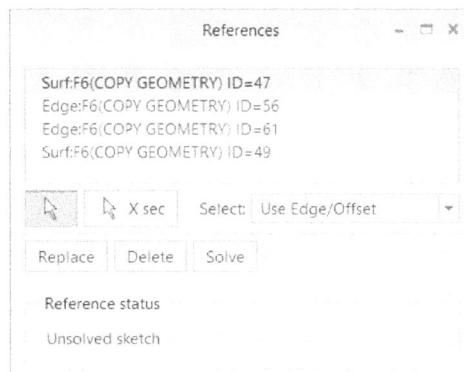

Figure 11–12

You can also select the orange phantom lines in the Sketcher window and manually delete them.

Coaxial Holes

For example, if datum axis features have been copied into a part using ⌐ (Copy Geometry), solid geometry is added and a Coaxial hole is created on a copied axis. If you want to eliminate the external reference in the part, you can redefine the hole and change it from Coaxial to Linear instead of deleting and recreating it (deleting the Copy Geometry feature causes the Coaxial hole to fail). You are then prompted to select two new dimensioning references. The system measures the distance from your selected references to the hole center and uses that value for the default distance. This technique enables you to sever the reference and easily maintain the same feature and the same location.

Once all of the child features have been redefined, the Copy Geometry feature can be deleted.

Copied Surfaces

Surfaces that have been copied into another part model usually present a challenge when you are trying to sever external references. You need to manually create a new surface (or series of surfaces), at an earlier point in the regeneration cycle than the protrusions and cuts that need them.

Depth Options

When a planar surface or datum plane in an external model is selected as the ⊥ (To Selected) or ⊥ (Through Until) depth reference, you can measure the distance from the sketching plane and use the ⊥ (Blind) depth option.

If a complex surface was used as the terminating surface, it can cause similar problems to those when using Copied Surfaces. You need to create a native surface at an earlier point in the regeneration cycle and select the new surface as the terminating surface.

Merged Features

A Merge By Reference feature cannot be converted to a Merge By Copy feature. The Merge feature can be made **Read Only**, which halts its associativity to the parent models. This also eliminates the need for the merged features to *see* the original models. This should only be considered as a temporary solution. It might be appropriate when sending a merged model to an outside source for review, preventing you from sending the part and assembly models.

Independent Copy Geometry Features

Changing a Copy Geometry feature from *Dependent* to **Independent** should be considered a temporary solution. It prevents the copied features from updating with any changes to the parent geometry, but the external references are still present.

Practice 11a	Severing External References

Practice Objectives

- Determine which features reference a Copy Geometry feature.
- Remove references to the Copy Geometry feature.
- Delete a Copy Geometry feature.

In this practice, you will investigate the external references using the reference viewer and use the appropriate tools to remove the references.

Task 1 - Open the model and investigate its external references.

1. Change the working directory to the *Sever_External_Links* folder.

2. Open **belt_cover.prt**.

3. Set the model display as follows:

   - $\times$ (Datum Display Filters): All Off

   - ⅔ (Spin Center): Off

   - (Display Style): ⬜ (Shading With Edges)

   The part and the Model Tree display as shown in Figure 11–13.

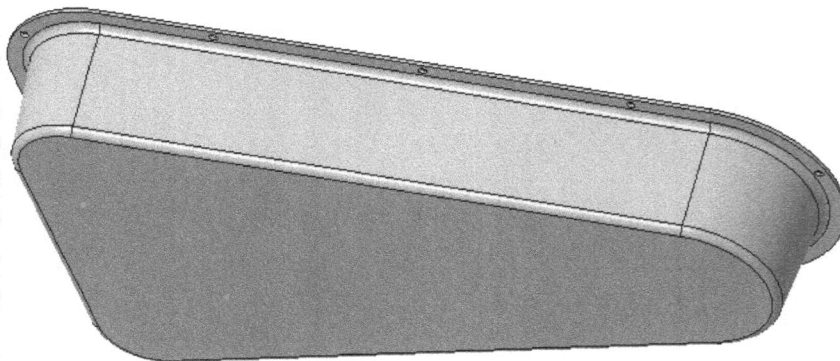

BELT_COVER.PRT
- ▸ 🗁 Bodies (1)
- ⬜ RIGHT
- ⬜ TOP
- ⬜ FRONT
- PRT_CSYS_DEF
- Copy Geometry id 39
- ⬜ MOUNT-COVER-IF
- ▸ BASE_FEATURE
- ▸ FLANGE
- Draft id 158
- Round id 189
- Shell id 292
- Curve id 383
- ▸ Pattern (PNT0)
- ▸ Pattern (A_1)
- ▸ Pattern (Hole)

Figure 11–13

Design Considerations

The design scenario is that this part is used in another assembly. It has been designed using an external reference that is indicated by the presence of the Copy Geometry feature that is listed in the Model Tree.

You will create a new part that is similar to the **belt_cover** part, except for a few dimensional changes. To complete this task, you must break the external references that exist in the part.

Task 2 - Create a different part and investigate the design.

1. Select **File>Manage File>Rename**. Set the new *Name* to **new_belt_cover** and select **Rename in session**, as shown in Figure 11–14.

Figure 11–14

2. Click **OK**.

3. Edit the definition of **BASE_FEATURE**.

4. Click in the graphics area and select ✏ (Edit Internal Sketch).

5. Click 🔄 (Sketch View) and the sketch for the **BASE_FEATURE** displays, as shown in Figure 11–15.

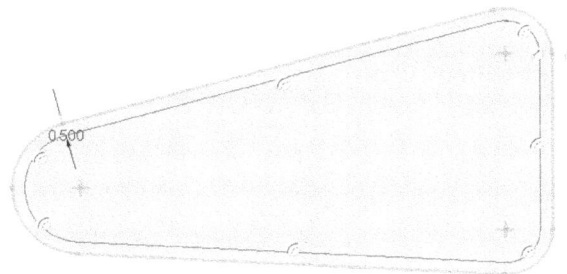

Figure 11–15

**Design
Considerations**

The only dimension that is available for you to edit is an offset dimension from an external reference.

6. Exit Sketcher and the *Extrude* dashboard without making any changes.

7. Return to he Default Orientation.

8. Attempt to delete the external reference by selecting the Copy Geometry feature, right-clicking, and selecting ✕ (Delete).

The Delete warning displays as shown in Figure 11–16. All of the features highlight in the display and in the Model Tree. The external reference is the parent to all of the features in the model.

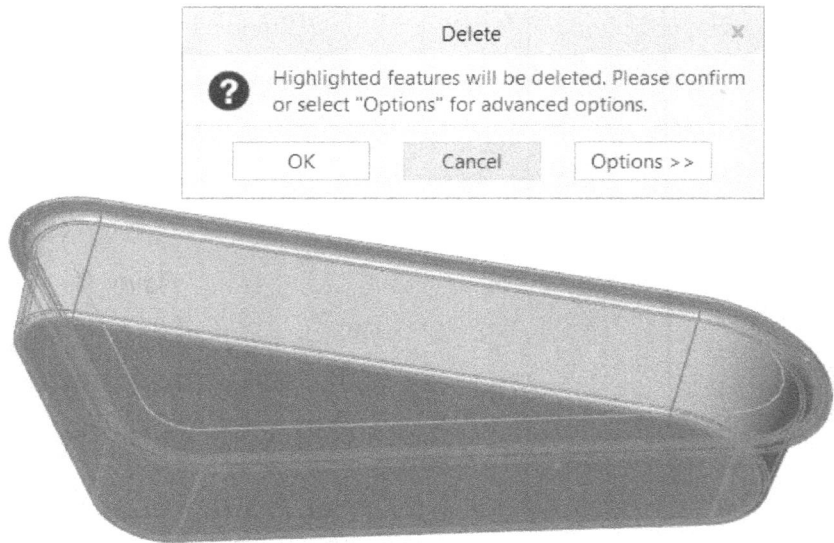

Figure 11–16

**Design
Considerations**

The base geometry that you need to change is controlled by an external reference, which is preventing you from making any dimensional changes to it. The external reference is also the parent of all of the geometry in the part, and it cannot be deleted. The external reference must be severed so that the part geometry is independent and modifiable.

9. Cancel the Delete command.

Task 3 - Investigate the external references.

1. Select the Copy Geometry feature in the Model Tree, right-click, and select **Information>Reference Viewer**.

2. In the *Reference Types* area, remove the check next to **System**. The Reference Viewer opens as shown in Figure 11–17.

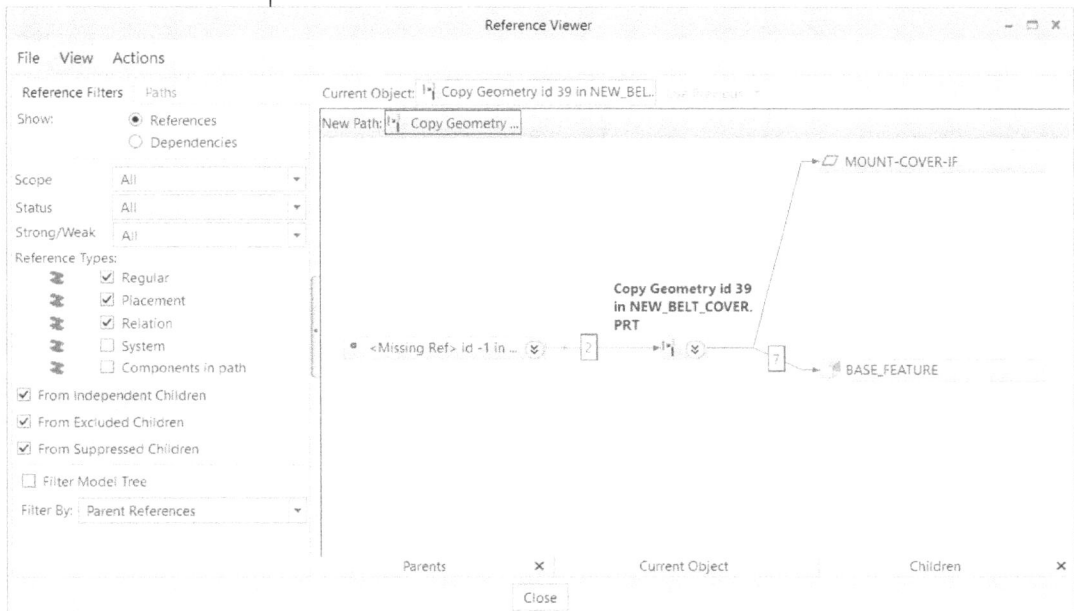

Figure 11–17

Design Considerations

The Copy Geometry feature has a missing parent and therefore will no longer update with any changes to the parent. Additionally, the parent and the Copy Geometry feature are no longer required because this new part will be used in a different assembly.

The Copy Geometry feature has two children: a datum plane named **MOUNT-COVER-IF** and an extrude feature named **BASE_FEATURE**.

3. Expand the **<Missing Ref>** node and note that the Copy Geometry feature references two references (indicated by the number 2), as shown in Figure 11–18.

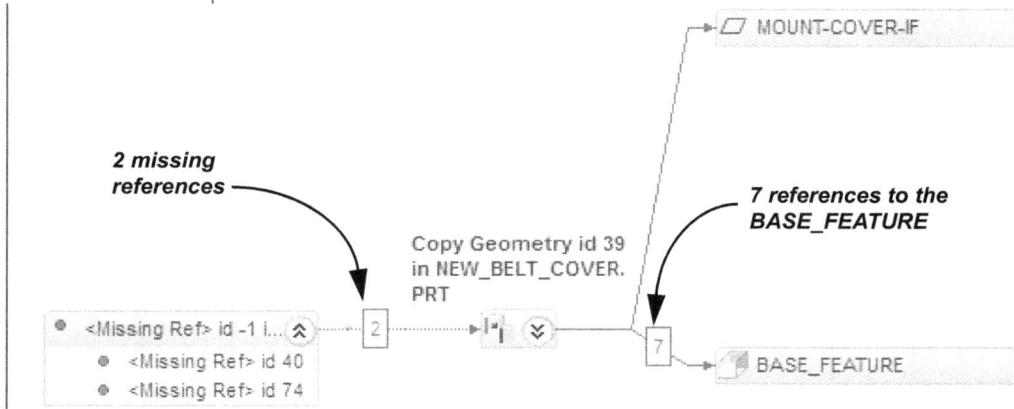

Figure 11–18

4. Close the Reference Viewer.

Task 4 - Investigate a reference using Edit Definition.

---

1. Edit the definition of datum plane **MOUNT_COVER_IF**.

2. View the reference used to create the datum plane and note that it references the Copy Geometry feature, as shown in Figure 11–19.

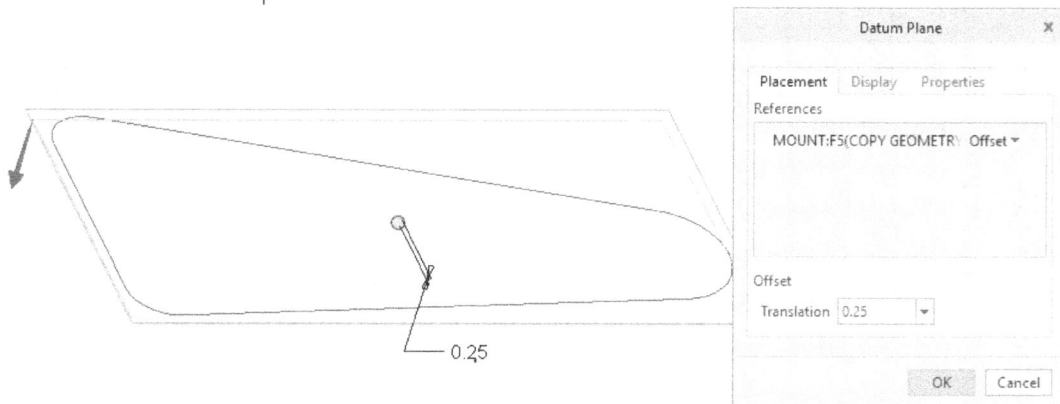

Figure 11–19

3. In the Datum Plane dialog box, click **Cancel**.

Task 5 - Measure the distance of an offset plane and redefine it.

Design Considerations

Datum plane **MOUNT-COVER-IF** is offset from a datum plane in the Copy Geometry feature. In this task, you will measure the offset distance of this plane from datum plane **FRONT**, and then redefine its reference. Datum plane **FRONT** is a default datum plane of the part and therefore a local reference.

1. Select the *Analysis* tab and click 📏 (Measure).

2. In the Measure dialog box, click 🗖 (Distance).

3. Click ⊕ (Expand The Dialog).

4. In the Model Tree, select datum plane **FRONT**, hold <Ctrl>, and select datum plane **MOUNT-COVER-IF**.

5. Click ⊕ (Expand The Results).

6. The *Distance* displays as **3.75** in the *Results* area in the dialog box, as shown in Figure 11–20.

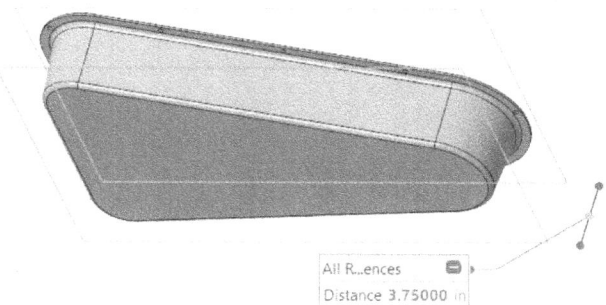

Figure 11–20

7. Close the Distance dialog box.

8. Edit the definition of datum plane **MOUNT-COVER-IF**.

9. Remove the Copy Geometry reference and select datum plane **FRONT** from the Model Tree as the new reference.

10. Select the drag handle and drag the plane "into" the screen.

11. Edit the *Offset* to **3.75**, as shown in Figure 11–21.

This ensures that the ***MOUNT-COVER-IF*** *plane is kept in the same location. You are only changing its reference.*

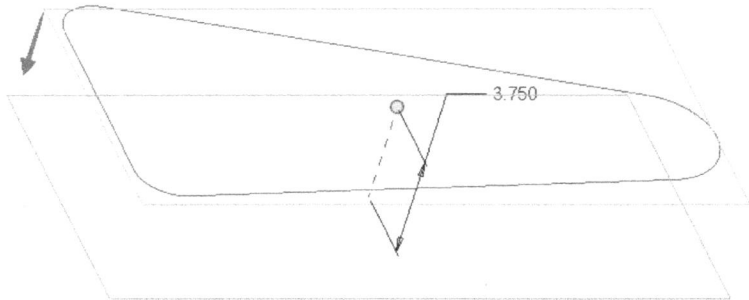

Figure 11–21

12. Ensure that the arrow points toward datum plane **FRONT** and click **OK**.

Task 6 - Review the references of the model.

---

1. View the references of the Copy Geometry feature and note that the **MOUNT_COVER_IF** plane is no longer listed as a child, as shown in Figure 11–22.

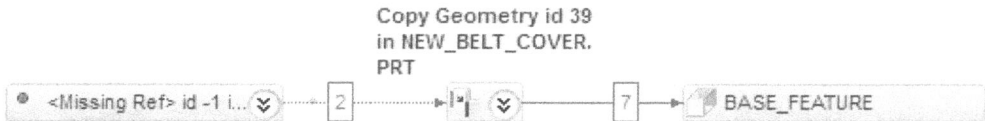

Figure 11–22

2. Close the Reference Viewer dialog box.

Task 7 - Sever the external reference in the base protrusion.

Design Considerations

In this task, you will break the external references of the **BASE_FEATURE**. The original section of the feature was created in the assembly by offsetting the edges of the existing geometry.

1. Edit the definition of **BASE_FEATURE**.

2. Click in the graphics area and select ✎ (Edit Internal Sketch).

3. The section contains an offset edge reference to the datum curve, as shown in Figure 11–23.

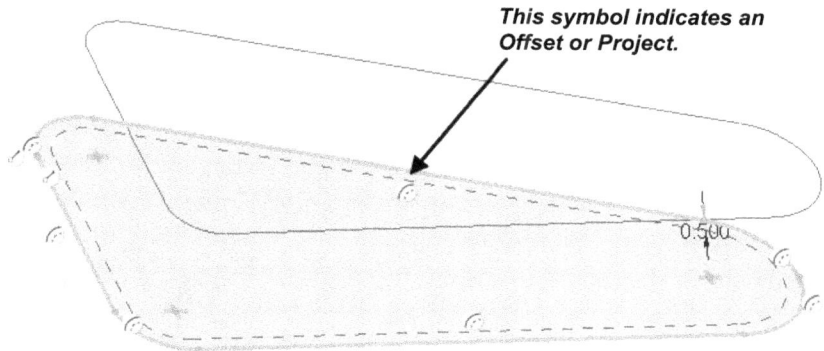

This symbol indicates an Offset or Project.

0.500

Figure 11–23

4. Click ▢ (References) in the *Sketch* tab.

5. Select the first COPY GEOMETRY feature that is listed in the References dialog box. Press and hold <Shift> while selecting the last COPY GEOMETRY feature. All of the COPY GEOMETRY features are selected, as shown in Figure 11–24.

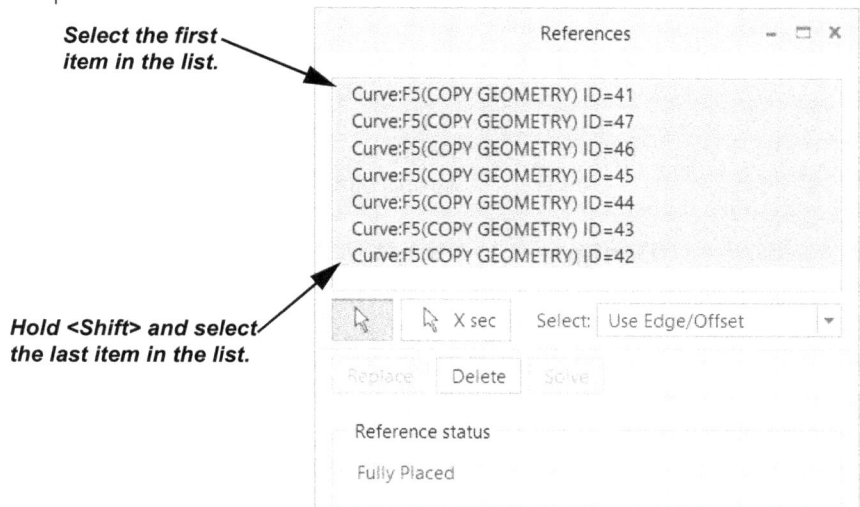

Select the first item in the list.

References ─ ▢ ✕

Curve:F5(COPY GEOMETRY) ID=41
Curve:F5(COPY GEOMETRY) ID=47
Curve:F5(COPY GEOMETRY) ID=46
Curve:F5(COPY GEOMETRY) ID=45
Curve:F5(COPY GEOMETRY) ID=44
Curve:F5(COPY GEOMETRY) ID=43
Curve:F5(COPY GEOMETRY) ID=42

Hold <Shift> and select the last item in the list.

☐   ☐ X sec   Select: Use Edge/Offset   ▾

Replace   Delete   Solve

Reference status

Fully Placed

Figure 11–24

6. Click **Delete**.

7. In the Model Tree, select datum planes **RIGHT** and **TOP** as the two Sketcher references for this section and click **Close**. The system adds dimensions to locate the section to the two datum planes that you selected, as shown in Figure 11–25.

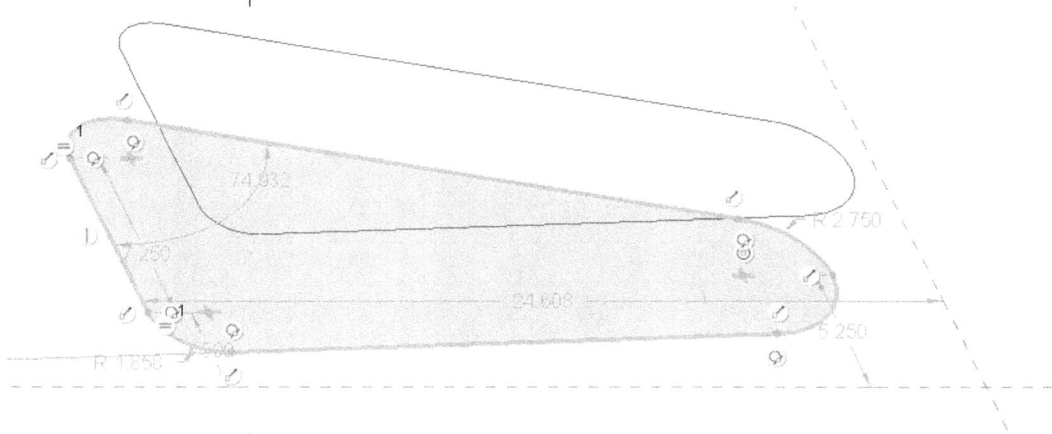

Figure 11–25

8. Drag a box over the complete sketch to select all of the dimensions, as shown in Figure 11–26.

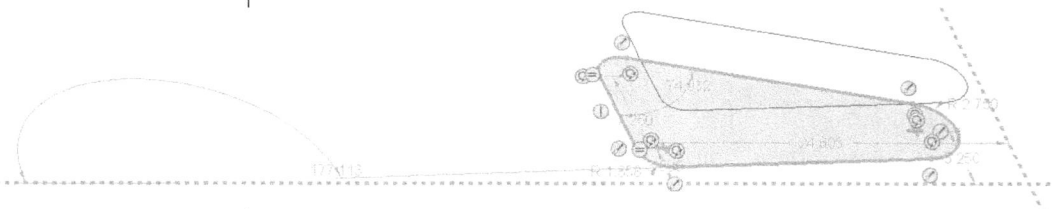

Figure 11–26

9. Press <Ctrl>+<T> to turn all of the selected dimensions into strong dimensions.

Design Considerations

In practice, you should ensure the resulting dimensions match your design intent, but we will leave them as is for this practice.

10. Complete the section and complete the change to the feature.

Task 8 - Review the references of the model again.

1. View the references for the Copy Geometry feature and note that it no longer has any children, as shown in Figure 11–27.

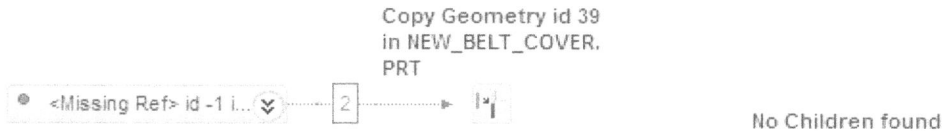

Copy Geometry id 39
in NEW_BELT_COVER.
PRT

<Missing Ref> id -1 i... ⊗ ----------- 2 ----------- ► |▸|

No Children found

Figure 11–27

2. Close the Reference Viewer dialog box.

3. Delete the Copy Geometry feature.

4. Click **OK** to complete the deletion. The external reference has been deleted successfully, as shown in Figure 11–28.

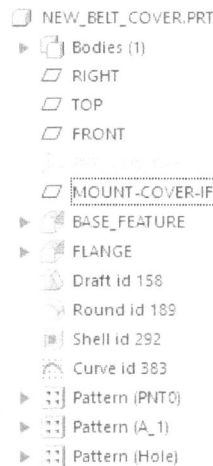

    ▢ NEW_BELT_COVER.PRT
    ▸ ▢ Bodies (1)
      ▱ RIGHT
      ▱ TOP
      ▱ FRONT

      ▱ MOUNT-COVER-IF
    ▸ ▰ BASE_FEATURE
    ▸ ▰ FLANGE
      Draft id 158
      Round id 189
      Shell id 292
      Curve id 383
    ▸ Pattern (PNT0)
    ▸ Pattern (A_1)
    ▸ Pattern (Hole)

Figure 11–28

Design Considerations

The part no longer has any external references. Any changes can now be made to the part as required.

5. Save the part and close the window.

Chapter Review Questions

1. The Model Tree can be used to determine when there is an external reference. The Model Tree in Figure 11–29 indicates that there are no external references.

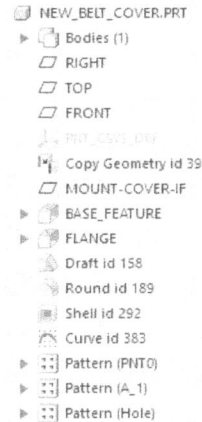

```
⌷ NEW_BELT_COVER.PRT
  ▶ ⌷ Bodies (1)
    ⌷ RIGHT
    ⌷ TOP
    ⌷ FRONT
    ⌿ PNT_CSYS_DEF
    ⌶ Copy Geometry id 39
    ⌷ MOUNT-COVER-IF
  ▶ ⌗ BASE_FEATURE
  ▶ ⌗ FLANGE
    ⌸ Draft id 158
    ⌇ Round id 189
    ⌸ Shell id 292
    ⌇ Curve id 383
  ▶ ⠿ Pattern (PNT0)
  ▶ ⠿ Pattern (A_1)
  ▶ ⠿ Pattern (Hole)
```

Figure 11–29

   a. True

   b. False

2. Which of the following cannot be done using the Reference Viewer dialog box?

   a. Investigate references and dependencies.

   b. Display the full reference path between components.

   c. Identify external references.

   d. Edit the definition of a component.

   e. Find all of the objects with external references.

3. Which of the following methods can be used to investigate external references? (Select all that apply.)

   a. Model Tree

   b. Model Information

   c. Reference Viewer

   d. Message window

4. Which of the following can be investigated and then broken or restructured? (Select all that apply.)

    a. Dependencies of reference models to independent Data Sharing features.

    b. Dependencies of mirrored models to their source models.

    c. Dependencies of replaced components.

    d. Dependencies of old assembly cuts.

    e. Dependencies to layouts.

Answers: 1.b, 2.d, 3.abcd, 4.abcde

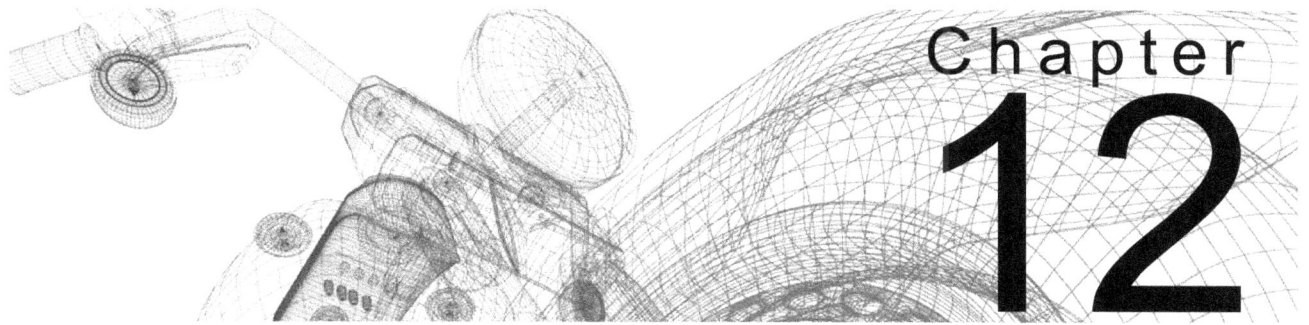

Intelligent Fasteners Lite

You can use the Intelligent Fastener functionality to automatically add screws, bolts, nuts, etc. to Creo Parametric assemblies. This chapter focuses on the standard (or Lite) version that is available with any Creo Parametric license.

Learning Objectives in This Chapter

- Understand how intelligent fasteners can speed up your development time by automatically assembling screws, nuts, bolts, and so on, to your assemblies using standard hardware.
- Understand the limitations of the standard Intelligent Fastener license.
- Assemble fasteners using datum points, axes, holes, or references.
- Update assembled fasteners.
- Pattern fasteners using reference patterns.

12.1 Intelligent Fastener Extension

The Creo Intelligent Fastener Extension (IFX) enables you to add screws, nuts, washers, etc. directly from a standard library. The two available IFX versions are *Standard* and *Advanced*. This course covers the standard license that is available with every seat of Creo Parametric.

The standard or Lite version of IFX enables you to assemble a screw on any point, axis or existing hole, or by selecting locating references similar to creating a hole feature. You can use the tool to automatically add nuts and washers. If the placement reference is part of a pattern, you can reference pattern the fastener.

For reference, the Advanced IFX license enables you to assemble dowel pins and screws and to customize fastener components.

To access the **Intelligent Fastener** functionality, select the *Tools* tab and use the options shown in Figure 12–1.

Only those options available with the Lite license will be covered in this guide.

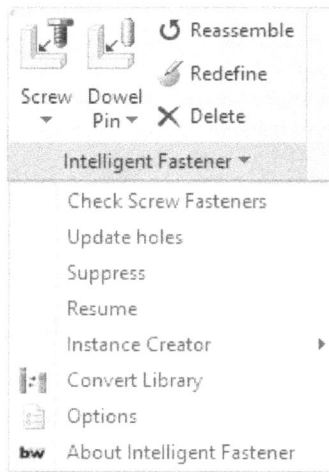

Figure 12–1

To assemble a standard fastener, expand ⬚ (Screw) in the *Tools* tab, and select either ⬚ (Assemble on reference) or ⬚ (Assemble by mouse click).

12.2 Assemble on Reference

Consider the simple assembly consisting of a container and plate cover, shown in Figure 12–2.

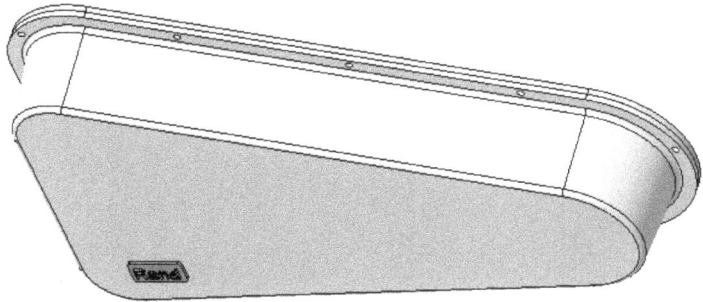

Figure 12–2

To assemble a standard fastener by selecting an existing reference, expand (Screw) in the *Tools* tab and select (Assemble on reference), as shown in Figure 12–3.

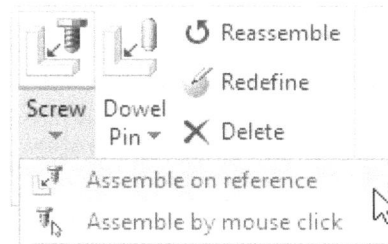

Figure 12–3

The Select References dialog box opens as shown in Figure 12–4.

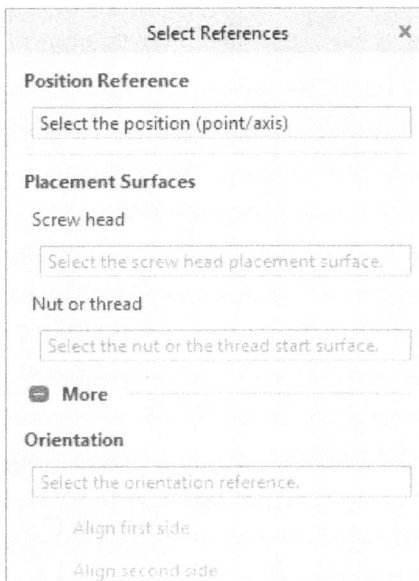

Figure 12–4

You can select a point or axis, or the surface of an existing hole, which will define the location for the fastener. Select in the *Screw head* fastener collector to define the start location for the fastener, as shown in Figure 12–5.

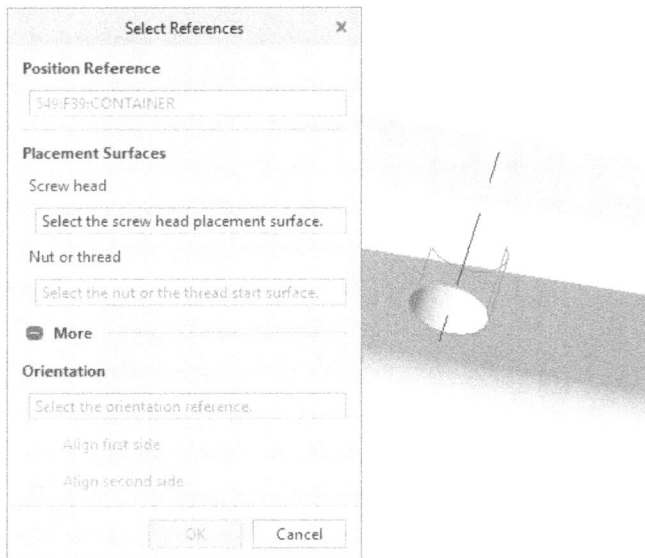

Figure 12–5

The type of fastener used will depend on the reference selected in the *Nut or thread* collector:

- Select two aligning surfaces to define a screw connection with thread.

- Select two opposing surfaces to define a screw and nut connection.

Two Aligning Surfaces

If two aligning surfaces are selected, the system automatically selects a threaded fastener, and opens the Screw Fastener Definition dialog box, as shown in Figure 12–6.

The mating surface of the adjacent component is selected as the Nut/Thread surface.

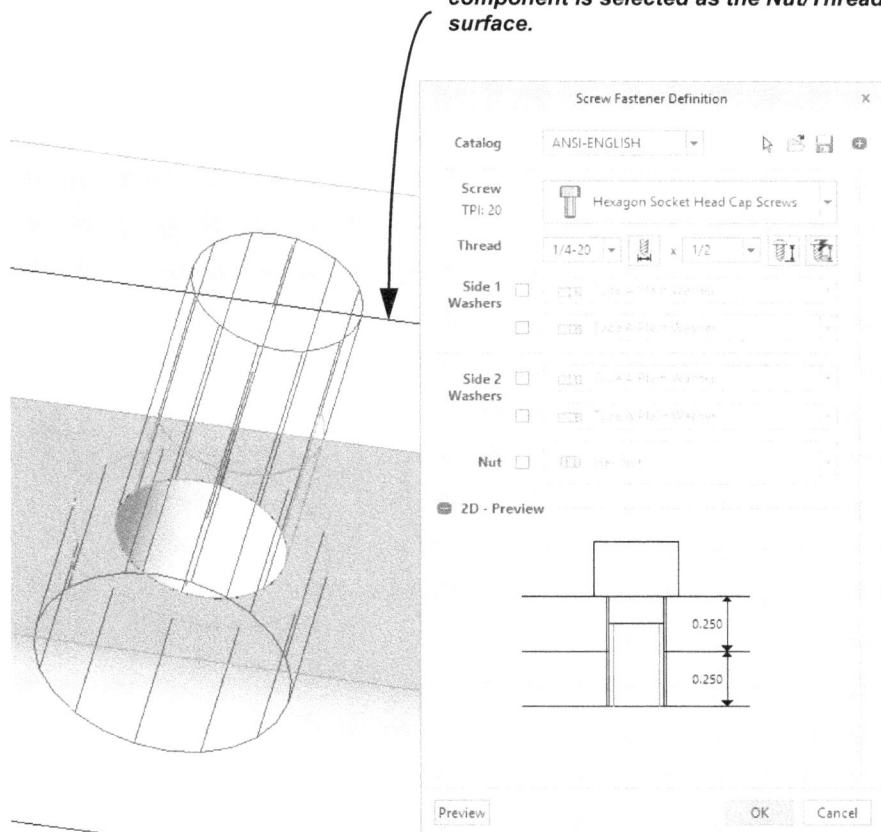

Figure 12–6

The Screw Fastener Definition dialog box enables you to define the specific characteristics of the fastener. Select the *Catalog* from which you will choose your fastener, as shown in Figure 12–7.

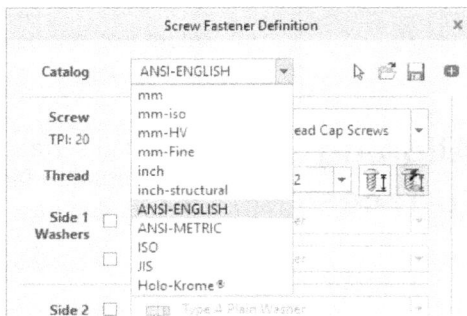

Figure 12–7

Select the *Screw* type and the *Thread* size and length, as shown in Figure 12–8.

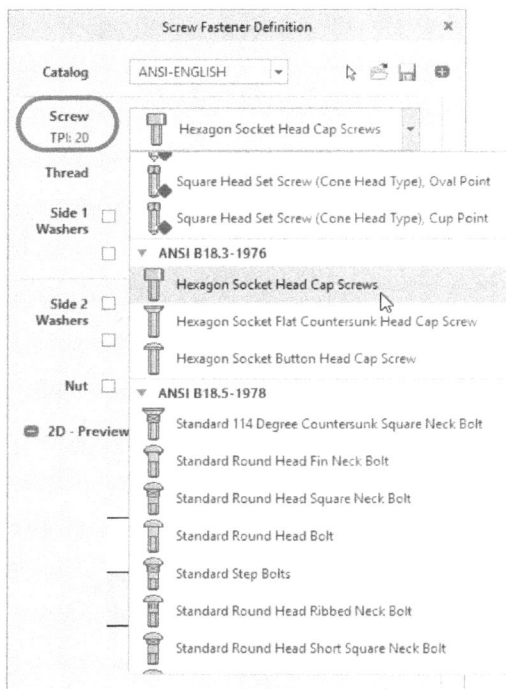

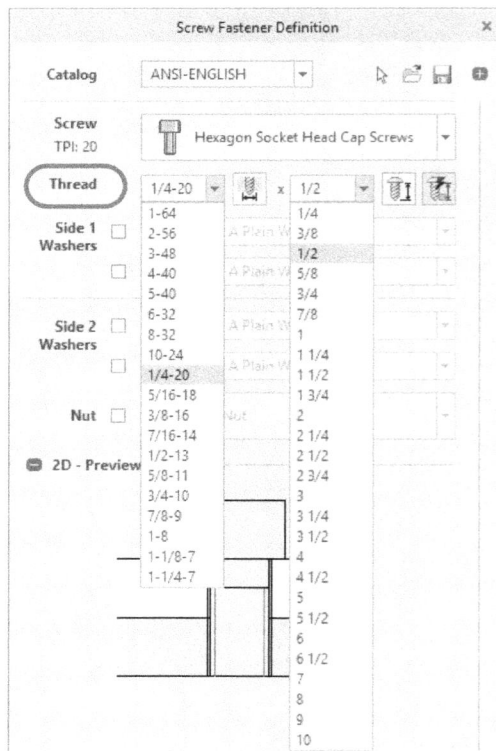

Figure 12–8

In the case where you are assembling a fastener to an existing hole, you can determine the correct fastener size by clicking ▨ (Measure Diameter), and selecting the surface of the hole.

In Figure 12–9, the selected *Thread* of **1-64** is smaller than the hole it is being inserted into, as indicated by the preview.

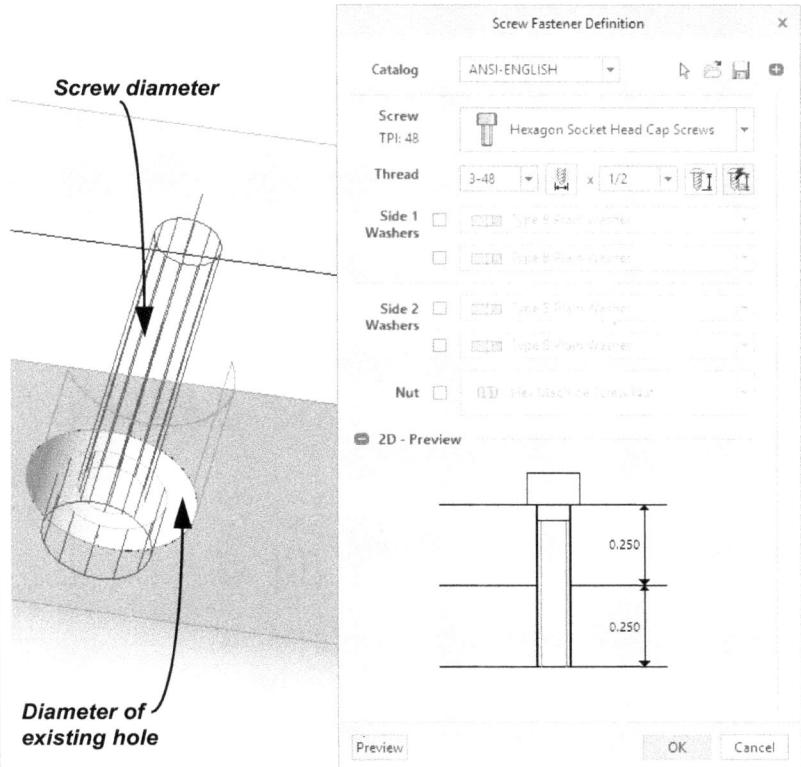

Figure 12–9

By selecting 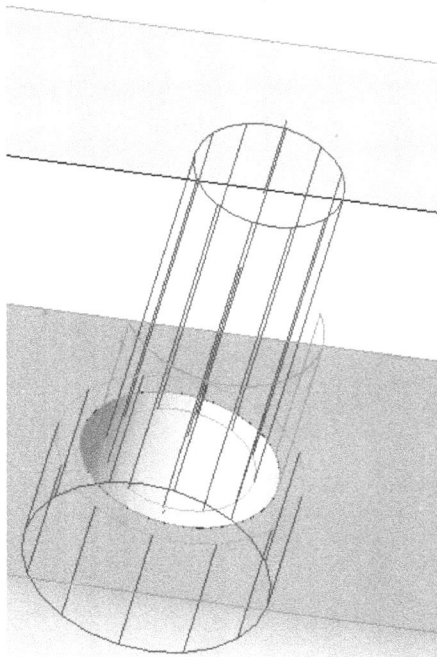 (Measure Diameter) and selecting the inside surface of the hole, Creo Parametric automatically changes the *Thread* to **10-24** to match, as shown in Figure 12–10.

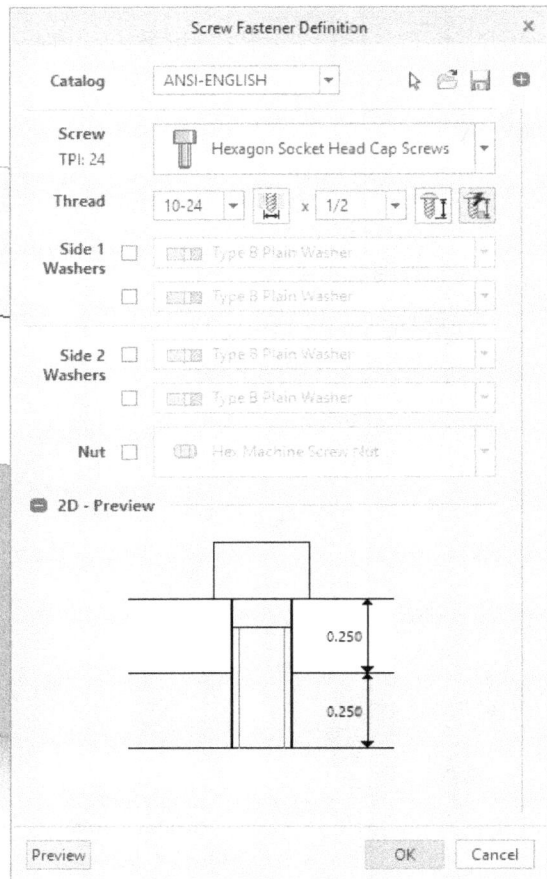

Figure 12–10

If you select a fastener depth that is too long, the

🔧 (Permanently Set Length) icon changes to 🔧. To automatically set the length to fit the depth of the geometry, click either 🔧 (Set length automatically) or 🔧 (Permanently Set Length).

In addition to the *Thread* and *Depth* options, you can also click

⊕ (Show/Hide Hole Layout) to expand the Screw Fastener Dialog box and control the resulting holes created in parts intersected by the fastener, as shown in Figure 12–11.

Note that if you assemble a fastener to an existing hole, countersinks and counterbores will not be cut into the surface of the part.

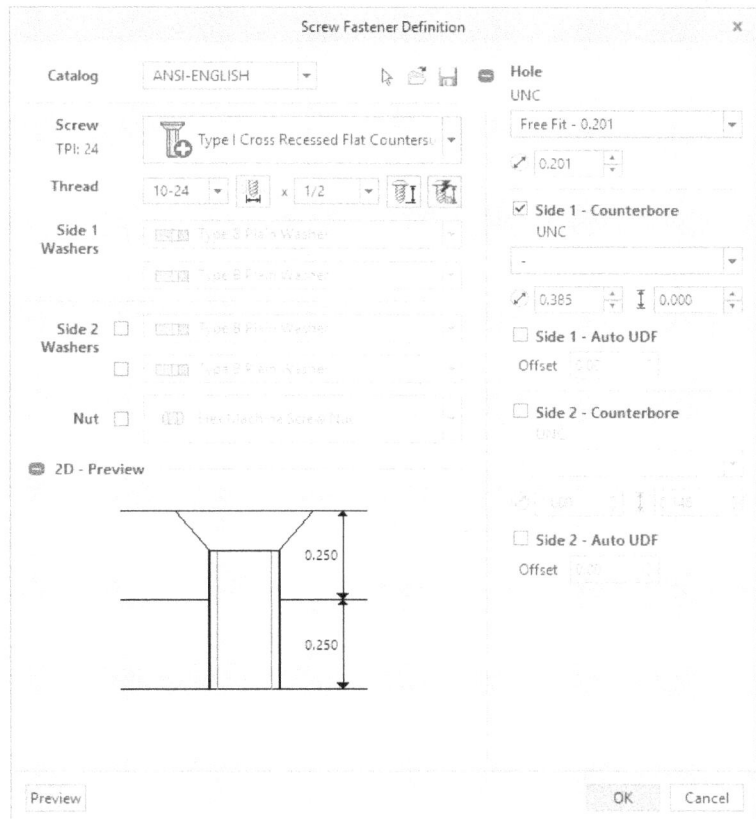

Figure 12–11

Two Opposing Surfaces

If two opposing surfaces are selected as references, the system automatically selects a screw and nut connection, and opens the Screw Fastener Definition dialog box, as shown in Figure 12–12. In this example, the fastener is assembled to an axis, rather than an existing hole.

The outside of the adjacent component is selected as the Nut/Thread surface.

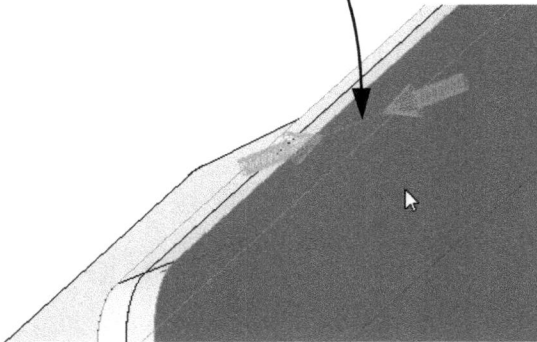

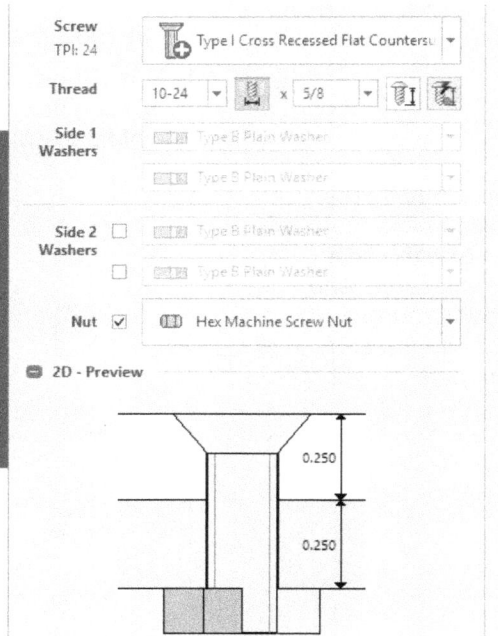

Figure 12–12

As shown in Figure 12–12, Creo Parametric adds a nut to the end of the bolt. In addition, a counterbore is defined based on the standard fastener. You can change the values if required.

Depending on your use case, you can also add a counterbore to the nut side of fastener assembly, as shown in Figure 12–13.

The Side 2 - Counterbore creates space to recess the nut.

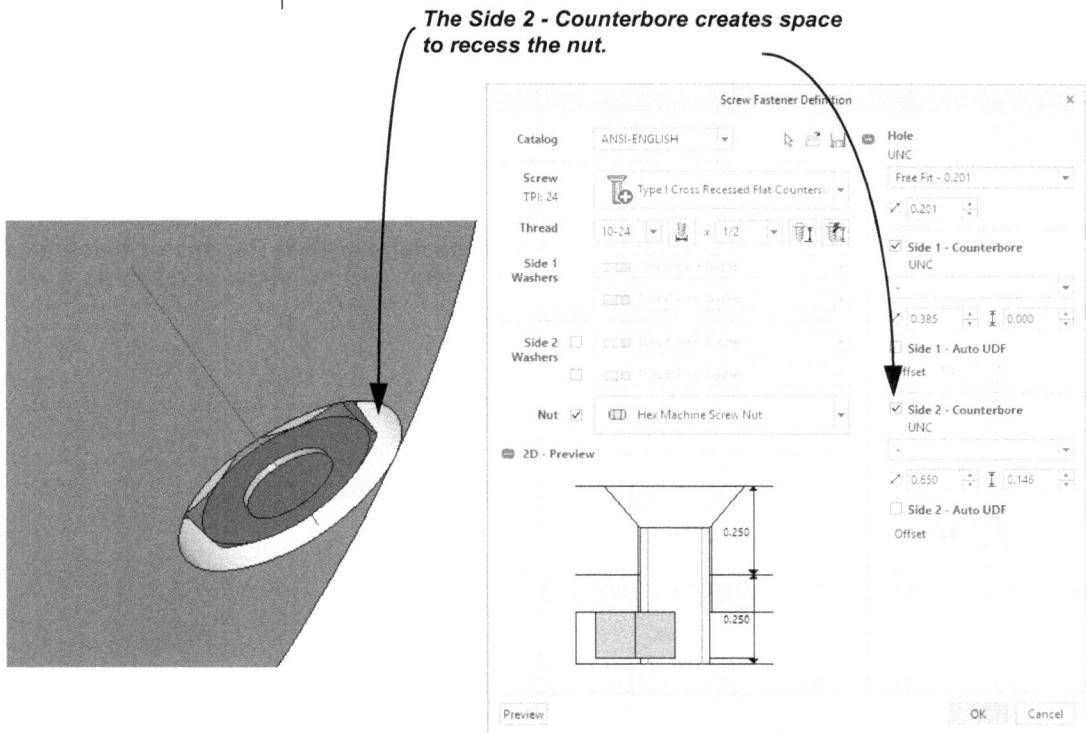

Figure 12–13

If the fastener is assembled to a patterned reference you will be presented with the Pattern Options dialog box, as shown in Figure 12–14.

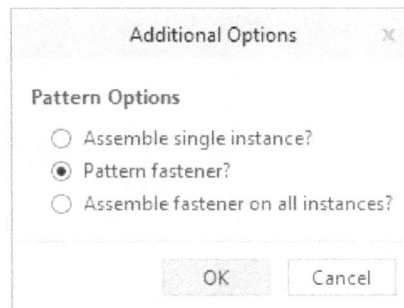

Figure 12–14

The options available are described as follows:

- **Assemble single instance?** - Ignore the reference pattern and assemble a single instance.

- **Pattern fastener?** - Use the existing pattern as a reference pattern.

- **Assemble fastener on all instances?** - Assemble individual instances of the fastener on each of the patterned instances.

Once the fastener is assembled, Creo Parametric automatically adds a standard annotation describing the required hole, as shown in Figure 12–15.

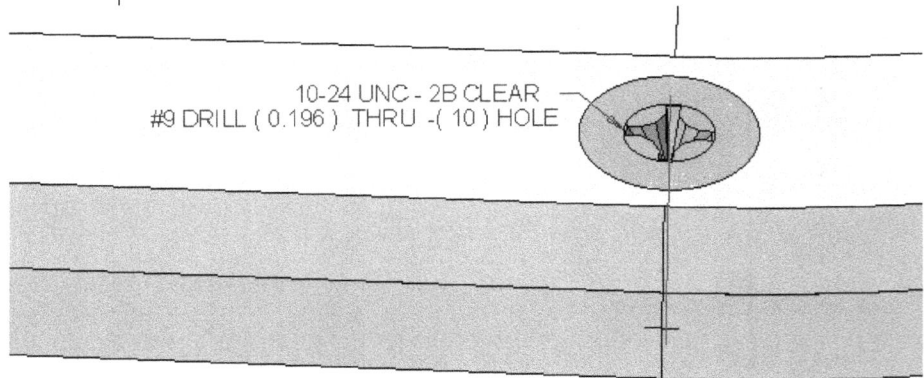

10-24 UNC - 2B CLEAR
#9 DRILL (0.196) THRU -(10) HOLE

Figure 12–15

If you open the components, the holes and counterbores you defined in the assembly will be present in the parts as well, as shown in Figure 12–16.

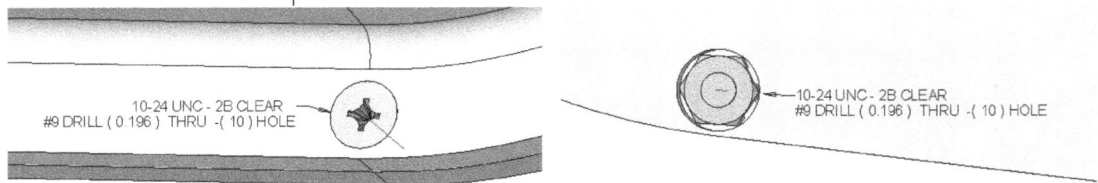

10-24 UNC - 2B CLEAR
#9 DRILL (0.196) THRU -(10) HOLE

10-24 UNC - 2B CLEAR
#9 DRILL (0.196) THRU -(10) HOLE

Figure 12–16

12.3 Assemble by Mouse Click

You can assemble fittings by reference as well. Expand
(Screw) in the *Tools* tab and select (Assemble by mouse click), as shown in Figure 12–17.

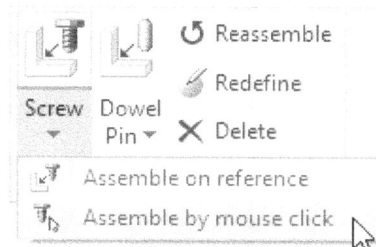

Figure 12–17

The Select References dialog box opens as shown in Figure 12–18.

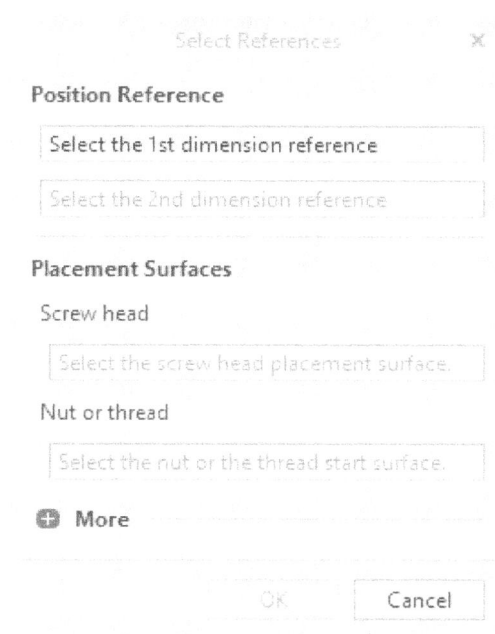

Figure 12–18

Select two perpendicular references to locate the fastener, then select the *Screw Head* and *Nut/Thread* reference surfaces. After defining options in the Screw Fastener Definition dialog box, the Mouse Click Location dialog box displays as shown in Figure 12–19.

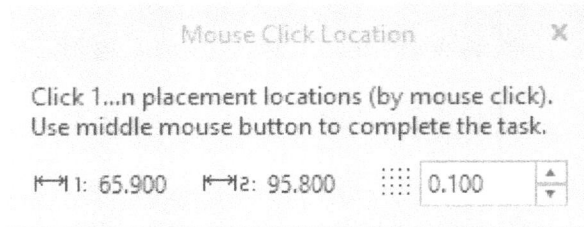

Mouse Click Location   ✕

Click 1...n placement locations (by mouse click).
Use middle mouse button to complete the task.

⊢—⊣ 1: 65.900   ⊢—⊣ 2: 95.800   ⠿ 0.100   ▲▼

Figure 12–19

You select a location on the placement surface, and Creo Parametric creates an Assembly axis on which the fastener is located. As you move your mouse across the placement surface, the dialog box displays the coordinates of the hole relative to the references you defined. The snapping interval can be changed in the dialog box on the right. You can select as many locations as required, and press the middle mouse button to complete the placement.

12.4 Inserting Heli-Coils in IFX

Heli-coil inserts provide protection and strengthening for tapped threads. The addition of a heli-coil helps to ensure bolt failure rather than damage to the material it is screwed into.

You can add a heli-coil insert on a screw fastener in the Screw Fastener Definition dialog box. Select **Insert** and select the HELICOIL type from the drop-down list, as shown in Figure 12–20.

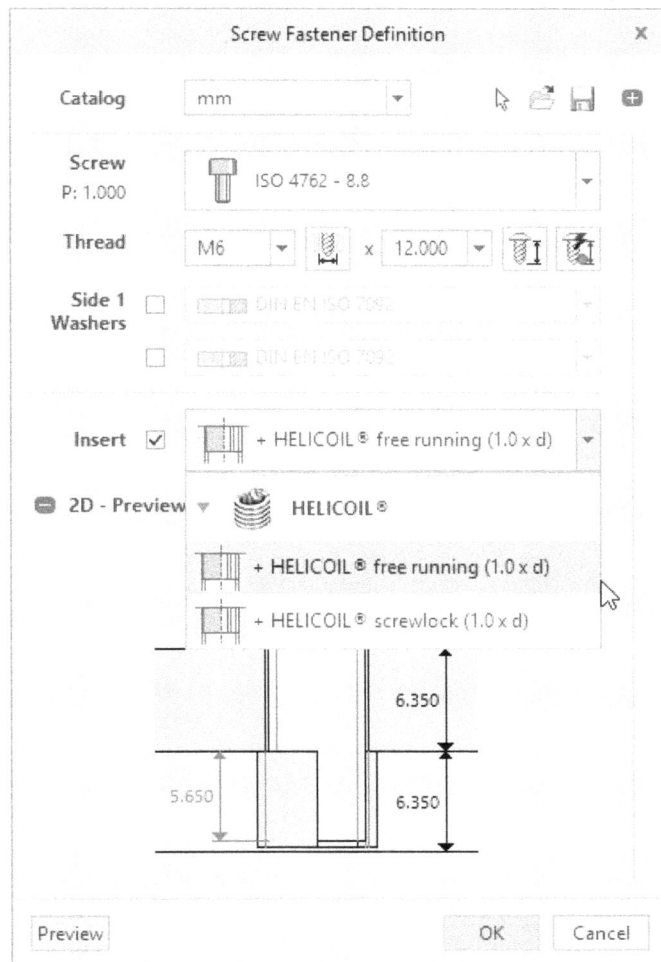

Figure 12–20

You can select the length from the dialog box shown in Figure 12–21. You can also right-click on the HELICOIL drop-down list and select the size as shown in Figure 12–22.

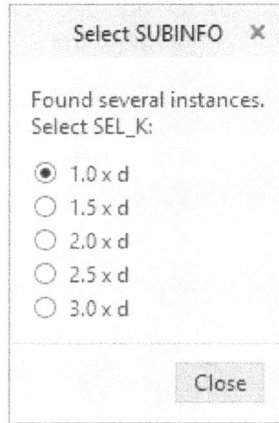

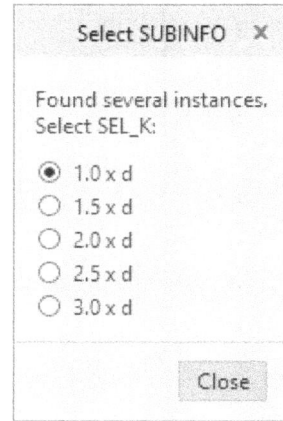

Figure 12–21   **Figure 12–22**

Figure 12–23 shows an example of HELICOIL, where the surrounding geometry has been hidden so the heli-coil is visible.

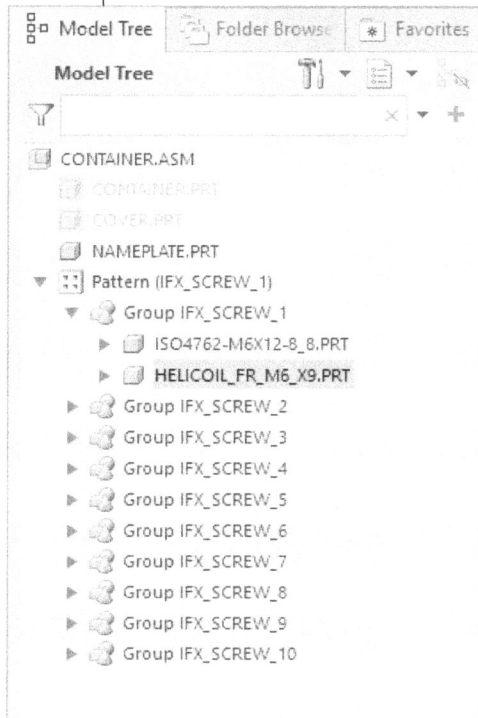

Figure 12–23

Practice 12a

Assembling Intelligent Fasteners

Practice Objectives

- Assemble a fastener to an assembly.
- Use the diameter of a hole to select a fastener.
- Change a fastener.
- Assemble a fastener using an axis.

In this practice, you will use various methods to assemble fasteners to an assembly.

Task 1 - Open an assembly file.

1. Change the working directory to the *Intelligent_Fasteners* folder.

2. Open **container.asm**.

3. Set the model display as follows:

    - ⅍ *(Datum Display Filters)*: ⁄ₒ (Axis Display) Only

    - ⌁ *(Spin Center)*: Off

    - ⎀ *(Display Style)*: ⬜ (Shading With Edges)

Task 2 - Add a screw to the assembly.

Design Considerations

In this task, you will add a screw to the assembly by selecting the surface of the hole in Figure 12–24 as a reference.

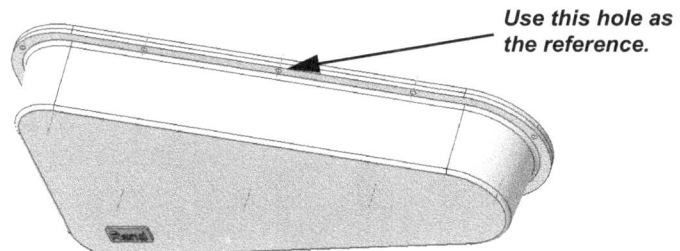

Use this hole as the reference.

Figure 12–24

1. In the *Tools* tab in the ribbon, expand ⌁ (Screw) and select ⌁ (Assemble on reference).

2. The Select Reference dialog box opens as shown in
   Figure 12–25. Select the highlighted surface as the *Position
   Reference*.

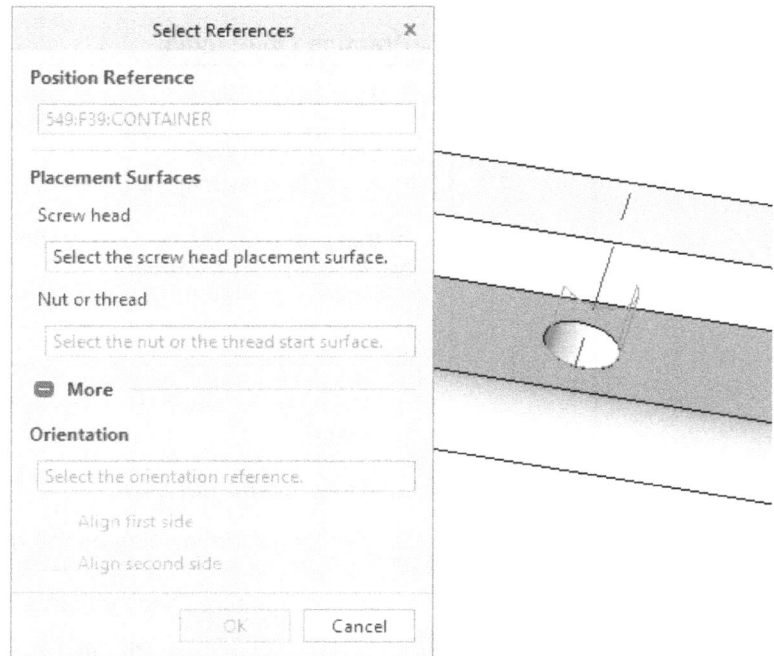

Figure 12–25

3. Ensure that the *Screw Head* collector is active and select the
   highlighted surface of the container component, as shown in
   Figure 12–26.

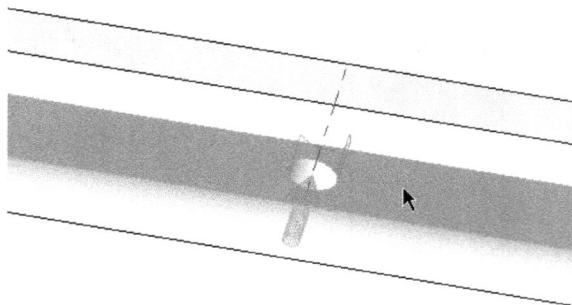

Figure 12–26

4. In the Model Tree, select **CONTAINER.PRT** and click
   ✎ (Hide).

Hiding the container part simply makes the selection of the cover surface easier.

5. Ensure that the *Nut or thread* reference collector is selected and then select the surface of **cover.prt**, shown in Figure 12–27.

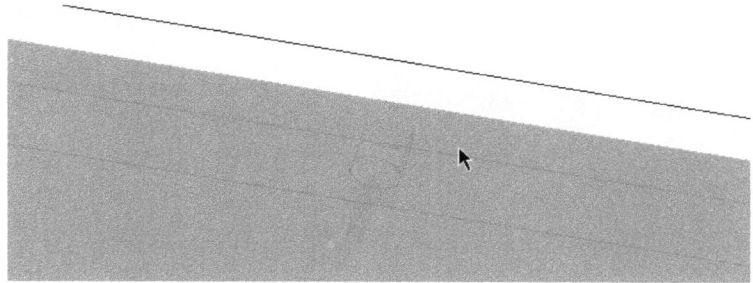

Figure 12–27

6. In the Model Tree, select **CONTAINER.PRT** and click ⊙ (Show).

7. Click **OK** in the Select References dialog box. The Screw Fastener dialog box opens as shown in Figure 12–28. Note that the dialog box might look slightly different depending on the last time it was used.

Note that the screw is too long, as indicated by the on-screen preview

and 🗝 (Permanently Set Length) icon.

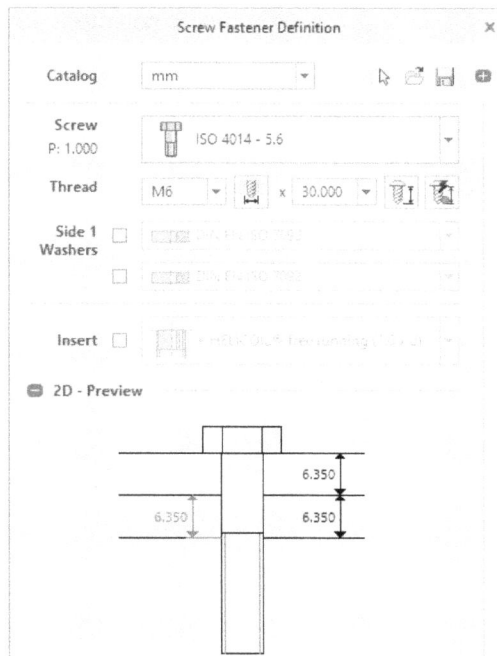

Figure 12–28

8. If required, select **mm** in the Catalog drop-down list.

9. In the Screw list, select **ISO 4014 - 5.6**.

10. If the screw geometry does not preview in the model, as shown in Figure 12–29, click **Preview** in the Screw Fastener Dialog box.

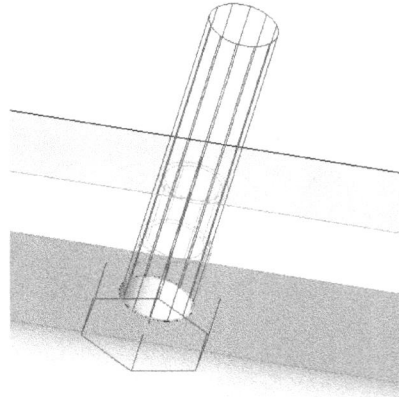

Figure 12–29

11. Click 📷I (Set length automatically) to automatically select a component that better fits the required length. The **M1.6x12** bolt is selected, as shown in Figure 12–30.

The bolt is still too long, and the diameter is not large enough to fit the hole. You will have to select a different Catalog to find a bolt that fits.

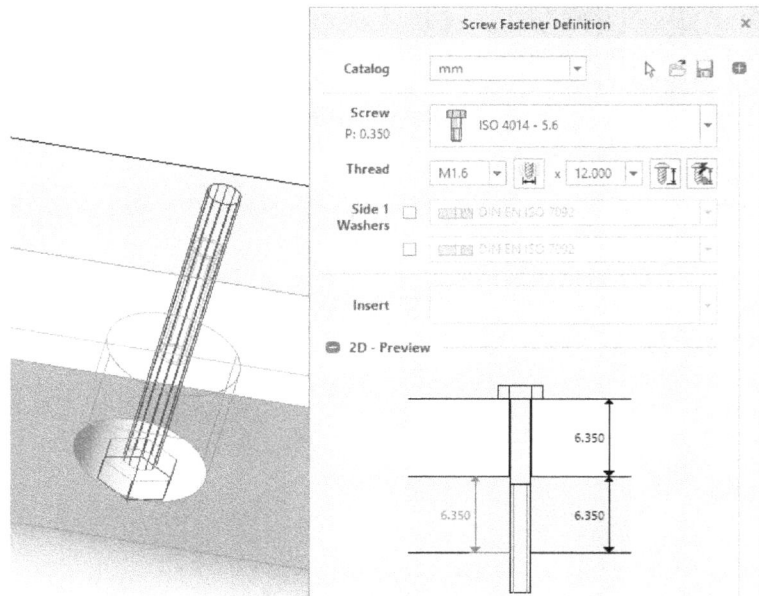

Figure 12–30

12. Do not close the dialog box.

Task 3 - Change the Catalog and select an appropriate fastener. Pattern the fastener on all holes.

1. In the Catalog drop-down list, select **ANSI-ENGLISH**.

2. In the Screw drop-down list, select **Hexagon Socket Head Cap Screws**, as shown in Figure 12–31.

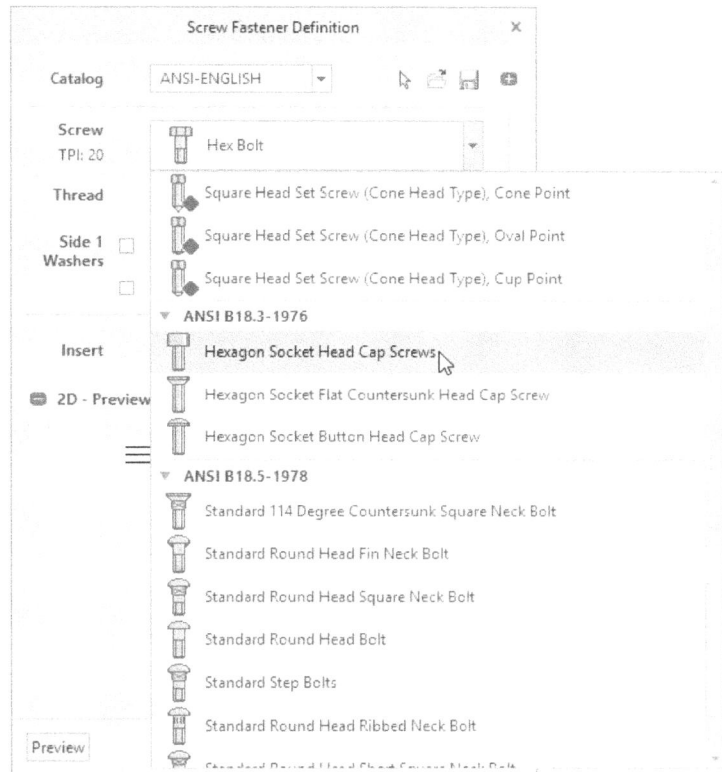

Figure 12–31

3. Click ▨ (Measure Diameter).

4. Select the diameter of the hole, as shown in Figure 12–32.

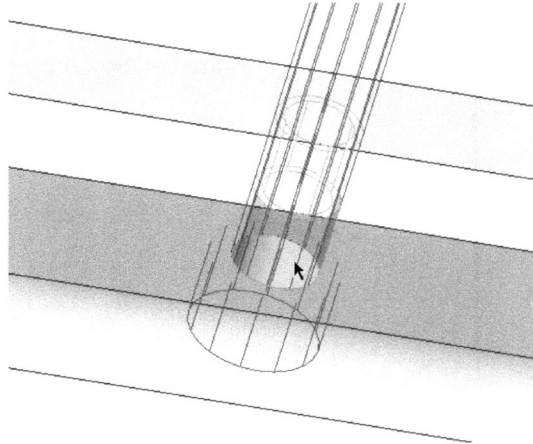

Figure 12–32

5. The *Thread* updates to **10-24** to match the hole.

6. Click 📷I (Set length automatically) and the length updates to **1/2**, as shown in Figure 12–33.

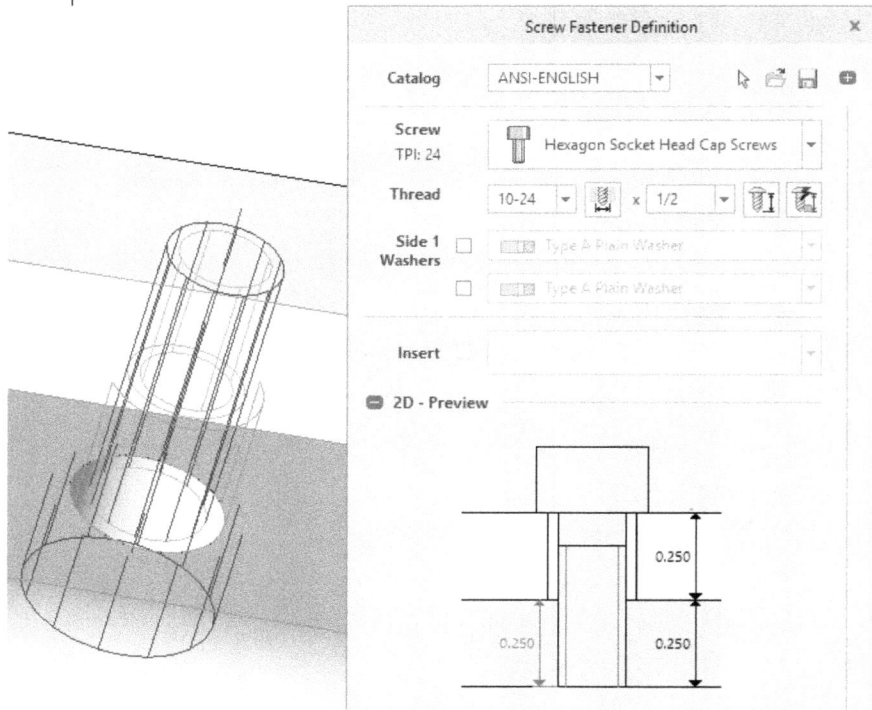

Figure 12–33

7. Click **OK** in the Screw Fastener Definition dialog box.

8. Ensure that **Pattern fastener?** is selected in the Pattern Options dialog box and click **OK**, as shown in Figure 12–34.

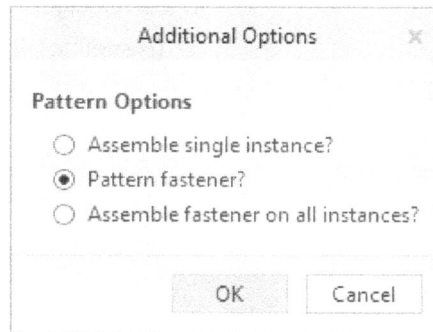

Figure 12–34

9. The fasteners are patterned as a reference pattern, as shown in Figure 12–35.

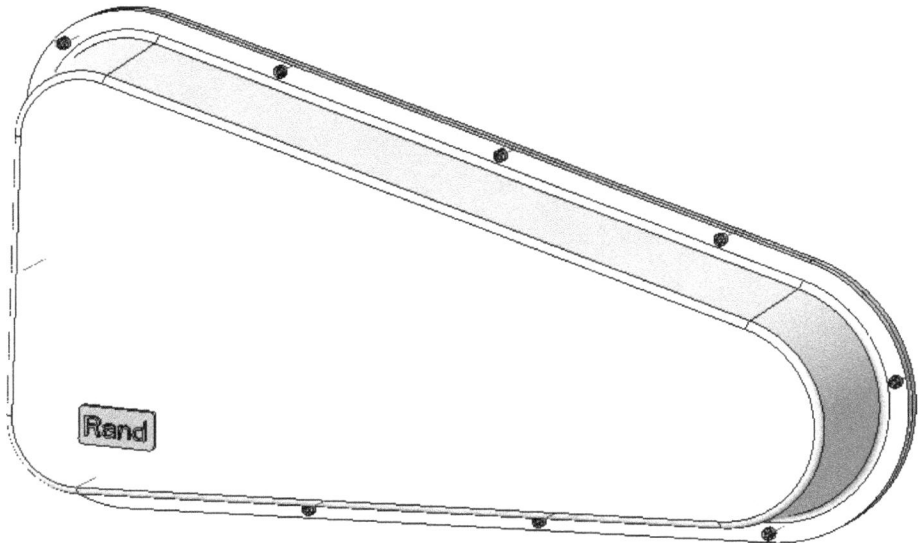

Figure 12–35

Task 4 - Change the fastener and update all instances.

1. Select one of the fasteners.

2. In the Intelligent Fastener group in the *Tools* tab, click
   (Redefine). The Screw Fastener Definition dialog box
   opens, as shown in Figure 12–36.

Note that if you select
(Edit Definition) in
the mini toolbar, you
would edit the
placement of the
fastener using standard
assembly functionality,
which is not what you
want in this case.

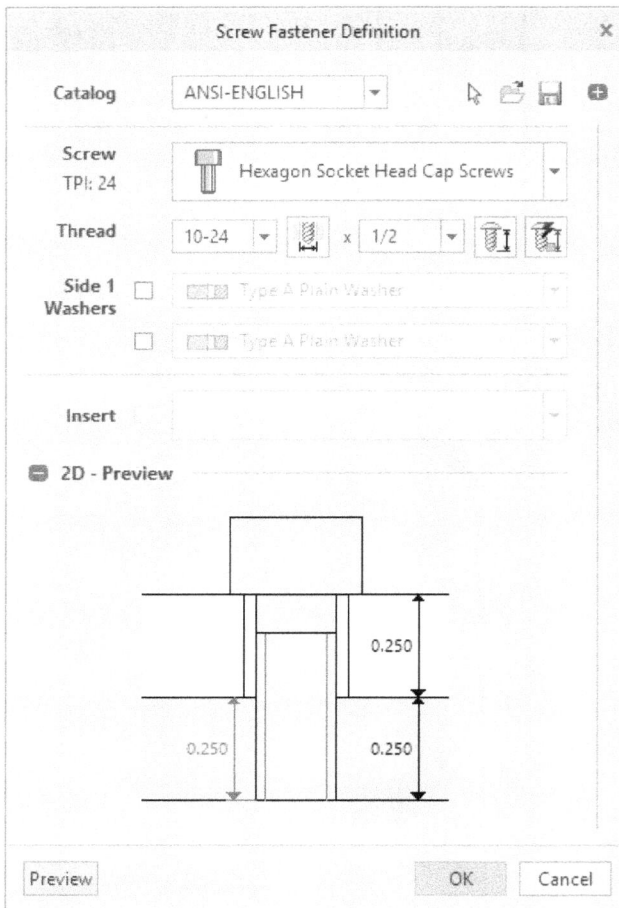

Figure 12–36

3. In the Catalog drop-down list, select **mm**.

4. In the Screw drop-down list, select **ISO 4017 - 10.9**.

5. Set the thread to **M5**. The Screw Fastener dialog box updates, as shown in Figure 12–37.

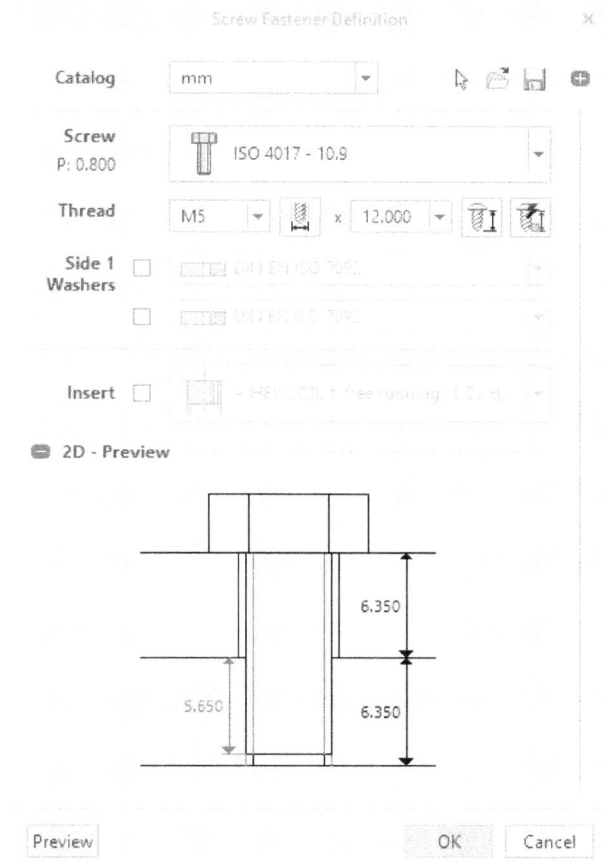

Figure 12–37

Task 5 - Add a Heli-coil.

1. Enable **Insert**, as shown in Figure 12–38, and note the preview of the Heli-coil in the dialog box and graphics area.

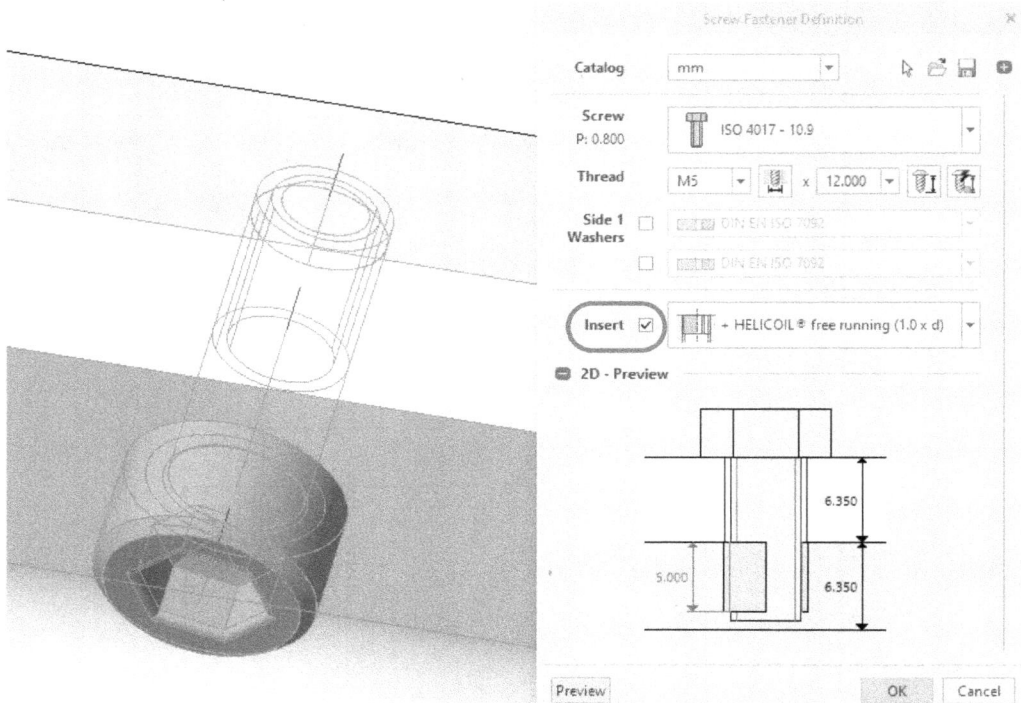

Figure 12–38

2. In the Insert drop-down list, select **HELICOIL screwlock**.

3. In the Select SUBINFO dialog box (shown in Figure 12–39), click **Close**.

This sets the length equal to the hole diameter.

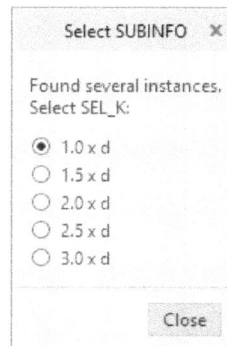

Figure 12–39

4. Click **OK** in the Screw Fastener Definition dialog box.

5. If a warning regarding threaded holes displays, dismiss it by clicking **Yes**.

6. In the Additional Options dialog box, ensure that **Pattern fastener?** is selected and click **OK**.

7. In the Model Tree, select **CONTAINER.PRT** and **COVER.PRT** and click ✎ (Hide) in the mini toolbar.

8. The screw and heli-coil display as shown in Figure 12–40.

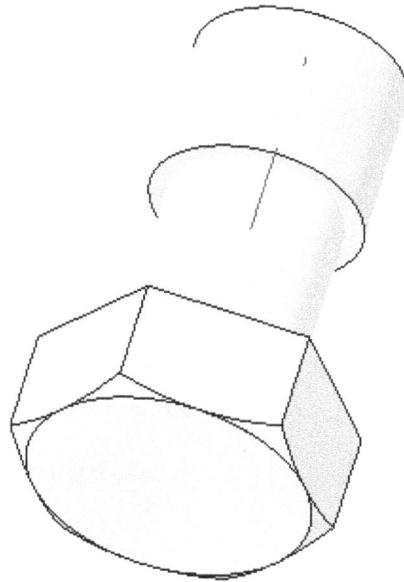

Figure 12–40

9. In the Model Tree, select **CONTAINER.PRT** and **COVER.PRT**, and then click ☺ (Show) in the mini toolbar.

10. Click on **CONTAINER.PRT** in the Model Tree and select 📂 (Open) in the mini toolbar.

11. Zoom in on one of the holes and note that no countersink has been added to the part, as shown in Figure 12–41.

Because the fastener was added to an existing hole, no countersink was added.

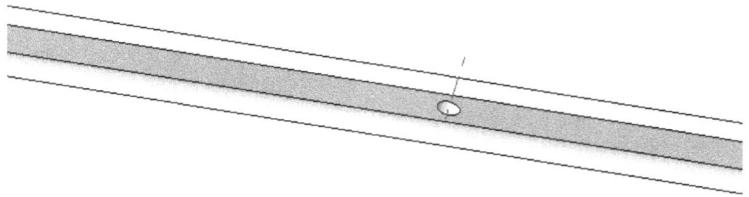

Figure 12–41

12. Close the CONTAINER part window.

13. Save the assembly and erase all files from memory.

Task 6 - Open another assembly and assemble a fastener to a pattern of axes.

---

1. Open **container_2.asm**.

2. Set the model display as follows:

   - (Datum Display Filters): (Axis Display) Only

   - (Spin Center): Off

   - (Display Style): (Shading With Edges)

3. In the *Tools* tab in the ribbon, expand (Screw) and select (Assemble on Reference).

4. The Select Reference dialog box opens, as shown in Figure 12–42. Select the highlighted axis as the *Position Reference*.

Use this axis as the reference

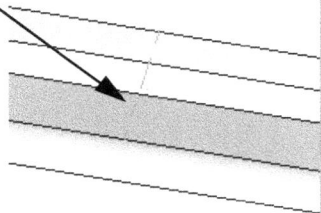

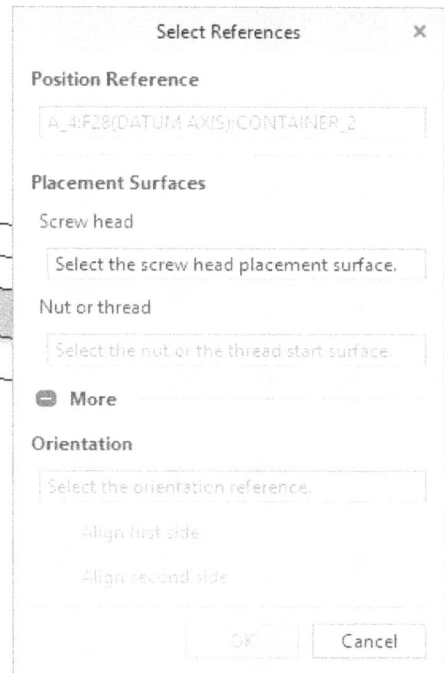

Select References	×

Position Reference

A_4:F28(DATUM AXIS):CONTAINER_2

Placement Surfaces

Screw head

Select the screw head placement surface.

Nut or thread

Select the nut or the thread start surface.

⊖ More

Orientation

Select the orientation reference.

Align first side

Align second side

OK   Cancel

Figure 12–42

5. Ensure that the *Screw Head* collector is active and select the highlighted surface of the **container_2** component, as shown in Figure 12–43.

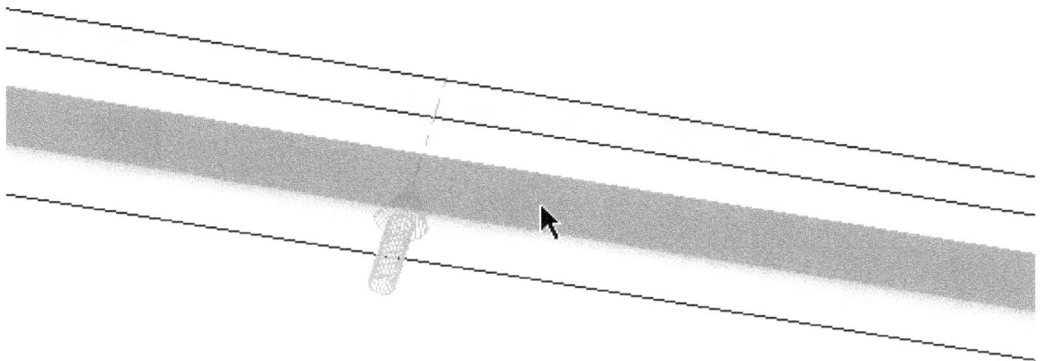

Figure 12–43

6. Ensure that the *Nut/Thread* reference, is selected. Spin the model and select the back surface of **cover_2.prt**, as shown in Figure 12–44.

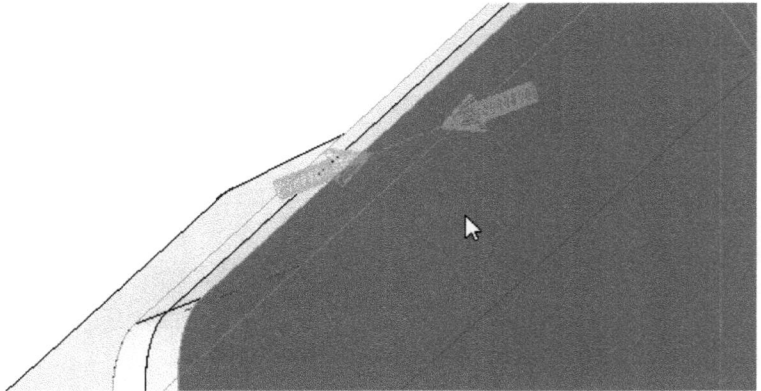

Figure 12–44

7. Press <Ctrl>+<D> to return to default orientation.

8. Click **OK** in the Select References dialog box. The Screw Fastener dialog box opens, as shown in Figure 12–45.

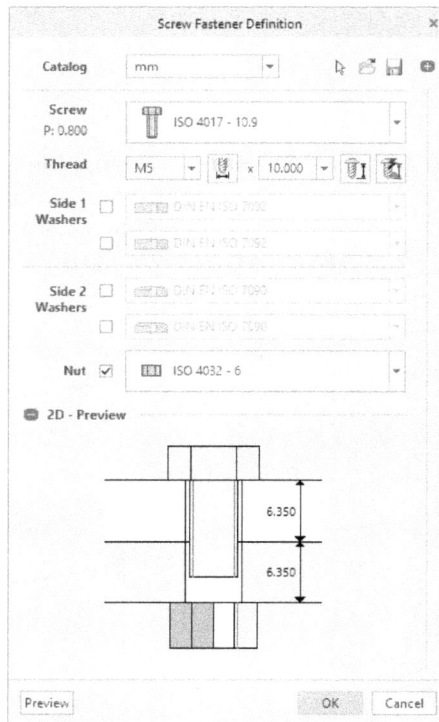

Figure 12–45

9. In the Catalog drop-down list, select **ANSI-ENGLISH**.

10. In the Screw drop-down list, select **Type I Cross Recessed 100 Degree Flat Countersunk Head Machine Screw**.

11. Set the *Thread* to **10-24**.

12. Click ⬆ (Automatically Set Length) and Creo Parametric updates the *Thread* length to 5/8, as shown in Figure 12–46.

The screw length is incorrect.

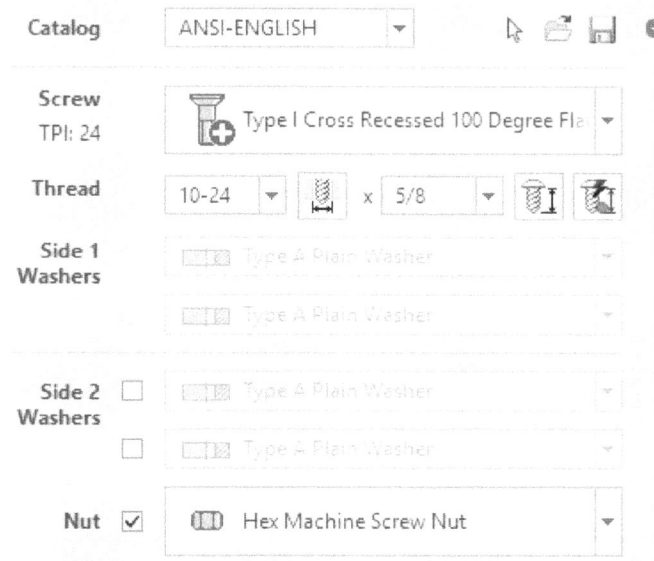

Figure 12–46

13. Set the *Thread* size to **1/4-20**. The screw is adjusted and is now the correct length, as shown in Figure 12–47.

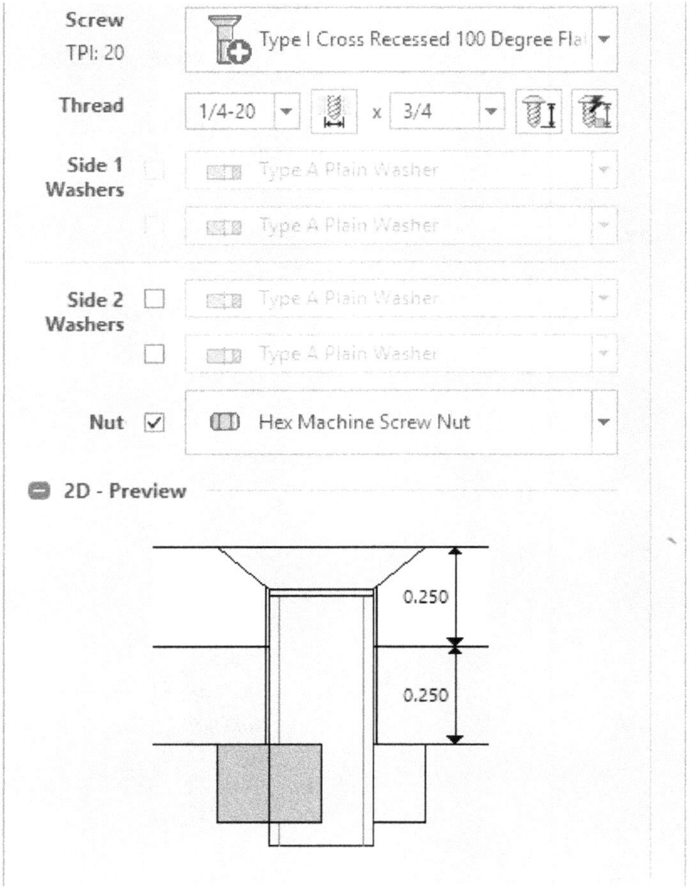

Figure 12–47

Task 7 - Add a counterbore for the nut.

1. In the upper-right corner of the Screw Fastener Definition dialog box, click ⊕ (Show/Hide Hole Layout). The dialog box updates, as shown in Figure 12–48.

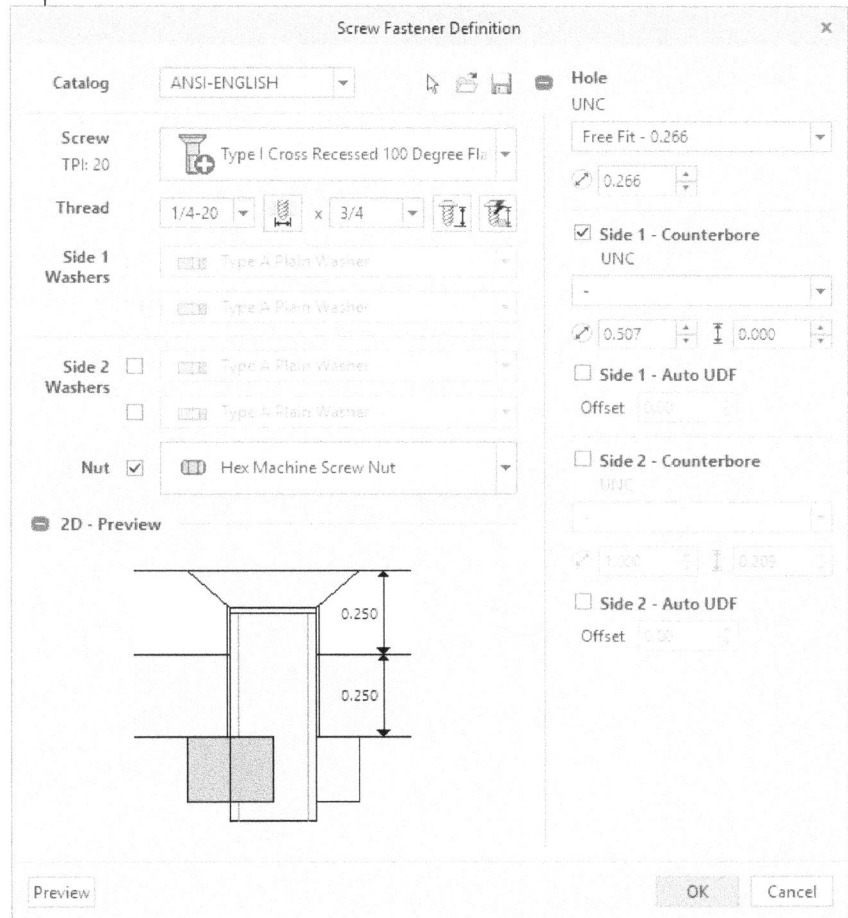

Figure 12–48

2. Change the *Thread* size back to **10-24** and the *Thread* length to **1/2**.

3. Select **Side 2 - Counterbore**.

4. Edit the diameter for **Side 2** to **0.450**.

5. Click **OK**.

6. Click **OK** in the Additional Options dialog box. The fasteners update as shown in Figure 12–49.

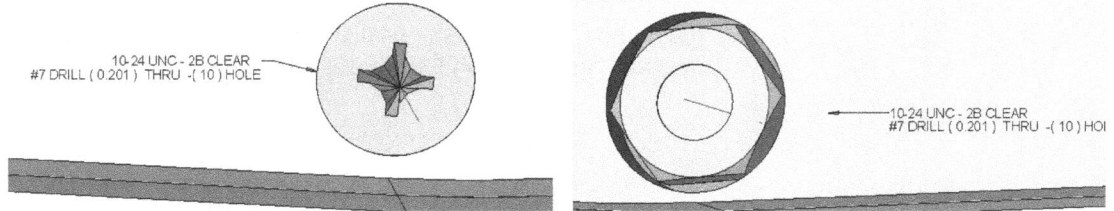

Figure 12–49

Task 8 - Open the parts to view the holes created.

1. Click on **CONTAINER_2.PRT** in the Model Tree and select
   (Open) in the mini toolbar.

2. Note the addition of the annotation calling out the hole, and the countersink to house the screw, as shown in Figure 12–50.

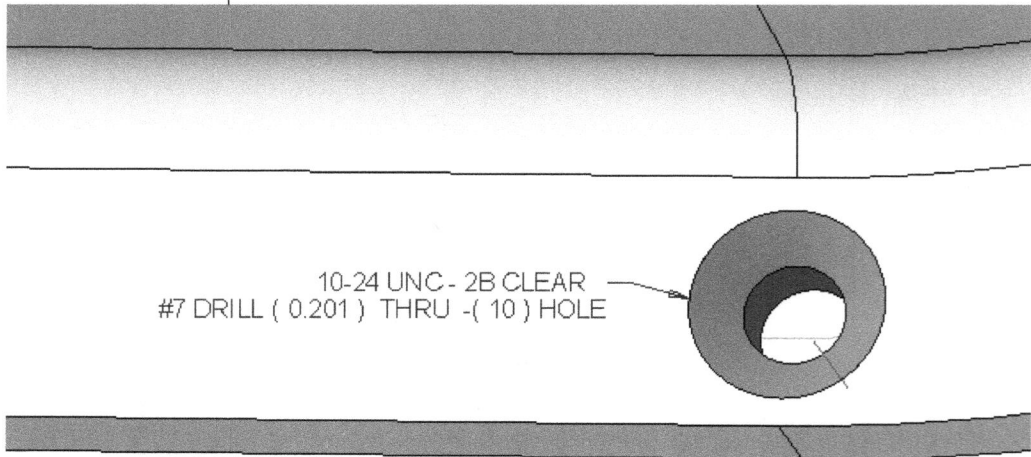

Figure 12–50

3. Close the window.

4. Click on **COVER_2.PRT** in the Model Tree and select
   (Open) in the mini toolbar.

5. Rotate the model and note that the addition of the counterbore holes, as shown in Figure 12–51.

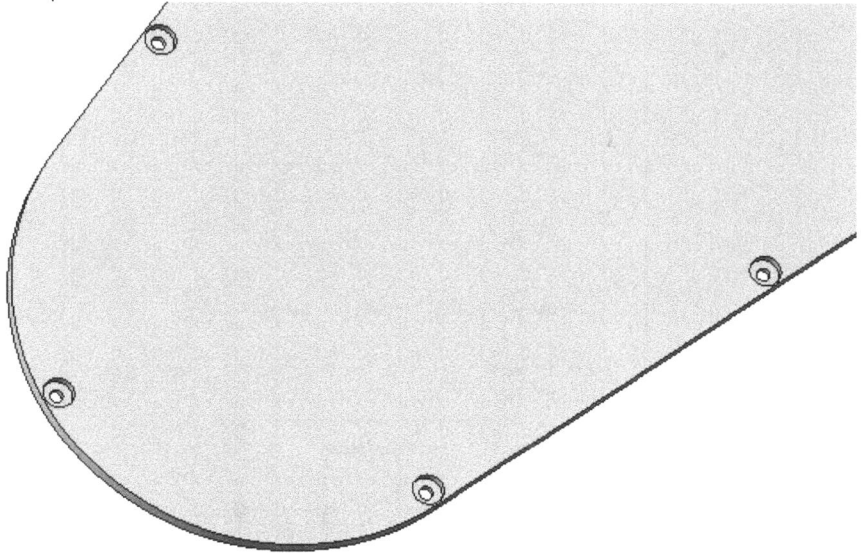

Figure 12–51

6. Close the window.

Task 9 - Change the fastener to remove the counterbore and add washers.

Design Considerations

The counterbore does not provide enough space for a wrench or socket. If its diameter were any larger, it would break through the side of the cover part. Change the fastener to two washers instead.

1. In the *Tools* tab, click ✎ (Redefine) and select a fastener.

2. In the Screw Fastener Definition dialog box, remove the check next to **Side 2 - Counterbore**.

3. Enable both **Side 2 Washers** and leave the default washer type as **Type A Plain Washer**.

4. Click ⬚ (Automatically Set Length).

5. The Screw Fastener Definition dialog box should display as shown in Figure 12–52.

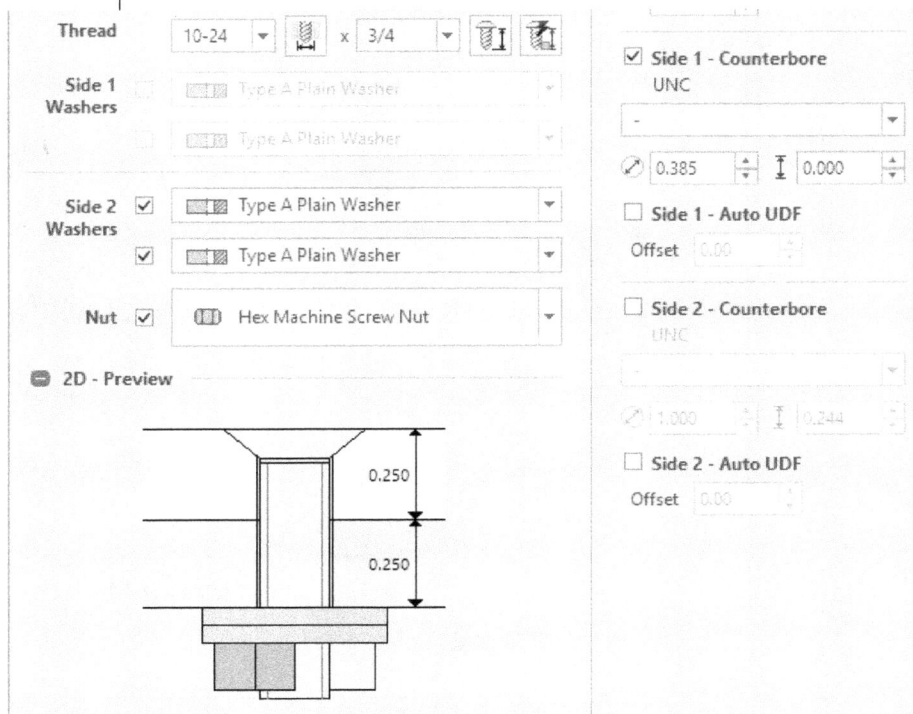

Figure 12–52

6. Click **OK**.

7. Click **OK** in the Pattern Options dialog box. The components update as shown in Figure 12–53.

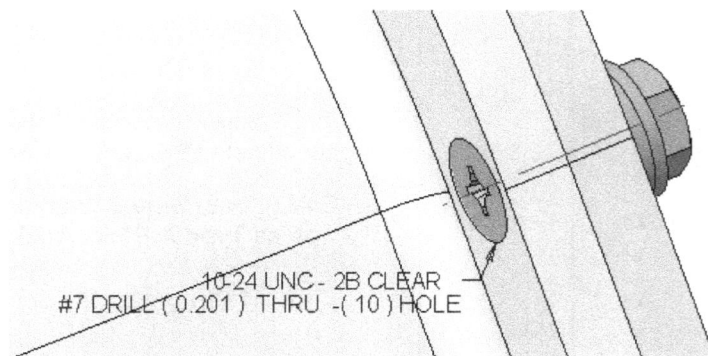

10-24 UNC - 2B CLEAR
#7 DRILL (0.201) THRU -(10) HOLE

Figure 12–53

8. Save the assembly and erase all files from memory.

Chapter Review Questions

1. Intelligent Fasteners enables automatic assembly for which of the following standard hardware? (Select all that apply.)

    a. Screws

    b. Bolts

    c. Washers

    d. Nuts

2. You can enter a thread diameter or use which of the following icons to select an existing hole surface?

    a.

    b.

    c.

    d.

3. When you select an existing hole to locate a fastener, Creo Parametric will automatically cut countersinks and counterbores in the parts intersected by the fasteners.

    a. True

    b. False

4. To add a nut to a fastener, what must the selected surface references be?

    a. Facing one another.

    b. Facing opposite to one another.

    c. From the same part.

Answers: 1.abcd, 2.c, 3.b, 4.b

Advanced Assembly Operations

Assembly models can be used to create new parts. There are two methods of creating mirrored parts and assemblies. In the first method, if the mirrored component and source component are required in the same assembly, you can create the mirrored component directly inside the shared assembly. In the second method, if you do not require the mirrored component and source component to be in the same assembly, you can open the source component and create the mirrored component directly, without the use of an assembly.

Learning Objectives in This Chapter

- Learn a method to mirror parts within the context of an assembly.
- Learn a method to mirror subassemblies within the context of an assembly.
- Learn a method to mirror a part or subassembly without creating an assembly.
- Use geometry in a part to add or subtract geometry in another part using the **Merge** or **Cut Out** options.
- Create an assembly and use the intersect subtype to generate a new part that results from the common volume of selected components.
- Learn the different option in the Drag dialog box that enables you to dynamically move, constrain, and create snapshots of an assembly.
- Learn to create equality or conditional relations for an assembly using operators, parameters, and functions.

13.1 Mirroring Components (Method 1)

New parts can be created by mirroring existing components in an assembly. The resulting part is a mirror image of the source component, and can be used in the existing assembly, opened in Part mode, or used in other assemblies. An example of a mirrored component is shown in Figure 13–1.

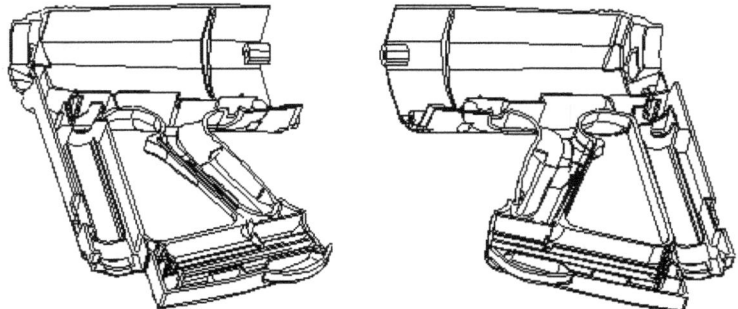

The model on the left was created in Part mode and then mirrored in Assembly mode to create a mirrored model.

Figure 13–1

Mirroring Parts

Depending on the mirroring options selected, you might not be able to delete the temporary assembly.

To mirror a component within the context of an assembly, the source component must first be inserted into the assembly.

If required, a temporary assembly can be used, in which to mirror the components. Once the component has been mirrored, the temporary assembly can be deleted. Once the assembly has been created, assemble the component to be mirrored.

How To: Mirror a Component in the Context of an Assembly

1. To mirror a component, click ⟩⟨ (Mirror Component) in the *Model* tab. The Mirror Component dialog box opens, as shown in Figure 13–2.

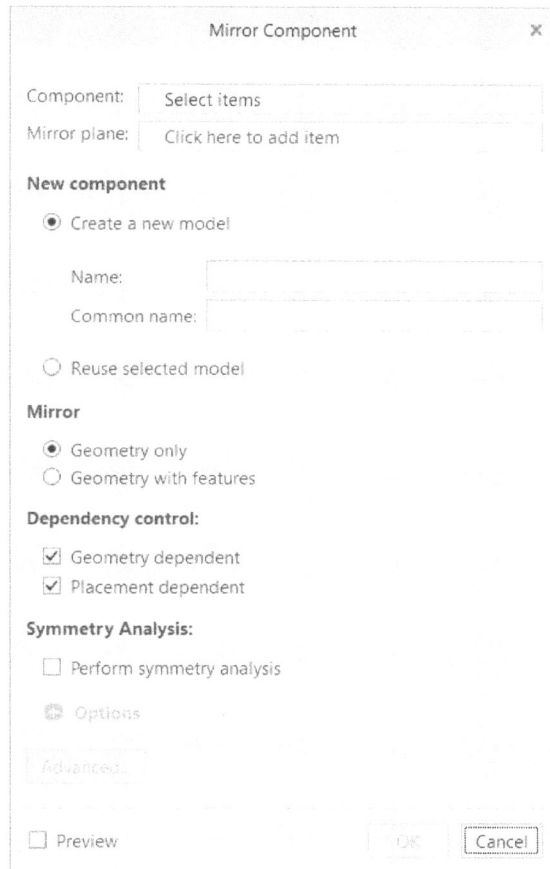

Mirror Component   ✕

Component: Select items

Mirror plane: Click here to add item

New component

◉ Create a new model

    Name:

    Common name:

◯ Reuse selected model

Mirror

◉ Geometry only
◯ Geometry with features

Dependency control:

☑ Geometry dependent
☑ Placement dependent

Symmetry Analysis:

☐ Perform symmetry analysis

⚙ Options

Advanced

☐ Preview   OK   Cancel

Figure 13–2

2. Select the component to be mirrored and the mirror plane, as shown in Figure 13–3.

Mirror Component   ✕

Component: 9003_RH.PRT

Mirror plane: Surf:F5(PROTRUSION):9003_RH ID=33

Figure 13–3

3. Enter a name for the new mirrored component, as shown in Figure 13–4.

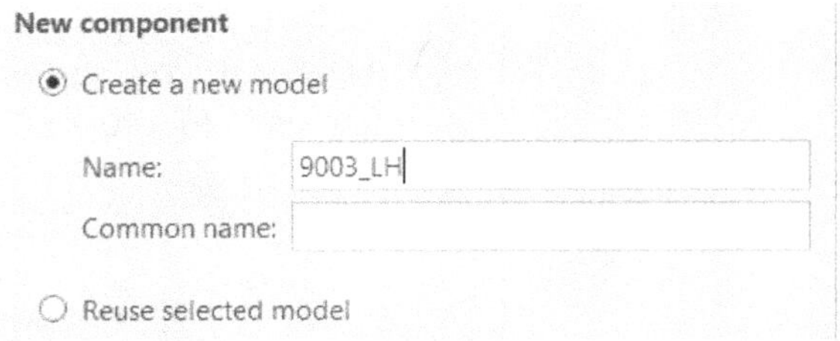

New component

◉ Create a new model

Name: 9003_LH|

Common name:

○ Reuse selected model

Figure 13–4

4. Specify the Mirror type for the new mirrored component. The available options are described as follows:

Option	Description
Geometry only	Mirrors the geometry without the structure of the source feature. You can specify both the geometry and placement dependency.
Geometry with features	Mirrors the geometry with the source feature structure. It copies all of the information to the mirrored part and the copy remains independent of the source part. Changes to the source part are not reflected in the mirrored part and the source part does not have to exist for the mirrored part to exist. Using this mirroring type, only placement dependency can be specified. You cannot specify geometry dependency because the models are independent.

Depending on the Mirror type selected, some options might be not be available.

5. Specify the Dependency Control, as described as follows:

Option	Description
Geometry dependent	Defines the part so that it references the source part for all of the information. Changes made to the source part are reflected in the mirrored part and the source part must exist for the mirrored part to exist.
Placement dependent	Makes the placement of the target component dependent on the placement of the source component.

6. Select **OK** to complete the mirror, as shown in Figure 13–5.

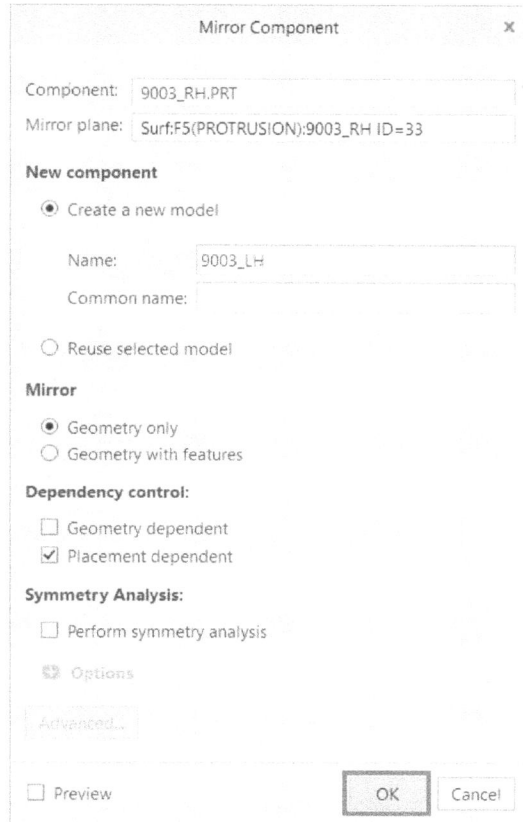

Figure 13–5

Two halves of an assembly are shown in Figure 13–6. The model on the left was created in Part mode and mirrored in Assembly mode to create the version of the model shown on the right.

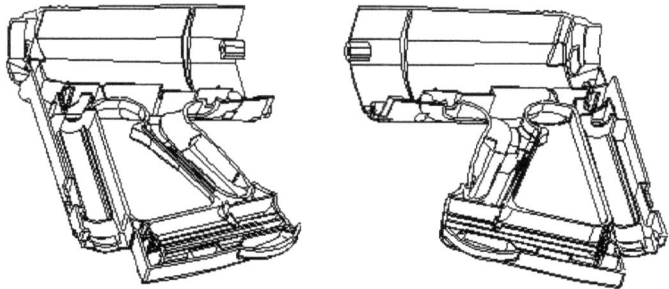

Figure 13–6

The two components are in the assembly as shown in Figure 13–7.

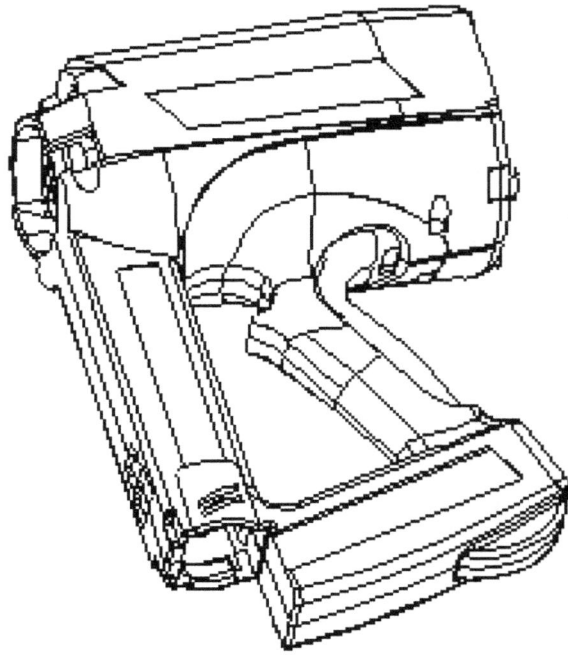

Figure 13–7

Mirroring Subassemblies

To mirror a subassembly within the context of an assembly, the source subassembly must first be inserted into the top-level assembly.

How To: Mirror a Subassembly in the Context of an Assembly

1. To mirror a component, click)|((Mirror Component) in the *Model* tab. The Mirror Component dialog box opens as shown in Figure 13–8.

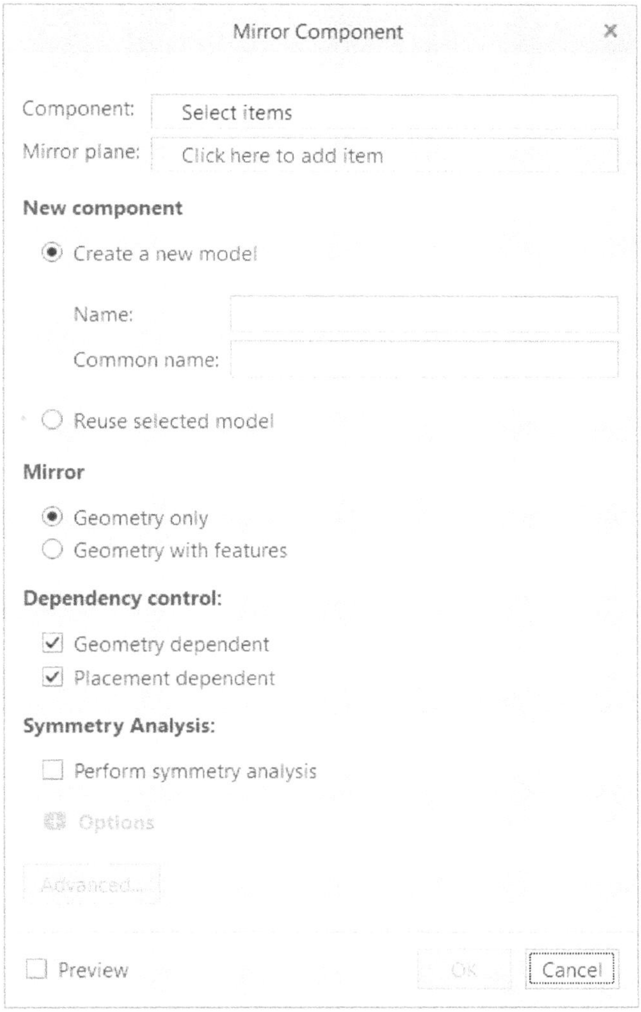

Mirror Component	✕

Component: Select items

Mirror plane: Click here to add item

New component

◉ Create a new model

     Name:

     Common name:

○ Reuse selected model

Mirror

◉ Geometry only
○ Geometry with features

Dependency control:

☑ Geometry dependent
☑ Placement dependent

Symmetry Analysis:

☐ Perform symmetry analysis

⚙ Options

Advanced...

☐ Preview   OK   Cancel

Figure 13–8

2. In the Mirror Component dialog box, select the component to mirror and the plane to mirror about. You can select **Create a new model** and enter a name, or select **Reuse selected model**. The **Perform symmetry analysis** option is used to check for potential reuse of symmetric component as shown in Figure 13–9.

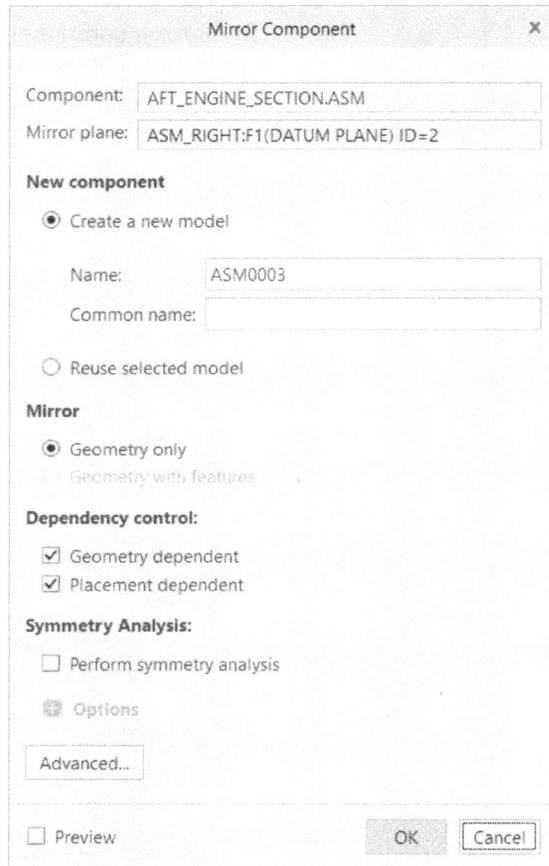

Mirror Component		✕
Component:	AFT_ENGINE_SECTION.ASM	
Mirror plane:	ASM_RIGHT:F1(DATUM PLANE) ID=2	

New component

◉ Create a new model

    Name: ASM0003

    Common name:

○ Reuse selected model

Mirror

◉ Geometry only

○ Geometry with features

Dependency control:

☑ Geometry dependent

☑ Placement dependent

Symmetry Analysis:

☐ Perform symmetry analysis

⚙ Options

[Advanced...]

☐ Preview   [OK] [Cancel]

Figure 13–9

3. Enter a name for the new mirrored assembly, as shown in Figure 13–10.

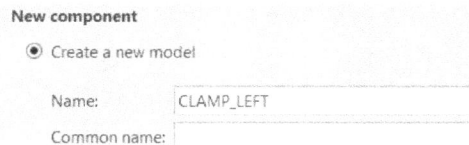

New component

◉ Create a new model

    Name: CLAMP_LEFT

    Common name:

Figure 13–10

4. Select **Advanced** to open the Mirror Subassembly Components dialog box, as shown in Figure 13–11.

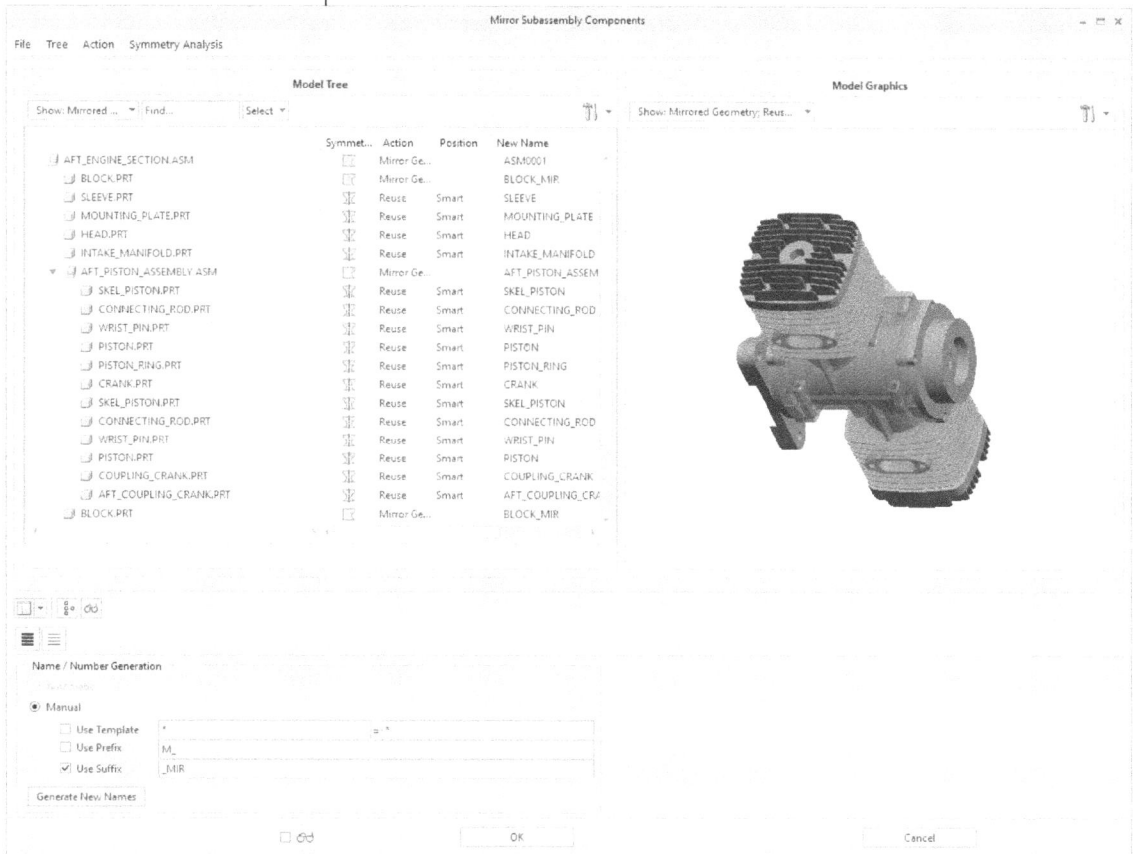

Figure 13–11

In the Mirror Subassembly Components dialog box, you can preview the results, adjust the name of components that are being mirrored, and decide on the appropriate action for the various objects.

For each object, you can set the *Action* to **Mirror Geometry**, **Reuse**, or **Exclude**. If you set the object to **Mirror Geometry**, it will be renamed. If an object is set to **Reuse** by the system and you edit the *New Name* field, the action will automatically change to **Mirror Geometry**.

Specify the columns as described as follows:

Option	Description
Action column	Enables you to define whether or not to include the component using the **Action** menu. If included, you can decide to assign a new name. The following options are available: • **Mirror Geometry:** (default) Copy the source component with a new name or right-click and select **New Name** to change the action of the selected component to **Mirror Geometry**. • **Mirror Placement:** Reuse the source component in the mirror assembly or right-click and select **Reuse** to change the action of the selected component to **Mirror Placement**. • **Exclude:** Excludes the source component from the mirroring operation. You can also right-click and select **Exclude** to change the action of the selected component to **Exclude**.
New Name	Enter the name in the *New Name* column. The *Use Template* area enables you to rename components based on specified criteria. The *Use Suffix* area enables you to append text to all of the component names.
Dependent Placement	Defines the placement of the target component as dependent on the placement of the source component for each component independently.
Dependent Geometry	Defines the component so that it references the source component for all of the information for each component independently. Changes made to the source component are reflected in the mirrored component and the source component must exist for the mirrored component to exist.

5. Click **OK** to create the mirrored component.

13.2 Mirroring Components (Method 2)

Mirrored parts can be created by mirroring the existing components directly in Part mode, without the need to create an assembly. The resulting part is a mirror image of the source component and can be opened in Part mode and used in other assemblies. Depending on the options used to define the mirror, the source part might or might not be required for the mirrored part to exist.

Mirroring Parts

How To: Mirror a Part

1. Open or activate the source part. Select **File>Save As> Mirror part**. The Mirror Part dialog box opens as shown in Figure 13–12.

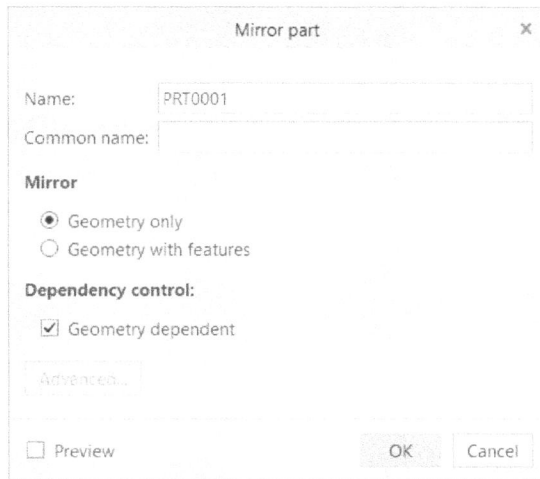

Figure 13–12

The source part is mirrored about the XY plane, based on the default coordinate system, to create the mirrored part.

2. Enter an appropriate name for the mirrored part using the *New Name* field.

3. Specify the Mirror type for the new mirrored component. The available options are described as follows:

Option	Description
Geometry only	Mirrors the geometry without the structure of the source feature.
Geometry with features	Mirrors the geometry with the source feature structure. This option copies all of the information to the mirrored part and the copy remains independent of the source part. Changes to the source part are not reflected in the mirrored part and the source part does not have to exist for the mirrored part to exist.

Specify the dependency control using the **Geometry Dependent** option. This option defines the part so that it references the source part for all of the information. Changes made to the source part are reflected in the mirrored part, and the source part must exist for the mirrored part to exist.

4. Click **OK** to create the mirrored component.

Mirroring Subassemblies

How To: Mirror a Subassembly

1. Open or activate the source assembly.
2. Select **File>Save As>Save a Mirror Assembly**. The Mirror Assembly dialog box opens as shown in Figure 13–13.

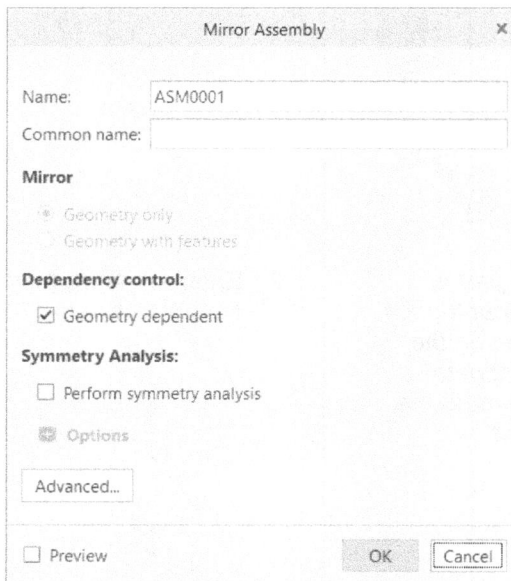

Figure 13–13

3. Enter an appropriate name in the *New Name* field.
4. Specify the dependency control as global for all of the components using the **Geometry dependent** option. This option defines the subassembly so that it references the source subassembly for all of the information. Changes made to the source subassembly are reflected in the mirrored subassembly, and the source subassembly must exist for the mirrored subassembly to exist.
5. Click **Advanced** to open the Mirror Assembly Components dialog box.
6. To complete the **Mirror** operation, you must specify an action and new name for each component in the subassembly. This is done using the Mirror Assembly Components dialog box, as shown in Figure 13–14.

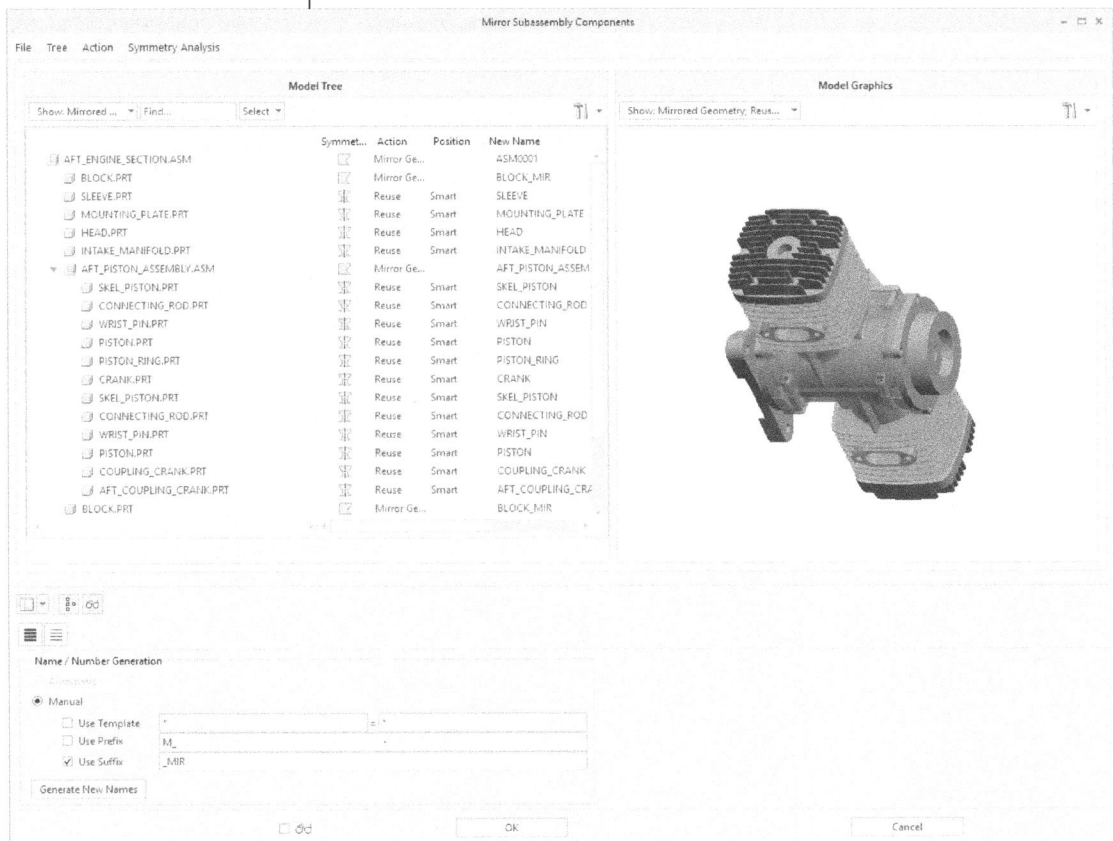

Figure 13–14

7. Specify the columns as described as follows:

Option	Description
Action column	Define whether or not to include the component using the **Action** menu. If included, you can assign a new name. The following options are available: • **Mirror Geometry:** (default) Copy the source component with a new name or right-click and select **New Name** to change the action of the selected component to **Mirror Geometry**. • **Mirror Placement:** Reuse the source component in the mirror assembly or right-click and select **Reuse** to change the action of the selected component to **Mirror Placement**. • **Exclude:** Excludes the source component from the mirroring operation. You can also right-click and select **Exclude** to change the action of the selected component to **Exclude**.
New Name	Enter the name in the *New Name* column. The *Use Template* area enables you to rename components based on specified criteria. The *Use Suffix* area enables you to append text to all of the component names.
Dependent Placement	Defines the placement of the target component dependent on the placement of the source component for each component independently.
Dependent Geometry	Defines the component so that it references the source component for all of the information for each component independently. Changes made to the source component are reflected in the mirrored component, and the source component must exist for the mirrored component to exist.

8. Click **OK** to create the mirrored assembly.

13.3 Boolean Operations (Merge, Cut, and Intersect)

The Boolean Operations of **Merge**, **Cut**, and **Intersect** enable you to add or subtract the geometry from one set of parts to another set of parts in the same assembly. The **Merge** option adds geometry and the **Cut** option removes geometry. The Intersect option adds the interfering volume between selected components to another component. Examples of a Boolean merge and a cut are shown in Figure 13–15.

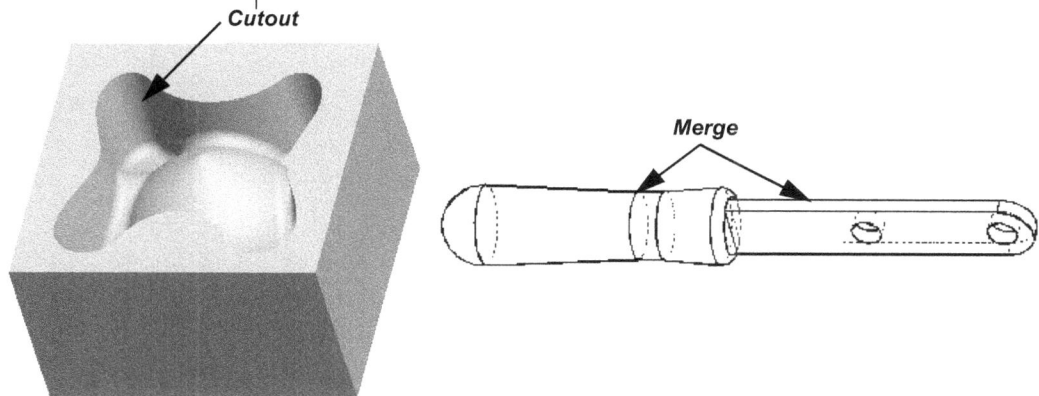

Figure 13–15

How To: Merge, Cut, or Intersect Geometry with Boolean Operations

1. To merge, cut, or intersect components, they must be assembled into an assembly. Constrain the components so that they are placed in the required location to perform the merge, cut, or intersect. Examples of assemblies that are used for Boolean Merge, Cut, and Intersect operations are shown in Figure 13–16.

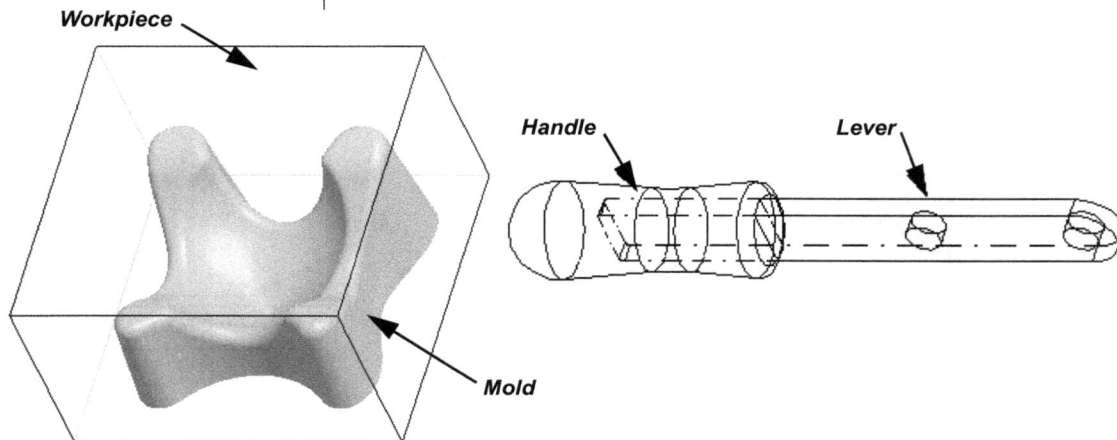

Figure 13–16

2. Select **Component>Component Operations**. The **Component** menu displays as shown in Figure 13–17.

Figure 13–17

3. Select Boolean Operations.
4. Select **Merge**, **Cut**, or **Intersect** to begin the operation, as shown in Figure 13–18.

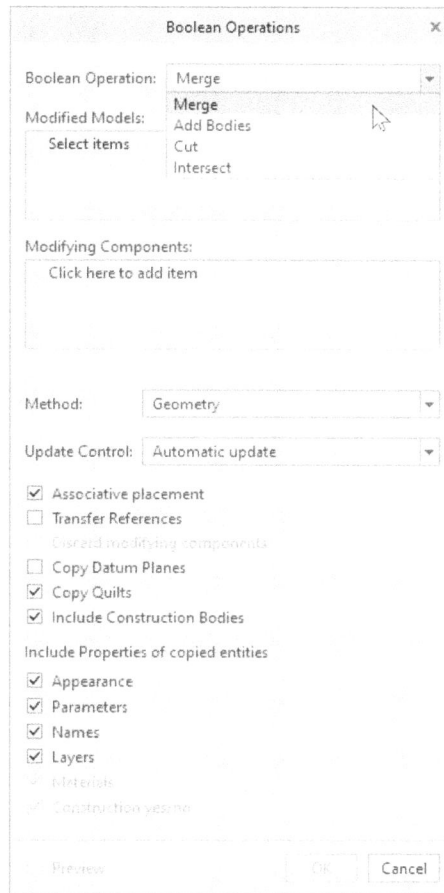

Figure 13–18

5. Select the references.

   To define the references for a merge or cut, select the parts you want to merge into or cut from in the *Modified Models* field. Then, click in the *Modifying Components* field and select the reference model for the merge or cut.

6. The Boolean Operations dialog box provides control over the update using either the **Automatic update**, **Manual update**, or **No dependency** option, as shown in Figure 13–19.

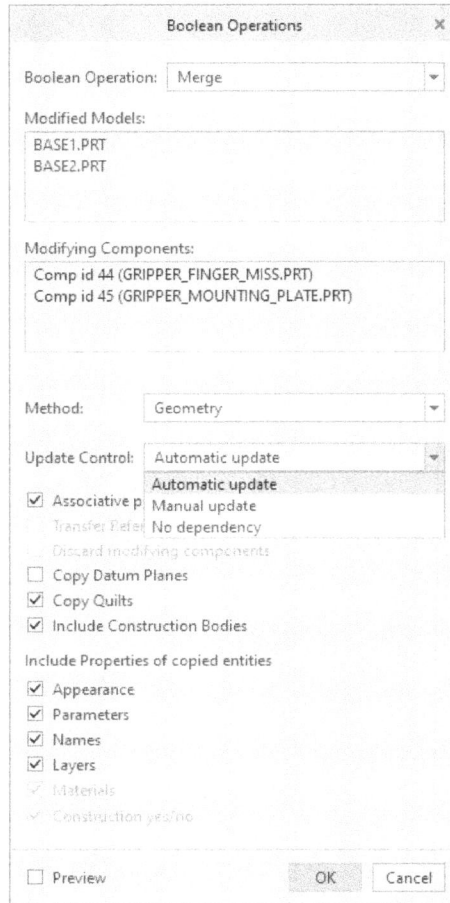

Figure 13–19

When the operation only involves a single modified model, you can clear the **Associative placement** checkmark. The **Discard modifying components** option becomes available, which enables you to remove the modifying components from the top-level assembly. If the removed components have children, the children will fail to regenerate. You can then select **Transfer References** and the references used to place the children are transferred to the merged part.

- **Reference**: Copies a component while maintaining a link to the original component. For example, a change in the original model updates in the merge or cut out feature. The **Copy** option copies component features and relations into another component without maintaining a link to the original model. Therefore, a change in the original model does not update in the merge or cut out feature. These options are the same for both **Merge** and **Cut Out**.

- **No Datums** (excluding datum planes) and **Copy Datums** (including datum planes): Copy the geometry from the first set of parts into the second set of parts. These options are only available by selecting **Merge>Reference**. Select **Done** to complete the operation.

7. Open the components in a separate window to display the geometry. A component before and after a **Merge** operation is shown in Figure 13–20.

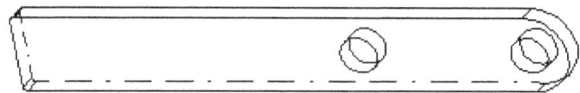

Before Merge operation

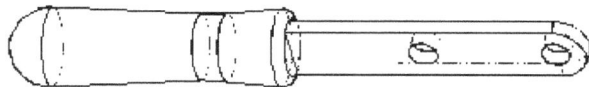

After Merge operation

Figure 13–20

A component before and after a **Cut Out** operation is shown in Figure 13–21.

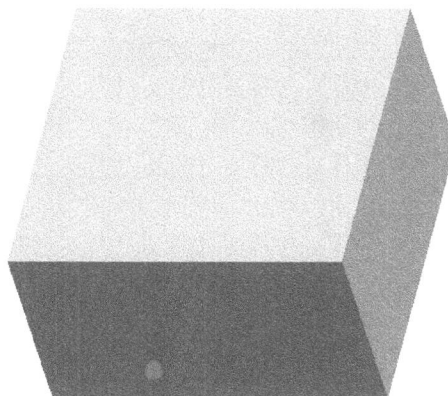

| *Before Cut Out operation* | *After Cut Out operation* |

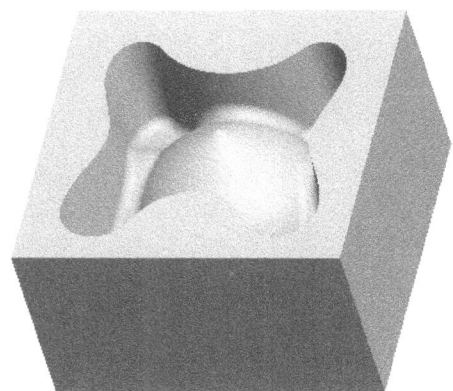

Figure 13–21

13.4 Part Intersections

Parts can be created from the intersection of components in an assembly. The new part results from the common volume of the selected components.

How To: Create an Intersected Part

1. To create a part from intersected components, they must be assembled into an assembly. Constrain the components so that they are placed in the required location to create the part. Two assembled parts are shown in Figure 13–22.

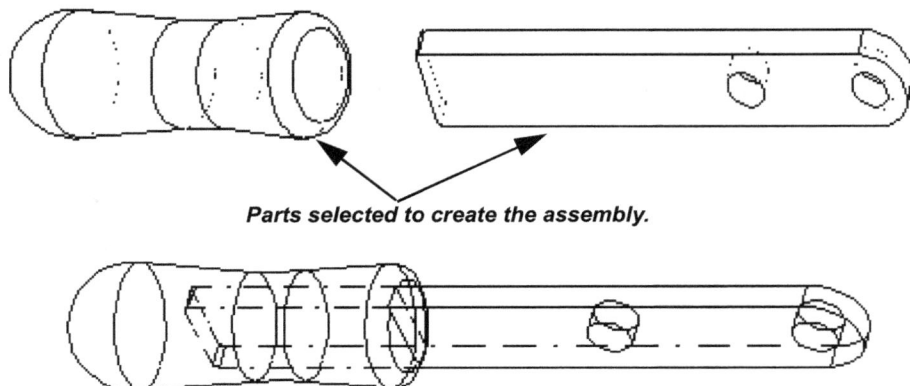

Parts selected to create the assembly.

Figure 13–22

2. To create a component by intersection, click ▣ (Create) in the *Model* tab. The Component Create dialog box opens. Set the *Type* to **Part**, the *Sub-type* to **Intersect**, and enter the name of the new component, as shown in Figure 13–23.

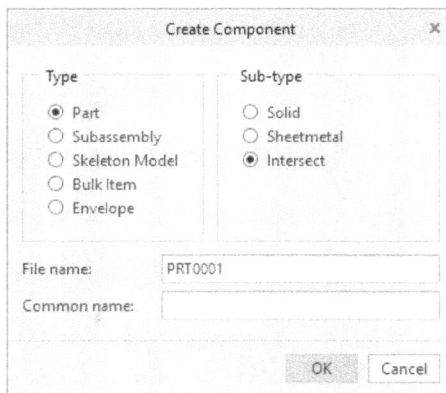

Figure 13–23

3. Select the parts to intersect. The part is created from the intersecting volume of the selected components.
4. Open the component in a separate window to display the geometry. The common intersecting volume of the two assembled components is the inside of the handle. The new part created using **Intersect** is shown in Figure 13–24.

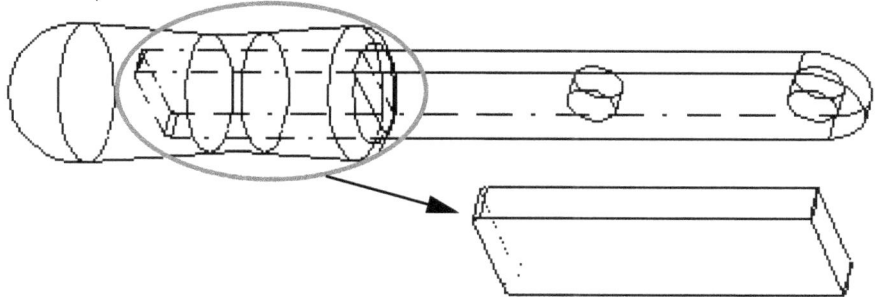

Figure 13–24

13.5 Dragging

The **Drag** tool enables you to dynamically move an assembly. This is useful when testing an assembly in various positions. Using the Drag dialog box, snapshots of the assembly in specific positions can be taken and saved to be recalled. These snapshots can also be reused in a drawing. The **Drag** tool is often used in conjunction with mechanism linkages to test the movement of an assembly, but it can also be used with assembly in which degrees of freedom remain.

How To: Drag an Assembly

1. To activate the Drag tool, click 🖑 (Drag Components). The Drag dialog box opens as shown in Figure 13–25.

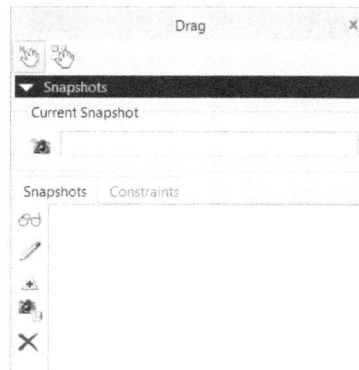

Figure 13–25

2. The assembly can be dragged using one of two methods:
   - Drag a Point
   - Drag a Body
3. Select the method using the options at the top of the Drag dialog box. The two dragging methods available are described as follows:

Icon	Description
🖑	When using **Point Drag**, the assembly follows the movement of the cursor as permitted by the assembly constraints and/or connections. Movements can consist of both translation and rotation. To use this option, select a point on the assembly and drag the cursor as required to translate and rotate it about the selected point.

When using **Body Drag**, the assembly follows the movements of the cursor as permitted by the assembly constraints and/or connections. Using this option, components can only be translated. When you drag a body, its position in the graphics window changes, but its orientation remains fixed.

Without adding additional constraints inside the Drag dialog box, the movements are controlled by any existing mechanism linkages and/or assembly constraints. For example, a packaged component to which some assembly constraints have been applied (such as Coincident, Distance, etc.), can only be dragged in its remaining degrees of freedom (DOF).

4. In the *Constraints* tab in the Drag dialog box you can control the Drag function by specifying the geometric constraints, locking and unlocking components, enabling or disabling connections, and selecting a specific Drag mode.

   The *Constraints* tab in the Drag dialog box is shown in Figure 13–26.

*The constraints defined from inside the Drag dialog box are only valid when the **Drag** tool is active.*

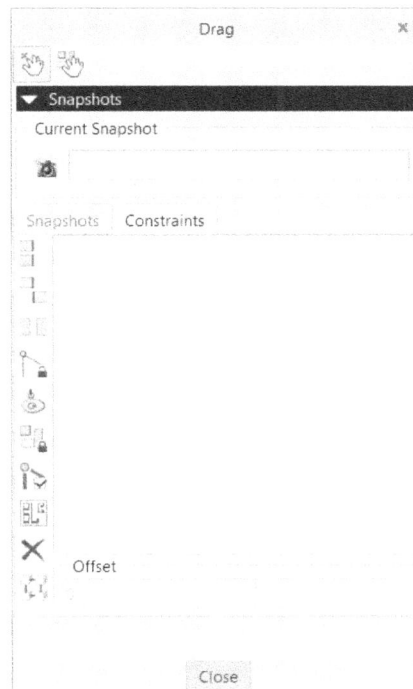

Figure 13–26

The *Constraint* tab icons are described as follows:

Icon	Description
	The **Align Two Entities** icon enables you to align two component surfaces.
	The **Mate Two Entities** icon enables you to mate two component surfaces.
	The **Orient Two Surfaces** icon enables you to orient two component surfaces.
	The **Motion Axis Constraint** icon enables you to fix a specific joint axis in its current position. You must select the connection icon for the item.
	The **Enable/Disable Cam Liftoff** icon enables you to maintain the connection between a cam and a follower, or it enables the follower to lift off from the cam at its peak motion.
	The **Body-Body Lock Constraint** icon enables you to temporarily lock a component in its current position relative to ground or another component. It is possible for the assembly to remain fixed if this option is used.
	The **Enable/Disable Connections** icon enables you to temporarily disable connections. This indicates how components would move relative to each other if they were one body.
	The **Delete Selected Constraints** icon enables you to delete any of the constraints applied in the Drag dialog box.
	The **Reconnect** icon enables you to force the mechanism to assemble using the previous options.

5. When a required model orientation is obtained, a snapshot or saved view, can be taken of the specific position. It can be recalled at any time and can also be used in drawing views. Saved snapshots are listed in the main window in the *Snapshot* tab in the Drag dialog box. The **Snapshot** icons are described as follows:

Icon	Description
	Enables you to save a snapshot. You have to enter a name for the snapshot in the *Name* field.
	Enables you to restore a snapshot configuration. To restore a configuration, select the snapshot in the list and click the icon.
	Uses part positions from other snapshots.

⊕	Enables you to redefine the snapshot configuration. To do so, drag the components to their new positions, select the snapshot in the displayed list, and click the icon.
📷	Enables you to indicate that a snapshot can be used on a drawing by putting an **X** in the *Asm State* column (as Explode State).
✕	Enables you to delete a snapshot. To do so, select it in the displayed list and click the icon.

Detecting Collision

Collision detection settings provide dynamic collision detection during dragging operations. To dynamically check for interference during the **Dragging** option, select **File>Prepare> Model Properties** and select **change** next to Collision Detection in the Model Properties dialog box, as shown in Figure 13–27.

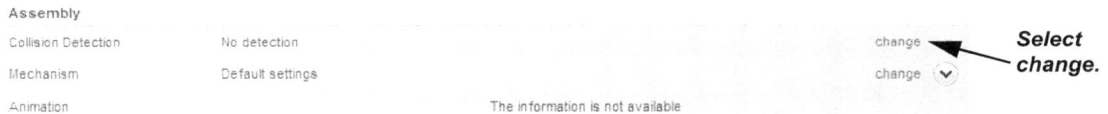

Assembly

Collision Detection   No detection   change ◄━━ *Select change.*
Mechanism   Default settings   change ⌄
Animation   The information is not available

Figure 13–27

The Collision Detection Settings dialog box opens as shown in Figure 13–28.

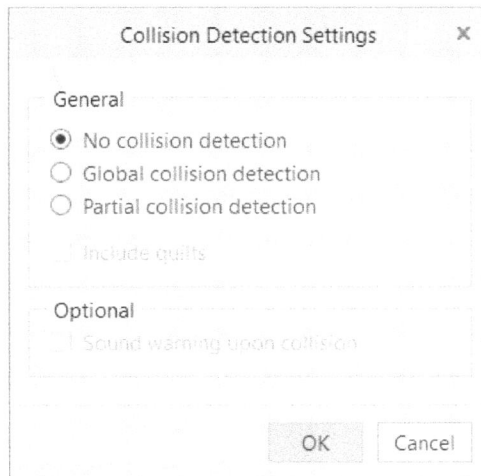

Figure 13–28

The General Settings control how the Collision Detection is calculated. You can select the following methods to drag a component:

- **No collision detection:** Permits a smooth dragging even in the case of collision.

- **Global collision detection:** Checks for any kind of collision in the entire assembly.

- **Partial collision detection:** Specifies the parts between which to check for collision.

In large assemblies the advanced collision detection options can cause very slow movement of the assembly.

Additional settings can be applied to the Collision detection when the **enable_advance_collision** config option is set to **yes**. The Collision Detection Settings dialog box with the **enable_advance_collision** config option enabled is shown in Figure 13–29.

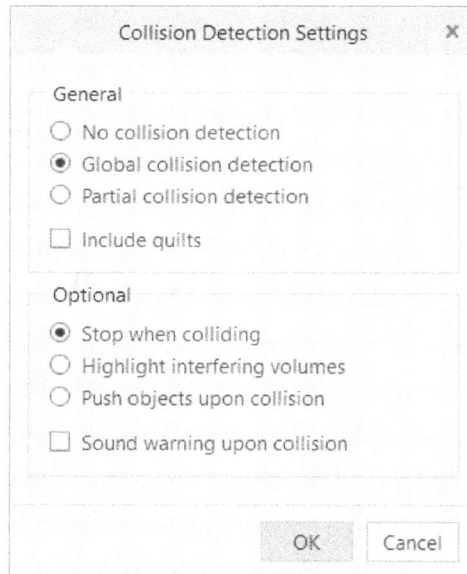

Figure 13–29

The Optional Settings enable you to control how Creo Parametric prompts you about a collision. For example, to sound a warning bell on collision, select the **Sound warning upon collision** option.

13.6 Assembly Relations

Creating assembly relations enables you to capture design intent.

Relations are user-defined mathematical equations that can be used to control geometry, as well as relationships between models in an assembly. All of the dimensions in a Creo Parametric model contain a symbolic dimension. An example of a symbolic dimension in a part is d6. If this part is used in an assembly, the same dimension is displayed as d6:#, where # is a session number for the component in the assembly. The session number enables the system to differentiate between similar symbolic dimensions in each assembly component. The symbolic dimension is used in relations to reference part and/or assembly dimensions.

Relations can be equality or conditional statements, as follows:

- Equality statements equate one side of the equation to the other.

  d36 = 2.75 + d20 * (1 - d42)

- Conditional statements use **If/Else/Endif** statements to equate a value based on a specified condition.

  If (d12 + d16) <= 10
  d3 = d6
  Else
  d4=d6
  Endif

Assembly relations cannot drive a part parameter that is already driven by a part relation.

An assembly consisting of a connecting rod and pin is shown in Figure 13–30. The symbolic diameter dimension for the pin is d6:72 and the symbolic diameter dimension of the bore in the connecting rod is d9:74. The design intent requires that the connecting rod bore remains 0.005 units larger than the pin diameter. The relation is written to capture this intent.

d9:74 = d6:72 + 0.005

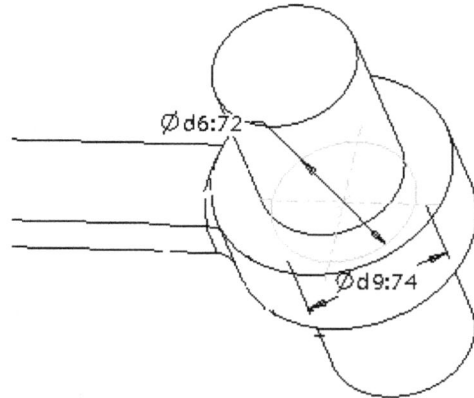

Figure 13–30

How To: Create an Assembly Relation

You can also click

$d=$ *(Relations) in the Tools tab.*

1. Click $d=$ (Relations) in the *Model* tab. The Relations dialog box opens, as shown in Figure 13–31.

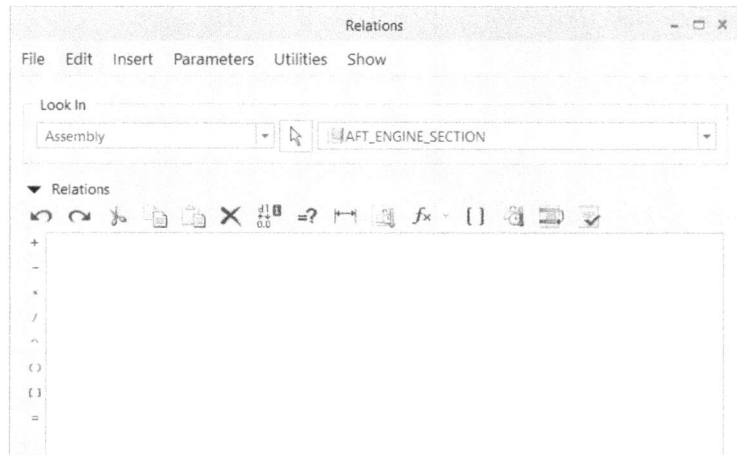

Figure 13–31

2. To select the type of geometry referenced by the relation, expand the Look In drop-down list, as shown in Figure 13–32. The option that is selected in this drop-down list determines where the relation is written.

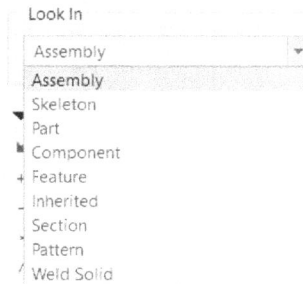

Figure 13–32

For example, if **Feature** is specified as the **Look In** option, you would select a feature in the assembly and enter the relation. The relation is then created in the part file and does not reference any assembly-level geometry or dimensions.

3. Relations should be preceded by a comment line. Comment lines provide information about the relations and help to organize them in the assembly. Relation comments are also valuable for downstream users of the model who do not know its original design intent. Comment lines must be preceded by the /* syntax, as shown in Figure 13–33.

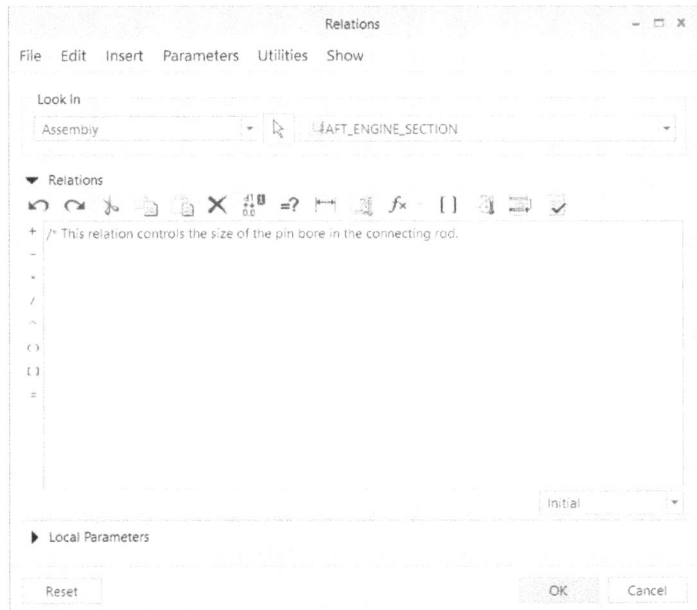

Figure 13–33

4. To obtain the required dimension symbol for the relation, select the part and feature for which you want to display the dimensions. All of the dimensions associated with that part and feature are displayed in their symbolic forms. You can toggle between the dimensional and symbolic display by clicking 🔲 (Switch Dimensions). The dimension symbols associated with two components in the assembly are shown in Figure 13–34.

*The Session Id can be obtained by selecting **Show>Session ID** in the Relations dialog box and then selecting the model.*

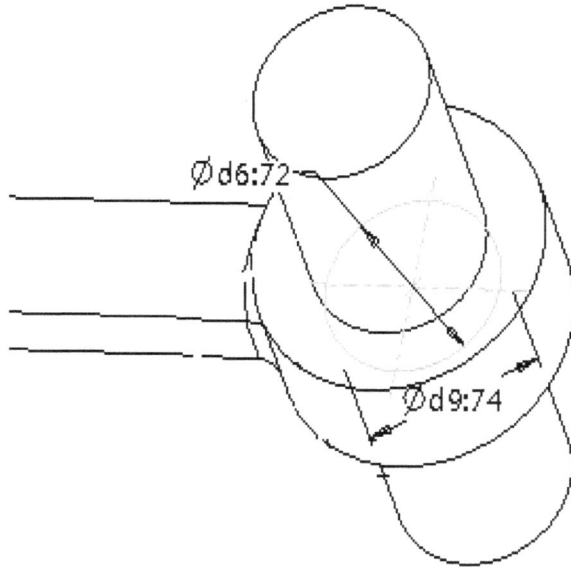

Figure 13–34

5. Equations can be entered manually or inserted directly from the model. To manually enter the relation, enter the operators, symbolic dimensions, and numerical values using the keyboard.

To directly insert the dimension symbol, select it on the model. The selected symbolic dimension is displayed in the *Relations* area in the Relations dialog box at the location of the cursor.

• The following can be included when entering a relation:
  • Symbols
  • Operators
  • Functions
  • Parameters

Symbols

The symbols described below can be used to write a relation, where # is the dimension symbol number that is applied to the dimension (e.g., d3, where #=3). If a negative value is possible, the dimension symbol must be preceded by a dollar sign (e.g., $d#).

Symbol	Description
d#	Part dimensions.
d#.#	Dimension in assemblies. The second # is the session id.
sd#	Sketcher dimensions (only used in Feature Relations).
kd#	Known dimensions in Sketcher (only used in Feature Relations).
p#	Number of instances in a pattern.
tp#	Positive tolerance values in a plus-minus format.
tm#	Negative tolerance values in a plus-minus format.
tpm#	Tolerance values in plus-minus symmetrical format.
rd#	Reference dimensions.

Operators

The operators described below can be used in relations. Some of these operators are also available in a toolbar on the left side in the Relations dialog box.

Operator	Description	Operator	Description
+	addition	**<**	less than
-	subtraction	**<=**	less than or equal
/	division	**==**	equal to
*****	multiplication	**!=**	not equal to
^	exponentiation	**&**	and
( )	grouping	**|**	or
>	greater than	**!**	not
>=	greater than or equal		

Functions

The functions described below can be used in relations.

Mathematical Function

sin ()	tanh ( )
cos ( )	sqrt ( )
tan ( )	log ( )
asin ( )	ln ( )
acos ( )	exp ( )
atan ( )	abs ( )
sinh ( )	ceil ( ) Smallest integer not less than the real value.
cosh ( )	floor ( ) Largest integer not greater than the real value.

Parameters

The parameters described in the following tables can be used in relations. User-defined parameters can also be used (e.g., ANGLE or DIST).

Predefined Parameters

PI (=3.1415...)	Mathematical constant.
G (= 9.8 m/sec2)	Gravity constant.
C1,C2,C3,C4 (= 1.0, 2.0, 3.0, 4.0)	Common parameters for all models in the current session that can be modified by relations.

Mass Property Parameters	**Description**
mp_mass	mass
mp_density	density
mp_volume	volume
mp_surf_area	surface area
mp_cp_x	x of center of gravity
mp_cg_y	y of center of gravity
mp_cg_z	z of center or gravity

The relation with a comment line and an equality statement equation is shown in Figure 13–35.

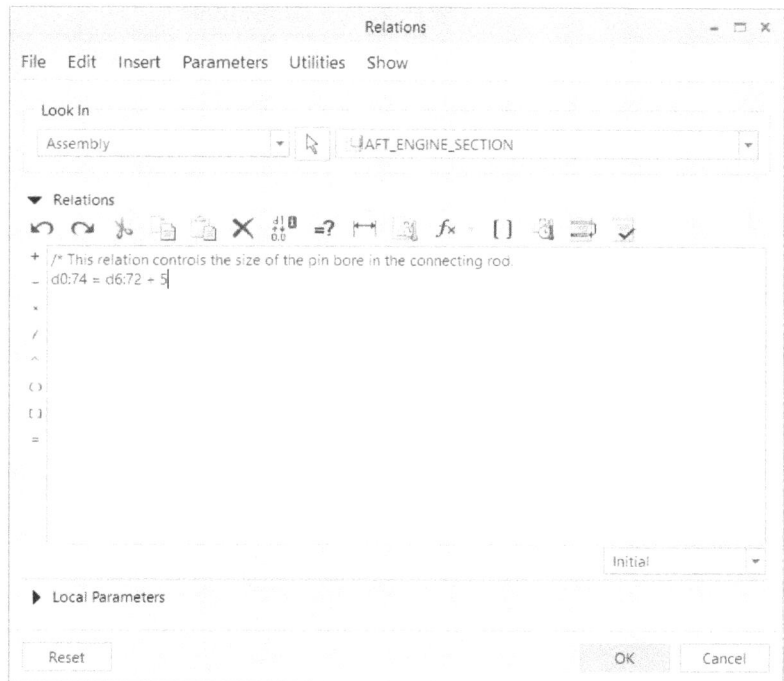

Figure 13–35

6. When all of the comments and relation statements have been entered, click **OK** in the Relations dialog box to complete the relation.

7. Click (Regenerate) to regenerate the model and update the geometry driven by the relation.

8. Flex the model by making dimensional modifications to determine whether the relation is correct and captures the required design intent.

Practice 13a	# Mirroring Components

Practice Objectives

- Create a mirrored part in Assembly mode.
- Create a mirrored part in Part mode.

In this practice, you will create a left-handed part from a right-handed part. This operation is performed using a temporary assembly and using the **Mirror** option. When both components are required in the same assembly, creating the mirrored component within the context of the assembly is the most efficient method. At the end of the practice, you will create the same mirrored component directly from Part mode to practice using this method of mirroring.

Task 1 - Open a part file.

1. Change the working directory to the *Mirroring_Components* folder.

2. Open **handle_right.prt**.

3. Set the model display as follows:

   - ⅍ *(Datum Display Filters)*: All Off
   - ⊱ *(Spin Center)*: Off
   - ▱ *(Display Style)*: ▱ (Shading With Edges)

   The part displays as shown in Figure 13–36.

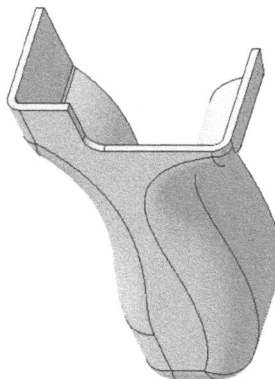

Figure 13–36

4. Close the window.

Task 2 - Create a new assembly.

In the next tasks, you will create the mirrored component in the context of an assembly. In this example, the assembly is only temporary, as it is only required to create the mirrored model. However, this method is very useful when both the source model and mirrored model are required in the same assembly.

1. Create a new assembly and set the *Name* to **Temp** using the default template.

2. Select **File>Options>Assembly** and ensure that the *Reference creation and backup control* section matches that shown in Figure 13–37.

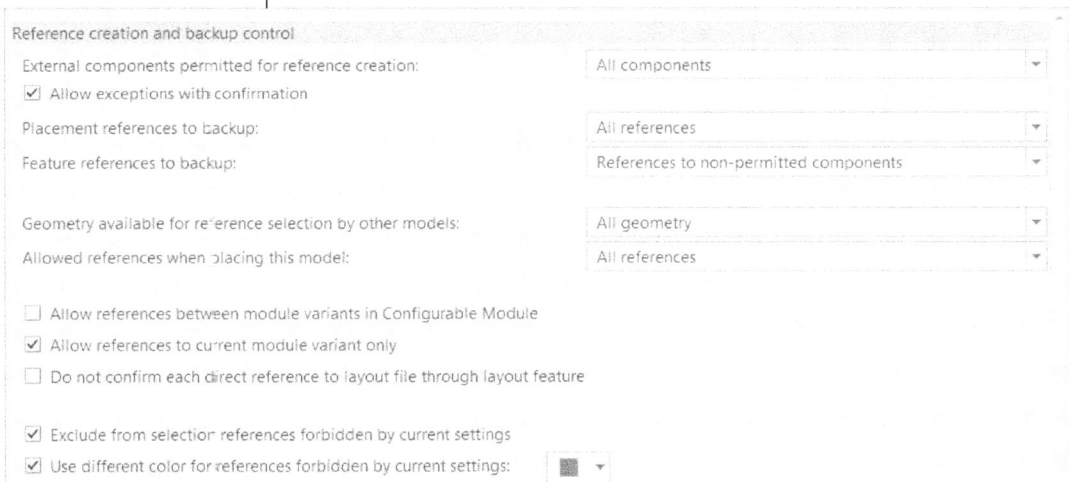

Reference creation and backup control

External components permitted for reference creation:	All components
☑ Allow exceptions with confirmation	
Placement references to backup:	All references
Feature references to backup:	References to non-permitted components
Geometry available for reference selection by other models:	All geometry
Allowed references when placing this model:	All references

☐ Allow references between module variants in Configurable Module

☑ Allow references to current module variant only

☐ Do not confirm each direct reference to layout file through layout feature

☑ Exclude from selection references forbidden by current settings

☑ Use different color for references forbidden by current settings:

Figure 13–37

3. Assemble **handle_right.prt** into the assembly without establishing any constraints.

Design Considerations

This component is left as packaged because this is only a temporary assembly that is used to create a mirrored version of the part file. Constraints do not serve a purpose and are not required.

Task 3 - Mirror the component by reference.

1. Click ⟩𝄁 (Mirror Component) in the *Model* tab. The Mirror Component dialog box opens as shown in Figure 13–38.

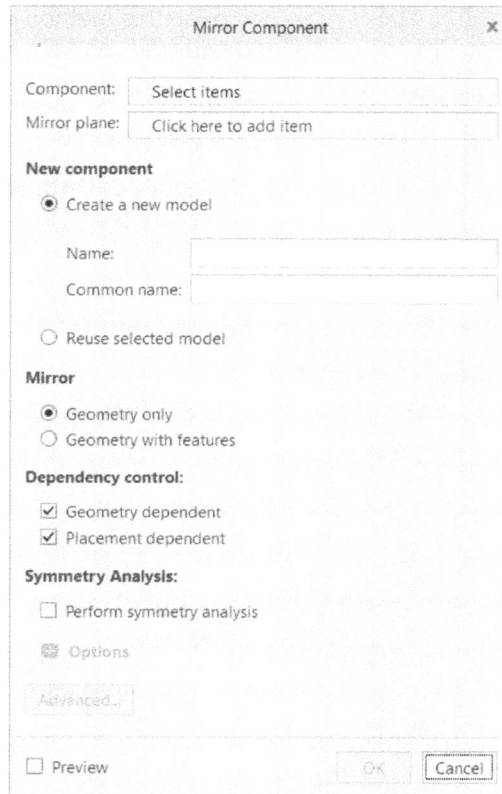

Mirror Component	×

Component: Select items

Mirror plane: Click here to add item

New component

◉ Create a new model

    Name: _____

    Common name: _____

◯ Reuse selected model

Mirror

◉ Geometry only
◯ Geometry with features

Dependency control:

☑ Geometry dependent
☑ Placement dependent

Symmetry Analysis:

☐ Perform symmetry analysis

⚙ Options

Advanced...

☐ Preview   OK   Cancel

Figure 13–38

2. Select **HANDLE_RIGHT.PRT** in the Model Tree.

3. Select the *Mirror Plane* field and select the planar surface of **handle_right.prt**, as shown in Figure 13–39.

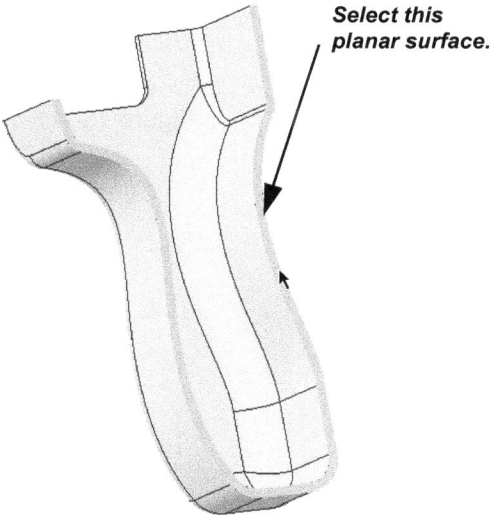

Select this planar surface.

Figure 13–39

4. Enter **HANDLE_LEFT** in the Name field as shown in Figure 13–40. Delete the common name if it auto-populates.

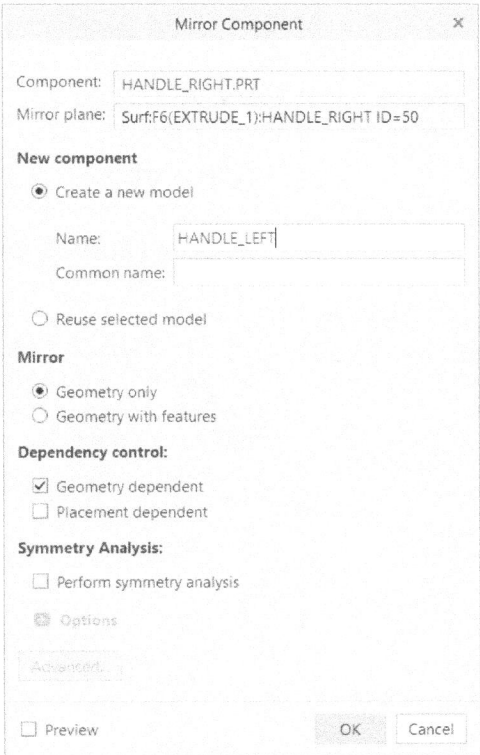

Figure 13–40

5. Ensure that **Geometry dependent** is selected in the *Dependency Control* area in the Mirror part dialog box.

6. Click **OK** to complete the mirror. The parts display as shown in Figure 13–41.

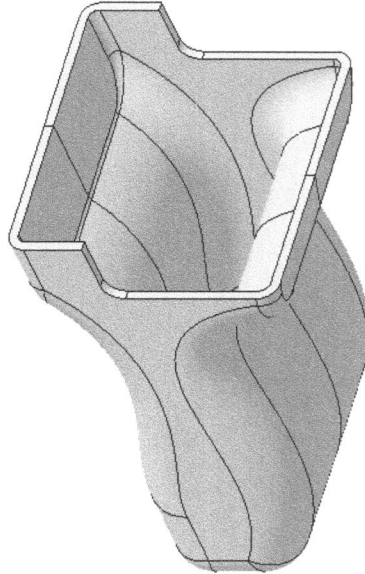

Figure 13–41

Task 4 - Open the mirrored part.

---

1. Open **HANDLE_LEFT.PRT** from the Model Tree.

Design Considerations

The left-hand version of the part displays as shown in Figure 13–42. The Model Tree indicates that the system created this geometry as a single merge feature. If the mirror was created using the **Include all Feature data** option, all of the features that existed in the source model would be listed in the target, and each feature could be manipulated individually as required.

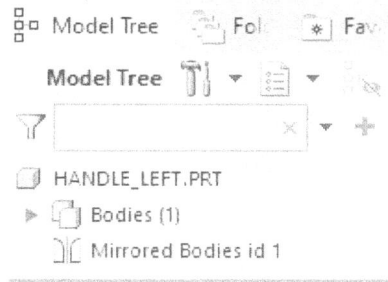

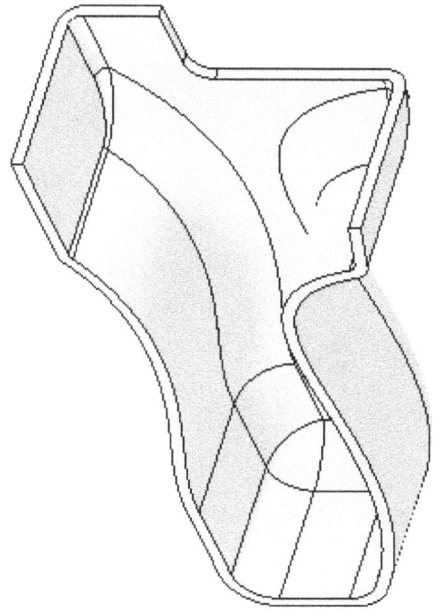

Figure 13–42

2. Save the mirrored part.

3. Close all of the windows and erase all of the files from memory.

Design Considerations

The temporary assembly has been erased. It is no longer required, now that the mirrored parts have been created and saved. When using this technique, it is important not to create any constraints or references to the temporary assembly file. Otherwise, the mirrored part might contain external references to the assembly and it cannot be deleted.

4. Open **handle_left.prt** to ensure that the part opens without the assembly.

5. Close the window and erase it from memory.

Task 5 - Create the same mirrored part using Save As.

In this task, you will create the same mirrored component directly inside Part mode. Using this method, creating a temporary assembly is not required.

1. Open **handle_right.prt**. Select **File>Save As>Mirror Part** to create a new part. The Mirror dialog box opens as shown in Figure 13–43.

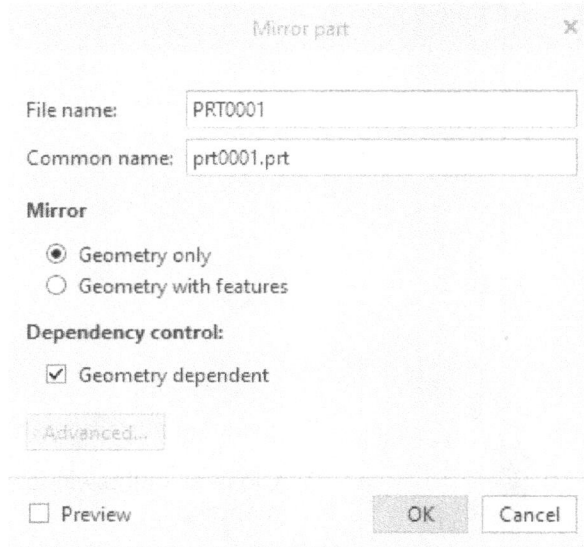

Figure 13–43

2. Set the *Name* to **HANDLE_LEFT2** and delete the common name.

3. Ensure that **Geometry dependent** is selected in the *Dependency Control* area in the Mirror part dialog box.

4. Click **OK** to complete the mirror. The new part window opens, as shown in Figure 13–44.

Using this method, you are not prompted to select a plane to mirror about. Creo Parametric automatically selects the XY plane, based on the default coordinate system, as the mirror plane.

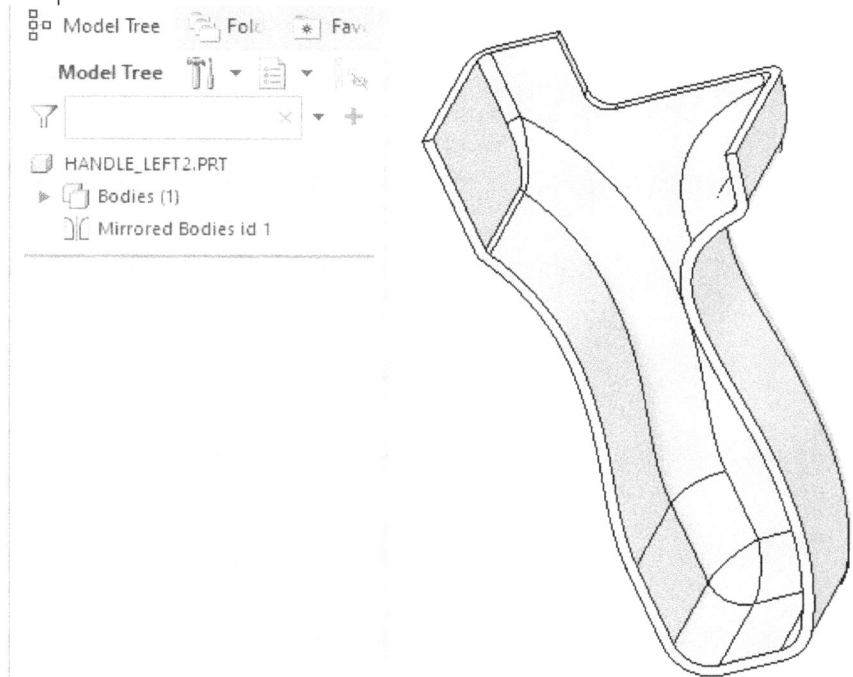

Figure 13–44

5. Save the mirrored part.

6. Close all of the windows and erase all of the files from memory.

Practice 13b | Assembly Merge

Practice Objective

• Create a single part file, merged from an assembly.

In this practice, you will create a weldment part by merging all of the components in an assembly. The resulting part represents the entire assembly in its welded state and can be identified as a single part number in the top-level assembly. Although the assembly consists of many components, these parts are all welded together during the manufacturing process. This is accomplished by merging the assembly. The merge is created using the **Reference** option so that changes made to the original assembly are reflected in the merged geometry. The model shown in Figure 13–45 is the final weldment part.

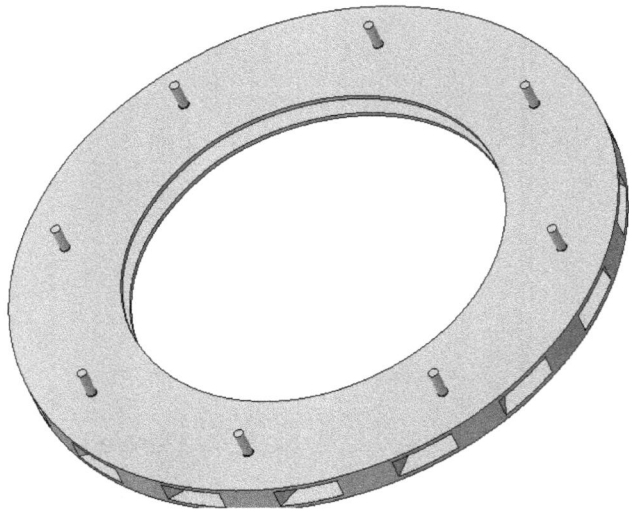

Figure 13–45

Task 1 - Create an assembly.

1. Change the working directory to the *Assembly_Merge* folder.

2. Create an assembly and set the *File name* to **temp**.

3. Set the model display as follows:

   • ⁺⁄⼂ *(Datum Display Filters)*: All Off

   • ⼂ *(Spin Center)*: Off

   • ⼂ *(Display Style)*: ⼂ (Shading With Edges)

Task 2 - Assemble the vane assembly as the first component.

1. Assemble **vane_diffuser.asm** using the Default constraint. The vane assembly displays as shown in Figure 13–46.

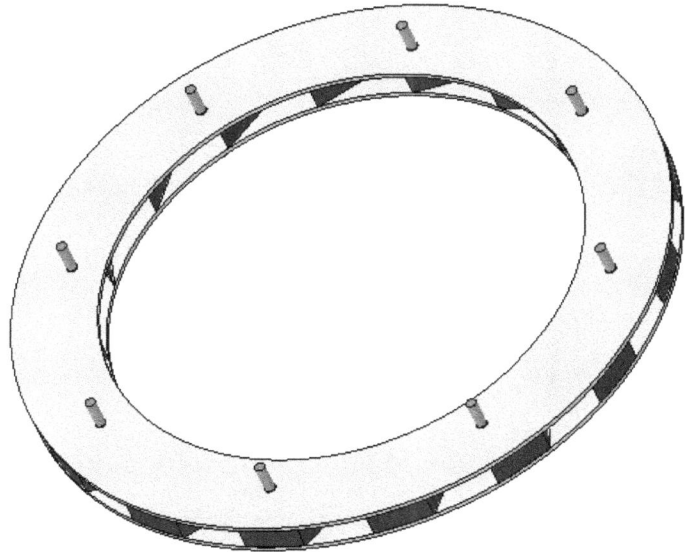

Figure 13–46

Task 3 - Create a new component.

1. Click ⬚ (Create) to create a new component.

2. Set the *Type* to **Part** and the *Sub-type* to **Solid**. Set the *File name* to **vane_weldment**, as shown in Figure 13–47.

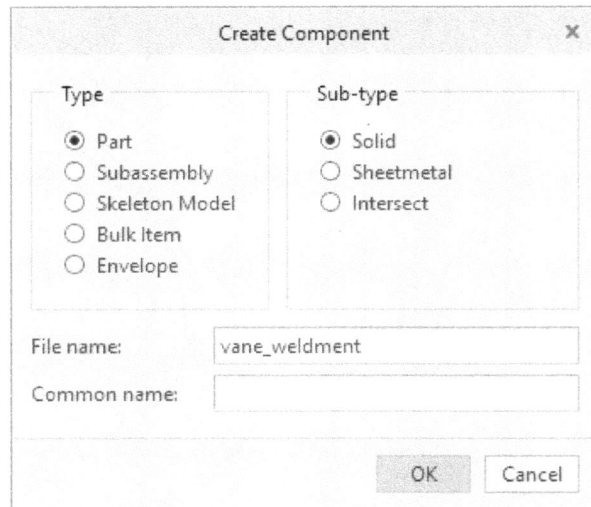

Figure 13–47

3. Click **OK**.

4. Select **Copy From Existing** and browse to select **start_part.prt**.

5. Click **OK**.

6. Constrain the new part using the Default constraint.

7. Click ✓ (OK).

Design Considerations

It is recommended that you use the default constraint for this operation as the merged geometry and copied geometry have their origins in the same relative location.

Task 4 - Copy the assembly geometry to the part model.

1. In the *Model* tab, select **Component>Component Operations>Boolean Operations**.

2. Select **Merge**, as shown in Figure 13–48.

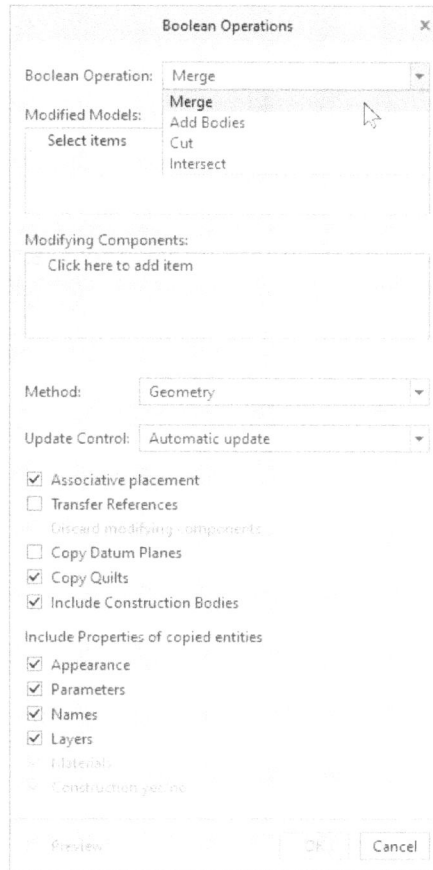

Figure 13–48

3. Select **vane_weldment.prt** as the component for the *Modified Models*.

4. Select in the *Modifying Components* field. In the Model Tree, expand **VANE_DIFFUSER.ASM** and both patterns of **VANE_STUD.PRT**.

5. Select the first **VANE_PLATE.PRT**. Press and hold <Shift> and select the last **VANE_STUD.PRT**, as shown in Figure 13–49.

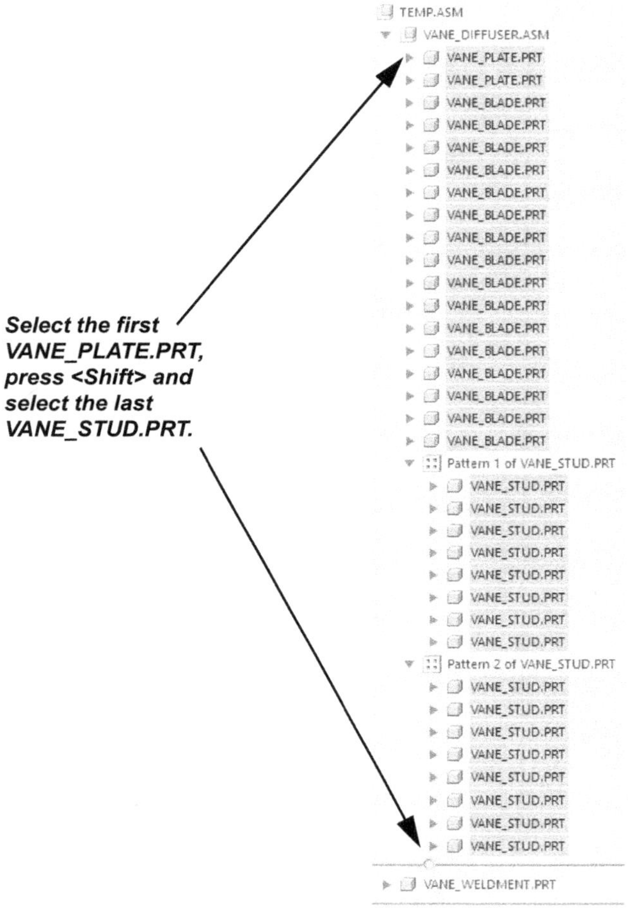

*Select the first
VANE_PLATE.PRT,
press <Shift> and
select the last
VANE_STUD.PRT.*

Figure 13–49

6. Set the options shown in Figure 13–50.

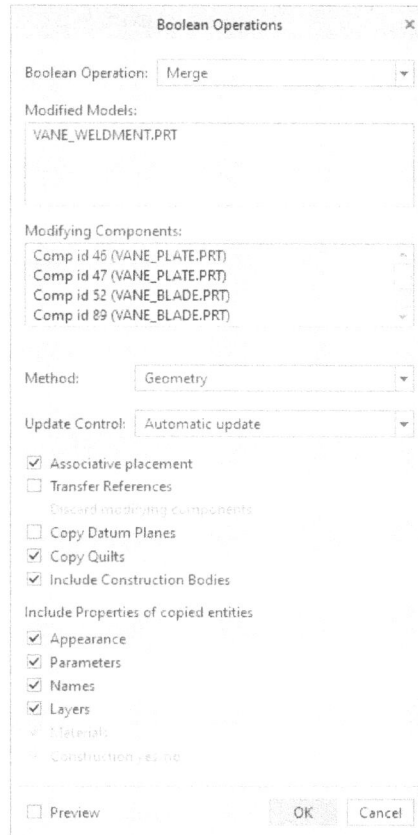

Figure 13–50

7. Select **OK** and **Done/Return**.

8. Open **vane_weldment.prt** and view the model geometry. The Model Tree contains 34 Merge features, as shown in Figure 13–51.

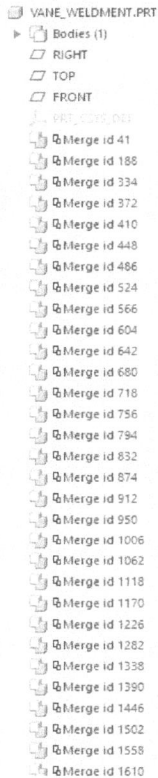

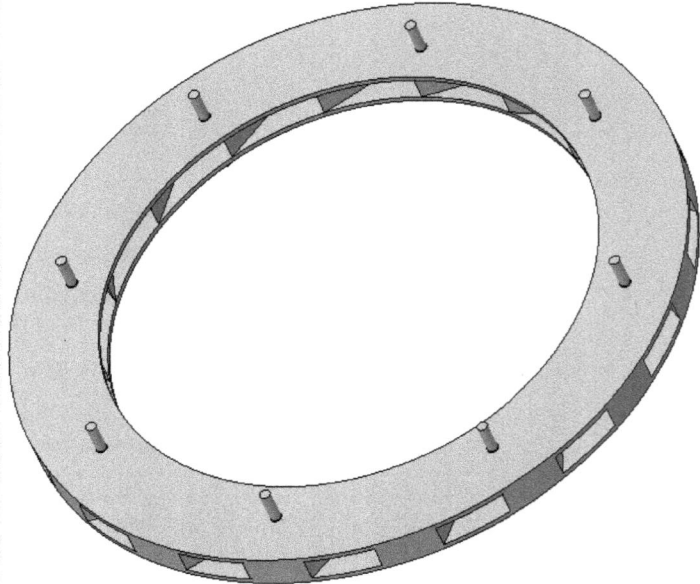

VANE_WELDMENT.PRT
▶ Bodies (1)
▱ RIGHT
▱ TOP
▱ FRONT
PRT_CSYS_DEF
Merge id 41
Merge id 188
Merge id 334
Merge id 372
Merge id 410
Merge id 448
Merge id 486
Merge id 524
Merge id 566
Merge id 604
Merge id 642
Merge id 680
Merge id 718
Merge id 756
Merge id 794
Merge id 832
Merge id 874
Merge id 912
Merge id 950
Merge id 1006
Merge id 1062
Merge id 1118
Merge id 1170
Merge id 1226
Merge id 1282
Merge id 1338
Merge id 1390
Merge id 1446
Merge id 1502
Merge id 1558
Merge id 1610

Figure 13–51

9. Save the part.

10. Close all of the windows and erase it from memory.

Task 5 - Modify assembly geometry.

---

1. Open **vane_diffuser.asm**.

2. Expand the first **VANE_PLATE.PRT** in the Model Tree.

3. Select **Protrusion id 39** and click ⟼d1 (Edit Dimensions) in the mini toolbar.

4. Change the *Diameter* dimension from *7.00* to **6.00** and the *Width* dimension from *1.25* to **1.75**. The dimensions display as shown in Figure 13–52.

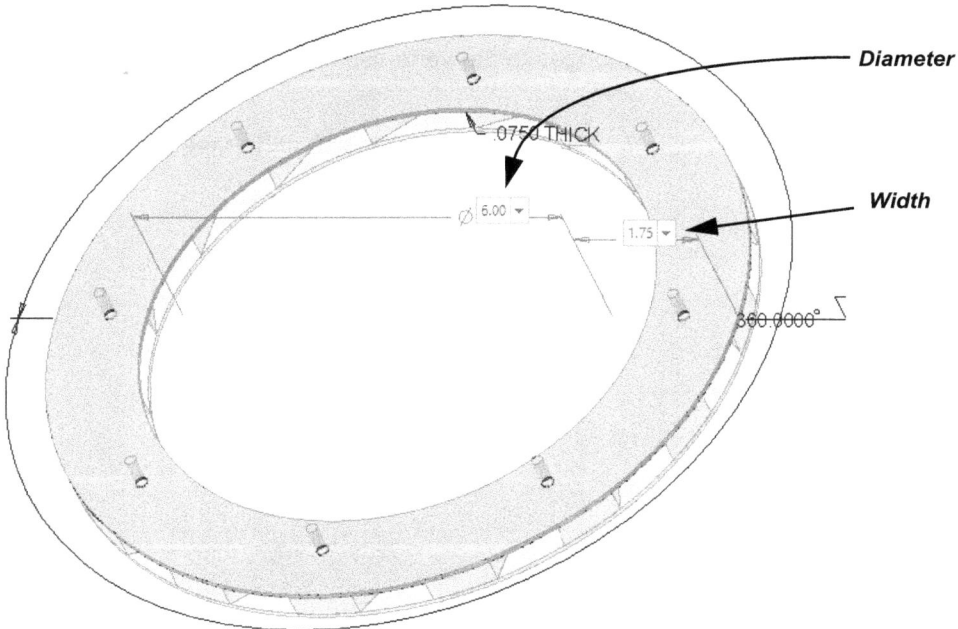

Figure 13–52

5. Regenerate the assembly. The model displays as shown in Figure 13–53.

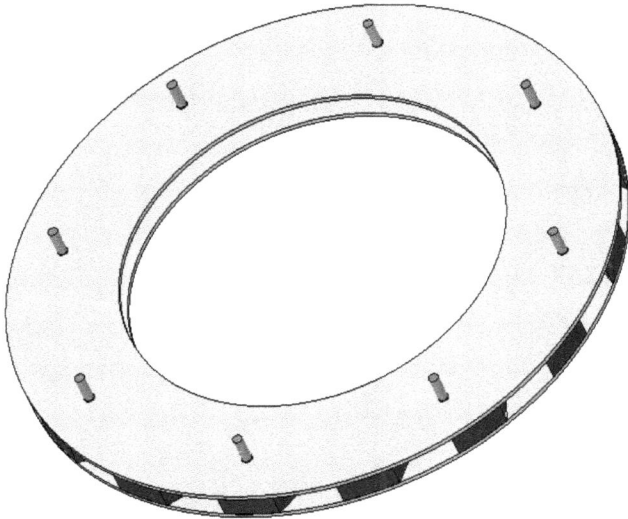

Figure 13–53

6. Open **vane_weldment.prt** and regenerate it.

Design Considerations

The dimensional changes have updated in the weldment part. This is because the merge was completed by Reference. Any changes to the vane assembly are reflected in the weldment part.

7. Close all of the windows and erase all of the files from memory.

Practice 13c

Mirroring an Assembly

Practice Objective

- Create a mirrored assembly in Assembly mode.

In this practice, you will create a left side assembly from a right side assembly. The operation is performed using the **Mirror Assembly** tool. This tool is available without needing to create a temporary assembly.

Task 1 - Open an assembly file.

1. Change the working directory to the *Mirroring_Assembly* folder.

2. Open **clamp_right.asm**.

3. Set the model display as follows:

    - ⚞ *(Datum Display Filters)*: All Off

    - ⚲ *(Spin Center)*: Off

    - ⬚ *(Display Style)*: ⬚ (Shading With Edges)

    - ⬚ (Annotation Display): Off

4. Select **File>Save As>Save a Mirror Assembly** in the menu bar.

5. Set the new assembly *Name* to **clamp_left**, as shown in Figure 13–54. Delete the common name if it populates.

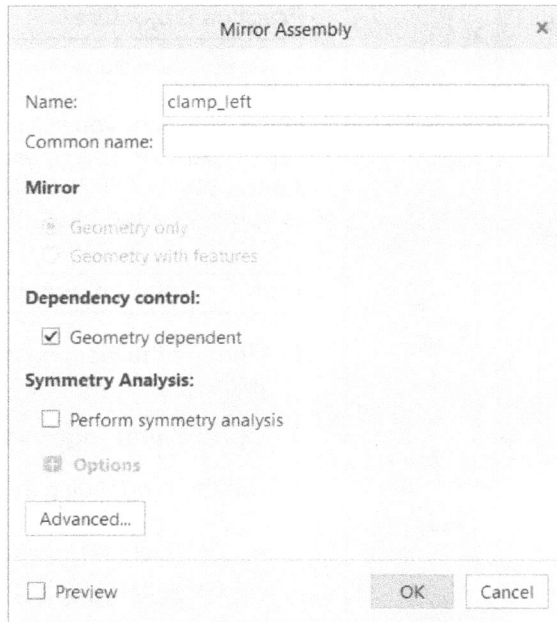

Figure 13–54

6. Enable Perform symmetry analysis, as shown Figure 13–55.

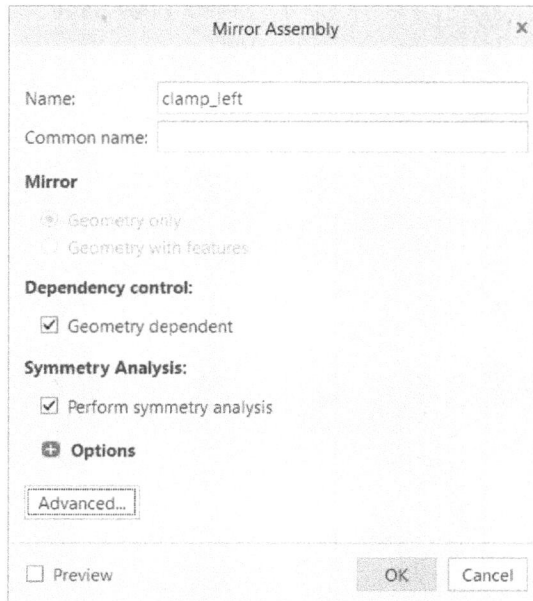

Figure 13–55

7. Click **Advanced**. The Mirror Assembly Components dialog box opens, as shown in Figure 13–56.

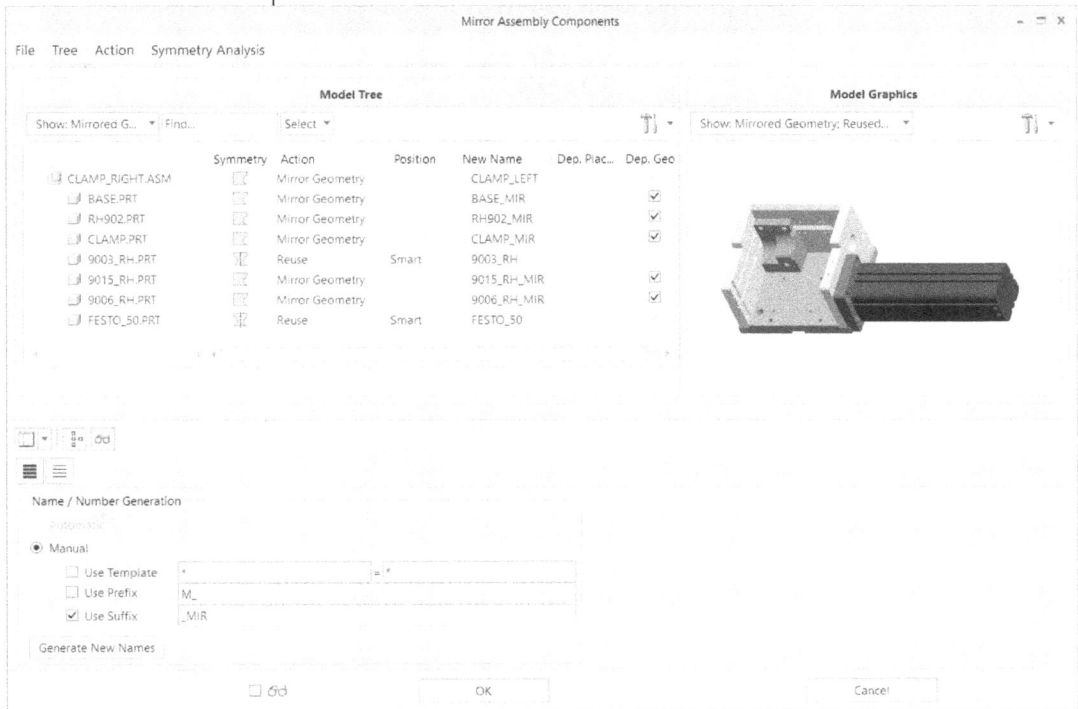

Figure 13–56

8. Note that the symmetry analysis for **9003_RH** and **FESTO_50** is set to **Reuse**. Select all models except for 9003_RH and FESTO_50 as shown in Figure 13–57.

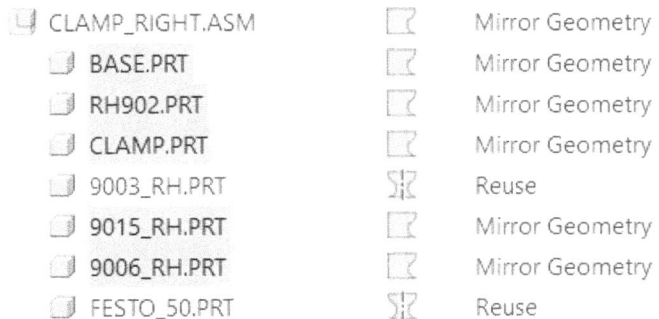

Figure 13–57

9. Enable **Use Suffix** and edit the suffix to **_LH**.

10. Click **Generate New File Names**. DO NOT click **OK**.

Task 2 - Reuse components.

In this task, you will set another part to be reused.

1. Select **BASE.PRT**, right-click, and select **Reuse**, as shown in Figure 13–58.

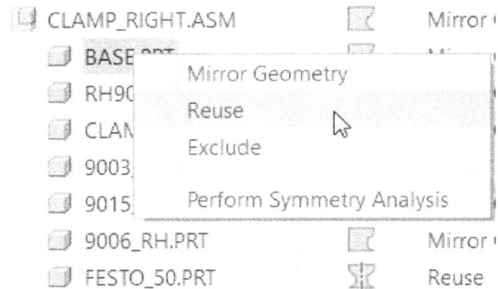

Figure 13–58

2. At the bottom of the dialogue box check ☿ (Preview)

3. In the Model Graphics section, show only Reused components as shown in Figure 13–59.

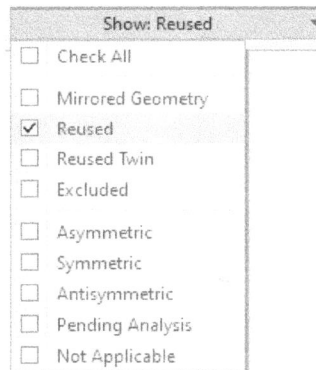

Figure 13–59

4. Rotate the model as shown in Figure 13–60. Note that **BASE.prt** is not oriented correctly in the mirrored assembly.

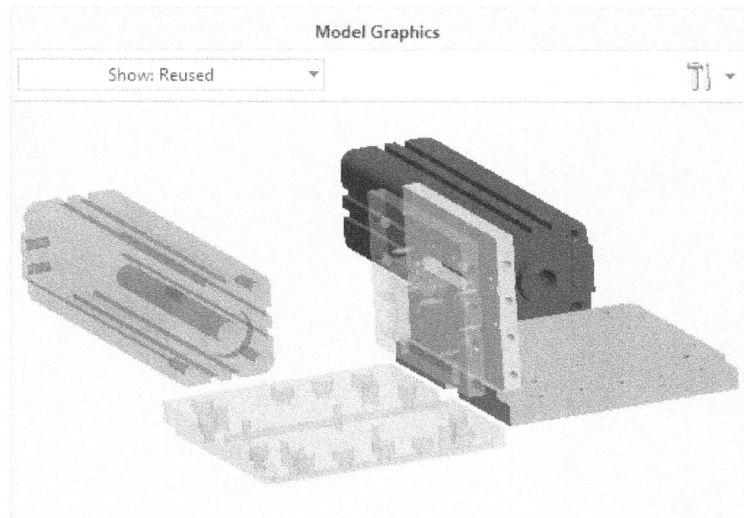

Figure 13–60

5. In the Model Tree section of the dialog box, change the position of **BASE.prt** from **XY_O** to **XY**, as shown in Figure 13–61. Confirm the part orients correctly.

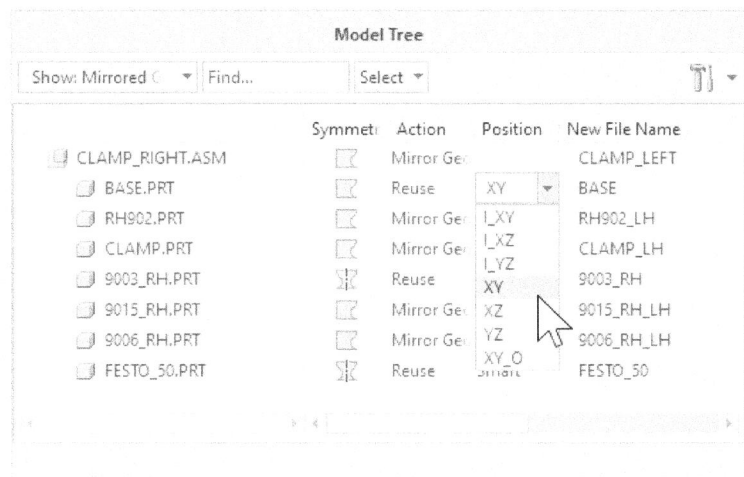

Figure 13–61

6. Click **OK**. The left assembly is created with the left components, as shown in Figure 13–62.

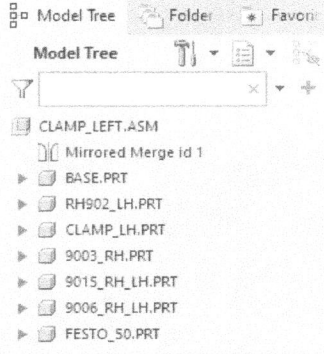

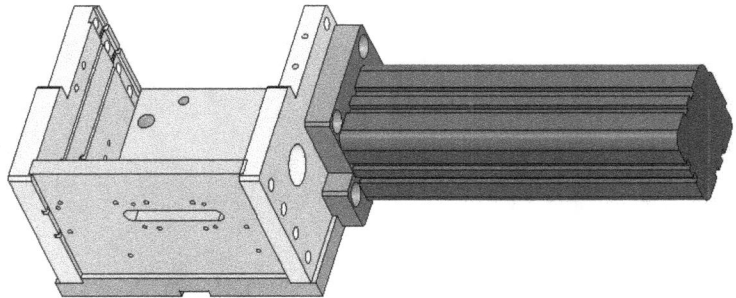

Model Tree · Folder · Favori

Model Tree

CLAMP_LEFT.ASM
  Mirrored Merge id 1
▶ BASE.PRT
▶ RH902_LH.PRT
▶ CLAMP_LH.PRT
▶ 9003_RH.PRT
▶ 9015_RH_LH.PRT
▶ 9006_RH_LH.PRT
▶ FESTO_50.PRT

Figure 13–62

7. Save the assembly. Close all of the windows and erase all of the files from memory.

Practice 13d	# Dragging Components

Practice Objectives

- Drag components.
- Change collision detection settings.

In this practice, you will use the **Drag** tool on a packaged component in an assembly. You will use collision detection to dynamically check for interference while dragging assembly components from different positions.

Task 1 - Open an assembly file.

1. Change the working directory to the *Dragging_Components* folder.

2. Open **slider.asm**.

3. Set the model display as follows:

   - ⅍ *(Datum Display Filters)*: All Off

   - ⤙ *(Spin Center)*: Off

   - ▱ *(Display Style)*: ▱ (Shading With Edges)

   The assembly displays as shown in Figure 13–63.

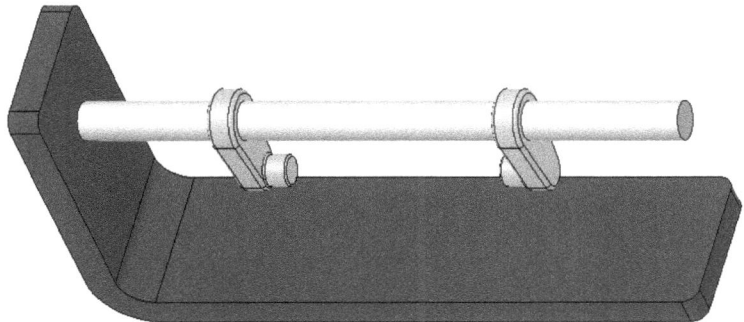

Figure 13–63

4. Click 🖐 (Drag Components). The Drag dialog box opens as shown in Figure 13–64.

If required, select here to expand the dialog box.

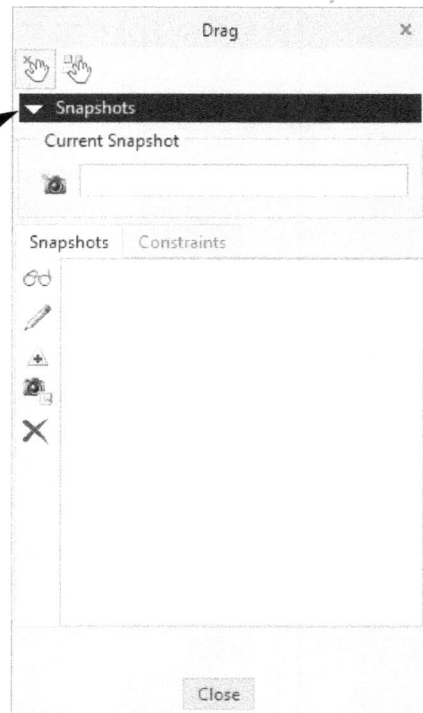

Figure 13–64

5. Select the slider on the right side and drag it along the length of the bar. The final position should be similar to the position shown in Figure 13–65.

Drag this slider back and forth.

Figure 13–65

6. Close the dialog box.

Task 2 - Change collision detection settings.

1. Click **File>Options** and select **Configuration Editor** in the PTC Creo Parametric Options dialog box.

2. Click **Add** and type **enable_advance_collision** as the Option *Name*. Set the Option *Value* to **yes**.

3. Click **OK**.

4. Click **OK** in the PTC Creo Parametric Options and **No** when prompted to save the configuration file.

5. Select **File>Prepare>Model Properties** and select **change** next to Collision Detection in the Model Properties dialog box, as shown in Figure 13–66.

Figure 13–66

6. In the Collision Detection Settings dialog box that opens, select the **Global collision detection** and select **Highlight interfering volumes**, as shown in Figure 13–67.

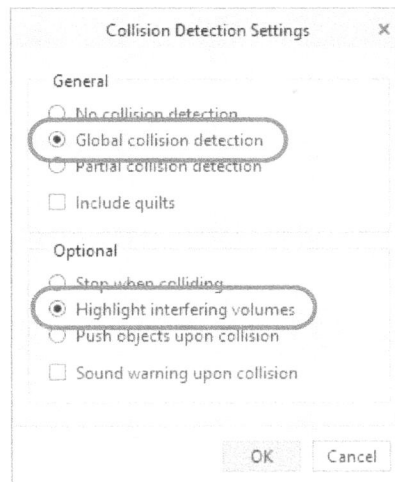

Figure 13–67

7. Click **OK**.

8. Click **Close** in the Model Properties dialog box.

9. Click 🖑 (Drag Components) and drag the slider to intersect the other slider. The interference displays highlighted in red, as shown in Figure 13–68.

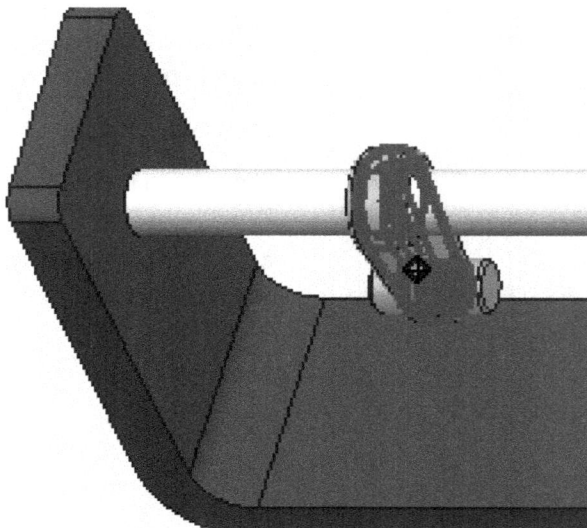

Figure 13–68

10. Drag the slider to the position shown in Figure 13–69.

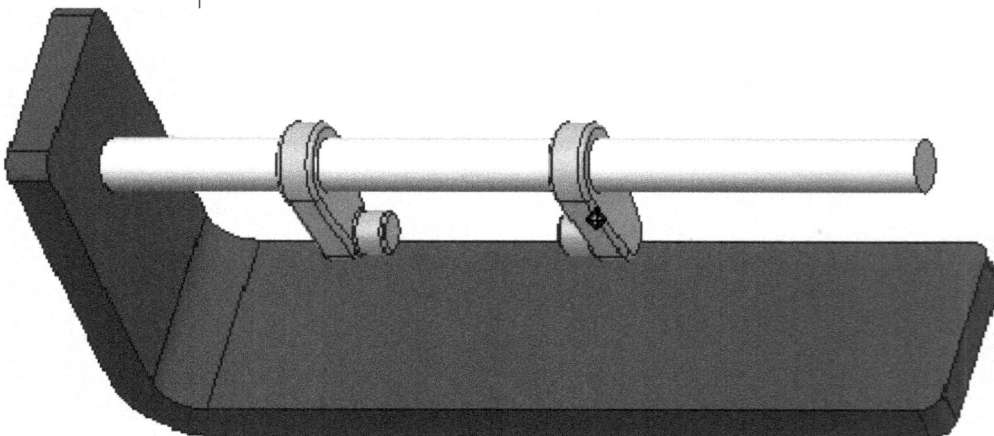

Figure 13–69

11. Change the collision detection settings to **Push objects upon collision**, as shown in Figure 13–70.

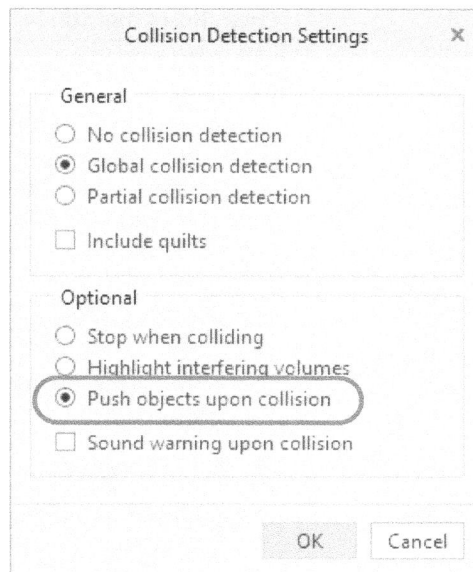

Figure 13–70

12. Drag the left slider and push the right slider to the positions shown in Figure 13–71.

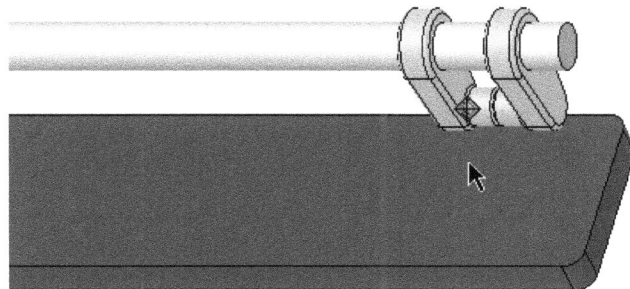

Figure 13–71

13. Save the assembly and erase it from memory.

Task 3 - Optional task.

1. If time permits, change the collision detection settings to **Stop When Colliding** and experiment with the slider positions.

Practice 13e | Assembly Relations

Practice Objective

- Create an assembly-level parameter and an assembly level-relation.

In this practice, you will create assembly parameters. You will then write relations that equate assembly dimensions to those parameters. The result enables you to drive the angular position and the diameter of a part by modifying the value of the parameters.

Task 1 - Open an assembly file.

1. Change the working directory to the *Assembly_Relations* folder.

2. Open **hinge.asm**.

3. Set the model display as follows:

   - *(Datum Display Filters)*: All Off

   - *(Spin Center)*: Off

   - *(Display Style)*: (Shading With Edges)

   The assembly displays as shown in Figure 13–72.

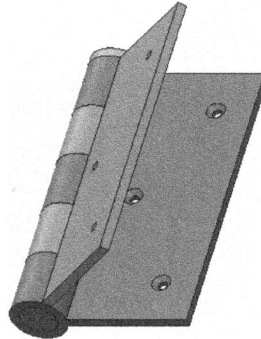

Figure 13–72

4. Click (Saved Orientations)>**FRONT** from the In-graphics toolbar.

5. Select **HINGE2.PRT** in the Model Tree and select ⃗d1⃗ (Edit Dimensions) from the mini toolbar. The **45 degrees** value displays. This is the angular value that positions the hinge relative to **HINGE1.PRT**, as shown in Figure 13–73.

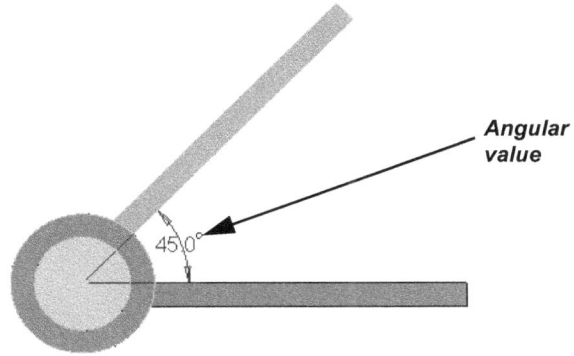

Angular value

45.0°

Figure 13–73

Task 2 - Create an assembly-level parameter.

You can also click

[ ] *(Parameters) in the Tools tab.*

1. Click [ ] (Parameters) in the *Model* tab. The Parameters dialog box opens.

2. Click ✛ (Add New Parameter) and set the following:

   • *Name:* **angle**
   • *Value:* **45**
   • Select **Designate**.

   The dialog box with the new parameter information updates as shown in Figure 13–74.

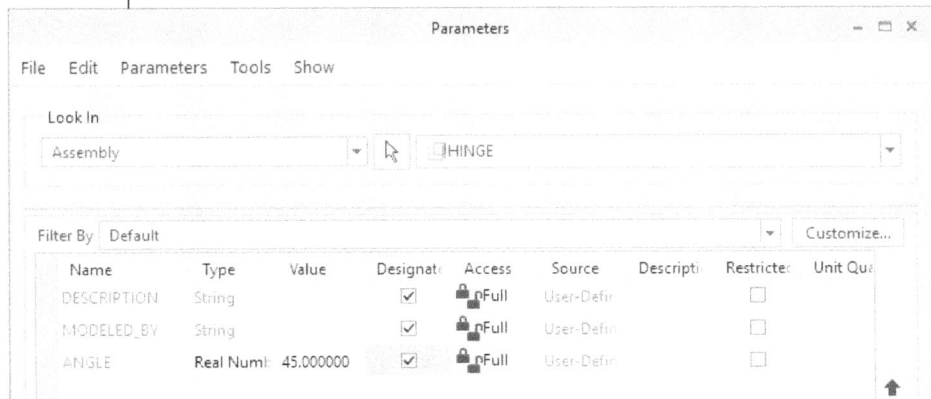

Figure 13–74

3. Click **OK**. Now that the parameter has been created, a relation can be created to associate the angular dimension with the parameter.

Task 3 - Create an assembly-level relation.

You can also click

d= *(Relations) in the Tools tab.*

1. Click d= (Relations) in the *Model* tab. The Relations dialog box opens as shown in Figure 13–75.

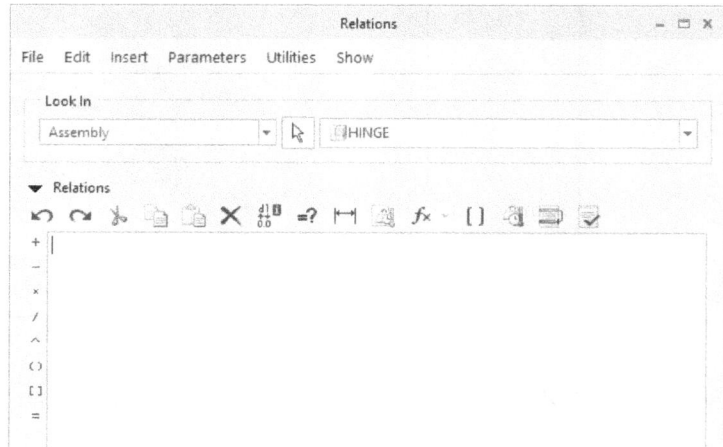

Figure 13–75

2. Select **hinge2.prt** and select the **d2:1** dimension symbol, as shown in Figure 13–76.

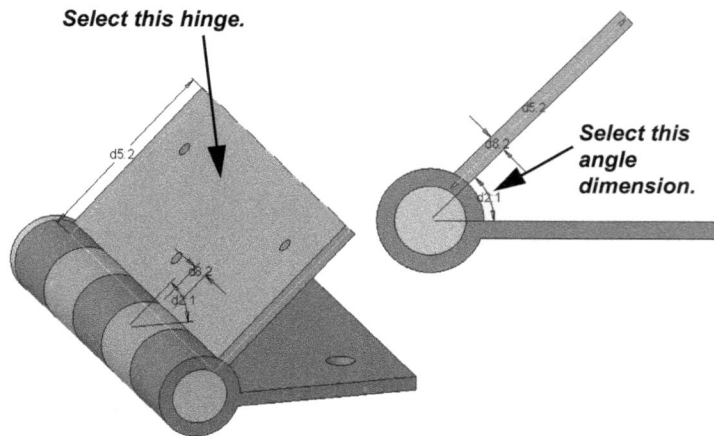

Figure 13–76

The selected dimension displays in the Relations dialog box.

3. Click the = icon.

4. Expand the *Local Parameters* area in the Relations editor and select **ANGLE**, right-click, and select **Insert to Relations**, as shown in Figure 13–77.

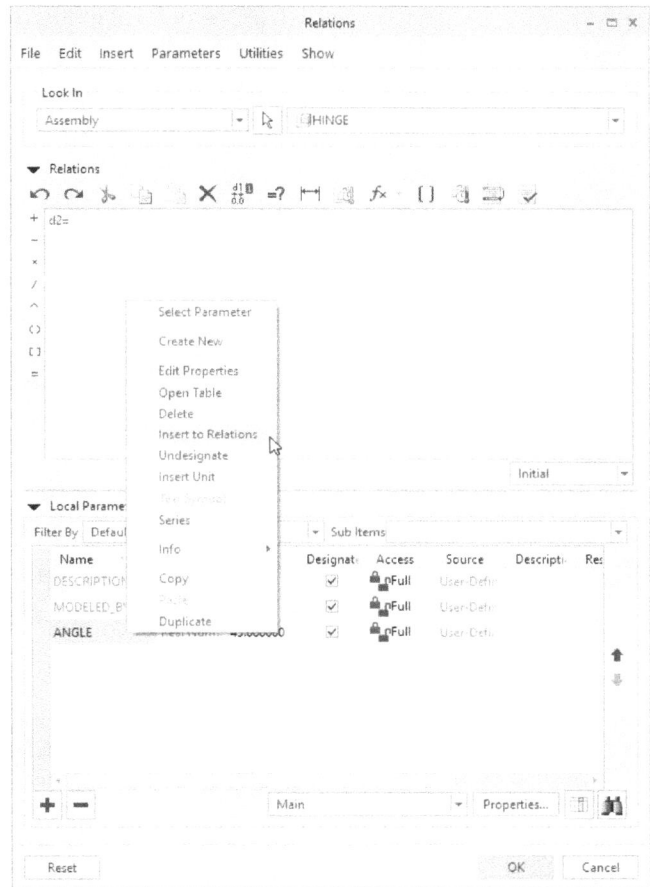

Figure 13–77

Design Considerations

It is considered good practice to always write a comment for all of the relations.

5. Enter the comment line shown in Figure 13–78.

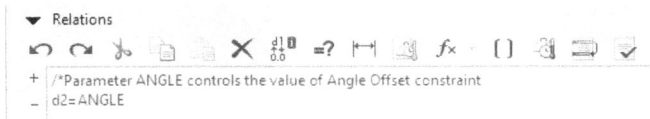

Figure 13–78

6. Click **OK**.

Task 4 - Edit a parameter value.

1. Select **HINGE.ASM** in the Model Tree and click

   [ ] (Parameters) in the mini toolbar, as shown in
   Figure 13–79.

Figure 13–79

2. Change the *Value* of the **ANGLE** parameter to **0**, as shown in
   Figure 13–80.

Name	Type	Value	Designate	Access	Source	Descripti	Restricted	Unit Qu
DESCRIPTION	String		✓	🔒 pFull	User-Defin		☐	
MODELED_BY	String		✓	🔒 pFull	User-Defin		☐	
ANGLE	Real Num	0	✓	🔒 pFull	User-Defin		☐	

Figure 13–80

3. Click **OK**.

4. Regenerate the assembly. The assembly displays as shown
   in Figure 13–81. The **ANGLE** parameter drives the angular
   assembly dimension as a result of the relation that you have
   written.

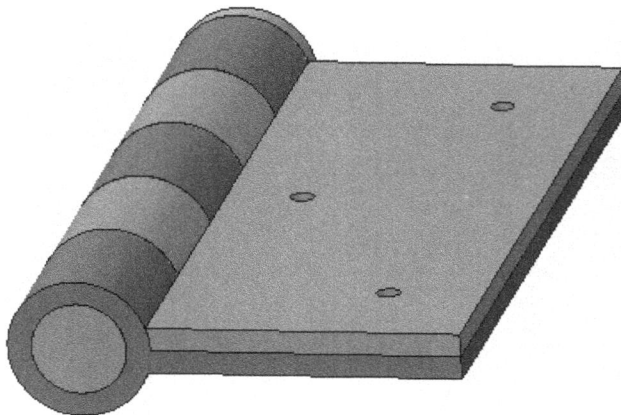

Figure 13–81

Task 5 - Add a column to the Model Tree.

Click 🔧 ˅ *(Settings)>*
Tree Columns.

1. Add a *Model Params* column to the Model Tree and display the **ANGLE** parameter, as shown in Figure 13–82.

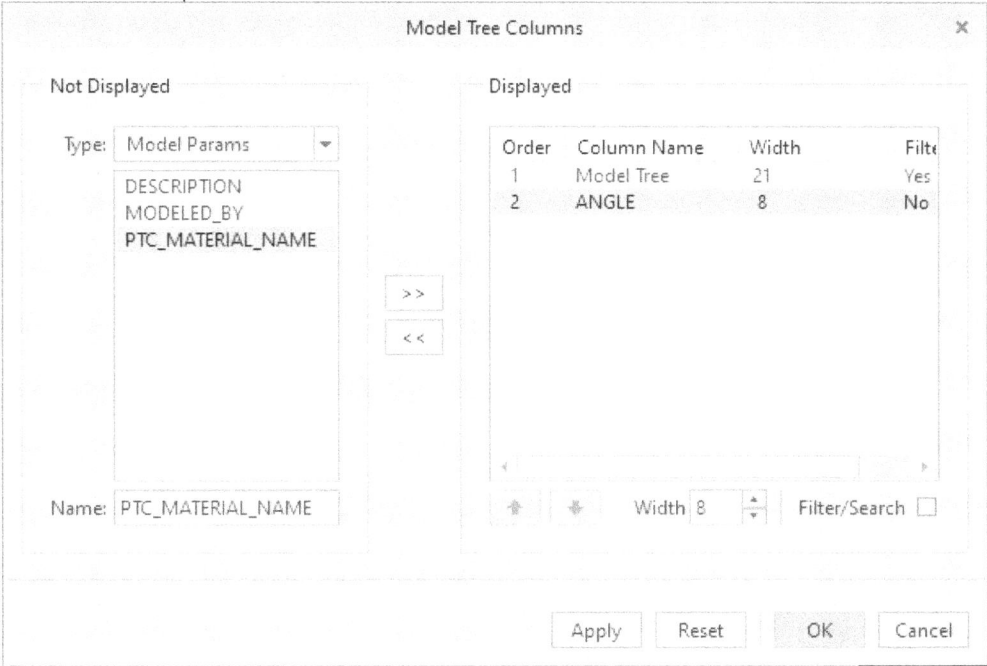

Figure 13–82

2. Click **OK**.

3. Edit the parameter *Angle* value in the Model Tree to **180**, as shown in Figure 13–83.

Figure 13–83

4. Regenerate the assembly. The regenerated assembly displays as shown in Figure 13–84.

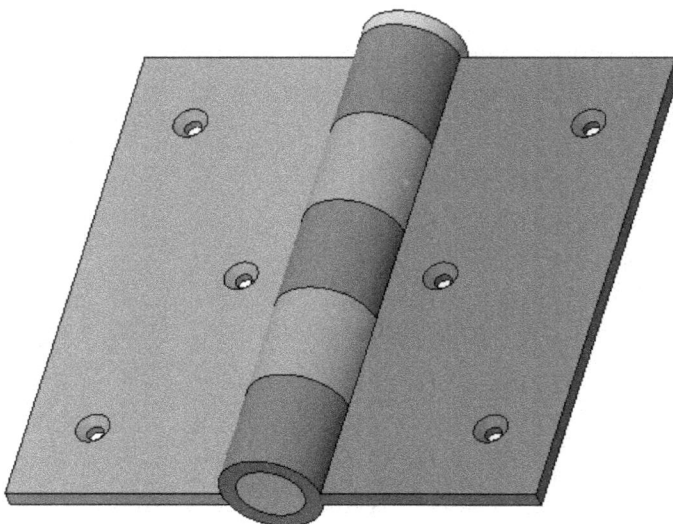

Figure 13–84

5. Save the assembly and erase it from memory.

Chapter Review Questions

1. To mirror a component within the context of an assembly, the source component must first be inserted into the assembly.

    a. True

    b. False

2. Once the component has been mirrored, the assembly cannot be deleted.

    a. True

    b. False

3. Which Mirror type option mirrors the geometry with the source feature structure? The option copies all of the information to the mirrored part and the copy remains independent of the source part.

    a. **Mirror Geometry Only**

    b. **Mirror Geometry with Features**

    c. **Mirror Placement**

4. When mirroring a subassembly, you can specify an action and new name for each component in the subassembly.

    a. True

    b. False

5. To merge or cut out components, they must be assembled in an assembly.

    a. True

    b. False

6. The Drag dialog box can be used to do which of the following? (Select all that apply.)

    a. Drag bodies.

    b. Constrain in the dialog box.

    c. Create snapshots.

    d. Take measurements.

7. Which of the following statements are true regarding relations? (Select all that apply.)

   a. Dimensions and parameters can be used in a relation to drive a value.

   b. Equations can be manually entered in the Relations dialog box.

   c. Equations can be created using a combination of manual entry and selecting dimensions directly from the model.

   d. Creo Parametric enables you to create both equality and conditional relations.

8. A comment line is required before entering a relation.

   a. True

   b. False

9. Relations must be verified before the model can be regenerated.

   a. True

   b. False

10. Which of the following can be included when entering a relation? (Select all that apply.)

   a. Symbols

   b. Operators

   c. Functions

   d. Parameters

Answers: 1.a, 2.b, 3.b, 4.a, 5.a, 6.abcd, 7.abcd, 8.b, 9.b, 10.abcd